Internet Marketing

FOUNDATIONS & APPLICATIONS

Second Edition

Carolyn Siegel
Eastern Kentucky University

Houghton Mifflin Company
Boston   New York

To Malcolm

V.P., Editor-in-Chief: George T. Hoffman
Development Manager: Susan M. Kahn
Development Editor: Jessica Carlisle
Senior Project Editor: Tamela Ambush
Editorial Assistant: Sage Anderson
Manufacturing Coordinator: Carrie Wagner
Marketing Manager: Mike Schenk
Marketing Associate: Lisa Boden

Cover image: Photodisc/Getty Images

Printed in the U.S.A.

Library of Congress Control Number: 2004116831

ISBN: 0-618-51999-8

23456789—MP—09 08 07 06

Contents

CHAPTER 3 Identifying Internet Users   52

CHAPTER 4 Taking Marketing to the Net   75

CHAPTER 5 Legal and Ethical Issues; Privacy and Security Concerns   101

Module II

Information for Competitive Marketing Advantage   159

CHAPTER 8 Using Data Tools to Enhance Performance   190

Module III

The Internet Marketing Mix   215

Module IV

Internet Marketing Action Plans   337

CHAPTER 14 Marketing Site Development:
Content, Design, and Construction   359

Preface

Within a remarkably short time, the Internet and World Wide Web have profoundly influenced the way we live, work, learn, and play. The changes are exhilarating and, at times, rather unsettling. When it comes to finding profitable applications for the Internet and Web, marketing is setting the pace—developing unique synergies, achieving operating efficiencies, serving existing customers more effectively, and searching out new online customers domestically and worldwide. Internet marketers are challenging traditional practices, models, and relationships, and rewriting the book on how marketing can be practiced in the opening years of the twenty-first century.

Purpose of the Book

There has never been a better time in the history of contemporary business to be teaching marketing. Yet at the same time, keeping up with the rapidly changing environment makes teaching Internet marketing an intimidating task. That's why this textbook was written, to organize the topic and present it in a framework that facilitates student learning. The basic structure of *Internet Marketing: Foundations and Applications,* Second Edition is organized in a highly approachable, traditional format of four modules and fourteen chapters that fit comfortably into a semester, quarter, or summer class schedule. It can be used in a traditional in-class setting, for totally online classes, or in a web-assisted course. The textbook is designed for an introductory course in Internet marketing and could even be used to teach marketing principles. The emphasis is on establishing the foundations of marketing and presenting current Internet marketing applications.

The Second Edition is thoroughly updated with many new cases, examples, activities, screenshots, and references. Exciting student features were added that make it more engaging and strengthen concepts introduced in the chapters. The Second Edition Instructor's Resource Manual (IRM) was updated, revised, and includes an expanded Internet Marketing Plan section. The IRM was written by the author and draws on her years of experience teaching Internet marketing and guiding students in the development of Internet marketing plans for small and mid-size local business clients.

Features of the Book

The textbook introduces foundation concepts and applications, and provides many examples of real world Internet marketing successes and failures. New opening case studies were written for each chapter in the Second Edition. The cases relate to the theme of the chapter and focus on how marketers deal with contemporary, real-world Internet marketing challenges. Short end-of-chapter cases were written for each chapter to highlight competitors of the company from the chapter's opening case. The competitive cases expand the focus from one company to the highly competitive environment facing Internet marketers. A new section called *Take Action!* was written for each chapter in the Second Edition. This feature challenges students to complete marketing tasks that can aid in the development of useful work skills. The tasks are developed around the premise that although students learn in different ways, active learning generally is more effective than passive learning.

CONTENT AND ORGANIZATION

Chapter 1, A Marketing Perspective in the Internet Age, defines Internet marketing and electronic commerce, and establishes similarities and differences with traditional marketing. It develops links from the Internet's past, showing how mankind's passion for communication, numeration, and industrialization led to innovations and discoveries that were essential to the Internet's creation. It establishes links to the Internet's present, explains how it was created and initially operated, and provides reasons why the release of the World Wide Web stimulated Internet commercialization. The chapter concludes by discussing effects of the Internet economy on business and society, and provides an initial look at how the Internet is changing society along with theories on what may be in store for Internet marketing in the future.

Chapter 2, Internet Fundamentals: Operations, Management, the Web, and Wireless, begins with a brief explanation of how the Internet works and why it operates so smoothly, even though no single entity, government, or organization governs it. Attributes that make the World Wide Web so conducive to marketing activities are discussed. The chapter wraps up by examining the potential and drawbacks of wireless connectivity.

Chapter 3, Identifying Internet Users, focuses on the types of buyers that are online and their distinguishing characteristics, and explores what buyers are doing online, which leads to a discussion of who's not online and why. Other types of behaviors that occur online, like anti-corporate activism, or behaviors that result from excessive Internet use, particularly social isolation and addictive behaviors, are presented within the context of why they concern Internet marketers.

Chapter 4, Taking Marketing to the Net, presents a simple classification system for business Internet activities, and explains how businesses are using the Internet and Web to market their products effectively. Next, the discussion widens to include other enterprises, particularly governments and non-profits, using online marketing to meet their goals. It presents examples of how individual sellers are using Internet marketing and describes external environmental factors that influence Internet marketing activities. These include the economic environment, technology, the social/cultural and natural environments, and government and legal factors.

Chapter 5, Legal and Ethical Issues; Privacy and Security Concerns, explains why Internet laws and jurisdiction are in such a state of flux and what remedies are being attempted. Internet marketers are confronted by important legal issues of jurisdiction, enforcement, taxation, privacy, and security. Ethical marketing behaviors are highlighted and the question of whether ethical marketing behaviors can be enforced on the Internet is debated. The chapter concludes with a discussion of online security problems and why they are of such pressing concern to buyers and sellers.

Chapter 6, Taking Internet Marketing International, discusses how international orientation affects Internet marketing strategy. It develops a global overview of Internet readiness, markets, and trends, and explains why marketing internationally is more complex than solely domestic Internet marketing. International Internet marketing strategies are identified along with differences among international Internet users. International issues that concern Internet marketers are identified and explained. This chapter is unique in that few Internet marketing textbooks examine the international environment at this depth, despite the fact that the majority of Internet users are from countries outside North America.

Chapter 7, Taking Marketing Research to the Net, emphasizes the importance of information and data tools to Internet marketing, identifies applied Internet marketing research methods, and discusses what they can do for online marketers. Primary marketing research methods that are used online are described and contrasted with their offline equivalents, including online focus groups, surveys, simulations, and observation. The synergy between offline/online research is pointed out. Evidence is provided to support calling the Internet a marketing research secondary source *gold mine.* Issues that concern Internet marketing researchers are presented.

Chapter 8, Using Data Tools to Enhance Performance, emphasizes the growing importance of collaboration between Internet marketers and information technology professionals. It presents data fundamentals and explores how data tools are being used to achieve marketing performance objectives. The chapter explores the marketing value of search engines and describes privacy-sensitive techniques used to develop consumer profiles and collect marketing data.

Chapter 9, Product in the Internet Marketing Mix, begins the discussion of the Internet marketing mix. It explains how the characteristics of products affect how they are marketed online. It identifies consumer products best suited to online marketing and describes how enterprise products are sold and developed online. The chapter concludes with a discussion of why Internet branding is so important and presents examples of how it can be accomplished.

Chapter 10, Price in the Internet Marketing Mix, identifies factors that affect how Internet prices are set. Internet price issues that concern consumers and enterprises are presented along with alternate Internet pricing models. Examples are given of the effects of online price transparency. It considers why some price strategies are successful online and others are not, and examines Internet payment alternatives for how buyers can pay for products online.

Chapter 11, Place in the Internet Marketing Mix, classifies online distribution (place) activities and explains how they are influenced by the Internet environment. It identifies online place issues that concern Internet marketers and characterizes successful online consumer channel strategies and the reasons for their success. Enterprise marketplaces and B2C channel issues are discussed. Etailing is introduced as an Internet marketing activity that is greatly expanding the reach of many traditional offline retailers.

Chapter 12, Promotion in the Internet Marketing Mix, identifies how marketing promotion is affected by the Internet and what online promotion issues concern Internet marketers and why. This includes spam (unsolicited commercial email) and intrusive web advertising such as persistent pop-ups and pop-unders (pop-behinds), and floating animation. The chapter deals at length with online advertising strategies and discusses why some are successful while others are not. Many examples are provided. The chapter concludes with an analysis of how sales promotions and permission marketing can be used effectively online.

Chapter 13, The Web Marketing Plan, introduces web marketing planning and identifies what should be included in a plan and why. It emphasizes the value of marketing planning and writing a marketing plan. Web marketing plan implementation and control are discussed, along with the role of a web marketing budget. An example of web marketing planning in a small business is developed throughout the chapter.

Chapter 14, Marketing Site Development: Content, Design, and Construction, examines issues that must be considered prior to website development, particularly as they focus on site content, design, and construction, including usability. It describes how website content and design advance site goals, and explains the impact of construction issues on website effectiveness.

CHAPTER PEDAGOGY

- *Format:* Streamlined organization of modules and chapters follows a familiar pedagogical framework that is readily accessible to instructors and students.
- *Opening Case:* Opening mini-case studies were written specifically for each chapter to encourage discussion related to chapter contents. The cases relate to the theme of the chapter and focus on how marketers deal with contemporary, real-world Internet marketing challenges. Each opening case links to an end-of-chapter competitive case study, which is also a new feature in the Second Edition. The general theme of the chapter is carried through to the cases and new student activity feature, *Take Action!,* and to the features *Check It Out* and *A Global Perspective.*
- *Competitive Case Study:* An exciting new feature was added at the end of each chapter. Short end-of-chapter cases were written for each chapter to highlight competitors of the company from the chapter's opening case. The competitive cases expand the focus from one company to the highly competitive environment facing Internet marketers. The subjects of both the opening and competitive cases can be used for projects that compare competitive market offers and strategies, and their respective successes and/or failures in the Internet environment.
- *Key Glossary Terms:* Important terms in each chapter are identified in bold and definitions are highlighted in the margin for easy reference.
- *Topic Updates:* Web icons found in each chapter direct students and instructors to updated information and expanded learning opportunities on the student website.
- *End-of-Chapter Review Questions:* Each chapter concludes with 15 self-test questions.
- *Chapter Summary Statements:* Summaries for each main chapter topic are helpful when students review for quizzes and exams.
- *Take Action!:* A new section called *Take Action!* was written for each chapter in the Second Edition. This feature challenges students to complete marketing tasks that can aid in the development of useful work skills. The tasks are developed

around the premise that although students learn in different ways, active learning generally is more effective than passive learning. The subject of each *Take Action!* feature relates to the chapter theme and cases. This feature challenges students to go online to perform research, evaluate the results of their research, and report their results and recommendations using standard business communication forms. Suggestions for using the *Take Action!* feature in class are presented in the Instructor's Resource Manual (IRM), which is available to adopters.

- *Website Links:* Websites used in each chapter are identified by their web address (URL).
- *Additional Internet Marketing Plan Emphasis:* Following the principle of the value of active student learning, few activities can be as potentially worthwhile as having students create an Internet marketing plan for an actual client. In response, the Internet marketing plan is given added emphasis in the Second Edition and in the accompanying Instructor's Resource Manual (IRM). The plan can be assigned as an individual or team project at the beginning of the semester. The IRM contains suggested assignments that guide students step-by-step from identifying a client to developing the plan and presenting recommendations.
- *International Orientation:* An international orientation is emphasized throughout the book, in addition to the international Internet marketing chapter. Many examples are used to reflect this emphasis.
- *Internet Marketing Ethics:* Ethical issues that confront Internet marketers are identified and discussed throughout the text.
- *Appendices:* Appendices, found only at the student website, are extremely student-centered and include URL Citation Style Guides, Evaluating Online Sources, Online Information Search and Retrieval, Internet Marketing Careers, and Creating a Web Page.
- *PowerPoint Slides:* Slides were created for each chapter to emphasize key points and are found on the instructor website.

A Fully-Integrated Package

Given the rapid pace of change, teaching Internet marketing can become a full-time job. That is why the supporting materials are so important to this book. The instructor and student websites, the Instructor's Resource Manual with Test Bank, and other supporting materials were developed by the author and tested by her undergraduate and MBA Internet marketing students. The website is overseen by the author, who is committed to keeping it current, relevant, and useful.

INSTRUCTOR WEBSITE

The instructor website is closely integrated with the textbook and uses the same format of modules and chapters as the book. The site is easily accessed, logically organized, easy to use, and rich in information and additional materials that aid instructors in keeping their Internet marketing courses current and interesting. It includes such resources as Ask Dr. Siegel, an online instructor resource manual, and PowerPoint slides. This site is frequently updated by the author.

STUDENT WEBSITE

The student website is an extension of the textbook and, like the instructor website, uses the same format of modules and chapters as the book and is frequently updated by the author. The student site includes the textbook appendices with hotlinks to websites, the complete glossary and flashcards, web updates, web links, ready notes, chapter outlines, chapter abstracts and learning objectives, and a resource center.

INSTRUCTOR'S RESOURCE MANUAL WITH TEST BANK

Available online and on disk, the Instructor's Resource Manual with Test Bank includes a Sample Syllabus, Chapter Abstracts, Chapter Outlines, Teaching Notes, Internet Marketing Applications, Suggested Answers, Web Updates, Mini-Case Notes, and the Test Bank.

Acknowledgments

Writing a textbook represents an enormous commitment. It's not the work of one person, although any shortcomings are the author's sole responsibility. The staff at Houghton Mifflin who worked so closely with me, particularly Editor-in-Chief George Hoffman, Development Editor Jessica Carlisle, and Senior Project Editor Tamela Ambush, deserve great credit for their professionalism, understanding, and tireless efforts guiding this book from concept to reality. Words cannot express my appreciation for their support and expertise. Thanks are also due to an outstanding group of colleagues whose comments and advice were extremely helpful. They include Sridhar Balasubramanian, *University of Texas;* Charlene Barker, *Spokane Falls Community College;* Paul Dowling, *University of Utah;* Larry Goldstein, *Iona College;* Cheryl Gruse, *DeVry College of Technology—Pomona;* Linda Ferrell, *University of Northern Colorado;* Theresa B. Flaherty, *Old Dominion University;* J. Morgan Jones, *University of North Carolina;* Jay Lambe, *Virginia Tech;* Carla Meeske, *University of Oregon;* Mohan Menon, *University of South Alabama;* George Milne, *University of Massachusetts;* Robert Moore, *Mississippi State University;* Deborah Moscardelli, *Central Michigan University;* Gillian Rice, *Thunderbird College;* Murph Sewall, *University of Connecticut;* Judith Spain and Norbert Elbert, *Eastern Kentucky University;* Fred Tennant, *Webster University;* E. Sonny Butler, *Georgia Southern University;* Wolfgang Grassl, *Hillsdale College;* Judith Grekowicz, *Kirtland Community College;* Susan Jones, *Ferris State University;* and Thomas Porter, *University of North Carolina, Wilmington.* I would also like to thank my students who inspired me to undertake this project. Over the past decade, they have tested the format of this book, its website, and projects many times over. Their input was critical to keeping everything clear, accessible, and student-centered. Thank you, one and all.

Finally, while writing this book has been a joyous task in many respects, it has also been extraordinarily intense and time-consuming. It could never have been finished without the complete and unselfish encouragement of my husband, Malcolm. Thanks also to Erik, Mark, and Stacey for your love and support.

Module I

An Introduction to the Internet and the Environment of Internet Marketing

Before the early 1990s, few people other than scientists, researchers, academics, and the military were even aware of the Internet. Their online world was black and white, with text and data transmitted in a noncommercial environment. That all began to change when the World Wide Web, the Internet's graphical service, was released in the winter of 1991–1992. Powerful user-friendly graphical browsers appeared in 1993 and quickly captured the public's imagination. Within five years, hundreds of millions of people worldwide, from children to seniors, were online communicating with friends and family, searching for information, playing games, and shopping in an environment rich in pictures, animation, colors, and sounds. Commercialization brought marketers online and today, Internet marketing occurs around the world and is taught in a growing number of colleges and universities in the United States and abroad. For most of us, the Internet has changed many aspects of our daily lives.

This book recognizes the breadth of Internet marketing and the importance of presenting it within the context of the greater Internet economy. In this economy, Internet marketing is directly affected by developments in electronic commerce and advances in information technology, as well as by environmental factors beyond marketers' control. It's also influenced by events in the past, which often have parallels in the present and sometimes provide insights into the future. Module I examines some of the important events and inventions that led to the Internet's creation, particularly in communication, numeracy, industralization, and computing. It explains how the Internet works and is managed, which buyers and sellers are online and what they're doing. The final chapters in Module I examine environmental factors that affect the Internet and Internet marketing. Together, these chapters develop a foundation for the discussion of Internet marketing models and the effective use of the marketing mix.

1

A Marketing Perspective in the Internet Age

LEARNING OBJECTIVES

» To develop a conceptual foundation for comparing traditional and Internet marketing
» To examine how human advances in communication, numeracy, and computing contributed to the creation of the Internet
» To identify the immediate precursors to today's commercial Internet
» To consider the current state of the Internet economy and theorize about its future

Google's Internet Marketing Advantage

There is a lot of **marketing buzz,** or interpersonal word-of-mouth discussion, about award-winning Google (*www.google.com*), one of the most familiar names on the Internet. Google is the reason why so many Internet users can quickly and easily find what they are looking for online. Its fast and accurate search process has made it the darling of the Internet world. Google was founded in 1998 by Larry Page and Sergey Brin, and the unique PageRank technology and hypertext-matching analysis that they devised powers the world's largest search engine. In an average day, Google accesses over eight billion web pages and processes in excess of 200 million search requests in over 30 different countries. The name *Google* is a variation on *googol,* a coined term for the number 1 followed by 100 zeroes, which refers to the company's mission to organize the vast amount of online information and make it accessible to users, typically within less than a second of their request. Known for its innovations, Google strives to identify and develop business opportunities and expand its brand franchise into new revenue-enhancing activities. In addition to searches, Google offers language translations, news

headlines, images, telephone book directories, access to non-HTML documents, and a massive archive of Usenet messages accumulated since 1981. Google markets its **scalable search technology** (search process rules that can be changed or expanded to accommodate new system requirements) to other businesses and has become the internal search engine of choice for many of the world's largest Internet portals and companies. Its innovative and nonintrusive advertising program is highly attractive to advertisers seeking access to Google's enormous user base. Why is Google such a success even though it was not one of the first search engines online? Accuracy, speed, and simplicity please Google's users, delivering what they want. Google satisfies advertisers by giving them eyeball access to hundreds of millions of potential customers who can easily link from Google's search pages to the advertisers' sites. Enterprises benefit by investing in Google's scalable technology, which gives them confidence that they can expand their present system when their needs change. Everyone benefits from Google's commitment to innovation that will help make the Internet become an even more valuable environment in the future.[1]

Marketing buzz
A considerable amount of interpersonal discussion (word-of-mouth) about a brand, product, person, marketing campaign, or related issue.

Scalable search technology
Expandable search process rules (algorithms) that can be changed and/or expanded to accommodate new system requirements.

Online
When users are connecting to the Internet they are *on the line,* which at the Internet's beginning was predominantly via telephone land lines.

Search engine
Software that is directed to conduct searches of online documents for keywords and to return a list of sites where the keywords are found, along with hot links to the sites.

Google is a great place to begin our study of Internet marketing. It's popular, successful, frequently in the news, and an excellent example of the exciting things happening **online.** Google illustrates many of the principles we'll examine at greater depth in subsequent chapters. Google's search technology is licensed by more than 125 corporate customers including EarthLink (*www.earthlink.com*), Palm (*www.palm.com*), Nextel (*www.nextel.com*), and Cisco Systems (*www.cisco.com*). It has been adopted by a large number of schools, universities, and other enterprises. Google is writing the book on how online search engines should operate and how Internet companies can successfully market their products. A **search engine** consists of software used to search online documents for keywords and to return a list of sites where the keywords are found, along with hot links to these sites.

Before 1993, the world didn't need online search engines and the term *search engine* didn't exist. Today, most Americans and hundreds of millions of other people worldwide know what a search engine does and use one on a daily basis. As a society, we have become quite dependent on the Internet, because it makes our lives more interesting, productive, and challenging. To marketers, the Internet has meant new jobs, different ways to market products, improvements on traditional marketing techniques, and the opportunity both to establish closer, more productive relationships with existing customers and to attract new ones. It has also meant coping with a volatile economic environment, accelerated technological change, and greater uncertainty.

From a traditional marketing perspective, Internet marketing is different and yet familiar. From a societal perspective, the Internet can be viewed within the context of humankind's historical and continuing search for more efficient ways to communicate, numerate, and develop machines to do our work. From an economic perspective, Internet commerce is growing despite dire predictions to the contrary during the recession at the turn of the century. For many marketers and their customers, the Internet will eventually become the principal, and possibly the only, marketing environment where their exchanges take place.

Chapter 1 begins building a conceptual foundation for studying Internet marketing. It provides some key definitions and examines how linkages to milestone events and inventions in the past cumulatively paved the way for the Internet's development and future. It considers how the Internet was created and the contributions of people whose vision and determination made it happen. Chapter 1 concludes with a look at the current state of the Internet economy and theorizes about the future of the Internet and marketing.

Defining Marketing in the Internet Age

Considering that web commercialization didn't gain momentum until after 1993, the Internet's impact has already been remarkable. Some people believe a revolutionary era in human history has begun; others dispute this view. If the Internet is *revolutionary,* then it will trigger radical changes in how business and marketing are conducted. If it is *evolutionary,* then many current business and marketing practices will quickly adapt to this different but still familiar environment.

THE INTERNET AND MARKETING

Internet
The world's largest network of interconnected (internetted) distributed computer networks.

The **Internet** is the world's largest network of interconnected (internetted) distributed computer networks. All computers and computer networks operating on the Internet must agree to abide by certain operating rules called TCP/IP protocols that allow computers to transmit data packets even though the data were created on different operating systems. TCP/IP communication rules facilitate seamless communication and data transmission across great distances in real or near-real time by computers and various other access devices, wired and wireless. The Internet may be the single greatest stimulus for marketing yet created.

Marketing
A broad range of activities that bring buyers and sellers together so they can make exchanges that deliver satisfaction and value to all parties.

Marketing is a collection of activities that bring buyers and sellers together to make exchanges that satisfy and give value to all parties. Marketing is a profession, a process, and a practice. It has been taught as an academic discipline for more than half a century. It began long before that, with the development of processes designed to clear product surpluses from markets and help balance supply and demand.

Practically anything can be marketed, from tangible goods to ideas, causes, places, groups, individuals, entertainment, information, and services. Marketing is performed by enterprises and individuals. In many enterprises, everyone from top management to office clerks is considered part of the marketing team. In others, marketers perform discrete marketing tasks in relative isolation from other functional areas. Marketers are suppliers, manufacturers, brand and product managers, distributors, wholesalers, retailers, promotion managers, and salespeople. Marketers initiate, plan, implement, and control processes that take products through their life cycle, from development to new product launch, management, and eventual discontinuation. Marketers seek to facilitate exchange by establishing profitable, mutually satisfying, long-term relationships with customers. Customers (buyers) are personal use consumers and enterprises of all types—businesses, organizations, educational institutions, governments, health care providers, and groups.

Marketers communicate information about products, negotiate exchanges, and transport, store, inventory, display, and transfer products to buyers. They gather information about markets and competitors, perform marketing research, and use the results to improve product offers and customer satisfaction. They promote products, price and sell them, and assume risks associated with exchange.

Marketers use an array of tools to accomplish their goals and facilitate exchange. These tools or marketing variables are referred to collectively as the 4Ps—product, price, place (marketing channels), and promotion. All are more or less adjustable and can be used by marketers to customize market offers. Over the years, successive attempts to replace the 4Ps with alternative concepts have failed to gain widespread acceptance. Because the 4Ps are enduring and still-valuable organizing concepts, they are used as organizing concepts in this book.

INTERNET MARKETING

Internet marketing
Marketing in electronic environments, primarily on the Internet, World Wide Web (WWW), intranets, and extranets.

Internet marketing, or emarketing, is marketing in electronic environments, primarily on the Internet, on one or more of its services (Web, email), or offline by enterprises that produce and sell Internet-related products. Like traditional marketing, the goal of Internet marketing is to facilitate exchange, build long-term customer relationships, and create value, which is the benefit or utility received from marketing exchange. Value is created for both buyers and sellers when traditional marketing is performed in electronic environments that reduce or greatly eliminate time and space constraints, facilitate personalization and customization, and allow the interoperability of computers and other devices.

Customer satisfaction is at the heart of marketing. Internet marketing adds to customer satisfaction by delivering time, place, possession, and form utility (value). *Time utility* occurs because web storefronts never close, information is available nonstop, and searches can be conducted and purchases made whenever the visitor is connected. The Internet is an always on *24/7/365* environment—24 hours a day, 7 days a week, 365 days a year. *Place utility* is provided by entertainment, news, weather, software, and other virtual products that can be delivered directly from the Internet to the visitor's computer screen or wireless device. Online visitors have worldwide access to stores and content. They also have seamless access to delivery services for tangible products purchased online. Buyers can take possession of purchased products with their credit card or online payment alternative, which creates *possession utility.* They benefit from *form utility* when products are customized or made available in the desired assortments or quantities. The Internet facilitates product customization on a scale that cannot be achieved offline.

Internet marketing is performed by enterprises that operate exclusively on the Internet (clicks-only enterprises) and by others that have both an online and an offline presence (bricks-and-clicks enterprises). Marketing is taking place in the infrastructure segment, where the Internet is being physically built out and maintained; in manufacturing where products that support online commercial activities are produced; and through ecommerce, where intermediaries sell products provided by other businesses, and manufacturers sell their own products. It occurs on **intranets,** proprietary (private) computer networks walled off from outsiders, and **extranets,** networks that allow selected external individuals or enterprises intranet access. Internet marketing can be targeted to local domestic regional, national, or global markets. Virtually anything that is marketed offline is now sold online, from thoroughbred horses and copies of the U.S. Declaration of Independence, to apparel, sports trading cards, automotive parts, carbon steel, bath soap, and electric power.

Some marketing tactics must be changed or new tactics developed to suit the online environment; others can be applied directly from traditional offline marketing practices. For example, printed cents-off coupons are distributed in freestanding inserts (FSIs) in newspapers, as cutout coupons in magazines, through direct mail and door hangers, in stores via shelf dispensers, and now downloaded and printed from websites such as MyCoupons (*www.mycoupons.com*) and HotCoupons (*www.hotcoupons.com*). Most retailers accept the printed web version as readily as traditional offline coupons. Some traditional grocery stores deliver coupons weekly by email to customers who willingly provide their email address. Just as offline coupons are susceptible to fraud, the same is a growing problem with online coupons. Some grocery chains have suspended acceptance of printed online coupons until effective security measures can be implemented to discourage coupon fraud.

The first attempts at Internet marketing on the Web in 1993 generally were sites offering static electronic versions of printed marketing brochures. The sites were

Intranet
A proprietary computer network that operates like the Internet, using TCP/IP protocols, but is closed to outside users and typically restricted to employees and approved visitors.

Extranet
A proprietary computer network that links several intranets and users.

virtual billboards for companies testing the new environment. Business sites typically encouraged visitors to go offline and contact a company sales representative by telephone or fax. They offered information but were not interactive.

Next to appear were storefronts and malls that tried to re-create land-based retail stores in the virtual environment. Some were interactive, and customers could send email to the company, comment on products, search online catalogs, and even participate in online surveys, but not purchase products online. Today, most brochure sites and many malls have disappeared, often replaced by transaction sites that offer information, are interactive, and sell products. These sites take advantage of the Web's unique characteristics and offer dynamic, engaging, constantly changing content.

Dot-com
Originally, any clicks-only online business with a .com in its domain name.

Amazon.com (*www.amazon.com*) was launched in 1995, along with many other **dot-com** businesses, trying to figure out how to grab part of the online market and be profitable. Originally, a dot-com referred to businesses that were solely online without an offline store, production facility, or office. Today, the term more broadly means the online operation of a clicks-only or bricks-and-clicks enterprise. A boom period continued from 1995 through late 1999, when all sizes and types of enterprises went online. Old-line brick-and-mortar retailers such as Wal-Mart (*www.walmart.com*) adopted dual distribution strategies, using their websites as complements to retail store sales. Others, such as Nordstrom (*www.nordstrom.com*) and J.C. Penney (*www2.jcpenney.com*), expanded into multichannel distribution using a website to complement both catalog and in-store sales. At the same time, the business-to-business (B2B) market expanded online. Businesses began selling products to one another, forming strategic online alliances, sharing databases, creating buying groups and trading exchanges, hiring employees from web résumé sites, and using the Web for in-house and outsourced employee training.

By late 1999 to early 2000, a brutal retrenchment began that ultimately forced many dot-coms out of business, while others scrambled to create profitable business models and find financial backing. Between January 2000 and October 2001, an estimated seven hundred mostly consumer-oriented dot-coms shut down. Even though this period marked the end of the Internet bubble, a period of wild speculation and inflated expectations, some dot-coms managed to find financing and profit. This type of cycle is not unprecedented; it has happened before in U.S. business history. Procter & Gamble began operating in the middle of the 1837 economic panic; 3M, General Motors, IBM, Sun Microsystems, Microsoft, and General Electric all started up during recessions. A period of rapid economic expansion makes it easier to find financing, even by companies lacking a sound business model. A period of economic downturn makes it imperative that a business manage its resources wisely, which can impose the discipline needed for sustainability.[2]

Terrorist attacks on September 11, 2001, in New York, Washington, D.C., and Pennsylvania dealt a blow to the U.S. economy and sounded the death knell for many fragile dot-coms. Others gained customers who feared crowded malls and sought safe shopping online. Immediately after the attacks, U.S. stock exchange activity was halted, most television and Internet advertising was suspended, web news sites were overwhelmed by visitors, some businesses closed, and the nation and much of the world viewed unfolding events amid rising anxiety, anger, and grief. An economy already in recession was further weakened. In subsequent weeks, unemployment rose, consumer confidence fell, and businesses struggled. Despite the uncertainty and faltering economy, there were bright spots. Forrester Research (*www.forrester.com*) and Jupiter Media Metrix (*www.jupiter.com*) stuck by estimates of an 11 percent increase in 2001 holiday spending online over 2000 spending. It forecast that many consumers would send gifts rather than travel over the holidays and that many gifts would be purchased online rather than in malls. Surprisingly, Forrester's online retail sales tracking service reported that even during the national emergency, people still shopped online. Between the time of the attacks and the next evening, over US$96 million in online sales were recorded. Within a short time after September 11, consumers and enterprises began returning to more normal online activities. Although growth forecasts were dampened, the survival of Internet commerce was never in doubt.[3]

Short-term disruptions, no matter how tragic or frightful, cannot stop the Internet's expansion or stem its increasing impact on business and society. In its short commercial history, people and enterprises have become dependent on its facilitation of communication, information, entertainment, community building, learning, and purchasing. The resilience and depth of the Internet economy, and increasing consumer and business dependence on it, underscore its essential role in contemporary life.

ELECTRONIC COMMERCE

Electronic commerce existed before the Web, primarily through Electronic Data Interchange (EDI)—that is, the B2B exchange of data over *proprietary* computer networks, email, and fax. EDI continues to be an important facilitator of B2B exchanges. However, the Web is the driving force of Internet commercialization and is where most consumer commerce and an increasing volume of business commerce occurs. Electronic commerce has many names, including **ecommerce,** ebusiness, web commerce, and etailing (electronic retailing). It is business activities conducted via the Internet, the World Wide Web, and other services such as email, and on intranets and extranets, by enterprises and consumers. It includes business transactions, information sharing, business relationship management, and the creation of online communities. Internet marketing is an important part of ecommerce.

Ecommerce
Business activities conducted on the Internet, the Web, and other networked electronic systems. Also known as ebusiness, web commerce, and etailing.

Links to the Internet's Past

It is good advice to look to the future, yet learn from the past. Many events, inventions, and discoveries from the past contributed knowledge and processes essential to the creation of the Internet and its commercialization (Figure 1-1). Changes happened slowly at first, thousands of years ago in isolated human communities. Later they spread across continents, triggering advances in how people lived and worked and in how societies and economies functioned. They led to major economic transitions, from subsistence agriculture practiced by nonindustrial farming societies, to industrialization and modern manufacturing in the nineteenth century, service economies in the twentieth century, and information economies in the twenty-first. Parallels can be found between what happened historically, what is happening today, and what may happen in the future. The constant is humankind's enduring need to

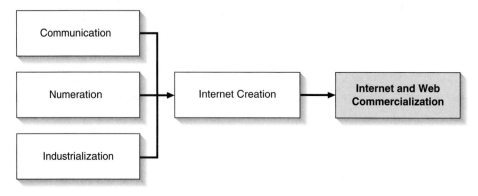

FIGURE 1-1 Historical Triggers
Human advances in communication, numeration, and industrialization triggered changes that created a need for marketing and for the development of knowledge that led to the Internet. People sought ways to communicate and share quantitative concepts, as well as to make work and life easier through mechanization.

communicate, numerate, and use machines to save labor and expand human potential. Historical events that triggered changes in business and society were responsible for the development of a need for marketing. If these changes had not occurred, marketing as we know it today wouldn't exist, and there would be no need for Internet marketing courses.

COMMUNICATION LINKS

Written communication is a fundamental human activity with an ancient history. Primitive people made cave drawings to depict incidents in their lives. The ancient Egyptians around 3000 B.C. created hieroglyphics: symbols and pictographs scratched or carved on stone walls and tablets.[4]

The Chinese compiled the earliest printed book around A.D. 868 but kept their invention secret for almost 900 years. The Egyptians developed papyrus rolls for writing in A.D. 800 to 900. Papyrus added mobility, and these rolls became the primary writing material for much of the known world. The word *papyrus* eventually evolved into the English word *paper*.[5] Today, popular writers sell digital books on the Internet that readers pay for electronically and then download and store them or print them from their own computers. Although some observers predicted that computers and the Internet would lead to a paperless world, that certainly has not happened thus far. Most people cling to the use of paper, preferring to print electronic files rather than read them online. Web retailers encourage customers to print order confirmations on paper, acknowledging the persistent desire of customers for tangible written proof of their purchase. Web content providers offer pages specially formatted for printing to accommodate those who dislike reading text directly from a computer screen, and inventors are still working hard to develop an acceptable device for reading digital text.

THE FIRST INFORMATION REVOLUTION

From the fourth through the fifteenth centuries, very few people other than clerics and nobles could read or write. Beautifully illustrated religious manuscripts were printed entirely by hand, laboriously copied letter by letter. The invention of the printing press that employed movable type, by Johann Gutenberg (c. 1398–1468) in Mainz, Germany, about A.D. 1445, triggered the first information revolution; the Internet triggered the second. Gutenberg's hand-powered press was modeled after a winepress, a clever adaptation of existing technology. Ink was rolled over the raised surfaces of handset letters and then pressed against a sheet of paper, parchment, or vellum. Some artisans continue to make hand-pressed books today, illustrating that old technologies can profitably survive in niche markets even when the mass-market technology has moved on.[6]

The mechanical press made it possible to print many copies of a manuscript relatively quickly, at an affordable price. Once books became more widely available, it grew popular and even fashionable for people to own them. An unexpected consequence was the dramatic increase in literacy rates and the creation of public libraries. Within thirty years, printed materials spread across Europe as the *divine art* of printing helped transform society. Printing was a driving force for the Renaissance, a period when learning, creativity, and artistry were valued and widely disseminated. Illiteracy was still common, but now ideas and information could be recorded and rapidly distributed among the increasingly more literate population. The dissemination of ideas prompted challenges to established organizations, religions, opinions, and practices. The pace of change in the sixteenth century was probably as breathtaking to scholars of that time as Internet-prompted changes are to us today.

From the mid-1400s until the late 1800s, few improvements were made to the basic Gutenberg press. It wasn't until 1874 that the first commercial typewriter was manufactured. Typewriters were ubiquitous in offices for more than a hundred years, until computers and printers began to replace but not entirely eliminate them.

INDUSTRIAL LINKS

Subsistence farming societies didn't need marketing. Primitive marketing began when product surpluses became routine and had to be reduced or eliminated. Prior to the mid-eighteenth century, economies were based primarily on agriculture, commerce, or small-scale labor-intensive manufacturing. Inventions during two industrial revolutions led to large-scale, mechanized manufacturing, and modern industries were born, along with modern marketing. British and U.S. inventions drove these revolutions, but the effects were felt worldwide.

The first industrial revolution began in Britain in the early 1700s. The second began in the United States after the Civil War and lasted until the early years of the twentieth century. Inventions revolutionized how products were made and how people worked and lived. Prices and costs dropped while output soared, and many unskilled laborers lost their jobs.[7]

The second industrial revolution (1875–1903) was dominated by inventions in the United States, particularly in electricity and chemicals. Inventions simplified long-distance communication and accelerated information dissemination, much as the Internet does today.

Industrialization had a negative side. Factories needed cheap, unskilled labor, and machine power meant that women and children could do work formerly reserved for men. As a result, many men lost their jobs to machines, and women and children were often exploited and forced to work under terrible conditions. Most factory workers endured squalid living accommodations in overcrowded cities. Disease, poverty, pollution, and lack of sanitation were unremitting.

Luddites
Laborers in England and the eastern United States in the early 1800s who protested industrialization.

Luddites were one group that opposed industrialization and rapid changes in society. They were named for a perhaps mythical textile worker, Ned Ludd, who reputedly dropped a hammer in a steam-powered textile machine to protest the loss of jobs to machines. For fifteen months from 1811 to 1812, these bands of English workers, fearful of losing their livelihoods, resisted the mechanization of the mills. Their revolt spread to the United States, where the execution of seventeen people in 1813 for violent protests essentially put an end to Luddite activities.[8]

Like the Luddites, some people today fear the Internet, believing it to be a threat to society, human interaction and civility, and traditional values. They protest such activities as online gambling and pornography, and they warn against the social isolation and possible addiction that comes with excessive Internet use. Sometimes referred to as neo-Luddites, their numbers are not large but their concerns merit consideration.

NUMERACY AND COMPUTER LINKS

Like written communication and industrialization, advances in numeracy contributed to the creation of computers and the Internet. Numeracy, or counting, began as primitive people developed a capacity for thinking quantitatively and expressing the results in numeric form. The abacus, a simple hand-operated counting machine, was first introduced in Babylonia (present-day Iraq) between 3000 and 2000 B.C. This earliest mobile mechanical counting device is still in use today. Almost 4,000 years passed before a reliable computing engine run by gears and wheels was proposed by Charles Babbage (1792–1871). Babbage is often called the father of modern computers for his model of a digital "analytical engine" designed to calculate Bernoulli numbers. This machine is considered the precursor to the modern digital computer. If Babbage's engine had been manufactured, it would have run on a plan written by Ada Byron, Countess of Lovelace (1815–1852), daughter of the poet George Gordon, Lord Byron. This was the first computer program, and Ada Byron was history's first computer programmer. In 1979, a programming language used on U.S. Department of Defense mainframe computers was named Ada in her honor.[9]

One of the first practical applications of labor-saving computer-like devices was Herman Hollerith's (1860–1929) system for recording and organizing data using a machine that sensed holes punched in cards.[10] His tabulation machine system, which later included card-feeding, -adding, and -sorting processes, revolutionized statistical computation. Hollerith's device was used to help analyze 1880 U.S. census data and saved the government two years and US$5 million, a very tidy sum in those days. Hollerith's Tabulating Machine Company evolved into the company that in 1924 changed its name to International Business Machines Corporation (IBM).

The world's first practical large-scale electronic digital computer was activated at the University of Pennsylvania in 1945. ENIAC (Electronic Numerical Integrator Analyzer and Computer) was originally designed to prepare firing and bombing tables for U.S. Army artillery in World War II. ENIAC was a monster. It had 19,000 vacuum tubes in 30 separate units, weighed over 30 tons, stood 10 feet tall, and was 150 feet wide. Six women acted as human computers, flipping ENIAC's switches and checking its settings. They were its software and its software engineers.[11]

Despite its vast size, ENIAC had less computing power than today's personal desktop computer. However, it was the first step in the development of the modern digital computing industry. Other important computer advances quickly followed.

Links to the Internet's Present

It has been over 550 years since Gutenberg invented the printing press that employed movable type. Great changes have marked the intervening centuries, including a huge increase in the world's population. The entire population of the known world in the 1400s was only 100 million more than the population of the United States in the 1990s. By the 1700s, world population had doubled to around 680 million; by the mid-1800s, it had increased to approximately 1 billion. At the birth of the Internet in 1969, the world population was around 3 billion. Today, it is estimated at over 6.4 billion.[12]

Another change is the availability and use of more channels for mass and interpersonal communication. By the 1930s, large numbers of people in the United States and other industrialized nations could read and write, as well as listen to radio, talk on a telephone, teletype messages, and (by 1939 in the United States) watch television. Today, people worldwide use the Internet as a multimedia communication channel to make telephone calls, listen to radio, download music and movies, watch television, video conference, fax messages, and send and receive email.

Innovations in the twenty-first century diffused rapidly within countries and across the world, spread by mass communication and transportation. Inventions from the first industrial revolution diffused slowly by today's standards and unevenly. Between 150 and 200 years passed before steam engines spread throughout Britain, France, Germany, the United States, and parts of Asia; the automobile took 40 to 50 years to diffuse, vacuum tubes about 25 to 30 years, and the transistor only 15 years.[13]

The same acceleration occurred in the **diffusion** of innovations in communication. The second information revolution (the Internet revolution) is diffusing far faster than the first (Table 1-1). Within five years of its release, the World Wide Web had spread

Diffusion
The process by which people adopt innovations, new products, and different ways of doing things.

Table 1-1 Technology Diffusion Rates in the United States[14]	
Invention	**Years to Reach Adoption by Fifty Million People**
Radio	38
Television	13
Personal Computer	16
Internet	5

around the world. People who were unaware of its existence in 1991–1992 were using it five years later to shop, learn, play, communicate, and work.

Another factor affecting the rate of Internet adoption is Moore's Law, which was articulated by Intel's Gordon Moore in 1965 and has so far held true. Moore's Law states that computing power (the amount of information stored on a chip) doubles every 18 to 24 months. This means that computers can steadily be made more powerful and cheaper, which increases the probability of finding commercial applications for new technologies such as artificial intelligence and virtual reality. Increased computational power lowers transistor and computer prices. Inexpensive computers and Internet-ready devices widen Internet accessibility and speed adoption (diffusion) worldwide. Escalating computational power also lowers prices for handheld devices, DVD players, smart appliances, digital cameras, PlayStations, and a myriad of other products. Advances in computer storage, graphics, and networking are occurring even more rapidly than Moore's Law predicts. Researchers at Intel and other companies are dedicated to reducing barriers to Moore's Law to ensure that it will continue to hold true in the years ahead.[15]

THE COLD WAR

Initial funding to support research on Internet feasibility was a direct result of cold war fears. The cold war began at the end of World War II and is often traced to a meeting at Yalta in 1945 between U.S. President Franklin D. Roosevelt, British Prime Minister Winston Churchill, and Secretary General of the Soviet Communist Party (USSR) Josef Stalin. The three signed agreements that many believe made overly generous concessions to the Soviet Union, in particular allowing them to achieve political and economic control (hegemony) over Eastern Europe.[16]

Growing mistrust between the United States and the USSR led to a nuclear and conventional arms race and to a period of apprehension and verbal rancor that lasted until the fall of the Berlin Wall and breakup of the Soviet Union in 1991.

During the forty-six years that the cold war lasted, both superpowers feared a nuclear attack by the other. The successful launch by the Soviets of the first Earth-orbiting artificial satellite, *Sputnik I*, on October 4, 1957, caught the United States off guard. The USSR was assumed to have the technical capacity to hit U.S. targets with nuclear missiles. Responding to national fears, then Senator Lyndon Johnson warned that the Soviets had jumped ahead of the United States in the space race and stated, "Soon, they will be dropping bombs on us from space like kids dropping rocks onto cars from freeway overpasses!"[17]

ARPA AND DARPA

Advanced Research Projects Agency
An agency that funded the ARPANet (Network), what has been called the first Internet.

It is popularly thought that the U.S. Department of Defense reacted to *Sputnik I* by forming the Advanced Research Projects Agency (**ARPA**) in 1958 to create a national nuclear-proof communication network (**ARPANet**). A broader and more accurate view is that ARPA's goal was for the military to fund research activities so that the United States could regain the lead in science and technology from the Soviets.[18] This included finding a way for scientists to share scarce computer resources. ARPA initiated and funded a monumental research effort to develop a way for geographically

ARPANet by 1971

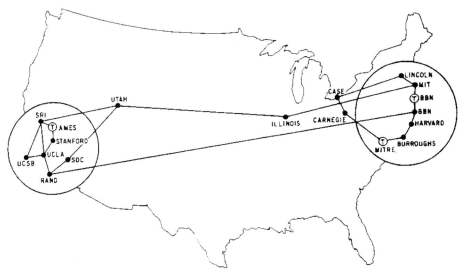

MAP 4   September 1971

Source: Salus, CASTING THE NET: FROM ARPANET TO INTERNET AND BEYOND, © 1995 Addison-Wesley Publishing Company, Inc. Reprinted by permission of Pearson Education, Inc. Publishing as Pearson Addison Wesley. http://www.cybergeography.org/atlas/arpanet3.gif accessed 10/03.

separated computers to communicate over telephone lines using a common operating standard called the Network Control Protocol (NCP). The outcome was ARPANet, a wide-area, packet-switching, resource-sharing communication network.

By 1969, four peer computer nodes located at the University of California Los Angeles (UCLA), Stanford Research Institute (SRI), the University of California Santa Barbara (UCSB), and the University of Utah were ready to be linked. UCLA's computers were the first to initiate a host-to-host data exchange. Ironically, when the UCLA researchers attempted a login with the SRI computers, someone accidentally typed in *log win* rather than login, which crashed UCLA's computers.[19] Computer crashes continue to plague users four decades later.

Within two years, a small network matrix of fifteen nodes connected twenty-three host computers at universities, the National Aeronautics and Space Administration (NASA), and research facilities around the United States. In 1972, ARPA was renamed the Defense Advanced Research Projects Agency (DARPA). That same year, the Internet went international with network connections through undersea Atlantic Ocean telephone cables linking the United States to University College of London, England, and the Royal Radar Establishment in Norway. The National Science Foundation (NSF) was also working on ways to connect supercomputers for academic research purposes through a reliable high-speed network **backbone.** NSF initiatives led to the development in 1986 of NSFNet, a major component of today's Internet.

The U.S. government funded many Internet-related inventions, including electronic mail (email). In late 1971, Ray Tomlinson, a computer engineer working for an

Backbone
The Internet's largest transmission lines that handle its major traffic flows.

ARPANet contractor, invented email, whose eventual importance even he didn't recognize. Email has been the single largest Internet service for more than a decade. Today, email marketing is a profitable area of online marketing.

ESTABLISHING STANDARDS: TCP/IP

TCP/IP Transmission Control Protocol/ Internet Protocol
Standards for data packet transmission on the Internet.

Several other important events rounded out the 1970s. In 1974, Vinton Cerf at SRI and DARPA's Robert Kahn proposed the system for addressing and forwarding data packets (Internet Protocol, or IP) and the flow control system (Transmission Control Protocol, or TCP). **TCP/IP** protocols became the common communication operating standards and rules for the Internet in 1983. Since January 1, 1983, traffic and services operating on the Internet matrix must voluntarily agree to use TCP/IP communication protocols. Because Internet-connected computers use TCP/IP, they can *talk* to one another, whatever their operating system or computer type. The Internet's birth date is often officially cited as 1983, when the TCP/IP protocols and standardization were adopted. However, a strong case can be made that it should be that day in 1969 when the first four computer networks were linked.

Civilian interest in the Internet in the 1980s accelerated as the matrix of networked computers grew beyond the research community to include public and commercial activity. In 1986, NSF opened its previously restricted NSFNet backbone to all users. By 1987, the number of Internet hosts had grown to over ten thousand.[20] Traffic increasingly moved onto the NSFNet, and in 1990, ARPANet ceased to exist.

THE WORLD WIDE WEB

Hypertext
Formatting language for creating web pages. Also known as HTML (HyperText Markup Language).

Browser
Web hypermedia application software that enables the user to view and retrieve WWW sites.

The Internet captured the public's imagination in the 1990s as its growth accelerated exponentially, but it was still only a text-based environment. Winter 1991–1992 is a key date in the Internet's commercial development. Sir Tim Berners-Lee, an English researcher, was working at the European Particle Physics Laboratory (CERN) in Switzerland in the late 1980s. A need to find information quickly prompted him to write a program that linked keywords to search for and retrieve information stored in computer files. His program, *Enquire,* was later expanded to handle finding and retrieving information in the CERN laboratory computers. This led to the design of a **hypertext**-linked information retrieval system called the World Wide Web. In December 1991, CERN's newsletter announced the Web's creation. Although hypertext was an Apple Macintosh innovation, Berners-Lee contributed the concept of an interconnected, user-friendly, global computer network accessible by anyone through a **browser** interface. He joined hypertext with the Internet's global matrix of networked computers in a hypermedia system. On June 30, 1993, CERN declared that WWW technology would be open (free to the public) and not proprietary.[21]

The Web is only one of many services that operate on the Internet matrix. It is the first global hypermedia sector (Table 1-2) and is where most Internet commercial activity and marketing occur. Users access the Web with a graphical browser (such as Internet Explorer, Netscape Navigator, Opera, or AOL) and then enjoy an easy

Table 1-2 Advantages of a Hypermedia System	
Open	An open system allows linking and data transfers to computer servers located across the hall or across the world in a matter of seconds by computers with different operating systems.
Interactive	Allows a user instant access to key words or topics within a document file, on different pages, or on different servers.
Dynamic	Changes can be made quickly on pages and sites; expansion is easy.
Media-rich	It is multisensory, supporting the use of text, graphics, animation, sound, and video on the same page and/or site.

point-and-click interface that simplifies navigation. Once the Web was released, the pace of Internet adoption increased dramatically, and many new milestones were reached.

Current Internet Indicators and the Future

The researchers who networked the first four computers in 1969 certainly did not envision commercialization in the Internet's future. However, within ten years of the release of the World Wide Web, the Internet had already made a significant impact on business and society in North America, Europe, and parts of Asia and South America. It had profoundly affected countries with high Internet adoption rates and countries where adoption was just beginning. Today's Internet economy is creating new jobs and transforming old ones. Internet use is changing how many people communicate, shop, play, work, and learn. It is also progressing unevenly with mixed results. Some businesses have already found ways to exploit the Internet successfully, whereas others are just beginning to move their business processes online. Initial predictions were that the Internet would transform business and marketing, making traditional methods obsolete. But although some sectors *are* threatened (for example, traditional travel agents), the extent of transformation has not been as drastic as forecast. Likewise, predictions of the death of all dot-com businesses during the economic downturn and 2001 recession were equally exaggerated. Businesses are adjusting to the Internet, and growing evidence suggests that the transformation is gathering steam and profitability is becoming more widespread.

INTERNET ECONOMY INDICATORS

The contribution of business activities in the ecommerce sector to U.S. gross domestic product (GDP) is still relatively small compared to the entire U.S. economy of over US$10.98 trillion (2003 estimate).[22] However, it is increasing in all sectors (Table 1-3) and, after only a decade of commercialization, represents around 10.6 percent of total U.S. GDP. B2B commerce continues to dominate, contributing between 93 to 95 percent of total ecommerce activity. This includes sales in the manufacturing and wholesale trade sectors, areas that were already heavily invested in EDI electronic

Table 1-3 Internet Economy Indicators 2002[23]

Sector	Percent of Total Sector Sales	Value (US$ billions)	Increase over 2001 Sales	Dominant Industries
Manufacturing	19.6%	$752	3.8%	Transportation equipment; beverages; tobacco; electrical equipment
Merchant wholesale trade	11.7%	320	12%	Drugs, druggist sundries; motor vehicles, parts, supplies; professional equipment and supplies
Selected service industries	0.9%	41	15%	Travel arrangements and reservations; securities and commodity contracts, brokerage; publishing; computer systems design
Retail trade	1.4	44	29	Nonstore retailers (catalog, mail-order, clicks-only retailers); motor vehicles and parts—top sellers are computer hardware, clothing and accessories, books and magazines

ordering systems. Consumer transactions are represented by services and retail trade. Each sector is dominated by a relatively small number of key players.

According to the Center for Research in Electronic Commerce at the University of Texas at Austin (UT), sales and marketing jobs have generated more Internet-related employment in the United States than other jobs, including those in information technology. In 2000, the Internet economy directly supported over four million workers, up from two million in 1999. These jobs were either newly created by Internet activity or shifted to the Internet when companies recognized the benefits of online operations. At that time, Internet commerce was the single largest area of job growth in the Internet economy.[24]

Although many jobs were lost because of the recession and sharp economic downturn in late 1999 through 2001 and immediately after 9/11/01, a recovery will increase hiring and new job growth, particularly as Internet use expands worldwide.

Several impediments are holding back growth in the consumer sector, in particular slow Internet access and security concerns. The problem of slow access is being resolved as more people sign up for faster connection alternatives when they become available. Security concerns are also lessening as more consumers report positive experiences with online shopping and as retailers strengthen security systems. Also encouraging is a Harvard University study reporting that most Americans have positive beliefs about the Internet and technology. This study concludes that the number of people using the Internet is likely to double or triple within ten years and that more people online will mean more sales.[25]

The status of the Internet economy in other parts of the world is mixed. Because data are collected using a variety of methods and different sample sizes, figures must be cautiously interpreted. However, all indicators are upward sloping, which

WEB UPDATE

For updates and
more on this topic,
visit the textbook
student website at:
http://college.hmco
.com/business/students
and select Siegel,
Internet Marketing, 2e.
**Internet Economy
  Indicators**

indicates growing use of the Internet worldwide and greater enterprise and consumer spending. For example, in Western Europe, paid online content revenue increased from £361 million (US$407 million) in 2002 to £544 million (US$614 million) in 2003 and is projected to rise to £2,366 million (US$2,670 million) by 2007. This amount is still small, but spending estimates thus far have proved far too conservative. Consumers in Europe are spending more online, an average £430 (US$485) per person compared to an average US$613 (£543) per person in the United States. Worldwide B2B revenues passed US$1.4 trillion in 2003 and US$2.7 trillion in 2004. In Australia, B2B ecommerce is growing about 33 percent per year, faster than projected, and represents more than 70 percent of all Australian online commerce revenues. Over 80 percent of all Japanese households are online, as are 79 percent of all businesses. The Internet economy, especially consumer sales, is growing more slowly in Africa, parts of Asia, and most of South America.[26]

INTERNET BUSINESS ADVANTAGES

It took over 550 years to get from Gutenberg to the Web but less than 10 years for the Internet economy to become an important economic factor in the United States and other countries. It is difficult to predict where the Internet is going, but it is triggering changes more rapidly than has any human invention in the past. The Internet provides opportunities for the development of new business models, companies, financing arrangements, corporate structures, and competitive relationships. For an established bricks-and-clicks business, the Internet opens a new channel of distribution, adds to its retail store and catalog sales, reaches buyers in other countries, and better serves its corporate clients. Many businesses have gone online to find new members of their marketing channels—suppliers, buyers, warehouses, retailers, or transport companies. Others are using the Internet to create buying groups or communities of businesses in the same industry. Some of these relationships are unique and probably could not have come into being without the Internet or a comparable electronic environment. The Internet simplifies communication and allows enterprises to create multifunctional teams of employees physically distant from one another.

Do all businesses belong online? Certainly not, but businesses that fail to have an online presence risk losing out to competitors who aggressively exploit the Internet's advantages (Table 1-4).

Are there disadvantages to being online? Absolutely. Many businesses that rushed to be the first online and were undercapitalized, had weak business models, were not committed to customer service, were poorly managed, or couldn't generate profits have been driven into bankruptcy, have merged with other firms, or have been acquired. Some businesses haven't figured out how to drive consumers to their websites, convert them into customers, and retain them. Others have failed because they lacked an order fulfillment infrastructure to support online sales. Some have experienced costly security failures or have failed to guarantee and protect consumer privacy. Many B2B exchanges failed because they couldn't generate a critical mass of participants.

Table 1-4 Business Advantages of Going Online	
Access	As more buyers go online, businesses with an Internet presence can enlarge their customer base. It is still early in the Internet's commercial history, and over 5 billion people are *not* online. Most of them will not go online in the immediate future, but those who do could become desirable customers.
Worldwide Exposure	Once a business goes online, it is an international business. This exposes buyers worldwide to the business's product offers. A business may choose not to engage in international marketing online, but for many it will be their best opportunity to attract international buyers.
Speed	Buyers can find products quickly and order online; some products can be delivered instantly online, others within twenty-four hours or less. Online ordering can significantly reduce ordering costs. This is a competitive advantage for Internet sellers.
Pricing Transparency	Comparison pricing can be conducted by the buyer independently or at a shopping site such as MySimon.com (*www.mysimon.com*) that searches the Web for products and retrieves pricing information. Pricing can become almost transparent since it is relatively easy to collect information. This is an advantage for businesses shopping online for raw materials, supplies, and parts. It is also a force that could keep prices competitive.
Reduced Inventory Costs	Online ordering in real time means that inventory holding costs can be reduced and that in many product categories, products can be made to order and delivered just in time (JIT), which eliminates holding costs. Extranets can be used to signal suppliers electronically when reorders are needed, which reduces inventory holding costs for buyer and seller.
Reduced Intermediary Costs	The elimination of intermediaries (*disintermediation*) is impractical for any tangible products that still must be transported from online seller to offline buyer. However, if customers buy directly online from a manufacturer, savings can result from the (potential) elimination of some intermediaries (wholesalers and retailers).
Reduced Supply Costs	Businesses can obtain supplies, materials, and parts faster online and often far cheaper than by traditional methods (see pricing transparency). Online businesses can join buying pools where demand is aggregated and group buying achieves lower prices.
Customer Satisfaction	Products that were mass-merchandized in the past can be customized through one-to-one online relationships with buyers. Mass customer support can be provided online. Businesses that satisfy their customers should have a competitive advantage. Better customer relationships can also improve B2B channel efficiency.

SOCIETAL EFFECTS

Like most technologies, the Internet is both praised and vilified. It is credited with creating a second information revolution. It is condemned for fostering antisocial and addictive behaviors. Which view one subscribes to depends greatly on one's perspective. To Internet users in the United States and other developed countries, the positives far outweigh the negatives.

The Internet was invented in the United States, yet this country's 300 million people are under 5 percent of the total world population of 6.4 billion. This can be an advantage if it means billions of possible future buyers eager to purchase U.S. products online. However, U.S. online sellers, both B2B and B2C, must overcome barriers to reach these internationals and convert them into buyers. If the Internet is perceived as an American-dominated technology, it could increase nationalism and protectionism in countries where anti-American sentiment is strong. Even though the Internet is a worldwide network, not all people embrace it equally, nor will everyone equally enjoy its benefits.

The Internet has the potential to encourage freedom of expression and free-market capitalism in nations that are not now democratic or capitalistic. Whether one regards democracy and capitalism as desirable also depends on one's perspective. However, completely shutting off Internet access to discourage change has proved difficult for those governments that have tried. The free exchange of information and ideas online, and people's exposure to goods and services unavailable in their home countries may encourage political and economic dissent, which some governments rightly fear.[27]

Because the Internet is borderless, taxing online sales and regulating online activities are highly complicated. Jurisdiction and control are controversial issues with no easy solutions. Considerable debate continues over such online activities as gambling, visual pornography, marketing to children, fraud, and unregulated pharmaceutical sales that are allowed by some countries and banned by others.

The Internet is changing the way many professionals work. Telecommuting is facilitated through some Internet services, particularly email and web mail. Hotels and airports are catering to persons who must connect to the Internet even while traveling, providing high-speed access and Wi-Fi hubs. The Internet is creating new jobs in occupations that didn't exist ten years ago—for example, webmaster/webmistress (site administrator), website designer, vice president for Internet marketing, and Internet marketing sales manager.

Learning is undergoing revolutionary changes. Distance learning means new ways of attending classes and earning academic degrees. The number of ecommerce and Internet marketing classes and majors at U.S. universities is growing. The United States, with its highly regarded universities, will gain export revenues by offering classes and degrees worldwide on the Web. The University of Phoenix (*universityofphoenix.com*), an accredited post-secondary education institution, has online classes for traditional, military, and corporate students and caters to working adults. Companies spent over US$60 billion on employee training via the Internet, intranets, and/or extranets in 2000. Education content, a US$4 billion market, is just beginning to migrate online. The Internet increases the flexibility and breadth of education for students of all ages.[28]

Digital divides are a continuing concern. Minority groups, the poor, people living in rural areas and in countries where electricity is expensive or undependable, and other vulnerable groups are at risk of being excluded from Internet access. This could lead to further polarization within and between societies and groups of people. An alternative view holds that as prices fall for Internet devices and access, and wireless becomes more widespread, more people who might have been disenfranchised will go online. Survey data support this view.[29]

Just as the first industrial revolution had its Luddites, contemporary neo-Luddites are raising moral and ethical arguments against the excesses of modern technology. They fear that the Internet and related technologies threaten our essential humanity and sense of community, and they urge great caution in accepting them. Others censure the Internet for making visual pornography widely accessible, allowing the sale of merchandise to children, encouraging gambling, offering child predators a new avenue of attack, providing a forum for hate groups, facilitating the activities of terrorists, and giving people an opportunity to become so engrossed in the online world that they shortchange their families, fall victim to temptation, or isolate themselves from offline social relationships.

THEORIZING ABOUT THE FUTURE

Making predictions about the Internet's future is risky. However, some predictions are more plausible than others. For example, far from being in decline, as some futurists predicted for the turn of the century, the United States is in a strong position to continue to exploit the Internet and benefit from its promise. The United States will retain its advantage if domestic research and development continue to produce innovations that move the technology in new directions and if the government refrains from imposing ill-conceived, heavy-handed restrictions. Tomorrow's Internet will be different from today's, and some advances are already anticipated. Let's look briefly at a few of them.

Speed Faster and more stable Internet connections via broadband and enhanced speed of traditional dial-up connections

Wireless Widespread adoption of wireless Internet access devices and use of Wi-Fi hotspots

Security Software that reduces security concerns and filters out spam

Speech Speech commands to replace typed commands

Visualization Visualization, virtual reality, and even holographic images so that customers can "feel" products through a sensory-activated mouse

Jobs New types of jobs and occupations created by the expanding Internet economy

Barrier-free access Easier Internet access for people with disabilities, and reduction in digital divides

Enterprises and consumers will continue to drive the Internet's growth; serving their needs more effectively and efficiently will drive its evolution. Businesses want the Internet to lower operating costs and increase revenues (and profits). Universities want the Internet to recruit students, deliver courses and programs, encourage alumni giving, and disseminate positive information about their programs and faculty. Hospitals want the Internet to market their services to consumers and medical practitioners, lower procurement costs, and deliver health information to patients and clinicians. Governments want the Internet to reduce procurement costs, provide convenient services to citizens, disseminate information and promote responsible citizen behaviors, and (in a growing number of cases) lower voting costs through online registration and voting. Marketers want the Internet to provide access to new markets and new customer-pleasing products, drive customers to purchase either online or offline, and create exchanges in an environment where buyers and sellers both benefit.

Summary

http://college.hmco.com/business/students

Defining Marketing in the Internet Age

Internet marketing is marketing in electronic environments, primarily on the Internet, on one or more of its services, or in offline sectors involved with Internet-related activities. Both traditional and Internet marketing focus on exchange, relationship building, and providing value. They perform the same functions, and often the same businesses are involved offline and online. Ecommerce is business activities conducted in electronic environments, including online on the World Wide Web, but also on other Internet services, extranets, and intranets. These activities include Internet marketing.

Links to the Internet's Past

Developments in written communication began with cave drawings and progressed through more mobile forms, including hieroglyphics and hand-printing methods. The first information revolution dates from the invention of movable type around A.D. 1445; Gutenberg's mechanical press provided multiple copies of a manuscript quickly and at a price more people could afford, which encouraged the spread of literacy. Two industrial revolutions moved nations to large-scale machine-intensive manufacturing, and modern industries were born, along with the modern marketing that was needed to facilitate transactions and clear markets of excess products. Charles Babbage proposed the precursor of the modern electronic computer, a digital "analytical engine" that would have run on a plan written by Ada Byron. Herman Hollerith invented a system for recording and organizing data using cards with holes punched in

them. ENIAC I was the world's first practical all-electronic, large-scale, general-purpose computer.

Links to the Internet's Present

The Internet's initial development is linked to the cold war, which began at the end of World War II. ARPANet was the first Internet. In 1983, a date often taken to mark the Internet's birth, the TCP/IP protocols were accepted as the communication operating standard for the Internet. Because all Internet-connected computers use TCP/IP, they can exchange data even if they use different operating systems. Sir Tim Berners-Lee at CERN created the World Wide Web; CERN released it as open software in the winter of 1991–1992. The Web and graphical browsers facilitated the development of Internet commercialization.

Current Internet Indicators and the Future

The Internet economy includes all activities related to the Internet that contribute to a nation's economy, often measured in terms of its gross domestic product (GDP). Internet economy sectors include manufacturing and wholesale trade (B2B sector), and services and retail (B2C sector). B2B continues to dominate Internet revenues. Businesses and other enterprises can profit from being online and can also suffer online problems. The Internet's effects on society will be felt in such areas as trade, expansion of freedom of speech and business activities, problems with taxation and regulation, encouragement of "portable professionals," revolutions in distance learning, digital divides, and neo-Luddite expressions of concern.

Take Action!

Let's assume that you have been hired by Google (*www.google.com*) and your job is to market the company's licensed software to universities in your area.

1. Carefully read about Google's Search Appliance (*www.google.com/appliance*) and construct a FAB matrix based on what you have learned. A FAB matrix is a table that identifies a product's features, attributes, and benefits. Features are listed at *www.google.com/appliance/features.html*. For example, one *feature* of Google's Search Appliance is that retrieved links can be viewed as HTML documents. The *attribute* of this feature (its characteristic) is that even if the original document is not in HTML, it will be reformatted automatically to HTML. The *benefit* (value to users) is that they can get a quick look at the document to see whether it is what they want without having to launch the original application, which can slow their search. Construct a table of five key features with their attributes and benefits. Keep your focus on marketing the product to universities, the target market.

2. Visit the list of Google's customers (*www.google.com/appliance/customers.html*) and select several that might help convince members of your target market that they should license Google's search product. Construct a table of Google's key customers, in which you identify their business type and cite relevant statements in their testimonials.

3. Write a fax to send to your target market. In the cover letter, highlight five key selling points based on what you have learned about Google's Search Appliance, its customers, and your market's needs. State that you are including the FAB matrix and customer list in the fax transmission. Consider how a fax differs from a telephone or face-to-face cold call. Identify advantages and disadvantages of a fax sales contact. Prepare a short email to your boss at Google in which you discuss the pros and cons of using a fax as a sales tool and make recommendations about using this method effectively.

Chapter Review Questions

1. Why is Google so popular? How can it maintain its competitive advantage?
2. How are traditional marketing and Internet marketing alike?
3. Why did some people fear industrialization during the first industrial revolution? Why do some people today fear the Internet?
4. What might have happened to Internet development if CERN had made the World Wide Web proprietary?
5. How was the effect of papyrus and the printing press on written communication similar to that of the steam engine on manufacturing and the economy during the first industrial revolution? Do you think the Internet will have equally sweeping effects? Explain.
6. Why did tiny *Sputnik I* cause such fear in the United States?
7. Why is it still important that all computers and devices connected to the Internet use TCP/IP?
8. What are the four sectors of the Internet economy? Which are business sectors, and which are consumer sectors? In what sector does Amazon.com operate?
9. What risks are associated with ecommerce?

10. Are all businesses experiencing the same level of benefits from the Internet?
11. How is the Internet potentially a force for democracy and free markets?
12. Explain why events that happened hundreds and even thousands of years ago contributed to the eventual creation of the Internet.
13. How can the United States export higher education?
14. Why is the United States expected to continue to lead the Internet revolution?
15. Do you think the Internet is revolutionary or evolutionary? Why should it matter? Explain your answer.

Competitive Case Study

Competing with Google

What exactly is a search engine? Generally, a search engine is a site that uses software to search the Web and retrieve pages that are indexed and stored in the engine's databases. When a user enters a request for information (a query) at the search engine site, the keywords are matched against the engine's keyword indexes. The best matches are returned to the user's browser and displayed on the user's screen, along with the page address and (typically) a very short description of page contents. Some engines search for content rather than keywords.

How important are search engines to Internet marketing? Surveys of web users consistently show that search engines are the top method for finding new websites. For the majority of users, they're essential to finding information in the growing clutter of web pages. Search engine marketing and the use of sponsored links is currently one of the hottest areas of Internet marketing promotion. Revenues from paid searches topped US$1.6 billion in 2003. This was 25 percent of all spending on online advertising, up from only 10 percent in 2001.

Search engines can be compared on a number of dimensions, including technology used, market share, number of pages indexed, speed, number of dead links, inconsistencies (search inaccuracies), comprehensiveness of results, usability, page freshness, time spent on site, and relevance of results. Measures are not available for all these dimensions, but those that are available and current indicate clearly that Google is staying ahead of the competition. For example, by May 2004, Google's global usage share topped 56.4 percent, trailed by Yahoo! (22.1 percent—*www.yahoo.com*), MSN Search (9.2 percent—*www.msn.com*), AOL Search (3.8 percent—*www.aol.com*), Terra Lycos (2.0 percent—*www.lycos.com*), and Altavista (1.7 percent—*www.altavista.com*).

Google also leads in the usage share of U.S. users. Its 32 percent of U.S. usage share leads Yahoo! (25 percent), AOL (19 percent), and MSN (15 percent). Even more striking, when share is computed in terms of the percent of searches actually powered by Google on its own site or licensed to other sites, its usage share is 76 percent of the U.S. audience!

Since 2001, Google has led the competition in the number of hits (pages) returned for searches. It also leads in pages indexed, at over 8 billion. Although bigger isn't necessarily always better, a larger number of indexed pages can increase the probability of finding the right information by widening the pool of sources searched.

Freshness is important to searchers because old, stale pages often provide less valuable information sources or lead to dead links. Fresher pages are less likely to contain errors or to misdirect users. MSN and HotBot, which both use Inktomi, have the freshest pages, followed by Google, AlltheWeb, Altavista, and Teoma.

Average time spent on a site in a month matters to advertisers, because a longer visit increases visitor exposure to sponsored links. It is also an indicator of a site's popularity. AOL users spend more time on the site (an average of 38 minutes), which is understandable because AOL is a multifunctional site that includes shopping, email, and other services along with search. Next are Google (28 minutes), InfoSpace (11 minutes), and Yahoo! (11 minutes).

Can Google maintain its competitive advantage? If its past performance is any indicator of its future, Google should continue to lead in innovation and customer satisfaction. However, no Internet company can rest on its laurels. The competition is ferocious, and technological advances could make Google's advantage evaporate quickly.[30]

CHECK IT OUT

Visit Google and check out several new features, including Froogle, pop-up blocker, auto web form filler, blogger button, and calculator. Consider how each of these features may or may not give Google a competitive advantage. Check out some of the competitors named in the case above and see whether they offer similar features.

A GLOBAL PERSPECTIVE

Visit Google Zeitgeist (*www.google.com/press/zeitgeist. html*) and look for popular queries in countries around the world. Compare them to popular queries from Google U.S. Zeitgeist in Google's trend report, which shows popular search terms in the United States and abroad. Through this page, Google taps into what it calls "the general intellectual, moral, and cultural climate of an era." Suggest ways in which an Internet marketer might make use of the Zeitgeist information.

2

Internet Fundamentals: Operations, Management, the Web, and Wireless

LEARNING OBJECTIVES

» To learn the basics of Internet operations
» To gain a perspective on how the Internet operates smoothly
» To identify attributes of the World Wide Web
» To examine the potential and drawbacks of wireless connectivity

Cisco Helps Build Out the Internet's Infrastructure

Cisco Systems (*www.cisco.com*) is the undisputed worldwide leader in the manufacture and sale of Internet data-networking equipment and software, and in related services. A good place to begin learning how the Internet works is with the role played by Cisco's many Internet-related products—routers, switches, remote access servers, concentrators, hubs, IP telephony equipment, wireless, security systems, and network applications. Cisco dominates Internet router sales with an over 80 percent worldwide market share. Its training, certification, and education programs are considered models for an industry where skills can rapidly become obsolete and technology inexorably advances. Cisco's primary customers are large enterprises and telecommunications service providers, but it also sells products for small businesses, governments, and consumers. Company income for the fiscal year ending July 2003 was US$3.6 billion on revenues of US$18.9 billion, continuing its recovery from a net income loss in 2001 caused by the recession. Although the company was forced to lay off employees during the downturn,

by 2003 the number of Cisco employees worldwide grew to 34,000, a 5.6 percent increase from the previous year.

A small group of Stanford University computer scientists founded the company in 1984, and its first products came to market two years later. Cisco's engineers collaborated in the development of Internet Protocol (IP)-based networking technologies, and its technology has driven Internet infrastructure advances. Although Cisco dominates its markets, it faces growing competition from established companies and start-ups. At the same time, it is forming alliances with other companies to develop software and standards for voice and data communication systems. Its joint offering with Oracle (*www.oracle.com*), the largest software provider for ebusiness, is aimed at providing integrated capabilities for communication—email, phone, web collaborating, web chat, and interactive voice response. Cisco is collaborating with IBM (*www.ibm.com*) to develop standards for self-diagnosis and self-healing in company information systems. As networks and systems steadily become more complex, simplifying and automating diagnostic and solution processes are essential to saving time, money, and effort. Technology developed by the two companies will be open, not proprietary, and they anticipate its adoption as industry standards. These activities may seem to be a long way from Internet marketing, but efficiently operating, healthy backend systems and an expanding, stable Internet are essential to Internet marketing operations and to successful long-term marketing activities.

Cisco also supports a vast training network that works with businesses to develop Internet and communication solutions. Cisco and the U.S. Small Business Administration (SBA at *www.sba.gov*) have developed training programs on "Internet Essentials for Growing Business Online," six online sessions for small businesses (*www.sba.gov/training/courses.html*). Cisco joined with other industry leaders to create the Open Mobile Alliance (OMA at *www.openmobilealliance.org*). OMA seeks to accelerate deployment of open standards for Internet mobile wireless IP networks, providing a seamless interface between the wireless industry and the Internet, and removing barriers to global wireless adoption.

Cisco uses its direct sales force, resellers, and distributors to sell its products in over 115 countries. Observers agree that Cisco listens carefully to its customers. It diligently collects customer feedback to make sure they are satisfied, and annual employee bonuses are tied to customer satisfaction ratings. Cisco employees are highly productive and have a strong incentive to keep the company customer-centered. The company's customer-centered philosophy was evident in its response to the September 11 attacks. Some of its largest corporate clients were displaced or seriously affected by the collapse of the World Trade Center towers. Cisco immediately sent employees to help clients restore their networks and get back online. Cisco's wireless office networks were used to restore phone and data service, protected by the company's security software and hardware.

Infrastructure
The physical equipment and software that make up the Internet.

It often surprises people to learn that the Internet is a tangible entity with a physical **infrastructure** that must be maintained and expanded in order to avoid slowdowns, down time, and frustrated users. Many companies in the United States and abroad manufacture and sell equipment and services that operate and extend the physical infrastructure. They include networking equipment manufacturers, access service providers, and telecommunications companies. Chapter 2 begins with a discussion of Internet operations. It examines how order is maintained on this enormous voluntary network of networks, how the Web operates and why it is attractive to marketers. The chapter concludes with a discussion of new technologies and the growing popularity of wireless.

Internet Operations: How the Internet Works

The Internet is composed of thousands of networks and millions of computers that operate within a loose voluntary association without a central governing authority. It is a dynamic open system, and more networks link to it each day, bound together by a common agreement to run on the TCP/IP common communication language protocol.

A HYPOTHETICAL EMAIL EXAMPLE

Email (electronic mail)
A message encoded by a sender and sent electronically to one or many receivers.

Internet service provider (ISP)
A business that provides Internet access for consumers and enterprises.

To help visualize how the Internet operates on a physical level, consider the data transmission process for a single hypothetical **email (electronic mail)** message sent from the United States to England (Figure 2-1). The same general process is used to send web pages and other files over the Internet, although each operates under its own protocols (operating rules) in addition to TCP/IP standards. To begin our example, a sender in the United States emails a friend in London. If the sender is at home, he or she typically uses a personal computer, modem, and standard telephone line to dial up (connect to) an **Internet service provider (ISP),** which provides access to the Internet. There are over 6,000 ISPs in the United States, an increase from only 90 in 1993. Some are small, local businesses with relatively low-speed Internet access. Many thrive in small niche markets where they also offer customized Web services to local businesses and enterprises. A handful of large companies with very high-speed Internet connections dominate the access market. The ten largest ISPs by subscriber numbers control over 63 percent of the U.S. Internet access market and include such familiar names as America Online (*www.aol.com*), Comcast (*www.comcast.com*), United Online (NetZero+United Online at *www.unitedonline.net*), EarthLink (*www.earthlink.com*), and SBC Communications (*www.sbc.com*). The largest ISPs by volume of traffic worldwide are South Korea's GNG Networks (*epidc.co.kr/english/index.asp*), MCI's UUNET (*global.mci.com/uunet/*), Japan's NTT Verio (*verio.net*), and Germany's Schlund (*www1.schlund.de/*).[1]

Small, low-transmission-capacity ISPs provide *indirect access* and must connect to a larger service provider, usually a regional service provider (RSP), that connects to the Internet backbone. National ISPs with high transmission capacity have *direct*

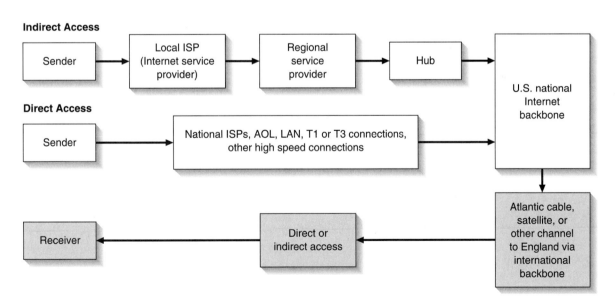

FIGURE 2-1 A Hypothetical Example: Routing an Email Message from the United States to England
Routers send data packets on the "best" paths (routes) from sender to receiver.

access and connect directly to the backbone. Even small ISPs typically offer several types of high-speed access in addition to dial-up service.

Bandwidth

The amount of data (communication signal frequencies) that can be transmitted through a communication line or channel per unit of time.

Bandwidth is transmission capacity—throughput, or the rate at which data (communication signal frequencies) flow per unit of time through a transmission line. A 56.6-Kbps (1 Kbps or Kb/s = 1000 bits, 1 kilobit, per second) analog dial-up modem transmits data at twice the speed of a 28.8-Kbps modem. A digital subscriber line (DSL) can transmit at speeds from 1.5 Mbps to 6.1 Mbps (1 megabit or Mb/s = 1,000,000 bits per second). Residential DSL is asymmetric (aDSL), with downloads faster than uploads, whereas enterprise DSL is symmetric (sDSL), with downloads and uploads at equivalent speeds. Bandwidth is often compared to a pipeline. Small ISPs, with very small data transmission pipelines, connect to RSPs with larger pipelines. Backbones have the largest pipelines of all and can transmit data much faster than smaller pipelines. Large text files and sound files, computer programs, streaming media, three-dimensional images, and virtual reality require greater bandwidth than text-only files.

Broadband

Very large-bandwidth communication lines with high-speed data transmission speed; for example, DSL and cable are broadband services.

The term *narrowband* is sometimes used to describe very small bandwidth transmitting text only. **Broadband,** on the other hand, means very large bandwidth with very high data transmission speed from 256 Kbps to 6 MHz (megahertz) and higher. Broadband can carry multiple signals, which means that audio, video, and other signals can be transmitted simultaneously. DSL and cable TV are broadband services. Two-way satellite Internet connections can transmit at 256 Kbps and higher; and wireless offers speeds of 11 Mbps and higher. Many marketers regard broadband as essential to making their websites more interactive, dynamic, and enticing to consumers. Consumers like it because they can go online with DSL or cable without tying up their home telephone. By 2000, more than two million DSL lines (up 435 percent from 1999) and almost four million high-speed cable connections (up 153 percent from 1999) were in use in homes in the United States. In 2004, the number of people in the United States with broadband at home increased to 45.2 percent, over 126 million people. Most U.S. workplaces have high speed connections. Canadian Internet users have more readily switched to broadband at home and now also consume more content than U.S. users. Around 53.6 percent of the 16 million Canadians online use broadband. Australians are also turning to broadband. Nielsen//NetRating reported a 150 percent surge in broadband subscriptions in Australia in one year (April 2002 to 2003); 1 million Australians now use broadband at home. Clearly, a "tipping point" is approaching at which the size of broadband-enabled target markets will free marketers from the restrictions of tailoring content to slow analog dial-up speeds.[2]

Most consumer Internet access in the United States is still by built-in dial-up modem on standard wire telephone lines from home at speeds less than 56.6 Kbps, but even dial-up speeds can be enhanced. Many ISPs are beginning to offer a higher speed dial-up service using compression and caching technologies to speed downloads to as much as five times the standard rate. Software enhancements compress text and graphical images before they are sent and cache (store) website elements so that when a user revisits a site, it doesn't have to be reloaded. This allows faster access for Internet users in areas that do not have standard broadband services and attracts those who are not willing to pay extra for DSL or cable. It requires a small software download and an easy setup using existing modem and software. The more the higher-speed connection is used, the faster it can become as more websites are cached (stored).

Internet access from an office, school, or other enterprise often is through a local area network (LAN) cable, most likely Ethernet, the industry standard LAN. If a LAN runs on part or all of a very fast connection line (a T1 or T3 digital circuit), it connects directly to the national Internet backbone without routing through an ISP or other intermediate service provider. A T1 transmits data at up to 1.544 Mbps, a T3 at up to 44.736 Mbps. An optical carrier line (OC) connects over fiber-optic cables at speeds from 51.84 Mbps (OC1) to 13.21 Gbps (OC 255). A gigabit (Gbps) is one billion bits. Higher-capacity OC lines are in development. Optical carriers accommodate very high-capacity connections and often are part of the Internet backbone. Backbone lines carry Internet traffic around the world, converging at network access points (NAPs) where data are exchanged peer-to-peer between major Internet service providers.

In the case of our email message, without the sender knowing it, his or her email is broken into small, independent digital units called *data packets,* each tagged with a unique identification number. Packets are routed along network transmission lines ranging from small-capacity lines leased by ISPs, through hubs (transfer points), to the major high-speed lines of national networks that interconnect to form the Internet's backbone. Many different routers (computers) in networks of various sizes must select the best paths for each packet to travel.

At some point, the data packets from the original email message leave the U.S. backbone (Figure 2-1). They may travel under the Atlantic Ocean on huge, armored undersea cable transmission lines or may be bounced from Earth-orbiting satellites to networks in England. Once the packets arrive, they are reassembled into the original email message, which the receiver can download and read. This process usually happens so quickly and seamlessly that sender and receiver have no idea what has occurred or where the data packets have traveled. However, sometimes parts of networks or whole networks crash (stop operating) or are removed from service for repair or maintenance, and data packets can be delayed, garbled, or even lost.

Because the Internet is a loosely distributed association where work is shared by many computers and networks, sections can go offline without bringing down the entire matrix. The Internet was built for **redundancy;** data can take multiple possible paths to a destination, and if the hardware fails in one section, it can be fixed or replaced without the entire matrix crashing. For example, in February 1999, a transatlantic cable was severed and its backup systems failed. This shut down Britain's largest network, the Joint Academic Network (Janet) and halted Internet communication with the United States for twenty-four hours. The rest of the Internet was unaffected, and other routes were used to bypass the downed network. In August 2003, the largest power outage in U.S. history struck New York City and much of the northeastern United States and southern Canada. Even though millions of homes, schools, and businesses lost power, there was no appreciable slowdown of Internet traffic. Websites being run from servers in darkened cities couldn't respond to requests to view their pages, but the Internet rerouted around unresponsive servers and continued to operate seamlessly.[3]

Redundancy
A property of systems, such as the Internet, where if one part slows down or stops, its function is redirected to other parts.

Fortunately, the Internet is robust, which is crucial to any marketer trying to conduct sustained business activities on its matrix. It is not, however, invulnerable.

Returning to our email example, if the receiver in London replies, his or her email's data packets will not travel exactly the same return route as the original data packets sent from the United States. Because of the Internet's design, there is no "right way" for data to get from a sender to a receiver. This means that every data packet typically takes a different route to its destination.

ROUTER, SERVERS, AND SOFTWARE

Routers

Sophisticated computers and the routing protocols embedded in the software that runs them; their job is to direct Internet traffic.

Routers and servers are essential to smooth Internet operations. **Routers** are sophisticated computers and the routing protocols embedded in the software that runs them. The Internet's millions of routers each connect two or more networks and direct the flow of data packets over those networks. They are sometimes called the Internet's traffic cops. Routers read each data packet's address to determine the packet's destination. Then they evaluate network traffic conditions on the networks to which they connect and decide what is the fastest and best route along which to forward the packet. Each Internet router can forward 10,000 to 200,000 or more data packets a second.

Servers

Computers, and the software that runs them, that serve data.

Servers serve data. They are computers and the software that runs them. Servers store files that other computers can access, and when a request for a file arrives, they *serve* the request by sending the file. At one time servers were very large computers; today, they are often the same size as the typical personal computer and, indeed, might be that same computer. Servers offer one or many services on the Internet, LANs, intranets, and extranets. For example, a web server provides web services, and an electronic mail server is a repository for email messages and a facilitator for email communication.

Routers, servers, and other machines require software to run them. Software is a set of programs that can run one, many, or millions of computers. Applications software creates files and documents and performs specific tasks for users—for example, word processing programs, spreadsheets, and presentation software. Systems software runs operating systems or support applications that manage the other programs in a computer or device; examples include UNIX, Windows, Mac OS X, and Linux. Internet software drives specific activities on the Internet or an Internet service such as the Web. Examples include programs for email, antivirus protection, HTML editing, web browsers, and instant messaging.[4]

INTERNET SERVICES

The Internet hosts many services (also called systems or sectors) that developed independently but run on top of the global matrix and adhere to TCP/IP protocols. Each service also has its own protocols, or rules, that direct its particular activity. Marketing activities occur on many of these services, in addition to the Web. The most popular services are briefly described in the following paragraphs.

ELECTRONIC MAIL (EMAIL)   Messages transmitted from one computer user to another via computer networks and the Internet. Simple Mail Transfer Protocol

(SMTP), Post Office Protocol (POP3), and Webmail are widely used. Marketing uses include email permission marketing, order confirmations, product promotion, and unsolicited commercial messages (spam).

USENET (USERS NETWORK)   A distributed bulletin board system where users with the appropriate software can read and post messages. It operates worldwide on the Internet and on many online services. The Network News Transport Protocol (NNTP) transfers Usenet communications. URLs that begin with *news* refer to Usenet groups. Newsgroups can be used for online marketing research and product promotion.

FILE TRANSFER PROTOCOL (FTP)   A set of message formats or rules that enable a user to transfer files to and from another computer over a TCP/IP network. FTP and its software can send, store, and retrieve data and can move files from one computer to another. Web pages typically are created on a host computer and then FTP'd to a server where the pages are stored and become accessible to multiple users via the Internet, an intranet, or an extranet.

TELNET   A remote login system that enables a user to connect directly to other computer systems on the Internet and access stored files.

CHAT OR INSTANT MESSAGING   A generic term for any service that allows logged-in computer or wireless users to have a real-time, online conversation much like a telephone conversation. Most messaging is text-based, but some also uses video and audio. Users may log into the same computer or chat on a network. Messaging can be used for marketing focus groups and product promotion.

VIDEOCONFERENCING   A computer-based online conferencing service that allows direct visual and/or audio connections between clients or multiple users. CU-SeeMe was the first videoconferencing tool. Videoconferencing can be used for marketing research, employee or customer training, education, and product demonstrations.

WORLD WIDE WEB   A system of servers that save and distribute documents formatted in hypertext markup language (HTML). It is a client-server hypertext distributed information retrieval service where most ecommerce and Internet marketing occur. HyperText Transfer Protocol (HTTP) governs World Wide Web functions and runs web email. Web browsers such as Internet Explorer, Safari, and Netscape Navigator are software applications that allow users to view text and graphics as well as to hear audio files and see video files.

INTRANETS AND EXTRANETS

Many enterprises have proprietary intranets (intraorganizational networks) and extranets (multiple intranets connected all or in part to other accepted intranets). Intranets are private networks that run the same type of software and adhere to the same protocols as the Internet and usually the Web. Access is restricted to authorized users.

Firewall
A combination of dedicated hardware and software with security systems that prevents unauthorized access and protects internal systems.

Most intranets have public Internet and Web access; some do not and are run solely within an enterprise. Intranets are sealed off from the public Internet by **firewalls,** dedicated hardware and software, combined with security systems, designed to prevent unauthorized access by external visitors. Firewalls protect databases, websites, and proprietary information and also monitor threats and activity patterns. They vary in cost and complexity, ranging from passwords or fairly simple IP address checks, which filter out unauthorized users, to extremely sophisticated, expensive hardware and software systems that create multiple layers of protection.

Because the Internet facilitates communication over great distances, irrespective of time or computer platform, employees can use a corporate intranet and a net-enabled desktop computer to share databases and information, file reports, make purchases, and access records. Teams can work collaboratively on projects despite geographical separation using email, chat messaging, videoconferencing, corporate web pages, and other Internet services. For example, Ford designers at plants around the world used a company intranet to collaborate on developing the 1996 Taurus. Intranets can reduce costs through workplace decentralization and decreases in paperwork. The software company PeopleSoft achieved significant cost savings by shifting its human resources processes to an intranet. Cisco Systems lowered the cost of processing expense reports from US$50.69 to US$1.90 per report by moving the process to its enterprise intranet. The return on its intranet investment was in the hundreds of millions of dollars.[5]

Intranets can save time by replacing physical face-to-face meetings that otherwise would require travel and can facilitate scheduling by maintaining centralized calendars. Although a growing number of enterprises consider intranets essential to their operations, most also acknowledge their drawbacks. Intranets can be costly to construct and maintain. They are susceptible to security breaches that can leave data exposed and vulnerable, and they are impersonal, which reduces or eliminates the synergy that can develop in face-to-face interactions.

Marc Andreessen, cofounder of Netscape, is credited with introducing the concept and term *extranet.*[6] An extranet is a part of a company's secure private intranet that is opened selectively to authorized users from outside the company. Users may be customers, suppliers, joint venture partners, vendors, or other businesses or enterprises approved for access. They can enter the extranet from the public Internet or from their own proprietary intranets. Like intranets, extranets also use Internet technology, which means they allow communication between computers regardless of operating system or program. Extranet firewalls are programmed to allow authorized visitors in and to keep unauthorized visitors out.

Extranets are being used for marketing and customer relationship management. For example, MasterCard Online (*https://hsm2stl101.mastercard.net/public/login/home.jsp*) is billed as a site *Where Members, Business Partners, and MasterCard Connect.* It is MasterCard's massive extranet portal that connects the company with over 25,000 users in 150 countries. Its payment card is accepted in over 22 million locations worldwide. Partner banks and other financial institutions that access MasterCard Online can use sixty products and services ranging from manuals and publications to security information. MasterCard Online began in 1995, but its greatest growth has been in the last several years.[7]

Consumers and enterprises alike are familiar with the United Parcel Service (UPS) extranet service whereby they can obtain package transit information online. Any public Internet user can visit the UPS website (*www.ups.com*), but only authorized customers who present a bona fide tracking number can enter the package-tracking system.

Companies or organizations that link their intranets can share information and work collaboratively to save time, effort, and money. They can share training programs and news of common interest. Inventory holding costs can be reduced, reorder times shortened, and paperwork reduced or eliminated if suppliers can directly access company sales data and initiate automatic product repurchases (*rebuys*) in real time. Extranets can be used to service customers faster and provide personalized attention. Authorized customers can access product catalogs on a company's intranet, which reduces the costs of producing and distributing hardcopies.

Along with their benefits, extranets also have shortcomings. Security is a top concern. The cost of implementing an extranet can be high, particularly if expensive, highly sophisticated security measures are required. Legal issues are another concern. Having an extranet can mean a significant increase in email and persistent electronic paper trails.

BARRIERS

Initially, the Internet was conceived of as an open environment where everyone would have access and information would be freely shared. Vinton Cerf, one of the Internet's founders, stated this philosophy in a speech titled "The Internet Is for Everyone: How Easy to Say—How Hard to Achieve." Cerf identified such barriers to Internet access as lack of affordable access, restricted access and censored content, undercapacity to handle anticipated traffic growth, overly complex and user-unfriendly Internet connecting devices, incompatible legal restrictions that hinder growth, lack of privacy and security, and irresponsible use. He called on everyone to work with the Internet Society and others to reduce the barriers and achieve the Internet's full potential. Cerf suggested that the Internet will advance democracy and extend voting franchises by opening access to these processes to more people. It will become the repository, he said, of "all we have accomplished as a society."

Cerf's vision is noble, but many barriers persist to this day. Recent data suggest that even in the world's most connected countries, many people remain unconnected, not always by choice. Governments that do not support free speech and democracy offline continue to exert censorship online, some more successfully than others. Furthermore, the disparities in economic wealth worldwide mean that fully industrialized countries with highly educated workforces benefit from Internet adoption far more than developing and transition economies. Most of the latter still lag in Internet adoption and use.

Evaluating Cerf's comments from an Internet marketing perspective reveals several contradictions. A completely free Internet is not necessarily in the best interests of Internet marketers seeking to generate revenue streams online. For example, many websites generate revenue by selling content subscriptions and others have customers willing to pay not to receive online promotions. Having *everyone* online would clog the Internet with large numbers of users unable and/or unwilling to purchase products or subscriptions. It would increase online clutter and weaken promotion effectiveness. Privacy is another contradiction. U.S. marketers doing business in the European Union (EU) must comply with restrictive privacy policies that could undermine their ability to collect meaningful customer information. Although privacy should be protected, Internet marketers must be able to collect enough relevant, timely information about customers to customize and personalize offers. Protecting children online is another contentious issue. Children, particularly in rich, developed countries, are marketing targets. At the same time, children must be protected from online pornography, pedophiles, invasion of privacy, and hard sell tactics.[8]

Despite these and other problems, the Internet will grow and evolve, perhaps not as purely as Vinton Cerf hopes, but in a form that supports commerce and still achieves some of the goals he envisioned. As for whether it *should* grow and evolve, most consumers and enterprises would greatly mourn its loss should the Internet cease to exist. It has become an inextricable and invaluable part of our society and economy, and its benefits already far outweigh its costs.

VULNERABILITY

The Internet is robust but not invulnerable. Concern about protecting the Internet from terrorists was growing prior to 9/11/01, even though no imminent specific cyberterrorism threat had been identified. For years, government officials, scientists, academics, and private industry groups had been debating how to protect the Internet against wide-scale attacks. Since September 11, talk about protection has assumed greater urgency.

Cyberterrorism is terrorism against the Internet, its networks, or linked computers with the intent of disrupting Internet communications, spreading fear, causing economic chaos, corrupting or stealing information, or otherwise compromising the system. It is violence designed to advance a political or social agenda and cause grave harm to its victims. Some attacks on specific corporate websites are called civil disobedience, and other attacks are senseless vandalism. However, these thoughtless and disruptive acts are not cyberterrorism, which is designed to have a far wider societal impact.

The complexity, size, and interdependence of the networks and computers that constitute the Internet's infrastructure and its open nature make it vulnerable. Small numbers of terrorists with knowledge and motivation could anonymously launch a remote attack. They could hijack computers and networks and then turn them against other computers and networks in coordinated "distributed denial of service" (DDoS) attacks designed to block legitimate traffic from reaching websites. They could spread computer viruses that quickly create havoc in infected systems, blocking email and crashing web servers. Terrorists can use the Internet to communicate among themselves and even launch offline attacks.

Malicious individuals and groups pose an asymmetrical threat that is difficult to track down, intercept, and eliminate. Enterprises with Internet-connected computers are urged to strengthen system security in order to protect their data and avoid being hijacked and used in DDoS or other attacks. Because the Internet is borderless, pre-

Cyberterrorism
Terrorism against the Internet, its networks, or linked computers with the intent of disrupting the Internet, the economy, and society.

WEB UPDATE

For updates and more on this topic, visit the textbook student website at: http://college.hmco .com/business/students and select Siegel, *Internet Marketing*, 2e. **Cyberterrorism, Web vandalism, and Internet vulnerability**

vention must extend to worldwide cooperation in the development and implementation of strategies designed to protect the matrix. Countries that do not cooperate could risk being disconnected. Unfortunately, regulations designed to protect Internet operations may also seriously restrict the free exchange of information that is its hallmark. A widespread terrorist attack on the Internet would be devastating to its commercialization in the short term and cost millions if not billions of dollars in lost revenues and repairs. It could disrupt transactions, slow or halt transmissions, block access, compromise payment security, expose data, and undermine confidence in doing business online. Lessons learned from the September 2001 attacks are galvanizing governments in the principal Internet-using nations to take steps to harden and protect the global network.[9]

Internet Management

Internet marketing occurs on a global electronic network shared by millions of computers and over 1.1 billion users worldwide. Given its size and distributed structure, it would be easy to assume that a powerful central international management system maintains the stability of the matrix, avoids chaos, and gets all members to cooperate and coordinate their efforts. Instead, Internet management is just the opposite. It is highly fluid, with changing contributors, and highly distributed, with shifting power centers.

Although the U.S. government funded and controlled the original military and academic Internet, its control began to diminish with NSFNet's privatization and the Internet's subsequent internationalization and commercialization. The U.S. government didn't disappear from Internet management, however. It continues to fund the next-generation high-performance Internet for academic research (vBNS and Internet2). It participates in international initiatives that deal with such cross-border Internet issues as jurisdiction, privacy, and cyberterrorism. It oversees issues related to U.S. Internet operations, including spam, taxation, gambling, online visual pornography, competitiveness, and domestic cyberterrorism. Nevertheless, throughout the 1990s and into the early 2000s, businesses, institutions of higher education, organizations, and volunteer technical committees took on more tasks that had formerly been the prerogative of U.S. government agencies.[10]

Today, the Internet is run by no single entity, yet it clearly is not unmanaged chaos online. Key U.S. government agencies continue to regulate U.S. online activities. The U.S. Federal Trade Commission (FTC) takes a lead role on most business issues. Other agencies actively involved with Internet activities include the U.S. Federal Communications Commission (FCC), the National Science Foundation (NSF), and the National Telecommunications and Information Administration (NTIA). The Federal Bureau of Investigation (FBI), the National Security Agency (NSA), and other agencies focus on issues of individual, enterprise, and national security. The Internet Fraud Complaint Center, a partnership between the FBI and the National White Collar Crime Center (NW3C), operates an Internet center where victims and others can report fraud.

The amount of management and control exerted by governments in other countries varies. Some are actively funding and managing large-scale Internet-connected networks. These include China's Cernet, SURFnet in the Netherlands, Britain's

SuperJANET, and GEANT in continental Europe. The EU has taken an active role in regulating businesses that collect consumer information online. The Australian government has been at the forefront of providing online service delivery.

Numerous businesses individually and collaboratively perform tasks that help run the Internet. They include telecommunications companies, hardware and software manufacturers, service providers, cable television companies, domain name registrars, and others. Businesses often contribute to the operations of the many voluntary professional committees that set technical standards, policy, and the Internet's future direction. Self-regulation plays an important role in addressing significant problems of Internet use, including privacy and free speech, and in reassuring consumers about the safety of doing business online.

Institutions of higher education play an important part in defining the role and direction of the next-generation research Internet. Their libraries are at the forefront of determining policy for the online management of data.

VOLUNTARY PROFESSIONAL TECHNICAL COMMITTEES

A number of voluntary professional committees run the technical side of the Internet. Much of the work is coordinated by the Internet Society (ISOC at *www.isoc.org*). Founded in 1992 and located in Reston, Virginia, USA, the ISOC is a nonprofit, nongovernmental, international organization that broadly considers Internet operating standards, public policy, education, and membership issues. Some have called it the conscience of the Internet for its concern about privacy, open access, Internet governance, and cybercrime. Members represent over 180 countries and include more than 150 organizations and 16,000 individuals. Industry members include network access providers (such as France Telecom, Nippon Telegraph and Telephone, SBC Internet Services, and Verizon Communications), product providers (such as Cisco Systems, IBM, Lucent Technologies, and Microsoft), domain registrars, publishers, educational institutions, research institutions, government agencies, and others. The ISOC is an umbrella organization that acts as a global clearinghouse for Internet information and education, and a facilitator and coordinator of Internet-related global initiatives. It is also the organizational home of the Internet Engineering Task Force (IETF), which sets standards including protocols for email and the Web, the Internet Engineering Steering Group (IESG), and the Internet Architecture Board (IAB)—groups responsible for developing the Internet's technical infrastructure.

Other voluntary committees contribute to maintaining order and standardization, and to planning for the Internet's growth. The Internet Research Task Force (IRTF at *www.irtf.org*) promotes research to further the Internet's evolution. Its research groups focus on the future of Internet protocols, applications, architecture, and technology. The Electronic Frontier Foundation (EFF at *www.eff.org*) is a nonprofit organization dedicated to protecting civil liberties, privacy, and freedom of expression on the Internet.

The World Wide Web Consortium (W3C at *www.w3.org*), with over 400 member organizations worldwide, is an industry-supported organization that develops standards for the World Wide Web, HTTP, HTML, and other Web protocols. Created in October 1994, the W3C is dedicated to maintaining Web interoperability and growth. It was established through the collaboration of CERN, DARPA, and the EU, and currently is spearheading efforts to create the Semantic Web (*www.w3.org/2001/sw/*) that will enable the current WWW to interconnect people and computers more effectively.

The Internet Corporation for Assigned Names and Numbers (ICANN at *www.icann.org*) was created by the U.S. government. It is a nonprofit corporation responsible for allocating IP addresses and managing the domain name system. ICANN accredits companies that register domain names for business and organizations.

SELF-REGULATION

Another mechanism for managing Internet activities is self-regulation, which frequently is undertaken to forestall the need for government regulation. TRUSTe (*www.truste.org*), an independent, nonprofit privacy initiative, began operations on June 10, 1997. It offers assistance to businesses developing website privacy statements, operates the online TRUSTe privacy seal program, and awards the TRUSTe hyperlink seal to sites with acceptable privacy practices. Its goals are to provide consumers with control over personal information collected online, to give web publishers a means of reassuring consumers that their privacy is protected, and offering government regulators evidence that business can successfully self-regulate. TRUSTe program sponsors include AOL, CommerceOne, Intel, Intuit, and Microsoft.

Another form of Internet self-regulation is industry-specific. The Verified Internet Pharmacy Practice Sites (VIPPS) program was implemented in the spring of 1999 by the almost one-hundred-year-old National Association of Boards of Pharmacy (NABP). NABP is the only professional association representing pharmacy boards in all fifty states of the United States, the District of Columbia, Guam, Puerto Rico, the Virgin Islands, New Zealand, nine Canadian provinces, and four Australian states (*www.nabp.net/vipps/intro.asp*). The VIPPS online pharmacy certification process was developed by a task force of state and federal regulatory associations, professional associations, and consumer advocacy groups. The VIPPS seal indicates that an online pharmacy has complied with VIPPS and NABP certification requirements for such standards as patient privacy rights and authentication and security of prescription orders. VIPPS-certified online pharmacies include Walgreens.com (*www.walgreens.com*), Clickpharmacy.com (*www.clickpharmacy.com*), Anthem Prescription (*www.anthemprescription.com*), Drugstore.com (*www.drugstore.com*), and Medco Health Solutions, Inc. (*www.medcohealth.com*).

A final example is the Better Business Bureau (BBB, *www.bbbonline.org*), which provides a BBBOnLine Reliability seal program. The program verifies that authorized

TRUSTe

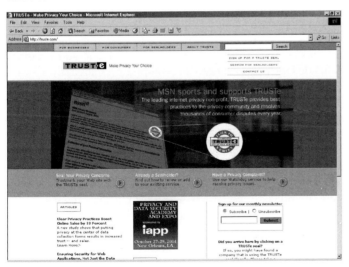

TRUSTe third-party seal program helps businesses address concerns about online privacy.

Source: TRUSTe and the privacy certification seal are registered trademarks at TRUSTe, Inc. Reprinted by permission of TRUSTe (www.truste.org).

businesses meet BBB membership standards and have the right to display the reliability seal. Its mission is "to promote trust and confidence on the Internet through the BBB*OnLine* Reliability and Privacy Seal Programs."[11]

Seal programs can be very reassuring to consumers. A seal from a reputable organization provides reassurance that a site is safe and reputable. Even a well-known retailer such as Walgreens, with more than 4,300 stores nationwide, benefits from its VIPPS certification, because consumers who shop the offline stores may still need reassurance about shopping the Walgreens website. The challenge for organizations issuing seals is to implement continuous member-monitoring programs to avoid allowing any certified site to undermine the seal's credibility by failing to maintain acceptable standards. The challenge for Internet marketers is to recognize that sites displaying seals have a competitive advantage over sites that do not. Prominently displayed seals on a site's homepage are always on 24/7/365 to remind visitors that the site is concerned about their well-being.

How the Web Works

HyperText Transfer Protocol (HTTP)
The rules or standards for exchanging HTML files, including web pages, images, text, sound, video, and graphics.

The World Wide Web (WWW, W3, the Web) is the hypertext (hypermedia) distributed information retrieval system where most public Internet marketing occurs. Like every system operating on the Internet matrix, the Web adheres to the TCP/IP protocol. It also requires a unique protocol, **HyperText Transfer Protocol (HTTP),** for exchanging HTML files, including web pages, images, text, sound, video, and graphics. Because so much Internet activity takes place on the Web, it is appropriate at this point to consider how the Web works and why it is an object of such intense marketing interest.

WEB PAGES

A web page looks like a standard computer application page but is distinguished by the arrangement of its text, graphics, design, multimedia elements, and hypertext links. Web pages can be made larger or smaller to fit a computer screen or the viewer's preferences. They can be scrolled down or sideways if the page doesn't fit on a single screen. The viewer can move backward and forward between pages linked in a multi-page website, store pages for later use, print pages, and easily move from one website to another. Most new computers have sufficient memory so that multiple web pages can be worked on or viewed concurrently. Web pages are often bright, colorful, interesting, useful, informative, entertaining, and highly creative.

Browsers make the Web user-friendly. A browser is a software program that reads hypertext and locates, retrieves, and views web pages. The most popular browsers (Internet Explorer, AOL, Netscape, Opera, and Safari) are graphical, but some people still use text-only browsers (such as Lynx) or turn off the graphics capacity in a graphical browser to speed download time. Text-only browsers download faster because they read text and ignore graphics or other multimedia-rich elements. Marketers should consider this when developing product pages and include text product descriptions where appropriate.

Web pages are written in a text-based document format known as the HyperText Markup Language (HTML) that creates a page's source code. The code tells a web browser where text and images should be placed on the page, what colors and backgrounds are used, and generally how the page is composed. HTML code is written with tags that indicate where page elements begin and end, and what the tag means. To view a page's source code, go to a web page and pull down your browser's *View* menu. Click on the word *Source*, and the source code should appear in a pop-up box.

Pages written in HTML usually contain links (hypertext connections or **hyperlinks**). Links help make the Web interactive and useful. A link is a connection from a word, image, or object to another area within a page, to another page within a website, or to a different website. The highlighted word is the most common link, although images and animations also can be used as links. A link typically is highlighted, colored, and underlined. When a user clicks on a link, the browser initiates delivery of the linked item, page, or site. HTML editing programs (such as Dreamweaver and FrontPage) simplify web page construction and eliminate the need for most page developers to write source code.

Web pages are stored as files on a web server. Servers send web pages in response to HTTP requests from remote browsers. Servers can run multiple software simultaneously. Some web servers, called *hosts,* store the web files being requested and send them when a request is received. *Client* servers are computers that request information.[12] To complicate matters, some servers can be both host and client.

Many web pages and websites are successful, others far less so or not at all. Some are very slow downloading, often because they contain an excess of animated graphics or large sound files. Some sites are so complicated and poorly organized that it takes too long for visitors to drill down to a destination page, so they click past the site. Content on some web pages is hard to understand or is not informative. Other pages are on websites that have moved without a forwarding address, have been abandoned, include links that do not work, or haven't been updated since 1993![13]

WEB ADDRESSES

A web page **address** is an important marketing tool for building awareness and directing visitors to a site. Just as people have an address that identifies the location of their home or business, all locations on the Internet and Web have an address. Addresses currently in use include email addresses, IP or Internet addresses, computer hardware addresses, and web addresses. Web pages are accessed using the Internet Protocol (IP) and a unique **Uniform Resource Locator (URL)** web address that a browser reads. A typical URL looks like *http://business.college.hmco.com/ students*. The anatomy of this address is explained in Table 2-1. Computers actually read a named address in four groups of numbers (from 0 to 255) separated by periods, such as 192.107.41.31. The numbered address tells a browser exactly where to locate the requested file in the domain and on a specified server.

Many addresses are dropping the http://www and using only the hostname and file location in their visible address. For example, the Weather Channel can be reached at *weather.com,* which is far faster to type than *http://www.weather.com/index.html* and more easily remembered. The Weather Channel registered many forms of its address, including both long and short forms, so that a visitor can type any of several address names and still be routed to the right location.

Hyperlinks
Links in web documents written in hypertext that, if clicked on, instruct the browser to retrieve information from that link.

Address
Numeric and/or named identifiers—for example an email address, IP or Internet address, computer hardware address, or web page address (URL).

Uniform Resource Locator (URL)
Address for a site on the World Wide Web.

Table 2-1 Anatomy of a Web Address	
A web address	*http://college.hmco.com/business/students/* is read by a web browser. The address provides the following information:
http://college.hmco.com	Protocol type (HyperText Transfer Protocol). Hostname: college.hmco.com, the Houghton Mifflin server where the file is housed. Its domain name is .com, which identifies a commercial address.
/business/students	In the directory (default folder) for business publications and the HTML file for students.

DOMAINS AND NAMES

Until 1984, all Internet (IP) addresses were numeric; each was a ten-digit number. People can easily remember the seven digits of their local telephone number and their nine-digit social security number. They are far less likely to be able to remember a solely numeric Internet address unless it is for their own website. Domain names were introduced to simplify Internet addressing by allowing the substitution of words for numbers, although each address has a corresponding number read by browsers.

The Domain Name System (DNS) established an hierarchical order for top-level and secondary-level domains. The original top-level domains (TLDs) were .edu, .com, .net, .org, .gov, .mil, and the two-digit Country Codes (CC). In many countries, second-level domains appear directly before the Country Code, so an address registered in England might read *www.hm.co.uk*, where the TLD, .com, comes before the Country Code.[14] The first registered domain was Symbolics.com (March 15, 1984); others quickly followed, including purdue.edu, ucla.edu, and mitre.org.[15] In October 2000, the number of registered websites passed 30 million and was forecast to exceed 60 million within eighteen months.[16]

Concern about dwindling numbers of the most desirable names, particularly dot-coms, led the Internet Corporation for Assigned Names and Numbers (ICANN) to pass a resolution that agrees to "the introduction of new TLDs in a measured and responsible manner." ICANN's goal is to increase competition and reduce profiteering by entrepreneurs that buy domain names to exploit their trademark or proprietary value and then hold the name ransom for sale to the highest bidder. Seven new names were added in November 2000, and by 2002, all were operational and accepting registrations. They are .aero (air transport industry), .biz (businesses), .coop (cooperatives), .info (unrestricted use), .museum (museums), .name (individuals), and .pro (accountants, lawyers, physicians, and other professionals). Although the new TLDs will ease the shortage of names, they add to the expense of registering all possible variations of an address.[17]

Registering a domain name once in the United States is not enough to secure the name worldwide. International companies are advised to register their domain names in all the countries where they operate and in the languages of the customers in their target markets. International domain names (IDNs) are now available in over 350 different languages. The proliferation of international domains has prompted some governments to consider breaking away from the U.S.-created ICANN and transfer international regulatory responsibility to the International Telecommunication Union that is affiliated with the United Nations.[18]

Domain names are valuable property and care should go into their construction and protection. For domain names to have marketing value, they must be carefully worded, descriptive, clear, memorable, and legally protected. They can contain any letter from a to z; numerals 1 to 9; and hyphens and underlines, though underlines cannot be directly under words. Letters can be lowercase or capitalized, but capital letters are more difficult to read. The numbers, letters, hyphens, and underlines must not exceed sixty-seven characters. However, the longer the name, the less likely it is to be remembered, and short names that evoke the image of the site are more engaging. Domain names should be registered as trademarks to protect them from legal challenge by others. Before registering, the name should be checked to see whether it is already trademark protected.[19]

In the earliest years of Web commercialization, it was not uncommon for speculators to purchase the domain names of well-known companies in the expectation that they could sell them in the future for a profit. Companies often had to sue to recover domain names that clearly were trademark infringements. Hasbro, Inc. was forced to sue to be able to register candyland.com. Hasbro won its case by proving that the pornography site registered at the Candyland address diluted the company's forty-seven-year-old trademark for the popular children's board game.[20]

Many recent cybersquatter cases involve celebrities. Actress Julia Roberts appealed to the World Intellectual Property Organization (WIPO) for control of the Internet domain name juliaroberts.com that had been registered by an accused *cybersquatter* (someone who registers famous names in "bad faith," to sell for profit or otherwise exploit). A WIPO arbitration panel extended commercial protection to Roberts as a famous individual whose name is her trademark. Similarly, Pierce Brosnan (007 in several *James Bond* films) appealed to the United Nations (U.N.) to reclaim the domain name of piercebrosnan.com. U.N. arbitrators ruled in his favor, stating that the cybersquatter "had no rights or interests in the name and was using it in bad faith." The U.N. copyright agency, begun in 1999, arbitrates domain name disputes and avoids costly litigation. By 2003, it had already settled ninety-one celebrity cases, finding for the celebrity seventy-seven times.[21]

The U.S. Anticybersquatting Consumer Protection Act of 1999 criminalizes the unauthorized use of trademark-protected names in Internet domain addresses. It remains to be seen how effective this will be in stopping a worldwide names market.[22]

Domain names don't last forever. Domain contracts can run from one to ten years. If some people have their way, domain names eventually will become irrelevant. Directory services are beginning to appear that sort out requests for site addresses by full company name, thereby eliminating the need for domain names. Alternatively, one company is offering extensions outside the ICANN naming system. New.net (*www.new.net*) sells domain names that can be activated at the browser or ISP level. New.net domain names exist alongside ICANN-sanctioned names. Their extensions include .shop, .xxx , .club, .ltd, .inc, .travel, .tech, .sport, .family, .law, .med, and .mp3. New.net claims a user base of over 175 million worldwide.

As the numbers of web pages and websites increase, it will become harder for marketers to penetrate the clutter and contact potential customers. Reaching existing customers is not as much of a problem. Online marketers already capture customer email addresses, store them in databases, and use the information to contact them periodically by email with reminders of the site and its offers. Because current customers are more involved with a site they've visited or bought from, they also are more likely to pay attention to television, radio, newspaper, magazine, or online advertisements that contain the site's URL. They may have bookmarked the site to facilitate an easy return visit.

Until 1999, domain names could be registered through only one company, Network Solutions Inc., which held a U.S. government-sanctioned monopoly on names ending in the domains .com, .net, and .org.[23] Today, ICANN-accredited and -qualified registrars operate worldwide. ICANN maintains a list of registrars, their country, and the TLDs they are authorized to register.[24]

Registering domain names is big business. Network Solutions, now a VeriSign company, registered only 13,000 domain names in 1993, 100,000 in 1995, and 1 million in 1997. Over 16 million names were registered in 2001 and by 2004, there were 34 million active domain names in its .com and .net registry. A web-hosting company that provides server space for web businesses can register a domain name for the businesses purchasing its services. Most businesses, however, go directly to a DNS registration company. Registering a domain name can cost as little as US$4.95. Companies often charge from US$35 to US$50 to register or reregister a .com, .net, or .org for one year and several hundred dollars for ten years.

PORTALS

Portals

Ports of entry to the Web; interfaces that offer links to websites.

Portals are ports of entry, gateways to the Web with links to websites that are of general interest (*generic or horizontal portals*) or are of special interest to like-minded people (*niche or vertical portals*). These gateways may be enterprise portals designed to operate on intranets or extranets, or public Internet portals. Generic portals include Netscape's NetCenter (*www.netscape.com*), Yahoo! (*www.yahoo.com*), and AOL.com (*www.aol.com*). Niche portals are like targeted cable television networks, such as Lifetime (women), CNBC (stock pickers), and ESPN (sports fans), that schedule programming to suit their audience's interests. Portal revenues come mostly from selling onsite advertising space. AOL, however, also profits from its subscriber base.

The first portals were the original online services (AOL, Prodigy, and CompuServe) that offered shopping malls, email, lists, search engines, and other services to subscribers. Netscape created one of the first portals at NetCenter. Today, many search engines have transformed themselves into portals in order to retain and enlarge their customer bases.

AOL's Netscape portal (*netscape.com*) has many of the same features as other generic public gateways. It offers links for general web searches as well as a weather search. The latest news is highlighted, with links to stories behind the headlines. It has a shopping center, web tools for booking airline flights, business information with a

AOL's Netscape Network Portal

AOL's Netscape Network Portal at *http://www.netscape.com*

Source: Netscape and the "N" Logo are registered trademarks of Netscape Communications Corporation. Used with permission by Netscape (netscape.com).

stock ticker, channels for special-interest links, a web calendar that can be personalized, and sports news. These features are designed to highlight deals and push visitors toward favored sites. Most portals encourage visitors to use them as their browser default (start) page, which is a savvy marketing tactic. Personalization is practically no-cost for the web host, a Netscape or Yahoo!. It builds a ready audience for content pushed from the host. It also pressures hosts to add new features and fresh content so the start page will not become stale. If it does, there's always another host eager to capture bored consumers looking for a more enticing personalized start page.

Portals exist for just about any known interest or target audience. For example, there are portals for kids (Alfy, The Web Portal for Kids at *www.alfy.com*), cowboys (the eCowboy Network for cowboys, cowgirls, rodeo, and country music at *www.ecowboy.com*), and health (Florida's e-Health portal at *www.floridahealthstat.com*). Must a marketer link his or her website to a portal? As the Web expands, interest-oriented portals may become essential entry points for consumers and enterprises overwhelmed by the myriad of websites facing them. On the other hand, portals have a tendency to get extremely cluttered, which can frustrate people who are trying to use them. They also pose a contradiction because most marketers want customers to stay on their sites (stick), whereas portals direct consumers to other sites. Finally, individuals can download software that allows them to create personalized portals. These portals are called blogs, weblogs, or web journals. Commercial portals may find that some of their strongest competition comes from bloggers who create highly personalized portals that attract like-minded individuals who share their interests. More will be said about blogs in later chapters.

Wireless Connectivity

Think back to Chapter 1 and our discussion of the development of written communication in ancient times. Initially, communication was place-bound, restricted to cave walls and stone tablets. As communication gained mobility with the invention of paper and later, Gutenberg's printing press, it initiated profound and unexpected changes in business and society. Something similar is happening today with the accelerating move toward wireless connectivity. We can only guess at where wireless will lead us, but if the past holds clues to the future, the path will lead in unexpected directions. Even if all the initial excitement and media hype about wireless subsides, enterprises and consumers will continue to enjoy the benefits of wireless and prepare for future refinements and new products.

Wireless
Generic term that refers to data transfer via radio or optical waves.

Wireless is a generic term that refers to the transfer of data between sender and receiver via radio (or optical) waves of different frequencies. Most Americans already use a variety of wireless devices, from their mobile telephones to remote, radio-controlled, keyless auto entry/security systems and optical light-sensitive television remote controls. In the case of mobile or cell phones, the phone's radio signal contacts the closest radio base station, which sends the call to a mobile switch. The signal may then connect to a fixed, wired receiver or be sent through a base station by radio signals to another mobile phone. This relay system is necessary because mobile phones have a limited range.

Wireless devices include both standard and Internet-compatible mobile telephones, where users can browse the Web on a screen roughly the size of a business card; wireless laptop computers and tablets; personal data assistants (PDAs); and game-playing devices. As the name implies, this technology frees users from cables, wires, and other hardware connection devices for short or long distances to transmit large or small amounts of data, on or off the Internet. Internet wireless users can connect over wireless local area networks (wireless LANs, or WLANs) to the Internet and/or to local hard-wired LANs (Ethernets) that connect to the Internet, intranets, or extranets. Workers can use their wireless devices to stay connected to their offices while traveling. Wireless-connected salespeople can enter orders from their cars, repair technicians can pick up work orders while on the job, travelers can check their email while flying cross-country, and home users can create wireless work and entertainment networks on and off the Internet using short-range radio signals.

Wi-Fi
High power wireless data transmission over long distances.

Bluetooth
Low power wireless data transmission over short distances.

Wireless is not one technology. Instead, it is a variety of related, complementary technologies that differ in their speed, range, power, and compatibility. The most familiar are **Wi-Fi** (the 802.11 protocol family, which includes several incompatible members), a high-power radio-based wireless Internet access alternative that can handle large amounts of data over long distances; **Bluetooth,** a low-power alternative that transmits data slowly over short distances; and ultra-wide-band technology (UWB), an ultra-low-power alternative that offers very secure digital radio communication not tied to any particular radio frequency. Analysts expect that products increasingly will use a combination of these types, exploiting the distinctive advantages of each and attempting to circumvent their limitations. WiMAX (wireless broadband) may eventually replace DSL and cable for broadband Internet access; mesh networks may greatly extend the geographical coverage of mobile phones; and cell phones routinely will be able to transmit large data files, including photographs.

Wireless has deeply penetrated the Asian market, is becoming established in Europe, and is making significant inroads in the United States. The United States is the most PC-centric industrialized nation in the world, yet by 2003 the number of wireless users, mainly of mobile telephones, topped 150 million, up from less than 5 million in 2000. However, the number of people in the United States using wireless PDAs, phones, or laptop computers to go online remains low. Only about 24 percent of Americans in mid-2004 used wireless to go online. Businesses are leading the way with wireless Internet connections, because mobile employees are more likely to use high-speed wireless Internet access provided by their employers.

Wireless is all the rage in Japan, where the popularity of Internet-connected wireless phones is credited with doubling Internet usage in 1999. Since then, over 50 million Japanese consumers have signed up for mobile Internet services and are now spending an estimated 300 billion yen (US$2.4 billion) annually on wireless data. Japanese teens and young adults like wireless because it is a fun, fast, fashionable, and relatively cheap means of communication. Nippon Telegraph and Telephone's (NTT) DoCoMo (*www.nttdocomo.co.jp*) markets wireless handsets using i-mode technology that enables users to press one button and go online through the company's wireless portal and to stay online as long as they wish. DoCoMo has captured over 70 percent of Japan's local wireless market with more than 33 million subscribers and is expanding globally. DoCoMo's subscribers can talk, send email, chat, and download content from more than 20,000 mini-websites created solely for i-mode. They can conduct financial transactions, order tickets, and make restaurant reservations. Handsets have small color screens for displaying text and graphics. The product suits the Japanese market, which is low on PC penetration. DoCoMo has also entered the U.S. market (*www.docomo-usa.com*) and, with its U.S. partner AT&T Wireless (*www.attwireless.com*), runs a showcase in New York City that features its wireless products including videophones.

South Korea's Samsung Electronics Co. (*www.samsung.com*) is making a major commitment to home networked wireless systems that link cellular telephones, computers, ovens, refrigerators, home security systems, and entertainment centers. The company has invested US$5 billion since 1998 developing appliances that can be controlled by a variety of wireless devices in a market projected to reach US$10 billion in 2004. Samsung's technology is already in place and being tested in 2,500 units in a complex of high-rise apartments in Seoul. Each apartment has a homepad portable flat-panel display monitor with icons for each room and wireless devices in the rooms. A special box on the television set sends and receives wireless signals that link DVD players and the television set to the Internet. Samsung, with Microsoft (*www.microsoft.com*), Intel (*www.intel.com*), Sony (*www.sony.com*), and others, is part of a sixteen-company technology alliance, the Digital Home Working Group, that is creating industry standards for compatible home networking devices.

Wireless holds the promise of bridging the access digital divide in developing countries. In Laos, the Jhai Foundation (*www.jhai.org*) has developed a robust PC with no moving parts that uses flash-memory chips to store data and is powered by bicycle-cranked car batteries. The PCs are used in remote Lao villages that have no electricity or technical support. Villagers log on to the Internet via wireless Internet cards that connect the computers to a hilltop solar-powered relay station that sends the signal to the Lao telephone grid and on to the Internet and Web. Villagers use the Internet to check crop prices, which guide their planting and marketing decisions. Groups from Peru, Chile, and South Africa have expressed interest in the Jhai wireless computer project.[25]

WI-FI, BLUETOOTH, AND HOTSPOTS

The radio-based technology that today is known as Wi-Fi was created by engineers at Harris Corp. in 1994. A decade later, what was once an obscure technology is the hottest thing in Silicon Valley and is increasingly popular worldwide. Large corporations are quickly moving to get their share of the market. Intel is spending US$300 million to promote its Wi-Fi Centrino chips; Cisco Systems already dominates the market for Wi-Fi access equipment; T-Mobile (*www.tmobile.com*) has become the leader in building public hotspots for wireless access. Wi-Fi chip sales reached US$40 million in 2003, up from barely US$1 million in 1999 when the Wi-Fi standards were finally adopted.

It is said that the term *Wi-Fi* was invented by the marketing departments of Wi-Fi equipment manufacturers. It is an abbreviation for *wireless fidelity,* just as *hi-fi* refers to high-fidelity audio equipment. Today it refers to any product tested and approved as Wi-Fi-certified by the Wi-Fi Alliance (*www.weca.net*). Wi-Fi-certified (also WiFi-certified) products are interoperable (compatible) with products from different manufacturers. This is a key point. The lack of interoperability had been a serious impediment to the adoption of wireless, because non-interoperable devices cannot exchange data. The Wi-Fi Alliance (*http://www.wi-fi.org*) is a nonprofit international association formed in 1999 to certify interoperability of wireless Local Area Network products based on IEEE 802.11 standards. It has 205 member companies from around the world and has certified 915 products as interoperable since certification began in March 2000. The goal of Wi-Fi Alliance members is to enhance the user's experience through product interoperability. The expectation is that user satisfaction will increase revenues and profits for equipment and software manufacturers and WLAN operators.

Bluetooth (*www.bluetooth.com*) is another wireless technology. Named for the tenth-century Viking king who unified Norway and Denmark, it is radio-signal-based and allows the close-proximity connectivity of Internet and non-Internet connected devices. It can coexist with Wi-Fi because the former is specifically designed for longer-distance Internet access, while Bluetooth is designed to allow wireless communication over short distances. New Wi-Fi products, particularly in the 802.11a range, help prevent interference between the two.

Bluetooth-equipped devices house a short-range radio chip. This means that a wireless computer with a Bluetooth chip inside can communicate with a Bluetooth-equipped printer. Hewlett-Packard (HP at *www.hp.com*) has started offering a Bluetooth-enabled dongle (enabling device) for its printers that could make the over 300 million existing HP printers Bluetooth-capable. The company has also launched a wireless printing platform for mobile phones that Nokia (*www.nokia.com*) will use in its cell phones. This includes Nokia's NGage handheld devices that offer games, MP3 music, FM radio, cell phone, and personal productivity software (address book, calendar) in the same unit. Bluetooth chips are expected to be installed in over 1.4 billion appliances by 2015.

Bluetooth is ideal for establishing quick networks in meetings or among workgroup members who need to share applications or exchange files when they are in the same room. In its worldwide distribution hubs, United Parcel Service Inc. (*www.ups.com*) is combining the technologies in what will be the world's largest wireless LAN and short-range wireless Bluetooth network. The project, which will cost slightly more than US$100 million, is expected to pay for itself within 16 months by enabling package sorters at the hubs to work more efficiently and by standardizing the company on single terminals and network systems.

Hotspots
Areas that offer wireless Internet access.

Hotspots (also hot spots) are areas where wireless Internet access is offered. Hotels, airports, malls, and Starbucks (*www.starbucks.com*) outlets are installing them in Japan, South Korea, Taiwan, Hong Kong, Singapore, and Australia, where Wi-Fi and WLANs are highly popular. Thousands of public wireless ISPs (WISPs) offer public wireless LAN access at indoor locations convenient to mobile workers, travelers, and consumers. In the United States, Portland is the top hotspot metropolitan area, followed by San Francisco, Austin, Seattle, and Washington, D.C. There are well over 20,000 hotspots in the United States and thousands more worldwide. Some hotspots offer free access as a loss leader, whereas others require that the user have a paid subscription to log on. In addition to Starbucks, public hotspots are in McDonald's (*www.mcdonalds.com*) restaurants, Borders (*www.bordersstores.com*) bookstores, Marriott (*www.marriott.com*) and Hilton (*www.hilton.com*) hotels, and other locations. Verizon (*www22.verizon.com*) offers portable Wi-Fi in major cities where its cell phone network reaches.

Hotspots appear to be popping up everywhere, but given that they have a very limited geographical coverage area, how can a user locate one? Most hotspots are not immediately recognizable, and no universal icon or symbol yet identifies them. T-Mobile signs are beginning to appear in some hotspot locations, particularly Starbucks, but this is the exception. Laptop users can turn on their computer and let it search for an access point, but this is an awkward strategy, particularly in urban areas where interference can return "false positives." Some companies are beginning to offer Wi-Fi-sniffing software, but initial tests indicate that this is a poor approach. The best way to locate hotspots is to go online to such search sites as Intel's hotspot finder (*http://intel.jiwire.com*), the Wi-Fi FreeSpot Directory (*http://wififreespot.com*), and the Wi-Fi HotSpotList (*wi-fihotspotlist.com*).[26]

THERE ARE DRAWBACKS TO WIRELESS

Although analysts and the media are very excited about wireless, it is important to remember the lessons of the bursting of the dot-com bubble and the subsequent shakeout. Irrational exuberance can lead to bitter disappointment. Today, some people regard the wireless boom and m (for mobile)-marketing with expectations of great profits, but all should realize that wireless has drawbacks too and just having a Wi-Fi chip in a laptop doesn't mean a consumer will search for and use a hotspot. Even Bluetooth, with its usable range of about thirty feet, has its problems. Reports are beginning to appear of *bluejacking*, where unsuspecting Bluetooth-equipped cell phone users receive surprise prank calls from similarly equipped Bluetooth users within their range. When Bluetooth is turned on, it automatically searches for similarly equipped devices and establishes a link. Pranksters can use the link to send calls.

Electronic interference from cordless telephones, microwave ovens, and other appliances, as well as signal overlap between Wi-Fi devices, can compromise the effectiveness of wireless devices using the 802.11b (the most widely used alternative) and 802.11g standards in the 2.4-GHz band range. This is a familiar problem to cell phone users who encounter *dead zones* where service is blocked by tall buildings or experience limited roaming areas.

More problematic for most users is whether their equipment ever attains the speed promised by manufacturers; the highest speeds typically require hardware from the same vendor. Slow connects will hinder the use of wireless for m-marketing.

Privacy and security are serious problems because wireless is more susceptible to intrusion than wired access. Wi-Fi Protected Access (WPA) is a secure standard that is just starting to appear in wireless products. It is now required for any new product seeking Wi-Fi Alliance certification. However, older products typically have weak shields against intruders.

Getting wireless systems to network can be an insurmountable challenge for the average homeowner. Documentation typically is unintelligible. The products often are difficult to mix and match, and figuring out how to connect routers, PC cards, USB adapters, and other kit elements can be beyond the ability of most adults, even though their kids can probably make it all work. Products, moreover, are sometimes faulty. Tech support for the products is also problematic and may be hard to reach, let alone understand.

Wireless Internet access can be slow and connections are sometimes finicky. The promise of ten-second movie downloads cannot be realized until connections become more reliable and more devices can accept fat, data-rich files. In short, running cables can be cheaper, more dependable, faster, and less annoying than going wireless.

Most companies with hotspots are not making money from the service. Any competitive marketing advantage they enjoyed from being a first mover quickly vanished as new entrants moved into the market. Consumers are not willing to pay for hotspot use, and frankly, many business users want to eat lunch away from the Internet and their email.

Some people are concerned about the fact that wireless devices can be equipped with a chip that links to the Global Positioning System (GPS) so users can be identified geographically whenever they connect. This presents opportunities for further invasions of consumer privacy as they go online. The Federal Communications Commission is requiring that all U.S. wireless handsets have precise positioning for 911 calls.

Wired and wireless will continue to coexist in North America, as many Internet users wait for prices to come down—and for the devices to improve—before converting. Yet even with all its problems, the market for wireless is very appealing. Large corporations such as Cisco Systems, Microsoft, and Intel are making sure they are not left behind as wireless gains momentum. This presents industrial and consumer marketing opportunities and marketing wireless products is a growth industry, at least for the present.[27]

Summary

http://college.hmco.com/business/students

Internet Operations: How the Internet Works

The Internet is a tangible entity with a physical infrastructure. Although most consumers in the United States still use a modem, standard telephone line, and ISP to connect to the Internet, this is beginning to change. Local area networks (LANs) connect users in businesses, schools, and organizations.

Data (email, web pages, and so on) are transmitted as small, independent digital packets routed along network transmission lines. When they arrive at their destination, they are reassembled into their original form. An important advantage of the Internet is its redundancy, which is vital to conducting online business activities because multiple routes for data transmission increase the probability that data will be delivered. Routers and servers are essential to smooth Internet operations and data packet transmission. Software includes programs, documents, and data that run one or millions of computers. The Internet hosts many services that developed independently but operate on the global matrix and adhere to the TCP/IP protocol. Many businesses and organizations support proprietary intranets and extranets, where many marketing activities take place. Security is a top concern with all Internet-based services. Although the Internet has been promoted as an open environment where information is voluntarily shared, significant barriers to universal access exist. The Internet is robust but not invulnerable. Cyberterrorism is a growing concern, and preventive measures are being taken by enterprises and governments in anticipation of future attacks against the Internet.

Internet Management

The Internet is run by no single entity, yet many individuals, organizations, enterprises, and governments contribute to its management, growth, and continued stability. The U.S. Federal Trade Commission has taken the lead on many Internet business issues. Self-regulation plays an important role in addressing significant problems of Internet use. First among the voluntary committees is The Internet Society. The World Wide Web Consortium develops standards for the World Wide Web, HTTP, HTML, and other web protocols. The Internet Corporation for Assigned Names and Numbers allocates IP addresses and manages the domain name system. Self-regulation is often undertaken to prevent the need for government regulation. TRUSTe, VIPPS, and BBBOnline are examples of industry self-regulation.

How the Web Works

Like every system operating on the Internet matrix, the Web adheres to the TCP/IP protocol suite. It also requires a unique protocol, HyperText Transfer Protocol (HTTP), for transferring files, including web pages. Special browser software locates, retrieves, and views web pages. Text-only files download faster than graphical files. Web page addresses are an important marketing tool. Many addresses are dropping the www and using only hostname and file location. Domain names were introduced to simplify Internet addressing by allowing the substitution of words for numbers. Domain names have sometimes been registered by speculators who planned to sell them in the future for profit. As the numbers of web pages and websites increase, it will become harder for marketers to penetrate the clutter and reach potential customers. Portals are generic or niche gateways to the Web. Portals pose a contradiction, for most marketers want customers to stay on their sites (stick), whereas portals direct visitors to other sites. Blogs are a form of individualized, personalized web portal.

Wireless Connectivity

Wireless is a generic term that refers to the transfer of data between sender and receiver via radio (or optical) waves of different frequencies. Most Americans already use a variety of wireless devices. The technology frees users from cables, wires, and other hardware connection devices for short or long distances to transmit large or small amounts of data, on or off the Internet. Wireless has deeply penetrated the Asian market, is becoming established in Europe, and is making significant inroads in the United States. It holds the promise of bridging the access digital divide in developing countries. Wi-Fi refers to any product tested and approved as Wi-Fi-certified by the Wi-Fi Alliance. Bluetooth is designed to allow wireless communication between chip-equipped devices over short distances. Bluetooth is ideal for establishing quick networks in meetings or among workgroup members who need to share applications or exchange files when they are in the same room. Hotspots are areas where wireless Internet access is offered. Hotels, airports, malls, and retail outlets are installing them. Wireless also has disadvantages, including privacy and security shortcomings, bluejacking, electronic interference, dead reception zones, unintelligible product documentation, defective products, and slow and sometimes undependable Internet connection. Hotspots are not generating revenue for most providers. Wired and wireless will continue to coexist in North America.

Take Action!

Let's assume you'll graduate soon, so it's time to begin the job search. Wireless appears to offer lots of marketing opportunities, and you believe T-Mobile (*www.t-mobile.com*) might be a good place to start.

1. You realize that you need to prepare for a job interview by familiarizing yourself with the company. Prepare a one-page bullet list of information about T-Mobile USA that you need to know before interviewing with the company. Focus on information relevant to your job search and the hiring situation. Visit T-Mobile online to obtain the information identified on the bullet list. When the list is complete, type it, single space, beginning with the most important information.

2. Use Google (*www.google.com*) to locate current news stories about T-Mobile with the search terms *T-Mobile News*. Alternatively, visit online news sources such as InternetNews (*www.internetnews.com/wireless/*), E-Commerce Times (*www.ecommercetimes .com*), and WirelessWeek (*www.wirelessweek .com*). Carefully check the sources to eliminate company press releases and anticorporate sites. Prepare a one-page, typed bullet list of current news stories headlines about T-Mobile.

3. Check to see what marketing jobs are listed on the T-Mobile site. Create a list of up to ten marketing jobs that might interest you. Consider why you are drawn to these jobs. Once you have narrowed the list, visit Monster (*www.monster.com*) and search for similar jobs in other companies. This is an effective way to gain insight into what is happening in the industry and into what the competition is doing.

Chapter Review Questions

1. What does Cisco Systems contribute to Internet operations?
2. Explain the difference between bandwidth and broadband.
3. What is Internet redundancy and why is it so important?
4. What is the marketing value of domain names?
5. How do portals invite behavior that is contradictory to how marketers want consumers to behave?
6. What barriers limit access to the Internet?
7. What effects will the growing numbers of web pages have on advertisers?
8. What are firewalls and what critical functions do they serve?
9. What is TRUSTe? How does it help manage the Internet?
10. Does the WWW operate on TCP/IP? Explain.
11. What is the difference between HTTP and HTML?

12. What is a cybersquatter? Is cybersquatting just good business or is it a serious threat to trademarks?
13. Cite four examples of TLDs.

14. Why do users like wireless? What might explain their low use of hotspots?
15. Why might senior citizens prefer wireless to PCs?

Competitive Case Study

Competing with Cisco

Cisco Systems dominates the market for routers and switches, essential hardware used to link computer networks and keep the Internet running smoothly. It is also a power in wireless connectivity. Still, Cisco has competition, principally among other hardware companies that manufacture networking equipment, such as Nortel Networks (*www.nortelnetworks.com/index.html*), Juniper Networks (*www.juniper.net*), and Extreme Networks (*www.extremenetworks.com*). Each has carved out a niche for itself, despite Cisco's dominance.

Customers are the driving force at Nortel Networks. The company is committed to delivering quality networking and communication services and infrastructure in more than 150 countries. Its product portfolio includes packet, optical, wireless, and voice technologies. Its goal is to deliver seamless, ubiquitous broadband connectivity. Wireless products sold by Nortel include cellular base stations and controllers. Customers include global communications carriers; regional, local, and wireless phone carriers; and corporations. According to the company, "People are our strength; innovation fuels our future; accountability brings clarity; and integrity underpins everything" (*www.nortelnetworks.com/corporate/cm/index.html*). Although Nortel doesn't sell its products directly online, it offers a partner locator service at *www38.nortelnetworks.com/nn/locator_2003/default.asp*.

CHECK IT OUT

Visit Hoover's Online at *www.hoovers.com* and locate Nortel Networks. Find the free company capsule view. What companies are Nortel's main competitors? Is Cisco among them? Compare Cisco and Nortel on fiscal year end sales, 1-year sales growth, net income, number of employees, and 1-year employee growth rate. Visit the Nortel website and determine what types of marketing jobs are available at Nortel. What skills are needed? Is experience required? What would a student have to do to prepare for a job at Nortel?

A GLOBAL PERSPECTIVE

Cisco Systems and Nortel Networks are both global companies. Judging on the basis of evidence from their websites, what countries are Cisco's principal target markets? What countries are Nortel's markets? Do they overlap in their market coverage? How accommodating are they to international visitors on their web homepages? Visit several of their country websites, and although the language is not English, look for consistency of web design, content, and technology. Do the companies localize their websites with local languages and images? What makes the international sites distinctively corporate sites? Is there a marketing advantage to this website consistency?

3

Identifying Internet Users

LEARNING OBJECTIVES

» To identify broad segments of Internet users
» To identify enterprise Internet users
» To identify consumer Internet users
» To understand what Internet users are doing online

Elearning: The University of Phoenix Online

The Apollo Group, Inc. *(www.apollogrp.edu)*, is a business that provides higher education and training opportunities for working adults through its subsidiaries the University of Phoenix (including University of Phoenix Online), the Institute for Professional Development, the College for Financial Planning Institutes Corporation, and Western International University. The University of Phoenix (UOP Online or Phoenix Online) was among the first accredited universities offering college degree programs totally online. It is the online unit of the nation's largest accredited university. The combined enrollment in all of Apollo Group's educational programs makes it the largest for-profit company of its type. At the end of 2003, Apollo's subsidiaries enrolled 211,300 students, up from just under 87,000 in 1999, on 74 campuses, 122 learning centers, and the Internet. Net revenues for 2003 (through November 30) were US$1.75 billion. Phoenix went online in 1989 and by 2003, degree enrollments had risen to 91,000 students, a 60 percent increase from 57,000 students in 2002. Net revenues for Phoenix Online were US$5.9 million, double the income from the previous year, and operating profit margins topped 30 percent. The company projects that Phoenix Online degree enrollments will increase another 50 percent in FY04. Phoenix Online delivers what working adult students want—convenience; online financial aid, book buying, counseling, and academic advising; quality instruction; and undergraduate and graduate degrees in education, nursing, and business. Classes are offered both totally online and through FlexNet, an option that combines online and classroom learning. Classes are small, around eleven students in each; emphasize interaction, writing, and application; and rely on email, threaded discussions, and text lecture files. Students can attend classes at times and places that fit their schedule, and they typically earn a degree in two or three years. Classes are offered one at a time, for five- to six-week periods, so that students can focus on a single subject with fewer distractions. Some educators scoff at the idea of a for-profit online university, complaining that quality suffers when students never meet their professors face-to-face. Others believe the best evidence of the quality of Phoenix Online is its profitability. "If they weren't doing a good job, if they didn't have a quality offering, they wouldn't be making any money." About 13 percent of the approximately 500,000 U.S. students earning a degree on the Internet are enrolled at Phoenix Online. Some analysts believe that at least half of all post-secondary students will eventually use the Internet to earn all or part of their degrees.[1]

Knowing who is using the Internet and how they are using it is an essential first step in developing effective Internet marketing strategies. The number of Internet users worldwide is expected to reach 1.46 billion by 2007, up from 533 million in 2001. Wireless Internet use will increase even more dramatically, from 4.5 percent of all users in 2001 to 46.3 percent in 2007. The dominant share of North Americans and Western Europeans online is eroding. In 2001, the North American–Western European share of worldwide Internet users was approximately 61 percent. Today, the growth in Internet adopter numbers is slowing in those regions as their markets approach maturity. Growth is accelerating in Asia, Latin America, and Eastern Europe as new adopters go online, often using wireless and broadband, skipping traditional personal computers and narrowband dial-up access. By 2004, the North American–Western European share of worldwide users had already dropped 3 percentage points to 58 percent, with Asia–Pacific's share rising to 33 percent, Latin America's to 8 percent, and Africa's to just under 2 percent. Within each of these regions, people increasingly are becoming dependent on the Internet at work, school, and home. They are also connecting at higher speeds. In 2003, high-speed broadband penetration was highest in Hong Kong (82 percent of its Internet-using population), dwarfing rates in the United States (33.8 percent of Internet users; 13 percent of all Americans) and Europe (28 percent of Internet users), although broadband use is accelerating in these areas. European broadband use jumped 136 percent from April 2002 to April 2003, driven by file sharing and downloads of music, film, and adult material.[2]

Internet User Segments

Even in countries with fully developed, highly industrialized, technologically sophisticated economies, some enterprises and consumers are not Internet users now and never will go online. Directing marketing efforts toward Internet *nonadopters* is a waste of resources for most marketers in most circumstances, particularly because the universe of Internet users is already large and expanding. There are some exceptions that will be discussed later in this chapter, but by and large, our marketing interest lies with *adopters,* current Internet users, and *laggards,* potential users that are slow to go online but will do so in the future, perhaps with some marketing encouragement.

Marketing niche
A marketing target group that is a smaller and relatively homogeneous subset of a larger group.

Consider all the types of people and organizations that comprise a complex society such as that of the United States. The entire society is the *universe* of potential Internet users. We can speak of the universe in marketing terms, noting, for example, that the United States generates a certain percentage of total worldwide ecommerce revenues. For strategic purposes, it is more effective to speak in terms of marketing to segments of the universe and, within the segments, of targeting relatively homogeneous subgroups or even smaller **marketing niches.** The members of a **homogeneous group** share characteristics that distinguish them from members of other groups. Prime targets for Internet marketing activities are two broad segments of Internet users: enterprises (including businesses) and consumers.

Homogeneous group
A group whose members share characteristics that distinguish them from members of other groups.

Enterprise
A broad segment that includes for-profit businesses as well as public sector governments, hospitals and clinics, universities, private nonprofit and nongovernmental organizations, religious institutions, and other groups.

B2B exchanges
Business-to-business marketing exchanges, wherein businesses sell to other businesses online or offline.

The **enterprise** segment is extremely broad and includes for-profit businesses along with public sector governments, hospitals and clinics, universities, private non-profit and non-governmental organizations (NGOs), religious institutions, and other groups. Many enterprises are run like businesses even though profit is not their primary organizational goal; many other enterprises must generate revenues and profits in order to survive.

A prime goal of most businesses is to facilitate revenue-generating, profitable exchanges that are the goal of marketing activities online and offline. These exchanges include business-to-business exchanges (**B2B exchanges**) business-to-consumer exchanges (**B2C exchanges**), and business-to-public-sector exchanges (**B2P exchanges**). Public sector exchanges are also made with businesses (P2B), other enterprises, and consumers (P2C).

Consumers are individuals or groups who purchase products for their own use, or for that of family, friends, or others, but not solely for business or enterprise use. Consumers significantly outnumber businesses and other enterprises online and offline. The United States, with an annual gross domestic product (GDP) of over US$11 trillion (2003 estimate), is often characterized as a consumer-driven society. Consumer spending in the aggregate constitutes two-thirds of U.S. GDP and drives enterprise planning, production, buying, and selling decisions. Internet commercialization spurred a boom in consumer-to-consumer exchanges (**C2C exchanges**), particularly on eBay (*www.ebay.com*) and other online auctions.

Enterprises Using the Internet

B2C exchanges
Business-to-consumer marketing exchanges, where businesses sell to consumers online or offline.

B2P exchanges
Business-to-public-sector marketing exchanges, where businesses sell to government and public sector enterprises.

Consumers
Individuals or groups who purchase products for their own or others' use but not solely for business or enterprise use.

Although businesses are a subset of the larger enterprise segment, we will consider them first because of their importance to Internet marketing activities, both as marketers and as targets of marketing activities. Although large corporations receive the most media attention, small businesses are embracing Internet use and attracting keen marketing interest. For many small businesses, the Internet presents a unique opportunity to serve existing customers better, expand their marketing reach, and compete in markets that were previously inaccessible.

BUSINESSES

A business is a legally incorporated enterprise whose activities are conducted primarily to make a profit. The U.S. Census Bureau counted 22.9 million businesses in the United States in 2002, including almost 6 million employer firms and 17 million non-employer firms.[3]

Caution must be exercised in applying these numbers because they are static, representing a snapshot at one point in time. In reality, the business segment is highly dynamic and exists in a constant state of flux marked by startups, subsidiary formations, closures, and business bankruptcies. The period after the 2001 recession was particularly volatile, with closures more common than start-ups. The reported number of U.S. businesses undercounts the total because it does not include the hidden, or underground, economy of businesses that evade taxes. It does include firms that employ more than one person (employer firms), sole proprietorships with no employees (non-

C2C exchanges
Consumer-to-consumer marketing exchanges, wherein individuals sell to other individuals particularly via online auctions.

employer firms) other than the owner–operator (for example, an independent real estate agent), part-time employees and hobby venturists, nannies, and over one million individuals in direct sales ventures such as Herbalife (*www.herbalife.com*) and Avon (*www.avon.com*).

Census Bureau data show that 99.7 percent of U.S. business are small, with fewer than 500 employees, yet they collectively employ over 50 percent of the nation's workers and create two-thirds to three-quarters of all new jobs. A small business is independently owned and not the dominant competitor in its field. The largest companies, with annual revenues over US$100 million, make up less than 1 percent of all U.S. businesses but represent over 40 percent of all employment and more than 60 percent of total business revenues. Midsize businesses constitute the remainder. Large businesses in industrialized nations were quick to use the Internet. They represent a highly diverse group, and although they have websites, they are not necessarily buying online or making transactions on their sites, although most do so. Many examples of large business Internet users are offered throughout the marketing strategy chapters later in this book.[4]

Small and midsize businesses also make significant contributions to the economies in other developed countries. In Australia, over 95 percent of all businesses are small, and in New Zealand, 96 percent of all businesses employ 19 or fewer full-time employees. Over 99 percent of the 2.2 million businesses in Canada are small and midsize enterprises (SMEs) with fewer than 500 employees. In England, 3.75 million active businesses are reported, and over 99 percent have fewer than 300 employees. Note that the definition of *small* varies between countries and within countries, as well.[5]

Small and midsize businesses are important to marketing students because they often are the first employers for new graduates and because many graduates hope eventually to become a small business owner. Small business ownership can be a lifestyle choice, a way to achieve the American Dream. It can also be the mechanism by which entrepreneurs can quickly take advantage of business opportunities, particularly online. For Internet marketers, small businesses can be profitable customers, clients, and suppliers.

BUSINESS COMPUTER AND INTERNET USE

Computer and Internet use are growing rapidly among small businesses. Results of the 21st Annual D&B Small Business Survey (2002) revealed that 85 percent of small U.S. business respondents had at least one computer, up from 80 percent in 2001, and that 71 percent of all small businesses had Internet access, up from 62 percent in 2001. Internet access was more common in larger businesses with six to twenty-five employees, home-based businesses, and B2B sellers; Internet use was more likely in such sectors as real estate, transportation services, and business services than in manufacturing, wholesale, retail, or construction. Small businesses represent a major opportunity for Internet marketers with the technical expertise to help small companies find profitable ways to market themselves online.[6]

Even for nonemployer small businesses, the investment in a computer and Internet access is small and falling. It is typically less than US$600 for an Internet-ready computer, under US$20 per month for enhanced-speed dial-up service, and as little as US$40 per month to rent web server space. Many small businesses have only one major customer, and increasingly, buyers such as Wal-Mart (*www.walmart.com*) and Meijer Stores LLP (*http://meijer.com*) require that their suppliers use electronic data exchange (EDI) on the Internet. By the end of 2003, more than 98 percent of Wal-Mart's EDI exchanges with suppliers were conducted on the Internet.[7]

NONBUSINESS ENTERPRISE INTERNET USERS

Eprocurement
Purchases made via Internet, intranets, or extranets.

Egovernment
Delivery of government information and services via the Internet, intranets, or extranets.

FirstGov

The federal government dominates the enterprise sector in the United States and many industrialized countries. In the United States, it is the largest single buyer, seller, and employer. From the beginning of Internet commercialization, the U.S. government has been a strong proponent of its adoption as well as one of its largest users. Popularized as the *Digital Superhighway,* the Internet was highly promoted by the Clinton administration for use by governments, schools, businesses, and citizens. It was viewed as a means for the federal government to achieve significant savings in online purchasing, or **eprocurement,** as well as bring government closer to citizens through **egovernment**—interactions with citizens over the Internet, intranets, or extranets. The Federal Acquisition Streamlining Act (FASA) of 1994, signed into law by President Clinton on October 13, 1994, mandates that the federal government use eprocurement to reduce paperwork, speed transaction times, and streamline purchasing procedures.

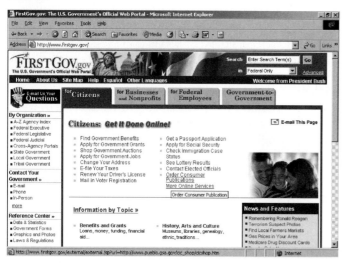

The United States government makes extensive use of the Internet to interact with citizens, businesses, and other enterprises. FirstGov is the portal to the U.S. government online.

Source: Courtesy FirstGov, www.firstgov.gov.

The highest rates of egovernment use are found in countries with the highest rates of overall Internet use, particularly the Scandinavian countries and North America. Research shows that citizen use of egovernment is highest in Denmark (63 percent) and Norway (62 percent), and Canadian egovernment use (51 percent) exceeds U.S. use (44 percent). Egovernment services lag in Britain, where it increased to only 18 percent in 2003. This compares to an estimate of 31 percent of egovernment-using citizens worldwide.[8]

City governments in all large and most midsize U.S. cities are heavy Internet users and typically have their own websites. Small cities are more likely to be part of a regional website than to have independent sites. Most regional administrative bodies have Internet connections, as do public utilities, airports, and similar facilities.

Internet use is almost universal in two- and four-year colleges and universities in the United States. Institutions of higher education support Internet use by their

Blue Grass Airport

Blue Grass Airport in Lexington, Kentucky, has its own website with information targeted to a broad array of users.

Source: Courtesy Blue Grass Airport, www.bluegrassairport.com.

American Red Cross

The American Red Cross uses its website to provide information, recruit volunteers, and solicit donations of blood, tissue, food, money, and supplies for emergencies worldwide.

Source: Courtesy American Red Cross, http://redcross.org.

students, faculties, and staff, and they also host complex, multipage information sites for such activities as student recruiting, distance learning, course registration, advising, and class scheduling. The University of Texas at Austin (*www.utexas.edu/world/univ*) maintains a linked list of regionally accredited four-year state universities and community colleges. Internet access in U.S. public schools grew from an estimated 3 percent in 1994 to 99 percent in 2002. The combined global market for education and worker training is estimated to be worth US$2 trillion, with the United States representing almost 40 percent of the market, or approximately US$70 billion.[9]

Medical professionals are active Internet users in the United States and other developed nations. This includes doctors, dentists, and personnel in medical schools, hospitals and clinics, and medical practices. For example, of the approximately 560,000 practicing physicians in the United States, nearly half participated in Internet-based meetings with pharmaceutical marketing representatives in 2003. Medical professionals around the world, even in developing nations, are online. A recent study in Nigeria found that almost 43 percent of currently enrolled medical and nursing students are computer literate and that 61 percent have used the Internet. The Health on the Net Foundation (*www.hon.ch*) maintains links to countries around the world that are encouraging the use of the Internet by their health care professionals and organizations.[10]

Large numbers of churches and religious organizations are online, including synagogues and mosques, Bahá'í Communities, the Society of Friends, religious schools, and university student religious groups. Charities large and small use the Internet, and environmental activists are online, as are human rights watchdogs and other groups. In short, it would be easier to list the types of enterprises that are *not* online than to catalog those that are Internet users.

Consumer Internet Users

Consumers are often called *personal use* consumers to differentiate their buying goals from those of enterprises and business buyers. The U.S. population of over 292 million is only 4.5 percent of the total world population of more than 6.4 billion, yet it is the most desirable consumer market in the world because of its size, high median income, relative homogeneity (including almost universal use of the English language), eagerness to spend, and receptivity to marketing. It is also currently the single largest market of Internet users in the world.[11]

Marketers have always been interested in the characteristics of the U.S. consumer market, and that remains true today as the market undergoes dramatic changes. Data from the 2000 census confirm that the U.S. population is aging, has become more ethnically diverse, and is no longer dominated by the traditional household of a husband, stay-at-home wife, and two or more children. In the 1950s, over 80 percent of all households were traditional; today, they represent only about 10 percent of all households. Only 25 percent of married couples have children at home, and that number is expected to drop to 20 percent by 2010. Growing numbers of nontraditional U.S. households are composed of singles, single parents, divorced individuals, empty nesters, and people of the opposite sex or of the same sex living together. More Americans are moving inexorably toward retirement as the **baby boom** cohort of people born between 1946 and 1964 ages, and there are fewer young adults ages 20 to 34, the prime years for building brand loyalty. The number of kids under 5 is shrinking as a percentage of the total population. At the same time, significant numbers of immigrants from China, Mexico, and India are refreshing the population and contributing to labor and consumer markets.[12]

Baby boom
Cohort of people born between 1946 and 1964.

INTERNET USER PROFILES ARE CHANGING

Early U.S. Internet users generally were highly educated (college and postgraduate), computer-savvy white males employed in professional, technical, or managerial jobs with higher than average incomes. U.S. Internet users today mirror the general population more closely, but not exactly. On a typical day, over 66 million Americans are online. The estimated overall number of Americans online is more than 63 percent of the adult U.S. population (those 18 years of age and older), but not all age groups are equally well represented. Around 75 percent of children between ages 12 and 17 use the Internet. Younger consumers are more likely to be online than retirees. Parents are more likely to be online than nonparents. In general, U.S. Internet users are still more highly educated; at least 32 percent have a college or postgraduate degree, compared with 22 percent of the general U.S. population. Even though 65 percent of all males in the U.S. population are online, they represent only 49 percent of total Internet users because there are more women proportionally in the general population, thus women make up slightly over 51 percent of all U.S. Internet users. More minorities than ever before are Internet users. However, whites still dominate the U.S. Internet-using population numerically and proportionally, with around 64 percent of Caucasians (whites) online compared to 63 percent of English-speaking Hispanics and 51 percent of African-Americans. More Americans still go online from home than from work or other locations such as school or Internet cafés. Out-of-home connections are more popular abroad than in the United States. Around one-third of American homes with Internet access have broadband connections. Higher-income consumers are far more likely to be online than lower-income consumers, and they spend more time online than other groups. Consumers in urban areas are more likely to use the Internet than consumers in rural areas.[13]

Several factors make it difficult to construct a profile of the average Internet user or to take a 100 percent accurate user tally. Most people go online from several different places—at home, at work, in school, in libraries and other public places, and by wireless. As a result, the same users may be counted multiple times, so the number of apparent Internet users is inflated. At the same time, the number of home Internet users is undercounted. Research that counts a single Internet-connected computer in a multiperson household may not capture how many people actually use it, how frequently they connect, or what they do online. This is also the case for the number of Internet users at work, because multiple users typically connect through the same host. Another problem is that research organizations use different parameters to describe groups under study. Definitions of *young* and *old* users vary. Some researchers count online populations as people 2 years old and older; others count users 18 years old and older; seniors may be 49–55 years of age in some studies and 65+ in others. Online demographic research is conducted within a highly dynamic environment where changes occur rapidly and often unexpectedly. New users go online easily and others go offline, which compromises the accuracy of user counts. These and other measurement problems have led to disparities in reported Internet demographics. Even so, trends clearly indicate that growing numbers of consumers of all ages throughout the world are becoming Internet users and, therefore, potential Internet marketing targets to their home-country marketers and international marketers.

Table 3-1 presents pertinent demographic data, compiled from multiple sources, about consumer Internet users in the United States. They represent increasing trends over time, with numbers that are growing but at a slower pace than in the period from 1999 to 2001.

Consumer Internet user demographics in Europe are also changing, and, just as in the United States, they more closely resemble the general population. More children are online in Europe (13.1 million), with Britain having the most under-18 Internet users (4 to 5 million). Children under age 12 are the single most rapidly growing Internet user segment in Europe. European families are going online more frequently, facilitated by broadband and flat rate access that replaces metered access where users must pay for using the Internet by the minute. Gender distribution is a noticeable difference between Internet users in the United States and in Europe. More European women are becoming Internet users, but even in Sweden and the United Kingdom (the countries with the largest numbers of women online), women represent only 47 and 45 percent of Internet users respectively. A continuing problem in Europe is the perception that the Internet is a man's world.[15]

Large numbers of non-English-speakers began using the commercial Internet around 1995. Initially, adoption occurred most rapidly in industrialized countries with

Table 3-1 Characteristics of U.S. Internet Users[14]

Characteristic	Number or Percent
Estimated Total U.S. Internet adult users (home, work, school)	151 million
Internet user access:	
Home	87 percent
Work	47 percent
School	99 percent
Internet café	25 percent
U.S. Internet users with broadband access	34 percent
Internet users online for more than 3 years	74 percent
Internet user gender:	
Male users as percent of all U.S. males	65 percent
Female users as percent of all U.S. females	61 percent
Gender distribution of total U.S. Internet population:	
male	49 percent
female	51 percent
Ethnic composition of U.S. Internet population: percent Caucasian Internet users of total white population	64 percent
Ethnic composition of U.S. Internet population: percent Hispanic Internet users of total U.S. Hispanic population	62 percent
Ethnic composition of U.S. Internet population: percent African-American Internet users of total African-American population	51 percent
Age distribution of U.S. Internet population:	
users ages 18–29 as percent of population 18–29	83 percent
users ages 30–49 as percent of population 30–49	73 percent
users ages 50–64 as percent of population 50–64	59 percent
users over age 65 as percent of population over 65	22 percent

high incomes and education levels but was slower in countries with low average incomes and education levels. North Americans from the United States and Canada dominated Internet and Web usage in the first decade of commercialization. By 2004, North America and Europe combined represented just under 60 percent of Internet users. This proportion will continue to fall as more Asian–Pacific, Latin American, and African consumers go online. Table 3-2 contains current country Internet usage data compiled from such sources as Nielsen-NetRatings (*www.nielsen-netratings.com*), the International Telecommunications Union (*www.itu.int/home/index.html*), local networked information centers such as Network Solutions (*www.networksolutions.com*), and ISPs. The United States remains the country with the largest total number of Internet users, but that lead will diminish as more Chinese and Indians go online. Both

Table 3-2 Top Countries by Internet Use—Penetration Rates and Populations[16]

Top 10 Countries by Penetration Rate	Percent	Top 10 Countries by Population	Millions
1. Sweden	76	1. United States	184
2. Hong Kong	67	2. China	68
3. Australia	64	3. Japan	59
4. The Netherlands	64	4. Germany	44
5. United States	63	5. United Kingdom	34
6. Denmark	64	6. South Korea	26
7. Iceland	60	7. France	22
8. Switzerland	59	8. Italy	19
9. United Kingdom	58	9. Canada	17
10. South Korea	56	10. India	16

China and India have populations of over 1 billion. More will be said about international Internet users and markets in Chapter 6.

Worldwide growth in numbers of Internet users increases the potential for reaching receptive international consumer markets. At the same time, more marketers are also going online. This hints at how crowded the selling space will become as adoption spreads. It presents a conundrum, for as much as marketers may want the revenues represented by having more potential consumers online, at the same time they will have to work harder to reach and keep them. For some U.S. marketers, the Internet may finally encourage them to abandon their domestic marketing myopia and pursue international revenues online. Others will use the Internet as a parallel channel to improve their service to existing customers in Canada and/or Mexico, our NAFTA partners. The majority will probably continue to use the Internet to service solely domestic customers, seeking efficiencies online but avoiding what they perceive as the problems associated with international Internet marketing.

WHO'S NOT ONLINE

The ideal of an Internet for everyone will never be achieved, even in the United States and other industrialized nations. Some enterprises and consumers are not online by choice. Others face barriers to becoming Internet users. It's the latter group that particularly concerns Internet marketers, because they represent lost potential customers.

Digital divide
A real or presumed barrier to Internet use and a gap between users and nonusers.

DIGITAL DIVIDES   The existence and extent of **digital divides,** real or presumed barriers to Internet use and gaps between Internet users and nonusers, continue to be debated. Several types of digital divides have been identified. One is between rich and poor countries—for example, between North America and Western Europe (richer, fully industrialized) and countries in South America or most of Africa (poorer, far less industrialized). The richer, more industrialized nations are being urged to help poorer nations become Internet users so they can take advantage of what the technology can do for their countries and people. The numbers of nonusers and the extent of the digital divide between rich and poor are controversial estimates. Internet user surveys typically fail to count the large number of people who use Internet cafés in poorer nations and even in some richer nations where personal computer ownership lags or local access costs are high. This undercounting somewhat misrepresents the digital divide between rich and poor and ignores relatively large numbers of Internet users at cafés and other communal locations. Despite the lack of an accurate assessment of the situation, in December 2003 the United Nations convened a World Summit on the Information Society to focus on the rich–poor divide. Delegates from 175 governments—over 10,000 participants—met in Geneva for three days. The results were a stated goal of "connecting 50 percent of the world's population by 2015," failure to explain how the goal would be achieved, and a plan to meet again in 2005 to continue discussions.[17]

Digital divides also occur between countries within regions. For example, Internet use in Europe is highest in the Scandinavian countries of northern Europe, lower in southern Europe, and lower still in parts of central and Eastern Europe. This results from wage disparities, differences in national wealth and technology adoption rates, and liberal telecommunications policies in the more affluent north. Education and in-school access, lower computer and Internet access fees, and business/government leadership are keys to solving the problem.[18]

Other divides exist within countries, most notably as a consequence of geography, socioeconomic factors, and age. Population concentrations in cities and densely populated suburban areas typically have better ISP service and the availability of DSL and cable, whereas some rural areas users can still connect only through costly long-distance hookups or satellite. This is becoming less of a problem in the United States but remains a considerable barrier in some other parts of the world, where rural areas lack any telephone access, wired or wireless. Free public Internet access, more Internet cafés, and wireless will help ameliorate this problem. Socioeconomic factors, principally wealth and education, significantly affect Internet use. Greater numbers of poorer, less educated people are becoming Internet users as governments and private donors make it a priority to extend access. Rapidly falling computer prices are also helping to close this gap. Families can buy computers for under US$500, and many schools have grant programs for low-income students. Another divide is age-related, the gap between younger and older consumers. The very elderly are underrepresented online in most countries. In the United States, this can be explained by their techno- and/or computer phobia, the fear of a loss of privacy or security threat online, insufficient funds to purchase a PC or ISP, disability, and/or lack of interest. Consumers over age 65 express the least interest in going online. This divide will resolve itself with time, as the more techno-savvy baby boomers age and become the Internet-using elderly.

A fourth divide in the United States exists between the general U.S. population and Native Americans. Many Native Americans live in remote, isolated rural areas not well served even by telephones, let alone by the latest Internet technology. This is an impediment to Internet use by Native American consumers and enterprises. Native

WEB UPDATE

For updates and
more on this topic,
visit the textbook
student website at:
http://college.hmco
.com/business/students
and select Siegel,
Internet Marketing, 2e.
Digital Divides

American access may be among the more intractable divides facing those who promote access equality. It will take a disciplined effort and sustained commitment by the U.S. government and corporations working with Native American leaders to make Internet access a priority and a reality. Yet failing to do so can only further disadvantage Native Americans in the emerging economy.[19]

OFF BY CHOICE   Countless businesses and millions of U.S. consumers will never use the Internet. Some businesses will not go online or create a website because they see little benefit and too many costs. Consumer nonadopters may not connect for many of the same reasons why many of the very elderly will not go online, believing the Internet poses a security threat or fearing that it can become an obsession and control their lives. Others simply prefer to live an unconnected life. Neo-Luddites harbor deep suspicion of the technology and of what they perceive as the Internet's threat to societal and individual values. Some consumers have shopped online, had a bad experience, and disconnected, citing privacy or security concerns, or dissatisfaction with online retailing. Many consumers simply prefer shopping in a conventional store. For them shopping is a social experience that cannot be duplicated on the Internet, at least not yet. Whatever nonadopters' reasons not to go online, marketers can still reach them with conventional offline marketing tactics.

RESTRICTED BY IMPAIRMENT   Consumers in the United States who have physical impairments (disabilities) spend more than US$175 billion annually. This includes over a million blind Americans, who need an audible translation of text embedded on web pages if they are to use the Internet. At least 8 percent of Internet users have a physical or learning disability; 4 percent are blind. For the blind, the Internet has the potential to deliver tremendous communication advantages. To facilitate their Internet use, the National Foundation for the Blind (*www.nfb.org*) is asking website owners to include text descriptors of all graphics so that screen-reading software can translate the text. The colorblind have difficulty deciphering colored graphics navigation icons that lack a text explanation. U.S. government agencies are making their websites accessible to the disabled, primarily by adding text for describing graphics, at a cost ranging from an estimated US$85 million to US$691 million. Barriers that have kept many disabled off the Internet are beginning to fall, but only slowly.[20]

What Internet Users Are Doing Online

Marketers are highly interested in what Internet users are doing online. Information about these activities can provide insights into potentially profitable gaps in the market, as well as reveal trends and behavior shifts that may represent opportunities or threats to current Internet marketing activities.

CONSUMER INTERNET BEHAVIORS

According to Pew Internet & American Life Project (*www.pewinternet.org*) tracking surveys, experience online and new applications motivate Americans to find new ways to use the Internet. Almost 75 percent of U.S. Internet users have at least three years

Table 3-3 Percent of American Internet Users Who Engage in Various Online Behaviors on an Average Day[21]

Behavior	Percent
Going online	66
Sending email	49
Using a search engine to find information	31
Getting news	26
Surfing the Web for fun	23
Looking for information on a hobby or interest	21
Checking the weather	20
Doing any type of research for their job	19 (2002)
Sending an instant message	14
Watching a video clip or listening to an audio clip	11
Sharing files from their computer with others	5
Purchasing a product	5

of experience online. That is good news for Internet marketers. More U.S. female Internet users are seeking health or religious information online; more males are looking for news (health, general, sports, or political news) and financial information. Internet use has increased among all minorities. More African-Americans are doing school research and seeking religious information online. More English-speaking Hispanics instant-message and download music than either African-Americans or whites. Wealthier and better educated users take advantage of a wider variety of Internet features, including online banking, egovernment, and auctions. Instant messaging appeals most to younger users, who are also heavy users of music downloads and/or file sharing. As expected, speedier connections and broadband increase online activities and the amount of time spent online. Financial activities and auctions are growing in popularity; email remains the single most engaged in online activity. Breaking news drives people online for more information.[22]

Table 3-3 identifies what American Internet users do on an average day, as determined by Pew tracking studies. Table 3-4 shows activities that have experienced significant increases since 2000. These data indicate that the prime activities of American Internet users continue to be communicating, seeking information and news, making transactions, and being entertained. Although numbers may differ, these are generally the same activities that engage most Internet users in other developed countries.

COMMUNICATING

The urge to communicate has been a dominant human characteristic since prehistoric times, as cave drawings illustrate. The Internet has made communication far easier and faster than ever before in human history. Although email is the single most heavily used

Table 3-4 Internet Activities with Significant Growth[23]

Activity	Millions	Percent Growth since 2000–2001
Banking online	34	127
Searching for religious/spiritual information	35	94
Buying/making a travel reservation	58	87
Participating in an online auction	24	85
Checking sports scores/information	52	73
Downloading music files	36	71
Buying a product	67	63
Looking for health/medical information	73	59
Using egovernment	66	56
Getting news	29	53
Seeking hobby information	22	47

Internet telephony
A technology that allows long-distance voice calls through the Internet, although frequently at reduced connection quality.

Internet service, interpersonal communication also takes place in online bulletin boards, listservs, and chat rooms and via instant messaging. Email is popular because it is fast, geographically unbounded, cheap, and reliable; its use is being degraded, however, by the glut of spam and the incidence of email-transmitted viruses. The convergence of telephone, Internet, fax, and wireless is moving communication toward a new form that creates a seamless integration of voice, text, and image. **Internet telephony** is showing signs of strength as a free or low-cost alternative to traditional long-distance calls over hardwires, although connection quality can be inferior to landlines.

Consumers are hooked on email. A Carnegie Mellon University study called *The HomeNet Project* reported that email is the driving force impelling many consumers to use the Internet. Heavy email use is also a predictor of whether people continue to use the Internet. The authors conclude that email is a self-reinforcing activity; the more consumers use it, the more likely they are to continue using it. Thus email becomes a social obligation—and one that women respond to more than men because of their greater propensity for creating and nurturing social networks. Senior citizens are highly motivated to use email to connect with children and grandchildren. Often, this is their primary reason for going and staying online. These results suggest the value of email as a marketing tool for nurturing customer relationships and brand building.[24]

As email volume increases, marketers will find it more challenging to cut through the clutter with meaningful, enticing marketing messages. It also sounds a cautionary note: Email marketers should avoid spam and promptly answer emails from customers.

For many college students and teens, email is both their most common Web activity and their primary reason for going online. Although email is used by all ages, chat rooms and instant messaging are most heavily used by teens and young adults under 25. This means that chat rooms are a good place to monitor teen trends, as well as to

WEB UPDATE

For updates and
more on this topic,
visit the textbook
student website at:
http://college.hmco
.com/business/students
and select Siegel,
Internet Marketing, 2e.
**Enterprise and Consumer
Internet Use**

keep an eye on how this market views products and competitors. Both chat rooms and email are popular marketing tools for religious groups, which use them to reach and recruit members. Instant messaging is all the rage among many teens, who often spend hours communicating with several friends simultaneously.

SEEKING INFORMATION

The Internet is a vast public library available at the mere click of a mouse. Although businesses and consumers use it extensively for gathering information and research, they are just beginning to show a willingness to pay for it. The marketing challenge is to convince them that content and/or service are worth the cost of a subscription or onetime charge. Whether consumers will pay for information depends on the value of the information and its timeliness, the convenience of receiving it online, the reasonableness of the price, and whether the information is available free elsewhere.

Online information seekers pose both an opportunity and a threat to traditional newspapers. More consumers are reading newspapers online. Online news is timely and is updated more frequently than hardcopy, can be customized to reflect the consumer's interests, and is available 24/7/365. Initial fears that virtual papers would mean the end of traditional ones appear to be unfounded. Indeed, many traditional newspapers have migrated to the Internet, where they are developing a strong following. Many newspapers are marketing information by offering free published articles for up to a week after their publication date. After that, buyers must pay for archived information.

College students regularly search the Web for information, browsing for topics of interest, conducting academic research, looking at news, researching and making travel plans, and reading magazines. Teens also use the Web for research and information. Consumers seek travel information online, researching destinations, comparing airfares, and booking trips and flights. Far more research travel information online and then go offline to finalize reservations, frequently using the online price to bargain for offline discounts. Travel agents are feeling the pressure of increased use of online bookings. Online sites rebounded from the effects of the September 11 terrorist attacks more rapidly than airline or agent sales, indicating that buyers responded to online incentives, including lots of fare discounts.

Seeking financial information online is very popular, and as the stock market slowly rebounded from the 2001 recession, so did online trading. Internet consumers go online to track and trade stocks and mutual funds and to check their bank account balances. Many younger people also are using financial websites. A financial site that is repositioning itself as a financial portal, The Motley Fool (*www.fool.com*), says it is online to "educate, amuse, and enrich." It combines information with communication (discussion boards), shopping, and entertainment to attract visitors and get them to stay.

Buyers' thirst for information presents an opportunity to attract them to and keep them on a website, get them to sign up for a permission email list, or sell them a content subscription. Offering content that buyers value and refreshing it on a regular basis can strengthen a relationship and increase sales. Content is king online, and information is the type of content that buyers value most. The downside is that too much content, the wrong content, or stale content drives users away from a site. Feedback from desirable users can be extremely helpful in determining what type and amount of content will be most attractive and how frequently it should be changed. Even better, if web marketers can get consumers to indicate what content they want on a site, they can be offered a homepage personalized with that content. This increases the value of the site and the probability of establishing a long-term relationship with the user. Content personalization is often found on ISPs, portals, and online news sources.

MAKING TRANSACTIONS

U.S. retail online sales for Q3 2003 were US$13.291 billion, up 27.0 percent from Q3 2002. This was 1.5 percent of all U.S. retail sales over the period and continues the relatively steady rise in Internet transactions since the Department of Commerce first began reporting Internet retail sales data in Q4 1999, when online retail sales were 0.7 percent of total sales. Even though consumer transactions are more profitable and sizable with each passing year, lots of prepurchase "window-shopping" still goes on, where buyers research products online and then make purchases offline. This also reflects continuing consumer concern about security and privacy (discussed in Chapter 5). It emphasizes the complementarity of online and offline marketing activities and indicates that online exposure to products, particularly by teens and preteens, can stimulate product sales.[25]

Online shopping habits generally mirror offline habits for men and women. Both value the Internet for its 24/7/365 time convenience, product availability, product/pricing comparison facility, and shop-at-home ease. Frustrations include shipping charges, spam, and concerns about credit card security. Men are more likely than women to be bargain hunters online, and men are more likely to fault online shopping because they can't touch or feel what they're buying. They are also more likely to purchase expensive products online, and they appear to have greater trust in Internet shopping generally.[26]

One of every five U.S. Internet users (more than 27 million) is a child between the ages of 2 and 17. Highly popular sites for preteens (2 to 11) are sponsored by Matell's DivaStarz (*www.divastarz.com*), which promotes its DivaStarz line of dolls, and Disney's multiple-player game site ToonTime Online (*play.toontown.com*). These companies successfully promote branded products online, which generates offline sales and/or pressure on parents to make online purchases. Older teens (12 to 17) are using Originalicons.com (*www.originalicons.com*), where they can download instant-messaging icons; Blunt Truth (*www.blunttruthgame.com*), an online game site that promises advertisers access to millions of users each month; and Teen People (*www.teenpeople.com/teenpeople/*). Teens are purchasing more online, thanks in part to prepaid credit and debit cards and other innovative online payment systems. Apple's iTunes (*www.apple.com/itunes/*) offers gift certificates and allowance accounts where parents can deposit money for their children to spend downloading music legally. Teen enthusiasm for online transactions is a strong positive indicator for future sales.[27]

The gay community is an often overlooked online market. About 80 percent of gay men are online, and an estimated 29 percent have been online for seven or more years. They use the Internet extensively for shopping, banking, entertainment, and community building. Homosexuals often have higher incomes and are better educated than the general population, are more likely to use broadband, and are a prime online marketing target for many businesses.[28]

Music is one area where online transactions are soaring. Although file swapping is rampant, especially among younger Internet users, the use of subscription and pay-per-song sites is exploding. Apple's iTunes digital jukebox software for Mac and Windows platforms is free and offers one-click access to downloads of over 400,000 tracks from the five major record labels and many independents. Within a week of the site's launch, over 1 million songs were downloaded legally at 99 cents each. By December 2003, the download number had risen to 25 million.[29]

BEING ENTERTAINED

When it comes to being entertained online, users are clever in satisfying their desires by visiting online marketers ranging from Disney (*disney.go.com/home/today/index.html*) to Playboy (*playboy.com*). Online entertainment can take the form of participating in online auctions, gaming, gambling, pursuing hobbies, listening to music, watching videos, engaging in chats, following sports, and surfing other pastimes. The convergence of personal computers and television illustrates the growing importance of the Internet as an alternative "entertainment channel." Yahoo! Movies (*movies.yahoo.com*), netflix.com (*www.netflix.com/Default*), and Moviefone (*www.moviefone.com*) are popular video and movie sites. Music site leaders in addition to Apple's iTunes are AOL Music Channel (*music.netscape.com*), MusicMatch Jukebox (*www.musicmatch.com*), and LAUNCH Music on Yahoo! (*launch.yahoo.com*). Children and men and women of all age groups are playing games online and their popularity is growing. In 1999, only 18 percent of Internet users played online games. This increased to 37 percent in 2003. Popular game sites include Yahoo! Games (*games.yahoo.com*), EA Online (*www.ea.com/home/home.jsp*), and MSN Games (*zone.msn.com/en/root/default.htm*).[30]

Other online entertainment pursuits, particularly gambling and visual pornography, are more controversial. Online gambling is a global business that includes sports and casino gambling. Despite the efforts of legislators in the United States to eliminate or regulate gambling, roughly half of Internet gambling revenues come from U.S. residents. By 2006, Internet gambling is projected to be a US$14.5 billion market. The good news for advertisers is that online gamblers are more likely to click on ads and re-member them, to sign up for email marketing, to open email promotions, and generally to find online ads less annoying. Although many parents and others promote zero tolerance for online adult content, it is a growing business. Estimates of annual revenues vary widely, with claims of anywhere from 30,000 to 60,000 adult content sites online. Consumers online are mirroring offline behaviors when it comes to gambling and adult content. They seem to value the 24/7/365 availability and convenience that online access offers, as well as what they construe as greater privacy and anonymity.[31]

OTHER BEHAVIORS

Ours is not a utopian world, online or off. Businesses and consumers can behave badly or have negative experiences in either environment. Some problems associated with Internet use affect marketing, directly and/or indirectly. For example, Internet-related social isolation can negatively affect marketing if the need or opportunity to make purchases is reduced. Customer complaints are another example. Legitimate customer complaints about business behaviors online certainly require a marketing response. However, anticorporate websites that post distorted negative attacks on a business can reach millions of people, reduce revenues, and undermine marketing efforts. Marketers can respond to some but not all online behaviors and must carefully weigh their responses to ensure their effectiveness.

SOCIAL ISOLATION   Two recent studies point to problems associated with extended Internet use. The HomeNet Project found that greater use of the Internet is associated with statistically significant declines in social interactions with family and friends and with higher levels of loneliness and depression. The Stanford Institute for the Quantitative Study of Society (SIQSS at *www.stanford.edu/group/siqss/*) study confirms these results and adds that high-wired adults have less time for shopping in stores, reading newspapers, or interacting with family and friends; they attend fewer social events; and 59 percent watch less television.[32]

These studies are disturbing for both societal and marketing reasons. From a societal perspective, dysfunctional effects directly related to Internet use could have a dampening effect on Internet adoption and lend weight to latent antitechnology biases. From a marketing perspective, dysfunctional effects could undermine marketing efforts aimed at getting consumers to use the Internet for commercial purposes. Study results appear to contradict a key benefit of Internet use where it facilitates communication contact with family and friends. However, communicating by email is not the same as going on a family picnic or spending an evening hanging out with friends. The reduction in shopping, of course, has obvious negative implications for marketing exchanges. Watching less television means consumers will be exposed to fewer advertising messages, which could curtail their receiving information about products and websites.

INTERNET ADDICTION   Although Internet addiction has been mentioned in the press, at this time it does not represent an official diagnostic medical category. Difficulty controlling Internet use can mask symptoms of serious underlying mental conditions. Studies on compulsive Internet use found that participants exhibiting such behaviors often also exhibit well-known clinically recognized disorders. It is likely that extended Internet use can exacerbate symptoms of already existing problems, particularly those associated with obsessive compulsive disorders (OCD).[33]

Behaviors often identified as addictive include excessive engagement with cybersex sites, overinvolvement with chat room socializing while avoiding face-to-face interactions, and obsessive online gaming or gambling to the extent that these behaviors dominate daily life. These behaviors can ruin lives and families when they become extreme.

It is not known to what extent the Internet may be affecting people who are already subject to problems with impulse control. If this emerges as a significant problem that involves large numbers of people, it could slow Internet adoption rates and affect marketing efforts. At this point, not enough evidence exists to indicate whether this is happening, and rushing to respond could have unintended consequences.

COMPLAINTS AND ANTICORPORATE ACTIVISM   Most reputable businesses work hard to ensure that buyers are satisfied with their purchases, yet buyers can still experience postpurchase regret (dissonance) or be seriously discontented with goods, service, and the purchasing experience. Thus websites have sprung up to channel consumer complaints to the offending source. Complaints.com (*www.complaints.com*) forwards consumer complaints directly to companies free of charge. Some sites survey discontented consumers about their product preferences and sell this information to interested companies. Most sites keep complaints private; others post them for all to see. Consumer complaints are a protected form of free speech, as long as the complainer is not knowingly trying to harm a business. Complaints about offline or online experiences can be lodged with these sites.[34]

Anticorporate activism is far more hostile than consumer complaints, because anticorporate websites give highly frustrated buyers an opportunity to vent their hostility against a corporate offender before millions of people worldwide. Angry customers provide only one side of a story, and companies often have difficulty dealing with the comments. Some have sued the owners of anticorporate websites for trademark infringement. Other site owners have been bought off by the company they are shaming. Sometimes a company will make amends in an effort to get an anticorporate website owner to shut down or moderate the intensity of the complaints it posts. For example, Fujifilm responded to an anti-Fuji site by offering a public apology to offended buyers for poor after-sale service. The company also severed ties with the agent responsible for the poor service. Anticorporate web protests are particularly effective because they are easy to create and can disseminate negative comments very rapidly. Software can help corporations track and monitor anticorporate site contents. Disgruntled employees often use anticorporate websites to vent their hostility toward their employers anonymously. Their comments, combined with those of angry buyers, can be extremely damaging.[35]

Consumer community
A group of people with a common purpose or interest who interact online to share information, support, and concern.

COMMUNITY BUILDING   A **consumer community** is a group of people with a common purpose or interest who interact online to share information, support, and concern. People often form highly personal commitments to online communities. Some consumer communities are maintained on business websites, but the business must be very careful not to intrude. Community members typically resent blatant marketing messages impinging on their space. Amazon.com (*www.amazon.com*) has created a community with its book-buying customers, soliciting their book reviews and involving them in recommendations. Kraft Foods' Interactive Kitchen (*www.kraft.com*) is a cooking website where consumers share recipes and email their *Wisdom of Moms* consumer comments for posting on the site. Kraft encourages consumer information sharing, while promoting company products in a low-key setting.

ENTERPRISE AND BUSINESS INTERNET BEHAVIORS

Enterprises and consumers exhibit some of the same Internet behaviors, such as using the Internet for communication, seeking information, and making transactions. Other behaviors are unique to enterprises, such as customer relationship management, workforce training, and various aspects of eprocurement, including Internet electronic data interchanges (EDI).

Enterprises and businesses are going online to reduce costs; to source supplies, parts, and materials; to increase operational efficiencies; to find new partners and customers; to recruit employees; to expand their marketing opportunities; and to keep up with the competition. They are liquidating inventory using online auctions such as eBay (*www.ebay.com*) and fixed-cost sellers such as Overstock.com (*www.overstock.com*); and they are using **B2B web exchanges** to buy and sell products. An exchange is a website designed to help businesses realize savings in transaction costs and greater efficiencies from online buying. Often small businesses pool their orders (demand aggregation) to increase their buying clout. They are forming online business communities and networking. Enterprise and business behaviors and use of the Internet will be considered throughout the remainder of this book, particularly in discussions dealing with marketing strategies and the 4Ps.

B2B web exchange
A website that facilitates B2B online buying and selling.

Summary

http://college.hmco.com/business/students

Internet User Segments

The two principal Internet user segments are enterprises, including businesses, and consumers. The enterprise segment is broad and includes for-profit businesses, public sector governments, hospitals and clinics, universities, private nonprofit and nongovernmental (NGO) organizations, religious institutions, and other groups. Many enterprises are run like businesses even though profit is not their primary goal; other enterprises must generate revenues and profits in order to survive. Enterprise exchanges take many forms, including B2B, B2C, B2P, P2B, and P2C. Consumers are individuals or groups that purchase products for their own use or for the use of family, friends, or others, but not solely for business or enterprise use. Consumers significantly outnumber businesses and other enterprises. Consumers often sell to each other online in C2C exchanges.

Enterprises Using the Internet

Large corporations receive the most media attention; small businesses are embracing Internet use and attracting keen marketing interest. For many small businesses, the Internet presents a unique opportunity to serve existing customers better, expand their marketing reach, and compete in markets that were previously inaccessible. Small and midsize businesses are important to marketing students because they often are the first employers for new graduates and because many graduates hope eventually to become small business owners. Small business use of the Internet is increasing and offers profitable opportunities for marketers. The federal government dominates the U.S. enterprise sector and is active in eprocurement and egovernment. Internet use is almost universal in two- and four-year colleges and universities in the United States. Medical professionals are active Internet users in the United States and other developed nations. Large numbers of churches and religious organizations are online, as are charities and other nonprofit groups.

Consumer Internet Users

Consumers are often called *personal use* consumers to differentiate their buying goals from those of enterprise and business buyers. The United States is the most desirable consumer market in the world because of its size, high median income, relative homogeneity (including almost universal use of the English language), eagerness to spend, and receptivity to marketing. It is also currently the largest single market of Internet users in the world. In both the United States and Europe, consumer Internet use profiles are changing, and users are becoming more like the general population. Some enterprises and individuals will never go online by choice; others are not online because of digital divides or impairments.

What Internet Users Are Doing Online

More U.S. female Internet users are seeking health or religious information online; more males are looking for news and financial information. Internet use has increased among all minorities. More African-Americans are doing school research and seeking religious information online. More English-speaking Hispanics use instant messaging and download music. Wealthier and better-educated users take advantage of a wider variety of Internet features, including online banking, egovernment, and auctions. Instant messaging appeals most to younger users, who are also heavy users of legal music downloads and/or file sharing. Financial activities and auctions are growing in popularity; email remains the online activity that is most heavily engaged in. The most popular consumer Internet activities are communicating, seeking information, making transactions, and finding entertainment. Other less desirable behaviors include gambling and seeking adult content. Social isolation can result from the ready availability of Internet diversions. Enterprises and consumers share some Internet behaviors—for example, using the Internet for communication, seeking information, and making transactions. Some behaviors are unique to enterprises, such as customer relationship management, workforce training, and various aspects of eprocurement, including Internet electronic data interchange (EDI).

Take Action!

Imagine that you have been hired by Phoenix Online to market its program to employees of the largest business in your state. The CEO of the business is committed to having her management-track employees continue their education with an MBA or (in some cases) complete their undergraduate degree. She has identified twenty-five employees who qualify for the program. The business will pay half the tuition of any employee who completes his or her MBA or BBA online within two years. You know that working professionals are often resistant to online education, so you will have to overcome the perception that traditional classes, where students meet the professor and other students face-to-face at least once a week, are better than online classes.

1. Perform a content analysis of the Phoenix Online site, looking for features and benefits that apply to your target market and will help overcome working employees' resistance. Begin by examining the Phoenix Online Frequently Asked Questions (FAQ) page (*degrees.uofphx.info/faq.jsp*).
2. Construct a FAB matrix for five key features that you believe make Phoenix Online attractive to working nontraditional students. A FAB matrix is a table that identifies a product's features, attributes, and benefits. In this case, the product is online higher education.
3. Write an email for distribution to the twenty-five employees. Use your marketing skills and the results of the FAB analysis to overcome objections to online education. Include all pertinent information that will help sell the product. Make the product attractive, but stick to the facts, and don't make promises that are unrealistic or unethical. Keep the email short, clear, simple, and persuasive.
4. Write a one-page fax to the CEO of the business in which you explain the purpose of the employee email and outline the next stages in your plan to "sell" Phoenix Online to her employees. Identify each stage, and briefly explain how it serves the general goal of better educating the employees so that they can become more effective managers. For example, the next stage might be to hold an information meeting for all twenty-five employees where you answer their questions. Consider how you will also use email, fax, and a website to market the program.

Chapter Review Questions

1. Should marketers target Internet nonadopters? Explain your answer.
2. In the United States, there are over 292 million people and millions of enterprises, including businesses. Explain this statement in terms of the universe, segments, and marketing niches involved. Provide examples of each.
3. How does eprocurement differ from offline conventional procurement?
4. Describe the following activities: B2B, B2C, B2P, P2B, P2C, and C2C.
5. Explain the following statement: The United States is a consumer-driven society. What is the relevance of this fact for Internet marketing?

6. Why is the U.S. government so eager to promote eprocurement?
7. Are newspapers facing extinction because of the Internet?
8. What makes communication such an important factor drawing users online?
9. Should richer nations help poorer nations go online?
10. What is Internet-induced social isolation?
11. Is Internet addiction a serious problem?
12. Should anticorporate websites be banned?
13. Are consumer web complaint sites a good thing for businesses? Explain.
14. What is community building on the Internet?
15. Do digital divides really exist?

Competitive Case Study

Competing with Phoenix Online

Does your university compete with Phoenix Online's courses? Chances are that it does, to a relatively limited extent, through classes that can be taken on the Internet, via an intranet or extranet, or on television (up- and down-link). It is less likely that your university offers a complete degree online. When it comes to publicly held for-profit university businesses, Hoover's Online (*www.hoovers.com/apollo-group,-inc./—ID__42338—/ free-co-factsheet.xhtml*) lists 11 competitors for Apollo Group, Inc., parent of Phoenix Online. For online education, a top competitor in "anytime, anywhere" educational delivery systems is DeVry (*www.devry.edu/ online/*), Inc., a North American higher-education holding company for DeVry University, Ross University, and Becker Professional Review. DeVry reported FY2003 revenue of US$706 million, with an almost 14 percent 5-year annual growth rate in revenue. Like Phoenix Online, it offers onsite and online courses and degrees in technology, business, management, and health through undergraduate, graduate, and lifelong-learning programs. DeVry began offering an online graduate degree program in 1998, nine years after Phoenix. DeVry projects con-

tinued earnings growth from "expanded enrollments, annual tuition increases, continued operating margin improvement, new programs, significant geographic expansion, increased student retention and attractive acquisitions." DeVry Online accommodates its primary target market of adult working students through online course syllabi and assignments, the DeVry virtual library, an online bookstore, course notes and lectures on CD-ROM and the Web, email and threaded conversations, and applications-oriented projects and exercises. Many public universities and private nonprofits have slowed their move into online degrees because of the high cost. Williams College rejected a partnership offer from a web-based learning company because breaking even would require enrollments of as many as 3,000 students per course. Others, such as the University of Maryland (*www .classearch.com/featuredschools/umuc/umuc_grad.cfm*), have offered online courses and degrees for years.[36]

CHECK IT OUT

DeVry Online offers an online demonstration of both a course and a laboratory. Visit DeVry and take the demo at *www.devry.edu/online/program_demo.html*. Run your cursor slowly across the elements in the class screen to observe their functions. Click on the items for more information. Do you believe the class structure would appeal to working adults? Would it also appeal to traditional full-time students? If so, under what circumstances? Compare the DeVry online demo to that of Phoenix Online (*www.uopxworld.com/main.asp*). What are the similarities and differences?

A GLOBAL PERSPECTIVE

Phoenix Online went international in 2003 and within six months was enrolling about 500 students a month. The company plans to offer classes in Spanish and possibly Mandarin Chinese. What international markets could be tapped by offering classes online in Spanish? Phoenix Online also offers courses for U.S. military personnel stationed in the United States and abroad.

4

.COM

Taking Marketing to the Net

LEARNING OBJECTIVES

» To develop a simple classification system for business Internet marketing activities
» To understand how other enterprises are marketing online
» To identify ways in which individuals are involved with Internet marketing activities
» To describe external environmental factors that affect Internet marketing

Why Isn't *Walmart.com* the Wal-Mart of the Web?

Wal-Mart Stores, Inc. (*www.walmartstores.com/wmstore/wmstores/HomePage.jsp*) has been called the 800-pound gorilla of retailing. It's the world's largest corporation by sales and the world's number-one retailer. It's bigger than Sears (*www.sears.com*), Kmart (*www.kmart.com*), and J.C. Penney (*www3.jcpenney.com/jcp/default.aspx*) combined, with more than 1.5 million employees worldwide, annual sales (2003) of US$244.5 billion, and a 12.3 percent one-year sales growth (2003). Wal-Mart has almost 5,000 bricks-and-mortar stores worldwide, including Wal-Mart Stores, SAM'S Club Members Warehouse, Wal-Mart Supercenters, and over 1,300 international outlets, principally ASDA in the United Kingdom and Wal-Mart de México, S.A. de C.V. It's also the number-one retailer in Canada and Mexico. According to the company, more than 138 million customers visit its stores each week. Fortune Magazine (*www.fortune.com/fortune/*) named Wal-Mart 2003's most admired company in the nation and the world.

The first bricks-and-mortar Wal-Mart store opened in 1962 in Rogers, Arkansas, USA. The first Wal-Mart web storefront (*www.walmart.com*) was launched in June 1995, relaunched in July 1996, and relaunched yet again in the fall of 1999.

The company spun off its in-house storefront operations in January 2000 to a new independent company, Walmart.com, of which Wal-Mart Stores, Inc. was majority owner. Other owners were its venture capital partner Accel Partners and Walmart.com employees. In 2001, Wal-Mart Stores bought out Accel and reintegrated Walmart.com into the parent company.

The strategy for the Walmart.com site is to "serve customers in a way they want to be served where they want to be served." Walmart.com's goal is to be *ecommerce for the masses* [italics added] by closely integrating the online storefront with offline stores. This includes a rollout of interactive in-store kiosks that give customers access to products not in the store and to a gift registry. Wal-Mart's commitment to *low prices always* is customer-pleasing, and its web storefront is an attractive alternative for people who like its low prices but hate shopping in Wal-Mart stores. Wal-Mart is a highly experienced retailer with instant name recognition that cuts through the online clutter. Returning products purchased online, with the exception of music downloads, couldn't be easier. Unwanted purchases can be returned by mail or taken to a local Wal-Mart store for instant credit. This **channel cohesion,** the integration of its online and offline channel operations, gives Wal-Mart a considerable advantage over clicks-only and most other bricks-and-clicks retailers. Wal-Mart has a highly diverse product base that facilitates **cross-selling,** identifying and suggesting related items to buyers, and it rarely experiences **stockouts,** the unavailability of products when buyers want them. Because its customer base mirrors the general U.S. population, over 60 percent should have computers for accessing Walmart.com. Wal-Mart brings unmatched offline clout to its web presence with an outstanding back-office system and compliant vendor relationships. The company demands that its suppliers communicate with it via its proprietary Internet EDI (Electronic Data Interchange), and over 98 percent do. It also demands cost cutting that can crush suppliers' profit margins.

Given all this, why does Walmart.com's online retail market share (9.12 percent) still trail far behind market leader Amazon.com (42.7 percent in 2003)? Amazon is a clicks-only online shopping mall, so all its business is online. Walmart.com is one channel of a multichannel retailer with a ubiquitous offline presence. Wal-Mart wants Walmart.com to be *ecommerce for the masses,* but it's not the masses that are online. Wal-Mart shoppers tend to have larger families, and they tend not to be in a hurry, often cruising Wal-Mart store aisles looking for bargains. In-store shopping becomes entertainment. This contrasts sharply with the typical hurried online shopper, who spends an average of only eight minutes and twelve seconds at a retail website. A Wal-Mart shopper is less affluent than the average online retail shopper and has less online experience. Walmart.com is somewhat dowdy, not trendy in its appearance or usability. Walmart.com CEO John Fleming admits that the site has not focused on marketing in the last few years, but this is changing. Traffic to Walmart.com is growing, averaging 3.5 million users a week (and 11 million per week during the holiday buying season in 2003). Its strength is the integration of its online and offline channels, product breadth, and low prices. Recent additions to Walmart.com include an opt-in email newsletter announcing price rollbacks, DVD rentals, song downloads, Wal-Mart branded computers, cheap Internet access, online prescription orders with offline payment and pickup, and online payment by personal check. Offline success obviously doesn't automatically guarantee success online, but it's far too early in the Internet's commercialization history to count Walmart.com out![1]

Channel cohesion
The integration and coordination of dual or multichannel (online and offline) marketing operations.

Taking marketing to the Net doesn't always turn out as expected, as shown by the Walmart.com example. Adapting marketing to the Internet environment is challenging. It requires developing new marketing methods to take advantage of the Internet's unique features and adapting traditional methods to drive traffic online. Chapter 4 examines how businesses, other enterprises, and individuals are taking marketing to the Internet with varying degrees of success. The chapter concludes by considering aspects of the external environment that affect Internet marketing directly and indirectly.

Business Internet Marketing Activities

Internet commercialization began with a bang, endured a media-frenzied crash, and is now on the way to recovery, perhaps eventually to exceed its original promise. The one certainty is that there will be many unexpected developments, as marketers find new ways to work in the expansive and challenging Internet environment.

Cross-selling
Identifying and suggesting related items (such as accessories and service contracts) to a buyer.

Stockout
The unavailability of a product when customers want to buy it.

Clicks-only
Businesses that market their products solely online on the Internet, World Wide Web, and/or intranets and extranets.

Bricks-and-clicks
Businesses that market their products online (clicks) and offline (bricks) using a dual or multichannel distribution strategy.

Shakeout
A financial upheaval marked by the failures of marginally financed, poorly managed industry members.

THE EARLY YEARS

Businesses that went online at the start of Internet commercialization were **clicks-only,** operating solely on the Net, or **bricks-and-clicks** with both offline (bricks) and online (clicks) operations. At the time, it was widely predicted that clicks-only businesses would miraculously reinvent marketing, eliminate distributors, reshape relations between buyers and sellers, make pricing transparent, reduce transaction and inventory costs, and attract hundreds of millions of new customers worldwide to the virtual environment. Clicks-only Amazon.com (*www.amazon.com*) was a model for the digital revolution. As commercialization progressed through the late 1990s, several thousand U.S. clicks-only dot-coms went online, investors often indiscriminately showered them with extravagant amounts of investment capital, share prices skyrocketed and created a speculative bubble, the stock market became overvalued, and the press helped create an almost manic enthusiasm for all things Web. It was a period of *irrational exuberance,* according to Federal Reserve chairman Alan Greenspan. His description of the U.S. stock market and overvalued technology and dot-com stocks in this manner almost immediately set off a dramatic stock market decline worldwide.[2]

The Internet bubble was bound to burst, and it did—with a resounding thud. Much has been written and said about the dramatic **shakeout** that began in mid-2000 and resulted in the shuttering of many businesses during and after the 2001 recession. A shakeout had been widely predicted, and when it arrived, the landscape quickly became littered with failed dot-coms. They included trendy United Kingdom apparel retailer Boo.com (which later resurfaced under new management at *www.boo.com*), toy seller Toysmart.com, price comparison site Brandwise.com, and online charity Hugging Hands International, among an estimated 700 to 1,000 others.[3]

Most failed dot-coms never showed a profit, and investors grew tired of waiting for profits to materialize. Others burned through their cash and never made it to their scheduled initial public offerings (IPOs). Internet retailers (etailers) were particularly hard hit.

The shakeout was brutal but not unprecedented. Consider what happened in the infancy of the U.S. automobile industry. In the first hundred years of U.S. automobile production, thousands of manufacturers turned out handmade and (later) mass-produced cars. Today, two major U.S. auto makers are left—Ford and General Motors, respectively number three and number one in worldwide sales (Toyota became number two in 2003). The first car to be produced in the United States was the Duryea. Other pioneer automobiles were the Haynes, Packard, Hudson, Nash, Maxwell, Willys-Overland, Kaiser, Frazer, and Studebaker. Most people have never heard of them; soon the same will be true of the recently deceased dot-coms.[4]

The great majority of original automobile pioneers simply closed their doors, others were bought out, and consolidation drastically reduced the number of competitors. Although obvious differences exist between manufacturing automobiles and operating profitable dot-coms, the similarity lies in the nature of American capitalism and free-market competition. Entrepreneurs are drawn to new industries whose early years tend to be highly speculative, volatile, and risky. Just as there was a shakeout in automobile manufacturing, there also was a shakeout in the early years of biotechnology and personal computers in the 1980s.

Large numbers of first- and second-wave dot-coms will fail, but several factors argue against the same drastic consolidation that led to only two surviving major U.S. automobile manufacturers. First, the cost of entry for a start-up dot-com is far lower than the cost of entry for an automaker in an industry that requires massive capital outlay. Thus the Internet environment is extremely attractive for entrepreneurs starting a small business. Second, an ever increasing number of dot-coms are actually bricks-and-clicks offspring of already profitable and well-established offline companies, so they benefit from their parent companies' expertise, established channels, recognizable brand names, financial stability, and loyal customers. Third, a growing number of dot-com survivors are profitable, and more are on the verge of profitability; these survivors have a higher probability of long-term success. Their success will attract a new wave of entrants that should be more web savvy, more risk averse, and better positioned to compete and profit. As the U.S. and world economies continue to recover, more venture capitalists will emerge to fund Internet ventures—perhaps this time with greater caution and success.

CLASSIFYING INTERNET MARKETING ACTIVITIES

The Internet is a dynamic, pluralistic environment where an abundance of marketing activities and actors pursue exchange goals. The challenge is to make sense of it. To that end, an organizing scheme can facilitate understanding and provide reference points for comparisons. Figure 4-1 presents a simple classification system for this purpose.

FIGURE 4-1

A simple classification system can enhance our understanding of marketing in the Internet environment and help organize comparisons. This system is based on a number of factors, including the marketer's home (solely online or both online and offline), served market(s), market coverage (from solely domestic and local to global), entity type, status, offer(s), site function(s), sector(s), and where fulfillment takes place.

HOME

First mover
The first business of its kind to take some innovative step.

Eziba

Eziba markets items handcrafted all around the globe to discerning customers worldwide.

Source: Copyright © 2004 by Eziba, Inc. Reprinted with permission, eziba.com.

Web drivers
Marketing activities designed to drive customers to a website—for example a mailed catalog that invites customers to purchase on a website or an online ad that viewers can click on to reach the advertiser's website.

Conversion rate
The proportion of visitors to a website who become customers—that is, who make a purchase.

Amazon.com was initially the model for a clicks-only business, where the Internet was its sole transaction home. Now, even Amazon.com mails catalogs. Amazon opened its virtual doors in July 1995 and was a **first mover** because it was the first business of its kind to set up shop on the Web in the first wave of commercialization. At one time, being a first mover was considered an advantage. Now its downsides are recognized, mainly in the high front-end marketing costs associated with building a brand name and in the delay of profits as available resources are used to expand the business rapidly. It's more likely that any true advantage will be enjoyed by the second, third, and subsequent waves that arrive after the first movers and learn from their mistakes.

Eziba.com (*www.eziba.com; ziba* is the Persian word for "beautiful") was launched November 9, 1999, initially as a clicks-only. It is a prime example of a business that evolved from a clicks-only to a multichannel marketer. First, the company introduced traditional mailed catalogs in 2000. Customers viewed products in the hardcopy catalogs and then purchased them online. In 2001 the company mailed 11 catalogs, including 4 during the holiday season, with a total circulation of over 7 million. Catalogs are highly profitable, cost-effective **web drivers** for Eziba. The company reports that catalogs have driven hundreds of thousands of customers to its website, resulting in a 22 percent increase in traffic. Catalogs are also credited with increasing the company's **conversion rate** (the proportion of visitors to a website who become customers and make a purchase) from 0.57 percent to 4 percent. In 2002 the company went a step further and opened its first retail outlet, the Eziba at ABC boutique in the ABC Carpet & Home store in New York City. Several more retail outlets followed in the New York area and Boston. As a company, Eziba is far, far smaller than Amazon, and rather than following the Amazonian mass-marketing strategy, Eziba is a *niche* marketer targeting select buyers who value handmade products from exotic parts of the world. Unlike Amazon, Eziba claims very low marketing expenditures were needed to build its brand name. Online sales have exceeded expectations. Not surprisingly, in 2000 Amazon.com invested US$17.5 million in Eziba. Like most clicks-only marketers, Eziba had to learn by doing. In 2000, it offered a US$20 online coupon that it later found customers could use repeatedly. When the company discovered the glitch, it gamely declared the promotion a success and let it run its natural course.[5]

E*TRADE, now E*TRADE FINANCIAL (*us.etrade.com/e/t/home*), was one of the first solely online financial brokers and a favorite of day traders who spent their waking hours in front of computer screens making massive numbers of small stock trades. E*TRADE aggressively and expensively marketed its services and brand name through such traditional promotion methods as placing advertisements in three straight Super Bowls, from 2000 through 2002. Its humorous monkey ads generated great marketing buzz and earned many advertising industry awards, including "best ad" recognition in *Time Magazine, USA Today,* WSJ.com Online, *Ad Age,* and *Adweek* and at the Cannes Advertising Festival. The ads introduced the company to over a billion Super Bowl viewers worldwide each year. Its January 2001 Super Bowl ad increased E*TRADE's top-of-mind brand awareness by 64 percent. Through the acquisition of online bank Telebanc, E*TRADE became the largest pure-play Internet bank in the United States, with electronic retail deposits that grew from US$1.1 billion at year end 1998 to US$2.6 billion a year later. By 2002, the diversified E*TRADE Financial group announced the most profitable year in its history, reporting total customer deposits of US$43.5 billion. Today the company markets products, content, and information to retail, institutional, and corporate customers from its website, automatic teller machines (ATMs), and banking centers and through its relationship managers and call centers. E*TRADE Financial is an example of a clicks-only business expanding offline and aggressively blending online and offline marketing in a **oneline marketing** strategy, with a seamless interface between what happens online in a web storefront and what happens offline in bricks-and-mortar stores, catalogs, etc. Offline promotions are used as web drivers. The company is using its website, banks, ATMs, and sales force to create a seamless flow of customer service.[6]

Although it is difficult to determine exactly how many businesses fit each category—clicks-only, bricks-and-clicks, or **bricks-and-mortar,** those businesses without any Internet activity (Figure 4-2)—it is safe to assume that bricks-and-clicks already far outnumber clicks-only for two principal reasons. First, more clicks-only businesses are evolving into bricks-and-clicks as they expand their marketing operations. Second, the entry costs for new clicks-only businesses will continue to rise, which makes this entry mode impractical for most start-ups. Because the majority of businesses already have a web presence, the most likely pool of late Internet entrants will be small businesses that previously were reluctant to test the electronic waters and new startups.

Oneline marketing
Integration of online and offline activities to develop synergy between the two, where the effect of the whole (online plus offline) is greater than the sum of its parts.

Bricks-and-mortar
Businesses without any Internet activity.

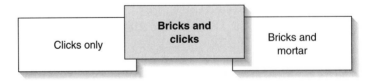

FIGURE 4-2 A Business's Home Makes a Difference
Clicks-Only Business has an Internet home, no offline selling; one electronic distribution channel.
Bricks-and-Clicks Business has both a web home and offline selling site(s) and/or catalog sales, at least two (dual) distribution channels and possibly more than two (multichannel), one being electronic.
Bricks-and-Mortar Business has no web home and sells only through offline stores and/or catalogs, single or dual distribution, none being online electronic.

SERVED MARKET(S)

Mass-market strategy
A marketing strategy that assumes a relatively undifferentiated, unsegmented, homogeneous market.

Segmenting
Dividing the homogeneous mainstream market into smaller, more homogeneous subgroups.

Market gap
A situation that exists when a product that customers want is absent from a market or is not in adequate supply; an unserved or underserved market.

A second way to classify Internet marketing activities is by served markets. A **mass-market strategy** assumes a relatively undifferentiated, unsegmented, homogeneous market such that the company can more or less standardize its offer for a mainstream of buyers. In its purest form, this strategy requires only one marketing program (the same product, price, promotion, and distribution system) for all. This standardization can result in significant economies. In reality, even mass marketers recognize that mainstream customers have different needs, so a mass marketer like Amazon also uses differentiated or niche marketing to reach special-interest customers. This is shown by its *Sell Yours Here* option for customers that want to sell items at a fixed price and avoid auction uncertainty.

Eziba is clearly a niche marketer, targeting a high-end Internet buyer looking for unusual, exotic products from artisans and craftspeople worldwide. It is **segmenting** the mass market, dividing the homogeneous mainstream market into smaller, more homogeneous subgroups and then aiming its marketing efforts at one or more promising groups. Online niche marketers often look for **market gaps,** unserved or underserved markets that present feasible profit opportunities because products that customers want either are absent from a market or are not in adequate supply.

To a great extent, buyers determine what products are sold, their prices, where they are sold (place), and how. Many businesses sell to a combination of buyers and thus have mixed target markets. Some etailers, such as Silly Goose Toy Store (*http://sillygoosetoys.com*), sell only to personal use consumers. Silly Goose was started by a *momtrepreneur,* a mom who identified a market gap for classic, high-quality children's toys and then filled it online.

BUSINESSES SELL TO DIFFERENT BUYER TYPES   Business-to-business (B2B) is an extremely active sector of online commercial activity with revenues that may exceed the B2C (business-to-consumer) sector's. Many B2Bs operate on proprietary extranets, so their activities are not as visible to the public and press as B2C transactions are. For example, FinancialMachine.com (*www.ecx.com/partners/fm*) is a B2B that offers credit products to online vendors, particularly small businesses with little online experience. Small businesses can purchase bank-approved merchant accounts that let them accept online credit card purchases and web-based payment transaction software that sets up shopping carts on a vendor's site. Its *QuickCommerce* option offers "everything you need to do business online."

Progressive Auto Insurance Co. (*www.progressive.com*) launched its B2C website in 1995 and within two years was offering real-time online auto insurance sales. Over a million unique visitors visit the site each month. Progressive uses its storefront to sell insurance online or connect consumers to the more than 30,000 independent insurance agents nationwide that sell its products. It offers automobile, motorcycle, homeowners, and other types of insurance online 24/7/365. B2Cs are more visible and more highly scrutinized than B2Bs, and they serve a greater number of buyers. Most people are far more familiar with a B2C such as Amazon.com than with any B2B.

Some businesses sell only to nonbusiness enterprises. For example, Tally's (*www.jvtally.com*) is a 125-year-old church supply house, a B2P business that sells to church clergy and laity. Another example is ElectionSupply.com (*www.electionsupply.com*), which sells reconditioned election equipment, vote recorders, ballot boxes, and voting booths to government buyers.

Many online businesses make offers to a combination of businesses, consumers, governments, and/or other enterprises. Dell Computer (*www.dell.com*) has consumer, business, health care, and government buyers, who may purchase the same products but in different quantities and on different terms. Like other hardware manufacturers, Dell sells computers B2B, B2C, and B2P. Its web storefront is particularly user-friendly, with a tutorial on how to order online, reasons why ordering online makes sense, and (for state government buyers) an interactive state map that links to personalized government pages. Small businesses are more likely to concentrate their marketing resources on a single niche.

MARKET COVERAGE

Coverage can be solely domestic (local, regional, and/or national), international (domestic plus at least one other country), or global (worldwide). A solely domestic local online marketer has the most geographically restricted market coverage. In this case, the marketer may use the Internet to communicate better with local customers, perhaps providing information about operating hours or product tips. An example is Dudley's Restaurant (*www.dudleysrestaurant.com*) in Lexington, Kentucky, USA. Its market is local, but even so, it sells gift certificates online for purchase by anyone with a credit card. Hillenmeyer's (*www.hillenmeyers.com*) is a 162-year-old landscape design, construction, and maintenance company that serves the bluegrass region of Kentucky with a regionally focused website filled with helpful tips relevant to its customers' needs. A leading national fashion retailer such as 103-year-old Nordstrom (*www.nordstrom.com*) shows its products to the world but ships only to its national domestic market. Finally, international and global marketers such as IBM (*www.ibm.com*) and Toyota (*www.toyota.com*) use their Internet presence in varying ways to serve international and (often) global markets. We'll learn more about international Internet marketing in Chapter 6.

ENTITY TYPE

Regardless of a business's home—clicks-only, bricks-and-clicks, or bricks-and-mortar—it still needs one or more legal licenses to operate. The most common legal organizational forms are sole proprietorships, partnerships, corporations (C or S), and cooperatives. Most small businesses are sole proprietorships, owned and operated by one person with no legal separation between owner and business. Partnerships are co-ownerships that can be general, with joint ownership and responsibility, or limited, with restricted ownership, responsibility, and liability. A corporation is a separate general-purpose legal entity where management is exercised by a board of directors elected by shareholders. A cooperative has members rather than shareholders and operates as a corporation.[7]

Entity type, particularly as it is related to size and organizational complexity, can significantly affect Internet marketing activities and even help predict whether a business is online. Many local small businesses, particularly those in services such as car detailing, dry cleaning, and child care may never go online with a website because they perceive the costs of doing so as greater than the benefits. However, others will conclude that not being online puts them at a competitive disadvantage, so they will create an online presence. They may use a static, information-only website or an interactive site with email, but not necessarily a site where they sell products directly. Others will take advantage of online marketplaces or auctions to sell products.

A survey of U.S. industrial small businesses indicates that by 2003, 80 percent were already involved in some form of ecommerce. Over half (51 percent) had a website; more than a quarter (27 percent) were selling on a website not their own or participating in an emarket exchange or other Internet activity. Many are aware of the challenges involved in ecommerce and want to learn how to drive web traffic (61 percent) and use (56 percent) **search engine marketing.** Search engine marketing consists of such techniques as keyword management by inserting HTML tags in a web page to obtain top ranking in a search engine list ranking and paying for a sponsorship or top listing on a search engine. Other concerns include generating sales leads online (53 percent), online promotions (52 percent), tracking the effectiveness of online marketing (49 percent), and security (40 percent). Many large businesses, such as Citigroup and Cisco Systems, recognize the value of the small business online market and are actively courting it. The SBA's U.S. Business Advisor has an e-services list of links with information for small businesses going online, including links to *E-Commerce 101 Primer* and *E-Commerce for Small Business.*[8]

STATUS

Most of the earliest commercial websites were passive, static, **information-only sites** with no email options or other interactive features. They displayed electronic catalogs, brochures, annual reports, and other printed materials that were digitized and stored in files on servers accessible to anyone with a computer, browser, ISP, and the patience to endure slow download times and text-only displays. Granted, most early Internet users had only text-only browsers and dial-up modems, so interactive features would have been wasted on them or—even worse—might have crashed their computers. These pioneer information-only sites did not sell online, and the information they provided was available offline in traditional formats. Many were online with no clear idea of how to use marketing strategically in the new environment. They went online to stake a claim or because they were keeping up with competitors that were probably just as ill prepared as they.

Most but not all information-only sites soon realized they were missing out on the Web's unique interactivity, so they added an email feature and thus became limited **interactive sites.** The next step for many was to become **transaction sites,** selling products (goods, services, content, digital files) directly from highly visible web storefronts closely watched by the general public, competitors, the press, government regulators, and investors. They also may use a web storefront to make offers on intranets and extranets. Businesses of all sizes are transacting business online, many quite profitably.

OFFER(S)

Today, Amazon.com is a Fortune 500 company. When it began in 1995 as a high-risk, doomed-to-failure, clicks-only bookseller, its chief executive officer (CEO) and founder, Jeff Bezos, chose to offer a single product category, a **tangible good** that he

---

Search engine marketing
Techniques such as (1) keyword management by inserting HTML tags in a web page to obtain top ranking in a search engine list and (2) paying for a sponsorship on a search engine or for a top listing.

Information-only sites
Primarily early websites that were static, offering information only without email options or other interactive features.

Interactive sites
Websites that added interactive email to their formerly information-only format.

Transaction sites
Websites that sell products from their online storefronts.

Tangible goods
Products that can be physically felt, stored, inventoried, mass-produced, tested in advance of purchase, and quality-controlled.

believed was particularly well suited to the Internet environment. In order to build a sustainable, valuable, and profitable company, Bezos dramatically expanded Amazon's offers, and the company now has millions of new and used items for sale on its site. According to the site, its offers include "apparel and accessories, electronics, computers, kitchenware and housewares, books, music, DVDs, videos, cameras and photo items, toys, baby items and a baby registry, software, computer and video games, cell phones and service, tools and hardware, travel services, magazine subscriptions, and outdoor living items."[9]

Services
Performances that cannot be stored, inventoried, mass-produced, transported, tested in advance, or quality-controlled through standardized methods.

Digital product
A product that is electronic; for example, music downloaded to a buyer's computer.

Online offers may be of tangible goods, **services, digital products,** or a mixture of a core product with associated services or digitals. Digital products such as ecards from Blue Mountain (*www.bluemountain.com*) illustrate why the Internet promised such radical changes in marketing. These products are purchased online and delivered electronically, directly to the buyer's or another recipient's computer, PDA, or other Internet-ready device. Some marketers specialize in one product category, such as books, whereas others become general mass merchants with multiple category offers. Product offers will be discussed further in Chapter 9.

SITE FUNCTION(S)

Some marketers are using websites as static billboards, encouraging visitors to window-shop online and then purchase offline. Others are running auctions, exchanges, shopping malls, or portals or are using sites to generate sales leads for their professional sales force. Offers are made and exchanges completed on *web storefronts,* where products are sold directly to buyers; at *web auctions* and *exchanges* on the Internet, intranets, and extranets; and on *push sites* that provide online product information designed to push consumers toward buying offline at traditional retail stores or to push enterprise buyers toward contacting an offline sales force or make a catalog purchase.

Rather than selling directly from a web storefront, some businesses act as managers for others' exchanges. eBay (*www.ebay.com*), a clicks-only business founded in September 1995, is the best-known example of an exchange manager that facilitates auctions for consumers as well as businesses and other enterprises. Asset Auctions (*asset-auctions.com*) is an enterprise market maker, a service that attracts sellers and buyers of surplus assets, including equipment, machine tools, aircraft, and industrial products. It hosts traditional auctions, private auctions, and an open-trading marketplace. Many marketing activities occur on B2B web exchanges, specialized businesses that use their software and management expertise to bring business, industrial, government, or nonprofit buyers and sellers together to negotiate sales, schedule payments, arrange deliveries, and provide after-sale service.

Selling is a highly visible, extremely important aspect of Internet marketing, which some analysts estimate is the goal of over 95 percent of online activities. Some transactions are made online, and others are made offline, driven by information obtained online. However, it's important to remember that a vast amount of marketing activity occurs in support of selling, before and after the sale. We'll learn more about marketing activities related to site functions in Chapter 11.

SECTOR(S)

The North American Industry Classification System (NAICS) replaced the Standard Industrial Classification (SIC) system beginning with the 1997 Economic Census. It was developed jointly by the United States, Canada, and Mexico to facilitate comparability in North American (NAFTA-related) business activity statistics. There are 20 NAICS sectors, subdivided into 96 subsectors (3-digit codes), 313 industry groups (4-digit codes), and (in the United States) over 1000 industries (5- and 6-digit codes). The sectors that are heavily represented on the public Internet are Retail Trade; Information, Finance and Insurance; Real Estate; Health Care and Social Assistance; Educational Service; Arts, Entertainment, and Recreation; Accommodation and Food Services; Transportation and Warehousing; Management of Companies and Enterprises; and Public Administration. Less well represented on the public Internet, but often heavily involved with intranets and extranets, are Agriculture; Forestry, Fishing, and Hunting; Mining; Utilities; Construction; Manufacturing; Wholesale Trade; Professional, Scientific, and Technical Services; Administrative and Support; Waste Management; and Remediation Services.[10]

Similarities can be found in how businesses within sectors use Internet marketing. For example, retail businesses are more likely to invest in web storefronts, whereas agribusinesses typically use B2B exchanges; universities share similarities in how they market distance-learning programs, which is different from how financial businesses market online banking services. Internet marketing sector examples are discussed throughout the chapters (Chapters 9 through 12) that focus on the marketing mix variables (the 4 Ps).

Fulfillment
Activities needed to fill an order and deliver the purchased product to the buyer.

WEB UPDATE

For updates and more on this topic, visit the textbook student website at: http://college.hmco .com/business/students and select Siegel, *Internet Marketing*, 2e. **Online Marketing Activities**

FULFILLMENT

If buyers never receive the products they purchase online, it will ultimately kill online sales. This emphasizes the importance of **fulfillment,** the "back end" of the order, which consists of those activities needed to fill the order and deliver the purchased product to the buyer. The fulfillment cycle for goods includes receiving customer orders, configuring the products ordered, invoicing (billing), shipping, delivering products to distribution centers or end users, and invoicing products to distribution outlets or end users. Goods ordered online must undergo a fulfillment process in order to ensure delivery. Services also must be processed, but those that are digital can be delivered electronically. Other digital products, such as music and videos, can be downloaded directly to the buyer's computer; however, they still must be processed, billed, and paid for. Fulfillment is a critical part of Internet marketing and will be discussed further in Chapters 9 through 12.

Enterprises Marketing Online

Governments and other enterprises use marketing online, sometimes in ways that directly parallel business Internet marketing activities and sometimes not. Many public sector and nonprofit enterprises operate like a business in that they must raise revenue in order to survive; however, profit is not their primary goal.

GOVERNMENTS AND THE PUBLIC SECTOR

The U.S. government is the largest single buyer in the United States, but it is also a big online seller. In FY2000, the U.S. government registered US$3.6 billion in online sales from its (at that time) 164 websites. It sold Amtrak tickets, houses that had been repossessed, stamps, reservations at national parks, and access to federal case and docket data.[11]

The General Services Administration (*http://gsaauctions.gov/gsaauctions/gsaauctions/*), the business side of the U.S. government, was a pioneer in using its website to sell excess and surplus federal assets. The general public can register at the site and bid electronically on office equipment, furniture, scientific instruments, heavy machinery, aviation equipment, naval vessels, vehicles (including crashed test vehicles), gold coins made into jewelry, and more.

The Department of Housing and Urban Development (HUD) sells HUD homes (*www.hud.gov/offices/hsg/sfh/reo/homes.cfm*) to real estate brokers and the public. HUD also uses electronic auctions to sell surplus properties. The Central Intelligence Agency (CIA at *www.cia.gov/cia/publications/factbook/docs/purchase_info.html*) sells its *World Factbook* online, and the Department of Commerce (*www.census.gov/statab/www/saorder.html*) markets *The Statistical Abstract of the United States* in print and electronic forms.

State governments are getting into the business of selling licenses online. The State of Hawaii (*www.hawaii.gov*) sells fishing, hunting, and professional licenses from its website, and New Mexico (*www.state.nm.us*) has online vehicle registrations. Many states list surplus property for auction on their websites. Police departments are also getting into online marketing. The New York City Police Department is one of 300 departments from throughout the United States that auction goods through the Property Room (*www.stealitback.com*), a California company that receives over 12 million unique visitors each month. Recent hot specials were bicycles, telescopes, gold coins, and computers of all types that were confiscated because of criminal activity or are unclaimed from burglaries.[12]

Governments are enthusiastic sellers online because of the Internet's convenience, which eliminates the need for buyers to travel to government offices; its almost universal reach; the savings that accrue from reduced printing and distribution costs; and the potential for downsizing as more services are offered online. Web interactivity and almost universal access in public libraries and schools brings government closer to its constituents.

Property Room

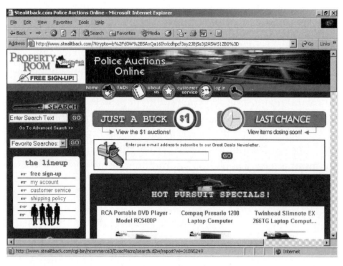

The Property Room connects law enforcement property rooms with online buyers through its auction site, *stealitback.com.*

Source: Copyright © 2004 by PropertyBureau, Inc. Reprinted with permission of Property Room, www.stealitback.com.

UNIVERSITIES AND ELEARNING

Before the Internet, universities marketed themselves to students primarily through printed materials, on-campus visits, and (for the more sought-after students) personal telephone calls. Today, the Internet is a prime marketing tool selling schools to Internet-savvy traditional and nontraditional students. American University's Kogod School of Business receives over 95 percent of its student applications online through its website (*www.kogod.american.edu*). The site was launched in 1999; since then it has recorded tens of thousands of unique visits. Kogod uses databases to manage its contacts with prospective students and follows up these contacts with emails, telephone calls, and mailed brochures. Its website uses the latest technology to provide an interactive homepage for prospective students and corporate recruiters that links them to needed information.[13]

Virtual college tours are replacing traditional campus visits for many students. Virtual tours save time and money, as well as help students narrow their college choice. They allow universities to market their programs using text, graphics, animation, and interactivity. For example, Duke University offers prospective students Duke 360 (*www.duke.edu/web/duketour/*), a panoramic tour of the campus using low- or high-bandwidth versions. A 1998 survey of college-bound high school seniors by a Baltimore higher-education marketing firm reported that 78 percent visited college websites, up from 4 percent in 1996. Online admissions are saving students and colleges time and money. It has been estimated that by 2003, well over 50 percent of all students applied for admission online. Some schools have gone to entirely online admissions and registration systems.[14]

Like many national athletics programs, the Duke University Blue Devils (*http://goduke.collegesports.com*) are online at their official site. They market Duke football, soccer, conditioning, baseball, and basketball camps. The Duke store sells a broad assortment of products, from apparel to watches. Customers can order online or by telephone. Successful national athletics programs often host elaborate websites that are informative and encourage interactions and transactions. They are a productive way to maintain ties with sometimes elusive alumni in long-term relationship management programs.

Colleges and universities are reporting excellent results from their online marketing efforts, including more admissions from previously untapped geographical areas. Accordingly, many schools are paying marketing consultants to redesign their websites and make them more appealing, easier to use, and more student-friendly. Institutions of higher learning will increasingly turn to Internet marketing as the competition for paying students intensifies.[15] The Internet's convenience and reach also attract corporate recruiters, who frequently use university websites to prescreen job applicants.

There were only 400 online corporate career-education universities in 1988; by 2000 the number had grown to more than 1,600. Corporate university elearning is a highly competitive and profitable industry. International Data Corp. (IDC) projected growth in the U.S. market for corporate classes from about US$1 billion in 1999 to more than US$11 billion in 2003, a compound annual growth rate of nearly 80 percent. Web-based instruction is highly cost-effective, shaving as much as 40 to 60 percent annually from corporate training budgets. IBM reported saving US$200 million in one year by purchasing online learning programs so that employees could train at their workplace computers.[16]

Online training and education have a number of important benefits. They can save time and money and can eliminate the disruptions caused when employees attend off-site training sessions. They also make training programs cost-effective for small and midsize businesses. Public and private universities recognize the value of online training and corporate education profits. The marketing of these programs will become more aggressive as the numbers of online competitors increase.

ARTS AND CULTURE

The Metropolitan Museum of Art's Met Store (*www.metmuseum.org/store/index.asp*) offers an extensive line of books and art-based objects in an elegant, multipage online catalog. The site has the latest in shopping basket technology, and online sales benefit the buyer as well as the organization. Not to be outdone, the Metropolitan Opera Guild (*www.metopera.org/guild*), the Kennedy Center for the Performing Arts (*www.kennedy-center.org/giftshop*), the San Francisco Opera (*www.sfopera.com*), and National Public Radio (NPR at *http://shop.npr.org*) also operate online stores. Sales of NPR's growing product line of books, apparel, recordings, videos, and other products help support NPR and its local affiliates.

Internet marketing vastly extends the reach of arts and cultural organizations, particularly those with national and international reputations, such as the Metropolitan Opera. It can also be used by local arts organizations seeking more timely communication with their patrons and the reduction or elimination of costly hard-copy catalogs and newsletters. It allows umbrella arts organizations such as the California Assembly of Local Arts Agencies (CALAA at *www.calaa.net*) to showcase member organizations and market the local arts concept. CALAA is a nonprofit membership organization representing California's 250 local community arts organizations (private) and arts-related local government agencies (public).

Arts patrons typically are better-educated, higher-income consumers who spend more time and money online. They are more likely than the general population to be regular Internet users with faster access. Arts organizations increasingly recognize the effectiveness of Internet marketing in reaching these target markets from web storefronts and by email. In addition to providing information online, which is what many visitors seek, organizations sell products from their gift shops and tickets for future performances, distribute digital newsletters and announcements, and/or provide online product catalogs that push visitors toward an offline purchase. Schoolchildren are another prime target market for many arts organizations whose goal is to develop future patrons. Arts organization websites often include pages specially designed for young people, to market the arts and the concept of participation. The National Gallery of Art (*www.nga.gov/kids/kids.htm*) has highly engaging interactive kids' pages that raise awareness about visual arts and the Gallery.

RELIGIOUS GROUPS

The Pew Internet & American Life Project reports that in the United States, more people go online for religious than for secular purposes, and large numbers of religious organizations use the Internet. Churches, synagogues, mosques, and other houses of worship use email to maintain contact with members and to reach non-members. They email newsletters, bulletins, and sermons. The Pew survey revealed that 80 percent of the churches and synagogues that participated in its study had websites at least a year old, and 83 percent say the sites are useful in getting visitors to attend services. The Pew study estimates that 28 million American "religion surfers" go online to obtain religious and spiritual information and interact with like-minded others.[17]

Religious marketing is an area that is often overlooked, yet its importance is growing in U.S. society, where religious groups must compete with a wide variety of secular activities. Not all religious groups show the Internet marketing savvy of the Fellowship Church, a mega-church in Grapevine, Texas, USA (*www.fellowshipchurch.com*). The church actively uses online marketing to advance its mission of connecting with the culture and with new technology. It provides secular services and press releases, along with the more expected sermons, Bible games, Bible reference materials, daily devotionals, education, and evangelism.[18] Visitors can order books, music, and videos from its online bookstore.

CAUSE MARKETING

Cause-related marketing benefits nonprofit organizations (NPOs) from private adoption agencies to community mental health/mental retardation boards, substance abuse programs, and Ronald McDonald Houses for families with seriously ill, hospitalized children. Tax-exempt public charities that solicit funds from the public are classified as 501(c)(3) organizations. NPOs can market themselves and their causes in several ways. They use their websites to attract volunteers, solicit donors, develop databases, increase the number of dues-paying members, and promote their goals. Some use their sites for charity auctions. Online donations are a growth industry. In 2000, less than 2 percent of charitable donations were received online; that proportion is expected to grow to 40 percent by 2005. Online fundraising after September 11, 2001 was unprecedented. Within weeks after the attacks, over US$100 million was raised online, mostly in small gifts of US$50 or under. Network for Good (*www.networkforgood.org*), a philanthropy web portal, generated over US$32 million in online donations in the two years after its launch in 2001 and raised US$17.5 million in 2003. The ephilanthrophy portal was founded by the Time Warner Foundation and AOL, Inc.; the Cisco Foundation and Cisco Systems, Inc.; and Yahoo! Inc. The Internet is credited with introducing many younger people to philanthropy. At the same time, philanthropic websites often fail usability criteria for their prime target audiences: Americans over 50, who are more likely to use slow dial-up connections and older computers, have difficulty reading small type size, and are still reluctant to use credit cards online.[19]

Nonprofits are finding that online retailing is highly profitable; among these nonprofits are such disparate organizations as the National Rifle Association (*www.mynra.com*), the American Civil Liberties Union (*http://forms.aclu.org/store/storemain.cfm*), and Save the Children (*www.savethechildren.org*). The consensus is that niche marketing on the Internet is even more profitable than traditional offline direct marketing.[20]

Some NPOs turn to affiliate marketing or "Shop-for-a-Cause" programs at so-called charity malls. Charities that sign up for these programs receive a donation (usually 5 percent of the purchase) for each purchase by a registered consumer at the website of an affiliated retailer. Portals such as GreaterGood.com (*www.greatergood.com*) and iGive.com (*www.igive.com/html/intro.cfm*) direct consumers to affiliated retailers that forward a portion of each purchase to a charity of the consumer's choice. These donations are not tax-deductible for the consumer. GreaterGood forwards donations to local and national charities, schools, and college scholarship funds. Affiliated retailers include Nordstrom (*http://store.nordstrom.com*), Lands' End (*www.landsend.com*), DisneyStore (*http://disney.store.go.com*), and Wal-Mart. Causes include Big Brothers Big Sisters, The Elizabeth Glaser Pediatric AIDS Foundation, and Make-A-Wish Foundation of America. At the Schoolpop website (*www.schoolpop.com*) consumers can designate a school they want to receive up to 20 percent of any purchase from a list of more than 300 affiliated online stores. Cooperating retailers include Amazon.com, Dell Computer, Office Max (*www.officemax.com*), and Barnes & Noble (*www.bn.com*). America's top ten charities, five of which are the Salvation Army (*www.salvationarmyusa.org*), the YMCA (*www.ymca.net/index.jsp*), Fidelity Investments Charitable Gift Fund (*www401.charitablegift.org*), the American Cancer Society (*www.cancer.org*), and the American Red Cross (*www.redcross.org*), are all online marketing services and causes.[21]

Schoolpop

Schoolpop is the top school support program in the United States, with over 60,000 school and nonprofit participants.

Source: Copyright © 2005. Reprinted with permission, www.schoolpop.com.

WEB UPDATE

For updates and more on this topic, visit the textbook student website at: http://college.hmco.com/business/students and select Siegel, *Internet Marketing*, 2e. **Enterprises Marketing Online**

Unfortunately, although the Internet is attractive for marketing an NPO, it also facilitates deception and fraud in the name of charity. According to the U.S. Federal Trade Commission (*www.ftc.gov/bcp/conline/pubs/tmarkg/charity.htm*), NPOs raised US$143 billion in 1995 and fraudsters collected around US$1.43 billion; by 2001, funds raised by NPOs increased to US$212 billion. This means that at least US$2.12 billion was probably diverted by fraud. Fraud was a problem even in the wake of fundraising for the September 11 terrorist attack victims and their families. Within days after 9/11, the National Fraud Information Center (NFIC at *www.fraud.org*) began receiving consumer complaints about phone calls and emails fraudulently soliciting money for rescue efforts, victims' families, and the hunt for Al-Qaeda terrorist leader Osama bin Laden. Legitimate fundraising groups such as the American Red Cross Liberty Disaster Relief Fund, the United Way September 11 Fund, and the Twin Towers Fund to aid the families of New York City workers killed in the rescue efforts lost millions of dollars in potential contributions. Individuals defrauded by cyber-thieves lost their money. Others lost their identity when swindlers emailed them asking for personal information to replace records supposedly lost in the World Trade Center building collapse.[22]

Individuals Marketing Online

Businesses, governments, and organizations are not the only online marketers. The low cost of setting up a website and the potential for reaching a large domestic or international audience are enough to encourage individuals to go online, marketing products and themselves. Individual sellers range from artists and athletes to lawyers and other professionals. Some do it all themselves; others seek the help of marketing consultants to design, construct, and maintain a website. Some market through cyber-malls; others sell treasures through an intermediary such as eBay. Some market solely online, whereas others use the Internet as one of several marketing channels. Although many engage in marketing online as a full-time business, others do it as a hobby or part-time venture.

PROFESSIONALS

Lawyers, doctors, dentists, consultants, psychologists, and other professionals have invaded the Web, marketing their services either directly from a web storefront or from a push site. Professionals can be located through search engines and sites that provide directories and locate local practitioners. Portals have sprung up to accommodate the search. For example, Lawyers.com (*www.lawyers.com*) is a lawyer-locating service that categorizes lawyers in terms of specialty and region. The American Dental Association (*www.ada.org/prof/index.asp*) has a dentist-locating service. Psychotherapist Search (*http://psychotherapistsearch.com*) is a national registry by state of psychotherapists, marriage counselors, family and child counselors, and various types of clinicians.

Although some professionals have marketed their services offline for years, this is still a controversial practice. Most professional organizations accept tasteful, low-key web marketing sites and online professional portals with links to practitioners by state or city. What most condemn are websites that make blatantly exaggerated claims and prey on vulnerable individuals in a time of personal crisis. Most professions self-regulate and can threaten decertification of members who use the online environment inappropriately. They have no direct control over nonmembers, however. Complaints against professionals can be made to professional organizations or to the appropriate federal government agencies.

ARTISTS AND CRAFTSPEOPLE

The visual richness of the Web makes it an exciting environment for individuals, arts organizations, government economic development agencies, and businesses to sell original works of art and copies online. ArtAmerica.com (*http://artamerica.com/a-@0000.shtml*) has links to individual artists displaying their work and selling it online. eBay provides a marketplace where individual artists can auction their own work or that of other artists. Artists of the Olympic Peninsula (*www.olympicartists.com/index.html*) market their art through an online cooperative. The collective accommodates artists (in other than the performing arts) who are seeking ways to broaden their customer base. Member artists must live on the Olympic Peninsula, the most northwest part of the continental United States.

Individual sole proprietor sites can be located through search engines by using product-specific keyword descriptors. A search for *handmade baskets,* for example, leads one to Baskets by Bernie (*www.basketsbybernie.com/default.htm*), who has been making unique baskets since 1978. Bernie (Bernadine) did not accept orders on-line as late as 2004, but she encourages interested visitors to contact her by email or telephone. Understandably, push sites are common among individual sellers who do not have the sales volume, expertise, or need to deal with the complexities of a store-front transaction site, or fear the risks of doing so.

FARMERS

Considering the vast number of websites and pages, finding small business and individual sellers online would appear to be an insurmountable task. However, with a bit of product-specific digging, they can be found. An example is fresh produce. Selling farm produce online should tax the limits of electronic technology, but a proxy exists at the Farmer's Market Online (*www.farmersmarketonline.com*). Individual farmers rent virtual *booth spaces* that are links to web pages where they sell directly to buyers. This is a small business version of a B2C or C2C web exchange.

CELEBRITIES

Celebrities and celebrity wannabes use the Internet to sell products, such as music CDs, videos, apparel, memorabilia, and tickets, as well as to fuel fan interest. Sports legends have launched personal web storefronts or joined sports malls. Sports memorabilia constitute an over US$2 billion industry, so using web storefronts could be good for the sports stars, as well as for the sites that host them for a small percentage of sales. Clicks-only sports malls have undergone considerable consolidation, and bricks-and-clicks sports retailers now clearly dominate the market, but most super-stars have their own web marketing sites. Golf phenomenon Tiger Woods (*www.tigerwoods.com*) has an official website with information about Tiger's golfing activities as well as an online store with co-branded apparel linked to Nike (*www.nike.com*) and memorabilia whose sale benefits the Tiger Woods Foundation. This foundation was established in 1996 to support programs designed to create positive environments for underprivileged youth. The online C2C sports memorabilia market invites fraud, however, because items such as autographed baseball cards and certificates of authenticity can easily be forged.[23]

Very few celebrities have the time or interest to maintain their own websites. Some celebrity sites are operated by the corporations that contract for their services. More interesting are the large numbers of individuals who create and maintain extensive celebrity sites where they sell posters and other products, show photos, host chat areas, and provide information about the celebrity. The celebrities that Internet users searched for most often on Google, Yahoo!, and Lycos in 2004 were Britney Spears, Shakira, David Beckham, Kobe Bryant, Eminem, Paris Hilton, Christina Aguilera, and Pamela Anderson.

Some celebrity sites take a highly creative approach. In 1994, for example, Detroit native Byron Allen launched a syndicated television program called *Entertainers,* a weekly interview program with celebrities. In 2000, Allen went online and created EntertainmentStudios.com (*http://entertainmentstudios.com*), where almost two million visitors each week can sit in on hundreds of archived celebrity interviews, read new interviews, and take virtual tours of stars' homes. Content is free and is drawn primarily from Allen's television program, but visitors are also attracted to other offerings: CDs, art, sports memorabilia, and a chat area.[24]

Environmental Influences on Internet Marketing

Marketing never occurs in a vacuum. To the contrary, marketing activities and ultimately marketing success are affected by what happens inside (*internal factors*) and outside (*external factors*) the business (Figure 4-3). *Internal factors* such as human resources, capital, and level of cooperation affect Internet marketing decisions. They are more controllable than external factors, but that doesn't mean marketers have control over them. Successful Internet marketing requires the commitment of top-management decision makers, as well as that of other key company members and teams. In larger businesses, this includes decision makers in finance and accounting, human resources, production, research and development, and purchasing. In smaller and midsize businesses, it means anyone whose work could affect or be affected by Internet marketing. It requires teamwork, particularly cooperation and collaboration between marketing and information technology professionals. Implementing, maintaining, and upgrading web marketing activities requires a resource commitment of people, money, equipment, and time. This can lead to turf wars unless a commitment to support Internet marketing efforts is developed and maintained.

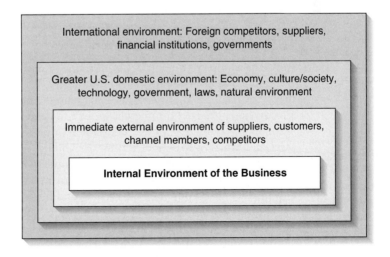

FIGURE 4-3 Environmental Influences on Marketing

Internet marketing requires skilled and committed people. Therefore, human resource departments must provide enough people with the skills needed to plan, implement, and control Internet marketing activities. Also required are clearly articulated goals and objectives to which Internet marketing must contribute, as well as marketing plans and production processes that produce products in sufficient quantity and quality to satisfy online buyers. Marketers can influence these factors, especially by making a compelling case that cooperation increases revenues and profits.

External factors are far less controllable. The immediate external environment includes businesses and people that interact closely and directly with the business. They are suppliers that provide raw materials, parts, equipment, supplies, and finished products used in business operations and sales. They are marketing intermediaries that transport products and perform warehouse and inventory control functions. Buyers are part of this environment, as are competitors and stakeholders.

The greater U.S. domestic environment directly affects the business and its Internet marketing activities. Although the largest corporations may influence some factors within this environment, most companies cannot. External factors are economic, technological, societal, cultural, natural, governmental, and legal.

Every business, whether or not it actively engages in the international Internet market, is affected by the greater global environment. Each country's own domestic environment contributes to the global environment. Since any business that has a website is an international marketer because of the borderless nature of the Internet, what happens in the global environment also affects each Internet marketer directly or indirectly. Some of these effects can be harsh, as when a government denies Internet access to its citizens or prohibits certain types of online marketing activities. All environmental factors require constant monitoring to determine when factors are turning against the marketing effort and when they present opportunities. This is particularly true of Internet marketing, which occurs in a highly volatile environment of its own, as well as being vulnerable to what is happening around the world. Several key U.S. macroenvironmental factors are examined in the following sections.

THE ECONOMIC ENVIRONMENT

Internet commercialization began during a period of great economic prosperity for the United States and many parts of the world. From 1993 until mid-2000, the stock market soared, productivity steadily increased, and consumer confidence was at an all-time high. Internet commercial growth seemed destined to expand forever. At the same time, computing power continued to observe Moore's Law, and computer prices fell steadily. ISPs and AOL in the United States converted to monthly access fees rather than charging by time used. Many services offered free email and/or Net access. For many marketers, a rosy economy meant it was comparatively easy to secure financing and purchase advertising and other promotions designed to get buyers to buy.

A contentious presidential election, impatience with unprofitable dot-coms, and a slowing economy thrust the U.S. economy into an economic downturn by late 2000 and into recession in mid-2001. An economic downturn has serious implications. For many Internet marketers, it was a knock-out punch. **Consumer confidence,** a key

Consumer confidence
A measure of the confidence consumers have in their economic future and in the nation's economy, often used as a predictor of future consumer buying.

indicator and frequently used predictor of consumers' willingness to purchase, fell proportionally and suggested harder times to come.[25]

Consumer confidence took a tailspin after the 9/11 terrorist attacks, falling to its lowest levels since the early 1990s. Consumer pessimism can delay or discourage purchasing. This negatively affects revenues online and off, creating a ripple effect that touches most sectors of the economy.

Marketers are particularly vulnerable to changes in the economic environment. Such changes may influence consumer and business confidence, purchasing, and spending patterns. Marketers can do little to affect consumer confidence as a whole. However, online marketers can reduce prices or make attractive offers that stimulate short-term sales. For the Christmas 2001 buying season, many etailers offered free shipping and handling for purchases over a minimal amount. Others used preseason clearance sales to boost site traffic. Online advertising expenditures were not increased, however, and in many cases suffered serious reductions. Despite the slowing economy, Christmas 2001 online sales grew over the previous year, and 2002 began strong. By Christmas 2003, the economy was in recovery and more consumers were shopping online. Online holiday spending in 2003 was US$18.5 billion, a 35 percent increase over the $13.7 billion spent during the 2002 holiday season. In the United Kingdom, sales during Christmas were also robust, soaring more than 70 percent over 2002 to £1.324 billion in December 2003.[26]

TECHNOLOGY

Technology is a double-edged sword. Keeping up with new technology is extremely expensive, and discontinuous innovations can threaten established ways of doing business. As wireless, handheld Internet devices become more popular in the United States, it will challenge marketers to redesign or re-create web storefronts to accommodate the smaller screens. New technologies on the horizon that could make online shopping more engaging for consumers include 3-D imaging, where consumers experience products in three-dimensional space, and sensations transmitted through a specially constructed intelligent mouse. As the viewer moves the cursor over an object, such as a sweater, the *feel* of the object is transmitted to the mouse, and the consumer experiences sensation. Like economic factors, technology requires constant monitoring.

THE SOCIAL/CULTURAL ENVIRONMENT

The social/cultural environment involves people interacting within families, communities, groups, and nations. People influence purchase decisions and other consumer behaviors. Families and reference groups exert perhaps the most direct influence. Consumer fears about Internet safety and security can seriously slow commercialization. Consumer adoption of new technologies will determine whether the Internet becomes like the telephone or television, a commodity with nearly universal access.

THE NATURAL ENVIRONMENT

It may be difficult to visualize a link between the Internet and the natural world, yet they are inseparably bound. The Internet relies on physical connections such as wires, telephone lines, cables, satellites, and other equipment that can be damaged or destroyed when natural or human-made disasters occur. Increased use of computers and of the Internet has been implicated in the natural gas and power shortage that struck California in early 2001. Widespread consumer and business Internet use added an estimated 10 percent to electricity demand. As demand grows, it may tax natural gas reserves and power supplies.[27]

Internet marketing can be seriously hampered by power shortages, particularly in the United States where the majority of Internet users rely on computers and modems to access the Web. Although Internet marketers can do little to increase power supplies, they may have an opportunity to aggressively market handheld wireless devices that operate independently of electrical power other than when they are recharging. Persistent power supply problems and rolling brownouts are serious threats to web commercialization.

Human-made disasters can be equally disruptive. When terrorist attacks felled the twin towers of the World Trade Center in Manhattan, high-speed switches and circuits in its basement and adjacent buildings were destroyed, along with computers and access lines throughout the stricken area. Financial firms at or near the Trade Center lost contact with customers and their own branches. Securities trading and data processing came to a halt for Bank of New York's (BoNY) headquarters and branches in the Trade Center area. Some Earthlink and AT&T WorldNet customers lost Internet access. As the crisis unfolded, the financial community closed ranks to cover liquidity shortfalls caused by losses at BoNY, Cantor Fitzgerald, and other firms. Internet companies offered free bandwidth to others so that they could maintain operations. Internet traffic was routed around the destroyed equipment. Many companies relied on mirror sites far from Manhattan to restore files and customer service. Although broadband and voice service in Washington, D.C., and New York City experienced delays, they continued to function despite extremely high traffic counts.[28]

GOVERNMENT AND LEGAL FACTORS

All businesses, online or off, are subject to government regulations and laws. These topics are considered in Chapter 5.

Summary

http://college.hmco.com/business/students

Business Internet Marketing Activities

Internet commercialization began with a bang, experienced a crash amid much media frenzy, and then began recovering. Businesses that went online at the start of Internet commercialization were clicks-only or bricks-and-clicks. Much has been written and said about the dramatic shakeout that began in mid-2000 and resulted in the shuttering of many businesses during and after the 2001 recession. The shakeout was brutal, though not unprecedented, and it was not the end of Internet commercialization. Similar events have occurred in automobiles, biotechnology, and personal computers. The Internet is a dynamic, pluralistic environment where an abundance of marketing activities and actors pursue exchange goals. A simple classification system can aid our understanding of Internet marketing. It is based on a number of factors, including the marketer's home (solely online or both online and offline), served market(s), market coverage (from solely domestic and local to global), entity type, status, offer(s), site function(s), sector(s), and where fulfillment takes place.

Enterprises Marketing Online

Governments and other enterprises are marketing online, sometimes in ways that directly parallel business Internet marketing activities, and sometimes not. Many public sector and nonprofit enterprises operate like businesses because they must raise revenue in order to survive, but profit is not their primary goal. Governments are enthusiastic sellers online because of the Internet's convenience, its almost universal reach, the savings that accrue from reduced printing and distribution costs, and the potential for downsizing as more services are offered online. Web interactivity and access in public libraries and schools brings government closer to its constituents. The Internet is a prime marketing tool in the selling of schools to Internet-savvy traditional and nontraditional students. Colleges and universities report excellent results from online marketing, including more admissions from previously untapped geographical areas. Online training and education have a number of important benefits. Internet marketing vastly extends the reach of arts and cultural organizations. In the United States, more people go online for religious than for secular purposes; large numbers of religious organizations use the Internet. Nonprofit causes use their websites to attract volunteers, solicit donors, develop databases, increase the numbers of dues-paying members, and promote their goals. Nonprofit online retailing is highly profitable.

Individuals Marketing Online

The low cost of setting up a website and the potential for reaching a large domestic or international audience are enough to encourage individuals to go online, marketing products and themselves. Lawyers, doctors, dentists, consultants, psychologists, and other professionals are attracted to the Web, marketing their services either directly from a web storefront or push site. Although some professionals have marketed their services offline for years, this is still a controversial practice. The visual richness of the Web makes it an exciting environment for individuals, arts organizations, government economic development agencies, and businesses to sell original works of art and reproductions online. Celebrities and would-be celebrities use the Internet to sell products, such as music CDs, videos, apparel, memorabilia, and tickets, as well as to fuel fan interest.

Environmental Influences on Internet Marketing

Marketing does not occur in a vacuum. Internet marketing is affected by environmental influences within and external to the company. Internally, management as well as people in other functional areas should be encouraged to cooperate, support, and sometimes participate in the Internet marketing effort. The immediate macroenvironment includes all the businesses and people with whom the business and marketer interact most frequently. The Internet effort is influenced by what happens in the greater U.S. macroenvironment, as well as in the global environment. Marketers must monitor the economic environment, the technology environment, the social/cultural environment, the natural environment, and government and legal environments.

Take Action!

You can help the owner/operator of a small coffee shop make several crucial decisions about Internet marketing. The coffee shop has been in business for over a year and draws customers from a 10-mile radius, mainly students and faculty at two small colleges, workers at two small industrial plants, professionals from the downtown, and older students and faculty from the public schools. Business is good, and the owner wants to add several Internet-connected computers to the shop, transforming it into an Internet café, the first in the area, although it was not the first coffee shop. She believes that Internet connections will attract older people (seniors) as customers and that they will use the shop to meet friends and send email while other customers are in school or at work. The owner and her four workers are very knowledgeable about the Internet and can help newbies (new users) go online and be comfortable there. She is even considering holding Internet introductory classes several times a month at the café. The café's computers and printers will be state-of-the-art with very fast connections. Her customers will be able to drink quality coffee, eat homemade sandwiches, and surf in comfortable surroundings for a modest charge per hour or a monthly membership fee. The shop is a popular place for local artists to display their work, which enhances the visual environment. The café also needs a website, where hours of operation can be listed, along with information about fees, classes, the coffee shop's menu (which changes seasonally), and perhaps a display of the art currently hanging in the café's art gallery. The owner projects café sales of nearly US$300,000 in year 1 and annual 15 percent increases thereafter.

1. Consider the environment in which the coffee shop/Internet café will operate, the multiple markets, dual product/service offer, and market coverage. Using what you have learned about the business, create a SWOT chart for it. A SWOT is a table with four cells that identify respectively **S**trengths, **W**eaknesses, **O**pportunities, and **T**hreats. Present your SWOT in a memo to the owner and briefly explain the contents of each cell. Focus in particular on what you believe are the opportunities in this business venture and the threats. Using a two-column bullet list, make several recommendations for seizing the opportunities and avoiding the threats.

2. Go online to Google (*www.google.com*) or use the map at CyberCafes.com (*www.cybercafes.com*) to locate several Internet café websites. Evaluate the sites and based on what you learn during your analysis, create a two-column bullet list of (a) features and content that should be on the owner's website and (b) features and content that should not be included. Attach this evaluation to the memo to the owner and SWOT analysis.

Chapter Review Questions

1. Explain what is meant by the following terms and give an example of each: clicks-only, bricks-and-clicks, bricks-and-mortar.
2. Why did so many dot-coms fail in 2000–2001?
3. Will dot-coms be consolidated like the automobile industry was after its early years and later shakeout?
4. What are the elements in the simple classification system for Internet marketing activities and actors?
5. What is a first mover and does a first mover really have an advantage?

6. What is a conversion rate and why is it important?
7. What is a digital product?
8. What is a web driver?
9. What is a market gap and why is it important to Internet marketing?
10. How are universities using the Web to market their programs?
11. Why would consumers respond to the shop-for-a-cause strategy?
12. Should all artists market their work online?

13. What external factors influence Internet marketing?

14. How can an economic downturn affect Internet marketing activities?

15. Why is technology a double-edged sword for Internet marketers?

Competitive Case Study

Competing with Walmart.com Is Easier Than It Appears

According to Nielsen//NetRatings and comScore Media Metrix surveys, walmart.com ranked 17th on the list of most visited U.S. web properties in December 2003 as accessed from home, work, and universities. The fact that walmart.com has expanded its offerings to include uploaded digital photo prints, DVD movie rentals, music downloads, email, and Wal-Mart Connect Internet service makes direct comparisons complex because so many different competitors are involved, from Amazon to Verizon. To simplify this comparison, walmart.com is classified as an **etailer** (online electronic retailer or department store). HitWise reported a surge in web traffic overall in December 2003, and etail accounted for 7.54 percent of it during the busiest month online of the entire year. In the HitWise (*www.hitwise.com*) list of most visited etail sites of December 2003, walmart.com ranks 4th, after eBay, Amazon, and Yahoo! Shopping. Following walmart.com are BestBuy.com, eBay Motors, Target, Dell Computer, Lower My Bills, Half.com (owned by eBay), CircuitCity.com, and Sears.com (12th), trailed by JCPenney.com (16th). However, these ranks must be viewed with caution, taking market share into account. In August 2003 (the prime back-to-school season, second only to December in sales), HitWise reported a 42.79 percent market share among etailers for Amazon, while walmart.com had a 9.12 percent share, followed by Target (7.48 percent), JCPenney.com (5.43 percent), and Sears.com (4.98 percent). Even farther down the list were Kmart.com (1.97 percent), Kohls.com (1.88 percent), Sam's Club (1.77 percent), and Macys.com (1.25 percent). With the exception of clicks-only Amazon.com, the Hitwise list included just bricks-and-clicks etailers offering a wide range of goods. The average Hitwise online etail shopper was in early mid-

dle age (26 percent were 35–44 years old), was a female (57 percent), used home access (69 percent), represented the upper middle class in socioeconomic status (38 percent had household income above $75,000), and spent 8 minutes and 12 seconds per etail visit. Many of these characteristics do not closely describe the average Wal-Mart shopper. Although Amazon still dominates the etail sector, walmart.com leads the remaining field. However, problems persist among the bricks-and-clicks, particularly as **channel-crossing customers** continue to experience problems with etailers ill-equipped to handle online purchase/in-store returns. Another issue is the absence of in-store web drivers; in some stores, it is almost as though the store's website doesn't exist. Website information continues to be absent on store signage, receipts, cash wraps, and shopping bags. In short, even though Wal-Mart dominates offline retail, it is not now the dominant player in etail and is itself among the pack of competitors chasing Amazon.[29]

Etailer
An online electronic retailer or department store

Channel-crossing customers
Customers who cross channels in their purchase activities, making a purchase online and a return offline, for instance.

CHECK IT OUT

Visit your nearest Wal-Mart store and look for web drivers. Are they on store signage, employee uniforms, shopping bags, shopping carts, cash register receipts, or in-store kiosks? Are the kiosks interactive and do they connect directly to walmart.com? Look for Wal-Mart advertisements (freestanding inserts) in your Sunday local newspaper. Do Wal-Mart print ads contain web drivers? If you see Wal-Mart television advertisements, look for web drivers. Be prepared to report your observations to the class, along with recommendations on how Wal-Mart can improve its store-related web drivers.

A GLOBAL PERSPECTIVE

Visit Walmart México (*www.walmartmexico.com.mx*) and click on English (unless you can read Spanish). How many Wal-Mart stores (units) are there in Mexico? In how many cities do they appear? Where are most of the company's units located geographically? When did the first Wal-Mart open there? What were last year's sales? Is the Mexico website an information-only, interactive, or transaction site? Compare the designs of the United States and Mexican websites. How are they alike? How are they different? Return to the walmart.com site and connect to the page for international sites. View the sites of several countries and describe how they are like or unlike the U.S. and Mexican websites. What insights have you gained about differences in international online markets as perceived by Wal-Mart?

5

Legal and Ethical Issues; Privacy and Security Concerns

LEARNING OBJECTIVES

» To understand why Internet laws are in a state of flux and what remedies are being attempted
» To learn what important legal and ethical issues confront Internet marketers
» To consider the right to and reality of online privacy
» To understand what online security problems concern buyers and sellers

Napster and Napster 2

Napster, founded in January 1999, was quickly embraced by music lovers who downloaded the free Napster MP3 file-sharing software, used it to search other MP3-enabled computers online for the music they wanted, and then transferred music files from those computers to their own computer hard drives. File-sharing music with others this way is piracy if the music is copyright protected and not paid for. Napster-users shared music files over the Internet without honoring the owner's copyright.

By December 1999, Napster had been sued by the Recording Industry of America (RIAA) for copyright infringement. This lawsuit quickly became the most celebrated online copyright case. RIAA claimed that losses through music file sharing cost the industry over US$300 million annually. In October 2000, Napster began developing a legal file-sharing system that would enable it to stay in business if the courts ruled against its free sharing system. On February 12,

2001, the Ninth Circuit U.S. Court of Appeals ruled that Napster violated copyright laws and had to honor copyrights or close—and close it did, at least in part because of the escalating costs of an appeal. This ruling marked the first time that an Internet service was shut down by a federal judge. Napster was not the only file-sharing site online, but as the most popular, it was an inviting target for the RIAA.

The record company's next tactic was to begin suing individual file swappers. Lawsuits were launched against music-swapping teens, college students, and grandmothers and against parents whose kids were file-swapping copyrighted music. Although many of these cases were later dropped, news of these actions sent a chill through the online file-swapping community.

Napster (*www.napster.com*) came back online on October 29, 2003. This time, the company hoped to duplicate Apple's iTunes's success in attracting paying customers. It wasn't the same old Napster, however, because Napster's name had been purchased in bankruptcy court for US$5 million. Its new owner, software maker Roxio, set out to capture the attention of a large number of the estimated 6 million online music file sharers and make money from music fans for whom the brand name *Napster* still resonated. Napster 2's marketing model is based on a product inventory of over 750,000 songs that can be purchased and downloaded legally by monthly subscription (initially US$9.95 per month) or by one-time purchase at 99 cents a track. Tracks can be burned to a CD, transferred to a portable player, or stored on the hard discs of up to three computers.[1]

Napster's story illustrates the evolving nature of the Internet's legal and regulatory environment. That environment all too frequently is a battleground between combative entrenched interests determined to preserve their markets, frequently without regard to their customers' best interests, and online companies that have sprung up in a marketplace that values such principles as electronic sharing and building communities. It also illustrates that although there are great advantages to doing business online, there also are drawbacks. Some of the most vexing challenges facing Internet marketers involve legal and ethical issues, and online privacy and security. This chapter begins with a discussion of various legal and ethical issues that confront Internet marketers. Privacy and security, the topics that round out the chapter, concern both buyers and sellers and have been identified as top reasons why some buyers swear they will never go online. Because the Internet's legal environment is dynamic and unpredictable, none of the information presented here should be taken as legal advice or legal opinion on any specific facts or circumstances.

Internet Laws and Jurisdiction

The Internet is a borderless virtual community, a worldwide network of internetted computer networks linking people and nations electronically. For an international body of Internet law to be effective, it must be accepted by the major internetted nations and then enforced either by existing international bodies such as the World Trade Organization (WTO) or the United Nations (UN) or by a new agency created specifically for the purpose. A patchwork of laws accepted by some (but not all) major and most minor connected nations will be unenforceable. It will also have a detrimental effect on the Internet's international commercialization. Currently, there is no body of internationally accepted Internet law. In its absence, laws dealing with specific Internet activities are being formulated piecemeal by legislatures, agencies, and courts in nations worldwide, but particularly in the United States and the European Union, and in Asia, principally by the Chinese government.

Peer-to-peer (P2P) computing
Sharing computer resources, data, and information by direct exchange of data, computer to computer, often by individuals sharing files online.

Judges often rule on Internet disputes using historical precedent derived from non-Internet business law cases and codes. Sometimes contradictory Internet laws are passed by legislatures in different countries, which adds to the confusion about what is and what is not legal, and where. New technologies, without direct existing equivalents, muddy the legal waters even further. An example is Napster and **peer-to-peer (P2P) computing,** where computer resources, information, and files are shared directly between peer computers, often by individuals sharing files online. Peer-to-peer computing captures the essence of what makes the Internet so exciting and unique. It also makes it more difficult to enforce copyright and other laws, because peer computers that are transmitting or sharing data can number in the tens or hundreds of millions and can be located in hundreds if not thousands of different legal jurisdictions.

THE INTERNET'S LEGAL ENVIRONMENT

The Internet's global nature strains traditional concepts of national and local-based laws. At the same time, the Internet also has the potential to facilitate the development of new international legal agreements and processes.[2] Why should anyone care whether nations collaboratively develop an integrated body of Internet law? As more consumers, businesses, and other enterprises become online buyers and sellers, maintaining order will be more difficult without an internationally agreed upon and consistently enforced set of rules. Web marketers must know where they are liable for problems that buyers have with their products, how they can resolve problems with buyers, and where they can seek redress should problems arise with their own purchases. They must know where to report and resolve fraud claims and disputes about product offers, online promotions, site content pirating, trademark and copyright infringement, anticorporate sites, and hacker attacks. Consumers must be protected from online swindlers and must feel confident that they can complete transactions in a private and safe online environment or they will take their business elsewhere and Internet commerce will suffer.

LAWS AND LEGAL SYSTEMS

Most marketplace problems can be resolved without legal action, and indeed, disputing parties should always attempt to negotiate or seek arbitration before resorting to the courts. For those issues that do require legal remedies, it becomes critical to know which courts have jurisdiction (whose laws are to be adhered to), what laws will be used to evaluate a dispute, and how difficult (in terms of time, money, distance, and convenience) it will be to reach the courts that have jurisdiction. The patchwork of laws and restrictions that Internet marketers face today adds to the cost of doing business online, makes many marketers reluctant to accept international orders, censors online content, and compromises the Internet's ability to host a truly safe, frictionless global commercial community.

Laws are commands created and declared by legislatures, enforced with regulations promulgated by agencies, and interpreted by appropriate courts. They are a form of social cement that binds a nation together with uniform standards, expectations, and sanctions and imposes order on international trade. U.S. courts have the power to interpret U.S. laws and to resolve disputes within U.S. borders and (in some cases) abroad via the privilege of extraterritoriality that places persons and businesses under their home country's legal jurisdiction. Each state has rights granted by the U.S. Constitution to create, declare, and enforce laws within its borders. U.S. businesses must comply with *commercial laws,* the legal rules and principles that regulate businesses and commercial transactions; *civil laws* governing private rights; and *criminal laws* governing crime and its prosecution. In addition, certain federal quasi-judicial agencies in the United States can make authoritative rules or regulations that have the force of law. For example, Federal Trade Commission (FTC at *www.ftc.gov*) and Federal Communication Commission (FCC at *www.fcc.gov*) rules regulate business activities in the United States. The FTC also collects consumer complaints and may use consumer complaint information in its investigations of business activities, although it does not resolve individual disputes.

In the traditional offline world, nations set up their own legal system within their geopolitical boundaries. National legal systems vary, though most are built on either common or case law (the United States and the United Kingdom and its former colonies), Roman or code law (France and former French colonies), or Islamic theocratic law (Iran). The world's most populous nation, the People's Republic of China (PRC), is a communist state with a unique legal system that incorporates custom alongside commercial, immigration, and criminal law. Despite these differences, a body of international business law has developed from mutually agreed upon rules and treaties that control the actions and rights of nations in areas where their interests intersect. This does not stop disputes from occurring, but it stops most disputes from escalating into trade wars or worse.

INTERNATIONAL RESPONSES TO INTERNET LEGAL ISSUES

Nations and organizations are struggling to find ways to deal with Internet legal issues. The United Nations (UN) Commission on International Trade Law (UNCITRAL at *www.uncitral.org/en-index.htm*) meets regularly to develop strategies and guidelines to encourage nations to harmonize and integrate their trade laws. UNCITRAL's Working Group on Electronic Commerce has produced a Model Law on Electronic Commerce (*www.uncitral.org/en-index.htm*) with legislative guidelines for governments to use when drafting Internet commerce laws. The committee is attempting to encourage coordination, cooperation, and the harmonizing of Internet commerce laws worldwide. Legislators in the following major Internet-using countries have already implemented provisions of the Model Law (the implementation date for each country is in parentheses): Australia (1999), France (2000), India (2000), Ireland (2000), Mexico (2000), New Zealand (2002), Republic of Korea (1999), Singapore (1998), South Africa (2002), and overseas territories of the United Kingdom, and in the Hong Kong Region of China (2000). Legislation influenced by the Model Law has been passed in the United States (Uniform Electronic Transactions Act, or UETA, 1999) and in Canada (Uniform Electronic Commerce Act, 1999) and many Canadian provinces. In the United States, UETA laws passed by Congress and 44 states state that existing contract law principles also apply online and recognize the legal validity of electronic signatures and transactions. UETA directly affects complex transactions online, including the sale of products such as insurance policies, but not wills and codicils, which require signed contracts.[3]

The World Trade Organization (WTO at *www.wto.org*) is the only international organization dealing specifically and directly with trade rules and trade disputes between nations. WTO agreements, negotiated and ratified by a majority of the world's trading nations, promote free trade, reduce tariffs, and settle trade disputes before they erupt into trade wars. In May 1998, its members adopted a declaration on global electronic commerce encouraging the practice of not collecting customs duties on products purchased online. A work group report in July 1999 concluded that most Internet purchases were services covered by the General Agreement on Trade in Services (GATS). These initiatives are not binding on members, however, so they have not brought clarity to the status of online activities. The WTO maintained its commitment to Internet commerce at its Ministerial meeting in Doha in 2001 and voted to continue customs duty moratoria on Internet purchases. The Fifth Ministerial meeting in Cancun in 2003 ended in no further action on electronic commerce. It has been discussed extensively by WTO members, but no decisive action other than banning customs duties has been implemented.[4]

The Organization for Economic Cooperation and Development (OECD at *www.oecd.org*) has issued reports on Internet taxation, hosted international forums on the global Internet marketplace, and formulated new guidelines for voluntary codes of conduct for businesses involved in Internet commerce. The United States was one of twenty-nine countries that signed the OECD guidelines. The guidelines "set out principles for voluntary codes of conduct" for businesses involved in electronic commerce; offer guidance to governments in evaluating their consumer protection laws regarding electronic commerce; and give consumers advice about what to expect and what to look for when shopping online.[5]

Delegates from fifty-two nations to the Hague Convention on Jurisdiction and Foreign Judgments (*www.hcch.net/e/workprog/jdgm.html*) have been meeting since 1992 to negotiate common Internet business jurisdiction rules and to try to formulate agreements on online copyrights, free speech, and ecommerce. They have been debating the very nature of the Internet, whether it consists of *stores* that buyers visit or of *traveling salespeople* who visit buyers. Depending on the outcome, consumers could have the right to sue foreign websites from the consumers' home country jurisdictions, which would be a nightmare for global U.S. web businesses.

If such a treaty is ever finalized and ratified, it will require participants to enforce each other's laws even if they contradict local (national) laws. All member states must agree to enforce so-called *white-listed laws*, whereas *black-listed laws* are issues that will be avoided, and the remaining, most contentious (gray) areas are where judgments will be made case by case. If this treaty is enforced, it will mean that countries with the narrowest, most restrictive laws, such as China and Morocco, will force other nations to enforce their laws. Advocates for free speech, librarians, online stores, and global ISPs oppose the treaty. Global web businesses fear they will have to continuously monitor each of their sites, which can number in the hundreds or more, to ensure that they are not breaking the laws or violating copyrights of any nation that has signed the treaty. A U.S. refusal to sign could seriously undermine the treaty because the majority of firms doing business on the Internet are based in the United States.[6]

A CONVENTION ON THE LAW OF THE INTERNET

Because the Internet is such a unique environment, some legal scholars recommend a separate jurisdiction for it, modeled on those created for Antarctica, outer space, and the high seas.[7]

Like the Internet, the high seas (oceans) are borderless, and many countries share a vital interest in what happens to them. The United Nations "Convention on the Law of the Sea," an international agreement on the oceans, their preservation, and commercial disputes, was implemented in November 1994 after negotiations that lasted more than fourteen years. The 150 countries that developed the Convention agreed that problems of the oceans are interrelated and have to be dealt with as a whole. The Convention contains traditional rules, introduces new legal concepts, and, perhaps most significantly, establishes a framework for the future development of rules.[8]

The Convention has not eliminated all disputes, but it has brought a level of harmony and cooperation to a highly contentious issue. Although a convention may be exactly what the Internet needs, it is doubtful whether nations, businesses, consumers, and others can wait fourteen or more years for a framework to be developed, approved, and implemented. In the meantime, a number of key legal issues vie for attention and remain unresolved.

JURISDICTION

Jurisdiction
The right and power to interpret and apply the law.

In what **jurisdiction** a dispute occurs determines which courts have the *right* to exercise authority, the *power* to decide the outcome, and *control* over issues and parties involved; it also determines which laws will prevail.[9] Before the Internet's commercialization, traditional jurisdiction was mainly consistent with geopolitical borders, except where stipulated by international agreements. Because the borderless worldwide Internet operates intrastate, interstate, and between countries, what courts and laws have jurisdiction is far more difficult to ascertain. For buyers and sellers, a home-country court and its laws typically are more desirable (and typically more favorable), less expensive, and more convenient than those of another country or group of countries, like the European Union (EU). Most businesses will understandably seek a home-country legal advantage.

The expansion of international business in the latter half of the twentieth century forced courts to face thorny cross-border jurisdictional questions. Sometimes they responded by extending their jurisdiction over defendants outside their own borders (extraterritorially), bringing cases back to their own home-country jurisdiction (forum) for consideration. On other occasions, they declined jurisdiction if it was determined that bringing a case back to their forum inflicted undue hardships on the parties or that courts in another forum were better suited to decide the case. Some courts have applied international jurisdiction case law to Internet jurisdiction disputes; others have tried to devise new jurisdiction tests.

Interactive business relations
The active selling of goods or services to buyers from a web storefront.

INTERACTIVE VERSUS PASSIVE RELATIONS   A jurisdiction test frequently used by courts is whether a website has interactive or passive business relations with visitors from its own or another state, province, country, or country group. A web storefront has **interactive business relations** when it actively sells to buyers, has two-way online communication as part of a business (transaction) relationship, and/or uses activities directly designed to solicit business from a target market. A 1-800 toll-free or fax number to take orders meets the minimum-contact standard of an interactive business site for many courts (see as follows). A web storefront has **passive business**

Passive business relations
Business relations that involve minimum contact with site visitors, not directly selling or interacting.

relations when it does not directly sell or have transaction-based interactions from the site. It may provide one-way information and even advertise, but it maintains a low level of business activity and does not have even minimum contact with visitors. The more interactively commercial a site is with citizens and enterprises in a particular jurisdiction, the more likely the site will be liable within that jurisdiction, even if the site is housed on a server in a different jurisdiction. The case most often used as an example of this "sliding scale of interactivity" principle is *Zippo Manufacturing Co. v. Zippo Dot Com, Inc.*[10]

Zippo Manufacturing Co. (the plaintiff) sued Zippo Dot Com (the defendant) for trademark dilution, infringement, and false designation. Zippo Dot Com, a California-based corporation, had registered various Zippo domain names and offered its services to customers on the Internet. At the time of the case, about two percent of Zippo Dot Com's Internet news service customers lived in Pennsylvania, headquarters of Zippo Manufacturing Co. Zippo Dot Com claimed a legal right to the domain names because Pennsylvania did not have venue jurisdiction over a California-based Internet company. The claim was denied on the grounds that the state of Pennsylvania's *long arm statute* extended to the Internet and thus, Zippo Dot Com was infringing on Zippo Manufacturing Co.'s trademark and intellectual property by interacting with customers in Pennsylvania.

In a related 2001 case, the California Supreme Court ruled that a Texas resident was *subject to suit* in California because his online activities had an effect there. The practice of enforcing personal jurisdiction over a nonresident who repeatedly solicits business in a state (forum) is known as the long arm statute. The implication for Internet marketers is that they could be hauled into court in any place where their site *has an effect*. Then there is the issue of where a court ruling would be enforced. For example, if a foreign court ruled against a U.S. company in an online trademark infringement case, would the United States enforce the court's ruling? It should be noted that after hearing the case, the California Supreme Court ruled that the defendant (Texas resident Pavlovich) did not commit an intentional harmful act aimed at California (*Pavlovich v. DVD Copy Control Association* [58] P.3d (2002).[11]

Internet jurisdiction risk
The legal risk that jurisdiction will be claimed by a foreign country even though the Internet business is not from that country.

INTERNET JURISDICTION RISK   A survey conducted by the American Bar Association and the International Chamber of Commerce in 2003 showed that U.S. companies have grown much more pessimistic about **Internet jurisdiction risk** than their European or Asian counterparts. Internet jurisdiction risk is the legal risk that jurisdiction will be claimed by a foreign country even though the Internet business involved is not headquartered there. The U.S. companies surveyed believe that Internet jurisdiction risk has worsened since 2001 and will be even worse by 2005. Companies are responding by targeting markets where there is a low risk of jurisdiction problems and avoiding areas where Internet jurisdiction risk is high. These companies fear litigation risk even more than differing legal systems in different countries. Media companies are particularly susceptible to Internet jurisdiction risk and typically change their online content accordingly to comply with local laws. This can have a chilling effect on Internet content and marketing decisions.[12]

Upload status
Data housed on a server in one jurisdiction is uploaded to a server in a different jurisdiction.

Download status
Data obtained from a server in one jurisdiction is transmitted to a visitor in a different jurisdiction.

UPLOAD/DOWNLOAD STATUS   Another jurisdiction standard used by some courts is **upload status** or **download status.** The country where a site's server is located is typically held to have jurisdiction. U.S. jurisdiction prevails when a buyer from another country makes a purchase from a U.S. site. If a U.S. consumer accesses a storefront in another country, jurisdiction is in the country where the site/server is located. By this standard, a nation (forum) clearly has jurisdiction over what its citizens upload and download from servers and ISPs within its borders.[13]

However, a recent case in Japan shows its courts assuming jurisdiction over Japanese citizens using a website hosted on a U.S. server. The case involved a Japanese citizen living in Japan who posted and sent pornographic images downloaded from a U.S. server to other Japanese citizens in Japan. He claimed, in a *server-is-elsewhere* defense, that he was exempt from Japanese law because the images originated from a U.S. server. The Japanese court claimed jurisdiction because he was a Japanese citizen living in Japan targeting buyers also in Japan. He was sent to jail for eighteen months.[14]

Some jurisdictional disputes can be resolved without going to court. In 1999, Amazon.com (*www.amazon.com*) was accused of selling hate literature online in Germany despite that country's ban on selling manifestos such as Hitler's *Mein Kampf.* The German Justice Ministry investigated the complaint. Amazon protested it was not violating German law because its German web storefront did not offer the materials in the German language to German buyers. However, German buyers were purchasing the books in English from Amazon's U.S. web storefront and having them mailed to Germany. An Amazon spokesperson ended the dispute by saying, "It's absolutely crystal clear that the German-language version is banned in Germany. It is not legally definitely clear to us what the status of the English version is. So to ensure that we're in compliance with the laws of a democratically run nation, we are not selling *Mein Kampf* into Germany from Amazon.com."[15] Amazon was well advised to avoid a confrontation with the German courts, which it probably would have lost. However, in doing so, the U.S.-based Amazon also complied with Germany jurisdiction control.

Yahoo! had a somewhat similar problem with France, which tried to extend its jurisdiction to the United States. A French judge in May 2000 ruled that Yahoo! had to find a way to prevent French users from seeing hate-related materials on its U.S. Web portal. Nazi-oriented auction items and related Internet links are illegal under French law. Yahoo! responded that it couldn't block French users from accessing its site and that to comply would mean removing all such items and links. In the end, a U.S. district court judge in November 2001 found that Yahoo! could ignore French law because if it complied, its right to free expression under the First Amendment to the U.S. Constitution would have been violated.[16]

The number of Internet jurisdiction disputes will surely rise until jurisdiction requirements are clarified and harmonized. The enormous challenge of doing this in a borderless electronic environment suggests that the issue will not be resolved easily. Too loose an interpretation of jurisdiction will mean that web storefront operators can be prosecuted in every forum where a buyer can access their site. If each nation assumes it can regulate the Internet because it has territorial standing, the Internet will be walled off into small fiefdoms, with laws and rules that make doing business online internationally a legal nightmare.

Nexus
A physical presence, such as a warehouse, retail store, and/or employees in a particular location.

NEXUS   Jurisdiction is more likely to be claimed if a website has a **nexus,** or physical presence—such as a commercial relationship with a warehouse, a retail store, an office and employees, or intermediaries—within a country or in a different country. Sites can limit their liability in a country by not having a nexus, by maintaining their domain name and site in English, and by not targeting the country's citizens. Nexus is key to the U.S. government's opposition to a 2004 World Trade Organization ruling on the legal right of offshore Internet gambling sites to target online U.S. consumers. It also affects the collection of sales and use taxes, and online content issues.[17]

RESPONSES TO CYBERCRIME AND TERRORISM

Despite the complexities of clarifying jurisdiction requirements, progress is being made in building common Internet criminal law against online crime (cybercrime). The Convention on Cybercrime (*http://conventions.coe.int/Treaty/en/Treaties/Html/185.htm*), a thirty-country work group composed of the United States, Canada, Japan, South Africa, and representatives of twenty-six Council of Europe member states, worked for four years and produced twenty-five drafts to develop the first international treaty on cybercrimes. The Convention covers crimes committed on the Internet and other computer networks, particularly copyright infringement, computer fraud, child pornography, and hacking. Its mission is to produce a common policy on such crimes, designed to protect society through the enactment of legislation and heightened international cooperation among nations and businesses. The treaty also provides guidelines on how the Internet should be policed within the jurisdictions of the signatories.

The treaty was signed in November 2001, but in order to be enforced, it had to be ratified by five members. This finally happened in March 2004, when Lithuania became the fifth ratifying country. The treaty is open for all nations to sign. The European Union intends to use this treaty as a foundation for drafting its own cybercrime laws. Some civil rights groups and ISPs oppose the treaty, citing its vague language, the lack of opportunity for public comment, and the heavy burden it places on service providers. The United States Senate has not ratified the Convention, although it has been asked to do so by the President.[18]

SHOULD THE U.S. POLICE THE INTERNET?

Passage of antiterrorism legislation that could make the United States the world's Internet police is a direct response to the terrorist attacks of September 11, 2001. The USA Patriot Act of 2001 (P.L. 107-56) contains provisions that greatly expand U.S. government monitoring of email, Internet, and cellular phone communications. This can include tracking what Internet visitors look at on a website if such surveillance is part of an ongoing investigation. The bill was signed into law by President George W. Bush on October 26, 2001. It has no direct equivalent in other nations. The law gives the U.S. government unprecedented access to electronic communication within the United States via its Carnivore and other surveillance technology. The act is designed to give the U.S. government access to terrorist email messages so that future attacks can be thwarted, and it takes advantage of U.S. dominance over major Internet backbone transfer points. Since more than 80 percent of Internet access points in Asia, Africa, and South America are routed through hubs in Virginia or California, the

United States can prosecute foreign hackers or others who use these hubs even if what is being communicated is legal in the country of origin. This includes gambling and adult content communications. The extent of this massive extension of U.S. sovereignty is clear from the following hypothetical example. An online seller housed on a server in China sends information to a buyer whose ISP is in China. Because the email travels from China to the Virginia hub and then back to China, while it is in the United States traveling along U.S. phone lines, it can be intercepted by U.S. government agents. If transmitting the information is in violation of U.S. laws, the sender can be prosecuted in U.S. courts. These provisions of the USA Patriot Act greatly expand U.S. jurisdictional reach.[19]

The law, whose official title is Uniting and Strengthening America by Providing Appropriate Tools Required to Intercept and Obstruct Terrorism, incited a heated debate over the expanded surveillance powers granted the government and the resulting erosion of privacy. Some of its provisions will expire in 2005, and others are yet to be implemented. An expansion of the act, known as the Domestic Security Enhancement Act of 2003 (Patriot Act II), would have broadened even further the government's right to intercept Internet traffic in a national emergency, with even less judicial oversight. Other countries are unlikely to be pleased with the intrusion of the FBI or of other U.S. government agencies into its citizens' data exchanges, and U.S. prosecution of foreign website owners could have a chilling effect on Internet commercialization. Patriot I and II could reinforce the image of a bullying United States trying to impose its values on the rest of the world.[20]

Legal and Ethical Concerns

Legal issues trouble online consumers and enterprises alike. Space constraints limit our discussion of Internet-related legal and ethical issues, but that does not diminish their importance. Consumers are concerned about the safety of online transactions, fraud and scams, and loss of privacy. Businesses are concerned about fraud and crimes against their property and about liability, contracts, taxation, and security and privacy. This section considers some prominent legal issues that currently concern Internet marketers and concludes with a discussion of Internet marketing ethics.

FRAUD

Fraud is a criminal act, the intentional exploitation of a person, group, or enterprise for gain. It is a perversion of the truth designed to convince the victim to surrender something of value, including personal information, or a legal right. Internet fraud is perpetrated through auctions, email, chat rooms, websites, and news groups. For example, consumer fraud occurs when a purchase that is paid for is never sent to the purchaser, when a merchant deliberately overcharges for a purchase, when a credit card number or identity is stolen, when a product purchased at auction differs dramatically from its description, when money is lost in get-rich-quick or work-at-home schemes, and when insurance or loan costs are inflated. Enterprises are vulnerable to the payment for orders by stolen credit cards, as well as to many of the same frauds committed against consumers.

How afraid should businesses and consumers be of the Internet? The incidence of personal, commercial, and criminal wrongdoing will certainly increase as more people go online. It is estimated that as many as 1.5 billion people will be using the Internet by 2007. Roughly 60 percent will be consumers; the remainder will be enterprises, including governments, businesses, and organizations. Many of these Internet users will be attractive targets for criminal activities.[21]

Some individuals and businesses will seek to exploit the Internet's unique characteristics, particularly its almost instantaneous communication and relative anonymity, just as others exploit consumers and enterprises offline. Clearly, Internet fraud and other online crimes are legitimate concerns, but the media often exaggerate their incidence, which fuels Internet fears. Some businesses make similarly extravagant claims about rising Internet crime in order to generate a market for their security products.

Not surprisingly, consumers are confused about the threat of doing business online. Research has shown that consumers' greatest fear is theft of a credit card number or other personal information while it is in transit to a website. In reality, credit card theft in transit is almost nonexistent. If it occurs, it tends to be from a website's own poorly protected computers or from consumer scams, where swindlers trick online consumers into revealing information. Shopping online at a reputable site carries virtually no monetary risk for consumers if they use credit cards, because the major credit card companies have a US$50 liability limit and most major bank credit cards have zero online liability. Likewise, the risk is reduced if consumers pay through PayPal (*www.paypal.com*) or another secure alternative payment system. Unfortunately, although victims may get their money back, doing so can often be time-consuming, and if identity fraud has been involved, it can be expensive and time consuming to restore a good credit record.

BUSINESS FRAUD   We have noted that consumer online credit card transactions have some protection, but most online businesses do not. It is estimated that about 3 to 4 percent of an online retailer's bottom line is consumed by fraud. Exactly how much fraud online businesses experience is not known, at least partly because many businesses do not want others to know how much they have lost. Average annual estimated losses for all U.S. businesses total around 6 percent of sales. Internet retail sales in 2003 (around US$55 billion) were about 1.9 percent of total retail sales. If the 6 percent rate is accurate, online business losses were around US$3.3 billion; if the 3 to 4 percent figure is accurate, losses were around half that amount.[22]

Phishing
High-tech scam span that deceives recipients so that they will disclose sensitive personal information.

CONSUMER FRAUD   The Federal Trade Commission (FTC) reports that its Consumer Sentinel (*www.consumer.gov/sentinel/*) complaint database received over half a million fraud and identity theft complaints for Calendar Year (CY) 2003. Internet-related consumer fraud was 55 percent of all reports in 2003, up from 45 percent in 2002. In 2003, the FTC received 516,740 fraud reports (up from 404,000 in 2002) for total reported losses online of US$437 million, a 40 percent increase over 2002. The average loss in 2003 was US$228.

Identity theft represented 42 percent of all complaints, up from 40 percent in 2002. Identity theft by **phishing** was significant. Phishing is a high-tech scam span that deceives recipients so that they will disclose sensitive personal information, such as their credit card or bank account number, Social Security number, or passwords.

Internet auction fraud accounted for 15 percent of all reported online frauds. Other top reported types of online fraud involved shop-at-home and catalog sales (9 percent), Internet services and computer products (9 percent), prizes/sweepstakes/lotteries (5 percent), foreign money offers and Nigerian letter scams (4 percent), advance-fee loans and credit protection (4 percent), telephone services (3 percent), business opportunities and work-at-home plans (2 percent), magazine and buyers clubs (1 percent), and office supplies and services (1 percent). Highest per capita fraud was reported in Washington, D.C. and surrounding areas, in Seattle/Bellevue/Everett, Washington, and in San Diego, California.

The increase in reported fraud must be viewed cautiously, because it may indicate that consumers are better informed about where they can report fraud, rather than indicating a sharp increase in its incidence. And certainly, some consumer fraud goes unreported because people do not know where to report it, they are ashamed to do so, or the amount is not significant enough for them to take the trouble to seek restitution.[23]

VULNERABILITY TO FRAUD

Some online consumers (and businesses) are more vulnerable than others to con artists who prey on their weaknesses, naiveté, carelessness, or greed. Others become susceptible when they are under stress. That is what happened almost immediately after the September 11 terrorist attacks, when swindlers began fake fundraising by email and from websites with fraudulent claims that they were raising funds for families of the victims or to stop terrorism. Normally cautious people were susceptible because their emotions overcame their good sense.[24]

Some businesses are more vulnerable to fraud or other crimes at least partly because they fail to take proper precautions against them. If they are victimized, they may decide not to report it in order to avoid having their insurance or merchant credit charges increased. Other businesses are attractive targets because they are highly visible or are in controversial industries such as tobacco or pharmaceuticals.

Governments, law enforcement agencies, corporations, and industry organizations are all becoming more visible and aggressive in the fight against cybercrime. In addition, the courts are gaining more experience in dealing with it, and consumers are becoming better educated about how to protect themselves online and where to report complaints. At the same time, individuals and enterprises are developing new and more sophisticated ways to perpetrate frauds and other crimes. It will require heightened vigilance, stricter enforcement, increased consumer and business education, better computer protection, and stronger commitment to ensure that the Internet will be a safer place in the future.[25]

AUCTION FRAUD

Industry-leading auction site eBay (*www.ebay.com*) recognizes that auction fraud puts its business model at risk. A classic auction house can be held liable if items sold on its site are not legitimate. However, if an auction site is a marketplace—an independent intermediary—then its liability is dramatically reduced or eliminated. In 2001, eBay survived a US$100 million class-action lawsuit that alleged it was liable for the sale of phony sports memorabilia in its auctions because it was an auctioneer. Plaintiffs argued that "eBay has facilitated, and continues to facilitate, a safe haven for the unscrupulous dealers perpetrating the forged collectibles scheme." The San Diego judge hearing the case dismissed it, finding that eBay was a marketplace, a venue where product sellers were responsible for authenticating their own product offers. eBay does restrict products auctioned and excludes drugs, alcohol, firearms, and body parts. Sometimes it also steps in to cancel auctions, as it did with the proposed auction of the prison ID card of Kevin Mitnick, a notorious computer hacker.[26]

eBay is responding to the threat of fraud in several ways. It has implemented an on-site self-monitoring program to reduce fraud and protect itself from liability for frauds perpetrated by those using its auctions. It is diversifying through joint ventures with other companies, acquiring new businesses, and expanding its fixed-price site, Half.com by eBay (*http://half.ebay.com/index.jsp*), in an effort to become an ecommerce portal. It is aggressively barring wrongdoers from its auctions and offers a Purchase Protection Program (*http://pages.ebay.com/help/confidence/purchase-protection.html*) that protects purchases for from US$200 up to US$500 minus a US$25 processing charge. eBay defines fraud as ". . . non-shipment or significant misrepresentation of items purchased on eBay."

WEB UPDATE

For updates and more on this topic, visit the textbook student website at: http://college.hmco .com/business/students and select Siegel, *Internet Marketing*, 2e. **Online Frauds**

FRAUD PREVENTION

Online businesses are responding to fraud and other cybercrimes. The non-profit Worldwide E-Commerce Fraud Prevention Network was formed in Fall 2000 with over 375 charter members, including American Express, ClearCommerce, and Expedia.com. In January 2001, it launched a merchant fraud prevention website where online sellers could find advice on safeguarding their website against online credit card fraud and learn about new fraud-preventing technologies. It also offered an online *Fraud Test* (*www .merchantriskcouncil.org/fraud.php*) for merchants, where they could take a survey that helped them determine how vulnerable they are to fraud. This body merged with the Internet Fraud Roundtable in 2002 to become the Merchant Risk Council (*www .merchantriskcouncil.org*). What can an online merchant do to protect itself against fraud? Some safeguards are

Safeguarding an Ecommerce Site

Here are some tips to help online storefronts protect themselves from fraud.

- Check credit card authorizations in real time to make sure the card is not stolen or lost.
- Verify the billing address with the issuing card company.
- Ask the buyer for the non-embossed credit card number code on the card.
- Use detection software to determine whether transactions warrant greater scrutiny.
- Check transactions against statistical profiles of fraudulent transaction.
- Hold orders that exceed a preset amount and check them for accuracy.
- Check suspect orders against an in-house or commercial database of past frauds.
- Check telephone numbers for authenticity.
- If an order is suspicious, call the customer to confirm it.
- Post cyber-shoplifting notices on the site, warning that fraud will be prosecuted.
- Track product deliveries.[27]

identical to what an offline merchant should do. Others are specific to the Internet. See the accompanying feature entitled "Safeguarding an Ecommerce Site" for some of these tips.

Consumers can guard against fraud by being vigilant and suspicious of unexpected requests for personal identification. They can use secure payment programs such as PayPal in place of credit cards or a program such as Verified by Visa (*www.visa.com.au/verified/safeshopping.shtml*), which gives shoppers a personalized number to use with their credit card online. Other smart web shopping tips are available from the U.S. Federal Trade Commission (FTC at *www.econsumer.gov/english/*), Visa and other credit card companies, or the National Consumers League (*www.nclnet.org/BeEWISEbroch.html*). These and other organizations are trying to educate consumers in order to encourage electronic transactions and discourage fraud. Unfortunately, most consumers are still unaware this information is available, and many others choose to ignore it.

PROPERTY PROTECTION

Fraud is not the only concern of Internet marketers. Crimes against property are also increasing. Property is something owned or possessed—for example, a trademark or website content.

COPYRIGHT   A copyright protects published or unpublished original, tangible intellectual property (not facts or ideas), such as a literary, musical, dramatic, artistic, or architectural work. Protection extends for the life of the creator plus fifty years. In the United States, copyright is covered in the Copyright Act of 1976, Title 17 of the U.S. Code. Copyrights can be registered with the U.S. Library of Congress (*http://lcweb.loc.gov/copyright*), but new works do not have to be registered, or even identified with a copyright notice, in order to be protected. The Digital Millennium Copyright Act of 1998 (Public Law 105-304) amends Title 17 and ratifies the World Intellectual Property Organization (WIPO at *www.wipo.org/index.html.en*) Treaty. It is designed to strengthen copyright protection of digital products and the right of transmission; however, its complexity is adding confusion rather than reducing it. Copyright violations can be prosecuted as criminal acts, but often are not prosecuted.

Most copyright disputes are about content (images, sounds, data, programs, games, music) copied from websites, text copied to bulletin boards, caching (storing pages or whole sites), and linking, primarily deep linking. *Deep linking* is a relatively new process that occurs when links to pages in a site bypass that site's front page so that visitors cannot tell who owns the site or the content. There is some disagreement about how much harm deep linking does. Web design expert Jakob Nielsen believes it should be encouraged because these links speed users directly to their goals and enhance overall usability.[28] Site and content owners disagree.

Entertainment companies such as Time Warner (*www.timewarner.com*) and newspapers such as the *New York Times* (*www.nytimes.com*) argue that they need greater protection for content on their websites because that content is so easy to copy. Even large corporations using the most advanced software cannot possibly search the entire Web for copyright infringers. Neither can small businesses or individuals find most copyright infringement. It is even more difficult to determine whether copyright-protected materials have been downloaded. An added complication is the doctrine of *fair use,* which allows a limited amount of copying for such activities as news reporting, research, and education. The goal of provisions for fair use is to protect copyright owners while still serving the public interest, but often neither goal is achieved.

Copyright infringement is a serious problem for web marketers, as shown by the chapter-opening case on Napster. To combat it, some trade associations aggressively search the Web for copyright theft. In early 2001, the Motion Picture Association of America (MPAA at *www.mpaa.org*) listened in on chat rooms and heard talk of DeCSS, software that descrambles (De) the Content Scrambling System (CSS) protecting Digital Video Disk (DVD) movies. The software, created by a fifteen-year-old Norwegian boy, enables any computer with a DVD drive to download and unscramble copyright-protected DVD movies, allowing them to be transmitted unscrambled anywhere on the Internet.[29] If DeCSS or comparable software becomes widely available, it could cost DVD copyright holders hundreds of millions of dollars or more in lost revenues.

PATENTS   The U.S. Patent Act is in Title 35 of the U.S. Code. The U.S. Patent and Trademark Office (USPTO at *www.uspto.gov*) is part of the Department of Commerce. A patent is an official document that gives the owner exclusive right, for a limited time, to a unique product made by an invention, to an invention process, or to a design. The U.S. is a "first-to-invent" country, not a "first-to-file" country. Many companies are disputing patent rights over Internet and web technologies, and some of these efforts threaten the adoption of the technologies and their improvement through widespread use. For example, Akamai Technologies (*www.akamai.com*) sued a competitor over content delivery patents and caching services. Amazon.com obtained patent rights for its one-click ordering technology, and the courts forced one of its competitors to switch to a two-click ordering process. This patent claim and threats to enforce it have angered those who advocate a free Web. Amazon.com was also granted patent rights for its affiliate program (*www.amazon.com/gp/browse.html/103 -2900406-7787819?node=3435371*), where a website that links to Amazon receives payment if a customer takes the link and makes a purchase from Amazon. Granting patents for what seem like widely used and unoriginal processes has led to harsh criticism of the Patent Office for not keeping up with technology.[30] Negative publicity about Amazon's one-click and affiliate patents, and the threat of possible boycotts, caused Amazon to modify its stance and call for reform in the patenting process.

Liberal interpretation of patent laws by the USPTO has resulted in a surge in the number of patents issued for business processes widely used by Internet storefronts. According to the USPTO, in 1991 only two Internet-related business method patents were granted. By 1999 that number had risen to 200; 2,517 were issued in the first half of 2000. By 2003, Internet-related patents represented more than 15 percent of all USPTO patents granted![31]

It is doubtful whether many enterprises will pay royalties for repeated use of patented Internet processes. Instead, these patents could constrict online business expansion and impede the spread of technologies needed to make commercialization more viable. Many such patents are being challenged in court.

TRADEMARKS   Trade and service marks are legal marks (words, phrases, symbols, product shapes, and logos) used to identify owners of goods or services within a country. Trademark protection comes from the Lanham Trademark Act of 1946. The USPTO registers U.S. trademarks for products used in interstate commerce. Internationally, countries have different trademark rules, and because there is no global trademark registration process, a company must register its trademark in each country in which it does business if it wants to protect it. Trademark law was simplified in 1999 with passage of the Trademark Law Treaty Implementation Act (TLTIA, PL105-330, 112 Stat. 3064 [15 U.S.C. 1051]), which was designed to harmonize U.S. trademark laws with those of other countries that also signed the treaty.[32]

Many businesses use trademark protection as grounds to force competitors to stop using similar-sounding names. For example, Reel.com (*http://reel.com*) claimed trademark protection for the name *reel*. It forced two competitors to stop using the name in their domain names or to license the name from Reel.com. On the other hand, trademark protection has been diluted on the Web by a Supreme Court ruling that limits trademark dilution claims, requiring proof that damage actually has occurred, and leaves the door open to limits on suits over domain names and metatags. In *Moseley et.al., DBA Victor's Little Secret versus. V Secret Catalogue, Inc., 01-1015,* the Court found that sexy-lingerie company Victoria's Secret was not harmed and therefore could not stop another lingerie retailer from calling itself "Victor's Little Secret."[33]

DOMAIN NAMES   A domain name is a form of trademark, an exclusive right to a unique address on the Internet's World Wide Web. Disputes typically arise over the second-level domain name, the name to the left of the top-level domain name (TLD; in most cases, the top-level domain name is .com, .org, or .net). Both the American Marketing Association and the American Medical Association might have used the second-level domain name *ama.* However, the American Marketing Association registered first and was awarded *www.ama.org*; the American Medical Association registered *www.ama-assn.org*. It does not take much thought to see which is the more user-friendly name. After several years, the American Marketing Association decided that its domain name was not sufficiently descriptive and changed it to Marketing-Power.com (*www.marketingpower.com*), although it maintains the registration on *ama.org,* which diverts to the newer domain name.

The U.S. Anticybersquatting Consumer Protection Act (ACPA, PL106-113 [1999]) protects trademark holders from those that register domain names in bad faith for profit or to divert profits from the legal holder. The maximum penalty is US$100,000 per domain name. A federal judge in Pennsylvania recently ordered a cybersquatter to pay the maximum fine for infringing on a trademark held by another company. Even James Bond is not immune from cybersquatters. Actor Pierce Brosnan, a movie James Bond, took a cybersquatter to the World Intellectual Property Organization (WIPO at *www.wipo.int*) of the United Nations, where arbitrators ruled that Brosnan had the legal right to *www.piercebrosnan.com* and that the cybersquatter had taken the domain name in *bad faith,* the controlling legal standard.[34]

Cybersquatters are more than a nuisance; they can cost a trademark owner lost revenues and bad relations with customers, along with the expense of having to ransom the domain name. Cybersquatting generally forces businesses to register multiple domain names so that visitors are not accidentally diverted to a site with a similar-sounding name. Registering sound-alikes is a favorite ploy of adult content (pornography) sites. Even the White House was victimized this way, and for years, visitors who mistyped the domain name immediately realized they were in the wrong place.

LIABILITY

Liability is a duty, responsibility, or obligation. Product liability entails being held responsible if one knowingly sells a defective and/or dangerous product. Marketers have a professional obligation to promote products that are not defective or dangerous. Businesses can be held liable for many things, from environmental contamination to employee harassment. An ISP can be held liable for the behavior of its customers—for example, copyright infringement by a site owner renting server space from the ISP—*if* the ISP knows the behavior is occurring and takes no action. Medical websites' liability risk increases if they provide specific information about a visitor's medical condition. Because there is no Internet liability law, courts often rely on existing law (for example, medical malpractice law in the case of medical websites) and try to make it fit the case. In response to growing incidents of destructive Internet viruses and hackers, companies and their executives that do not make a satisfactory effort to protect their networks and ensure reasonable security may be liable to civil and even criminal penalties.[35]

The FTC is the government watchdog agency that looks for online scams and frauds. Its Internet Coordinating Committee holds surf days when members search the Web for work-at-home, fix-your-credit, college scholarship, and travel scams. The FTC issues warnings to sites that are liable for prosecution; often the sites shut down before being investigated further. The Securities and Exchange Commission (SEC at *www.sec.gov*) monitors online investment offers.[36]

CONTRACTS AND DIGITAL SIGNATURES

A contract is a binding agreement between two or more parties that spells out their responsibilities in a particular situation. In the United States, a highly litigious society, legal contracts are the accepted way of defining a business arrangement. One difficulty in completing contracts online has been the inability to provide, for the parties to the contract, authenticated signatures that cannot have been forged or copied. This has been addressed by the Electronic Signatures in Global and National Commerce Act (ESIGN), which became effective October 1, 2000. The law allows **digital signatures** to have the same authority as traditional signatures on paper documents. A digital signature is an encrypted certificate that verifies authenticity. Encryption software such as Pretty Good Privacy (*www.pgp.com*) can create a digital signature, which is technically a 128-bit hash or key combination of encrypted letters, numbers, and symbols that represent a signature. Two keys are needed to operate the system. The signature owner uses the private key to sign a document, and the key owner provides the public key to those who need to authenticate his or her signature. Signed documents are compared with the key to authenticate the signature.

Critics say that the digital signature is more a seal than a real signature and that there is no guarantee that the person sending the signature is the bona fide signer. At least one virus has surfaced that tries to steal digital signature hashes from computer files.[37]

Digital signature
An encrypted certificate consisting of code that verifies authenticity and has the same authority as traditional signatures on paper documents.

Fifteen U.S. states adopted digital signature laws before the federal government finally acted. ESIGN brings consistency because it requires states to adopt certain standards if they intend to implement digital signature statutes. ESIGN does not apply to all documents; court orders, product recalls, and insurance cancellations are still exempt.[38] Given the present technology, signatures that are written or faxed may still be preferable to digital signatures.

CONSUMER COMPLAINTS AND CORPORATE BASHING

Most marketers would prefer to receive no consumer complaints. Some complaints are justified, however, and can provide valuable feedback; others are not justified. In either case, consumers will tell far more people about a bad experience than a good one. Positive word of mouth (WOM) can increase sales; negative WOM can destroy them. The Internet has made it incredibly easy to create anticorporate gripe or suck sites to disseminate negative and sometimes defamatory statements to a worldwide audience with relative impunity. Most complaints center on bad customer service, product dissatisfaction, or missing parts. Some sites are run by disgruntled employees or encourage inflammatory comments from them. The consensus is that it is a big mistake for a web storefront owner to do nothing about online complaints. Suck sites are growing in number, scope, and popularity. Examples can be found by using any popular search engine and typing in "I hate" and the company name. At least in the United States, the First Amendment right of free speech sometimes protects angry individuals seeking to inflict damage on a company.[39]

Companies have taken legal action against online corporation-bashing sites when their trademarks are linked to or stored on the sites. Others have bought out the owners and shut down the offending sites. Buying a domain name to shut it down does not stop the site owner from opening another such site unless the terms of sale prohibit such activity, at least for a period of time after the sale.

TAXATION

The U.S. Constitution gives the federal government and the states the right to levy taxes on citizens, businesses, and organizations. Taxes redistribute income and provide services for the common good, such as defense. The sales tax is a state taxing device. The United States does not have a national sales tax or a value-added tax (VAT) like that used in Europe. The Internet Tax Freedom Act (ITFA) of 1998 (PL105-277), which postponed any tax on Internet access until October 21, 2001, was based on the concepts that information should not be taxed and that infant online businesses should not be weakened by being taxed. Two relevant U.S. Supreme Court rulings in 1967 and 1992 found that state and local governments (forums) do not have the authority to collect taxes on nonstate (remote) retailers without a physical presence, or nexus, within the forum's borders. This presence can be a warehouse, retail outlet, or business office. The ruling took into consideration the over 7,500 different taxing jurisdictions in the United States.

Because ITFA allows taxes to be collected at the sales destination, not the point of sales origination, even allowable taxes on Internet sales are often lost. If this system were changed to sales origin taxing, it could introduce competition in local taxation with the result that states would compete for Internet businesses by lowering their tax rates.

Most cash-strapped states and many bricks-and-mortar retailers favor sales taxes on Internet purchases. In 2002, representatives from thirty-two states approved model legislation that would create a uniform system for taxing Internet sales by 2005. The Streamlined Sales Tax Project (SSTP) will establish one tax rate for products and services sold online. They argue that states need the tax revenues, that not taxing Internet sales discriminates against offline sellers that collect sales tax, and furthermore that it is unfair to the poor and others who are not online because they do not have access to tax-free online sales. It is estimated that without a tax on online sales, the fifty states could collectively lose over US$45 billion in Internet sales tax revenue in 2006. In the meantime, California and New York have added lines to their income tax forms where tax payers must report the amount of their out-of-state Internet purchases. At least nineteen other states are taking similar action. This is predicted to be the beginning of a tidal wave of Internet taxing efforts.[40]

In November 2001 the U.S. Congress extended the tax moratorium an additional two years until November 1, 2003. President Bush signed the bill, although he would have preferred a longer extension. In 2004, Congress passed another four year extension.[41]

GAMBLING AND VISUAL PORNOGRAPHY

Gambling is a popular activity offline in casinos, lotteries, horse and dog racing tracks, and sports betting. It is subject to federal and state laws, and is highly regulated. Internet gambling attracted around 25 million customers in 2000, generating an estimated US$1.2 billion in revenues, an increase of 80 percent over 1999. Online wagers in 2003 were estimated to be from US$4.2 to US$6.1 billion, collected by over 1,800 offshore websites. Revenues are forecast to reach US$10 billion by 2005. Internet gambling is global, but 50 to 70 percent of its revenue is from U.S. customers. It has become a highly contentious issue in the United States and abroad.[42]

At issue is whether the U.S. government can ban online gambling because it bans the use of interstate telephone lines (wired and now wireless) for transmitting gambling information, except for horse racing wagers. As a result, gambling sites targeting U.S. consumers are mostly offshore, operating from ISPs in gambling havens such as Costa Rica, Antigua and Barbuda, and various other Caribbean countries where online gambling is legal and warmly welcomed for the jobs it creates and its contributions to local economies. Many of the estimated 1,800 gambling sites worldwide have established commercial operations in offshore host countries.

U.S. casinos and other legal gambling operations oppose online gambling for the most part, because they are losing customers to the sites. However, some U.S. gambling businesses realize that stringent laws against online gambling could restrict their own access to a highly lucrative Internet business opportunity. States are losing taxes to online offshore gambling sites. Social agencies criticize the ease with which gambling addicts and children can access online games.

A new avenue of attack has opened to stop U.S. gamblers by banning the use of credit cards to pay for action at offshore sites. A bill introduced in the 108th Congress

(2003) as S.627 and HR 2143 IH, the Unlawful Internet Gambling Funding Prohibition Act, was designed to prevent the use of bank credit cards for unlawful Internet gambling and other purposes. Even before this Citigroup Inc., the world's biggest issuer of credit cards, had agreed in 2002 to stop processing online gambling transactions; PayPal quickly followed suit. Yahoo! has announced that it will no longer accept gambling advertisements.

Congress's actions provoked a response from tiny Antigua and Barbuda, a Caribbean nation whose economy is closely tied to online gambling. Antigua challenged the U.S. position at the WTO. In 2004, the WTO issued its first finding on an Internet-related dispute when it ruled that the U.S. policy banning online gambling is in violation of international trade law. As expected, the United States is appealing the WTO's ruling.[43]

ONLINE ADULT CONTENT

Like online gambling, online adult content (visual pornography) is also under attack, particularly by individuals and organizations committed to making online child pornography less accessible and to making all adult sites inaccessible to children. It is difficult to determine the total revenue generated by online adult content sites because many of them want to maintain a low profile, some are very small, and they can enter and exit this high-profit-margin business very quickly. Offline pornography in the United States is estimated to be around a US$10 billion industry. According to Forrester Research, adult content sites generated more than US$800 million in 1998. In 2003, adult content grew to an estimated US$1 billion industry online, which will increase to US$5 to US$6 billion by 2007. An estimated one in four Internet users visits the over 1.3 million sites featuring adult content, which offer more than 260 million pages of erotica. As in the case of gambling, some major credit card companies are putting a stop to customer charges at adult content sites. They claim that these sites encourage fraud and that it is too costly to continue doing business with them.[44]

Unfiltered reports of what people search for at search engines such as MetaCrawler's Metaspy Exposed (*www.metaspy.com*) clearly indicate the popularity of sex sites. A Google search for *adult content* returned 6.02 million hits. Spam email is often used to lure people to these sites. Domain names with naughty four-letter words draw in crowds of **type-in consumers** trolling for pornography by typing in keywords that they expect will link to adult content sites. Adult sites claim **conversion rates,** that is, the proportion of site visitors converted to subscribers, of 1 in 36 and higher. Several large, privately held companies dominate the industry. Three of the sites claim annual gross incomes of US$100 to US$150 million.[45]

Why are online pornography sites so popular? They offer convenience and anonymity, satisfy visitor curiosity, and provide entertainment for those who like erotic content in their own home. Sexual imagery draws consumers; technology and content get them to return. Although the United States still hosts the greatest number of pornography sites, sites in Europe and Asia also are booming. Playboy Online (*www.playboy.com*), a wholly owned subsidiary of publicly traded Playboy Enterprises, Inc., is one of the few branded adult sites and the number-one lifestyle and entertainment destination for men. On the Web since 1994, its network of branded sites gener-

Type-in consumers
Consumers who search for pornography by typing in keywords at a search engine site that they believe may lead them to adult content sites.

Conversion rate
The ratio of website visitors who become subscribers or buyers to the total number of visitors to the site.

ated US$5.6 million in revenue in the first six months of 1999. Playboy Online's net revenues for the fiscal year ending December 31, 2001, were US$27.5 million, a 9 percent increase over the previous year; by 2003, online revenue had grown to US$39 million. In 2002, Playboy Enterprises derived 55 percent of its revenue from the entertainment and online divisions, the remainder from publishing and licensing. Playboy Online is forecast to generate 13 percent of company revenues in 2004. The site registers several million visitors each month. Playboy also has a members-only subscription site, Playboy CyberClub, where, for US$60 per year, over 100,000 members can participate in online chats and exclusive events and have access to Playboy's programming library.[46]

INTERNET MARKETING ETHICS

Ethics is a system of moral principles, rules of conduct that a society develops over time. It consists of the standards of right and wrong, and of good and bad, that parents teach their children and that adults enforce for others through sanctions on unethical social behaviors. Although societies share many ethical principles, what is ethical in one country is not necessarily so in another. Even within countries, different subpopulations can disagree about moral principles. The situation becomes even more complicated on the Internet, where there is no code of *cyberethics.* Principles of ethical online social behaviors are still evolving, and people from many different cultures interact without their country of origin necessarily being identified.

The U.S. Department of Justice and the Information Technology Association of America (ITAA) have formed a Cybercitizen Partnership (*www.cybercitizenship.org*) to develop a curriculum to teach schoolchildren the ethical use of technology. In light of a recent survey of more than 47,000 elementary and middle-school students who revealed that they do not consider hacking a crime, this effort is obviously needed. Internet ethics is not taught in schools, yet many schools are dealing with specific Internet ethical and legal situations, particularly copyright infringement and plagiarism, hacking, cyberpornography, and hate email. Some students perceive the Internet's anonymity as protection against any consequences of their own online actions.[47]

The speed of Internet communication and its reach, relative anonymity, and low cost tempt some to engage in questionable behaviors. Areas of Internet marketing concern include conducting marketing research online, the marketing of professional services, marketing to children and other vulnerable groups, marketing restricted products, and unsolicited commercial email, or **spam.**

Spam
Unsolicited commercial bulk email.

ONLINE CONSUMER RESEARCH   A vast amount of online consumer research is being conducted by marketers and others. The ease of collecting information online, coupled with the large numbers of consumers in chat rooms, makes the Internet an attractive place for sociologists, psychologists, anthropologists, and consumer behavior researchers. At this time, no widely accepted guidelines for conducting online consumer research exist. Some key ethical questions that Internet researchers are debating will be addressed further in Chapter 7.

THE MARKETING OF PROFESSIONAL SERVICES   The ease with which lawyers and health professionals market themselves online can put them in conflict with the stated ethics of their professions. Professional organizations develop codes of ethics that members must adhere to or face sanctions for violating. Ethics rules govern the marketing of legal services through websites and email. Although rules vary from one state to another, most bar associations strictly prohibit false or misleading statements, exaggeration, or puffery. Comparative self-laudatory advertising is prohibited, and soliciting legal work in person or by email is considered inappropriate behavior.

The American Marketing Association has a Code of Ethics for Marketing on the Internet. The statement reiterates this body's commitment to ethical professional conduct in all aspects of marketing. It warns marketers to do no harm online; to protect the rights of privacy, ownership, and access; and to abide by all applicable laws and regulations. If members fail to adhere to this code, the American Marketing Association vows to suspend or revoke their membership.[48] Chances are that any marketer who violates these standards may already be in far more serious trouble with his or her employer and possibly the law.

Other professional organizations have also issued Internet marketing guidelines. The Electronic Retailing Association (*http://www.retailing.org/new_site/memresources/ policies_procedures/code_ethics.htm*) has Online Marketing Guidelines for online advertising and email. The guidelines encourage fair, ethical, and responsible Internet marketing with the goal of promoting consumer confidence in ecommerce. The Interactive Direct Marketing Association (*www.the-dma.org*) has Online Privacy Principles and Guidance for email marketing and online data collection from children. These and other marketing organizations have a vested interest in promoting ethical behaviors by their members. Otherwise, government may lay a heavy hand on their activities, using laws and regulation to gain compliance. Although these organizations' efforts are commendable, they cannot control nonmembers, and the sanctions they apply to members often are not stringent enough to guarantee widespread compliance.

MARKETING TO CHILDREN AND OTHER VULNERABLE GROUPS   Online hard-sell advertising to children and other vulnerable groups is unethical and, in some cases, illegal. Children and impaired adults typically are unable to discern the differences between advertising and entertainment, and they are vulnerable to high-pressure personal data collection techniques. Children are more likely than adults to provide personal information online, particularly when offered a free gift for the information. The Children's Online Privacy Protection Act (COPPA) clearly defines rules that website marketers must follow when targeting children under thirteen. The FTC enforces COPPA and prosecutes violators.[49]

MARKETING RESTRICTED PRODUCTS   Critics complain that alcohol and tobacco companies are using the Web to promote their products to children and youth. These companies' websites are designed to attract youthful visitors, who can easily enter the sites by lying about their ages and can then purchase tobacco products without even being asked their age. The Robert Wood Johnson Foundation (*www.rwjf.org*) funded research that tracked and analyzed the online marketing of these products. The research revealed that alcohol companies are using online marketing tactics designed to appeal to teens and college-age drinkers. Cigarette companies are less aggressive in establishing a web presence marketing to youth, but chat rooms and bulletin boards appeal to a pro-smoking culture that glamorizes the products. Cigar sites target older consumers. Websites are proliferating for all these products. In January 2000, there were an estimated 80 U.S. websites selling tobacco. By 2001, the number had grown to 200. A 2003 study found that children could buy cigarettes online 92 percent of the times they tried. An increasing number of kids are going online to buy tobacco as cigarette taxes drive prices up and it becomes more difficult to buy the product offline without showing proof of age. Adults are also seeking discount tobacco sites, thereby reducing tax collections at offline sites.[50]

Online Privacy

Contrary to public perception, the U.S. Bill of Rights does not contain a statement guaranteeing the right of personal autonomy or of information privacy. The right of *personal autonomy* is contained in the due process clause of the Fourteenth Amendment, but it is very narrowly defined to protect privacy of family, marriage, motherhood, procreation, and child rearing. Further extensions of this right of privacy have been attempted under other amendments to the U.S. Constitution but have not been adopted. The right of *privacy in access to personal information* (what information can be collected and distributed by others) is contained primarily in enacted legislation. The key legislation that speaks directly or indirectly to online privacy includes the Fair Credit Reporting Act of 1970, the Privacy Act of 1974, the Electronic Communications Privacy Act of 1986; the Telephone Consumer Protection Act of 1991, the Children's Online Privacy Protection Act of 1998 (COPPA), the Gramm-Leach Bliley Act (the Financial Modernization Act of 1999), and the Health Insurance Portability and Accountability Act of 1996 (HIPAA). The Federal Trade Commission has narrow regulatory responsibilities to enforce privacy promises made in the marketplace.[51]

The most onerous privacy invasion involves collecting personal information from children. Public outcries about harmful marketing and data collection practices led Congress in 1998 to pass the Children's Online Privacy Protection Act (COPPA), which went into effect April 21, 2000. Websites collecting information from children under the age of thirteen must comply with FTC regulations restricting the collection of personally identifiable information without a parent's consent. The FTC can impose civil penalties up to US$11,000 per violation. COPPA shouldn't be confused with the Child Online Protection Act (COPA), which was ruled an unconstitutional violation of First Amendment free-speech rights on June 22, 2000. COPA required websites with commercial content to bar underage readers from access to any material that might be "harmful to minors." This exceedingly broad law would have required storefront operators to censor site content according to the most severe conservative standards in order to avoid criminal liability.[52]

EXPECTATIONS OF PRIVACY

Despite the patchwork of privacy laws, most Internet users expect their personal information privacy to be secure. What most don't understand is that whenever they send or receive information or messages (data) online, those data pass through multiple computers and systems. Any system administrator can read a message and/or store it. Any workplace system administrator can monitor workers' emails. Any website administrator, ISP, or telecom transfer point administrator can invade the user's privacy, and with the USA Patriot Act, a government agency can do the same. Website owners taking orders online often store information that buyers willingly reveal in exchange for product ownership or to gain access to a website. Advertising spyware collects information about users without their knowledge. Postings to listservs, discussion groups, and chat rooms, as well as domain registration, are public activities and can be read and disseminated by third parties according to the Electronic Communications Privacy Act of 1986 (Public Law 99-508). However, this confusing law, which gives so little privacy protection to stored messages, does give privacy protection to messages in transit. Finally, swindlers are also hard at work, primarily using email techniques, trying to deceive Internet users into revealing personal information about themselves.

Almost without exception, no Internet activity can be assumed to be absolutely private. Some activities, particularly using public access points like cybercafes, must be assumed to be completely unprotected unless the user determines otherwise from the site operator and is confident of the operator's veracity. Even if a person has never been an Internet user, there is usually some information about him or her online and publicly accessible. A quick Google search can return a non-Internet user's phone number and address. Many businesses can be hired to perform a comprehensive online search designed to uncover personal information.[53]

Consumers have good cause to worry about their online privacy. Businesses can change their privacy policies almost instantaneously. They can go from claiming they do not sell consumer information to third parties, to selling it. Some sell it even though they claim otherwise. Many bankrupt Internet businesses are finding that their only valuable asset is consumer information, which they are selling despite prior promises that they would not do so. Vast amounts of data are being collected and stored. These data warehouses are vulnerable to theft. Health sites collect confidential data on medical conditions, etailers collect credit card information as well as addresses, and financial services sites collect Social Security numbers and account information. In the wrong hands, these data can expose consumers to unwanted marketing solicitations as well as to fraud. Despite the huge quantities of detailed information being collected, most businesses do not have the capacity to turn it into useful marketing information. They are wasting a valuable resource and scaring consumers at the same time. They are also provoking more congressional interest in regulating online data collection.[54]

Cookies
Small data files placed on a user's hard drive without the user's knowledge or consent by a website's server and used for information gathering and tracking.

THE EUROPEAN PRIVACY DIRECTIVE

The European Union (EU) has a more stringent policy about online privacy than the United States. Its *Directive 2002/58/EC Concerning the Processing of Personal Data and the Protection of Privacy in the Electronic Communications Sector* states that businesses targeting customers in the EU must use an opt-in standard for email marketing. This means that companies must obtain customers' permission before emailing them. The EU Directive also prohibits the transfer of personal data to other locations without adequate safeguards and requires sites to inform visitors before placing **cookies.** More will be said about online privacy and the EU in Chapter 6.[55]

Disclaimer
A disclosure made by a website owner about how information is collected and used; may also contain a disavowal of liability, particularly for the content of external links.

DISCLAIMERS   A **disclaimer** is a statement made by a website owner that explains how and what personal information is collected, used, and disseminated by the site. It often also contains a disavowal of liability for the content of linked external sites. A privacy disclosure should address the four substantive "fair information practice" principles of notice, consent, access, and security. Most website disclaimers do not contain this detail.

Many disclaimers are on a website's home (front) page or linked to a separate disclaimer page within the site. There are few guidelines on what should be in a disclaimer, nor is it clear how effective disclaimers are in limiting liability, particularly in foreign jurisdictions. A web storefront might restrict its liability with a disclaimer, but that disclaimer must be carefully worded and placed, because opinions differ on what is acceptable. A national domestic disclaimer placed on or linked from a web storefront page might state that the site accepts orders only from certain U.S. states. An international disclaimer might state that the site accepts orders only from U.S. citizens in the continental United States. Unfortunately, it is not always clear where a buyer is located, and sometimes buyers are not truthful about themselves or their locations. Thus, although disclaimers should be used, they cannot be relied on exclusively to filter buyers and protect sellers. Most website marketers post disclaimers, but most visitors do not bother to read the statements carefully, if at all.[56]

CAN-SPAM

Almost everyone hates spam. Unsolicited commercial bulk email (UCE), or spam, is a growing problem that now represents close to 70 percent of all email sent. It may cost over US$9 billion annually in the U.S. (US$2.5 billion in the EU) in lost productivity as workers struggle to delete spam from clogged email boxes. Spam irritates consumers and employees, overwhelms ISPs, and crashes servers under its volume. ISPs use *blocklists* to identify known spammers and block their messages. Content filtering helps clear some spam. But overall, nothing seems to stop the flow, not even the first federal antispam legislation. The Can-Spam Act, formally titled the Controlling the Assault of Non-Solicited Pornography and Marketing Act of 2003, went into effect in January 2004, but initial reports indicated that it was having little effect. Can-Spam requires that spam emailers include in each message a working email return address, a valid Post Office address for the company sending the spam, a relevant subject line that identifies the spam as such, and a working opt-out offer. The FTC is directed to establish a national do-not-spam list like the do-not-call list for telemarketing. Some spamming activities carry penalties of jail time and multimillion-dollar fines. With Can-Spam, the federal government joins at least thirty-four states that have already implemented antispam laws, some much harsher and more stringent than the federal law.

Beside being irritating and expensive to deal with, Spam is sometimes used to commit fraud. Work-at-home scams are often conducted by email. For example, two con men recently received prison sentences for harvesting consumer email addresses and using them to spam offers of a job stuffing envelopes at home. More than 12,000 people responded and paid a US$35 processing fee for information they never received. Identity fraud by phishing is growing, and more Internet users are experiencing a "joe job," wherein spammers use a victim's email address to send out millions of spam emails. Nigerian email letter fraud reached an all-time high in 2003.[57]

WEB UPDATE

For updates and more on this topic, visit the textbook student website at: http://college.hmco .com/business/students and select Siegel, *Internet Marketing*, 2e. **Spam and Other Invasions of Privacy**

EMAIL SCANNING

Google made one of its few missteps when it released details of its Gmail (*http://gmail.google.com/gmail/help/about.html#ads*) free-email service in early 2004. Individuals using Gmail will have their email scanned so that Google's data-mining software can pick out key words that will be used to target Gmail users with targeted advertising messages. Ads will appear as sidebars in email messages, much like the advertising sidebars that appear on Google search pages. Gmail will have many attractive features that may tempt users to surrender their privacy in exchange for a slick product. Privacy and consumer groups quickly attacked Google for what they claimed was an unprecedented invasion of online privacy. Given consumers' proven willingness to reveal information about themselves online, Gmail stands a good chance of being highly successful. Google, in the meantime, will collect a massive amount of information that most advertisers will find highly attractive.[58]

REGULATING PRIVACY

Self-regulation often is undertaken by professional organizations, businesses, and industries to avoid government regulation. It is also designed to provide ethical boundaries in ambiguous circumstances and, sometimes, to calm consumer fears. For example, to allay consumer fears about privacy of medical information online, the American Medical Association "has developed principles to guide the development and posting of website content, govern acquisition and posting of online advertising and sponsorship, ensure site visitors' and patients' rights to privacy and confidentiality, and provide effective and secure means of e-commerce."[59]

PRIVACY SEALS   TRUSTe (*www.truste.org*) is just one of several organizations working to develop online privacy policy standards. It is an independent, nonprofit privacy initiative whose goal is to build Internet users' trust and confidence in online activities. Websites that earn and display the TRUSTe Privacy Seal pledge to give Internet visitors notice, choice, access, security, and redress with regard to their personal information. TRUSTe has launched an effort to control spam and is developing guidelines for wireless privacy standards.[60]

Security

Security means protection against an attack or theft. Online security means protecting the safety of online banking and credit card transactions, keeping invaders out of websites and databases, vaccinating computers against virus- and worm-infected email, and stopping such cyberterrorism as denial-of-service (DOS) attacks.

HACKERS

Hackers
People who break into computers to steal and/or corrupt data.

Hackers were initially identified as Internet scoundrels who broke into computer systems to prove the owners needed stronger security or defaced web pages to protest perceived social injustice. **Hackers** today are more often seen as vandals, malicious individuals and groups that target businesses and break into computer systems to steal or corrupt data, or release programs that inflict damage, often for financial gain. The programming community still tries to make a distinction between hackers and *crackers,* the original subset of mischievous programmers, but this distinction has faded as hacker incidents have become more extreme and costly. A third subset of this group consists of *tame hackers* who are hired by companies to test their Internet security.

Internet vandals attack websites to breach their security defenses, penetrate a site to change prices and content, steal credit card numbers or data, do damage, and brag about their vandalism. They have struck the *New York Times* as well as Microsoft, where they took advantage of an employee's mistake to infiltrate the corporate site and penetrate protected source code. They are particularly attracted to online banking software, web registration forms, and other sources of consumer data. They attack applications software and force their way into corporate databases. DVD Jon, the young Norwegian hacker who devised and posted a DVD DeCSS decoding program when he was fifteen years old, is reported to have cracked the code for Apple's iTunes Music Store, but only for the Windows version. The program, which was posted online, enables users to bypass Apple's antipiracy software and download music free.[61]

Hackers were responsible for releasing the 2001 Code Red and Nimda mass mailing worms that cost an estimated US$3 billion in lost productivity. The Computer Security Institute and Federal Bureau of Investigation (FBI) estimate losses due to hacker-caused security breaches in 2002 at more than US$456 million. Losses are difficult to calculate because many attacks are never discovered, and when they are, site operators often do not report them for fear of negative publicity. Site attacks are becoming more organized, with gangs operating from the Ukraine and Russia gaining access to consumer credit cards by exploiting vulnerabilities in server software. Recently, the FBI and U.S. Secret Service reported the theft of over a million card numbers from more than forty victim sites. The attackers informed the sites that card numbers were stolen and then tried to sell security services to the operator to prevent future attacks. Some stolen numbers may have been sold to organized crime members.[62]

DENIAL-OF-SERVICE (DOS) ATTACKS

Denial-of-service (DOS) attack
The blocking, by vandals, of legitimate users from accessing a website by overloading it with traffic designed to tie up or crash its server(s).

Denial-of-service attacks (also called Distributed Denial-of-Service, DOS, DoS, and DDOS attacks) occur when vandals block legitimate users from accessing a website by overloading it with traffic designed to tie up or crash its server(s). The traffic can come from unsuspecting computers that have been taken over specifically to launch DOS attacks (a joe job). In February 2000, massive DOS attacks were launched against E*TRADE (*www.etrade.com*), Yahoo! (*www.yahoo.com*), Buy.com (*www.buy.com*), CNN.com (*www.cnn.com*), and Amazon.com (*www.amazon.com*). Legitimate traffic trying to access the sites got the equivalent of a busy signal. Business losses were in the millions of dollars. These attacks sent a clear message to site operators that security is a growing concern and must be increased to prevent future lost revenues and, more critically, lost consumer and business confidence. It was also a chilling warning that computers connected directly to the Internet can be used by cyberterrorists to launch a DOS attack, often without the owner's knowledge. Such attacks began appearing in 1981 and have gotten progressively worse. In 2003 a DOS attack launched against Microsoft knocked its servers offline for two hours. ISPs that use blocklists are also being targeted for DOS attacks.[63]

CYBERTERRORISM

Since 9/11 discussions about cyberterrorism have taken on a new urgency. A terrorist cell could launch a cyberattack designed to halt sections of Internet traffic or worse. Attackers could penetrate data warehouses and create havoc with credit card numbers or financial information. They could breach security systems that operate dams, power grids, and emergency services. The United States as a society and its economic system are dependent on electronic networks for communication and transactions. The Internet is its own worst enemy in that there are manuals and guidebooks online that describe in detail how such attacks could be launched. Any war on terrorism must include cyberterrorists among its most critical targets.

VIRUSES

Viruses—programs designed to penetrate and infect a host computer or network—are another security problem for individuals and networks and could be part of a cyberterrorist attack. Often launched from infected email, viruses have also been known to travel between documents in Excel and Word 97.[64]

Some viruses are merely nuisances; others can crash a hard drive or steal data. Some viruses reproduce by using the victim's address book to send infecting emails to unsuspecting recipients. Viruses are expected to be a continuing problem that requires monitoring and the use of up-to-date antivirus software to protect individual computers and networks.

CONSUMER RESPONSIBILITY FOR ONLINE SECURITY

As more consumers use broadband, online shopping and online banking will increase. Up to 56 million consumers will be using online banking by 2008. However, studies indicate that even experienced online consumers continue to express concern about online privacy and security, an issue that directly affects their decisions about online activities and spending.[65]

Consumers bear some responsibility for their own online security. Several strategies will help keep them safe online, although there will always be some risk. Consumers can learn some smart online shopping tips at various government and organization websites. The FTC has a page with shopping tips for the global market and the National Consumer League has a pdf file titled "Be E-Wise: How to Shop Safely Online." Here are some questions to ask: (1) Is the business well known? Is it affiliated with trade groups or self-regulation associations? Does the website have VeriSign (*www.verisign.com*), BBBOnline (*www.bbbonline.org*), TRUSTe (*www.truste.com*), or other reliability and security seals posted on the front page? (2) Is sufficient information given about product prices and conditions? Buyers should print product prices and conditions in case a dispute arises. (3) Are transaction prices clearly stated in U.S. currency denominations? If prices on foreign websites are not stated in U.S. dollars, the buyer should contact the seller and determine how exchange rates are calculated. (4) Are security seals posted on the site? Before placing an order, buyers should look for the closed-lock icon on the lower browser screen, which signals that ordering information is encrypted. (5) Does the site have a clear privacy statement? Is collected information sold to third parties? Is there an opt-out box to avoid future contacts? The buyer should click the opt-out box if future contact is not wanted and refuse the sale of personal information to third parties. (6) How strong is the company's commitment to customer satisfaction? How are complaints resolved? (7) Buyers should carefully review all monthly credit card and debit card billing statements and ensure that online purchases are accurately billed. They should look for unauthorized purchases or overcharges and report them to the credit-issuing company, bank, and/or consumer fraud protection organizations.[66]

Consumers and businesses should make their computers as secure as possible. This includes installing routers and antivirus software and keeping the software up-to-date. Scans should be run on a regular basis, and any evidence of viruses or ping attacks (in which intruders try to take over a computer) must be dealt with promptly.

All Internet users should be on the alert for suspicious email and never *ever* open attachments until they have been scanned for viruses—and even then only if the sender is known.

All Internet users must never assume privacy online. If at all possible, consumers should avoid sending personal information wirelessly.

Finally, Internet users should be suspicious, cautious, and prepared. At the same time, they should not be paralyzed by fear. As consumers take more responsibility for their own online security, governments, businesses, and organizations are actively combating those elements that are trying to make the Internet a no-man's land.

Summary

http://college.hmco.com/business/students

Internet Laws and Jurisdiction

For an international body of Internet law to be effective, it must be accepted by the major internetted nations and then enforced. In its absence, often contradictory laws dealing with specific Internet activities are being formulated by legislatures, agencies, and courts around the world. Because of the growing numbers of consumers and enterprises going online, Internet laws are needed to maintain order. Many organizations are trying to deal with Internet legal issues. Some recommend a separate jurisdiction for the Internet, similar to those created for Antarctica, outer space, and the high seas. Jurisdiction determines which courts have the right to exercise authority. Many U.S. companies believe Internet jurisdiction risk has increased and will continue to do so. Two frequently used tests for jurisdiction are whether the website has interactive or passive business relations with visitors and a site's upload or download status. Some jurisdiction issues are resolved without litigation. Jurisdiction is more likely to be claimed if a website has a nexus (physical presence) in a location. Some progress is being made in building common Internet criminal law against online crime (cybercrime). Passage of the USA Patriot Act could make the United States the world's Internet police. Despite the relatively low incidence of online fraud against consumers, fear of fraud cost businesses many lost online sales. Auction fraud, consumer-to-consumer, is the top complaint. Businesses also experience online fraud, but how much is not known at least in part because many businesses do not want others to know how much they have lost.

Legal and Ethical Concerns

Consumers are concerned about the safety of online transactions, unresponsive sellers, fraud and scams, and loss of privacy. Fraud, security, and privacy are also matters of concern for marketers, along with protection of their property, the issues of liability, contracts, and taxation. Some online consumers (and businesses) are more vulnerable than others to con artists. Industry-leading auction site eBay recognizes that auction fraud puts its business model at risk. Online businesses are responding to fraud and other cybercrimes. Most copyright disputes are about content copied, text on bulletin boards, caching, and deep linking. Some companies are disputing patent rights over Internet and web technologies. The Federal Trade Commission (FTC) looks for online scams and frauds. Cybersquatters are being sued for registering domain names in bad faith. Digital signatures have the same authority as traditional signatures on paper documents, with some exceptions. Companies can take legal action against online corporation-bashing sites if their trademarks are linked to or stored on the sites. The Internet Tax Freedom Act of 1998 postponed levying any tax on Internet sales. Most states and bricks-and-mortar retailers favor collecting sales taxes. Those seeking to encourage Internet commercialization argue for leaving the Internet tax-free. Online gambling is aggressively marketed through advertisements on search engine sites, travel sites, and other web locations and by email. Online adult content sites are also under attack for encouraging child pornography and giving children access. Problem areas in online ethics include marketing research online, the marketing of professional services, marketing to children and other vulnerable groups, marketing restricted products, and unsolicited commercial email.

Online Privacy

The most onerous practice involves collecting personal information from children. The Children's Online Privacy Protection Act (COPPA) requires sites that collect information from children under the age of thirteen to comply with FTC regulations restricting the collection of personally identifiable information without a parent's consent. Most Internet users do not realize that whenever they send or receive information/messages (data) online, that information data passes through multiple computers and systems where it can be viewed and stored. Almost without exception, no Internet activity can be assumed to be absolutely private. The European Union (EU) has a more stringent policy about online privacy than the United States. A privacy disclosure disclaimer should address the "fair information practice" principles of notice, consent, access, and security. Spam irritates consumers, overwhelms ISPs, and costs businesses by clogging employee email boxes and sometimes crashing servers. The Can-Spam Act went into effect in January 2004, but initial reports indicated that it was having little effect. Spam is sometimes used to commit fraud. Self-regulation is often undertaken by professional organizations, businesses, and industries in an effort to avoid government regulation. It is also designed to provide ethical boundaries in ambiguous circumstances and, sometimes, to calm consumer fears. TRUSTe is just one of several organizations working to develop online privacy policy standards.

Security

Online security means protecting the safety of online banking and credit card transactions, keeping hackers out of websites and databases, vaccinating computers against virus-infected email, and stopping such cyberterrorism as denial-of-service (DOS) attacks. Hackers today are seen as vandals, malicious individuals and groups that target businesses and break into computer systems to steal or corrupt data, or release programs that inflict damage, often for financial gain. Losses are difficult to calculate because many attacks are never discovered, and when they are, site operators often do not report them for fear of negative publicity. DOS attacks occur when vandals block legitimate users from accessing a website by overloading it with traffic designed to tie up or crash its server(s). Viruses are programs designed to penetrate and infect a host computer or network.

Some viruses are nuisances; others can crash a hard drive or steal data. Viruses are expected to be a continuing problem that requires monitoring and the use of up-to-date antivirus software to protect individual computers and networks. Consumers bear some responsibility for their own online security. Several strategies can help keep them safe online, although risk will always exist.

Take Action!

You can help website owners understand how to use their privacy statements as marketing tools and help educate visitors in the process. Although consumers are very concerned about their privacy, they tend not to read website disclaimers and privacy statements. Part of the reason has to be the length of the statements and the complexity of the language. Visit several high-traffic websites and evaluate their privacy statements. For example, visit Napster 2, Apple's iTunes Music Store, and other music download sites.

1. Using what you have learned from evaluating the sites, construct a table that lists the sites you have visited and the points on which you have evaluated their privacy statements. Develop a six-slide PowerPoint presentation that might be given to a client who is considering how to rewrite her or his website's privacy statement. One of the PowerPoint slides should contain the table. You might consider these points in making the evaluation:

   a. Is the privacy statement link clearly visible on the website's front page, or is it stuck at the bottom of the page where it probably won't be seen without significant scrolling down?
   b. Does the link to the privacy statement page work?
   c. Is the length of the statement appropriate, or is it too long?
   d. How complex is the language? Can it be read and understood by the "common man"?

2. On the basis of your evaluation and the PowerPoint presentation, prepare a short (no more than two-page) memo that summarizes your findings. Include in your memo recommendations for what an effective privacy statement should contain. Present these recommendations in bullet form. Conclude the memo with your analysis of why a privacy statement can be an effective marketing strategy.

Chapter Review Questions

1. Why are internationally agreed upon Internet laws needed?
2. How legitimate are fears about doing business online?
3. What international organizations are working to develop Internet laws?
4. Why is jurisdiction an important Internet marketing issue?
5. Why should a website operator be concerned about copyright infringement?
6. What should a web storefront do to guard against fraud?
7. What is ethics and why is it important online as well as offline?
8. Why are patents for online business method processes potentially damaging to Internet commerce?
9. What can marketers do to reassure consumers about online privacy?

10. Are disclaimers a foolproof way to escape liability? Explain.
11. How do digital signatures work?
12. Should Internet sales transactions be taxed?

13. Should consumers be allowed to gamble online?
14. Is spam unethical? Is it illegal?
15. What is a DOS attack, and how can it hurt a web storefront?

Competitive Case Study

Napster 2 Faces a Harsh Competitive Environment

Piper Jaffray reports that online music market revenues will grow to about US$240 million by 2006 as legal music downloads crowd out illegal music file swapping. As a result, many companies are jumping into the sector. First was Apple's iTunes Music Store, which initially sold only to owners of its Mac-based iPod. A Windows-based version was released on October 29, 2003. Less well known sites such as MusicMatch (*www.musicmatch. com*), Rhapsody (*www.listen.com*), and BuyMusic (*www .buymusic.com*) offer downloads under a similar plan, and the widely known brands Amazon, Dell, Wal-Mart, and Sony have also entered the sector.

One key to success will be having inventories that represent all five major music groups: BMG, EMI, Sony, Universal, and Warner. Another will be the site's approach: whether it offers downloads with rights to record or burn copies; streaming music, which is real-time listening as often as desired after a subscription fee is paid; or custom radio with preprogrammed music. Product mix, and particularly access to single tracks or albums, device, price, and usability are other competitive factors.

Although Napster 2 was to be the nemesis of Apple's iTunes Music Store (iTMS), by early 2004 iTunes was outselling Napster 2 by a 5:1 margin. In Napster 2's first launch week, iTMS sold 1.5 million downloads while Napster 2 had 300,000. Fans have purchased and downloaded over 17 million songs from iTunes since its April 2003 launch, and it has an 80 percent market share.

Consumers appear to be buying into the idea of paying for music downloads. Jupiter Research found that of 2,500 adult Internet users, 35 percent were willing to pay up to US$1 for a song, which helps explain why most downloads are kept below that price point. A Pew Internet & American Life study reported that illegal online music file swapping fell over 50 percent after the introduction of iTunes in the last six months of 2003. This probably reflects both the popularity of iPods and iTunes and the chilling effect of the music industry's lawsuits against file swappers. Use of file-swapping websites also declined from November 2002 to 2003 with Grokster taking the biggest loss (59 percent).[67]

CHECK IT OUT

Visit Napster 2 (*www.napster.com*) and the iTunes Store (*www.apple.com/itunes/store/*) to see what is happening on the sites. How are their offers alike? How do they differ? Compare their usability. Of the two, which might you prefer to use? Why? Can peer-to-peer file transfers be stopped? Is the shrink-wrapped music CD doomed? Extend your analysis to your local Wal-Mart store. Visit the music department and look for indications that Wal-Mart is heavily promoting its online music download service. Now go online to Wal-Mart's music store (*http://musicdownloads.walmart .com/catalog/servlet/MainServlet*) and compare its offer to those of Napster 2 and iTunes Store. In the long run, who might gain competitive advantage in this highly competitive sector? Why?

A GLOBAL PERSPECTIVE

Visit the iTunes Music Store in the United Kingdom (*www.apple.com/uk/itunes/*), Australia (*www.apple.com .au/ilife/itunes/*), and France (*www.apple.com/fr/itunes/*). Is Apple using a standardized approach, or is it localizing to each market? Compare the sites in terms of design and product offer. Are they the same, or can you find differences?

6

Taking Internet Marketing International

LEARNING OBJECTIVES

» To develop a global overview of Internet readiness, markets, and trends
» To identify international Internet marketing strategies
» To develop an understanding of differences among international Internet users
» To appreciate the importance of key international issues that should concern Internet marketers

Yahoo! Worldwide

Yahoo!, founded in 1994, is an old company by Internet standards. Stanford Ph.D. students David Filo and Jerry Yang began Yahoo! as a hobby. It went commercial as a pioneering information directory, evolved into an Internet portal, and is now a worldwide communications, commerce, and media services company that claims top Internet brand recognition worldwide. As a portal and trading platform, it draws over 237 million unique visitors each month and reaches over 70 percent of U.S. workplaces. FY2003 sales were US$1.6 billion, an increase of 70.5 percent over 2002. The company employs 5,500 people, up 52.8 percent from 2002. The first quarter (Q1) of 2004 was the most successful in company history, with revenues rising to US$758 million, from US$283 million in Q1 2003; the second quarter reached another record with revenues of US$832 million, up from US$321 million (Q2 2003). Terry S. Semel, the company's CEO since 2001, has plans for Yahoo! to become a worldwide digital theme park, an Internet destination where users willingly pay for broadband connections, digital music and movies, premium email with expanded storage space, job search, and other enhanced interactive and (increasingly) broadband-based services. There are no guarantees that this strategy will succeed. Yahoo! has stumbled in the past. It was forced to close five of its European auction sites in 2002 because its international expansion strategy proved too costly. On the positive side, the company pioneered Internet search results advertising, which is now the most rapidly growing Internet promotion form. In 2003, Yahoo! acquired Overture Services, Inc., a pioneer in paid inclusion (also called pay-per-click or pay-for-performance) ads that appear during an Internet search and create revenue when visitors click on them. Purchasing Overture better positions Yahoo! to compete with Google and the expected Microsoft algorithmic search technology being readied for release. Although Yahoo!'s twenty-five international sites (offered in thirteen languages) draw millions of visitors worldwide, its estimated 21.1 percent share of the international market trails Google's 56.4 percent market share. Non-U.S. operations are responsible for around 13 percent of Yahoo!'s revenues. Its international plans extend beyond search and include premium email. In early 2004, the company added Russian-language email services, and it is planning similar product rollouts in Eastern European and Southeast Asian languages, including Polish, Turkish, Bahasa (the national language of Indonesia), Thai, and Vietnamese. The Russian-speaking market includes 2 to 3 million Russian émigrés living in the United States and around 35 million others living outside Russia. Russian-language speakers are an emerging Internet niche market for Yahoo! Around 10 million Russians already use the Internet and email is the favorite online activity of 90 percent of them. Along with pushing its premium email, Yahoo! is also introducing new anti-spam and anti-spyware tools in its existing and new email markets. Yahoo! has already established its brand name in developed Internet markets, and it recognizes the potential profitability of emerging markets.[1]

Because the U.S. Internet market is so large and profitable, it's easy for U.S. marketers to concentrate on it to the exclusion of marketing to the rest of the world. However, many large companies are profitably targeting other fully developed markets such as Canada and Western Europe, big emerging markets such as China and Brazil, highly Internet-savvy small countries such as Israel, and niche markets such as Russian-language-speaking email users. Many small and midsize businesses that benefited initially from unsought contacts with international Internet markets have become actively international. This chapter examines some of the features of international Internet marketing, including Internet readiness and trends, international strategies, and some differences among international markets. The chapter concludes by identifying issues that should concern any enterprise marketing online.

Identifying International Internet Markets

International telecommunications arguably began in 1801 when the optical telegraph networks of Sweden and Denmark were manually linked. The International Internet dates from 1973 when the first international connection was made between ARPANET in the United States and University College of London (England) via Norway's NORSAR (*www.norsar.no/NORSAR/*). NORSAR was the first non-U.S. node on the network that was the Internet's predecessor. Today's Internet—that international matrix of networks, fiber-optic links, undersea cables, land-based routers and switches, satellites and mobile base stations, and wired and wireless devices—links the world electronically, making distant markets far more accessible than at any time in the past.

Almost from the beginning of Internet commercialization, some businesses took advantage of the Internet's unique global reach to initiate, expand, complement, and/or maintain their existing international marketing activities. Others entered international markets later and sometimes failed, at least temporarily. This happened to eBay in Japan, where it began operations in 2000, only to pull out in 2002 after acknowledging that revenues didn't meet expectations. Many analysts consider eBay the savviest of all Internet-only companies. Why, then, did it fail in Japan? Several reasons are usually mentioned. It entered the market late behind first mover Yahoo! and couldn't overcome Yahoo! Japan Corp.'s auction market leadership. eBay also suffered from a Japanese cultural aversion to used goods. eBay remains committed to overseas expansion and is looking for growth in the rapidly emerging China market. By 2004, its international sales were 30 percent of its transaction revenues. Unlike Yahoo! and eBay, some companies have avoided internationalizing their websites or considering international opportunities because they are satisfied with domestic revenues, fear international risks and entanglements, and/or are too busy refining their domestic Internet marketing strategies. But ignoring the international Internet environment carries its own risks, for much of what is happening internationally affects all Internet buyers and sellers.[2]

THE NETWORKED READINESS INDEX (NRI)

On the surface, it appears that Internet commercial activity still occurs only in the world's most highly developed industrialized regions, principally North America, Western Europe, and parts of Asia/Oceania. This impression is highly misleading, however, because considerable activity is occurring worldwide, often in unexpected places. Businesses and consumers are finding new and often unexpected ways to go online, even in countries where computer ownership, telephone access, and Internet readiness are low. **Internet readiness (IR)** is a measure of how well prepared a country, region, or area is to use information and communication technologies (ICT), make Internet access widely available, and participate in Internet-related commercial and public activities. Readiness is an indicator of Internet receptiveness and competitiveness, but it should not be the only indicator used in assessing international marketing opportunities.

Internet readiness
A measure of how well prepared a country, region, or area is to make Internet access and activities widely available.

The World Economic Forum (WEF at *www.weforum.org*), an independent international organization, has been issuing reports on global competitiveness since 1979. Since 2001, it has also produced a Global Information Technology Report. Its 2003–2004 report is the combined effort of the Forum, the World Bank's Information for Development Program (InfoDev at *www.infodev.org*), and international business school INSEAD (*www.insead.edu*). The 2003–2004 Report's Networked Readiness Index (NRI) measures "the degree of preparation of a nation or community to participate in and benefit from ICT developments." ICT stands for information and communication technology, a key catalyst for organizational transformation and sometimes disruptive change, particularly in banking, airlines, and publishing. ICT adds value to the marketing of such consumer products as television sets, cameras, cars, and mobile telephones, and it enables companies to develop new distribution channels, create new products for new markets, and offer enhanced customer services. It is a useful indicator of country-level Internet competitiveness and marketing opportunities.

The Networked Readiness Index is an important tool because it provides a benchmark for comparing networked readiness among the world's leading economies and captures trends in emerging countries as governments and businesses increase their commitment to ICT, and more enterprises and citizens go online. The index has three components: a country's ICT *environment* (market, political/regulatory, infrastructure), the *readiness* of key stakeholders (individuals, businesses, governments) to make decisions that support ICT, and ICT *use* by these stakeholders.

Of the 102 countries evaluated in 2003–2004, the United States is identified as the most innovative in the use of information and communication technology. This reflects the quality of its scientific research institutions, numbers of new patents issued, extent of government online services, and number of business computers per 1,000 inhabitants. Rounding out the top 10 (2 through 10) are Singapore, Finland, Sweden, Denmark, Canada, Switzerland, Norway, Australia, and Iceland. Ending the list are Haiti, Ethiopia, and Chad. The inclusion of a large number of developing countries makes this report one of the most comprehensive of its kind.

The NRI certainly contains some surprises, among them tiny Israel (13). Its ranking is explained by the country's highly skilled workforce and active support of Internet use and ebusiness. Another surprise is Estonia (25), the leader in Eastern Europe. Most Estonians didn't have a telephone in 1991 when the Soviet Union ended its rule. Since then, a technology revolution has transformed Estonia and today, over half the country's population bank online, government websites are heavily used, and the 70 percent of Estonians with mobile phones can use them as debit cards at gas stations, restaurants, and hotels. Not surprisingly, *E-Estonia* (*www.vm.ee/eng*) is attracting foreign investors drawn to its technology-friendliness, wireless infrastructure, and business opportunities.

The top 25 listed countries are further divided into regional groupings that include the Americas (U.S. and Canada), Western Europe (14 countries, Scandinavia being the leader), Asia and Oceania (Singapore leading 7 countries), the Middle East and North Africa (only Israel), and Central and Eastern Europe (only Estonia). Although South America is not highly rated, the leaders are Chile (32), Brazil (39), and Mexico (44). Russia is only 63rd, but that is up from 69th place in 2001–2002. The "most ready" Asian countries are Malaysia (26), Thailand (38), India (45), and China (51). Thailand's ranking reflects a government initiative that began in 1996 (updated in 2002) to improve computer and Internet literacy among its citizens. The strategy includes selling personal computers for US$250 and notebook computers for US$500, wiring thousands of schools, and offering Internet services throughout rural areas. The results are already impressive. Over 12 percent of Thai websites now sell products online, and Internet access has spread outside the capital, Bangkok, reaching over 50 percent of Thailand's rural areas.

Although it was not included in the NRI, the world's most isolated country, North Korea, is beginning to emerge from its hermit-like state and cautiously embrace the Internet. The government has launched mobile phone services in its main cities, is developing broadband services to stimulate business activity, and has announced plans to link its domestic intranet, the Kwangmyong, to the global Internet network. At a connect cost of US$10 per hour, an Internet café in Pyongyang is too expensive for most citizens to use, but it is used by visitors, diplomats, and journalists.[3]

THE *ECONOMIST* E-READINESS INDEX

The Economist has published an annual e-readiness ranking of the world's largest economies since 2000. This ranking is a composite derived from nearly 100 quantitative and qualitative criteria in six categories: technology infrastructure, general business environment, consumer and business adoption of ebusiness, social/cultural conditions that affect Internet use, and the availability of ebusiness support services.

The 2004 ranking identifies four tiers of e-readiness. The *First Tier* contains the top 25 highly developed Internet countries that are all moving ahead rapidly in ICT. Denmark is the leader, earning 8.28 of a possible 10 points. The *Second Tier* is led by Estonia (26), the leader among Eastern European countries that were part of the European Union's eastward expansion. Second Tier countries have rapidly growing e-services but lack dense communication and Internet infrastructures. The Latin American countries Brazil (35), Argentina (37), and Mexico (40) are in this tier. The *Third Tier* is a mix of developing countries from Columbia (41) to Russia (55) and includes India (46) and China (52), along with Bulgaria (42), Thailand (43), and Romania (50). The *Fourth Tier* contains countries struggling to enter the Internet age, from Ecuador (56) to Azerbaijan (64).

The United States was the undisputed e-readiness leader when these rankings were begun in 2000. Each year since, other countries have advanced, and in 2003 the United States lost its top spot to Sweden. In 2004, the United States fell to 6th behind Denmark, the UK, Sweden, Norway, and Finland. Rounding out the First Tier are Singapore (7), the Netherlands (8), Hong Kong (9), Switzerland (10), Canada (11), Australia (12), Germany (13), South Korea (14), Austria (15), Ireland (16), Belgium (17), France and New Zealand (19), Taiwan (20), Spain (21), Israel (22), Italy (23), Portugal (24), and Japan (25).

The United States obviously remains a leader on all readiness dimensions, and it still has the largest single Internet market. However, its relative decline indicates how rapidly other countries are progressing with accelerated penetration of high-speed Internet infrastructures, wireless, and advanced ebusiness services. The rankings overall are highly consistent with other attempts to measure Internet readiness, adoption, and use. The conclusion is that with few exceptions, nations worldwide recognize that the Internet can stimulate their economies, make government more accessible, lower business transaction costs, advance entrepreneurship, and enrich their citizens' lives. Many governments, even in some of the world's poorest countries, are making considerable progress in getting their businesses and citizens online—and in the process, are helping to reduce international digital divides. They are creating marketing opportunities for companies in many different industry sectors, and the governments themselves are prime marketing targets for many Internet-related products.[4]

THE ITU MOBILE/INTERNET INDEX

Internet marketers worldwide recognize the growing importance of mobile telecommunications and the wireless Internet. An International Telecommunication Union (ITU at *www.itu.int/home/*) index provides useful insights into this market. ITU is an independent international organization within the United Nations system that traces its origins and objectives to the establishment of the International Telegraph Union in 1865. Its mission is to bring together governments and the private sector to coordinate telecommunications networks and service operations, and to advance international communications technologies. ITU forecasts that the convergence of mobile and the Internet (wireless Internet) will be a major demand driver in the twenty-first century. Wireless can bridge digital divides and help countries go online quickly and cheaply despite their weak telephone infrastructures and low computer use. For this reason, wireless has been called a *leapfrog* technology.

The ITU 2002 Mobile/Internet Index measures adoption rates of mobile and Internet technologies in over 200 economies. It uses twenty-six different indicators, including the quality and extent of technology infrastructures and networks (fixed lines and mobile subscribers, PCs, bandwidth, 3G or third-generation wireless deployment), usage rates (roaming, ISPs, costs), and market conditions (private and public involvement, market structure).

According to ITU, mobile/Internet leaders are (1 through 10) Hong Kong (China), Denmark, Sweden, Switzerland, the United States, Norway, South Korea, the UK, the Netherlands, and Iceland. This index also illustrates how markets often take different paths. For example, the Philippines (33) is doing well in mobile use but not in Internet penetration. India is advancing rapidly in Internet use but not in mobile. China (47) has overtaken the United States as the market with the greatest number of mobile users, but not percentage of users. Countries with strong prospects for high mobile Internet use are Romania (37), Peru (39), and the Dominican Republic (41).

Marketing opportunities in mobile include hardware, software, access, and such unexpected new revenue sources as **ringtones** (various sounds, including music, emitted by wireless devices to announce incoming calls) and **wallpaper** (images used to decorate mobile receiver screens or computer monitors). Ringtone sales reached US$3.5 billion in 2003, up 40 percent from 2002. They average about US$4 per download, and in 2004, ringtone revenues exceeded revenues from legal online music downloads. Yahoo! India is a key player in ringtone downloads, with about one million in 2003. Mobile music downloads, including ringtones and their successors, could represent 20 to 30 percent of all music sales by 2006, and marketers are already trying out ringtone promotions. Teens regard ringtones and wallpaper as fashion statements. They are enthusiastic mobile users and ringtone downloaders, particularly in South Korea and Japan, where this age group dominates mobile use. Their phone bills reflect significant levels of "flirtatious and frivolous" downloads of cartoons and avatars. An **avatar** is an animated cartoon-like or lifelike figure that represents a person while he or she is in a chat room, playing games, or text messaging. Text-messaging teens in Tokyo are known as the thumb generation, or *oyayubi sedaim,* for their dexterity in using their thumbs to text-message rapidly on phones, wireless email devices, and other handheld gadgets.[5]

Ringtones
Sounds emitted by wireless devices to announce incoming calls.

Wallpaper
Images used to decorate mobile receiver screens or computer monitors.

Avatar
The body or representation of a person in a virtual community; an animated, cartoon, or realistic figure that represents the user in chat rooms, games, or messaging.

Nokia

Ringtones, wallpaper, and avatars are hot products for mobile teens worldwide but particularly in Asia.

Source: Reprinted with permission, www.nokiausa.com/usshop.

WEB UPDATE

For updates and
more on this topic,
visit the textbook
student website at:
http://college.hmco
.com/business/students
and select Siegel,
Internet Marketing, 2e.
**Internet and Mobile
   Markets**

THE INTERNATIONAL INTERNET POPULATION

Although it is impossible to count how many people are active Internet users world-wide, several organizations track usage patterns and capture trends. Their estimates generally have been conservative. According to the Computer Industry Almanac, Inc. (*www.c-i-a.com*), the world Internet population in 2004 was 945 million and will rise to 1.46 billion by 2007. This is up from just over 500 million in 2002. The United States remains the country with the largest number of people online, but even so, it represents only 19.7 percent of all Internet users worldwide. Sometime in the next decade, there will probably be more mainland Chinese online than Americans.

In 2001, the fifteen top Internet-using countries accounted for over 80 percent of all Internet users; that fell to 61 percent in 2004. This indicates how rapidly Internet use is growing outside the original highly developed Internet markets and suggests that these markets are becoming saturated. Countries with over 50 percent of their populations online include the following; the estimated number of active users, in millions, is provided in parentheses: Canada (20.5), Denmark (3.7), Finland (3.3), Germany (41.9), Hong Kong, China (4.9), Iceland (0.2), Ireland (2.1), Israel (3.0), Italy (28.6), Japan (77.9), New Zealand (2.3), Portugal (6.1), Singapore (2.5), Sweden (6.1), Switzerland (4.7), Taiwan (13.2), the UK (34), and the United States (186).[6]

Even though online populations are growing internationally, only about one-third of U.S. Internet businesses actively target them. This reflects the desirability of the affluent, Internet-savvy U.S. market. It also emphasizes how much easier and cheaper it is to market in one's own country where the language(s) and culture are familiar, there is a single currency, deliveries and returns are relatively simple, and online and offline marketing are complementary. For many businesses, this justifies staying exclusively domestic but ignores the real risk of losing customers to international Internet marketers from other countries.

ONLINE LANGUAGE COMMUNITIES

There are exceptions, but most countries are not *monolingual.* Their citizens and other residents speak, write, and read more than one primary language; thus they are *bilingual* or *multilingual.* An example is Switzerland with its four official languages: German, spoken by 63.7 percent of the population, French (19.2 percent), Italian (7.6 percent), and Romansch (0.6 percent). Multilingualism typically grows with population migrations and declines when societies demand that new arrivals communicate in one official language.

Rather than being confined within a country's borders, languages know no such boundaries. Rather, a *language community* is made up of a significant number of people who share a primary language regardless of where they live in the world. An **online language community** is a significant number of people who communicate in the same primary language electronically on the Internet or other network. They often represent profitable niche marketing opportunities, as shown by the example of Yahoo! targeting the Russian-speaking online community for its new email services.

Differences in size between offline and online language communities provide insights into how Internet adoption is proceeding and into the changing dimensions of online populations. For example, Chinese is the world's most prevalent language

**Online language
community**
A significant number
of people who com-
municate in the
same language elec-
tronically on the
Internet or other
network.

IBM

IBM is an example of a company that uses local languages on its various country websites. Site designs are instantly recognizable as belonging to IBM, but site languages differ.

Source: Reprint Courtesy of International Business Machines Corporation copyright 2004 © International Business Machines Corporation.

offline. It is the primary language of 14.4 percent of the world's population, followed by Hindi (6.0 percent), English (5.6 percent), Spanish (5.6 percent), Bengali (3.4 percent), Portuguese (2.6 percent), and Russian (2.8 percent). Online, the numbers are different. European non-English languages are the primary language of 37.9 percent of the world's online populations, followed by English (35.8 percent), Chinese (14.1 percent), and Japanese (9.6 percent).

In 1996, English was the primary language of 80 percent of the online population. By 2004, that had declined to 35.8 percent. The turning point was the year 2000, when non-English-speaking Internet users for the first time outnumbered English speakers. This was just the beginning of the proportional decline in both the number of English-speaking Internet users and the dominance of English-only web pages. English is still the primary language of business worldwide, but at the same time, customers want to be spoken to online in their own language. Failure to do so can be commercial suicide.[7]

International Internet Marketing Strategies

International Internet marketing
Marketing via electronically mediated environments, particularly the Internet and World Wide Web, to more than one country.

International Internet marketing is international marketing in electronically mediated environments on the Internet and World Wide Web, intranets, and/or extranets, making offers to and accepting them from more than just the marketer's domestic (home) market. An **international Internet market** is external to the marketer's home country and may consist of consumers, enterprises, or both. A market may be a country, segmented groups within a country, a region or group of countries, or a mass market or niche market of buyers, such as members of a language community.

Variables in the marketing mix are adjusted more or less to serve the international target market. For an international market to be viable in marketing terms, it must be reachable online and large enough to make targeting profitable. Its buyers must have

International Internet market
An Internet market external to the marketer's home country.

sufficient resources to make purchases, the authority to do so, a mechanism to make payment (credit, check, money order, PayPal account, or the like), and a means for taking delivery. These requirements can eliminate large numbers of consumers in very poor countries and remote regions.

Going international is not strategically appropriate for all bricks-and-mortar businesses, nor is it necessarily the right move for all web marketers. However, the borderless global nature of the Internet means that even solely domestic online marketers with no desire or intention to use the Internet internationally must address the issue of international access, if only to state clearly that they do not accept international orders. Many of these businesses will never take advantage of the Internet's global reach; others are not doing so now but may in the future. All are exposed to the international Internet environment once they go online to do business.

FACTORS AFFECTING INTERNATIONAL STRATEGY

Internationalization was not an issue at the beginning of Internet commercialization. The United States led the world in creating and commercializing the Internet, and international buyers and sellers were not important because there were so few of them. But in less than a decade, the picture changed dramatically.

Many factors can influence international strategy. *Current strategy* is a key factor. International marketers offline are more likely also to be international marketers online, usually targeting those key markets that they currently serve and others that are in their expansion plans. Small and midsize solely domestic marketers may find internationalization beyond their capacities and needs, particularly if they exclusively serve local home-country selling areas. Microsoft (*www.microsoft.com/worldwide/*) is a prominent international marketer offline and online; a local computer repair shop that makes onsite repairs solely within a small city market is not.

Exactly what the firm markets—its *market offer*—also influences international strategy. Culturally sensitive products (such as entertainment, advertisements, fashions, and some foods) often are more complex and challenging to market internationally. Cultural differences affect preferences in apparel color, placement of keys on a computer keyboard, the language of a word processing program, and how many golf balls go in a pack (because certain numbers are construed as inflicting bad luck in prime target markets). Some offers are clearly specific to one market. For example, U.S. patriotic apparel and artifacts, pins, flags, and other tangible items were marketed heavily on U.S. websites to U.S. buyers after September 11, 2001. They were appropriate for this market but are far less so for international markets, particularly today.

Customer demand is closely related to market offer. If demand is exclusively home-country local, then Internet marketing and websites will be local. If demand is international, then Internet marketing and websites are likely to be international and to be offered in languages to accommodate important markets. Sometimes a major customer drags its suppliers online, forcing them to become international Internet marketers. General Electric's (*http://ge.com/en*) former chairman and CEO Jack Welch made it clear that he wanted GE suppliers to be online in order to do business with the huge industrial conglomerate. This had a considerable impact on GE's suppliers, but because most were not ready to make the move, GE had to back off this demand, at least temporarily. Wal-Mart has been far more successful in demanding that its suppliers go online and communicate with the company via its own software. If they want to do business with Wal-Mart, they have no choice.

Management is another powerful influence. Proactive internationally oriented managers are more likely to promote international Internet marketing strategies, and their commitment will cause resources to be allocated accordingly. An internationally oriented ebusiness manager can be an irresistible force moving a company toward international markets online.

Competitors can spur Internet marketers to internationalize. Fear of being left behind by the competition is a potent motivator, as is waking up to offshore Internet marketers competing for a company's local customers. Because nearly all large businesses and a growing majority of small and midsize businesses are already online, failure to have a website sends customers a negative signal about the business, implying that it is slow to adopt new technologies and serve them electronically.

Economic conditions, in both domestic and foreign served markets, can encourage or discourage internationalization. A home-country economic downturn or recession can encourage marketers to develop international revenue sources to hedge against losses at home. International marketers spread the risk by offsetting losses in one market with gains in others. *Government encouragement*, particularly through a tax moratorium or special financing opportunities, can also stimulate online exporting.

Finally, *serendipity* is a factor. Unexpectedly receiving that first unsolicited international order can lead a marketer to believe that the bottom line can be enhanced with relatively little effort, which can often prove to be the case.

RISK FACTORS

International Internet marketing is certainly not without risk. Savvy Internet marketers identify risk factors and develop strategies to reduce their probability and minimize their effects. The risks associated with international Internet marketing are related to such factors as business size, industry, markets, competition, and offer.

The risk of *overexpansion* arises when a business enters too many international markets too rapidly. Websites that must be localized for all or many of its new online markets can be extremely costly. This can result in large cash drains, insufficient human resources to maintain the expansion, and (ultimately) collapse. It can strain fulfillment and result in frustrated rather than satisfied buyers. Take the case of the original Boo.com, a European online apparel retailer. Despite being called a cool dot-com in 1999, the company was a dead dot-com by May 2000. Poor planning led to the site's being launched simultaneously in fourteen countries, each with different issues related to taxation, currency, language, and business practices. Going international using sponsored links on an international Google site or selling through one of eBay's international auction sites obviously carries less of an overexpansion risk than the approach taken by Boo.

The Internet's accessibility increases the risk of *brand dilution*, particularly for luxury products. Overexposed brand names risk diluting their luxury image and lowering their brand equity. This is one reason why high-end fashion designers such as Burberry Group (*http://burberry.com*) initially resisted selling online from its website.

Instead, would-be shoppers were advised to use the site's store locator to find offline shops where Burberry products are sold.[8] However, even Burberry now sells a limited inventory online while still maintaining its store locator service.

Overestimation of expected revenues can result in insufficient consideration of the costs of international expansion and its financial risk. Revenue estimates tend to be influenced by the degree of enthusiasm for internationalizing—greater enthusiasm often leads to greater overestimation. This is linked to the associated risk of *underestimation*. It's easy to underestimate the cost of competing in international markets. For large businesses targeting multiple international markets, it can take US$15 to $30 million or more to create, launch, and maintain a single web-selling site. Each additional site adds to the costs. Obviously, costs are far less for smaller single website businesses, but international expansion still can be unexpectedly expensive. For example, BlueTie, Inc. (*www.bluetie.com*) sells secure, web-based messaging and collaboration software to individuals, small and midsize businesses, health care organizations, and service providers. Its sixty employees are based in Rochester, NY, USA and in other cities across the country. The company was founded in March 1999. In 2001, Canadian and Australian companies unexpectedly began ordering products from BlueTie's U.S. website. The orders were unsolicited but welcome. The downside was serving them, which was complicated by customers coming from four different time zones, using different day and time formats. It is estimated that it cost the company in the six figures to fix its site to accommodate international orders.[9] Costs are more predictable if marketing is through a trading platform such as Google, eBay, or Amazon. However, costs are associated with sales volume and transaction fees; subscription or advertising fees can exceed profits.

Regulation risk can be higher in international markets, because each country market that is served exposes the marketer to another government and its regulations. Some governments are far more intrusive than others, and their regulation of Internet commerce restricts marketing activities and adds costs. On the other hand, some governments are eager to advance Internet technology and offer incentives to cooperating businesses.

Every Internet marketer considering going international should carefully assess the risks and costs, and then weigh them against potential benefits. Unfortunately, costs are often difficult to forecast, and benefits can be even more elusive. However, if projected costs are greater than potential benefits, the best action may be to stay solely domestic. Because change is swift and inevitable, particularly online, risk assessments should be conducted regularly to ensure that potentially profitable international Internet opportunities are capitalized on and that losses, when they occur, are minimized.

TARGET, REACH, INTERACT, AND TRADE

The challenge for Internet marketers going international is to effectively and profitably develop strategies to *target, reach, interact*, and *trade* with offshore buyers. Once the decision is made to go international, *target* markets must be selected and strategies developed to *reach* buyers in the key markets. This is becoming more difficult as the Web gets cluttered with billions of pages, as email spam increases, and as more buyers go wireless, which necessitates web pages designed to accommodate smaller screens and different software standards.

If products are sold from a website, the site must be prepared to *interact* with non-English-speaking buyers and with buyers speaking non-American English. Localizing a site and hiring local customer service representatives can be costly. An alternative approach is to sell through online malls, via online auctions, or by purchasing sponsored links that direct visitors to an existing domestic website that has international purchasing instructions.

Finally, methods must be implemented to facilitate cross-border online *trade.* This includes addressing logistics and shipping requirements for moving tangible goods into offshore markets and handling returns. It means finding satisfactory and secure payment mechanisms that protect both buyer and seller and accommodate currency conversions, currency rate fluctuations, privacy concerns, and cross-market price variations. It also means overcoming government-implemented barriers designed to protect online local home-country sellers and give them an advantage over others.

ENTRY APPROACHES

Businesses can quickly go from being solely domestic to being international marketers just by going online. This is one of the most remarkable advantages of the Internet: worldwide market exposure often at relatively little cost. Most Internet start-ups and small businesses with web storefronts could never achieve equal international exposure offline. Even so, many U.S. businesses refuse unsolicited international orders.

Some domestic websites are *passively international,* with a one-site-fits-all strategy based on the home-country strategy. They accept unsolicited international orders that happen to turn up, and if this begins to occur frequently, they may become actively international. Another approach excludes international sales online but uses websites and email to inform international buyers, promote offers, and drive buyers toward bricks-and-mortar outlets, catalog sales, and/or a professional sales force in their local markets.

The most committed international Internet marketers are *actively international.* This approach requires a strong commitment to develop, maintain, and extend an international buyer base. It requires deciding where and how to target offers, and it entails making decisions about website design and maintenance, cultural and linguistic adaptations, currency and size conversions, product standards, ISP hosting, shipping, and how to comply with local legal and regulatory restrictions. It also requires developing strategies for promoting the site in international markets.

Some businesses target online foreign markets independently, without partners. Others recognize that local partners are extremely important in helping them penetrate the market, hire local employees, obtain financing, avoid cultural mistakes, and gain acceptance. Yahoo! Japan Corp. (*www.japancorp.net/*), Japan's top Internet portal, is a joint venture partnership of Yahoo! Inc. (33.5 percent owner) and Japan's Softbank Corp. (42 percent owner). Another approach is to enter a market by acquiring foreign-owned or foreign-targeted companies. Some businesses use a combination of strategies. To enter the Taiwan market, eBay acquired a Taiwanese online auction operator, NeoCom Technology Co. For China, eBay purchased a 33 percent stake in

EachNet, a U.S. company based in Delaware that hosts the largest online trading community in China. EachNet operated throughout China with a variety of partners, who became eBay partners through the acquisition.[10]

Localized Internet marketing strategy
Adapting web pages and email to local languages and cultures targeted in each served international market.

Actively international approaches also vary. A **localized Internet marketing strategy** adapts marketing offers to accommodate local preferences and customs in each served international market. It includes creating web pages and emails, sponsoring links and promotions in local languages, and adapting them to local cultural preferences. This is a customized approach consistent with believing buyer groups are heterogeneous with many different needs, wants, and preferences. A localized strategy can be used for one or many markets.

Glocal strategy
Localization applied globally by adapting websites, email, and promotions to key target market local cultures but trying to maintain some standardization.

A **glocal strategy** is an approach that localizes and makes site, email, and promotion adaptations to appeal to local markets, but standardizes where feasible. Coca-Cola (*www2.Coca-Cola.com*) is an example of a company with a glocal strategy. Coca-Cola opened its first international plants in 1906. Today, its international sales account for over 70 percent of its income. The company states, "we 'think global and act local,' because we need to listen to all the voices around the world asking for beverages that span the entire spectrum of tastes and occasions." Coca-Cola produces almost 400 different beverage brands in more than 200 countries, with strategic business units (SBUs) making localized decisions in the Americas, Asia, and Europe/Africa. The company has websites in over thirty countries (*www.coca-cola.com/worldwide/flashIndex1.html*) adapted more-or-less to each local market or market group. Localized websites exist in the major Internet countries as well as in such emerging markets as Argentina, Brazil, China, Hungary, Peru, Russia, and South Africa.

Although Coca-Cola is a local marketer, it also standardizes on its country websites. The sites show graphics of the company's trade-dress-protected bottle, and Coca-Cola red is either a prominent background color or a contrast color. Generally, the language used on the site reflects local preferences. Coke's Netherlands site (*www.coca-cola.nl/*) is in both Dutch and English; its site in Poland (*www.cocacola.com.pl/u235/navi/71*) is predominantly in Polish. Its Japanese (*www.cocacola.co.jp/index3.html*) site has English category headings with Japanese text. All sites are alike in that they rely heavily on a youth orientation, music, and graphical intensity; most use flash technology. Coca-Cola has made a considerable effort at the SBU level to adapt website look, sound, and content to local tastes.

Global marketing
Offering an undifferentiated marketing mix to perceived homogeneous markets worldwide.

Finally, a *global strategy* actively seeks international buyers but still standardizes, treating all markets with a more-or-less culture-neutral approach. **Global marketing** is offering an undifferentiated marketing mix to homogeneous markets worldwide. Although the terms *international* and *global* are often used interchangeably, they are different. For most marketers, global marketing is an unrealized ideal. Harvard Business Professor Emeritus Theodore Levitt was the first to propose that widespread access to communication, transport, and travel were driving buyers worldwide toward wanting and accepting the same product offers. Levitt believed that this movement toward *converging commonalities* would allow marketers to standardize their offers rather than require them to adapt to local preferences. The benefits are obvious. They range from economies of scale in production to advantages in distribution, promotion, and management. The Internet has undermined the globalization concept to a certain extent, making it possible to mass-customize offers and personalize customer contacts effectively and efficiently. At the same time, it has been extremely effective in spreading information about product offers available on websites hosted in other countries. If Levitt had been able to predict the invention of the World Wide Web and its commercialization, he would have added the Internet to the forces driving converging commonalities and homogeneous markets.[11]

International Internet Users

Although there are many similarities among Internet users worldwide, there also are some notable differences. It is impossible to identify all user characteristics in every major and emerging Internet market, but looking at some notable features can help us develop a useful perspective for identifying viable international opportunities.

FINDING BUYERS

Search engines and directories are popular worldwide. Buyers can find websites anywhere by searching one of the popular search engines, a localized Yahoo!, Google, or a home-grown, country-specific search engine. Local search engines can be found at Search Engine Colossus (*www.searchenginecolossus.com*), the International Search Engine Directory, which has links to search engines from 195 countries and 55 territories. The popularity of search engines increases the value of purchasing ad space or sponsored links on major international engines. For example, Google.es (*www.google.es*) is estimated to reach over 60 percent of Internet users in Spain; Yahoo! (*http://es.yahoo.com*) reaches over 70 percent. An Internet marketer targeting buyers in Spain is well advised to consider using search engine marketing strategies to find buyers there.

Many businesses target their current international buyers. For example, country-of-origin log file data and careful study of Internet demographics helped Yahoo! determine where it needed localized websites. Lands' End (*www.landsend.com*) was mailing hard-copy catalogs to customers in England, France, Germany, and Japan before it constructed web storefronts and warehouses in those countries. Amazon.com (*www.amazon.com*), eBay, AOL (*www.aol.com*), and other Internet "pure plays" (clicks-only businesses) used a U.S.-extension strategy, launching websites first in the United States, where their buyers were concentrated, and then targeting countries with large numbers of buyers rapidly going online. B2B marketers with international customers and suppliers are more likely to target current markets where they already have significant operations with offices, plants, warehouses, and sales forces. Extranets also offer cross-border opportunities to market to offshore suppliers, customers, and partners.

DEMOGRAPHICS

Slightly more women than men are online in the United States, but the gender gap persists in other parts of the world. Although European men still dominate Internet use, the gap is closing—except in Italy, where 41.7 percent of men are online compared to 21.5 percent of Italian women. Internet use by women continues to grow outside North America and Europe. For example, Taiwan has gender parity, with

25.1 percent of men and 23.5 percent of women online. Figures vary widely by country, but generally, men have been online longer than women, and higher education still is a predictor of Internet usage.[12]

BROADBAND

Broadband adoption is supported strongly by many governments, but not in the United States, although some have called for the government to subsidize it as a national policy. Even though broadband is still expensive in the United States compared to the rest of the world, many Americans are finally signing up. By 2003, 23 percent of U.S. Internet users were on broadband; in late 2004, that number had grown to around 51 percent. That compares to over 50 percent of Internet users on broadband in most Western European countries, over 53.6 percent in Canada, over 80 percent in Hong Kong, and over 70 percent in South Korea. The impact of broadband is significant. Consumers with broadband purchase as much as 30 percent more than narrowband-using consumers, spend more time online, spend less time watching television, use the Internet more often, and visit more sites. Speedier connections also increase music and movie downloads.[13]

OUT-OF-HOME ACCESS

Having electricity and a telephone connection is no longer a requirement for Internet access. In remote villages in Laos, the Jhai Foundation (*www.jhai.org*) has helped engineers create a machine with no moving parts that uses flash-memory data chips, a liquid crystal screen, and a 486-processor, and is powered by a car battery run by bicycle cranks. It connects via wireless Internet cards to a solar-powered hilltop relay station that links to a nearby town computer with Internet access. The system enables villagers to determine the price of rice in the local market town before deciding whether to bring their crop to market. They use the Internet to talk to relatives abroad and find partners to help them market their handwoven textiles. People from eighty-five countries have expressed interest in the low cost, sustainable Jhai PC and communication system.

Projects in other developing countries are also designed to connect rural areas. In India, soybean farmers in remote villages log on to check soybean futures at the Chicago Board of Trade and to check local soybean prices electronically. This information helps them decide when to bring their crop to market. They are part of the echoupal initiative of ITC Group (*www.echoupal.com*) that provides a computer and Internet access for farmers in India. In Hindi, a *choupal* is a gathering place; an *e-choupal* is an electronic commerce hub. Around 3,000 echoupals were operating in Indian villages by 2004. Children in these villages are learning how to use the Internet. Indian businesses are beginning to recognize opportunities in emerging rural village markets.[14]

PIRATES!

Pirates
Internet users who illegally download copyright-protected electronic files, principally music, software, and videos, without paying the copyright owner.

The United States has its problems with music pirates and Internet piracy is growing even more rapidly internationally, from Germany to Indonesia. **Pirates** are Internet users who illegally download copyright-protected electronic files, mainly music, software, and videos, without paying the copyright owner. The illegal downloading of music is rampant throughout Europe and Asia, fueled by teens and college students. European tenacity in clinging to free file sharing is perhaps understandable because KaZaA, the most popular software for file sharing, was developed by a Swede and three Estonians. The European market for music is second only to the U.S. market, with annual sales of around US$11 billion and legal download sales of over US$30.5 million. Germany is the market most affected by music piracy and the government is cracking down on it. The chief offender in Asia is China, where piracy is an organized business rather than a matter of friends swapping files P2P. The culture there is deeply rooted in counterfeiting. In Singapore, a recent survey found that 75 percent of the population have no objection to pirated files. While legal download services such as Apple's iTunes (*www.apple.com/itunes/*) are credited with declining rates of piracy in the United States, similar effects have yet to be seen in places where legal download services are not well established.[15]

International Issues

The complexity, cost, and risks of going international should give pause to Internet marketers considering it. At the same time, international opportunities and profit potential should motivate them to seriously consider doing so. This section examines some key international issues that can affect international online marketing success.

LANGUAGE

Over 64 percent of the Internet's worldwide users do not speak English. Europeans are the second largest bloc of Internet users and 37.9 percent of them speak European, non-English languages. Non-English-speaking buyers may have sufficient language skills to understand an English-only website, or they can use online translators such as those offered by Google Language Tools (*www.google.com/language_tools?hl=en*) or AltaVista's Babel Fish (*http://babelfish.altavista.com*). Even so, the importance of using the languages of local target markets is emphasized by Forrester Research, which reports that visitors stay twice as long on sites written in their native language and adapted to their culture. Nine out of ten non-English-speakers prefer their own language on websites, even when English is their second language. However, if the purpose of a U.S. website is to attract suppliers or partners, then having an English-only site is more appropriate.[16]

Grouping within language communities is intuitively appealing, but important variations exist even within what is seemingly the same language. Differences between American, British, Australian, South African, and other forms of English are well documented and include spelling (color or colour), meaning (car trunk or boot), and pronunciation (*patriot*, with **a** as in gate versus *patriot*, with **a** in sat), which can be a problem for voice recognition software. At the same time, global English is still the predominant business language worldwide, and using it on a website is a relatively rational choice unless the site is targeted to a group for whom English is clearly not appropriate.

Putting an American spin on English can be detrimental. American slang and obviously U.S.-centric English should be avoided on offshore-targeted websites because many international users are sensitive to perceived U.S. Internet dominance and to the perceived heavy-handed export of American culture and politics. Nonetheless, the use of American English to describe technical specifications is preferred in non-English-speaking countries because it is authoritative and represents expert judgments.

Language is the most obvious difference between home-country and international markets. Translating pages and whole sites into other languages can help make offshore customers feel welcome, but the cost of translation can be high. It is not necessary to translate everything and marketers are well advised to streamline and edit before translating. Generally, the fewer words, the lower the translation cost. Size is also an issue in markets where wireless is popular. Small screens, often no larger than two inches square, discourage reading large amounts of text. Large text files are also a problem for markets where average download times are slow, often only 28.8 bps. The cost of translating email is far less, as little as 15 to 18 U.S. cents per word, which is an incentive to marketers seeking a low-cost method for promoting online offers internationally using wireless.

Translation takes place on many levels. It can be as superficial as translating one page for offshore visitors or as deep as offering a fully translated mirror site localized to each served market. To be effective, translation should include content text as well as frequently asked questions (FAQs), feedback forms, product specifications, privacy statements, security warnings, shopping cart instructions, contact information, and the like. It also requires registering with popular local search engines in target markets and using local-language keyword descriptors for metatags. In most cases, easily misunderstood colloquialisms, slang, buzzwords, and idioms must be avoided unless they have been adopted locally. Web marketers can lingualize their sites using translation software, a linguistic translator, or a native speaker, or by hiring a multilingual content management firm. These alternatives are costly and, however painstakingly prepared, will be incomplete if they ignore cultural differences.

Another important aspect of language should also be kept in mind: Language is a product. Asians spend an estimated US$20 to $30 billion each year on English lessons. For many Asians, instruction via the Internet is much cheaper than private instruction or face-to-face classes. Most English elearning sites are 24/7/365 operations with human instructors available to interact with students as needed. This requires streaming audio and video technologies that are found in many Asian businesses but in very few homes. Online English instruction represents a profitable marketing opportunity for U.S. universities.[17]

OTHER CULTURAL ISSUES

Online culture
An extension of offline culture that includes the look and feel of a website, acceptable colors, measures, and even how much text or animation is acceptable on a page.

Culture is composed of behaviors, customs, beliefs, coping mechanisms, art, rituals, language, and other factors that characterize a group of people and distinguish it from other groups. **Online culture** is an extension of offline culture that includes the look and feel of a website; acceptable colors, measurements, and standards; manner of using body parts, politics, humor, history, children, animals, flags, women, acronyms, and abbreviations; and even how much text or animation is acceptable on a web page. It also influences appropriate responses to email marketing, online promotions, and pricing strategies. Sites can be *culturally neutral,* avoiding cultural nuances and attempting to appeal to cultural universals; *culturally local,* targeting locals with specific cultural nuances; or *culturally U.S.-centric,* deliberately reflecting U.S. culture.

Businesses that target online international audiences and yet ignore cultural differences risk offending international buyers. For example, in North America and Western Europe, dogs are pets, often regarded as family members. In France, dogs can sit at the table with their masters in fine restaurants. Their images on web pages convey warm, friendly messages in these cultures. Putting a dog picture or icon on a website targeted to Asia conveys a distinctly different impression, however, because in some parts of Asia, dogs are food.

Black is a popular background color on U.S. websites, where it is regarded as a sophisticated web color, conveying a sense of style, mystery, or high fashion. But black is a sinister or unlucky color in Asia, Europe, and Latin America, and its use on a website communicates a far different message than intended. Red is a lucky color in parts of China, yet overdoing red in web design can be insulting to the target audience if it is interpreted as patronizing. Red should not be used in onscreen text targeted to China because it is negatively associated with the Cultural Revolution; black, white, and green are unlucky. Lucky colors in India are yellow, red, and green; white and black are unlucky. Germans, on the other hand, prefer cool colors: blues and grays with red accents. Blue is the most culturally acceptable web color internationally.[18]

Numbers likewise have different meanings. For example, web marketers targeting North America, Australia, and much of Western Europe should avoid the number 13, which is perceived as unlucky, as is 666. Japan's Nippon Airlines does not use seats numbered 4, 9, or 13. *Four* has the same pronunciation as the Japanese word for "death"; *nine* sounds like "agony" or "torture." *Four* is also unlucky in China because it is similar to the word for "death," and *eight* is lucky because it sounds like the word for "wealth" or "riches."[19]

Answering email requests for information from internationals requires understanding how people expect to be addressed. While Americans tend to be informal, often using first names, to reply to an email using a first name in Asia is insulting. The use of family names and courtesy titles requires reformatting order boxes and other HTML forms created for Western-style names. In China, it is difficult or impossible to distinguish between male and female names, and married names may not be used. A married woman may use Madam or Mrs. with her maiden name. This seriously complicates email marketing and personalization efforts, unless they are directed by native speakers who understand local cultural nuances.[20]

Measurements and numbers vary between markets. A woman's size 9 medium shoe in the United States is a size 7.5 in the United Kingdom, a 41 in Europe, an 8.5 in Australia, and a 30 in Japan. Currencies vary, but online currency converters are easily linked to a web page and major international credit card companies make conversions for charges with their cards. Dates and time are not reported consistently. What is the date 01/12/07? Is it the twelfth of January 2007 or the first of December 2007? It all depends on who is reading the date. In the United States, it is read as January; in other parts of the world, it is December. The ISO 8601:1988 International Date Format is year-month-day, so the January date would be written 2007-01-12. However, most websites ignore this format and use the local one. In Mandarin Chinese[21], the same date is:

二零零六年一月一号

Picturing body parts online is taboo in many markets. Naked foot bottoms are unacceptable screen images for Belgians. A pointing finger, that common web icon, should not be incorporated into sites targeted to Portugal because a finger is commonly used to beckon a prostitute. Women's arms, legs, or other body parts should be avoided on web pages targeted to Muslim countries.

Culturalization
Localizing a website to conform to cultural standards and preferences in the targeted market(s).

A fully internationalized website requires **culturalization,** localizing the site to conform to cultural standards in the targeted market(s). It is a costly process to create a localized site, and to maintain and update it. Internet marketers that localize in several countries risk incurring costs that can rapidly drain cash reserves. Grouping by culture is a tricky business. French culture in Montréal, Canada, is quite different from French culture in Paris, France, or former French colonies in Africa. That is why so many web marketers still use countries as the level at which localization decisions are made and regard customizing in terms of language as the first localization task.

GLOBAL SQUABBLES OVER INTERNET GOVERNANCE

The 2003 United Nations World Summit on the Information Society presented the most substantial challenge yet to U.S. control over key Internet resources, principally how to run the top-level domain name addressing and numbering system. The UN debate targeted ICANN, the privately run Internet Corporation for Assigned Names and Numbers that operates under authority of the U.S. Department of Commerce. Many countries are unhappy with what they perceive as U.S. domination of Internet addresses and believe that responsibility should be shifted to the ITU, a multilateral UN agency. Meanwhile, the United States is unwilling to allow countries with questionable records of Internet censorship (specifically, China and some African and Middle Eastern nations) to participate in Internet governance for fear that their involvement will jeopardize free speech and technical innovation. A UN working group is studying the issue and will report recommendations in 2005. This dispute is the tip of an iceberg of discontent that threatens to engulf the Internet and jeopardize its cross-border commercialization.[22]

CROSS-BORDER SPAMMERS

Asia has emerged as a key link in the international spam chain. Massive quantities of spam are spewing from Asian servers. Although the United States remains the top country for spam operators, not far behind are China, South Korea, Brazil, and Taiwan. As many as 80 percent of U.S.-based bulk email spamming services use servers in China to mass-mail messages and therefore, avoid U.S. and European anti-spam laws. Tracing, identifying, and prosecuting spammers outside the United States and Europe is extremely difficult. Spam has spread to cell phones and text-messaging devices. NTT DoCoMo, the largest cell phone carrier in Japan, reports that about a sixth of its customers receive from one to five cell phone spams daily. Spam is also increasing on blogs, online chats, and web log comments.

The Spamhaus Project (*www.spamhaus.org*), a volunteer group based in London, tracks spammers to help ISPs and others block their output. It claims that 90 percent of all spam sent to the United States and Europe is generated by about 200 spammers identified on its Register of Known Spam Operations (ROKSO at

Zombie drone

A computer that has been taken over and used by hackers to launch spam or a DDOS attack.

www.spamhaus.org/rokso/index.lasso). Its list of the top spamming countries for 2004 included (numbers 1 through 10) the United States, China, South Korea, Brazil, Taiwan, Argentina, Canada, Russia, Hong Kong, and Italy. Some spam is sent by **zombie drones,** computers that have been taken over by hackers without the owner's knowledge or permission to launch spam or a distributed denial of service (DDOS) attack against other computers. The 2003 Mydoom/Novarg worm launched zombie drone spam attacks.[23]

GAMBLING

Online gambling is a multibillion dollar industry that operates through about 1,800 web casinos; Britain and Asian countries lead the way. The Interactive Gaming Council (*www.igcouncil.org*), based in Vancouver, British Columbia, claims that Internet casinos are a legitimate industry and should not be restricted. Meanwhile, projected growth of Internet gambling is fastest in Asia, where users should exceed those in the United States by 2006.

Even though most gambling sites are located on web servers outside the United States to avoid U.S. laws, at least 40 percent of all online gamblers are Americans. Online gambling is under attack by the U.S. government, religious groups opposed to gambling, collegiate athletics associations, and conservative activists. They helped pressure the U.S. Congress to ban credit card payments for electronic gambling. U.S. casinos, on the other hand, see the Internet as a future revenue source. In early 2004, the U.S. government began seizing cash from television and media companies that sold advertising to online casinos for "aiding and abetting" the casinos' online operations.

U.S.-based Harrah's Entertainment, Inc. has eluded U.S. restrictions by opening a subscription gambling site in the UK through its Harrah's Online Ltd., an indirect, wholly owned subsidiary of Harrah's Entertainment, Inc. Its site, LuckyMe (*www.luckyme.co.uk*), charges a monthly fee of £10 to £50 (US$18 to US$92); is targeted to women aged 28 to 47; and accepts subscribers only from England, Scotland, Wales, and Northern Ireland. Britain is well positioned to become the world center for gambling. Its offline betting shops already have excellent reputations for honesty. Its gambling industry is large and respectable, and the country's betting tax has been repealed. Annual British gambling turnover is around £15 billion (US$28 billion), about a third from foreign bettors. Britain controls around 75 percent of the cross-border betting market. The country also has betting exchanges—online auction platforms where gamblers betting for or against specific outcomes are matched. Betfair (*www.betfair.com*), the largest exchange and the world's largest online betting company, managed more than £1.5 billion in exchanges in 2002. Bettors can also use Betfair in Chinese, Danish, Finnish, German, Greek, Italian, Norwegian, and Swedish.

In 2003, the World Trade Organization (WTO) upheld the complaint of Antigua and Barbuda, small Caribbean nations, that U.S. bans on Internet gambling were illegal. The WTO determined that the U.S. ban on Internet telephone and other remote gambling services violated its WTO commitments. The United States had argued that the bans were legal under WTO rules that allow countries to make exceptions for laws to protect public morals and public order. The United States is appealing the WTO ruling.[24]

GOVERNMENT INTERVENTION

Although the Internet is described as borderless, it is inextricably bound to countries and to their governments, legal systems, and regulatory controls. Any Internet marketer doing business internationally must be aware of the changing legal environment in each market targeted (see Chapter 5). This is an area where legal outsourcing—that is, engaging local legal experts to advise on marketing decisions—and constant monitoring are necessary. Ignorance of the law in international markets is not defensible and can be a costly mistake.

Governments administer local export laws, tariffs (taxes), and customs standards and set documentation requirements. Express delivery and freight-forwarding companies can help marketers deal with these matters in the majority of the world's markets. Exporters of tangible goods in particular need expert assistance and should consider outsourcing. Specialized software vendors can help by providing documentation and regulatory information for most markets.

Governments can prohibit the sale and distribution of certain products within their borders, and they sometimes try to do so in other countries. Consider the Yahoo! case in France, where a U.S. site was told by the French government that it had to install filtering software on its California (USA) site to prevent French citizens from participating in online auctions of Nazi memorabilia.

Governments can prohibit their nationals from doing business with other countries. The U.S. government enforces embargoes and sanctions that restrict or prohibit trade with such countries as Cuba, North Korea, Libya, Sudan, and Syria. These bans extend to online sales.[25]

While U.S. businesses fear government overregulation, Europeans are concerned about underregulation. Europe has a much greater level of government intervention than the United States, and of course this sets the stage for conflict between the two. European countries are far more restrictive about promotions; for example, many will not allow advertising to children. Small businesses are aggressively protected from pricing, distribution, and product advantages enjoyed by large businesses. The EU has a Telecommunications Anti-spamming Act that permits email marketing only if it is clearly identified as marketing material and if companies get the recipient's permission to send it prior to doing so. If enforced, this almost impossible requirement could be devastating to U.S. email marketing. The Chinese government also closely monitors and regulates business. It bans most online advertising, and what is allowed must be licensed by the State Administration of Industry and Commerce (SAIC). China censors website content. Although China promises great opportunities, it has a highly regulated, volatile, and risky business environment.[26]

Governments also censor what their citizens do online. This is the case in the United States with the USA Patriot Act. Singapore has been selective in blocking access to certain websites. China uses the Internet to exert control, monitoring its citizens in chat rooms and on websites, as well as using the Web to spread propaganda and denounce political activists. China blocks some Western periodicals and frequently will not let its citizens read *Time* or the *New York Times* online. It has even occasionally blocked Google. The Chinese government has been accused of launching cyberattacks against Falun Gong sites in Canada.[27]

European Union (EU) privacy standards are far more rigorous than those in the United States. U.S. marketers routinely collect personal consumer data electronically (see Chapter 7), share it with other companies, and use it to personalize online advertisements and offers and for email permission marketing. The EU's 1998 Directive on Privacy Protection requires that everyone, regardless of nationality, doing business online or offline in the fifteen EU member countries comply with the EU's strict privacy regulations or be prohibited from collecting and transferring data about EU buyers. The EU law requires anyone processing such data to permit consumers to see, change, and/or delete data about themselves.

In effect, the EU is attempting to force EU privacy restrictions on other countries, including the United States, mandating that other countries adhere to EU privacy laws in their own markets. This means that a European consumer who makes a purchase on a U.S.-hosted website is protected by the EU directive, and theoretically, the U.S.-based host is liable in European courts for invasion of that consumer's privacy.

Some U.S. businesses have protection under voluntary *safe harbor* provisions; many do not. Safe harbor provisions, which were negotiated between the U.S. government and the EU, are agreements that allow U.S. businesses to self-regulate and declare that they are abiding by the EU standards, thereby receiving protection from prosecution or litigation in Europe. The U.S. Department of Commerce maintains a safe harbor list (*http://web.ita.doc.gov/safeharbor/shlist.nsf/webPages/safe+harbor+list*) of companies that are in compliance. A company also can be approved by the TRUSTe EU Safe Harbor Web Privacy Program (*www.truste.org/sealholders/faq_eu_safe_harbor.php*). The EU directive sets a dangerous precedent of imposing Internet laws on other countries. And the EU is not alone; Canada and Argentina have passed similar laws.[28]

Summary

http://college.hmco.com/business/students

Identifying International Internet Markets

There are many different ways to identify developed and emerging Internet markets. The Networked Readiness Index (NRI) evaluates countries on their information and communication technology levels. Of the 102 countries evaluated in 2003–2004, the United States is recognized as the most innovative in the use of ICT. The ITU Mobile/Internet Index measures adoption rates of mobile and Internet technologies in over 200 economies. Mobile/Internet leaders are Hong Kong, China, Denmark, Sweden, Switzerland, and the United States. The convergence of mobile and wireless Internet will be a major demand driver. *The Economist's* e-readiness ranking of the world's largest economies identifies four tiers of e-readiness. The United States was the undisputed e-readiness leader when these rankings were begun; it is no longer. Many governments, even in some of the world's poorest countries, are making considerable progress in getting their businesses and citizens online and, in the process, are helping to reduce international digital divides. The world Internet population is expected to rise to 1.46 billion by 2007, up from just over 500 million in 2002. The United States remains the country with the largest number of people online. Online language communities can be profitable niche marketing opportunities.

International Internet Marketing Strategies

The variables that make up the marketing mix can be adjusted more or less to serve international online target markets. Going international is not strategically appropriate for all bricks-and-mortar businesses or for all web marketers. Factors affecting international strategy include current strategy, market offer, customer demand, management, competitors, economic conditions in domestic and foreign served markets, government encouragement, and unsought orders (serendipity). Risk factors include overexpansion, brand dilution, overestimation, underestimation, and regulation. The challenge for Internet marketers going international is to effectively and profitably develop strategies to target, reach, interact, and trade with offshore buyers. Entry alternatives include being solely domestic; being passively international, with a one-site-fits-all strategy; and being actively international, using a localized "glocal" or a global approach.

International Internet Users

There are many similarities among Internet users worldwide, but there also are notable differences. Buyers can find websites anywhere by using one of the popular search engines, a local Yahoo!, Google, or a local country-specific search engine. Many businesses have no trouble identifying their international Internet target markets because they simply target their current international buyers. While slightly more women than men are online in the United States, the gender gap persists in other parts of the world. Broadband adoption is supported by many governments, but not in the United States. In parts of Europe and Asia, broadband adoption by Internet users is well over 50 percent. The impact of broadband is significant. Having electricity and a telephone connection is no longer a requirement for Internet access. The United States has its music pirates, but the problem of piracy is growing even faster internationally, from Germany to Indonesia.

International Issues

Language and culture are key issues that must be addressed by Internet marketers targeting international markets. Over 64 percent of the Internet's users do not speak English. Grouping markets simply in terms of their use of the same language is not always as effective as it appears. Language is the most obvious difference between domestic and international markets, but online culture, which is an extension of offline culture, is another important influence on international Internet marketing. Cultural factors include colors, measurements and standards, and the use of body parts, humor, history, children, animals, flags and symbols, and other factors that define a society. Some governments believe that authority over Internet domain naming and numbers should be moved from U.S. to United Nations control. Asia has emerged as a key link in the international spam chain. The World Trade Organization has ruled that U.S. bans on Internet gambling are illegal. Governments are a powerful influence on Internet marketers. More online censorship exists in Asia than in other regions. Differences in privacy standards, particularly between the European Union and other countries, are a contentious issue.

Take Action!

Tom handcrafts western saddles and sells them from his workshop store in Denver, Colorado, USA. His customers are pleasure riders from the western United States looking for fine-quality leatherwork, a comfortable, centered seat, and attractive tack. Last year, he went online with a web storefront for his business, Tom's Custom Saddles. Almost immediately, he began receiving orders from the site, including one for his most expensive chestnut leather saddle. Tom was startled by the customer's location—Peterborough in

England. Of course Tom is familiar with England's rich equestrian tradition, but this first international order was an eye opener for him. Suddenly, he realized the full implications of the term *World Wide Web*. Tom has decided that he can significantly increase his revenues by opening a new market for his products and actively selling to the UK. Tom could enter the market by using one or more of the merchant services offered through malls or trading platforms at Amazon UK (*www.amazon.co.uk*), eBay UK (*www.ebay.co.uk*), or Yahoo! UK (*http://uk.yahoo.com*). Alternatively, he could test the waters by purchasing sponsored links at Google UK (*www.google.co.uk*) or Yahoo! UK (*http://uk.yahoo.com*). Tom needs help making this entry decision.

1. Go to Google UK AdWords (*https://adwords.google.co.uk/select/*) and evaluate Google's offer. Create a two-column table. Use the first column to identify key issues that Tom must consider and the second column to indicate how AdWords handles the issue. Some of these issues are the number of countries (markets) reached by AdWords, costs, the number of lines of text allowed, whether or not graphics are allowed, and currency considerations.

2. Go to Yahoo! UK Shopping (*http://uk.shopping.yahoo.com/submit_products.html*) and evaluate Yahoo!'s offer. Create a second table using the same format and issues as the Google UK AdWords table, but for Yahoo! UK Shopping.

3. On each site, run a search for products like Tom's to identify competitors. Print copies (screenshots) of the web homepages of two sites with competitive offers.

4. Create a series of PowerPoint slides to compare the two offers. Use bullets and include tables where appropriate. Conclude the presentation with an analysis of the competition and with recommendations for Tom's site. Be prepared to deliver the presentation in class.

Chapter Review Questions

1. Why is it understandable that some U.S. Internet marketers remain solely domestic?
2. What is ICT? What is its importance to Internet marketing?
3. What does mobile have to do with Internet readiness?
4. Explain the grouping of economies into four tiers in *The Economist's* e-readiness rankings.
5. How many people use the Internet worldwide?
6. What factors affect how businesses go international?
7. Identify risk factors involved with internationalizing.
8. Why are projects like those run by the Jhai Foundation potentially of value to Internet marketers?
9. What are some compelling reasons not to use a black background on an international website?
10. Identify international entry strategies for Internet marketers.
11. Contrast local and global strategies.
12. What type of international Internet marketing strategy is Coca-Cola using?
13. Would U.S. online buyers benefit from EU-style privacy regulations?
14. What is global English?
15. Identify some cultural factors that should be considered in designing international websites.

Competitive Case Study

Yahoo!, Google, and . . . Zhongsou.com?

China Search Online (*http://page.zhongsou.com*), or Zhongsou.com, was launched in 2003 to compete directly with Yahoo! and Google. The company claims that it has solved the difficult problem of accommodating elements of the Chinese language, such as homophones and regional accents, to online text search. Competition in the emerging Chinese search engine market is heating up. Baidu.com (*http://baidu.com*) and 3721.com (*http://3721.com*) recently fought it out legally in the Beijing No.2 Intermediate People's Court over counterclaims of infringement on protected search engine technology. Baidu.com says that it is the world's largest search engine, with over 300 million Chinese-language website pages and over 60 million page hits daily. It reaches more than 95 percent of China's Internet users, over 80 million people. Baidu.com has a market share of 48.2 percent in China's search engine traffic, whereas Google.com has only a 29.8 percent share. The value of China's search engine market was estimated at US$100 million in 2004 and is expected to double by 2006. Zhongsou .com, Baidu.com, and 3721.com are the three largest domestic search engine companies in China. All are profitable from paid sponsored link revenues. Yahoo! purchased the 3721 network in November 2003 for US$120 million, so in this case, what appears to be a home-grown competitor is not. Baidu is seen as a prime acquisition target for Google. Google China went online in February 2004.[29]

CHECK IT OUT

Company press releases are a source of valuable information. Yahoo!'s press releases (*http://docs.yahoo.com/ info/pr/releases.html*) provide a window into the company's activities, its goals, its accomplishments, and its relationships with other companies. Check out Yahoo! by reading some of the company's recent releases. What companies are Yahoo!'s joint venture partners? What marketing programs are they initiating? What are Yahoo!'s plans for international expansion?

A GLOBAL PERSPECTIVE

Print a screenshot of Yahoo!'s U.S. homepage (*www .yahoo.com*), preferably in color, and compare it with screenshot prints of any three other Yahoo! country sites (but not sites in double-byte-language countries such as China). The list of country sites is at the bottom of Yahoo!'s front page. Select ten points of comparison on the U.S. homepage that are key indicators of Yahoo!'s design, content, interactivity, or features. For example, a design element is blue print on a white background. An example of a content element is listing search categories such as *Arts & Humanities.* A search box is an interactivity element. *Personalize My Yahoo!* is a feature. On the basis of this comparison, what do you think Yahoo!'s strategy is— local, global, or something in between?

Module II

Information for Competitive Marketing Advantage

Information fuels the new economy and plays an essential role in developing and maintaining a sustainable competitive marketing advantage. Collecting, evaluating, and applying information faster and more effectively than the competition can be the defining advantage in today's marketplace and the means for successfully managing customer relationships in the long run. The Internet's unique reach, speed, and interactivity make continuous data gathering feasible. Computers allow the mining of data on a scale unimaginable just a few years ago. At the same time, the massive collection of consumer data through marketing research and operational data tool activities is heightening the debate over the erosion of privacy online and threatens the expansion of Internet commercialization.

Data are the building blocks of the information age. Sophisticated software collect, compile, organize, and refine data, extracting information that can be converted into knowledge. Marketing knowledge of customers and prospects, competitors, industries, and the environment can be applied toward improved decision making and, ultimately, enhanced profitability. At the same time, the overwhelming volume of data being collected threatens to compromise marketing decision makers and compromise their decision-making abilities.

Marketing research and operational data tools are the subjects of Module II. Marketing research includes such methods as surveys, conjoint analysis, focus groups, brainstorming, consumer panels, and secondary research. All are being conducted online via the Web and email with methods adapted from traditional offline marketing research. Online marketing research has gained acceptance within professional research communities as studies report high levels of validity, reliability, and projectability. Professional validation of Internet marketing research along with its lower costs, greater reach, and faster response times are compelling reasons why more marketing research activities will continue to move online.

Operation data tools are the companion side of the information equation. These tools compile data into databases and warehouses, facilitate data analysis and mining, allow marketing intelligence gathering and web profiling, and collect even more data from behavioral tracking devices like cookies and bugs. They are even more controversial than marketing research because they collect far more data, are operational 24/7/365, and while most tools are not transparent, they have become lightning rods for online privacy advocates' complaints.

7

.COM

Taking Marketing Research to the Net

LEARNING OBJECTIVES

» To explore the basics of marketing research
» To understand how primary marketing research is conducted online
» To appreciate the breadth and depth of secondary marketing research available online
» To identify issues that arise in connection with Internet marketing research

WPP and Millward Brown Research Consultancy

The companies that make up WPP Group PLC (*www.wpp.com*), the world's second largest advertising and communication services conglomerate (340th in Fortune's Global 500), include leaders in advertising, public relations, branding, health care communications, promotion and relationship marketing, and information and consultancy services. WPP had year-end 2003 sales of US$7.3 billion. Its companies serve 300 of the top Fortune Global 500 companies, operate in 106 countries, and employ over 70,000 people in 1,400 offices worldwide. Ogilvy & Mather Worldwide, J. Walter Thompson Company, Young & Rubicam, Hill & Knowlton, and The Kantar Group (*www.kantargroup.com*) are all WPP brands. Kantar was formed in 1993 to consolidate WPP's Information, Insight, and Consultancy Group of research companies. Kantar member Millward Brown (MB at *www.millwardbrown .com*) is a leading global market research company known for its applied qualitative and quantitative research projects. It operates in thirty-six countries, and by 2004 it had already undertaken over 700 major Internet projects. MB was the first to test the branding effect of online banner ads, the first to test the effectiveness of superstitials

and interstitials, and the first to research the effectiveness of Big Impression ads. MB's *IntelliQuest* unit conducts marketing research for the technology and Internet industry; its *Precis* unit focuses on public relations; and Kantar Media Research (*KMR* Group) supplies media measurement services and software. A recent MB IntelliQuest study surveyed Internet users at work using a LightSpeed Consumer Panel (*www .lightspeedresearch.com/panels/*) in cooperation with the Online Publishers Association (*www .online-publishers.org*). Among its findings: Male (77 percent) and female (68 percent) workers are more likely to go online before lunch; for over 25 percent, the Internet is the only media they use at work; Internet users at work are more affluent (annual incomes ≥ US$75,000) and better educated than those who do not use the Internet at work; average income levels are less among those who use the Internet at night; working women frequently check the weather at work, and if they shop online, they do so at night; and in every surveyed online activity, the more tenured Internet users (online ≥ 7 years) had higher usage levels than the least tenured users (online ≤ 4 years). Perhaps surprisingly, 74 percent of workers say the Internet has improved their at-work productivity; 56 percent use the Internet at home for business.[1]

Millward Brown is just one of many research consultancies that have taken marketing research to the Internet. They range in size from global giants, such as Millward Brown, to very small owner-operator research shops. Marketing research conducted on and about the Internet ranges from enormous, highly sophisticated, multicountry projects that cost millions and even hundreds of millions of dollars to run, to extremely small question pop-up customer surveys that cost only several hundred dollars. Marketing research may be proprietary and company-specific, or it may be public and freely disseminated online. Internet marketing research (Chapter 7) and customer-centric information tools (Chapter 8) are used daily to help solve marketing problems and make important contributions to advancing marketing knowledge.

Marketing Research Basics

The importance of research to the marketing profession began emerging after World War II, when the rapidly expanding postwar consumer market created the need for a more systematic, substantial understanding of buyers, competitors, and marketplaces. Marketing researchers developed new methods to apply the research process to areas of marketing interest and attempted to create predictive models. The development of computers and software facilitated the rapid analysis of complex data and propelled marketing research in new directions. Now, the Internet is providing a highly conducive environment for conducting marketing research on a grand scale while realizing the benefits associated with its unique characteristics. Marketers are also developing new customer-centric information tools that track online behaviors and mine vast databases for relationships that refine and extend marketing offers.

Marketing research
Research conducted to obtain objective, meaningful results that can be used to solve applied marketing problems or expand basic marketing knowledge.

Marketing research is the systematic and objectively planned collection and analysis of meaningful data (results) that are transformed into information communicated to decision makers for use in solving applied marketing problems, answering marketing questions, implementing effective marketing plans, and extending marketing knowledge. Research can be used to describe, predict, and prescribe. *Descriptive research* identifies and describes such things as products, buyers, competitors, behavioral intentions, and market situations. *Predictive research* assesses and forecasts trends, demand, actions, or events. *Prescriptive research* recommends a course of action. Most marketing research is *applied research* directed toward solving contemporary marketing problems experienced by enterprises, as opposed to *basic research*, which is designed to expand the boundaries of marketing knowledge. **Internet marketing research** is marketing research conducted on and/or about the Internet, the World Wide Web, or other Internet sectors. **Marketing researchers** are the individuals and enterprises that perform marketing research on and off the Internet. Sometimes called the scientists of the business world, marketing researchers are asked to provide the right data at the right time so that an enterprise can take advantage of opportunities and avoid failures. Some marketing researchers work in-house for companies that maintain their own marketing research department. Others work for consultancies or as individual entrepreneurs, contracting out their research expertise.

Internet marketing research
Marketing research conducted on and/or about the Internet or any of its sectors.

Marketing researchers
Individuals and enterprises that perform marketing research.

RESEARCH WITH AN APPLIED FOCUS

Marketing as a discipline is known for its applied problem-solving research that focuses on creating a better understanding of the interactions of the marketing mix variables (the 4Ps of product, price, place/distribution, and promotion) with buyers (consumers, enterprises), competitors, markets, and the marketing environment. The level of analysis varies and may be the industry, sector, market, niche, individual enterprise, product type, brand, buyer, usage situation, or other focal point. The scope ranges from the micro perspective of the individual customer to the macro global level of all Internet users.

Small and midsize businesses typically spend comparatively little on marketing research, and many spend nothing at all. Enormous customer-centric consumer products companies such as Procter & Gamble (P&G at *www.pg.com/main.jhtml*) spend hundreds of millions of dollars each year on marketing research aimed at better understanding why consumers purchase P&G products, how they use and store the products, why they prefer P&G products to those of competitors, how they respond to P&G promotions, and related matters of marketing interest. P&G pioneered marketing research with its creation in 1925 of a Marketing Research Department. Through the remainder of the twentieth century, the company maintained one of the most sophisticated marketing research programs in the world. P&G, with net sales of over US$51.4 billion in FY2004, spent more than US$1.65 billion on research and development (marketing research expenses were several million dollars), compared to around US$4 billion on advertising and promotion.[2]

P&G has been conducting marketing research online since 1998. Today, the company conducts virtually all of its concept and new product testing online, at one-hundredth of the time and one-hundredth of the cost of offline testing. Whitestrips is an example of how P&G used a website as a low-cost way of researching consumer response to a new product. P&G initiated a highly successful online test market in August 2000 for a new home tooth-whitening product, Crest Whitestrips. The product's retail price was set at US$44; consumer acceptance was unknown. Rather than running an expensive, time-consuming test market offline in the traditional way, P&G marketing researchers went online, offering the strips initially only at the U.S. Whitestrips.com (*http://whitestrips.com/*) website. Supporting television and print advertising from August to May 2000 were effective web drivers that encouraged potential buyers to visit the site. Customers who requested a product sample from the website and agreed to receive product updates by email were contacted regularly to see whether they had used the product, how they liked it, and whether they would repurchase it. In the eight-month test market period, P&G sold 144,000 whitening kits directly from the site. It recorded a 12 percent conversion rate of site visitors making an online purchase. Confident of the product's reception, its price, and the marketing message, P&G introduced Whitestrips into stores in May 2000 and by late July recorded sales of nearly US$50 million. This climbed to US$178.2 million by year end 2003, roughly a 60 percent market share of what is now a growing US$300 million market. The product is no longer sold by P&G directly from the site; instead, visitors to the Whitestrips informational site are directed to retailers where an online purchase can be made. P&G is credited with singlehandedly carving out a new market segment,

P&G's Whitestrips.com

P&G's Whitestrips.com is now an attractive, information-only site that drives visitors to make purchases at cooperating etailers or offline.

Source: Copyright © The Procter & Gamble Company. Used by Permission.

targeted principally to women ages 35–50 and to teens. Consumers can still participate in test-marketing P&G products at the company's *Try and Buy* website (*www.pg.com/products/try_buy.jhtmlth*).[3]

Basic research, primarily carried out by university-based researchers, is also conducted and often reported online. Sources for basic research articles include the *Journal of Marketing Research*, the *Journal of Consumer Research*, and the *Journal of Advertising Research*. KnowThis.com maintains an online list of links to academic marketing journals at *www.knowthis.com/publication/journalsonline.htm*. Another set of academic journal links is offered by Tilburg University (*www.tilburguniversity.nl/faculties/few/marketing/links/journal1.html*). Some academic journals are now published solely online.

IDENTIFYING RESEARCH METHODS

Why conduct marketing research? Good research collects reliable data that can provide valuable information to improve marketing decisions and, ultimately, generate greater profits and better satisfy customers. The benefits of good research typically far outweigh its costs. However, good research sometimes delivers results that decision makers choose to ignore, which can have serious repercussions. Bad research poorly conceived, executed, and evaluated produces flawed information that compromises decision making and misleads decision makers. In other cases, marketing research is not feasible because of cost, time, or knowledge constraints. Even if systematic, procedurally appropriate research is not used, marketers can still gain useful information through careful observations of website visitors, customer preferences and purchase patterns, customer feedback, competitors' website offers, and the marketplace.

Marketing research results can be used for many purposes. The opening case showed how research conducted by Millward Brown was designed to help illuminate how people use the Internet at work. Online research can be used to test new products, as shown in the Whitestrips example. Other uses are to identify and target online markets, develop effective communication campaigns, obtain feedback on marketing campaigns, test website usability, and measure the progress of the implementation of a marketing plan.

Primary research is original research designed to answer a precise marketing question or solve a specific marketing problem (see Figure 7-1). It requires the collection of *primary (original) data* that are directly related to the question or problem and use qualitative or quantitative methods, or a combination of the two. **Qualitative primary research** is original research in which in-depth subjective methods are used

Primary research
Original investigational research designed to answer a precise marketing question or solve a specific marketing problem.

Qualitative primary research
Original research that consists of collecting qualitative (sometimes called soft) data from relatively small numbers of participants via in-depth subjective methods.

FIGURE 7-1 Marketing Research Methods
Internet marketers use a variety of marketing research methods online and offline.

to obtain *qualitative data* by examining the opinions, behavioral intentions, behaviors, statements, and/or beliefs of the participants (who are also called subjects or respondents). Popular methods include focus groups, brainstorming, interviews, and content analysis of online communications in chat rooms and on message boards, blogs, and feedback forms. Qualitative primary research is often labeled *exploratory research* because it is frequently performed to explore an array of issues or areas of interest and to identify issues that can be studied using quantitative methods. Because they reflect subjective (not objective) opinions and beliefs, qualitative data are sometimes called *soft data*. **Quantitative primary research** is original, objective research that consists of collecting numerical *hard data* for statistical analysis and generates information that is projectable (generalizable) to a population. Surveys (questionnaires), experiments, and observations are popular quantitative research methods.

Secondary research utilizes qualitative or quantitative studies previously conducted and published by others or draws on reports and data generated in-house for other purposes. Some studies compare the results of large numbers of secondary studies on the same topic. This type of *meta-analysis research* uses quantitative methods designed to improve objectivity, generalizability, and precision. Secondary research usually is less expensive than primary research, but sometimes it is not totally applicable because it was originally designed for other purposes, samples, or times. Secondary research consists of collecting *secondary data*.

Researchers sometimes use multiple methods in the same study. Employing several methods increases costs but often produces more substantive, objective, well-rounded results that provide an internal check on the methods used. For example, to find out why website visitors are abandoning their shopping basket orders before completing the transaction, researchers might use (1) a *pop-up survey* administered to every *n*th site visitor to the site's homepage, (2) *click stream analysis* (an operational data tool) to determine at what point most consumers abandon their baskets, (3) *email interviews* with every *n*th person who abandons a shopping basket to ask them directly

Quantitative primary research
Original, objective research that consists of collecting numerical data (sometimes called hard data) for statistical analysis.

Secondary research
Previously collected and published research found in-house or obtained from other sources.

what it would take to get them to complete their purchase, and (4) a *literature search* of previously published research on the topic to identify trends in shopping basket abandonment.

Marketing research is conducted online by many individuals and enterprises, including businesses, governments, universities, private nonprofit research centers, and nongovernmental organizations (NGOs). Some enterprises outsource marketing research by hiring consultants or research firms to perform the research for them; others do it in-house. Research is conducted on a regular basis or periodically as needed to solve a particular problem, deal with an emerging marketing crisis, or take advantage of an opportunity.

Marketing research on consumers, such as the P&G Whitestrips website marketing study, should contribute to the development of **consumer insight,** an in-depth understanding of what consumers need and want, as well as their product preferences and perceptions, past market behaviors, and possible future actions. Likewise, B2B marketers use research to develop insights about business buyers and markets, competitors' offers, and product gaps. One obvious difference between research on consumer and research on business buyers is that there are far more consumers than businesses. An online consumer survey may require a thousand or more respondents (subjects) to meet the statistical standards that govern research, whereas a business survey may involve only several hundred or even fewer. The online consumer research industry is far more visible than its business equivalent, which is more likely to produce proprietary results that are rarely if ever published. Many research consultants and companies have both consumer and enterprise clients; others focus entirely on one type.

Consumer insight
An in-depth understanding of consumers' needs and wants alternately change to wants, behaviors, and preferences.

THE RESEARCH PROCESS IS SYSTEMATIC

Both online and offline applied marketing research require the same careful, systematic process (Figure 7-2). The first step (*a*), clearly stating the problem or question, is often the most difficult. For example, a company facing an unexpected decline in website sales may use marketing research to find an answer to the question *Why have sales from our website declined in the past quarter?* Systematic research is needed to develop an explanation that can be substantiated and used with confidence in making decisions about how to do a better job satisfying consumer needs and increasing sales.

Once the problem is stated clearly and concisely, a research plan (*b*) is developed for answering the research question. The plan is a blueprint for how the research will be conducted. It states *who* is responsible for conducting the research, *when* the

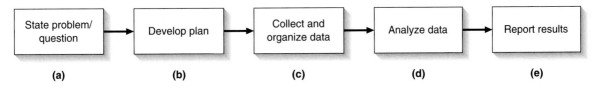

(a)   **(b)**   **(c)**   **(d)**   **(e)**

FIGURE 7-2 The Research Process
Marketing research is a systematic process.

research will take place, *what* methods will be used, *how* the data will be collected, *how much* is budgeted, *what timetable* will be followed, and *who* (departments, individuals) will receive the results. The plan governs data collection (*c*), the third step of the marketing research process. The Internet has made data collection far easier, faster, and cheaper than comparable offline methods. Data can be collected online in real time, with results input directly into data sets that can be grouped and analyzed electronically. The development of highly sophisticated operational data tools has created rich new data sources and complex data-mining methods. Next, data are analyzed (*d*) and transformed into usable information. Information is evaluated and transformed into knowledge for generating a report (*e*) that states the problem, addresses the research question, presents information, and provides recommendations on a course of action. At this point, it is up to decision makers (marketing managers and others) to evaluate the recommendations and implement appropriate responses.

THE ADVANTAGES AND DISADVANTAGES OF ONLINE RESEARCH

Even though taking marketing research online has many advantages, it is not appropriate for all marketing research methods, problems, researchers, subjects, or situations. However, most research experts agree that the benefits of conducting marketing research online far exceed its disadvantages. The clearest advantages of conducting online marketing research are related to ready access to samples, speed and time, convenience, cost, and technology. Its limitations include nonrepresentative samples, costs, technical obstacles, click-aways, and dishonesty.

The Internet's unique structure means researchers can increase sample sizes cheaply and quickly. Research consultancies such as Millward Brown can create a randomized sample of several thousand survey respondents drawn from hundreds of thousands or even millions of people who have voluntarily opted in to become panel members. Samples and subsamples of these magnitudes tend to wash out extreme deviations from the norm. Because of the Internet's reach, samples can easily be formed to include multinational and multiethnic participants. Researchers can use the Internet to contact respondents later for follow-up questions, something that is exorbitantly expensive—and rarely attempted—offline. Multiple contacts can verify responses and form the basis for longitudinal (long-term) studies that retest the same people (or others like them) repeatedly over long periods of time.

Speed is a significant advantage of online research. Surveys can be emailed anytime, received almost immediately, and replied to in real time. It is not uncommon to have results available in less than twenty-four hours, which provides a significant time advantage over traditional mailed surveys. Web surveys are available for respondents to complete 24/7/365.

Convenience is another advantage that online research offers. Online focus group members can participate from home, work, or public wi-fi facilities at airport or hotel cyberports, or via handheld device connecting from an airplane or train. They do not have to travel physically to a focus group location. Costs are reduced if facilities do not have to be provided or travel reimbursed.

Technology is also an advantage. Web surveys can be tabulated continuously as respondents submit them and analyzed by sophisticated software. Web and email survey returns are faster and response rates are higher than for traditional offline methods. Focus group responses can immediately enter databases electronically, which reduces the errors that tend to occur with mechanical data entry. The Internet's electronic reach means that consumers worldwide can participate in research activities; traditional methods are far more place-bound.

Online research also has drawbacks, however. One obvious drawback is that online samples are not completely representative of the population at large. The differences are dwindling, however, and online and offline populations have become almost mirror images of each other. Online research excludes those who do not use the Internet unless an effort is made to include them using traditional methods. The problem of nonrepresentativeness has declined now that about 75 percent of the U.S. population uses the Internet. In addition, Internet-based marketing research can reach certain underrepresentated groups that are far more difficult to contact via traditional offline channels.

Another disadvantage is cost. For example, both online and offline focus groups are expensive, because while travel and facility costs disappear online, technology costs can be high. Email surveys often require the rental of email address lists from a list broker and permission to distribute the surveys and collect returns. Larger numbers of surveys may be needed because spam blockers and email filters may block email surveys, or email survey recipients may mistakenly identify the message as spam and delete it. Web surveys have setup and operational costs. Other technical obstacles include networks that go offline and software that crashes and prematurely terminates online sessions.

Other disadvantages also exist. Participants in online focus groups or survey respondents may get bored with all the typing required or find it stressful to keep up with a typed conversation and hence may *click away*, terminating the session by clicking off the site. It is far easier to leave an online focus group than physically to leave the room while a traditional focus group is in progress. Finally, online anonymity may encourage participants to take on personas and make responses that are dishonest or misleading. Even with these disadvantages, online marketing research is a growth industry, where the benefits outweigh the costs for most marketing research in most situations.

Conducting Primary Marketing Research

Marketing is an information-intensive activity. Marketers regularly gather information to monitor what is happening to their product offers, customers, and competitors and to the environment. Primary research can employ qualitative and/or quantitative methods.

QUALITATIVE RESEARCH METHODS

Qualitative methods, particularly focus groups, brainstorming, interviews, and communication content analysis, help marketers to learn in-depth what consumers think and to understand their perceptions of product offers, their reactions to proposed new products or changes in existing offers, and their responses to competitors' offers. Most popular traditional qualitative marketing research methods have been adapted for Internet use.

Focus groups
Qualitative marketing research that uses small numbers of subjects for directed moderated discussions of a marketing topic; also known online as cyber groups, egroups, virtual groups, and focus chats.

ONLINE FOCUS GROUPS   **Focus groups** are the most popular primary qualitative research method. Online they are also called cyber groups, egroups, virtual groups, and focus chats. The focus group method was developed in 1941 by Columbia University's Robert King Merton, who asked participants in studies of preferences among radio programs to remain after the sessions and *focus* on what they liked or disliked about the programs.[4]

The first online focus groups were formed in 1994 and used chat room technology. A small number of consumers, usually seven to fourteen, assembled online and chatted about marketing topics in real time with one another and a moderator. Responses were typed and appeared onscreen, identified by the contributor's name or alias. Text-only focus groups are still used, but focus group technology has advanced and now may include text, sound, and images pushed to participants' browser screens by the moderator.

Focus groups are used for every imaginable topic, from learning how participants use a product to what they like and what they do not like about banner advertising or a particular website. They are used for new product concept testing, website usability assessments, and determination of product pricing preferences. It is very risky to rely on insights gained from only one focus group because the results represent subjective opinions from a small number of people. Results from multiple groups provide a better perspective, but they still reflect a small sample that is representative only of the Internet-using population at that time.

Online focus group participants can be recruited through email announcements and pop-up website online intercepts; they are selected from prescreened pools of volunteers who may receive small regular or periodic cash incentives for participating. Opt-in volunteers complete online registration forms and provide demographic (age, marital status, household income, education), lifestyle (products used, hobbies, vacation preferences), and transaction (product preferences, brand preferences, purchase situation) information.

Some online marketing research companies maintain enormous pools of prescreened subjects from which they can quickly draw a focus group subset. Greenfield Online (*http://greenfield.com*), a business unit of Greenfield Consulting Group, has over 3.4 million double opt-in panelists, including multiethnic and multinational participants, and runs focus groups through its iTracks (*http://greenfield.com/ products/fieldwork/qualitativehosting.asp*) research tool. Subjects are selected for a group because they share characteristics relevant to the topic being researched—such characteristics as age, gender, purchasing habits, attitudes, lifestyle, or product usage. Greenfield Online offers graphics, videos, 3-D, and other enhancements for testing consumer responses. Greenfield is a member of the Millward Brown family of research companies.

Focus group members log on from their homes, work, or other locations and go directly to a website secured from unwanted visitors. Because the groups are conducted entirely online, participants can be anywhere in the world. Once selected for a group, they are given a valid password to enter the firewall-protected chat room. Once logged into the virtual facility, they see either an online chat message board (for text-only focus groups) or a screen that is split for text, graphics, and video. Split screens display product pictures, product concept drawings, print or video advertisements, or even animated 3-D images. Typed discussion occurs on the other half-screen. *Real-time* focus group sessions typically last 60 to 120 minutes and cover thirty to forty-five prepared questions. *Message board* focus groups can last several days, so participants can consider their responses and build on posted discussion threads. A trained moderator directs the discussion, begins new threads, maintains focus, and (if necessary) expels rowdy participants. The moderator elicits comments about what consumers think and feel. Technical support behind the scenes makes sure the software and the session run smoothly. One clear advantage of online focus groups is that researchers can communicate with the moderator at any time to interject questions or change direction. Internet video conferencing can transmit focus group discussions in real time for analysis in remote locations.

A recent study by the Qualitative Research Consultants Association (QRCA at *www.qrca.org*), a nonprofit organization that promotes qualitative research, concluded that many companies already use online focus groups, and their numbers are increasing. QRCA researchers compiled a list of the advantages of using online focus groups. They include having a wider market for obtaining subjects, greater access to difficult-to-reach groups (gays and lesbians, college students, mothers with babies, and others), anonymity that can encourage more candid responses, greater cost-effectiveness through the elimination of travel and facility rentals, and rapid reporting of results (clients can receive full transcripts of a session almost immediately after it ends).

Online focus groups also have disadvantages. Among them are the lack of nonverbal communication cues (body language and other visual and auditory responses), shallowness of responses, difficulty in following the discussion when subjects talk (type) over one another, nonrepresentativeness because Internet access is not universal, and the fact that anonymity can encourage dishonesty. A person whose real identity is not known may not hesitate to invent one and give dishonest responses.[5]

Live video cameras (cams) will eventually make possible the observation of nonverbal communication, thus overcoming the absence of nonverbal cues, and voice commands will eventually replace typing. Those who do not use the Internet will continue to be excluded, even though the Internet population closely mirrors the offline population and is growing. Videocams may reduce the "false identity" problem, but dishonest responses can never be completely eliminated online or offline. Recruiting larger numbers of participants can minimize the effects of discrepant response, but this increases costs.

Still other shortcomings were not mentioned in the QRCA study. Given the current state of technology, a skilled technician must be available to resolve technical problems whenever a group is conducted, which increases costs. Online group moderators must have both technical and moderator skills, and when these skills are deficient, group outcomes can be flawed. Responses are typed, which excludes some disabled consumers and people who can't type. Even reasonably good typists may tire if the session is too long, which can lead to premature departures (click-aways) from the group. Message board sessions can drive off participants who lose interest.

The low cost of online focus group sessions, as little as US$3,500 per session, makes them highly attractive. However, it is unlikely that online focus groups will ever completely replace offline groups, because in some cases it is extremely important to see focus group participants' facial expressions and body language as they make or hear others' comments. Some topics are better suited to either offline or online sessions, so both will certainly continue to be used.

Brainstorming
A marketing research method that encourages group participants to spontaneously generate ideas about issues or problems.

ONLINE BRAINSTORMING   Brainstorming, or the spontaneous generation of ideas, encourages group participants to share opinions and come up with creative responses to issues or problems. This technique was developed in the 1930s by Alex Osborn, long before the Internet's creation, let alone its commercialization.[6]

Online brainstorming uses the same techniques as its offline equivalent but allows for the development of ideas over several hours, days, weeks, and sometimes months. Participants are invited to join a brainstorming session through approximately the same selection process used for focus groups. Participants are given a password that admits them to a private firewall-protected website. A trained facilitator (moderator) begins a discussion thread to focus participant ideas and postings. For example, the facilitator might type *Describe the perfect home entertainment center, one that suits your every home entertainment need.* Participants begin typing their ideas as rapidly as they can. They are identified by self-selected nicknames. For example, Big Momma types *It's got to be big enough for a really, really big TV.* Billy Boy types *It takes up a wall in my family room, floor to ceiling.* Daddy O types *It has a special shelf to store movies so you can see the title on the end of the box.* Tiny types *It has an Internet connection so I can watch TV and surf the Net at the same time.*

The facilitator monitors the session and can enter the idea generation stream at any point to guide the expression of ideas or ask new questions (start a new thread). For example, the facilitator may interject with such questions as *Where exactly do you store movies in your home entertainment center? How tall is the center? Where does the TV sit? Where is it in your house? How does it make you feel when you're using it? What slogan would you use in advertising the entertainment center in television and print advertisements?* Each participant adds a thought or opinion to the threads at his or her leisure. Contributions are visible to all participants, and they are encouraged to build on previous ideas. Contributions can be monitored by others without participants' knowledge. Responses are identified by participants' nicknames (pseudonyms), by a first and last name, by initials, or by an alias developed specifically for the brainstorming session.

Greenfield Consulting Group's (*www.greenfieldgroup.com/ideastation.asp*) IdeaStation is an interactive, real-time brainstorming system. It uses a threaded response format wherein participants can build on ideas. The moderator can add graphics, audio, or video, and sessions can build in visits to websites so participants can review and comment on their content or usability. Online brainstorming has been used for many purposes. For example, consumers were invited to generate ideas for new products and brand direction for a major U.S. beverage maker. More than a thousand ideas were contributed by three hundred consumers over a four- to five-day brainstorming period. Their ideas helped the company decide on product names, descriptions, and how to market the products.[7]

Online brainstorming is subject to many of the same problems as online focus groups. The researcher is still dealing with a small group, typically numbering in the low teens, and it can be very costly to run multiple sessions. The ideas may be useful, or they may not be, and interpretation is highly subjective. Screening is required to keep the group in line and avoid negative comments that can stop the session dead in its tracks. The facilitator must be trained to be firm in handling—or even disconnecting—raucous participants. Technical problems can interrupt a session, and there is no way to stop a member from clicking away before a session ends.

Voice Over Internet
Transmitting voice calls and fax over the Internet.

ONLINE INTERVIEWS   Initially, slow dial-up speeds hampered the use of online interviews. Now, thanks to greater use of high-speed dial-up and broadband access, and to such advances as **Voice Over Internet (VoIP or VOIP),** transmitting voice or fax over the Internet, online interviews are more feasible and cost-effective. Greenfield Group offers a variant on the face-to-face interview that combines personal telephone calls with websites where participants can view and experience various marketing offers while being interviewed. WETI, Web-Enabled Telephone Interviews (*www.greenfieldgroup.com/weti.asp*), generally last from thirty to sixty minutes, during which the moderator and participant view the same site. The moderator can push visual stimuli to the participant and then ask questions about them. This technology reduces interview costs, expands the participant base worldwide, saves time, and eliminates travel expenses.[8]

The video online interview (VOI) is a tool often used by executive recruiters and for online chats with business executives. Interviews can be simultaneously broadcast (multicast) to different locations as well as taped for playback. If bandwidth capacity is not high enough, however, images are warped and jerky, and a several-second delay distorts sounds. These problems will be resolved as bandwidth increases and video online systems improve.

ONLINE CONTENT ANALYSIS OF CHAT, BLOG, FEEDBACK, AND SEARCH

Online content analysis
A qualitative research method that systematically examines, categorizes, and analyzes online communication.

Online content analysis is a qualitative research method that systematically examines, categorizes, and analyzes online communications, such as statements made in chat rooms, on interactive blogs, on website feedback forms, on search lists, and in other forums where large numbers of Internet users communicate. Statements can be written (text), verbal (audio), or even graphical images. The researcher creates a dictionary with rules (mathematical algorithms) that cluster words and phrases into preestablished categories. Constraints clarify how the statements are classified. Items are coded and placed in the categories, and statistical analysis explicates relationships and trends. Software can be used to implement the algorithms, group statements, and analyze results. The hope is that online content analysis will lead to predictive accuracy in spotting gaps in a market, product usage trends, and commercial opportunities. Content analysis software is already used online to analyze **word bursts,** words or phrases that appear frequently in online communications.[9]

Word bursts
Words or phrases that appear frequently in online communications.

Chat room
A place online where people can communicate with others by typing messages that are displayed on their screens almost instantaneously.

A **chat room** is a website or service where participants can communicate with others by typing text that is displayed almost instantly on other chatters' screens. Some rooms also facilitate graphics, sound, and videos. These online forums are active 24/7/365, and participants use them to discuss a myriad of topics. Researchers can content-analyze discussions in Usenet groups, Yahoo! chat rooms, and other forums to develop consumer insight, spot trends, uncover problems, identify opinion leaders, and track discussion threads. The unobtrusive nature of the research is a considerable advantage. Participants do not realize their comments are being observed and recorded, so the assumption is that their statements are more valuable because they are speaking freely. However, anonymity can lead some participants to assume personas unlike their real selves and to make statements that they would never make using their real names. Furthermore, even though chats are public forums, performing this type of research without participants' knowledge has serious privacy and ethical implications. Marketing research companies claim they don't use high-tech tracking to discover the real identities of chat participants, but unscrupulous researchers have no qualms about doing so.

Blog
A journal or diary published online.

Blogger
An individual who creates and/or hosts a blog.

Some of the same people who chat also provide feedback to **blogs,** online journals or diaries where the owner records his or her thoughts, posts images, collects feedback, and provides links to other sites. The most popular blogs are interactive and encourage feedback from readers. Like chats, statements by the **blogger** (the individual who creates and hosts a blog) and blog discussants can be content-analyzed.

Website feedback forms are another mechanism for collecting communications—in this case, the comments of visitors to a website. These forms typically require the respondent to provide a working email address for a reply, so anonymity is not present. Email feedback collects statements from people who are motivated to communicate with the enterprise, and thus they may represent extreme or unique views, particularly negative ones. Communicating via feedback form is more likely to have a narrowly company-, problem-, or website-specific focus. Important information can be culled from comments when they address website functionality, such as *Your navigation buttons aren't working* or *The link to the homepage from the shopping basket page is broken.*

Search engine buzz
Words or phrases used frequently as descriptors on search engines.

Search engine buzz, words or phrases used frequently as descriptors for search engine searches, are often reported on the major engines. Google compiles and offers them in its Zeitgeist (*www.google.com/press/zeitgeist.html*), which lists search patterns, trends, and surprises. Yahoo! has its Buzz Index (*http://buzz.yahoo.com/*) of top searches, as does Ask Jeeves (*www.jeevesiq.com/docs/about/jeevesiq.html*). Trend spotters frequent these sites looking for interest patterns.

Google Zeitgeist

Google Zeitgeist is full of interesting information that may interest marketers.

Source: Copyright © 2004 by Google.com. Reprint with permission.

Communication researchers, particularly in chat rooms and on blogs, seek out opinion leaders and monitor their comments because opinion leaders have a powerful influence on others. An opinion leader can sway many times more people than an ordinary discussion participant. Sophisticated mathematical algorithmic models identify opinion leaders by the quantity and content of their postings. Comments to Howard Dean's *Blog for America* (*www.blogforamerica.com*) during the 2004 presidential primary were carefully analyzed for insights into voter preferences and future behaviors. Chat analysis has been used extensively in online financial discussion groups to measure consumer interest in various companies and their stocks. It has been used to analyze consumer comments about automobiles at Edmunds.com's Town Hall (*http://townhall.edmunds.com/TH/townhall*) to learn what brands consumers cross-shop and the features they most value. Conversation-tracking software identifies the most relevant conversation threads and develops consumer profiles from the content. Chat analysis has even been used to evaluate chat library reference services where library patrons can converse online with a librarian in real-time, asking questions and receiving reference guidance.[10]

QUANTITATIVE RESEARCH METHODS

Quantitative research methods include surveys, which are by far the most popular primary research method. Surveys are highly versatile and can accommodate variable numbers of subjects from a handful to thousands or more.

Survey

A primary quantitative marketing research method that uses a set of questions to collect specific information from respondents.

ONLINE MARKETING SURVEYS   A **survey** (or questionnaire) is a quantitative research method that uses a set of questions to collect specific information from respondents who may be site visitors, buyers, businesses, institutions, organizations, or others. The first recorded U.S. survey was the 1790 United States Census. Although census surveys have been conducted every ten years since, survey research did not become popular, particularly in marketing, until after World War II, when the growth of the mass market and the need to understand consumer behavior spurred the development of more sophisticated survey forms and statistical methods to analyze results. Today surveys are ubiquitous and consumers are hard-pressed to escape them, particularly when they pop up unexpectedly on their browser screen. Surveys are administered on the Web and by email, which includes web mail, as well as on intranets and extranets. *Inside Research,* a marketing research industry newsletter, estimates that 23.6 percent of all marketing research spending in 2003 involved Internet surveys, up from 10 percent in 2000. It is projected to rise to 33 percent by 2006.[11]

Email surveys are sent in an email message, which is also returned to the sender by email. Alternatively, email recipients may be directed to a website where they complete the survey. The hot link to the survey site is included in the email invitation. Members of research panels, such as those run by Greenfield Online, allow panel members to sign up for website surveys if they fit the characteristics required. Many web surveys are pop-ups that appear on the visitor's computer screen in a separate minipage. Others are embedded within a web page, and sometimes the visitor must answer survey questions in order to gain access to a site. The latter type of survey, which demands information as the price of entry, is irritating and can elicit retaliatory trash answers rather than useful data.

Online standardized form surveys are simple to take, code, and analyze. They are very inexpensive compared to mail and telephone surveys, both of which have declining response rates. Questions can be closed-ended (preprogrammed numerical or restrained choice) or open-ended (unrestrained written comments). Survey software can be programmed to intercept every nth site visitor to draw a random sample of a predefined population. For example, while writing this chapter, an online pop-up survey

WEB UPDATE

For updates and
more on this topic,
visit the textbook
student website at:
http://college.hmco
.com/business/students
and select Siegel,
Internet Marketing, 2e.
Online Research

at the weather site Intellicast.com (*www.intellicast.com*) appeared. The survey contained two categories of questions. The first had seventeen questions about using the site in planning activities or hobbies; the second (thirteen questions) asked about using the site for business applications. Each question had a five-point Likert-type scale with responses for using the site that included *Never, Several Times a Year, Several Times a Month, Several Times a Week,* and *Almost Daily.* The survey took less than a minute to complete, and when it was submitted, a thank-you screen popped up and stated that the survey information would be used to help Intellicast "prioritize and focus its effort on new products, content, and applications that meet your interests." Closing the survey page returned the recipient to the weather forecast page; thus survey respondents never leave the host site.

Response rates for online surveys are higher than for traditional surveys. They can be as high as 95 percent returns versus an average of 5 to 15 percent for mail surveys and about 14 percent for telephone surveys.[12]

The cost of administering an online survey is significantly lower than that of traditional surveys. Harris Interactive, Inc. (*www.harrisinteractive.com*) reports that whereas a traditional large-scale telephone survey can easily cost US$300,000 or more, a comparable online survey can cost US$50,000 or less. The SBA (*www.sba.gov*) estimates that small businesses can conduct telephone surveys for anywhere from US$5,000 to US$25,000. An online survey costs far less. A typical mail survey costs around US$1.56 per survey; a fax survey costs US$0.56, and both email and web surveys cost an estimated US$0.01 per participant. Zoomerang (*www.zoomerang.com/login/index.zgi*), a MarketTools, Inc. business unit, offers free use of a simplified version of its powerful Internet-based survey software. Users can design a simple survey, distribute it, and analyze results in real time. An online tutorial (*http://info.zoomerang.com/quicktour.htm*) explains the process. The company also sells more complex versions of its software and professional assistance. By 2003, the company had launched over 500,000 of its surveys. Match.com (*http://match.com*), a subscription-based online dating service, used Zoomerang in 2003 for a gift-giving survey of its members. Over 85 percent of survey respondents reported that gifts are important clues to a person's personality and that Valentine's Day gifts indicate the giver's generosity (42 percent), creativity (64 percent), and loving nature (53 percent).

Online surveys produce results rapidly. For example, worldwide marketing research consultancy Harris Interactive surveyed one thousand consumers for an advertising client and returned results in twenty-four hours, a response time impossible to match using traditional mail survey methods.[13] An online survey can be transmitted to participants in real time (almost instantaneously) when an existing email distribution list is used. With mail surveys, by comparison, it may take a month or more to send the initial surveys, collect the first wave of returns, send out reminder postcards (or a second mailing), and then wait for the second wave of returns. With email surveys, reminders are sent easily and quickly, and follow-up questions can be used. Online surveys are flexible and can be modified for different subsets of the respondent population. Survey data can be entered into a database automatically and without input errors, and computations are continuously updated.

Experience has shown that online product-specific survey results are more trustworthy than opinion surveys, which can attract participants with radical views. Although there were initial concerns about reliability and validity, recent research indicates that offline and online surveys are comparable on these measures.

Despite the enthusiasm for online surveys, some cautions are in order. The hardware and software can be costly, at least initially. Because online surveys are self-administered, any confusion over instructions can result in incomplete or inaccurate data collection. Because many web surveys use convenience samples, self-selection bias can skew results. Participants must be online, which eliminates those who are not; therefore, results can be generalized only to populations currently online. Consumers are more likely to disconnect from overly long surveys. Multiple surveys can be taken by the same person, unless stringent admission controls are in place.

Web surveys should be designed without graphically intense formats that slow download times and discourage respondents from completing them. Surveys that require linking to multiple pages also should be avoided, because they can frustrate respondents who are using slow modem connections. To ensure privacy, a *clear form* or *reset* button should remove input data after the completed survey is sent. Encryption should be used for the secure transmission of responses. Surveys should be encrypted and most use HyperText Transfer Protocol over Secure Socket Layer (HTTPS). Returned surveys should also be encrypted by HTTP over SSL.

Just as in offline surveys, there is a debate over whether to offer incentives. Some surveys offer respondents money, prizes, tee shirts, or other small incentives to participate. It is unclear whether consumers who participate in online surveys without incentives differ significantly from those who participate only when incentives are offered.

SRI Consulting Business Intelligence (*http://www.sric-bi.com/VALS/*) has been collecting Values and Lifestyles Survey (VALS) data online since the mid-1990s and offline since 1978, when the first VALS survey was introduced. VALS2, released in 1989, is the model for online VALS. VALS data are used to identify adult consumer target markets, to position products, to match consumer types with media preferences, and to aid in the development of marketing strategies and new products. Adult participants are typed by their resources (demographics) and lifestyles (psychographics) into mutually exclusive groups that provide insight into factors that motivate purchases. Participants self-select to take the VALS online survey. Their only reward is learning their VALS type—actualizer, fulfilled, achiever, experiencer, believer, striver, maker, or struggler. Meanwhile, SRI is collecting an enormous amount of data that are highly attractive to consumer product marketers.

Survey results are also sold by commercial research firms. Syndicated online research is jointly sponsored by businesses in the same industry with similar research interests, which thus share the cost of what is often a very expensive activity. The level of analysis typically is the industry or sector. Although participants share the data, reports are tailored to the specific needs of each sponsor. Maritz, Inc. (*www.maritz.com*) and Forrester Research (*www.forrester.com*) are two companies that perform and sell syndicated research.

ONLINE PANELS   Online panels, or epanels, take several forms. Sometimes panels are called group interviews or even focus groups, but this is misleading. Many online panels use surveys to generate reviews and therefore, act as a quantitative research method. However, panels may also collect consumer opinions by monitoring chat room and online discussions and asking visitors to post open-ended opinions to research questions, which are qualitative methods. Online panels are something of a hybrid method, but they are considered here because their principal research method is the survey.

Most online panels are opt-in. Individuals are recruited by email, are intercepted when they visit a website, or click through from a pop-up advertisement. Many panels use a *convenience sample,* selecting participants because they are available. Some research firms maintain large pools of willing prescreened participants, often hundreds of thousands or even millions of consumers. Because demographic and behavioral information is collected from these panel members, a *purposive sample* can be drawn. A purposive sample is a group with specific characteristics that are found in the population being studied. For example, a panel may require that participants be housewives, 25 to 45 years old, college educated, and with two children living at home. A different panel might require college students, males and females, 18 to 22 years old, and not living in a dormitory or at home with parents. Companies with large numbers of panel members can select a stratified random sample of panelists from their member pools. Only consumers with characteristics appropriate to the research topic are allowed to complete the surveys. For example, Greenfield's Health & Wellness panel (*www.greenfield.com/panel/americas/healthcare.asp*) of more than 3.1 million U.S. member households and over 3.4 million globally is used to survey consumers with any of twenty-two different disease states that require specific medications. A stratified random sample of these pre-identified sufferers can be quickly recruited to participate in marketing studies for pharmaceutical companies, health care groups, or wellness organizations.

ONLINE REVIEWS   Online reviews, a far less rigorous, nonscientific variant of the panel, still can offer insights into what consumers are thinking and doing. Consumers self-select to provide written opinions of products using a variety of responses, which can be as simple as a yes/no response to the question *Would you recommend this product to others?* Responses often are in the form of stars, from five or more stars (an exceptional rating) to a zero or no stars. Alternatively, reviews can be extended written summaries of product use. Comments are often aggregated, analyzed, and the results sent to client companies. Representative comments are posted on the host website. Epinions (*www.epinions.com*) has collected over a million consumer reviews of over two million products in more than thirty product categories from books and movies to cellular telephones and ski resorts. It provides both monetary and nonmonetary incentives for consumers if their reviews are read by site visitors.

CONJOINT ANALYSIS   Participants in conjoint or tradeoff analysis are exposed to a situation where they have to make choices, trading off factors to reach a desired end. This method can help determine what people value in different product features or service attributes. It is often used in automobile feature testing to find out what features consumers are willing to give up in order to get something they value more, perhaps forgoing a car compact disc player for side panel air bags. Outcomes help guide new product design, decisions about redesigning or repositioning old products, and pricing. Conjoint was first used in marketing research in the mid-1960s and is based on psychometric research conducted at Bell Labs, Princeton, and other academic institutions. Conjoint analysis is used in the travel industry to determine how much consumers are willing to pay for a ticket in order to get more leg room on an airplane. It is used in pharmaceuticals to determine whether consumers prefer aspirin or acetaminophen, gel caps or uncoated tablets, for pain relief or to reduce inflammation.

Sample sizes for online conjoint analysis studies can be relatively small, from 200 to 300 participants. ConjointOnline (*www.conjointonline.com*), a unit of Kingsley Research, Inc., has been conducting online conjoint analysis interviews since 1992. Online conjoint analysis is also used to match midlevel career changers to job types. Like other online primary research methods, these methods claim to be better, faster, and cheaper than their offline equivalents.

Lands' End (*www.landsend.com*) uses conjoint analysis in its *My Personal Shopper* feature. Consumers call up the web page (*www.landsend.com/cgi-bin/vpsEntry .cgi?sid=8900065977889191090*) and use conjoint to register their *Quick Preferences* and create their own personal profile of apparel preferences. The Personal Shopper database uses this information to make decisions about what apparel choices should be pushed to the consumer's browser screen. The first question asked is about *size* (regular, petite, plus, or tall); next is *occasion*, work or leisure; and then, body shape. The next screen begins the tradeoff by asking the consumer to select options. Two alternative apparel choices, A and B, are shown on the screen. The consumer then selects one of the following alternatives on each of the following six screens.

- I like A, I would not wear B
- I like A somewhat more than B
- No preference
- I like B somewhat more than A
- I like B, I would not wear A

The next screen shows a different pair of outfits for A and B and offers the same set of responses to choose among. After progressing through the six choice screens, the consumer is asked to select from among sets of "special considerations." These include types of fabric preferred, colors, and styling. Finally, the Personal Shopper pushes some suggestions to the consumer's screen. Of course, *My Personal Shopper* is not a real person. It is a sophisticated software program that trades off the consumer's choices to arrive at optimal product alternatives. Data collected from large numbers of conjoint choices can be used in product development and promotion.

Secondary Marketing Research Online

The Internet makes so much secondary data available that it is a virtual gold mine of information for marketing research. At the same time, there is far too much information for most people to sort through, so it is a challenge to find what is needed. Small and midsize businesses can perform secondary research online, although many pay someone else to do it instead, if they do it at all. Because most secondary research involves previously published studies, care must be taken to avoid copyright infringement.

THE BASICS OF SECONDARY RESEARCH

Secondary research uses internal information as well as external research published by others, public data sources, and various directories, rankings, and periodicals. It can save time and money, but it can also be unusable if the information is old, is inaccurate, is at the wrong level of analysis, uses a different subject group from what is needed, or comes from unreliable and/or biased sources. Secondary research results often provide direction for the development of primary research. The basic research process is the same for both primary and secondary research.

Anyone conducting online secondary research must carefully check sources. Appendix B on the textbook website considers source accuracy at length, so only a few cautions will be offered here. With any data downloaded from the Web, it is a challenge to determine reliability and value, and whether the information can be used with confidence. Anyone can publish almost anything on the Web with relatively little effort. Currently, there are no standards or fact editors, so evaluating the reliability of information is absolutely essential. The Web is an endless trough of information, yet not all web-based information is worth having or using.

The quantity of information online also presents a problem. There is a vast and growing information glut: at this writing, there are an estimated several billion unique publicly accessible web pages and five billion pages in the invisible Web, or **deep Web.** Even the best search engine can access less than one percent of the accessible pages. Deep websites are inaccessible to most search engines and to the public because they are on intranets or extranets. Some deep websites use technology that search engines cannot penetrate, while others are blocked because a subscription or registration is required to access protected pages. Quality and quantity issues force many companies to turn to professional data librarians, whose efforts still must be guided by a marketing research plan.

Deep Web
Websites inaccessible to most search engines.

DeepPlanet (*http://aip.completeplanet.com*) searches much of the deep Web. It calls itself the front door to the deep Web.[14]

SECONDARY RESEARCH METHODS

Secondary research results are available in a variety of forms. They are published in academic journals; released by governments, universities, foundations, or think tanks; archived by professional associations; or disseminated by organizations. Traditionally, a researcher identifies useful secondary sources, contacts the sources or accesses them in an online library or other facility, *pulls* the content to his or her computer, and evaluates the contents for applicability to the research problem. Alternatively, the source is identified and linked through a search engine or other intermediary.

eMarketer

eMarketer pushes secondary research data to willing opt-in recipients.
Source: Courtesy eMarketer.com.

A second method takes advantage of the Internet's unique interactivity. For example, research companies such as McKinsey & Co. (*www.mckinseyquarterly.com*) and eMarketer (*www.emarketer.com*) *push* opt-in emails or newsletters with announcements about current research to interested opt-in email users. Pushed content is designed to motivate the receiver to click through to the website and buy the report and/or establish a relationship with the research company that may someday result in a transaction. Most research newsletters are sent on a monthly or bi-weekly schedule and are powerful promotion tools for the owner's research products.

SECONDARY RESEARCH SOURCES

Despite obvious shortcomings, online secondary research can uncover studies, reports, and databases that provide valuable information for use in making marketing decisions. Marketers have a broad array of online secondary sources to use, including governments, businesses, professional groups, and organizations.

Government sources   The U.S. government, the largest data collector in the world, hosts a vast number of web pages with free information and some that require a subscription and nominal fee. FirstGov (*www.firstgov.gov*), the U.S. government web portal, has links on the homepage to business statistics, trade information, patents, copyrights, and government resources. It hosts gateways (portals) for citizens, businesses, and governments. EDGAR (*www.sec.gov/edgar.shtml*) is a popular site for business students looking for SEC filings.

State and local governments often provide useful information from their websites. The Library of Congress has a meta-index for state and local government information (*www.lcweb.loc.gov/global/state*) as well as state links. The European Union's website (*www.europa.eu.int*) offers news, activities, and official documents. The United Kingdom's open.gov.uk (*www.open.gov.uk*) is a portal to all its government sites and "the easy way to government information and services online." It promises citizens that they will be able to do all their business with government online by 2005. The Australian government portal (*www.australia.gov.au/*) is a massive site with links to all aspects of Australian business and society and to Australian Commonwealth government information.

International sources   Most international organizations offer data and documents online as well as links to other resources. Notable among this group are the United Nations (*www.un.org*), the Organization for Economic Cooperation and Development (*www.oecd.org/home/*), the World Trade Organization (*www.wto.org*), the World Bank (*www.worldbank.org*), and the International Monetary Fund (*www.imf.org*). Other websites provide information for the public sector, nongovernmental organizations (NGOs), and for nonprofit marketers.

Periodicals and other business sources   Although some online periodicals require subscriptions, many still offer some free content at the entry level of their site. *Brandweek* (*www.brandweek.com*) has media news, directories, and links to other marketing publications. Some information is free; access to other pages requires a paid subscription. Other sites with current business news include the *Wall Street Journal Online* (*www.wsj.com*), *Advertising Age* (*www.adage.com*), and the *New York*

Times Online (*http://nytimes.com*). Current company information is available from such sources as Hoover's Online (*www.hoovers.com*) and CorporateInformation.com (*www.corporateinformation.com*). Many businesses offer free information online as an incentive designed to pull visitors deeper into their site. Dun & Bradstreet (*www.dnb.com/us/*) has a resource center with timely information as well as the list of D&B D-U-N-S number holders. Internet.com (*www.internet.com*) concentrates on Internet and IT information.

Universities   Many universities host data-rich research center sites. Purdue University's CIBERWeb (*http://ciber.centers.purdue.edu*) hosts a portal with links to U.S. Centers for International Business Education and Research (CIBER). Many universities store working papers online. Vanderbilt University's Sloan Center for Internet Retailing has eLab (*http://elab.vanderbilt.edu*), founded in 1994 to study the marketing implications of web commercialization. It is a particularly rich site for marketers. The University of Texas hosts Advertising World (*http://advertising.utexas.edu/world/index.asp/*), which calls itself *The Ultimate Marketing Communication Directory*.

Professionals and professional organizations   Professionals and professional organizations often publish secondary research online. A portal for online marketing professional associations, maintained at Tilburg University (*www.tilburguniversity.nl/faculties/few/marketing/links/journal1.html*), has U.S. and international links of interest to marketing professionals. Some associations offer reports and publications; others sponsor meetings and seminars. Many have links to related marketing sites and job listings.

Online Marketing Research Issues

Conducting marketing research online raises a number of important issues. Internet marketers who perform, access, or purchase research online ignore these issues at their peril.

RISKS

Marketing researchers face risks involving samples, content, methods, bias, and results. If these risks are not avoided or at least anticipated and accounted for, the consequences can be research results that are worthless at best and at worst, are seriously misleading.

Sample risk   Sample risk is the danger of collecting information from the wrong respondents—people or businesses that do not represent the market or have extreme and unique views. A variant is collecting information from such a small number of people that results are skewed or collecting information from too large a sample and being overwhelmed by the quantity of responses. Marketing research conducted on samples of Internet users automatically runs the risk of being unrepresentative of the entire population. Convenience samples can be risky if they are not representative of the population being studied.

Content risk   Content risk occurs when researchers ask the wrong questions or too many questions, causing participants to click away, or ask too few questions or questions that do not cover the topic adequately.

Methods risk   Methods risk occurs when an inappropriate research method is used or the right method is used incorrectly.

Bias risk   Bias risk occurs when data are mishandled such that they are no longer reliable. Bias can be minimized by using sufficiently large, appropriate samples.

Results risk   Results risk is the danger of collecting a large amount of information and not being able to make sense of it, trying to analyze it statistically but using the wrong test or using the right test and misinterpreting the results, or conveying the results to the wrong decision maker.

Small or midsize Internet marketers may have no choice but to perform their own online research. If so, they can help avoid or minimize risk by seeking assistance from a local small business development center (SBDC) or from the marketing department in a nearby comprehensive university, or by hiring a reputable marketing research consultant. SBDCs typically have staff members who can advise clients about acceptable research methods. Marketing majors may be able to help develop and administer an online survey, run an online focus group or brainstorming session, evaluate complaints collected in a *suggestion box* located on the owner's website, or conduct secondary research. Another alternative is to go online and look for research tutorials or books on Internet marketing research at an online bookseller. StatPac (*www.statpac.com/surveys*) has a free tutorial on questionnaires, survey design, and marketing research. SurveySite (*www.surveysite .com*) offers online demonstrations of various marketing research methods. Listing these sites, of course, does not represent an endorsement of their services.

MARKETING RESEARCH ETHICS

The ease of collecting information online, coupled with the large numbers of available research participants, makes the Internet an attractive place for sociologists, psychologists, anthropologists, and marketing researchers. At this time, no widely accepted guidelines for conducting online consumer research exist. However, several professional research organizations are sufficiently concerned about enforcing ethical research behaviors that they have codified rules of ethical conduct for their members.

Internet marketing research ethics
A set of guiding principles that govern individual and group marketing research behaviors online.

Internet marketing research ethics is a set of guiding moral principles or values that direct individual and group marketing research behaviors online. Many ethical concerns are related to collecting data from chat rooms. Because so much research is being conducted online and more is expected, it has been suggested that a warning label be developed to alert participants in public chat rooms that researchers are present. An ethical warning label would be required on any site where observations or other forms of online research take place. The Association of Internet Researchers (*www.aoir.org*), an academic association of Internet researchers from many disciplines and countries, is one professional organization currently debating ethical issues of online research. Here are some key ethical questions that Internet researchers are debating:

Information status   Is the information posted in online support groups public or is it private? Should researchers enter archived chats without informed consent?

Identification   Should researchers make their presence known in chat rooms? If so, will their presence compromise the postings and change participants' responses and reactions?

Scientific soundness   How scientifically sound are data collected from chat rooms where participants are anonymous and/or create new identities for themselves? Does the environment distort participants' behavior?

Information use   If a company sponsors a chat room in order to collect information, should the company warn participants that their comments are monitored? For example, do pharmaceutical companies hosting support group chat rooms for patients with the condition the pharmaceutical is treating have an obligation to inform the chat room moderator and/or participants that the group is being studied?[15]

Several professional organizations have issued guidelines for online marketing research. The Marketing Research Association (MRA) has an Expanded Code of Marketing Research Standards (*www.mra-net.org/codes/index.cfm*) and an Internet Ethics Guide (*www.mra-net.org/codes/internet_ethics_guidelines.PDF*). The MRA expects members to conduct research in an honest and ethical manner; instill confidence in research and encourage public cooperation; instill confidence in the business community that research is done in a professional and fair manner; carry out every research project in accordance with the code; and respect the general public.

The Council of American Survey Research Organizations (CASRO at *www.casro .org*), has published an extensive Code of Standards and Ethics for Survey Research (*www.casro.org/codeofstandards.cfm*). Like the MRA, CASRO requires that members respect respondent confidentiality and privacy, avoid harassment, not use unsolicited emails or subterfuge to obtain survey participants, and adhere to the code.

Even if a researcher is not a member of these organizations or of the American Marketing Association (*www.marketingpower.com*), he or she should adhere to the same ethical research standards. A small business owner sending an email customer survey should respect customer privacy, guarantee anonymity, not use the survey as a selling tool, and never survey children without the permission of their parents. Unfortunately, it is unrealistic to expect universal compliance with ethical Internet marketing research guidelines. For those who behave in an unethical manner, the burden is on offended consumers and enterprises to report such practices and file complaints with the Federal Trade Commission (FTC Consumer Complaint Form at *https:// rn.ftc.gov/pls/dod/wsolcq$.startup?Z_ORG_CODE=PU01*), the Better Business Bureau Online (*http://bbbonline.org/consumer/complaint.asp*), or TRUSTe's Watchdog Dispute Resolution (*http://truste.org/users/users_watchdog_intro.html*).

RELIABILITY, VALIDITY, PROJECTABILITY, AND SAMPLING

Evidence is growing that when it is conducted rigorously with attention to the size and representativeness of the samples employed, Internet marketing research can be equivalent to traditional research in reliability, validity, and projectability. These issues were a serious concern when Internet marketing research was in its infancy and its methodological rigor was unproven. After countless studies, they are less of a concern now.

Reliability
A measure of precision of measurement used in survey research.

Reliability is a measure of measurement precision. Used in survey research, it is the extent to which independent, comparable measures are the same from one administration of the survey or test to the next. The extent of a method's reliability depends on how much variance is due to random, chance errors and how much is due to imprecision in the survey itself. Reliability tends to increase as more items are added to a survey or scale. Hence a dilemma: Using too many items may result in participant burnout and exit (click-away). Too few items and the survey will not provide the information needed.

Validity
A measure of how accurately what was supposed to be measured by a survey actually was measured.

Validity is a measure of how accurately what was supposed to be measured actually was measured. A valid measure shows differences in observed scores that are true differences and nothing else. A valid measure is also reliable. A reliable measure is not necessarily valid.

Measures that are valid and reliable, assuming that the sample is properly drawn, exhibit **projectability.** Marketing research results from projectable measures can be generalized, or projected, to the population under study. Projectability is achieved when the sample used in the study is representative of the universe, and reliability and validity are high.

Projectability
A property of research results that they can be generalized, or projected, to the population under study.

A population is every member of a particular group. If the subject of a marketing research study is Internet users in the United States and Canada, the population is the number of Internet users in these two countries at the time of the study. Obviously, it is neither desirable nor feasible to survey all these users. Therefore, researchers select a subset of the population called a **sample.** A sample will be far smaller than the original population. Samples yield estimates of the opinions or behaviors of a far larger population. Thus, to ensure that the sample is representative of the population, it is essential to be very careful in selecting it.

Sample
A subset of a population under study.

Representativeness is the key to obtaining a sample from which inferences can be drawn about the population. The way a sample is drawn has a greater effect on the sample's representativeness than does its size. However, as sample size increases, generally the margin of error decreases and the sample becomes more representative of the population. That is why samples of fewer than 2,000 can be used to make predictions about the entire U.S. population of over 293 million, with a +/– 3 or 4 percent margin of error. Although a sample of Internet users today is not representative of the entire U.S. population, as Internet users come to mirror the entire population more and more closely, an online random sample eventually will be generalizable to the entire U.S. population. When that happens, even more marketing research will move online.

Random samples are representative when they are drawn in such a way that all members of the target market are equally likely to be selected. Most Internet samples are not random. Instead they are *convenience samples*—that is, individuals selected because they are conveniently available. The exception is random samples drawn from panel member subsets at Greenfield and other research companies. Because their panel members are prescreened, a large pool of representative participants can be formed. For example, Greenfield can select random samples for surveys from its representative pool.

The issue of *sample size* involves the number of responses needed to obtain repeatability. Samples that are too large inflate research expenses. Samples that are too small distort and undermine confidence in results. Some samples can be as low as several hundred people. Sample sizes of a thousand or more are often used online to provide repeatability. Because the cost of adding participants is low online, sample sizes can be larger, and that typically increases confidence, Ceteris paribus (other things being equal). Sample size calculators are widely available online.

IN-HOUSE OR OUTSOURCED

Some businesses and enterprises are large enough to have full-time staff researchers, so marketing research is planned and implemented *in-house.* Others need to *outsource,* hiring marketing research consultants or companies that offer a limited or a full range of research services. Marketing research in the United States currently is an over US$6- to $7-billion industry involving more than 2,000 firms. Online marketing research revenues grew steadily from US$3.5 million in 1996 to around US$300 million in 2000. Spending in 2001 was estimated at US$1.49 billion. By 2005, online marketing research was expected to represent 50 percent of all marketing research revenues, or about US$4 billion.[16]

Decision rules can help indicate whether marketing research should be conducted and, if so, by whom. Generally, Internet marketing research should be conducted when the benefits from the research are greater than the costs of conducting the research—that is, $R = BR > CR$, where R = Conduct Internet marketing research, BR = Benefits of doing the research, and CR = Costs of doing the research. The difficulty lies in trying to calculate the benefits and costs. This is one reason why a surprisingly large number of companies marketing online do not have active marketing research programs. Factors affecting the decision to perform online marketing research include the following:

Market size   Typically, the larger the market, the more likely it is that marketing research will be conducted. Internet marketers with very small markets are far less likely either to run extensive research in-house or to outsource. Small business owner/operators rarely have the money, expertise, or time to conduct marketing research. What they can do is listen carefully to customer feedback, respond quickly to customer email, and visit competitors' websites to see what they are doing. Alternatively, they can use a service such as Zoomerang.

Costs   The costs of conducting Internet marketing research will typically be greater than the benefits for businesses with very small markets and small profit margins. The cost of running an Internet survey is far less than that of conducting a traditional survey, but hiring a marketing research consultant can still be an expensive proposition. Marketing research consultants provide estimates of proposed projects, which can be helpful to a business trying to decide whether the research costs are justified.

Benefits   The greater the estimated benefits to be derived from the research, the more likely marketing research will be conducted. Unfortunately, because it can be extremely difficult to calculate expected benefits, the benefit side of the cost/benefit equation is far less precise than the cost side.

Competition   The more competitive the market, the more likely marketing research will be needed. When competitors are performing Internet marketing research, it exerts pressure to conform and do the same.

Customers   If the business is losing customers, experiencing a high rate of shopping basket abandonment, receiving a growing number of customer complaints, experiencing a growing rate of product returns, or otherwise having customer problems, marketing research is needed. It is also needed if a decision has been made to enlarge the customer base or attract new customers.

If the decision is made to outsource Internet marketing research, the next step is to hire a marketing research consultant or full-service marketing research company. Such consultants and companies can provide advice about doing research online, or they can actually plan, implement, and evaluate the research. They should be hired when their expertise is needed, when there is not sufficient time or resources to do the work in-house, when an outside objective perspective is needed, when there is disagreement in-house about the type or extent of research that is warranted, or when an expert is required to lend credibility to the research.

Finding the right research consultant or company can be a challenge. So many of them are available both online and offline that it is easy to be overwhelmed in trying to sort out the choices. Good places to start include local SBDCs, universities, local associations of marketing professionals, marketing research associations such as the MRA and CASRO that have online directories of their members, and referrals from other businesspeople. Marketing research suppliers are online in large numbers. Their websites can be extremely helpful if they provide examples of the type of research performed and case studies of client work. Past clients can be useful in recommending the consultant, or not. Once a list of possible consultants or companies is compiled, each should be contacted to initiate a discussion of research objectives, the deadline for completing the research, expectations of outcomes, costs, responsibilities, and terms. Client references are a must for checking out the consultant. Terms include deadlines for specific parts of the work, payment schedules, reporting schedules, and the like. When a hiring decision is made, a contract typically is written specifying the terms and conditions of the research. It should be signed by those with the authority to do so. Work should be monitored. Specifications for delivery of the final report should be among the terms negotiated.

Summary

http://college.hmco.com/business/students

Marketing Research Basics

Marketing research is the systematic, objectively planned collection and analysis of information that is communicated to decision makers for use in solving marketing problems, answering marketing questions, and writing effective marketing plans. Research *describes*, *predicts*, and *prescribes*. Most marketing research is *applied research* dealing directly with real-world marketing problems, as opposed to *basic research* that expands the boundaries of marketing knowledge. Marketing research results can be used to segment target markets, develop effective marketing communications campaigns, expose opportunities and risks, forecast trends, test market products, set benchmarks, obtain feedback, track competitors, measure the progress of a marketing plan, and market products more effectively. Marketing research is conducted by businesses, governments, universities, private nonprofit research centers, individuals, and organizations. Some businesses hire consultants to perform research for them; others conduct research in-house. Consumer marketing research should contribute to the development of consumer insight, an in-depth understanding of what consumers need and want and of their product preferences and perceptions, past market behaviors, and possible future actions. Online and offline research requires the same careful, systematic process—state the problem/question, develop a plan, collect and organize data, analyze data, and report results. The advantages of conducting online marketing research are largely related to sample, speed and time, convenience, cost, and technology. Its limitations include nonrepresentative samples, costs, technical obstacles, click-aways, and the possibility of respondent dishonesty.

Conducting Primary Marketing Research

Qualitative primary research involves mining *qualitative data* from participants' opinions, behavioral intentions, and beliefs. Quantitative primary research is empirical and generates projectable numerical data, sometimes called *hard data.* Popular qualitative research methods include focus groups, brainstorming, interviews, and communication content analysis. Focus groups are the most popular primary qualitative research method. Online focus groups have advantages and disadvantages. Brainstorming, or idea generation, encourages participants to share opinions and suggest creative responses to issues or problems. Online interviews today are more feasible and cost-effective than traditional interviews because of the widespread use of broadband and improved technology. Content analysis is a qualitative research method that systematically examines, categorizes, and analyzes online communications, which may include statements made in chat rooms, on interactive blogs, or on website feedback forms, searches, and other forums where large numbers of Internet users communicate. Statements can be written (text), verbal (audio), or even graphical images. Surveys are the most popular primary quantitative research method. Online surveys take one of two forms, email or web-centric. Online surveys have higher response rates than other types of surveys and produce faster results. Online panels use surveys as a research

method. Online reviews, a far less rigorous, nonscientific variant of the panel, still can offer insights into what consumers are thinking and doing. In conjoint or tradeoff analysis, subjects are exposed to a situation where they have to make choices, trading off various factors to reach a desired end.

Secondary Marketing Research Online

Secondary research utilizes published qualitative or quantitative studies conducted by others, or reports and data generated in-house for other purposes. It is usually less expensive than primary research but sometimes is not fully applicable because it was originally designed for other purposes, samples, or times. Secondary research collects *secondary data.* The Internet is a virtual gold mine of secondary data for marketing research, but there is far too much for most people to sort through, and readily finding what is needed is a challenge. Secondary research uses internal information as well as external research published by others, public data sources, and various directories, rankings, and periodicals. It can save time and money, but it can also be unfulfilling if the research is old, inaccurate, or at the wrong level of analysis or if it was conducted on a different subject group from what is needed. Secondary research results often provide direction for the development of primary research. Marketers have a broad array of external secondary sources from which to choose, including governments, private companies, professional groups, and organizations.

Online Marketing Research Issues

Internet marketing research that is outsourced to research companies or conducted in-house by marketing professionals is less risky than research performed by those without training, experience, or assistance. Risk can be related to the sample, content, methods, bias, and results. An alternative is to go online and look for research tutorials or books on Internet marketing research at an online bookseller. Internet marketing research ethics is a set of guiding moral principles or values that direct individual and group marketing research behaviors online. The principal concerns are about protecting the privacy of participants, using data responsibly and securely, complying with laws that restrict research involving children and young people, and using sound scientific methods so that results can be reported and applied with confidence. In-house researchers should adhere to the same principles even if they are not members of an association for research professionals. Evidence is growing that when Internet marketing research is conducted rigorously and with careful attention to sample size and representativeness, it can be equivalent to traditional research in reliability, validity, and projectability. Some businesses and enterprises are large enough to have full-time researchers on staff. Others need to outsource, hiring marketing research consultants or companies that offer a full range of research services. Generally, Internet marketing research should be conducted when the financial benefits expected to accrue from the research are greater than the costs of conducting the research, a relationship often summarized with the equation $R = BR > CR$.

Take Action!

You work for the Blue Knob Crafts Cooperative marketing the work of its over one hundred potters, weavers, woodworkers, basket makers, and other creative members. Members' products are functional and highly desirable. They include wrought iron decorative candlesticks, rag rugs, handwoven baskets, carved wooden bowls, stoneware plates and pots, and broomcorn brooms. Blue Knob sponsors craft fairs in the spring and fall to sell members' work. The fairs attract buyers from a five-state area. You believe that Blue Knob members will sell more products if they better understand their customers. This insight will guide them when they talk about their products at the fairs. They need to know what product information will resonate with buyers. The annual Cooperative meeting is coming up, and you will be presenting information about buyer types that you have developed with the assistance of the VALS (*www.sric-bi.com/VALS/*) framework. It's been a while since you worked with VALS, so you need to visit SRI Business Intelligence to refresh your knowledge.

1. Prepare a one-page introductory handout for Blue Knob members that contains a bullet list of important points about VALS: what it is, its history, and other relevant information. Keep your focus and make sure the list includes information that will be useful to Blue Knob members, makes your marketing goal clear, and avoids jargon.

2. On the basis of your knowledge of the Cooperative's customers, you believe they generally fit the VALS categories of *believers* and *makers*. Carefully read the descriptions of these segments, and identify one characteristic for each that can be used in promoting Blue Knob products. Develop a marketing message for each characteristic— that is, what a Blue Knob member might emphasize about a product. For example, a psychological characteristic of one of the VALS groups is a preference for practical, functional products. Therefore, stress how products can be used to help solve everyday problems. Develop a role-playing scenario wherein a Blue Knob member plays the role of a potential customer and you are the seller. Using the characteristics of a VALS group, guide the buyer-seller conversation to emphasize the points that will make the product more desirable.

3. The VALS data are helpful, but you believe it would be even more valuable to develop a customer survey for the Cooperative's website. Given that the overall goal of the survey is to develop greater consumer insight, what five survey questions should be asked of site visitors? Write the survey and be prepared to defend the inclusion of each question.

Chapter Review Questions

1. What is Internet marketing research?
2. Why is *applied* marketing research so important to Internet marketers?
3. What are some advantages and some disadvantages of online marketing research?
4. Why do marketers need both qualitative and quantitative research?
5. Can all marketing research be performed online?
6. Describe how an online focus group is conducted.
7. Why are qualitative research results more challenging to analyze than quantitative results?
8. What cautions should marketers exercise in using online surveys?
9. What ethical issues should concern Internet marketing researchers?
10. Should incentives be offered to consumers taking an online survey? If so, what form should they take (i.e., money, products, discount coupons for a future purchase)?
11. If the owner of a small web storefront cannot afford marketing research, where can he or she go for assistance?
12. Why is survey research such a popular online marketing research method?
13. How might a web marketer find a marketing research consultant?
14. Is the Internet a secondary source gold mine or an information quagmire? Explain.
15. What are some of the risks that Internet marketing researchers face?

Competitive Case Study

Forrester Research, Inc.: Serving High-Tech And Internet Companies

Although Forrester Research, Inc. (*www.forrester.com*) is far smaller than Millward Brown, it serves the same target market as MB's IntelliQuest (*www.intelliquest.com*) unit, principally high-tech and Internet companies. Forrester performs research on the effect of technology on business for over 1,800 clients in marketing and information technology companies. The company's revenues in 2003 were US$126 million, with a one-year sales growth of 30 percent. For five consecutive years, Forrester has been ranked among the top 75 of the Forbes 200 Best Small Companies. Its research studies are widely quoted, and the company is seen as a leader in its field. Forrester provides free research on its site, but its goal is to sign the visitor on as a client. Registered guests can also subscribe to a free industry-specific email newsletter. Recent Forrester research reveals a lot about what's happening in the tech industry. For example, the company reports that B2B eprocurement (online

purchasing) is experiencing a resurgence of interest; it predicts that Google's hold on the market will weaken as the search engine industry becomes more competitive; and it notes that despite the efforts of credit card companies to get clients online to maintain their check balances and perform other self-serve activities, only 36 percent have enrolled for online services and 81 percent report that they will never do so! By releasing the results of these and other studies online, Forrester is effectively marketing its research services and adding value to its brand name.[17]

CHECK IT OUT

PaidSurveys.com (*www.paidsurveys.com/?campaign=dougstreet*) takes a different approach to online surveys. It is a survey portal with links to twenty-five survey companies that actively seek participants. Visit PaidSurveys to see what types of incentives it offers survey takers. With all the interest in getting consumers to participate in online surveys, is there a risk that some will become survey junkies? Will they make it their life's work to go from one survey company to the next, completing survey after survey? How can companies control online survey junkies? Should they? Why?

A GLOBAL PERSPECTIVE

Marketing researchers in the United States are not alone in going online. Marketers in other countries recruit participants for online surveys. Visit the UK site A Penny Earned (*www.apennyearned.co.uk/surveys_uk.html*) and evaluate some of the many opportunities that exist for getting paid to take online surveys. Some surveys offer cash incentives. What are some other incentives? Are surveys restricted to UK citizens? Judging from this site, how actively are Europeans conducting marketing research online?

8

Using Data Tools to Enhance Performance

LEARNING OBJECTIVES

» To learn some data tools fundamentals
» To explore how data tools are being used to achieve marketing performance objectives
» To consider the marketing value of search engines
» To understand why some data tools are criticized

IBM Offers Information Solutions

Anyone who emails, shares files electronically, uses a search engine, makes a website purchase, creates and runs a website, operates a wireless network, runs an email marketing campaign, places third-party cookies, writes a blog, web conferences, or sends requisition lists over a proprietary supply chain extranet is assisted at some point by an IBM Intel-based UNIX server or other IBM hardware or software. International Business Machines Corporation (IBM at *www.ibm.com*) is the world's largest information technology company, the largest technology services provider and financier, and the world's second largest software provider. IBM, one of the most influential companies in the world, reported year-end 2003 sales of over US$89 billion. The company employs more than 319,000 workers worldwide. It has been named the world's third most valuable brand and is one of the most trusted. The company has pioneered information handling and technology throughout its over 100-year history. IBM's predecessor, C-T-R, was created through acquisitions that included Herman Hollerith's Tabulating Machine Company. Hollerith was the inventor of the punch card data-recording system used in the first automated U.S. census. During World

War II, IBM collaborated with Harvard University to develop the Harvard Mark I computer, the first machine to execute long computations automatically. In the same year that the first four Internet nodes were connected, IBM dramatically changed the way it sold its hardware, software, and services by unbundling components and marketing them individually. This strategy is credited with helping stimulate the development of the multibillion-dollar worldwide software and computer industry. The company took a beating in the 1990s when it underestimated the Internet's impact, but it reinvented itself in the early 2000s as a customer-centric business selling integrated business solutions and ebusiness hardware and software. Its open-structure UNIX-based eServers support the type of technology infrastructure that websites and trading platforms must have in order to be customer-centric. IBM's Business Consulting Services Unit, the world's largest consulting and services organization, helps businesses use information technology to improve their performance. As expected, IBM reports considerable savings from its own intranet, extranet, and public Internet sites. Its on-demand supply chain saved the company

US$5.6 billion in 2002 and reduced the time needed to place requisitions with suppliers from two to three weeks to two hours; its over 9,000 monthly web conferences avoided US$50 million in costs; 70 percent of all its customer contacts are online, where customers use IBM.com for product information, installation and service information, software update downloads, beta-code and software fixes, and problem tracking, as well as to communicate with company technicians. Over 40 percent of its training is online, and IBM.com is the company's lowest-cost sales channel, averaging US$63,000 in sales per minute from the site. IBM is the leader in almost every market in which it competes, and its familiar logo is ubiquitous worldwide.[1]

Chapter 7 examined how online marketing research collects primary and secondary data. Chapter 8 continues the discussion by exploring how data collected from marketing research and other sources are put to work improving marketing performance. It begins with some basic information and then offers examples of how data tools can help achieve performance goals. Search engines are singled out for their data-organizing value and their ability to present marketers with self-selected segmented audiences. The chapter concludes by identifying some data tools that are harshly criticized. This chapter is not designed to offer an in-depth, technical examination of complex data tools and information technology. Instead, it presents a framework for considering how these tools are used to improve Internet marketing performance and facilitate better customer relationships.

Data Tools: Why They Matter

In the 1800s and early 1900s, a local storekeeper lived in the community he served and probably knew what each customer wanted as soon as he or she entered his store. From years of being neighbors with and serving the same customers, he knew their names and family members, their ages and genders, what they did for a living, where they lived, what they purchased, how much and how often, and whether they paid cash or had to be carried on the books until the next payday. Because he had a lifelong relationship with these people, marketing was one-to-one, up close, and personal. Knowledge of his customers guided the shopkeeper's marketing efforts, and without realizing it, he was collecting and storing data and applying customer relationship management principles long before the terms were invented. The storekeeper was a human computer, and his mind was its exceedingly efficient processor.

The storekeeper probably had at most several hundred customers, so record keeping and information management were relatively simple. His performance goals were also simple, primarily to keep his customers satisfied and to make a living. His customer knowledge (insight) was a powerful tool that helped him retain their loyalty and, when appropriate, *up-sell* (encourage the purchase of higher-priced products) and *cross-sell* (encourage the purchase of related products). This insight helped him to identify and attract new customers and to defend his business against competitors. He also had a store of data about his suppliers and business customers, although they were far fewer in number than his consumer customers.

Data tools
Software, programs, and systems that collect and manage data and generate knowledge in a format that can be applied to marketing performance issues.

Data
Distinct sets of information or values formatted as text, numbers, sounds, images, or other elements translated into a storable form, typically electronic.

Data collection
The systematic gathering of data via marketing research and other methods.

Database (DB)
An electronic filing system of related data organized in fields, records, and files that are stored and processed using computer software and programs.

Relational databases
Databases where data are organized in tables whose rows and attributes share common elements that can be flexibly related.

Times certainly have changed. Performance goals have become much more complex, and achieving them has become much more difficult. Contemporary enterprises increasingly rely on **data tools,** a variety of software, programs, and information systems and technologies that collect and manage data and generate knowledge in a format that can be applied to marketing performance issues. Output is typically in report form that includes text, tables, charts, and graphics. **Data** (plural) are distinct sets of values formatted as text, numbers, sounds, images, or other elements translated into a storable form, typically electronic. **Data collection** is the systematic gathering of data via marketing research and other methods. Related data are maintained in a **database (DB),** an electronic filing system of related data typically organized in fields, records, and files that are stored and processed using computer software and various programs. A traditional telephone directory is an offline hardcopy manually accessed database composed of text files with names, addresses, and telephone numbers. Many telephone directories are now available online in hypertext form at such sites as Verizon's SuperPages.com (*www.superpages.com*). *Hypertext databases* organize large amounts of digital information, but not for numerical analysis. Numerical databases are compiled so they can be analyzed statistically.

The first step in compiling an electronic (digital) database is to identify its purpose and design, including defining what data must be collected. Data are collected from many sources (such as marketing research, in-house sales records, supplier purchase orders, website tracking and server logs, and advertising metrics) and formatted for input. Data are cleansed to remove obvious errors or omissions and are organized into fields (single pieces of data), records (complete sets of fields), and files (collections of fields) to be stored until needed. Electronic DBs are routinely edited, refined, transformed, cleansed, purged, retrieved, sorted and resorted, and stocked. They can be accessed using database management programs housed on a single computer or server or on huge mainframe computers. They can be contained within that single computer, shared by many computers within an enterprise, or transported on intranets, extranets, and the Internet to other servers and computers. Databases have countless uses. For example, they are used in automatic teller machines, airline reservation systems, inventory management systems, university registration systems, hospital patient records, and electronic libraries. Even very small businesses can benefit from collecting customer or supplier data, maintaining them in simple DB programs, and using them to improve performance. For example, a sales database can generate a list of email addresses of a company's most loyal customers for an email promotion designed to clear inventory. Supplier databases can generate restocking schedules to ensure that requisitions (purchase orders) are emailed in time to avoid stock-outs.

Relational databases are currently the preferred database format. In a relational DB, data entries are organized into tables whose rows and attributes share certain common elements that form the basis for aggregating data across different tables. One ubiquitous common element is a customer identification (ID) number. An ID number appears in virtually all customer files and is the element that allows files in different tables to be linked. Customers can be tracked by ID number through tables that contain data such as purchase records, payment methods, purchase dates, shopping areas, product preferences, and media habits.

Marketing data
Data collected from and about markets, segments, customers, suppliers, partners, and competitors, as well as from in-house records with marketing applicability.

Database marketing
The use of databases to generate information for marketing purposes.

Marketing data are data collected from and about markets, segments, competitors, suppliers, partners, and customers, from relevant in-house records, and from other areas of marketing interest. **Database marketing** uses information drawn from marketing DBs for such marketing purposes as identifying best customers, tracking suppliers and orders, identifying customer groups that are receptive to advertising messages, identifying new product opportunities, testing price points, retaining customers, and adjusting distribution schedules to accommodate customer buying patterns and production schedules. *Information technology* (also known as information services or management information services) consists of all the computer-based data processing and management in an enterprise, in marketing as well as finance, human resources, production, and other areas.

How many data are there? Researchers at the University of California at Berkeley estimate that around 5 exabytes (5.36 billion gigabytes) of data were created in 2002, compared to 2 exabytes in 1999. This is roughly equivalent to half a million libraries the size of the U.S. Library of Congress. Over 90 percent of all new data are stored on hard disks. Each year the amount of information produced increases by 30 percent; the United States is the world's largest producer, generating 40 percent of the global total of new data each year. With a world population of over 6.4 billion, this means that almost 800 megabytes of new data are produced per person each year. Obviously, there are wide margins of error in these calculations, but the message is clear: The mountain of data is rising dramatically.[2]

DATABASES CAN INFLUENCE MARKETING PRACTICES

Databases are most valuable when they provide knowledge in an understandable form that can be used to improve marketing performance. Usable databases can be powerful instruments of change. A case in point is the misguided practice of treating all customers the same. All customers should be treated *fairly*, but not necessarily equally. Databases have made it easier to identify a company's best customers, as well as its least productive ones, by examining their purchase histories. By concentrating marketing effort on those best customers who have purchased the most and have the highest potential to buy more, a company should be able to improve its marketing performance.

Knowledge about best customers is applied through loyalty programs such as the one used by Chico's FAS, Inc. (*www.chicos.com*), the hottest specialty retailer in the United States. Chico's sells exclusive private-label, sophisticated, and distinctive casual women's clothing and accessories through a chain of over 536 specialty stores in 46 U.S. states, the District of Columbia, the Virgin Islands, and Puerto Rico and on the Web. Fiscal year (FY) end 2003 sales topped US$768 million, an increase of 44.7 percent over FY end 2002. Each Chico's store averages a 32 percent profit margin. The target market is mature women (ages 25-35) with moderate to higher incomes. Chico's customers are invited to enroll in its Passport Club, which has almost a million members and is the heart of the company's marketing effort. Its best customers earn their way into permanent Passport Club membership by spending US$500 in total purchases. Members receive a lifetime 5 percent discount on every subsequent Chico's purchase, along with invitations to special parties and events,

Chico's

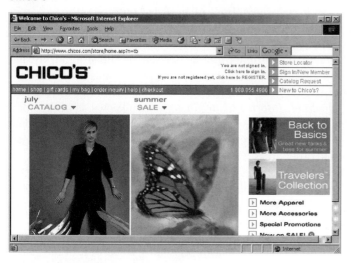

Chico's FAS rewards its best customers with a variety of special offers.

Source: Reprinted by permission of Chico's Retail Services, Inc. Ft. Myers, FL., www.chicos.com.

private discounts, exclusive sales, promotional offers, special offers on their birthday, and free shipping and handling on all web purchases. Passport Club members shopping Chicos.com sign in with their membership number and information about them is retrieved from Chico's customer database. The company makes sure that Passport Club members receive the same rewards whether they are shopping online or offline in a seamless *oneline* strategy. Loyal Passport Club members generated 74 percent of Chico's business in 2003. Although Chico's does not separate catalog and Internet sales numbers, together they were 3 percent of Chico's 2003 net sales, an increase of US$6.7 million (up 41.8 percent) over FY 2002. Increased web page counts are credited for the increase, along with more catalog mailings and television spots.[3]

MANAGING DATABASES

Database management system (DBMS)
Programs that systematically store, process, modify, and retrieve data from databases.

It's implausible to think that any large twenty-first-century company would manually manipulate enormous databases. Instead, they increasingly use **database management systems (DBMS).** A DBMS (also called an information management system or a knowledge management system) consists of programs that systematically store, process, modify, and retrieve data from databases. The file-saving system on a personal computer is a very simple DBMS, invisibly saving digital data, retrieving it on command, and accommodating real-time changes and re-storage. Although the large-scale DBMS industry is dominated by IBM, Oracle (*www.oracle.com*), and Microsoft (*www.microsoft.com*), many small and midsize vendors sell proprietary DBMS systems in an ever-expanding market.

DBMS software can run on personal computers, but in large enterprises it is more commonly found on huge mainframe computers, and sometimes supercomputers, that allow hundreds or even thousands of users to access the DBMS simultaneously. DBMS programs vary in price from extremely expensive custom products to inexpensive off-the-shelf packages.

Database management software can affect performance by speeding up marketing processes, improving data accuracy, increasing the breadth and depth of data available for analysis, and making data access simple for non-technical employees. One disadvantage is that many DBMS programs are highly complex, and successfully managing them can be a daunting challenge. DBMS maintenance is often outsourced. The systems can be unpredictable, and people still must interpret and apply the output. Data must be entered and often converted from incompatible formats, which can be time-consuming and costly. Bad data cannot be made better, even with a smoothly running DBMS. This proves yet again the old GIGO adage: *garbage in, garbage out*. A DBMS can easily produce a glut of information, far more than can be reasonably evaluated and used. Operating costs can be more than most small and many midsize businesses can afford. For a growing number of businesses, however, the benefits outweigh the costs, and being online with a selling, content, or service site necessitates having a DBMS. An alternative is to subscribe to merchant services that include a DBMS along with other marketing services.

Like many etailers, Chico's operates multiple databases that seamlessly link its online and offline data. Chico's operates a *sales database* for collecting, storing, and retrieving such data as customer identity, sales history (online and offline), products purchased, products returned, purchase dates, payment options, shipping dates, and other relevant sales data. These data are used in determining when a customer has reached the US$500 spending threshold and thus becomes a permanent Passport member eligible for the 5 percent discount and future customized offers. It's less obvious, but the company probably also has a *site tracking database* for site-specific information about who visits the site, page views, where the visitor was directly before visiting the site, and where he or she goes after leaving it. Site tracking logs can be mined to identify the site's most popular pages. The company currently asks for a customer's email address in order to send an email purchase confirmation, and these data could be used if Chico's launches an email newsletter in the future. The company encourages visitors to sign up to receive a hardcopy catalog, and in addition to asking for the visitor's name, address, phone number, and email address, the form also asks how he or she heard about Chico's (television, magazines, friends and family, don't know). Surprisingly, the form does not ask whether the visitor was directed by a search engine. These tracking data can direct decisions about allocating promotion budgets to the media that customers use most. Customers can make purchases online, so transaction software is required to operate its shopping bag system and interact with the sales database. Behind the scenes, the company has an *inventory management system* with databases for managing inventory levels and supplier orders. Its *product database* contains a catalog of digital images and text descriptors, along with stock numbers and other information to track inventory levels and display onsite product pictures.

DATABASE SOURCES

In-house database
A database built from a company's own data.

Compiled database
A database made up of data collected by external sources and, if proprietary, sold.

Not all databases are alike and many alternatives exist for obtaining them. Businesses can create **in-house databases,** built from their own data, or obtain **compiled databases,** which consist of data collected by others and, if proprietary, sold. Often, they use both. If Chico's was selecting a site for a new store, the company might purchase a compiled demographic database to determine whether the region under consideration has a sufficiently large group of potential customers of the right age and income to support a Chico's store.

In-house databases have some important advantages. In-house data typically have greater depth and breadth as they include records for buyers who already have a purchase history with the company, buyers who have not purchased recently, and prospects who have visited but have not yet purchased. In-house data are assumed to have greater immediate potential for use in retention, up-selling, and cross-selling, because past purchase behavior generally is a good predictor of future purchase behavior. This obviously is not the case for all customers all the time, but it is more often the case than not—and particularly so for loyal customers. In-house data can be compiled from many sources, including existing company records, marketing research, website tracking, online advertising results, and supplier records. A company has greater control over the quality of its own data, and if it has good **database hygiene,** then in-house data should be more accurate and current, and should have fewer omissions and mistakes than compiled DBs. Unlike compiled databases, in-house DBs can match online and offline sales. Another advantage of in-house databases is that the company's familiarity with its customers, products, and purchase situations can add a valuable perspective about what data should be collected and how they should be used. In-house databases can be built by the company's own employees, outsourced to suppliers, or compiled and reported by subscription merchant services such as Yahoo! Small Merchant Services (*http://smallbusiness.yahoo.com/merchant/*).

> **Database hygiene**
> Process for maintaining accurate and current data in databases.

Compiled databases also offer certain advantages. Using one can identify new targets for businesses seeking to expand their customer reach. Such DBs are already compiled and available, and regular updates can be purchased. It often costs less to purchase a compiled database than to collect and process in-house data. Compiled DBs often use multiple data sources that include public records, private sources, and overlays of customer response data. They may contain predictive scores based on data mining or survey data.

Many databases are available online, and of course they are subject to the same problems that plague secondary data in general. They are free on many government and some organization websites, and many are sold by online proprietary services. Proprietary databases can be leased from their owners or purchased. They may contain niche and/or mass market data. SK&A Information Services, Inc. (*www.skainfo.com*) illustrates the type of data available online. The company leases its databases of key health care decision makers for direct marketing to hospitals, pharmacies, group practices, nursing homes, and other facilities. It offers what it claims are the most comprehensive lists and databases available of health care professionals.

Any Internet marketer considering the purchase of proprietary databases should carefully evaluate the seller's reputation and check client references. The database broker's salespeople should be able to provide complete information about advantages or disadvantages of the databases, data sources, database hygiene records, accuracy, costs, and terms of use. Database suppliers should be able to provide predictive scores for customer response rates. Compiled DBs are frequently used in financial services and by retailers seeking to drive traffic to a website through mass email marketing.

DATA WAREHOUSES

> **Data warehouse**
> A central repository (storehouse) for corporate-wide databases; an organizing framework, and a database system for extracting and managing large quantities of data.

A **data warehouse (DW)** is a central electronic repository (storage place) for corporate-wide data in databases. A warehouse is a framework for organizing the databases and a DB system that allows the extraction and management of large quantities of data. It is often distributed on many computers, housed on mainframe computers, and accessed through servers, although the process is transparent to the user. It must have a flexible structure to accommodate multiple users and different methods for slicing through the data. The warehouse is stocked with databases collected from marketing, finance, and other functional areas; data derived from in-house transaction and inventory records; and data compiled from external suppliers. A production data warehouse may be separate from a transactional data warehouse used for nonproduction purposes.

Data warehouses are extremely complex and technically challenging to construct. Once the design is agreed on, DBs are gathered from multiple sources and compiled by database aggregators. The databases are transformed to a common platform. Inconsistencies in data formats and coding are removed, and the databases are loaded (populated) into the warehouse. User interfaces are installed that allow marketers and others to query the data and request responses to hypotheses. The warehouse should be closely monitored and regularly cleansed and updated. Enterprises of all types—businesses, governments, universities, hospitals, organizations, and nonprofits—have data warehouses.

Some warehouses are massive. One of the largest belongs to France Telecom (*www.francetelecom.com/fr/*), with 29.2 terabytes (29,991 gigabytes) of raw data running on an Oracle System. This warehouse holds three times as much printed material as is stored in the U.S. Library of Congress. By January 2005, an estimated 43 percent of all data warehouses will be larger than 1 terabyte (TB), the equivalent of 1,000 copies of the print *Encyclopaedia Britannica.* At the same time that data storage costs have declined, greater amounts of data are being stored, and large amounts of *dormant data* are never retrieved. The effect is likened to human arteries clogged with cholesterol and headed for a heart attack.[4]

Marketing queries to a warehouse start with a hypothesis (H); for example, *H1: Customers 45 to 65 years old who purchased infant gifts from our website last holiday season are most likely to respond to email offers of toddler products for this holiday season.* The task is to identify customers from last year who fit the profile. The query to the warehouse is designed to produce an email list of customers 45 to 65 years old with the requisite transaction history. The generated list is used to send a promotional email offer to those customers who gave permission (opted in) last year for the company to contact them in the future. The offer refers directly to last year's purchase, has links to products that make great toddler gifts, offers a discount if a purchase is made before December 1, and offers free shipping for orders ≥US$50.

Selected areas in corporate data warehouses are often opened to the company's suppliers, partners, and customers via extranets. Sharing data can help the company and its partners work out solutions to product or production problems. Corporate customers access warehouses to make better-informed purchase decisions, obtain detailed product specifications, and check delivery schedules.

Jiffy Lube International, Inc. (*www.jiffylube.com*), now a Shell Oil Company (*www.shellus.com*), constructed a data warehouse to speed the integration of its online and offline marketing efforts. The company began its data warehouse project in 1998. Three people made up the planning team—the head of strategic marketing, a senior IT analyst, and an enterprise data administrator. It took seven months to plan the warehouse and longer to load 35 million vehicle records. During the process, Jiffy Lube's parent company, Pennzoil, purchased Quaker State, and the warehouse had to be expanded to fold in Quaker State's records. The data warehouse's more than 50 million records are used to profile Jiffy Lube's best customers. Service centers use the Jiffy Lube website to send direct mail to prospects in their service districts who match "best customer" profiles. Website visitors are invited to provide their email addresses so that they can receive the latest news and maintenance tips. Jiffy Lube is the largest franchising business in the fast oil change/fluid maintenance industry.[5]

DATA MINING

Data mining
Analytical methods that systematically sift through databases looking for predictive relationships and statistically significant patterns and correlations that have previously gone unrecognized.

Data mining (also called machine learning, expert systems, and knowledge discovery) is a class of machine-driven analytical methods that shift through (drill down) into DBs and data warehouses seeking predictive relationships, hidden patterns, and plausible relationships. Mining is used to uncover useful consumer information from website transactions and visits. Software (neural networks, association rules, and genetic algorithm software) systematically sifts through large databases, extracting statistically significant patterns and correlations. Data mining can substantiate an educated guess about a marketing relationship or, using automated discovery, search for previously unrecognized relationships. It is a descriptive and predictive tool, and a general approach that uses different methods for a variety of marketing purposes that ultimately should improve marketing performance.

The data-mining process creates its own theory about why a relationship exists. Take the case of an etailer that wants to use data mining to reduce online credit card fraud. One approach is to develop a *descriptive* profile of credit card users who are most likely to use fake or stolen cards and then use this profile to stop fraud by denying service to any customer who fits the fraud profile. The *predictive* profile is created from credit card purchase patterns of known credit card fraudsters. Data-mining techniques are used to compile the profile and then apply profile characteristics to identify others who share them and therefore have a higher probability of committing online credit card fraud. In other cases, data mining can be used to answer such questions as *What is the probability that a customer who fits this profile will:*

- purchase at least $500 in apparel from our online spring catalog?
- respond to our email promotion of US$25 off an online purchase of US$100?
- click through to a game site from a banner advertisement?
- respond to a free shipping offer for an online purchase of US$100 or more?
- return online purchases?
- respond to a cross-sell offer?

Mining requires drilling down through multiple layers of data. Customer transaction data are searched to create profiles of customer purchase behaviors, including lapsed customers who have not purchased recently and those least likely to purchase. Mining creates models for segmenting customers and forecasting attrition and retention rates. It can indicate what websites have prime advertising space for reaching a target market, pricing opportunities, cross-selling and up-selling potential, and how to personalize offers effectively. By separating best customers from others, marketers are able to offer different levels of service based on predicted buying potential and thus operationalize the 80-20 rule. Vilfredo Pareto (1848–1923), an Italian economist, observed in 1906 that in Italy, 80 percent of the land was owned by 20 percent of the population. This ratio was later applied to business in a number of ways, including the prediction that 20 percent of customers produce 80 percent of revenues. The 80-20 ratio also has been applied to gardening and scientific discoveries, among other applications.

Until recently, highly trained statisticians were needed to operate most large-scale Unix-based database-mining software. Much of it was proprietary, customized, costly, and difficult to create and run. Now, cheaper, off-the-shelf software allows English-language queries so that data can be mined from desktop computers. Thus customer service representatives, telemarketers, and salespeople in large companies can access company databases and mine them, often in real time while still on the telephone with customers, interacting with them by email, or on the Web using live chat or instant messaging.[6]

Companies that already had massive databases, particularly large retailers such as Wal-Mart (*www.walmart.com*), are leaders in data mining. Wal-Mart popularized the use of data warehousing and now runs one with over 500 terabytes (1 TB is 1 trillion bytes of data characters). To appreciate the size of this warehouse, compare it to the U.S. Internal Revenue Service's relatively puny 40 TB warehouse. Wal-Mart centralizes corporate-wide data from all its stores and mines those data extensively. The results allow the company to predict sales of every product at every store, which gives Wal-Mart tremendous clout with suppliers, huge savings in inventory holding costs, and maximum returns from promotional spending. Customer-focused Wal-Mart tailors inventory to specific markets, and its customers enjoy lower prices that result from distribution efficiencies and tailored merchandise mixes that satisfy local preferences. The company also is championing **RFID,** miniature, low-cost Radio Frequency Identification sensor chips embedded on pallets, cases, and products that track them electronically as they move through distribution channels and create an on-the-fly up-to-date inventory. These *smart tags* are already being used by businesses and are under analysis for use by the U.S. government in homeland security. Shell Oil Company is using them to track the status of pumps at Shell gas stations. RFIDs are a primitive, first-generation application of **sensor networks,** which are low-cost, low-power, single-task miniature computers that create their own nodes and networks across a geographical area and can collect, process, store, and disseminate data. Sensor networks create their own intelligent environment. As they are deployed worldwide, they will create a massive extension of the Internet as miniature sensors are embedded in things that move, grow, make noise, heat up, or cool down. Sensors create their own networks and can run computations. They could be used to track individuals by their shopping habits.[7]

J. Crew (*www.jcrew.com*) uses data mining to track visitor movements (clickstreams or virtual tracks) on its website and to predict product recommendations in real time to up-sell and cross-sell while visitors are still browsing its website. J. Crew's data mining also provides recommendations for making its web storefront design more effective, as well as improving marketing and merchandising strategies. Site marketing managers receive daily reports on website traffic patterns, customer demographics, transactions, and responses to marketing campaigns. The company operates almost 200 retail stores, a catalog, and 70 outlets in Japan, in addition to

RFID

Miniature Radio Frequency Identification sensors (chips) placed on pallets, cases, and products that track them electronically through distribution channels.

Sensor networks

Low-cost, low-power, single-task miniature computers that create nodes and networks across a geographical area and can collect, process, store, and disseminate data.

Jcrew.com. FY 2003 sales were US$766 million. Internet sales for the first nine months of 2003 were US$82.5 million, down about 9 percent over 2002 because of a companywide restructuring.[8]

DATA MATCHING

Collaborative filtering

A data-matching tool that produces personalized product recommendations based on the similarities among customers with similar tastes and buying habits. Also called community knowledge or social filtering.

Collaborative filtering (also called community knowledge or social filtering) is a data-matching tool that makes custom product recommendations based on the preferences and/or purchases of customers with similar tastes and buying habits. It is a more specific tool than general data mining. Collaborative filtering is used for cross-selling and up-selling by Amazon.com (*www.amazon.com*) and others. A recent example at Amazon.com began when the customer, who purchased a copy of the book *Mr. Midshipman Hornblower* by C. S. Forester, returned to Amazon and was greeted by name (personalization) with a recommendation that because he had recently purchased *Hornblower,* he would also enjoy *Master and Commander* by Patrick O'Brian. The recommendation was based on *n* other customers who purchased both books and reported enjoying them. Collaborative filtering automates collective word of mouth by extracting data from massive customer databases. The more preferences and purchases housed in the DB, the greater the likelihood of making a good match and facilitating a sale.

One of the problems with collaborative filtering is the need for huge amounts of data in order to make meaningful comparisons and wash out anomalies. Another is that many customers simply ignore recommendations and others regard them as a self-serving ploy by the site owner. Because recommendations are matched to previous purchases or expressions of interest, they reflect no information about the reason for the purchase. Purchase reasons differ and range from restocking for the buyer's personal use to unique gifts for others. Unless gift information is gathered (for example, that gift wrapping or a gift card was requested), that information won't be in the database.

Dynamic content

Web page content produced on demand that differs by user or user type.

DYNAMIC CONTENT

Early web pages were mostly static; content did not change, and the same page was always delivered from the server, regardless of who requested it or when. Today, **dynamic content** has become much more common. Such web pages are produced on demand from databases with page content that differs according to what user or user type requests the page, the time of day, or the point in the update cycle. Language is one rule that can trigger a database to send a customized web page. If a site visitor's language preference is French and the website offers pages in French, then that is what is served to the visitor. Other examples include frequently updated pages that are generated *on the fly* to provide the most current information and pages that contain different product prices being tested for customer responses. Survey systems with dynamic content can be built into websites and emails. URLs ending in .asp, .cfm, .cqi, .dhtml, or .shtml often identify dynamic content.

Dynamic content can be an effective tool for increasing sales. It is also very demanding of server and database space and can slow page delivery times, although accelerator programs are available. Dynamic content is used on news sites, auctions, and

WEB UPDATE

For updates and more on this topic, visit the textbook student website at: http://college.hmco .com/business/students and select Siegel, *Internet Marketing,* 2e. **Online Data Tools**

B2B exchanges and in catalogs. It is used at Amazon.com to retrieve requested books or videos, at Charles Schwab (*www.charlesschwab.com*) to retrieve customer data and stock reports, at FedEx (*www.fedex.com*) to track orders, and at Lands' End (*www.landsend.com*) to display products from the catalog. Some search engines have difficulty creating links to dynamic content changes.

Using Data Tools to Improve Performance

Most Internet marketers will tell you that their top goal is to improve performance, but performance objectives and measurements are defined in different ways. For goods-selling sites, performance objectives may be to increase sales (clear inventory) and decrease marketing costs (holding and fulfillment), so measures are needed for sales, returns, costs, conversion rates, inventory levels, customer satisfaction, and related factors. Performance objectives at content sites may be to increase readership, downloads, subscriptions, and stickiness (time spent on the site), while reducing cancellations. Measures track interactions on the site and specific page views, as well as purchase behaviors. For sites that seek to generate sales leads, performance objectives may be to increase information downloads, newsletter subscriptions, and offline contacts, so measures may track content use, contacts, and leads that close. Related objectives are to make email campaigns more effective, sell more advertising, find better ways to spend advertising dollars, or improve yet other performance outcomes. Another category of performance objectives is broader and seeks to do nothing less than establish, maintain, and nurture long-term customer relationships.

WEB ANALYTICS

Web analytics

Software and systems for studying how visitors interact with a website and what impact it has on them.

When the performance objective is narrowly defined and website-specific—particularly to improve customer interactions with a website—many marketers turn to **web analytics.** These are tools that help marketers understand what is going on at their website. Because it is a generic term, *web analytics* means different things to different people. Web analytics software and systems use server logs, cookies, and other data-gathering tools to collect, analyze, and report data that measure site activities. Some web analytics programs are off-the-shelf, and others are custom-built. They vary in complexity, measures, results, and price. Most are designed to study how visitors and customers interact with a specific website, not websites generally, and what impact the site has on them. Web analytics programs can build highly detailed profiles of site visitors (linked to customer databases), sort unique from returning visitors, determine how visitors reached the site (direct link, search engine referral, banner ad click through, or other method), identify keywords used in searches for the site, track what site pages they visit and how long they stay, identify where they go after leaving the site, check to see that all site pages are working, and track returns from expenditures on search engine marketing, banner ads, email campaigns, and other online promotions.

Web analysis service providers (WASPs) can be hired to extract useful information from web log data. They can perform cross-site customer behavior analysis, as well as in-site tracking. WebSideStory (*www.websidestory.com*) is one of many companies that perform on-demand web analytics. Their software and services can measure marketing ROI, help marketers improve targeting and conversions, identify online opportunities to enhance revenue, and provide the accurate site traffic numbers that advertisers need to make purchase decisions.

Black & Decker Corporation (B&D at *www.blackanddecker.com*) contracted with NetIQ (*www.netiq.com*) to run a number of web analytics studies on its website. One was designed to provide insights into how B&D could increase visitor registrations. The company's information-only site supports consumers through their various home improvement projects, and having visitors register to receive additional information is an important step in the company's effort to develop a long-term relationship with them. Web analytics reports allowed B&D's marketing staff to monitor closely how visitors used the site. The performance outcome, to increase site registrations, depended on getting more visitors to click on the registration button, complete a registration form, and send it to the company. During the test period, the team moved the registration button to different locations on the B&D homepage and tracked visitor responses to each move. By analyzing the number of registrations in each location, they identified the highest-yield location and placed the

Black and Decker

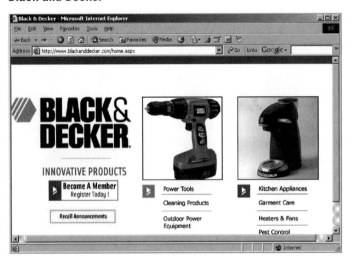

Web analytics tools helped B&D place its registration button in the best location on its web page—and thereby increased registrations.

Source: Copyright © 2000–2004 The Black & Decker Corporation. All Rights Reserved. Reprinted with permission, www.blackanddecker.com.

button there. As a result of this change in the button's location on the web page, on-site registrations increased 40 percent![9]

B&D successfully used web analytics to achieve its performance objective, but the promise of web analytics to boost returns on investment (ROI) can exceed the reality. The programs can produce overwhelming amounts of the wrong data—information that is of little value in actually improving performance by linking marketing actions to ROI. Information overload can impede rather than facilitate improved performance. Reports are not always accurate or reliable. Different software running on the same database can produce different results. Programs are often highly complex, laden with interfaces that are difficult to understand and well beyond the technical ability of many small businesses to implement and run. Web analytics programs require a huge amount of data: an estimated terabyte of data per year per client. Web analytics requires people who can connect analysis to marketing solutions and website improvements. They must be able to identify what needs to be tracked, how to measure it, how to interpret results, and how to apply these results to specific site improvements.[10]

eCRM

e-Customer relationship management (eCRM) A broad strategy that uses software and automation to create a seamless interface between offline and online systems to improve customer interactions across multiple channels.

A growing number of companies are looking for broad performance solutions from **e-customer relationship management (eCRM),** a broad strategy that uses software and automation to create a seamless interface between offline and online systems to improve customer interactions across multiple channels. It is a holistic view of customer-focused activities that reflects the basic marketing concept of putting customers first, wherever they are found.

eCRM, when it works, enables customers to interact seamlessly with the business on the Web, by email, through call centers, with field sales representatives, and in stores—a oneline strategy. Every **customer touchpoint**—all the "places" where customers interact with the business on a website, by email, through call centers, by meeting with sales representatives, and elsewhere—is managed to create a unified, seamless experience. The top sellers of eCRM software and technology are Oracle, Siebel Systems (*www.siebel.com*), and Pivotal Corporation (*www.pivotal.com*).

Customer touchpoint Any point at which customers interact with the business on a website, by email, through call centers, and elsewhere.

Advocates say that a successful customer-centric eCRM program can provide a matchless depth and breadth of timely customer information. Some organizations have used eCRM to shorten their sales cycle, increase order size, boost sales per customer, increase response rates to advertising messages, lower customer acquisition costs, reduce service response times, encourage customer feedback, personalize and customize marketing communications, and increase customer retention. However, evidence suggests that the greatest performance gains will accrue to those companies that are already customer-centric and successful at managing their customer interactions. These companies are the ones that will use the Internet to incorporate their online channel into the unified experience that already exists in their other channels. They will use the Internet to increase the number of customer touchpoints and expand opportunities to create and nourish relationships with customers.

Early adopters of eCRM software and sales force automation were very large companies in financial services, computer software, and telecommunications. Spending on CRM, including eCRM, in 2001 was around US$61 billion. This is forecast to rise to US$148 billion in 2005, when eCRM spending should reach US$10.39 billion. In FY 2003, small and midsize businesses, with less than US$50 million in annual assets, spent over US$1 billion on eCRM systems, but eCRM is used by only a tiny fraction of them. CRM spending by the U.S. government for both traditional and online systems is forecast to increase from US$260 million in FY 2002 to over US$590 million by FY 2007. Much of this spending will be for interagency CRM rather than for systems that interact with citizens.

Like many other data tools designed to improve performance, eCRM has its problems. Its cost and complexity are obvious, although cost is coming down and the user-system interface is improving. Because eCRM software must be linked to existing back office systems, problems with integration and interoperability are bound to arise. Employees often don't buy into eCRM, which undermines its effectiveness. It is also not unusual for more attention to be paid to the technology than to customers and how better to serve them. A surprising number of companies merely pay lip service to the concept of customer service and relationship management and still perpetuate a company-first model. This is becoming more risky as savvy Internet marketers recognize that online customers shop around and that there will always be a competitor eager to convert them. Perhaps most troubling, IBM found that only about 15 percent of the companies that implement CRM do it right and that for most of them, their customers really don't see any improvement in service or interactions with the company. For companies that do succeed with eCRM, the greatest value appears to be in improving presale and postsale customer interactions.

Despite all the enthusiasm for eCRM, this is a technology whose time has not yet come for most businesses. At the same time, it is clear that the fundamental principle of eCRM is sound, and most businesses should recognize that the messages customers are sending cannot be ignored. According to a Consumer WebWatch (*www.consumerwebwatch.org*) study, customers want ease of navigation, trustworthiness, frequent updates, identified information sources, and information about who owns and financially supports the site. They want shopping baskets that work, secure transactions, and information that can be found without excessive searching. They want a seamless interface between the Internet and offline touchpoints. Most emphatically, they want someone to respond to their emails and feedback forms, and they expect timely responses, which some companies still can't seem to provide.[11]

CUSTOMERS AREN'T GETTING RESPECT

According to research company The Customer Respect Group, Inc. (*www .customerrespect.com*), many large businesses are still not treating their website customers with respect, despite all the talk about eCRM and the billions of dollars spent on it. As late as 2003, some 21 percent of the largest one hundred companies in the United States did not respond to online customer inquiries, and 10 percent still did not have a privacy statement on their website. This behavior ignores numerous studies revealing that online customers want answers to their questions and insist on knowing how their personal data are used. It is particularly shortsighted considering how many customers use the Internet as their primary tool for gathering product information and conducting product research. Consumers spent over US$90 billion online in the United States in 2004, and that expenditure is forecast to rise to US$130 billion by 2006. At least 10 percent of all sales start on the Internet; 80 percent of all business professionals use the Internet to gather product information; over 51 percent of U.S. online households purchase online; more than 60 percent of customers will not buy from a company that isn't open and honest about how their personal data will be used; and privacy concerns discourage about 82 percent of Internet users from giving personal information to a website.

The Customer Respect Group annually evaluates over 1,000 websites in 16 different sectors to measure how customers are being treated. Its research considers over sixty different attributes to arrive at a website's *Online Customer Respect* score of 0 to 10 points, with 10 the highest possible score. The attributes are grouped into sets that measure *simplicity* (navigation ease), *privacy, customer-centric attitude, transparency, responsiveness,* and *principles* (respects customer data). On the basis of its research, The Group has developed a series of rules for online customer respect. It advises companies to focus on their key message, the one *reason why* customers should buy and come back; to make it easy for customers to find information quickly; to provide an online contact method; never to send any email without the customer's permission; to be open and honest about collecting personal data; to articulate an understandable privacy policy; never to share personal data without the customer's consent; to reply quickly to online inquiries; to personalize and customize online communication with customers; and to treat online and offline customers the same—as though each one were the company's only customer.

Most industry sectors are not showing their online customers respect. The airlines sector has an average customer respect score of only 6.2 out of 10; 8 percent of the companies in the sector have no online contact option; 33 percent take more than four days to respond to inquiries; 91 percent use cookies, but only 28 percent explain why and how they are used. Northwest Airlines has the top score in the sector, 7.8 out of 10. In the 2003 study, Procter & Gamble had the highest score (8.4) of all companies in the packaged-goods sector, where the average score was 7.2. Nike topped the apparel sector (9.5), and Steelcase, Inc. (8.9) led the furniture and home equipment sector.[12]

STRIVING FOR A GREAT CUSTOMER EXPERIENCE

Procter & Gamble Company (P&G at *www.pg.com*), the top U.S. consumer packaged-goods maker, strives to treat its online customers with respect. The company uses an integrated team approach to creating and operating customer-centric websites. Its goals are to provide a great online experience for visitors, sell more P&G products, and increase profits. P&G is a leader in the innovative use of IT, and its corporate IT department of 4,500 employees represents almost 5 percent of the company's total workforce. Around 800 of P&G's IT staff are assigned directly to one of the P&G operating business units—health care, beauty care, baby and family care, snacks and beverages, or fabric and home care. This reflects the company's strategy of increasing IT brand and marketplace responsibilities. Many of its IT professionals are directly involved with making interactive marketing work technically, from designing web marketing sites to operating email newsletters, managing onsite chats, developing online communities, collecting customer website information, and installing in-store Internet kiosks.

A recent visit to P&Gs Olay website provides insights into how the IT-marketing team collects data and implements customer-centric processes. Olay (*www.olay.com*) is a global site with map links to mirror sites in thirteen other countries. A recent visit began with a pop up that asked every *nth* visitor to *Please help us improve our site.* This visitor feedback (primary quantitative research) request was powered by interactive marketing agency imc^2's (*www.imc2.com/Index.aspx*) WebIQ software. The visitor could opt out; however, if the visitor opted in, he or she was asked to browse the site as usual but to expect pop-up questions while doing so. The next screen asked participants for additional demographic information, including the number of Olay site visits made, gender, age (13–17, 18–24, 25–34, 45–54, 55–64, or 65+), brand of facial moisturizer purchased in the past six months, purchase frequency, probability of purchasing an Olay product, main reasons for visiting the site (professional opinion, seeking coupons, general information, to sign up to receive newsletter or free samples, etc.), and finally, two sections of five-point Likert-scaled questions designed to evoke perceptions of the brand and depth of brand loyalty. The response categories were exact, and failure to respond within the survey's parameters meant having to return to the unanswered category and try again.

Olay

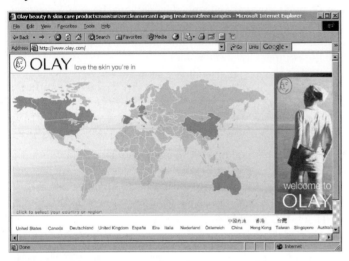

P&G's Olay website is a team effort directed at providing a customer-satisfying experience.

Source: Reprinted by permission, www.olay.com.

While the visitor was browsing the site, more pop-ups appeared, asking specific questions about whether the visitor found what he or she was seeking, how easy it was to navigate the site, degree of overall satisfaction with the site, likeliness of purchasing an Olay product in the next six months, and whether a visit to the site changed the visitor's opinion of the product. Questions were also asked about the visitor's race, household size, annual household income, and about how the visitor first became aware of the Olay website (television, radio, print ad, mail ad, email ad, banner ad, search engine, product packaging, in-store display, URL type-in, or word of mouth). The participant was asked to give permission for an email re-contact within the coming months. Under the surface, site tracking was recording page views and paths.

Another method for customer relationship management is Club Olay (*www.olay.com/clubolay/intro.htm*), a highly successful activity that collects data and adds customer value. Club Olay is an online opt-in community with over 4 million members. Membership is free and benefits include information, free samples, a monthly email newsletter, special offers, and skincare technology tips. P&G uses Epiphany (*www.epiphany.com*) customer relationship management software that reports and analyzes customer data from Club Olay and helps build product penetration among brand-loyal customers. Epiphany managers analyze primary research results from focus groups, surveys, and visitor feedback responses, as well as syndicated data from other sources and inventory data from P&G's internal database system that helps the site's managers track visitors and develop insight, including ideas for new products. Data from the Olay site are shared with other P&G units in company databases (warehouses) that span geographic areas and product lines. P&G shows customers respect on its websites, while also making the sites data collection magnets.[13]

ONLINE COMPETITIVE INTELLIGENCE

Companies can learn what their competitors are doing by studying their websites, using search engines to locate articles and news about them, monitoring chat room comments, reading blogs, and searching U.S. government websites that regularly file business regulatory documents. This is the *competitive intelligence* process, and it is legal and ethical as long as publicly published and available sources are the only ones used.

Performing competitive intelligence online is easy. Many companies will perform it for a business, for a fee. Successfully analyzing and applying competitive intelligence, particularly to enhance performance and gain competitive advantage, is far more difficult. The ease of collecting competitive intelligence online also means that companies are exposed to others' espionage and thievery because of the ready access of analytical tools and the openness of the Web. The Society of Competitive Intelligence Professionals (SCIP at *www.scip.org*) claims that pharmaceutical companies are the best at collecting, analyzing, and distributing competitive intelligence information.

Competitive marketing intelligence is both (1) a process for collecting, transforming, storing, and retrieving marketing data about the competition and (2) data that can be transformed into knowledge to be applied in making marketing decisions. In most large businesses, gathering marketing intelligence is a continuous process. Data can be gathered in a variety of ways. A panel of customers, company employees, or automated software robots can visit competitors' websites and systematically analyze all aspects of those firms' marketing activities. The analysis tests online ordering processes, checks site navigation and downloads, monitors delivery costs, and investigates how returns are handled. Site visits are often conducted on a daily basis if marketing offers frequently change. A company's online press releases and posted job openings are a rich source of information about its strategies. Chat rooms and message boards are fertile ground for collecting consumer comments. The caveat is that these data are difficult to interpret, are highly subjective, and (although they can provide useful insights) should not be the sole input to marketing decisions.[14]

Competitive marketing intelligence
A *process* (system for collecting, transforming, storing, and retrieving marketing data about the competition) and *content* (knowledge relevant to marketing decisions).

Value-Added Search Engines

Finding information online before the advent of search engines was problematic at best and impossible at worst. The situation has improved but still leaves a lot to be desired. Search engines have become extraordinarily popular data tools, and that has made them extremely valuable for online marketing because they can deliver access to self-segmented niche markets. Many search engines were developed in universities and then migrated to the Web, where some have become very successful businesses in their own right.

SEARCH ENGINE BASICS

When a visitor queries a search engine with a keyword, it triggers a search of the engine's databases, and a list of relevant URLs, or *hits,* is returned. Search engines build their DBs in a variety of ways. *Automated crawler* engines such as Google (*www.google.com*) use software to crawl (search) the Web seeking new pages, page titles, metatags, and other elements. *Human-organized* directories such as the Open Directory Project (*http://dmoz.org*) recruit Net-citizen volunteers to conduct searches and organize data. Other engines, such as MSN Search (*http://search.msn.com*), are *hybrids,* presenting results both from human-powered listings and crawlers.

Search engines use different weighting (ranking) algorithms to assign value to URLs according to their relevance to a keyword or the popularity of a site (measured by links to it). Some search engines accept **paid inclusions,** where a company pays the engine to accept any number of its individual pages or its entire site for indexing in the engine's databases. This gets a site listed quickly and improves its rank. Other engines *deep crawl,* drilling down deep into a site to access pages that were not submitted. Google and AllTheWeb (*http://alltheweb.com*) deep crawl. All major engines support metatag description tags and keywords in HTML code that are used

Paid inclusions
Pages or entire websites indexed in a search engine's database because a company has paid for them to be included.

to catch the attention of spiders, crawlers, and bots. Engines differ dramatically in the number of sites indexed in their databases, their ranking algorithms, retrieval speed, and the relevance of the sites listed.

Paid listings
Short text ads that a company pays a search engine to display linked to the advertiser's site on the engine's results page.

Most engines accept **paid listings,** short text advertisements that are hotlinked to the advertiser's website and appear at the top and/or sides of a search engine's results page. Advertisers pay the search engine for these sponsored ads, which are also known as search-related or pay-per-performance advertising. Paid listings generated US$2 billion in advertising revenues in 2003, about 25 percent of all online advertising sales, and should generate US$7 billion by 2007. Growth will continue at a compound annual rate of 20 percent through 2008.

Google, the top search engine in the world, has a 65.1 percent market share, followed by Yahoo! at 21.5 percent. Google has over 6 billion indexed items in its databases, including over 4.5 billion web pages, 880 million images, and 845 million Usenet messages. Users appreciate Google's effective, clean, and simple presentation; 89 percent report "strongly positive" experiences using it.

Search engines have many limitations, and the most serious is not being able to accurately interpret the meaning of many queries. Search engine bots cannot enter stored databases and are confused by frames and dynamic content pages. They typically search only the public Web and cannot enter the deep Web, intranets, or extranets. However, most intranets and extranets have internal search engines, often with site-specific technology licensed from Google.[15]

AN EXCEPTIONAL TECHNOLOGY

More than any other current Internet technology, search engines represent a killer technology that is exceptionally rich with opportunities, something that Amazon.com recognizes. Amazon formed a separately branded and operated subsidiary, A9.com (*http://a9.com*), in 2003 to develop its own search engine portal. A9 will help Amazon's own customers *find, discover,* and *buy* and will enable the company to license its technology to other companies. There will be a market for the product *if* it is a significant improvement over existing engines. A9's data are from Google, the massive Amazon.com website, and Amazon's Alexa subsidiary. The beta version of A9 shows some novel features, including book excerpts from Amazon's *Search Within a Book* feature that are matched to a search query. Like the Amazon site, A9 will emphasize personalization. What Amazon, Google, Yahoo!, and others are seeking is market leadership in the lucrative paid-search market. We will have more to say about paid search in Chapter 12.[16]

RSS FEED

Rich Site Summary (RSS)
A method for distributing syndicated web content.

News search and indexing is another area of growing marketing interest because it delivers self-segmented audiences. **Rich Site Summary (RSS),** also called RDF Site Summary and Real Simple Syndication, is another way for a website to interact with users and market its products by distributing links to its syndicated content. Users can opt in to receive the content automatically or manually. RSS content is registered with an RSS publisher, who is the distributor. Yahoo! (*http://news.yahoo.com/rss/*) is an RSS publisher and already offers RSS feeds in a growing number of categories. RSS content is created by newspapers, blogs, broadcasters, and others. It can contain text, graphics, and links. There are already tens of thousands of RSS feeds covering topics from sports to *Star Trek*. The advantage of RSS is that spam filters don't block it because it isn't sent by email. It is 100 percent opt in, which means that recipients want to have the interaction, and thus they belong to a self-selected interest group or market niche. The challenge for Internet marketers is creating content that is a *must have* for readers.[17]

Data Tools: A Lack of Respect?

There are two sides to using data tools. Marketers like them because the information they yield can be used to develop customer insight and to improve offers, track where consumers go online, and target large self-selected niche markets for advertising messages. On the other hand, some organizations criticize the tools and the marketers who use them for undermining privacy and degrading the online experience. Many consumers don't like them because the tools are invasive and threaten their privacy. Most consumers, however, don't realize how much personal data is already being collected about and from them. Almost 60 percent of adult Internet users do not realize that even those sites with privacy policies collect information about them and often share it with third parties.[18]

COOKIES, BEACONS, BUGS, AND SPYWARE

Cookies

Small text files placed on a user's browser often without the user's knowledge or consent by a website's server and used for information gathering and tracking, and to guide page customization.

Cookies are HTTP text files that are placed on a user's browser, often without the user's knowledge or consent, by a website's server that enable marketers to track where consumers have been on the Web and to customize web pages. Most cookies are small; others can be huge. Most cookies are persistent (permanent or stored) and last until they expire or the user trashes them. Others are transient and last only for a single session (visit) in temporary memory until the user's browser shuts down. Cookies are delivered from a server to the user's computer and sent back to the server whenever the user revisits the site. The site's web server determines whether or not a site cookie is on the user's computer. If it is, the cookie is accessed, and the data affects the content sent to the user's computer. A cookie stores *direct data,* information the user provides that is recorded automatically. If the user makes a purchase, the cookie records transaction data. Cookies also collect and store *indirect data*—clickstream records of where the user went on the site, how much time was spent at each click, and the user's computer information.

Some consumers and privacy advocates hate cookies because they fear that too much information is being collected surreptitiously. Other consumers love the convenience of cookies. Cookies can eliminate the need for passwords, registrations, and subscription codes, and this relieves consumers of having to write down or memorize a long series of numbers and type them in when asked. Cookies can capture a surprising amount of information. Amazon.com is very open about the information collected from cookies and other analytical tools. Amazon cookies include the IP address that connects the user to the Internet, the user's email address and Amazon password, computer and connection information, browser type and version, computer operating system and platform, user's Amazon purchase history and full URL clickstream path getting to and through Amazon, cookie number, products viewed or searched for at Amazon and zShops visited, Amazon auction history, and the user's telephone number if it was used to call 1-800.[19]

BEACONS AND BUGS

Web beacons (bugs)
Single-pixel electronic GIF images placed by third-party media and research companies.

Web beacons (bugs) are single-pixel electronic GIF images, generally used with cookies, placed by third-party media and research companies on a website or in email. Third-party beacons (also called pixel tags or clear GIFs) greatly increase the number of websites from which data can be collected or, in the case of email, where spam can be sent. The cookie on a user's hard drive is read whenever the user clicks on advertisements or views pages where advertisements are placed by a third party such as DoubleClick. That is where the beacons appear. Web beacons collect Non-Personally Identifiable Information (NP-II)—for example, a user's cookie number, the time and date when a page was viewed, and a description of the page where the web beacon is placed.

What sets web beacons or bugs apart from standard cookies is the ability to track cookies on more than one site. The original website that placed the cookie may partner with hundreds of other websites. As the user links to other websites, the beacons record the visits and send cookie information to the third party.

Yahoo! (*http://privacy.yahoo.com/privacy/us/pixels/details.html*) plants web beacons to report aggregate information about users, including demographic and usage data and unique visitor counts. They are on pages within the Yahoo! site as well as on sites owned by Yahoo! partners. Data from the beacons affect what offers Yahoo! delivers. It also lets Yahoo! tailor its web content and advertisements. Yahoo! does not share personal information about users with its partners. It also stipulates that partners must disclose in their privacy policies that Yahoo! beacons are placed on their sites. Users can opt out of Yahoo!'s web beacon program.

Network advertisers claim that the information collected by web beacons enables them to make offers that are more relevant to visitors. Beacons are also useful tools for measuring the effectiveness of online promotions. However, advertisers also acknowledge significant privacy concerns, which is why the Network Advertising Initiative (NAI at *www.networkadvertising.org*) was formed to fight spam and protect legitimate email.

The *spam beacon* is a variant of the website bug. It is embedded in email. When the recipient opens or previews the email, a signal is sent back to the spammer confirming that it has reached a valid email address. Thus the email address owner has sent a signal that he or she is ready to accept spam. There is no defensible marketing use for the spam beacon.[20]

SPYWARE AND ADWARE

Spyware
A broad category of software secretly placed on a user's computer that surreptitiously gathers information and reports it to a remote location.

A more malicious variant of the type of software that runs cookies and beacons has evolved to plague Internet users and exacerbate privacy concerns. **Spyware** refers to a broad category of software that is secretly transferred to a user's computer in downloaded shareware or freeware, through email or from web pages as a hidden bundled component, or when the user unwittingly agrees to accept the software as a condition of downloading music or other files. Spyware quietly tracks the user's online actions and collects and transmits information about the user without his or her knowledge to a remote location. This tracking software can dig into the user's hard drive and covertly send passwords, email addresses, and even stored credit card numbers and bank account information. Spyware also can be sent through peer-to-peer sharing of illegally copied music files. As independent programs, spyware can monitor, track, and report just about anything that occurs on the infected computer and may contribute to the computer's instability. It is a live server working within the unknowing user's computer. Research conducted by the Cyber Security Alliance (*www.staysafeonline.info*) in late 2004 found that of the population studied, two-thirds were not protecting their computers from spyware and other malicious software, and 80 percent of their computers already housed spyware.

Adware is a variant of spyware, although not all adware is spyware. Adware, or ad-serving software, also places software on a user's computer and gathers information secretly from the user's computer, primarily tracking Internet behaviors, and reports it for advertising purposes. Adware is shorthand for *advertising supported software.* The information reported is used primarily to direct specific advertising to the user's browser based on the user's browsing habits. Media attention has alerted many Internet users to adware and as a result, programs that cleanse computers of adware and spyware have become extremely popular. Spybot (*www.safer-networking.org*), for example, has been recognized by various computer industry sources for its privacy software that stops unsolicited commercial email messages (spam) and deletes adware and other pernicious files. Responding to growing complaints about software that not only tracks and reports information, but also hijacks computers, interest is growing in the United States Congress to regulate or even try to ban such software outright.[21]

Adware
A variant of spyware that gathers information secretly from the user's computer primarily for advertising purposes.

SERVER LOG FILES

Server log files
Plain-text files not really readable by humans that gather website traffic data.

Most web servers log (record) every request they receive in **server log files.** These files are not really readable by humans but must be read by third-party parsing/reporting programs that decipher the puzzling lines and code. The files (numbers and letters) usually end in .log. A file requesting data from a web server might look something like

eku.edu/webadmin/home/pub.p/marketing/public_html-[12January/2002
:05:47:52-0800] "GET/~marketing/text/if HTTP/1.0" 200 193847 "www
.bizcommkt. com:88/~marketing/" "Mozilla/1.12I (X11; I; NEWS-OS 6.1
.1 news5000) via proxy gateway CERN-HTTPD/3.0pre5 libwww/2.16pre"

The reporting program pulls out user name or machine identification number; web file or place requested; whether the request for information was successfully filled or a 404 error message was sent; size of the file transferred; browser used; date and time when the request was logged; and whether a proxy server was used, which indicates the presence of a firewall.

Server logs are traffic counters. Marketers can use them to help build site traffic, but clickstream data can be misleading because they cannot distinguish whether a visit is unique or a repeat, and they do not record traffic from files that are cached (stored). Nevertheless, they are useful in tracking what users do while they are on a site, and they can compare trends in site visits over time. Log file records can be obtained from a system administrator or ISP.[22]

GMAIL AND GOOGLE DESKTOP

In early 2004, Google announced a new free email service called Gmail (*https:// gmail.google.com*). It was almost immediately attacked by privacy advocates and consumer watchdogs because the company's computers will scan incoming and outgoing Gmail and deliver ads depending on the content. The ads and email surveillance are tradeoffs for 1 gigabyte of free storage space. Google also says it will retain copies of the email even if a user cancels the account, which means it will have a massive amount of archived email that might become available to the government. If Google is successful in implementing Gmail, it could be used as a model for other email providers.[23]

Google Desktop Search (*http://desktop.google.com*) is yet another innovation from Google that, while it has great advantages, is also perceived as a significant privacy threat. Desktop Search was introduced in October 2004 as a revolutionary way for users to harness Google's highly successful search technology for their own computers. Once downloaded, the software allows the user to search his or her email files, history of web visits, and chats. It can call up web pages even when the computer is not Internet-connected. Google Desktop Search finds documents in Outlook, AOL Instant Messenger, Internet Explorer, Word, Excel, and PowerPoint. It blends into Google's technology and the links returned are displayed in a typical Google page format. Privacy advocates are concerned because of the direct link established between a user's personal computer and Google itself, virtually moving a personal desktop to the Internet and possibly making personal information readily accessible to third parties.

Summary

http://college.hmco.com/business/students

Data Tools: Why They Matter

Enterprises increasingly rely on data tools, databases, and data collection. Relational databases are the current preferred database format. Marketing data are collected from and about markets, customers, competitors, and other areas of marketing interest. Databases are valuable only if they provide knowledge in understandable form that can be used to improve marketing performance. Usable databases can be powerful instruments of change. A DBMS systematically stores, processes, modifies, and retrieves data from databases. Some databases are created in-house; others are compiled. A data warehouse is a central electronic repository for corporate-wide databases. Data mining is sifting through databases and data warehouses to discover predictive relationships, hidden patterns, and previously unrecognized relationships. Collaborative filtering is a data-matching tool. Dynamic content adjusts page content according to what user or user type requests the page, the time of day, or the point in the update cycle.

Using Data Tools to Improve Performance

Web analytics tools help marketers understand what is going on in their website. eCRM is a broad strategy that uses software and automation to create a seamless interface between offline and online systems to improve customer interactions across multiple channels. Many large businesses are still not treating their website customers with respect, despite all the talk about eCRM and the billions of dollars spent on it. Companies can learn what their competitors are doing by studying their websites, using search engines to locate articles and news about them, monitoring chat room comments, reading blogs, and searching

U.S. government websites that regularly file business regulatory documents.

Value-Added Search Engines

Search engines are extraordinarily popular data tools, and this has made them extremely valuable for online marketing because they can deliver access to self-segmented niche markets. Automated crawler search engines such as Google use software to crawl (search) the Web seeking new pages, page titles, metatags, and other elements. Human-organized directories such as the Open Directory Project recruit Net-citizen volunteers to conduct searches and organize data. Other engines, such as MSN Search, use both of these approaches. Some search engines accept paid inclusions. Most engines accept paid listings. Search engines are currently the Internet technology with the greatest marketing potential. Rich Site Summary (RSS) is another way for a website to interact with users and market its products by distributing links to its syndicated content.

Data Tools: A Lack of Respect?

Cookies are small HTTP data files that are placed on a user's hard drive, without the user's knowledge or consent, by a website's server and that enable marketers to track where consumers have been on the Web. Some consumers and privacy advocates hate cookies because they fear that too much information is being collected surreptitiously. Other consumers love the convenience of cookies, which reduce the need for passwords, registrations, and subscription codes. Web bugs or beacons are single-pixel electronic GIF images placed by third-party media and research companies on a website or in email. They greatly increase the number of websites at which data can be collected and to which spam can be sent. Spyware is software that lurks on the user's computer and secretly reports tracking information to third parties. Adware is a variant of spyware that gathers and reports information for advertising purposes. Server logs are traffic counters. Gmail has been attacked by privacy advocates and consumer watchdogs because Google's computers will scan incoming and outgoing email and deliver ads depending on the content. Google Desktop Search has also been criticized because it creates a direct link between a user's personal computer and Google itself, virtually moving a personal desktop to the Internet and possibly making personal information readily accessible to third parties.

Take Action!

Let's create a scenario that you are working part-time in your university's career center. You have been asked to research Monster.com (*www.monster.com*), the leading worldwide career network.

1. Read Monster—About Us at *http://about.monster.com*. Watch the video of founder Jeff Taylor telling the Monster story. Prepare a memo to the Career Center's Director in which you identify five reasons why students at your university should use Monster.com's services prior to graduation.
2. Monster.com uses monsterTRAK (*www.monstertrak.monster.com*) to collect data and create its database. Monster is accessed more than 50,000 times each day; it targets over 2,800 university and college career centers, MBA programs, and alumni associations and is used by over 600,000 employers. Student résumé databases contain over 630,000 files. Consider the huge data requirements of this site. Create a schematic drawing that illustrates the relationships among data, data sources, data collection, and databases. Draw lines that indicate how Monster makes the connection between employers and applicants.

Chapter Review Questions

1. What are data tools and why do contemporary enterprises increasingly rely on them?
2. What is a database?
3. How are databases used?
4. How can databases affect marketing practices?
5. Explain how a personal computer is a simple DBMS.
6. Identify the advantages of in-house databases.
7. Should all customers be treated equally?
8. Why must databases be cleaned regularly?
9. How can Amazon.com make a product recommendation when a customer makes a return visit to the site?
10. What is the difference between paid listings and paid inclusions?
11. Contrast standard cookies and web beacons or bugs.
12. Why can't a marketer just read a server log?
13. What are customer touchpoints and what role do they play in eCRM?
14. Why is it important that customers be shown respect by websites?
15. Explain privacy concerns that arise from spyware, adware, and Google's Gmail and Desktop Search.

Competitive Case Study

Microsoft versus Linux and IBM

Microsoft Corporation (*www.microsoft.com*) is the world's top software company, known for its Windows operating system and Office Suite of business software, including Word, Excel, and PowerPoint. The company's FY 2003 sales were US$32.19 billion; it has over 55,000 employees worldwide. Whereas IBM has embraced the free Unix-based Linux operating system and created a Linux portal (*www-1.ibm.com/linux*), Microsoft has not. IBM is moving toward a Linux operating system for its desktop computers and servers, which will also affect its web access and viewing tools. IBM made the decision at least in part because Linux is open-source, which means that developers around the world can use the Linux source code to create new applications, including databases. Microsoft is in a fierce battle with Linux in the office and home computer operating systems markets. Microsoft's product advantages are interoperability, software application support, and value. Because Linux is open-source, its operating system is very enticing to governments and information technology experts, es-

pecially compared to Microsoft's operating system, which is perceived to be expensive and *buggy* (susceptible to security breaches). IBM's support of Linux evokes memories of bitter battles between IBM and Microsoft in the past.[24]

CHECK IT OUT

What makes Linux so attractive to IBM and so threatening to Microsoft? Check out Linux by visiting the IBM Linux page (*www-1.ibm.com/linux*). What companies are using Linux? Read several case studies and consider how Linux and IBM are offering solutions to business problems.

A GLOBAL PERSPECTIVE

How worldwide is IBM.com? Visit its *Select a Country* page (*www.ibm.com/planetwide/select/*) and select several countries to visit. Perform a content analysis of these country sites. What are some of the similarities and differences you observe? Is IBM taking a standardized approach to marketing on the Internet or is it more localized to country preferences?

Module III

The Internet Marketing Mix

The marketing mix or 4Ps of product, price, place (distribution), and promotion are known to anyone that has ever taken an introductory marketing class. Although many attempts have been made to replace or expand the Ps, they've endured as an effective method for organizing the major tactical tools marketers can deploy in a competitive marketplace. Just as the 4Ps have an enduring place offline, their importance online is equally compelling. Many dot com failures can be attributed to weak or non-existent attention to the planning, implementation, and control of the marketing mix, and the essential details that mean the difference between profitability and bankruptcy.

Module III begins with Chapter 9, Product in the Internet Marketing Mix. The next three chapters focus on the remaining 4Ps, their fundamentals, and Internet applications. Although Internet marketing is still very young and highly dynamic, successful Internet marketing mix models are emerging and providing lessons for others trying to find marketing success online.

Product in the Internet Marketing Mix

LEARNING OBJECTIVE

» To understand the fundamentals of Internet products
» To become aware of consumer products marketed online
» To consider enterprise products marketed online
» To become familiar with Internet brand issues

Amazon: More Than Just Books, and Toys, and Music, and . . . ?

When the speculative Internet bubble burst in 2000, Amazon's CEO Jeff Bezos went from "Internet poster boy to Internet Piñata." Net entrepreneur Bezos launched Amazon.com (*www.amazon.com*) in 1995 as "the Earth's biggest bookstore," a direct challenger to traditional bricks-and-mortar retail book sellers. The company is named symbolically after the river that carries the largest volume of water on Earth. Amazon.com went public in 1997 with a US$24 billion market capitalization on annual sales of less than US$600 million. By 2000, its losses were over US$1.4 billion, and in October 2001, its price per share dipped to a low of US$5.51. Bezos's initial strategy was to get big quick, acquire other companies, maximize cash flows (not profits), and expand product offers. As the largest first-mover cyberbrand of its kind, Amazon's size made it far more difficult for second- and third-generation companies to compete. Amazon's current business model is based on low prices, huge selection, availability, convenience, and lots of good product information, and it styles itself "Earth's most customer-centric company." Amazon's strategy is paying off. Sales rose from US$86 million in 1998

to over US$5.26 billion in 2003, when it showed its first full year of profitability (US$250 million). Amazon's percent of sales spent on marketing has declined steadily since a high of 12 percent in 1999, although the company remains a heavy advertiser. Better yet, it has dramatically increased the efficiency of its distribution system and cut its operating costs. Amazon's strategy includes moving aggressively outside the United States, selling everything everywhere. The company operates websites in Canada, the UK, Germany, France, and Japan. Like most businesses, Amazon has also made its share of mistakes. In 2002 it was criticized for making "faux" recommendations to potential buyers for apparel, recommendations not based on its collaborative filtering process. This temporarily undermined the credibility of its recommendations, although some retail experts have doubts about the value of recommending purchases on the basis of collective purchasing patterns. Delivery delays plagued the company during the 2003 holiday season; however, its sales volume was enormous. In one day in took in and processed over 2 million orders. Despite these problems, Amazon is one of the ten most trusted Internet brands and has received the highest customer satisfaction scores seen in retail. Amazon sells a

amazon.com.

Amazon.com, one the world's best-known, most trusted, and most customer-pleasing Internet brands.
Source: Courtesy of Amazon.com, Inc. All rights reserved.
www.amazon.com.

huge assortment of new and used products, including books, CDs, DVDs, videos, toys, tools, electronics, health and beauty aids, prescription drugs, gourmet foods, film processing, and more. It collects a 15 percent fee for every used book sold from its site. Amazon caters to customers by offering free shipping on certain orders over US$25. In 2001 it allied with the Borders Group Inc., the second largest offline book retailer, and now operates the online Borders site. Other businesses have set up shop on Amazon. Featured partners include Office Depot, Toys "R" Us, Babies "R" Us, and Target. Amazon processes their orders for a fee (typically 10 to 15 percent, with as much as a 70 percent profit margin for the partner). This eliminates inventory risk but adds delivery risk, because order fulfillment is not from Amazon's

warehouses. Apparel shoppers can purchase from Gap, Lands' End, and Nordstrom through Amazon's apparel store. Individual sellers and small businesses can sell their products through Amazon's *Sell Your Stuff* program. The company is an innovator in email marketing, running several hundred multiple concurrent campaigns each quarter. Its advanced technology pioneered customer recommendations, single-mouse-click ordering, *Search Inside the Book,* Gold Box specials, and the Amazon Honor System. In early 2004, Amazon launched a jewelry store, which drew 100,000 orders while it was still in beta test. Its low margins (as little as 13 percent on some pieces) will drive growth. Amazon's independent search engine unit launched an expanded Amazon/A9 search portal in 2004 with a discount offer for searchers who also made purchases on Amazon. The discount for registered A9 users is activated when they use Amazon's shopping cart. A9 is unique in its ability to organize information and websites for users. As it continuously reinvents itself, Amazon is poised to be like its namesake the river, moving the largest volume of products on the Internet.[1]

Product offer
The total value proposition presented to buyers for their consideration and to initiate an exchange.

The breadth and depth of Amazon's online product offers are remarkable. The **product offer,** the total value proposition presented to buyers for their consideration, is at the core of the marketing exchange process. The offer includes the product itself, as well as other tangible and intangible elements that affect its attractiveness, including its price and availability. An increasing number of offers are made on the Internet, the worldwide electronic bazaar that never sleeps, where products and brands are on display in profusion, and marketing exchanges can be made 24/7/365. In this chapter we discuss product basics, the types of products sold online, and brand building.

The Fundamentals of Internet Products

The Internet is a transformational technology. It is part of a major economic disruption, one of five great economic turning points over the past 250 years that have propelled society and commerce to enormous advances. Each disruption was also marked by a speculative bubble followed by bust, recovery, and vibrant growth. These turning points were the First Industrial Revolution's canals and turnpikes (c.1771), followed by steam and railroads (c.1829), steel and electricity (c.1875), the automobile, oil, and mass production (c.1908), and now information and telecommunications (c.1971).

Each proceeded initially by the building of a physical technology infrastructure, followed by experimentation in how to use it, and commercialization—the development of a wide array of profitable products and delivery systems dependent on and associated with the infrastructure. Some of these products were true innovations that collided with existing products and hastened their obsolescence. For example, nationwide electrification allowed General Electric (*www.ge.com*) to build a market for the labor-saving electrical home appliances that replaced ice boxes (pre-electric refrigerators), which required blocks of ice for cooling, and supplanted manual scrub boards for washing clothes and linens.[2]

The Internet's speculative bubble broke in 2000, but within two years, recovery was well under way in the form of growing commercial activity. Between 2001 and 2002, online sales (in manufacturing shipments, merchant wholesale trade, retail trade, and selected services) outperformed these sectors in the general U.S. economy on a percentage basis. Although revenue estimates vary depending on the data sources and research methodology used, revenue trends are all upward, with sales rising every year and continually exceeding forecasts. Online retail sales in 2003 rose to an estimated US$114 billion (5.4 percent of total retail sales), a 51 percent increase over 2002 that far surpassed forecasts. Sales were expected to grow an additional 27 percent in 2004 and to exceed US$133 billion by 2005. Large numbers of buyers obtain product information online and use it offline to guide purchase decisions, an activity that is not reflected in online or offline sales reports. Over 75 percent of new-car buyers research cars online before making their purchase offline. Many come to the car dealership clutching printouts to use in their negotiations. Top-selling products online are travel, clothing and clothing accessories, computer hardware, books and magazines, and electronics. Travel is the single largest sales category and represents around a third of all B2C sales. The product categories that have experienced the greatest online sales growth are health and beauty, apparel, and flowers, gifts, and cards. Both new and used products are selling briskly. As much as 25 percent of all sporting goods sold online are used. Used cars are the second largest product category of products sold on eBay (*www.ebay.com*).[3]

The U.S. Department of Commerce reports that in 2002, B2B sales continued to dominate online commercial activity, generating 93 percent of online revenues. Revenue increases were concentrated in five industry groups led by transportation equipment, followed by beverage and tobacco products and then by computer and electronic products, as measured by the value of product shipments. Merchant wholesalers' online sales were concentrated in pharmaceuticals and druggist sundries, motor vehicles and parts, and professional and commercial equipment and supplies. By 2004, the leading product category in U.S. online B2B sales was motor vehicles and parts, representing over 27 percent of total online sales (more than US$274 billion). Around a fifth of all motor vehicles and parts trade was expected to be online by 2005. This sector also represents the largest group of online advertisers. Worldwide B2B sales are also increasing, from US$280 billion in 2000 to US$823 billion by 2002, and exceeded US$2.7 trillion by 2004.[4]

Product
A good, service, idea, information, entertainment, or other item of value.

UNDERSTANDING PRODUCT

Product is the marketing mix variable that determines to a significant extent how strategies are developed for price, place (distribution), and promotion. A product can be a good, service, idea, place, person, information, entertainment, organization, or other item of value offered in trade for something of value from the buyer, principally cash, credit, or other acceptable exchange unit, including other products in a barter exchange. Product is a bundle of benefits that creates value for buyers, seller, and intermediaries. Marketing mix decisions are product-specific, yet marketers rarely have authority to make all product decisions independently. Marketers often contribute essential information about buyers' responses to product offers, their product preferences, and demand forecasts.

Two key criteria in understanding product are *buyer* and *use.* Key questions are *Who is the buyer?* and *How will the product be used?* Buyers are consumers or enterprises, although sometimes the distinction blurs. Buyers focus on product benefits. Consumers want to know what's in it for them if they purchase and use this product. They want products to meet their needs and wants, satisfy their desire to take possession and own something of value, and send signals about their preferences, buying power, and social standing. Consumer products have psychological and symbolic benefits that affect the buyers' self-image, status, and perceptions of worth.

Enterprise buyers, particularly businesses, want to know how products will solve their enterprise-related problems—for example, how products will shorten delivery times, improve safety, or increase profit margins. Enterprise products are inputs to production processes, used in operations, and purchased for resale. They generate revenue and, it is hoped, profits. Even with these differences between them, consumer and enterprise buyers sometimes purchase the same products, such as computers and software, airline tickets, and office products. At other times they buy radically different products. Even when they purchase the same products, there are significant differences in the quantities they purchase and in the purchase and repurchase schedules, purchase processes, price paid per unit, and delivery terms.

Products are composed of multiple layers, and each layer adds value and an opportunity for marketers to connect with buyers. The layers are the *core product* (functional elements, design, benefits offered, needs satisfied, and patent protection), *packaging* (brand name, style, quality, product features, package, packing, trademark, trade dress, price, and image), *support* (delivery, credit, warranty, guarantee, installation, after-sale service, repairs, spare parts, and training), and *product potential* (proposed product extensions, modifications, improvements, repositioning, and rebranding).

Successful marketers determine what buyers most value and deliver it. In some cases, such as perfume, packaging may be more important than the core product; in other cases, such as mainframe computers, support may be a prime purchase consideration. If a buyer has no prior experience with a product and if product cues are lacking, there is a risk of postpurchase dissatisfaction (dissonance) based on unmet expectations. This is where online customer recommendations can help minimize risk, but they cannot completely eliminate it. Some products are high-risk, whereas others pose low or no risk. The challenge for marketers is to minimize risk while maximizing purchase and repurchase probabilities.

CATEGORIZING PRODUCTS

Various frameworks have been developed for categorizing products in an effort to understand them better and assess how buyers perceive and value them. This knowledge can lead to more effective and profitable product marketing. One popular framework

Goods
Tangible products that can be felt, stored, inventoried, produced in quantity, transported, pretested, and quality-controlled.

categorizes products as *goods* (tangibles such as a candle or forklift), *services* (intangibles such as a haircut or accounting audit, a performed service), *digitals* (digital products such as music and software), or a combination of these forms.

Goods are tangible physical products that can be felt, stored, inventoried, mass-produced (produced in quantity), transported, tested in advance of purchase, and quality-controlled. Examples include apparel, automobiles, and computers. Product fulfillment for goods adds costs (inventory, shipping, and handling) and lengthens the time between purchase and when the buyer can take possession. This can be a problem when the buyer wants or needs the product immediately. Presenting goods online for buyer inspection is a significant challenge. Consumer goods are commonly shown in small thumbnail pictures, presented several to a web page. One-dimensional images are not a good substitute for being able to *experience products*—to see, touch, smell, or taste goods. Pictures of goods can be enlarged and rotated online, which makes their presentation on a web page superior to the flat, static pictures in a hard-copy catalog. At apparel site Landsend.com (*www.landsend.com*), clothing can be fitted to a consumer's self-created virtual model. Apparel colors can be changed and the model rotated so that the consumer can see how he or she will look wearing the item, assuming that the model has been created using accurate dimensions. Some sites try to solve the "experience problem" by offering to send potential buyers free product samples, such as a fabric swatch from an apparel site or a food sample from a candy site.

With few exceptions, most goods sold offline are also sold online. This includes

Lands' End

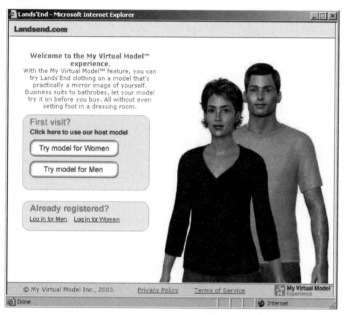

Lands' End's *My Virtual Model* enables customers to *try on* apparel, which adds an experience dimension to the product purchase and helps reduce the risk of a poor choice.

*Source: © Lands' End, Inc. and My Virtual Model[a] 2003. Used with permission. (*www.landsend.com*).*

Durables   Goods that have relatively long life spans and can be used over and over. A clothes washer is a consumer durable that can last several decades, depending on its maintenance and use. Sears (*www .sears.com*) sells durable washing machines online with delivery scheduled from a Sears warehouse via UPS, the USPS, or Sears Home Delivery.

Nondurables   Goods that are rapidly used up and must be replaced on a regular and fairly frequent basis. A bottle of shampoo can be ordered online from Reflect.com (*www. reflect.com*).

Disposables   Expendable nondurables that are used once and then discarded. Drugstore.com (*www.drugstore.com*) sells disposable paper cups and plates.

Perishables   Nondurables with a short life span that is subject to decay or deterioration even if the product is not used. Ice cream is sold by Schwan's (*www.schwans.com*), a company that has been home-delivering fresh frozen food since 1952 and now has online ordering for direct-to-home delivery.

For goods that are not sold online, their offline sale can be facilitated when a website displays the product, provides useful information about it, and drives buyers to telephone a salesperson for more information or visit an offline store to make a purchase. This is certainly the case with large, custom-made industrial and defense goods (capital products) such as aircraft or naval vessels that require negotiations over the specifications for their construction. It is also the case with customized enterprise computer systems—computers and other equipment that must be adapted to the unique needs of the business. In these cases, products presented on a website are designed to drive customers or prospective customers to contact the offline sales force. Increasingly, sales of new cars and trucks are completed offline with price and specification information obtained online from manufacturers' sites (Ford Motor Company at *www.ford.com* or General Motors at *www.gm.com*) or from online car-buying guides such as Edmunds (*www.edmunds.com*).

All retailers must deal with returns, overstocks, closeouts, and remainders. Many bricks-and-clicks retailers allow store returns of goods purchased online, an advantage for the buyer *and* seller because it gets the customer into the store where more offers can be made. Other returns are sent back by delivery carrier. Generally, it is too costly to restock returns, so they are sent to the retailer's own outlet stores (on- and offline) or sold to such companies as It'sGottaGo.com (*www.itsgottago.com*), an ecommerce marketplace that sells closeouts and used products at auction. Overstock.com (*www.overstock.com*) sells name brands at clearance prices, sometimes as much as 70 percent off list. Some returned goods, as well as overstocks and seasonal leftovers, are sold on eBay and other auctions.

Services
Nonphysical products, performances that cannot be stored, inventoried, mass-produced, transported, pretested, or easily quality-controlled.

Services are nonphysical (intangible) performances that cannot be stored, inventoried, mass-produced, transported, tested in advance, or controlled through standardized quality control methods. Services typically are inseparable from their performance; service consumption often cannot be delayed beyond the time of its delivery. The customer more or less participates in the service performance and does not have ownership of it. Examples include a haircut, an automobile tune-up, and shoe repair. Although many services, such as marriage counseling and dating services, are delivered online, more are delivered offline, and many are a mixture of online/offline delivery. A haircut cannot be delivered online, but a hairdresser appointment can be scheduled online. A customer can evaluate an assortment of haircut styles online, select one, and print it for his or her stylist to copy at the time of the haircut. Industrial equipment maintenance can be scheduled online, but servicing the equipment must be performed offline. Some computer repairs can be completed online; for example, new printer drivers can be downloaded and installed in the user's computer. Tax preparation services are offered online, as is online filing.

Digital products
Products that are created, transmitted, and/or stored electronically in bytes (binary digits), including digital cash, digital music, and information.

Digital products are created, transmitted, and/or stored electronically in bytes (binary digits). Examples include digital cash, digital music, electronic airline tickets, and software. Most digital products are not unique to the Internet but are particularly well suited to Internet purchase and delivery. Content of all types is an online product increasingly valued by both consumers and enterprises.

Mixed products are combinations of the foregoing forms. Examples include an oil change (good and service), a computer operating system upgrade pushed from a software vendor's site (digital product and service), video training lessons that accompany an exercise machine (digital product and good), and a restaurant dinner (good and service). A popular combination is an online service manual for a refrigerator (good). More marketers are providing online service manuals and parts lists for consumer and enterprise goods, which reduces the cost of providing this information in printed form and requires fewer live customer service representatives.

ADVANTAGES OF MARKETING PRODUCTS ONLINE

The advantages of marketing products online can be viewed from the perspective of buyers and from that of sellers. From the buyers' perspective, *availability* is an advantage; products that often are not available in local offline stores can be found online. This makes online shopping particularly appealing to buyers who live in remote or rural areas. Some products are offered only online, which confers a clear availability advantage. Because the product *assortment* is larger online, the buyer has broader and deeper choices. *Comparison shopping* is much easier and faster online, and because there are more sellers, there are more product choices to compare. Buyers have greater access to product *information,* particularly product specifications, parts lists, and service manuals. Buyers have access to product *reviews* and other buyers' experiences with the products, along with *recommendations.* Online information can be brought to an offline sales negotiation, as in the case of automotive products and home sales. New product information can be disseminated quickly via email and newsletters. Most online product sales are *untaxed,* unless the company has a nexus in the buyers' home state; this freedom from taxation is a price advantage. Buyers appreciate the *time* and *place convenience* of window shopping products 24/7/365. Many online offers can be *customized* and *mass customized,* which can create products that are constructed to buyers' specifications. Online auctions facilitate the purchase and sale of vast numbers of *used products. Customer service* can be immediate and interactive for buyers on broadband, because they can interact with customer service personnel at the same time they are viewing products on the website using instant messaging or telephone. Online *product simulations* enable buyers to experience how apparel will look on their body type or how a custom-made part will fit into a production process.

A prime advantage for marketers is that they can broaden their *customer base* by offering products online and worldwide 24/7/365. This offers the opportunity for them to *clear inventory* more quickly because they are reaching a far broader and larger buyer base. Excess inventory can be sold online through overstock and liquidator intermediaries, on-site clearance, and at auction. Furthermore, marketers can provide more *product information* in greater depth and at a *lower cost* in an HTML or .pdf file than in a four-color print catalog. This *cost shift* moves the cost of reproducing product information to the downloader and can reduce the need for live customer service representatives. Online information can be a *driver* to offline sales. *Product test markets* online typically cost less, can involve more participants, and collect results more quickly. *Dynamic product offers* can be tailored to visitors, they can be changed quickly, and the results can be analyzed in real time. These offers can be used to up-sell and cross-sell. Data collected online can be used to identify *new product opportunities.*

DISADVANTAGES OF MARKETING PRODUCTS ONLINE

There are disadvantages to marketing products online, and some products, such as music, are far better suited than others to the Internet environment. Perceived *security and privacy risks* associated with online product purchase can dampen product sales. This increases the importance of providing a secure transaction process and ensuring that buyers know security measures are operational. *Purchasing process breakdowns* often lead to shopping basket abandonment and lost sales, which can be avoided by constantly assessing the usability of shopping basket software. Product *quality* is difficult to assess in the absence of prior experience and/or *sensory cues.* Because the Internet environment currently lacks sensory cues except for sound, buyers can't touch, feel, smell, or taste products. When sensory cues are important, marketers must develop appropriate strategies to provide them, such as sending free samples on request, listing testimonials of satisfied buyers, offering downloadable coupons to encourage offline product trial, or providing virtual models or simulations so buyers can simulate the product experience. Simulations can be used with industrial products to demonstrate products being used. Product *pictures* are often small and static, which can misrepresent the product, and colors are easily distorted by buyers' computer monitors. This can be addressed by improving resolution, offering larger view links from the thumbnails, and providing access to a service representative who can answer questions and address these issues. *Product returns and redress options* are important but can be complicated and frustrating to the site visitor. They must be clearly and accurately explained online. Browsing or *window shopping* itself can be frustrating, particularly if it means a lengthy or fruitless search. This problem can be remedied by licensing an internal search product from Google (*www.google.com*), Yahoo! (*www.yahoo.com*), or other such company. *Excessive product information* can overload and frustrate shoppers. Eliminating this problem requires usability testing by current or prospective buyers, efficient information organization, and skilled editing.

PRODUCTS FOR A MASS MARKET OF ONE

Mass-marketing strategy
A marketing strategy that assumes a homogeneous market with undifferentiated buyers who will accept standardized products and have the same general marketing mix preferences.

A **mass-marketing strategy** assumes that the market is relatively homogeneous, composed of buyers who generally share marketing mix preferences for products, price, place/distribution, and promotion alternatives. *Standardized products* are mass-produced, uniform products. Buyers have limited alternatives for such standardized products as canned foods and computer printer paper. Limited variations of a product are often produced so that buyers will have some choices. For example, Procter & Gamble (P&G at *www.pg.com*) offers several alternative Tide (*www.tide.com*) laundry detergent formulations, including powder and liquid, with and without bleach or bleach alternative, and Tide HE (high efficiency). Buyers can select from among these limited alternatives. Although Tide isn't sold from its P&G website, visitors can access valuable information about fabric care and laundry basics there. Many standardized products are sold online at other sites, such as Walmart.com (*www.walmart.com*) and General Electric's ColorXpress (*www.gecolorxpress.com*), which offers industrial OEM buyers an inventory of over 20,000 colors and special effects for plastics, paints, textiles, and inks.

Customized products are truly unique. The manufacturer works directly with the buyer to produce an original, unduplicated product. Examples include a hand-tailored shirt and process-specific industrial polymers. Many custom manufacturers are online, but to deliver customized products, many typically must still meet the client face-to-face, at least initially. In the case of hand tailoring, the initial contact must be offline, but once the tailor has the client's measurements, subsequent reorders can be taken online. Toys can be custom made totally online. ToyBuilders.com (*www.toybuilders.com*) turns imagination into reality by letting customers design their own board pieces for Monopoly, Clue, Chess, Checkers, various role-playing games, and even their own toys. Some game pieces incorporate photographs of the customer's family members. Prospective customers can see product samples online to help them create designs, and then rapid prototyping machines capture the designs and translate them into finished, custom-made products. Customers can see a three-dimensional model of their order before they give final approval for its manufacture. The advantages of online customized products are convenience, timeliness, and availability. The disadvantages include not being able to touch or interact with a tangible product until the finished product is received.

Mass-customized products give buyers options, while avoiding the higher costs of true customization. **Mass customization** produces a large quantity of *semicustomized* products very quickly because options are limited and products are produced in part in advance of the final customization and held in inventory. Buyers are involved in the manufacturing process, providing input to final product design. Examples include Reflect.com cosmetics and fragrances and Dell (*www.dell.com*) computers. Manufacturers have the flexibility to offer mass customization online backed by modular product design, flexible manufacturing processes, intelligent manufacturing systems, computerized order management, information systems and databases, and delayed assembly.[5]

Mass customization is particularly well suited to the Internet with its worldwide reach, interactivity, 24/7/365 access, and speed. A mass-customized product is often developed from visitor responses to preprogrammed closed-ended questions. Visual images can be used to add greater depth to the choices. The fact that touch and smell are not yet available online currently limits the use of these senses in customizing consumer products, but careful choice of keyword descriptors can give buyers verbal cues to tactile and fragrance features. Consider Reflect.com, the site that allows customers to design their own perfumes and cosmetics. The site was launched in September 1999 as a separate and privately owned P&G joint venture; P&G has a 65 percent ownership. A visitor to the site is guided through a series of questions that builds a profile for when the perfume will be worn (occasion) and preferences for top, middle, and bottom notes (fragrance shades). The quality of these descriptions and evocative pictures accompanying the text help overcome the absence of smell. Buyers have a limited number of choices to make, which ensures a manageable number of different perfume formulations. Once purchased and named by the customer, the customized perfume is elaborately packed, shipped without charge, and unconditionally guaranteed. Rather than incurring the cost of returning merchandise, a customer who is not

Mass customization
Allowing consumers to customize a product within manufacturer-set options.

satisfied gets to keep the fragrance and try again. Marketing research has shown that the site has the highest conversion rate (browser to buyer) of any online beauty site and a lower shopping basket abandonment rate than similar sites. The industry's abandonment rate average is from 65 to 85 percent. Buyers appear quite willing to spend more for these fragrances.[6]

Consumers designing their own fragrances at Reflect.com pose less of a threat to cannibalize offline retailer sales of P&G products than if P&G sold its existing standardized perfume products directly from its website. Avoiding confrontations with offline distributors provides an incentive for manufacturers to adopt a mass-customization approach online, if it's appropriate to their products. Reflect.com's mass-customized Internet-only perfume is a high-margin product because it is premium-priced, the process eliminates traditional intermediaries from the distribution channel, and products move quickly out of inventory, reducing inventory holding costs. Reflect.com minimizes buyers' product purchase risk by making the promise, "Free recustomization—money-back guarantee—no product returns necessary."

Online mass-customization is offered for a wide variety of products, including soccer uniforms (custom and stock uniforms from CustomJersey.com at *www.customjersey .com/soccer.html*), bicycles (HubBub Custom Bicycles, fitting, and refitting at *www.hubbub.com*), and photo watches (Pet Connection at *www.petcollection.com*), among others. Personalization, or one-to-one marketing, is not mass customization. It uses technology, particularly cookies, collaborative filtering, and customer databases (stored or collected in real time) to personalize electronic commerce interactions between a marketer and each customer (see Chapter 8). It appears as a line on the front page welcoming a customer back to the site by greeting him or her by name.

SEEKING INTERNET PRODUCT OPPORTUNITIES

New products are the lifeblood of an enterprise, and the Internet offers a platform where consumers and enterprises can collaborate in their development. The new product development process is a series of steps from scanning the market for product gaps to commercialization, bringing a new product to market. New products are expensive, time-consuming, and risky to develop. It is not unusual for a new product to cost a large or midsize business from US$20 million to over US$100 million to commercialize. It is estimated that the average cost of developing a new prescription drug is around US$850 million. In addition to the cost, the failure rate of new products is extremely high; three out of every four new products fail. Close to 50 percent of the cost of developing and commercializing new products is never recovered.

Marketing activities already occurring online can lessen costs and risks, and can shorten the time to commercialization. Online chat rooms and consumer panels can be used for opportunity scanning, determining what the competition is offering and listening to what consumers are saying about existing products and product gaps; online focus groups are used for idea generation and screening (see Chapters 7 and 8). Online concept testing and test markets can be conducted on restricted websites. Commercialization and new product launches can be announced online, they can be supported with online promotions, and sales can be tracked to evaluate results.

New blockbuster products are rare, although their promise is intoxicating. Enterprises can achieve greater actual profit and encounter less risk by making good products better. As a result, most new products are modifications of existing products or *continuous innovations*—that is, tweaking some product feature and calling it *new and improved*. Some new products are *product line extensions,* such as the addition of the *Wall Street Journal Online* to the Dow Jones stable of print publications. Others are *repositioned products,* products that have changed their features, functions, target markets, or marketing strategies. For example, Yahoo! is being repositioned as a shopping portal. Very few new products are so radically different and unique that they can be labeled *discontinuous innovations.* Email is such a unique product. People had to learn a new way of communicating, and for many, it was a very frustrating process at first.

How different are online products from offline products? A close look at most consumer and enterprise products reveals that they are the same online and offline. Lands' End drifter sweaters sold online are exactly the same as drifter sweaters sold in a Lands' End print catalog, at a Lands' End Inlet store, or at a Sears store in a local mall.

Have some existing products been modified because of the Internet and the Web? Absolutely! This is readily apparent when on-screen announcements pop up during a television program and encourage viewers to visit the channel's website to learn more about the topic. Stories in the *Wall Street Journal* print edition refer readers to the *Journal* website, where they can participate in a chat on the topic. It is evident in the replacement of hard-copy airline tickets by electronic tickets and of paper checks by online bill payment. Many university libraries are dropping subscriptions to traditional hard-copy journals and are instead subscribing online to their electronic versions.

Are there products whose existence is inextricably linked to the electronic global marketplace? Without the Internet, there would not be Internet service providers (ISPs); Internet routers, web servers, and related hardware and software; dial-up modems and DSL; web directories, search engines, spiders, and bots; web browsers; Flash and related products; HTML editors; animated .gifs and .jpgs; streaming audio and video; ecards, ebooks, elearning, emagazines, etickets, and ecash; and so on. The Internet and the Web have stimulated the creation of many products whose existence depends on a global electronic marketplace.

Are any Internet product opportunities still available? Again, the answer is a resounding yes! Transformational technologies such as the Internet promote the development of new products designed to take advantage of its infrastructure and benefits. An example is downloadable music, which was an early Internet success for peer-to-peer (P2P) file sharers using Napster (*www.napster.com*) and similar sites. Apple Computer, Inc. (*www.apple.com*) recognized a product gap when legal challenges forced the original Napster to shut down in 2000 and the Recording Industry Association of America (RIAA at *www.riaa.com*) began suing individual P2P downloaders for illegal file sharing. Apple released its controversial "Rip. Mix. Burn." iTunes music software in 2001. In early 2003, Apple CEO Steve Jobs unveiled the first legal digital music store, the Apple iTunes Music Store, supported by a massive television and print campaign whose message was "Buy. Mix. iPod." iTunes initially contained a music library of over 200,000 legally downloadable songs that could be purchased for US$0.99 each. By early 2004, iTunes had sold over 25 million tunes and over 150 million by late 2004! Companies such as Rhapsody.com (*www.rhapsody.com*), which promises "Brings the Celestial Jukebox to Life," also recognized the opportunity and took a different approach, offering music download subscription services.

Apple's strategy was to use iTunes to sell its remarkable, innovative, ground-breaking iPod hardware, although the iTunes Store is itself a web destination. Apple introduced the iPod in 2002, and by 2004 it had sold over 3 million units. By early 2004 the third-generation iPod was released, and competitors were still struggling to create comparable models. iPod is a portable music player that operates on Mac and Windows PCs and can play regular MP3 files from any source. Its advantages are simplicity, massive storage capacity (30 gigabytes on top-of-the-line models), elegant design, low price, long battery life, thinness, light weight, and compatibility (usable on Macs, Windows PCs, and televisions and in cars).

Apple continues to introduce extensions to its iPod line, including cheaper models with more storage capacity, the iPod Mini, and (in cooperation with BMW) the *iPod Your BMW* plug-in (*www.apple.com/ipod/bmw/*). The 3.6-ounce business-card-size iPod Mini was a *BusinessWeek* 2004 Best Product Design winner. Apple's intention is to make Macs the *digital hub* for a full range of devices from camcorders, digital cameras, and video to digital music. iTunes now offers live performance recordings, rehearsal outtakes, and other unique products that traditional music retailers don't carry. Other companies are using iPods as the basis for some interesting products of their own. iPodlounge (*www.ipodlounge.com*), the site for "All Things iPod," launched in 2001, by early 2004 was receiving over 5 million visitors each month looking for iPod accessories and software. The site is an independent clearinghouse for iPod information, offers product reviews, hosts a 23,000-member iPopdlounge community, and posts pictures of iPods in use around the world. Well over 200 iPod accessories are available—voice recorders, headsets, portable speakers, digital photo adapters, and more. More than 100 software applications turn the iPod into everything from a videogame player, voice memo recorder, map reader, bible reader, appointment book, weathercaster, and lyric writer to Google-getter. When a product like the iPod captures buyers' imaginations, it stimulates the development of other products that augment the original. It also invigorates the competition.[7]

INTERNET PRODUCT DECISIONS

Internet marketers make many product-specific decisions and for bricks and clicks, they can be complex. For example, the initial decision is whether or not to sell products online. If not, then the website can drive offline sales, so decisions focus on what products to highlight and how, what information to provide, how to drive visitors to the website to access information about these products online, and how to give them an incentive to go offline to complete the purchase. For clicks-only sellers, decisions include what products to sell, in what form (standardized, customized, mass-customized), how to show products, how frequently to change inventory, and how to deal with stockouts, surpluses, and returned products. Bricks and clicks must also decide whether to integrate product offers across multiple channels or to offer web-exclusive or store-exclusive products. There is no standard "right answer" to any of these questions, and all such decisions must be made by balancing buyer demands with enterprise resources and goals.

WEB UPDATE

For updates and more on this topic, visit the textbook student website at: http://college.hmco .com/business/students and select Siegel, *Internet Marketing*, 2e. **Online Products**

Consumer Products Marketed Online

Most consumer products that are marketed online are the same products marketed offline. Others are modified or are innovations that have been adjusted to the Internet environment. Still others exist exclusively because of the Internet.

PRODUCT TYPES FROM A CONSUMER PERSPECTIVE

U.S. consumers obviously spend considerable time, effort, and money shopping. Their personal high debt load attests to their commitment. Consumer spending (primary demand) is an essential contributor to the nation's economy, accounting for two-thirds of U.S. gross domestic product (GDP), and also stimulates derived demand for industrial production. Melvin Copeland recognized the importance of consumer shopping in a 1923 *Harvard Business Review* article, where he proposed a classification system for merchandise sold in retail stores. His system is based on buyer habits, the consumer's view of the purchase of *convenience, shopping, specialty,* and *unsought* products. Copeland's classification system is still used today with modifications, which consist principally of including products that were not available in the 1920s and expanding the definition of the term *product,* which in Copeland's time was taken to mean just tangible goods. This framework is useful in organizing observations about online consumer product offers.[8]

CONVENIENCE PRODUCTS   *Convenience products* are staples, emergency, and/or impulse products. Many convenience products, particularly staples, have thin profit margins. They are commodities whose only differentiating feature may be the product's marketing. Profitability requires high sales volumes and tight controls on costs, particularly inventory holding costs. High shipping and handling costs, and the eventual collection of sales tax, are working against their online profitability. However, consumers value convenience, and this is the basis for optimistic forecasts about the growth of convenience product sales online, over time.

At first glance, convenience grocery products do not appear particularly well suited to online marketing, yet they are sold online to a limited extent in the United States and more successfully in the UK and parts of Europe. Consumers and businesses in Connecticut, New York, the greater Washington, DC, area, Massachusetts, and Chicago can shop online for convenience products at Peapod, Inc. LLC. (*http://peapod.com*). Founded in 1989, Peapod offers packaged food staples, household items, health and beauty aids, fresh meat and deli items, produce, and bakery goods for local delivery in the markets served. Buyers select and pay for products online and register for a delivery time. The store has competitive prices and weekly specials and accepts manufacturers' coupons. Its trained shoppers handpick items from the customer's list at free-standing central distribution warehouses maintained by partner supermarkets also owned by Netherlands holding company Royal Ahold (*www.ahold.com*). Drivers deliver the order directly to the customer's door during the requested delivery time. The shopper's list can be saved on the Peapod server and modified until it is ready for checkout. A modest delivery charge is added to each order. The advantages of using Peapod include top-quality products, opportunities to save money, convenience, first-rate customer service, and the ability to shop from work or home, day or night.

The online ordering and subsequent delivery of convenience products is a considerable advantage for many customers; prime targets are busy professionals, people who are disabled, the elderly, and customers who are in ill health. The biggest problems are low margins and high delivery costs, which cannot entirely be passed along to customers. Maintaining quality will be a continuous challenge. Having a stranger pick standardized and often branded canned goods or milk off a shelf is not a problem, because there is little product variability. It can be a liability, however, when the products in question are fresh produce, meat, or other perishables. The customer must rely on the selection skill of the shopping surrogate, the availability of top-quality products, and delivery without spoilage.

Peapod

Peapod's "Pod Bugs" deliver convenience products purchased online and effectively promote the product offline. Have you seen a Pod Bug in your neighborhood?

Source: Copyright © 2005 by Peapod, LLC. Reprinted with permission, http://peapod.com/corpinfo/GW_index.jhtml.

Emergency products are purchased infrequently and in response to an unusual situation. A hurricane approaching an Atlantic beach community sends consumers rushing to the nearest hardware store to purchase plywood sheets to board up windows. This is a crisis emergency with delivery urgency. Products must be obtained without delay, which means consumers do not have the time to go online, order plywood sheets, and wait two weeks for delivery. Noncrisis emergency products, however—precautionary products appropriate for regular delivery—are offered online. A San Francisco, California, resident can go to EarthquakeStore.com (*www.earthquakestore.com*) and purchase emergency earthquake supplies and a personal survival kit for the next big one. Hand-crank emergency AM/FM radios that play on spring power are sold online, as are emergency power generators and solar-powered flashlights. Convenience and availability are two clear advantages of purchasing these products online.

Impulse (spur-of-the-moment) purchases require little thought, search, or buyer involvement and provide instant gratification. Examples include candy, gum, and magazines at the grocery checkout lane and that soft drink beckoning from an icy tub next to the counter in a gas station. Marketers are finding ways to tempt consumers with online impulse products. Amazon.com uses collaborative filtering techniques (see Chapter 8) to push product recommendations to a visitor's screen and cross-sell them. Its *Your Gold Box Offers* is another example of encouraging an impulse purchase. Products are pushed to the user's computer, paired with discount coupons good for sixty minutes after the coupon is activated.

SHOPPING PRODUCTS   When consumers spend more time, effort, and money searching for, comparing, and selecting, they are said to be searching for *shopping products*. These products include high-ticket items such as washing machines and furniture, as well as airline tickets, compact music discs, videodiscs, and computer games.

Consumers are more involved with these products because they cost more, they are not as readily available, and there is a greater risk in making a poor choice.

Homogeneous shopping products are very similar to one another but still have some characteristics that justify search and comparison, particularly price, design, content, functional features, and availability. Small television sets are *commodity products;* there is not much to distinguish one 13-inch color television set from another. When faced with homogeneous commodities, consumers look for points of differentiation, and price often is the key. A price-conscious consumer might compare prices on 13-inch televisions at Sears.com, BestBuy.com (*www.bestbuy.com*), and CircuitCity.com (*www.circuitcity.com*), looking for the lowest price and/or free shipping and handling. This is easy to do using any of the popular price comparison shopping robots (shop bots). The ease of making price comparisons is one clear advantage offered by Internet shopping.

Heterogeneous shopping products have features that are important enough for price to be less important, because consumers willingly shop around to find a product with the desired features. A consumer shopping for an expensive large-screen projection television set probably wants to compare several brands in terms of sharpness and number of lines of horizontal resolution, color reproduction, screen size, front or rear projection, analog or digital, front-to-back size, sound system, and more. A shopper may visit many sites seeking product descriptions, detailed product specifications, complete ordering and shipping information, and return instructions. By shopping around, he or she can compare product attributes and make an informed decision. The Internet excels at offering product information far beyond what is typically available offline. An added advantage is offered when the online retailer also has a personal shopper at a 1-800 telephone number or by instant messaging waiting to answer questions. Contrast this with what often happens offline, where untrained, uninformed, and often uninterested salespeople know less about a product than does the customer trying to purchase it.

Maytag (*www.maytag.com*) sells washing machines online through online partners, but the orders are filled by independent Maytag dealers and local retailers nearest the buyer. Consumers traditionally shop around for new automobiles. Although most new cars and trucks can be ordered online, they must be delivered and serviced by dealers near the buyer's home. This is an example of the **B2B2C model.** That is, the online business sells to a consumer who takes delivery of the product from a local business. Some online shopping products are under attack. Tobacco products are readily available online, to the distress of smoking foes. The Ojibwas Trading Post (*www.ojibwas.com*), operated by the Ojibwas Indian Tribe, is located (as stated on the website), "on Sovereign Indian Territory. All transactions are initiated and concluded on Indian Territory and governed by Indian Law and applicable Indian Treaties." The site's front page contains the Surgeon General's health warning and a pop-up screen asks visitors to self-certify that they are 21 years of age or older. Critics complain that this type of age filter is ineffective in stopping underage buyers. International websites such as Switzerland's Yesmoke.com (*www.yesmoke.ch*) offer foreign and premium U.S. brands, often at prices far lower than those charged locally offline. As a bonded warehouse, YesSmoke exports its products with a *duty-free-sales-only stamp.* Each carton is shipped individually, which reduces the product value and the chance that it will be taxed in the receiving country. Individual ship-

B2B2C model
Businesses that allow consumers to place orders online but the purchased product is delivered offline by local affiliates, which avoids antagonizing dealers and local retailers.

ping also raises delivery costs. Other frequently criticized but readily available online shopping products are X-rated videos and adult content sites, gambling, and prescription pharmaceutical products, which are far too easy to purchase online without a prescription or bona fide examination by a physician.

Airline tickets and travel services are shopping products particularly well suited to online marketing. Airline tickets are a high-cost, perishable service product purchased by consumers and enterprises. Online sales cut ticket printing and distribution costs and eliminate travel agent commissions. The forecast is that within the next several years, over 50 percent of all travel bookings will be made online. More than US$35 billion in trips were booked online in 2003. Southwest Airlines (*www.southwest.com*) was the first airline with a website, and by 2000, approximately 30 percent of the carrier's total sales (about US$1.7 billion) were booked online through southwest.com. Its booking cost per ticket is only US$1.00, compared with US$10 per ticket for travel booked through a travel agent.

Airline tickets and services are also sold by airline-affiliated sites such as Travelocity (*www.travelocity.com*), which had a 20 percent market share in 2003 (sales of US$3.9 billion), compared to market leader Expedia's (*www.expedia.com*) 40 percent share (US$7.7 billion). They are also sold by agencies known as *bucket shops* that purchase blocks of spare seats from airlines and then resell them. Priceline (*www.priceline.com*) is an independent agency that operates this way. Online sales work well for simple itineraries, easily scheduled point-to-point flights. Complex travel plans may require a travel agent's help. Booking flights online can be a hassle, with too many confusing screens and pages for the average buyer, consumer *or* enterprise purchaser, to negotiate. Computer crashes in the middle of ordering can leave the buyer frustrated and uncertain whether the purchase registered. Unless buyers are convinced that the transaction will save them money, the effort and frustration of completing arrangements online can easily lead to shopping basket abandonment.

Some digital shopping products are not selling well online. Although a majority of online shoppers have heard of ebooks, only a very small number report that they are *very likely* to purchase one. Drawbacks include price (ebooks cost about the same as hardcopy books) and mode of delivery (the buyer must read the book online or download and print it). However, even with these drawbacks, in the nine months ending in September 2003, ebook sales increased 32 percent to US$7.6 million and were forecast to exceed US$10 million in 2004. Sales will be increased by the advent of improved high-resolution paper-like electronic displays, including a prototype developed by the E.Ink Corporation (*www.eink.com*). They also may get a boost when more publishers take college textbooks online. Pearson PLC announced in 2004 that it was going online with 300 of its most popular college textbooks, which would be sold online at half the price of hardcopy versions. This could eventually threaten the US$3.4 billion U.S. college textbook market, particularly the sales of used books. Piracy of web-based books is a huge concern.[9]

Online banking offers advantages for consumers by eliminating long teller lines and the inconvenience of having to do business during "bankers' hours." The service makes it easier to transfer funds, review accounts, and pay bills. Growth in electronic billing is increasing at a steady rate. This is attributed to an increase in targeted consumer promotions by online financial institutions. Consumers are beginning to adopt this digital service, and the forecast is for continued rapid growth, from 18.6 million households in 2001 to 49 million in 2006. Sweden leads the world in online banking services, which are used by about a third of its population. Its online banks offer a full range of competitive services, forcing traditional banks to improve services offline.[10]

SPECIALTY PRODUCTS   Consumers are more highly involved with *specialty products* and with trying to locate them. Specialty products are more difficult to find than shopping products, so search is an important component of the purchase process. These are often unique products, available in very limited numbers or found at only a few retailers. Consumers are often so happy to find them that price is not much of an issue; their relative scarcity adds to their value. Because they are more costly and less readily available, they often convey non-verbal messages suggesting that the buyer is of high social status. Examples include expensive high-fashion designer clothing and jewelry, luxury automobiles, and handcrafted furniture.

Ashford.com (*www.ashford.com*) targets upscale consumers and corporate clients, offering luxury and premium-quality jewelry, handbags, women's scarves and men's ties, watches, and fragrances from among more than 400 luxury brands and 15,000 products. High-resolution product pictures are used throughout the site. Most products carry an extended Ashford warranty and a thirty-day return privilege. Same-day shipping is offered for in-stock products ordered before 4:00 P.M. EST. Orders of US$100 or more receive free shipping.

Bricks-and-mortar specialty retailers often are shopping destinations. Shoppers will travel considerable distances to purchase a certain type of professional photography equipment, jewelry, or a designer handbag from a specific retailer. Tiffany & Co. (*www.tiffany.com*) is a destination upscale jewelry retailer online and off. Because it accepts orders online, it reaches consumers who might find it difficult or impossible to visit one of its bricks-and-mortar locations. Tiffany has a limited number of stores in North America, Europe, and Asia; however, unless a buyer lives in a large urban or affluent area, there will not be a Tiffany nearby.

Music123.com (*www.music123.com*) offers specialty products that *shouldn't* work well online, but do. Music123.com is the online retail outlet for Zapf's Music, established in 1928. The site went online in early 1999 and initially offered over 10,000 musical instruments, accessories, software, and sheet music from manufacturers that typically are highly restrictive in awarding franchises. Generally, musicians want to test an expensive instrument before purchasing it. In this case, they are willing to forgo testing in exchange for product selection. International buyers shop Music123.com to purchase instruments not readily available in their home countries and to obtain brand names known for quality and performance consistency. Today, the site offers over 125,000 products and states that it offers the lowest prices, expert advice, service, selection, and convenience.[11]

UNSOUGHT PRODUCTS   Some products are *unsought*. These are products consumers avoid, search for out of necessity, or are unaware of because the products are new to the market or unknown. Funeral caskets are an unsought product readily available online from such retailers as American Casket Store (*www.thecasketstores.com*) and Funeral Depot (*www.funeraldepot.com*), which both offer free next-day casket delivery. Casket shopping online has benefits. The online customer does not have to visit a funeral home, which many people find upsetting. Buying a casket online in an impersonal environment not laden with emotion may encourage a more objective purchase decision. It avoids the up-selling attempts of a salesperson trying to lay a guilt trip on the buyer for selecting a cheaper model. Whether consumers will seek caskets online is another matter, particularly because most do not shop for a casket offline before it is actually needed. Other examples of unsought products sold online are life insurance and long-term care insurance, and cemetery plots. Although unsought consumer products may be among the least well suited to web shopping, some will be profitable. Product avoidance offline is probably a good predictor that online offers will be equally unpopular unless there is a clear online advantage. Finding unsought products online is not as much of a problem as it was in the past because of vastly improved search engines.

CONTENT PRODUCTS

Content is one of the most sought-after products online, and much of it is still not paid for, although this is changing. Even unsought product content sites exist online. Legacy.com (*http://legacy.com/legacyhome.asp*) performs a unique digital service. Founded in 1998, the company is backed by investors including the Tribune Company and Gannett Co., Inc., the largest newspaper group in the United States. This site's mission is to provide space for the recently bereaved to celebrate the life of their loved one, posting obituaries, tributes, eulogies, photographs, and memorials. For under US$200, a *Legacy Life Story* is posted online permanently; temporary listings cost less. Potential customers can learn about the service from newspaper obituary writers, funeral directors, and word of mouth. If family and friends cannot attend a funeral, an online memorial tribute to the deceased enables them to share their emotions. Each listing also includes directions to the funeral service and mentions any charities designated by the family for memorial donations.

Other areas of highly sought after product content are health data, particularly among the growing numbers of older Net users; magazines; weather reports; and even baseball, which is now is heard on over 200,000 online radio broadcasts. Many users pay for adult content and gambling. Paid content in 2003 generated an estimated US$2 billion in sales, an increase of 30 percent over 2002. It is purchased by consumers and enterprises.[12]

Enterprise Products Marketed Online

An enterprise is a group of similar entities producing, supplying, purchasing, and/or servicing products. Enterprises can be businesses, governments, hospitals, universities, and other organizations that purchase products for the enterprise and not personal use. Many types of entities exist within each enterprise group, and they purchase and sell a wide array of products used to make other products, to run their operations, or to resell. United States B2B online spending in 2003 was around US$482 billion, a 242 percent increase over 2001. Worldwide, the total value of B2B product exchanges far exceeds B2C exchanges.

MARKETPLACE EXCHANGES

More businesses than ever before are purchasing and selling products online, typically over established proprietary networks or auctions such as eBay Business (*http://business.ebay.com*) and, far less often, over general, independent B2B marketplaces or exchanges. This is not what was originally predicted; in fact, B2B exchanges were forecast to become the backbone of online B2B enterprise. Exchanges were promoted as intermediary businesses that matched buyers and sellers, created liquidity, and reduced trading costs. Before the dot.com bubble burst, there were an estimated 2,000 B2B exchanges; the best estimate is that only a third were left by 2004.

Probably the most successful proprietary network is Wal-Mart's (*https://retaillink .wal-mart.com/home*) Retail Link that grants approved suppliers access to the Wal-Mart and Sam's Club computer information system (CIS). Retail Link has product sales reports, online supplier agreements, and information about doing business with the company and how to manage sales, inventory, and communications. Wal-Mart has an over US$250 billion annual turnover on its proprietary B2B systems. Suppliers must use its system if they want to sell products to Wal-Mart.

Some B2B exchanges have succeeded. WorldWide Retail Exchange (WWRE at *www.worldwideretailexchange.org/cs/en/index.htm*) was established in 2000 by seventeen international retailers and suppliers and now has sixty-four members from Africa, Asia, Europe, and North and South America. Their combined annual sales are approximately US$900 billion, with over US$1.5 billion reported in savings from WWRE activities through mid-2004. The exchange's goal was to simplify and automate supply chain processes and reduce inefficiencies. This is not a general exchange but an independent company established by retail and related manufacturing business members.

Another survivor is Exostar (*www.exostar.com*), which was created by some of the largest businesses in the aerospace and defense industries. Like WWRE, Exostar provides supply chain solutions that improve business processes and enhance relationships among trading partners. It has over 13,000 trading partners, including Boeing (*www.boeing.com*), Lockheed Martin (*www.lockheedmartin.com*), Raytheon (*www .raytheon.com*), and Rolls-Royce (*www.rolls-royce.com*).

An estimated 84 percent of large businesses go online to purchase and sell products, including services. The remainder and many small and midsize businesses have not gone online to buy products for a variety of reasons, and some may never do so. Many are satisfied with their existing product procurement methods and don't want to take the risk of dealing with unknown suppliers or buyers. Others have not gone online because online procurement is still too complicated, they don't believe they have the time to do so, and/or they fear insecure online transactions. Larger companies increasingly require their suppliers to be online, but for many small suppliers it means connecting electronically to their prime or sole buyer's extranet.

Online B2B buying is understandably more focused on goods than on services, on commodities than on other products, and on process efficiencies. Even though many companies were initially disappointed with online product procurement, they realize they will be using electronic methods far more in the future. Benefits include faster order times, convenience, and cost and time savings. Other benefits come from collaborating with online partners to develop new products, to outsource product manufacturing, to plan and forecast product demand, to direct logistics, and to manage customer relationships.[13]

One of the hottest B2B sectors is used vehicles and parts. Online used-car auctions are rapidly growing in popularity. Many used-car dealers bid on General Motors–certified used lease return cars at GMAC's SmartAuction (*www.gmonlineauctions.com*); others use eBay auctions. Used-car auctions are an US$81 billion business, and online auctions are a growing part of the market. Some 300,000 sold from the GM site in 2002, about 40 percent of the company's total used-car sales.[14]

CLASSIFYING ENTERPRISE PRODUCTS

Rather than being categorized in terms of shopping behaviors, enterprise products are classified in terms of how they solve problems. The principal categories are raw materials and parts, equipment and supplies, finished goods, services, and digital products, services, or information.

Raw materials and parts are used as production inputs. For example, iron ore and scrap are raw materials in steel production, and windshields are needed for automobiles. Raw materials include *soft goods* (agricultural commodities), such as the raw wheat, barley, and oats essential to the production of cereals, and the chemicals used in the production of pharmaceuticals. *Hard goods* used in producing machines, instruments, and consumer durables, such as the steel used in the manufacture of automobiles, are also raw materials. Most raw materials are sold via long-term contracts lasting a year or more, so buyers shop for these products less frequently.

Some raw materials are sold directly from corporate websites, and many are sold through online exchanges. Exchanges typically are private, independent public exchanges or consortia exchanges. The complexity of managing an exchange and the difficulty of finding sufficient numbers of buyers and sellers to make them functional have resulted in many failures. One survivor is the Noble Group Alliance's RawMart.com (*www.rawmart.com*), a commodity exchange matching buyers and sellers for raw materials used in agribusiness, chemicals, energy, metals, minerals, plastics, pulp, and paper. RawMart is a global exchange that operates in English, Chinese, Russian, Japanese, Spanish, Portuguese, and Korean. It facilitates buyer/seller exchanges in more than six hundred industrial raw materials and commodities groups, meeting materials and logistics needs through market exchanges.

Partially or completely finished parts are used in the production of components such as computer chips and the picture tubes in television sets. Buyers and sellers of electronics parts are linked on electronic portals such as Electrosupport Online (*www.electrosupport.com*), a member of PartsLogistics.com (*www.partslogistics.com*). Electrosupport Online provides direct access to wholesalers, distributors, and manufacturers of a wide variety of electronics parts. PartsLogistics.com does the same with a wide variety of industry parts, products, and services. These exchanges make finding an outsourcing partner for product manufacturing anywhere in the world much easier than in the past.

Equipment and supplies are products used to run a business or organization. A metal stamping machine is equipment used to stamp out automobile body frames; paper and printer cartridges are expendable office supplies that must be replaced on a regular basis.

Finished goods, services, and *digital products* are products manufactured or purchased for resale by wholesales and retailers and/or destined for eventual purchase by personal use consumers. Capital equipment goods include tools and equipment used in production and the buildings where production occurs. GE Healthcare (*www .gehealthcare.com*), which offers health care facilities and products for sale and lease, customizes products to suit the buyer's needs. Expendable supplies are purchased to run an enterprise; they include operating and maintenance supplies. Consumers and enterprises can go online to purchase home office supplies from Office Depot (*www.officedepot.com*), which also provides small business services in marketing, communication, management, and human resources. Finished products for resale are what wholesalers and retailers purchase to sell to consumers and other businesses.

Services are nontangible products or performances, including equipment repairs and maintenance, training, assembly line redesign, and other activities that contribute to production and operations.

Information products are found in abundance online, and many businesses, as well as other enterprises, purchase information from various vendors. These products include competitive marketing intelligence, research reports, market analysis, economic forecasts, and trend analysis.

OTHER ENTERPRISE PRODUCTS

The U.S. government is one of the Internet's largest sellers and one of its largest buyers. For the year 2000, the U.S. Treasury Department's TreasuryDirect (*www .treasurydirect.gov*) reported revenues of US$3.3 billion from the online sale of U.S. savings bonds, T-bills, and Treasury notes. Other government products for sale include gravesite flowers at U.S. military cemeteries overseas from the American Battle Monuments Commission (*www.abmc.gov),* real and personal property from the General Services Administration's Office of Property Disposal (*www.gsa.gov*), military trucks from the Department of Defense (*www.govliquidation.com*), and luxury goods confiscated from drug dealers by the U.S. Marshals Service and tax-defaulted property (*www.bid4assets.com*). The Federal Deposit Insurance Corporation (FDIC at *www.FDICSales.com*) auctioned US$21.8 million in loans assets in one month in 2004. Just like other enterprises, some government agencies use eBay to sell surplus goods.

Critics of U.S. government online product sales believe the government is violating federal law that prohibits it from competing with the private sector in selling products directly to consumers. Some government products, such as surplus U.S. Coast Guard cruisers, are not found in civilian stores. Their sale could be considered for the common good, because it is better to sell them, returning the profits to the U.S. Treasury, than to have them rust away. Other products compete directly with businesses, however, and this causes concern. One very large target is the federal-government-owned, self-supporting postal corporation. The U.S. Postal Service (*http://usps.com*), which has changed its domain name from .gov to .com, directly competes with UPS (*www.ups.com*), Federal Express (*www.fedex.com*), and other carriers. Critics believe it has an unfair advantage in that the federal government is there to bail out the USPS if needed.

Government procurement online is a multibillion-dollar business involving purchases of almost every type of good and many services. The U.S. government and most state governments are establishing processes whereby vendors can bid for state purchasing contracts online. The National Association of State Procurement Officials (*www.naspo.org*), a nonprofit organization of the central purchasing officers in all fifty U.S. states, the District of Columbia, and U.S. territories, publishes a vendor guide for small businesses to help them bid on state purchasing contracts. Products are purchased to solve such problems as feeding federal prisoners at institutions nationwide and keeping government printers stocked with paper. The federal government has established FedBizOpps (*www.fedbizopps.gov*), the point of entry for government procurement information, to streamline the bidding process and encourage small and midsize businesses to participate in bidding for contracts over US$25,000.

Virginia has made great progress in moving toward a fully electronic procurement system. By 2004, the eVA site (*www.eva.state.va.us*) already had over 409,000 orders, 22,822 registered vendors, 965 e-Mall vendor catalogs, 9121 users, and US$4.1 billion spent. As the site proclaims, EVA is *Virginia's Total e-Procurement Solution.* Recent transactions included finding a vendor to install a Lucent telephone system in two middle schools in Fauquier Country, a roof replacement in the state Department of Transportation, and janitorial supplies at the University of Virginia.

Goods confiscated by local police are increasingly being sold online. PropertyBureau .com (*www.propertybureau.com*) is one outlet, eBay is another. The State of Oregon disposes of more than 98 percent of its surplus property on eBay, grossing around US$8.5 million annually.

Organizations purchase many of the same products as governments. Universities and other enterprises purchase products directly from retailers such as OfficeDepot.com or purchase through state contracts if they are public institutions and the orders are large. OfficeDepot.com illustrates the blending of products for use by consumers and enterprises.[15]

Online Brand Basics

Brand
A name, symbol, design, or other element that personifies and differentiates one product or entity from another, identifies ownership, and provides tangible and intangible meaning.

A **brand** personifies what is branded, identifies ownership, and represents tangible and intangible associations. It is a promise, feeling, unique name, symbol, design, reputation, or other element that differentiates one product, company, or other entity from another. A **brand name** is the spoken part of a brand; it is used, for example, when someone says "*Amazon*" or "*eBay.*" A **brand mark** is the unspoken part of a brand: the Macintosh Computer apple or Target's red bull's-eye (*www.target.com*). A **service mark** is a trademarked brand identification for advertising services where there is no tangible commodity. A service mark is typically designated SM. Examples include Prudential Insurance's signature Rock of Gibraltar and the Travelers red umbrella logo for its insurance products before the company was acquired by Citigroup.

Registered brands provide legal protection for product assets. They represent huge investments for many enterprises, and their management is a key marketing responsibility. Brands must be built and maintained; if they are not, they can easily fade away

Brand name
The spoken part of a brand, used, for example, when a person says "*Amazon*" or "*eBay*."

Brand mark
The unspoken part of a brand, such as the apple on a Macintosh computer that identifies it as an Apple product.

Service mark
A trademarked brand identification for services.

or be overtaken by aggressive competitors. Brand names have resonance. They convey emotional messages and help build *brand loyalty*. When buyers are loyal to a brand, perceive its quality, and repurchase, it increases the brand's equity. *Brand equity* is a measure of a brand's extra financial worth and market power created by buyer loyalty.

In many cases, a corporate name is the company's brand name. Where would Starbucks (*www.starbucks.com*), Lexus (*www.lexus.com*), Amazon.com, and Yahoo! be without their distinctive, instantly recognized corporate brand names? The corporate brand extends to its products, as in Starbucks flavored or bottled coffees. Although branding is commonly associated with consumer products, it is also important to enterprises; Boeing and General Electric are examples. A quality brand is more important than price in many enterprise transactions.

A well-known brand such as Amazon.com or eBay is a beacon drawing buyers to the company's website and products. Experience with the brand reassures buyers that the business is reliable, safe, and trustworthy. It also saves buyers time, because they know what to expect at the site and can avoid having to shop around for an alternative. Branded products can provide the same benefits. In an electronic environment where there is often a high degree of uncertainty, a brand name is a cognitive anchor, a point of recognition. When buyers need a product, store, information, or entertainment, they often seek a brand they know and trust. Loyal Wal-Mart customers offline are drawn to Wal-Mart.com, loyal Target customers seek out Target.com, and Google's users turn to it first when they seek information.

FIRST-MOVER CYBERBRANDS

Cyberbrands
Brands created from scratch for such Internet-only pioneering companies as Amazon.com, eBay, and Yahoo!.

Many of the biggest brands on the Internet today were also among the first movers online. Some were pure **cyberbrands,** brands that existed only on the Internet's World Wide Web, including such pioneering clicks-only companies as Yahoo!, eBay, and Amazon.com that built their online brands from scratch. Because they existed only online, they could not rely on existing brand names, awareness, and previously formed associations with buyers.

Most major first-mover cyberbrands spent hundreds of millions of dollars on advertising and promotions and used press releases, media interviews, and virtually any marketing communication device and channel that would create buzz about the brand and raise initial awareness of their new online businesses. AOL aggressively marketed its name through direct mail, sending its software to millions of potential subscribers on floppy disks and later on CDs. It continues this practice today. Yahoo! was everywhere initially—in television commercials, magazine advertisements, and print articles. Amazon was relentless in advertising itself in the traditional media as well as online.

The success of the first cyberbrands is reflected in their rank in the initial e-Branding Index, a benchmark study of top Internet brands. Not surprisingly, the top five brands in 2000 were AOL, Yahoo!, Amazon.com, Netscape (purchased by AOL in 1998 for US$4.2 billion), and eBay. Their efforts obviously were successful because by 2003, AOL was 64th on *BusinessWeek's* list of the world's top 100 most valuable brands (cyberbrands as well as bricks and clicks); others that made the list were Yahoo! (65) and Amazon.com (74).

BusinessWeek's ranking is based on an evaluation of how much the brand name drives sales, market leadership, stability, and cross-national appeal. That same year, a survey of 4,000 branding professionals named Google, the world's leading search engine, the year's top brand. Google was recognized by these professionals as the brand with the greatest impact, followed by Apple for its iPod. These brand rankings parallel website traffic counts. The top parent companies for website traffic in May 2003 were Microsoft MSN (1), AOL (2), Yahoo! (3), Google (4), eBay (5), and the U.S. Government (6). These rankings were unchanged a year later. The limitation of equating traffic with brand value is that not all traffic is equally valuable. More useful measures of brand value differentiate the site traffic of most-valuable visitors from that of least-valuable web surfers.[16]

BRICKS-AND-CLICKS BRANDS

Bricks and clicks faced a different challenge when they initially went online. They had to decide whether they would use the same brand name offline and online in an *integrated, one-brand-name strategy.* AT&T, IBM, Dell, and others created websites with immediately identifiable name brand URLs. Wal-Mart and Target followed them with integrated online/offline brand names. Most bricks and clicks with well-established, highly regarded offline brand names rely on them to build online website awareness and traffic.

Other bricks and clicks, such as Procter & Gamble, have adopted a *mixed-brand-name strategy.* There is a P&G corporate site and other sites named for products or brands, such as Tide. Co-branding came later. For example, Amazon.com and Toys "R" Us formed a ten-year alliance in August 2000 that expanded Amazon's product offer into toys without adding the expense of building inventory. Toys "R" Us benefited from being on a high-traffic site and escaping the expense of maintaining its independent website. Co-branding can be mutually beneficial, but it can also lead to conflict. In 2004, the Toys "R" Us online unit sued its partner, Amazon, claiming that its original agreement was for Amazon to sell only Toys "R" Us toys and baby products. Toys "R" Us claims that Amazon is allowing third parties to sell these products on Amazon's shopping mall and is seeking the return of US$200 million in exclusivity fees. Amazon responded that the claim was without merit.[17]

DOMAIN NAME BRANDING

Brand building online begins with selecting a domain name. The domain name should be either the name of the business or a meaningful, short, descriptive name associated with characteristics of the product or company. Domain names identify brands online. They create awareness as well as addresses. Yahoo!, eBay, and Amazon are businesses with .com domains that identify them as commercial enterprises. They are coined names that were created and "built," having had no initial meaning in the marketplace. Short company names are integral parts of their complete domain names.

Bricks and clicks with highly regarded, well-known brand names wisely obtained identical domain names. IBM, AT&T, Dell, and others were able to do so. Some companies had to pay off cybersquatters to claim appropriate domain names. This is less of a problem today, since the enactment of anti-cybersquatter legislation.

Having the right domain name is not enough to guarantee success in web marketing, and having the wrong name can be overcome with smart marketing. Pets.com, a great name for a pet supply storefront, is highly descriptive, easy to remember, and short. Unfortunately, the name alone could not keep the company solvent. Boo.com (*www.boo.com*) is not descriptive and sounds more like a Halloween party store than an apparel site. It failed once and later reopened, under new management, as Fashionmall.com. On the other hand, eLuxury.com (*www.eluxury.com*) is a website with a highly descriptive domain name that immediately creates an image of the products and lifestyle it sells. Because eLuxury.com is so descriptive, it also helps establish a *brand personality,* the public face presented to site visitors. Unfortunately, eLuxury.com and the other e-brands run the risk of overloading consumers with the letter *e*.

Similar-sounding brand names and URLs make it difficult for buyers to cut through the online clutter and find what they need. Word repetitions make it hard to differentiate among SmartShip.com, GoShip.com, Accuship.com, ShipNet.com, ShipChem.com, Shipper.com, and ShippingAuction.com.[18]

A brand needs a great name. Most large and midsize companies, and many small ones as well, turn to professional naming experts to develop an appropriate brand or company name. The same holds for domain names. Branding is considered such a vital part of product marketing that an over-US$2 trillion industry has developed around brand creation and maintenance. Brand naming and management often includes hiring domain name consultants. As might be expected, many domain-naming businesses are online, offering their services to startups as well as established enterprises.

BUILDING BRAND AWARENESS

"If you build it, they will come." But if you name it, buyers will not come unless they are aware that the brand exists. Brand awareness is often built through online and offline cross-media promotions working together. Initial brand awareness can be developed through campaigns with advertising, direct marketing, sales promotions, online advertising, email marketing, and search engine placements. A recent study reports better brand recall from search engine listings than from online button or banner ads.[19]

Awareness is built through press releases, events, appearances on talk shows, community involvement, and encouraging positive word of mouth. Some online marketers use *viral marketing* to build awareness. They enter chat rooms, discussion boards, listservs, and other areas where they can build positive buzz about a brand. An increasing number of websites post *Tell a Friend* suggestions in the hope that a satisfied customer will email the site's address to a friend. Brands can be built and nurtured through online communities—groups of people who share interests and meet online to discuss them. Positive word of mouth among such individuals builds brand awareness. Opinion leaders in these groups can be especially effective brand advocates. Advertising is still very important to online brand building. Researchers have found that greater brand awareness is related to multiple exposures to banner advertisements, sparing use of animation, longer exposure to the advertisement, larger advertisements, and uncluttered banners. Slow-loading online advertisements lessen brand impact.[20]

Online advertising can play a key role in brand building, despite rising consumer frustration with their numbers and intrusiveness and with the proliferation of online advertising clutter.

Awareness is not the only goal in brand building. It is important to associate the message with the brand, to make an attractive and meaningful brand promise, and to move the consumer toward interest in the brand. Interest should lead to a belief that the brand is the right one to satisfy a need or solve a problem. Purchase intention and, it is hoped, purchase should follow. Online advertising is used throughout this process, reinforcing the brand message and reiterating the brand promise.

Brands are not built overnight, and they cannot be created with a massive one-time advertising expenditure. Brand building requires careful planning that reflects

- Knowledge of the company, product, or other entity to be branded
- Knowledge of the target market(s), consumers and enterprises—their needs, wants, and problems
- A clear understanding of how the brand will benefit the target market—that is, the *reason why* it should be purchased and repurchased
- Knowledge of competing firms—their brand(s) and the promise(s) they make—and of information that differentiates the brand from those offered by competitors
- Monitoring of brand perceptions in order to discern when brands lose their luster and "brand aid" is needed

MAINTAINING THE BRAND

Positive brand images are built through positive experiences and impressions. Customer relationship management is important to brand building. Providing a good website experience and product satisfies consumers, adds to brand equity, and encourages buyers to return. It also stimulates positive word of mouth, which can be far more powerful in building a brand than any advertising campaign. A website is a gateway to a company's brand and its public face. Given the branding importance of a site, the following actions are recommended.

- Create an inviting homepage.
- Keep content fresh, useful, and helpful.
- Provide clear navigation links that work.
- Provide a useful internal product search engine when needed.
- Use interactivity sparingly and only where it is appropriate.
- Offer user-friendly shopping baskets and ordering forms and secure means of payment.
- Answer customer email promptly.
- Avoid the use of senseless animation that slows download time.
- Offer easy, convenient product returns.
- Protect and guarantee customer privacy.
- Handle customer complaints carefully and sensitively.
- Listen to customer feedback, and follow through on useful suggestions.
- Build trust through honest transactions.

- Avoid 404 error messages that blame the customer for reaching the wrong page.
- Never indulge in overpromising.
- Deliver quality products, as promised.
- Use every touchpoint (point of contact) with customers and prospects as an opportunity to project a positive image of the brand.

BRAND RISKS

Unfortunately, the more well known the brand, the more likely that it will become a target for hackers, complaints, and theft. High-visibility brands are tempting targets for hackers and those who would steal images, content, and designs. An entire site can be stolen or defaced in several minutes. Theft of intellectual property is a significant problem because it is so easy online. The threat is that images, design, and content associated with one brand can turn up on an imposter's site. Visitors to the imposter's site can be deceived, have a bad experience, and then tell others about it through negative word of mouth. This can be highly destructive to the legitimate brand.

Another risk is from co-branding. A bad match in a co-branded product or company can be a disaster. At the least, any co-branding effort must be thoroughly evaluated for the effects it may have on both brands. For every good co-branding experience, there are several bad matches.

Brands are vulnerable to complaints, derogatory comments, and even defamation at online "suck sites" and from negative comments in chat rooms, blogs, discussion boards, listservs, and other public forums. It does not matter whether such comments are accurate. If they are widely disseminated, they can undermine the brand's value.

Although Internet marketers should constantly monitor the Web for brand abuse, there are far too many sites and pages for most marketers to monitor them effectively. Brand risks can be reduced through the use of security software and technology to uncover piracy, copyright infringement, libelous postings in discussion groups, and similar problems. Companies such as Cyveillance (*www.cyveillance.com*) and Cobion Internet Security Systems (*www.cobion.com*) are active in this field. Cyveillance lists Nextel, InterContinental Hotels Group, Goodyear, Nintendo, and Dow Jones Indexes among its online clients. It uses automated intelligence gathering and human analysis to protect its clients' brands by locating stolen content and monitoring discussion groups.

Summary

http://college.hmco.com/business/students

The Fundamentals of Internet Products

The Internet is a transformational technology responsible for the creation of some innovative and many improved products. Sales of B2B products continue to dominate online commercial activity. A product can be a good, service, idea, place, person, information, organization, or anything offered in exchange for something of value. It is the offer made to a market— a bundle of benefits—that creates value for buyers. Products are composed of multiple layers. Buyer and product use are two key considerations. Consumers use products to satisfy their needs and wants; enterprises use products to solve problems and carry on their activities. Products sold online can be tangible goods, intangible services, digital products, or a mixture of these forms. There are both advantages and disadvantages connected with marketing products online. Mass customization makes it possible to produce a large quantity of products quickly, because buyer options are limited and products often are semiproduced in advance of final customization. Personalization, or one-to-one marketing, is different from mass customization. The Internet offers a platform where consumers and enterprises can collaborate in the development of new products. Internet marketers make many product-specific decisions.

Consumer Products Marketed Online

The popularity of online shopping is growing, as are sales. Convenience, shopping, specialty, and unsought products are available online. Convenience products are purchased frequently and are readily available in many different locations. Often they are disposable, are low in cost, and require minimal purchase effort, search, or product comparisons. To be profitable, marketers of convenience products must sell high volumes and maintain tight cost controls. Grocery products are sold online, but thus far, their online marketing has met with only limited success in the United States. Bricks and clicks have an advantage selling convenience products online because of their established brand names, their up-and-running processes, and the option of providing for in-store returns. Shopping and specialty products require more effort to find and purchase. Shopping products include books, airline tickets, consumer durables, and education. Shopping products are the product type best suited to online sales. Consumers are highly involved with specialty products and with trying to locate them. Specialty products are unique or hard to find. Unsought products are products that consumers avoid, search for only out of necessity, or are unaware of because the products are new to the market or simply unknown. Content is one of the most sought-after products online.

Enterprise Products Marketed Online

Enterprises include businesses, organizations, hospitals, universities, and governments. More businesses than ever before are purchasing and selling products online, but they typically do so over established proprietary networks or auctions. Enterprise products are categorized in terms of how they solve problems. They include raw materials and parts, equipment and supplies, finished goods, services, and information products. The U.S. government is one of the Internet's largest sellers and one of its largest buyers. Organizations purchase many of the same products as governments.

Online Brand Basics

Brands represent huge investments for many enterprises, and their management is a key marketing responsibility. Brands constitute legal protection of product assets and act as a key communication tool and a way to differentiate products from competitors. Brands must be built and maintained. Many of the biggest brands on the Internet today were also among the first movers online. Bricks and clicks faced a different branding challenge when they initially went online. Domain names can create brands. Cyberbrands exist only online. Some companies integrate their offline and online brands. Others use a mixed branding strategy. A brand means little without brand awareness. Brands are built through positive experiences. A website is a gateway to a company's brand. Brands can be built and maintained through online communities, advertising, and other means. The better known the brand, the more likely that it will become a target for hackers, complaints, and theft.

Take Action!

The Internet is particularly well suited to the mass customization of products. At the same time, there is a big difference in how various websites implement the process and even define the term. Your company has been hired to create a customer-centric website for a business that mass-customizes cosmetics and fragrances. Reflect.com is the industry leader in this product category and the benchmark against which your client is compared.

1. Visit Reflect.com and evaluate the site for (a) overall site usability, (b) clarity of instructions, (c) number of product options available, and (d) risk reduction strategies used. Prepare a set of PowerPoint slides that report your results for each item evaluated.

2. Select any product from the categories listed on the site's front page. For that product, create a FAB table in which you identify three or four *Features, Attributes,* and *Benefits.* Format the table so that it can be displayed on a transparency.
3. On the basis of your evaluation, write a memo to your client with a series of recommendations on what a customer-centric site should offer.

Chapter Review Questions

1. What is a product offer?
2. How do enterprise buyers differ from consumer buyers?
3. Explain the different product states. Which product types are sold online?
4. Which has larger sales online, B2C or B2B?
5. What are product layers?
6. What are some advantages of products marketed online—for buyers and marketers?
7. Why do you think P&G did not give its company name to Reflect.com?
8. How different are online products from offline products?

9. Cite the different types of consumer products, and compare them in terms of how involved consumers are with their purchase.
10. Should tobacco and alcohol be sold online?
11. What enterprise product types are sold online?
12. What is keeping some businesses from trying e-procurement?
13. How is the U.S. government marketing products online?
14. What are some of the Internet's top cyberbrands?
15. Why is brand such an important consideration in Internet marketing?

Competitive Case Study

An Amazonian-size Task Facing B&N Online

Barnes & Noble, Inc. (B&N at *www.bn.com*) is the top bookseller in the United States with 2004 sales of US$5.95 billion, a 12.9 percent increase from 2003 sales. The company has 43,000 employees and operates over 653 superstores and about 190 mall bookstores. B&N went online in 1997 in partnership with Bertelsmann (*www.bertelsmann.com*), a worldwide media company, largely to compete with Amazon.com. B&N, Inc. bought out Bertelsmann in May 2004 and took the B&N

web company private. B&N integrates its online and offline operations and offers same day home delivery in Manhattan, New York City, and store pickups for online purchases. It also accepts payment by cash or check rather than just by credit card. Research indicates that multichannel retailers tend to do more business than single-channel retailers such as Amazon. First-quarter 2004 net sales at B&N.com were a loss of US$9.8 million, a 26 percent improvement over losses in Q1 2003. This compares to Amazon's Q1 2004 sales of US$598.7 million, an increase of 15.7 percent over Q1 2003. B&N.com obviously is having difficulty competing directly against Amazon.com. One way B&N is trying to differentiate its product offering is by promising same-day delivery in certain locations. Amazon has matched this by conducting a test of same-day delivery in Manhattan. This is a risky decision; costly same-day delivery was responsible for a number of dot.com bankruptcies. B&N and Amazon have a rocky history, including a 1999 law suit filed by Amazon against B&N.com for "maliciously copying" Amazon's patented one-click purchase process. The suit was settled in 2002 for undisclosed terms.[21]

CHECK IT OUT

It has been claimed that B&N.com is a clone of Amazon.com. Check it out. Evaluate the two sites on such factors as product offerings, delivery terms and rates, and special customer-centric features. What is your conclusion?

A GLOBAL PERSPECTIVE

Amazon has entered international markets with sites in a number of other countries. The company believes that an aggressive international strategy is essential to its continued growth. Has Barnes & Noble taken the same approach? Review B&N's section on International: Delivery Time and Shipping Rates. Does it ship purchases to international buyers? Does it appear to have websites in other countries?

10

.COM

Price in the Internet Marketing Mix

LEARNING OBJECTIVES

» To identify factors that influence Internet pricing
» To learn about online price issues that concern buyers
» To consider Internet pricing models
» To examine Internet payment options

"I Got It on eBay!"

eBay (*http://ebay.com*) has 125 million registered users worldwide, and in 2004 around half of them used the company's global trading platform to generate sales of over US$20 billion. That's an astonishing figure not fully captured by eBay's over US$3 billion consolidated net revenues for 2004, which are forecast to be over US$9 billion by 2010, with more than half coming from eBay's international websites. Net revenue has averaged a compound annual growth rate of around 80 percent for the past 5 years, and in 2003 profits rose 176 percent. eBay's revenues are from listing and transaction fees and from advertising. More than 45,000 different categories of merchandise are sold on eBay by individuals and families and by for-profit and nonprofit enterprises large and small. Merchandise is old and new; in-season and season remainder; returned, refurbished, and confiscated by law enforcement agencies; obscure and highly popular; goods and services; sold for profit and for charities; and sold at negotiated auctions and for fixed prices with the *Buy It Now* option. eBay has trading center websites in twenty-eight different countries,

often through arrangements with joint venture partners or by acquisition. eBay's newly acquired EachNet (*www.ebay.com.cn/*) is China's largest ecommerce site. International eBay sites are tailored to accommodate local tastes. For example, the French eBay (*www.ebay.fr*) sells lots of wine, and *kimchi* (fermented cabbage) is a popular auction item in South Korea (*www.auction.co.kr/default.html*). In 2002, eBay spent US$1.4 billion to purchase PayPal (*www.paypal.com*), an electronic banking system that speeds transactions and provides payment security for the parent company and others. By almost every measure, eBay is one of the world's fastest-growing and most successful businesses, which is remarkable considering that it happened within a decade of eBay's 1995 launch as a first-mover cyberbrand. eBay does not hold auction inventory or move goods, but it does a remarkable job satisfying its customers. It has an impressive 88/100 buyer satisfaction score, compared to an average of 78 for the online auction house category as a whole. eBay experts teach others how to auction at eBay University (*http://pages.ebay.com/university/*) *Selling Basics* and *Beyond the Basics* seminars on the road and online. Its feedback forums and seller ratings systems promote self-governance. Manufacturers, liquidators, and retailers use eBay as a sales channel. Disney (*www.disney.com*), Sears (*www.sears.com*), and other large corporations sell on eBay, which has caused some smaller sellers to complain that they are being crowded out. At the same time, large companies have found that they cannot profitably dump large quantities of a single product on eBay because doing so dramatically lowers per-unit price. eBay operates most efficiently at the beginning and end of the product life cycle (PLC). Popular and scarce new products often are purchased at the beginning of their PLC and then auctioned on eBay at a higher price to buyers eager to own them. A recent example is the iPod mini at the very beginning of its life cycle, when it was difficult to obtain in some markets. At the end of

their PLC, products are sold at a discount to clear inventory. Used products are a lucrative market of their own. Although eBay has been exploited by frauds and pranksters, it is a remarkably efficient community, and because its eBay police closely monitor transactions, the company has been able to maintain its reputation and keep users' trust. As eBay has racked up its own profits, it has also given rise to an entire class of entrepreneurs—individuals and small businesses that operate on eBay part-time or full-time for their owner–operators, and larger companies such as AuctionDrop Inc. (*www.auctiondrop.com*) that provide a service to people who want to sell on eBay but don't want to do it themselves. eBay is also a great source of entertainment for countless users caught in its web of transaction excitement.[1]

eBay has been a unique online success almost from its inception. It began as a negotiated-price trading center and now also offers fixed-price products for customers who either don't have the time or lack the inclination to auction. Price is one of the most dynamic and least well understood variables in the marketing mix, but its importance is beyond question. Basic information, issues, and models related to Internet pricing are considered in this chapter, along with payment options.

The Fundamentals of Price

Marketing is the functional business activity directly responsible for generating revenue, and price is a key marketing mix tool used to achieve revenue goals. Most consumers use price as a determining or contributing factor in deciding whether to make a purchase. Product quality and value are principal concerns of others, followed by price. However, when quality is not clearly evident, price frequently becomes a surrogate cue for it. Most businesses use price as a revenue-generating tool and as a means of competing strategically; but they also want a fair price for products they purchase and sell. Some organizations and governments constrain price and require lowest-bid purchasing.

Price is often a lightning rod for complaints. Consumers complain because they believe prices are unfair and too high (rarely are they too low). Businesses complain because competitors undercut their prices, because they believe they are paying too much for their own purchases, or because they can't get others to pay enough for their products. Government wants to encourage competition and ensure that prices respond legitimately to market demand. Marketers complain about the difficulty of setting the right price—one that is low enough to attract buyers yet high enough to hit revenue, margin, and profit targets. Price is a highly flexible variable; it can be changed quickly to respond to changes in demand, seasons, competitors, the economy, government regulations, and societal tastes. It can be changed instantly, in real time online, to respond to competitors' price changes and to demand. Price is complex and generally misunderstood, and its value as a dynamic marketing tool is often ignored. Marketers have responded to the Internet environment in several ways, sometimes with seriously flawed price models that justifiably failed. Others are taking advantage of the Internet's reach and sophisticated data tools to sharpen their price targeting, using differential pricing, dynamic pricing, and price testing. Most have simply moved their offline prices and pricing models online.

PRICE AND DEMAND

Price
How much buyers must give up of something they value in order to take advantage of a market offer.

Price is how much buyers (consumers and enterprises) must give up of something they value in order to take advantage of a market offer, primarily to possess and use a product. It is a measure of the *value* that buyers associate with a product and of their demand for it. Once buyers accept a price, sellers take payment in the form of something that both they and buyers value. In the United States, credit cards are by far the preferred payment mechanism. Other options are cash, debit cards, smart cards, online hybrid payment options, and barter or countertrade. Around 90 percent of online consumer purchases are still made directly or indirectly with credit cards.[2]

Price allocates products, determining who can buy, possess, and use them, and clears markets via the law of supply and demand. When demand increases, more products are sold, reducing existing inventory. When existing inventory falls to a designated point, typically it is replaced through restocking and, ultimately, increased production.

Most consumers are *price sensitive* with convenience and shopping products, highly aware of price changes, unwilling to pay above what they think is a fair price, and suspicious of product quality if price is too low. Because convenience and many shopping products are widely available online, consumers can shop around fairly easily, seeking the best price by visiting various online sellers or using a shopping search engine.

Perhaps surprisingly, however, many consumers do not shop around and willingly pay a higher price in return for something they value more (such as convenience, reliability, or familiarity) or out of brand loyalty. An example is Tesco (*http://tesco.com*), the largest supermarket chain in the UK and the world's largest online grocer. Tesco reaches 96 percent of Britain's population with its "online order and offline delivery" service. Its original selling advantage was low prices, or buyers' perception of low prices. Experts warned Tesco managers before its 1995 website launch that customers would not pay extra to order online and have their groceries home-delivered. These experts were wrong. Today, Tesco fills over 120,000 online orders each week for customers who willingly pay between £3.99 and £5.99 (about US$7.26 to US$10.90) per delivery regardless of order size. This means the company collects over US$45 million annually in delivery fees alone. The fee covers both the cost of the shopping surrogate who hand-fills the order and the cost of delivery.

Tesco's customers are willing to pay more for the convenience of online grocery shopping. They feel safe purchasing from a reliable, trusted brand—a local company that has long been a familiar part of their everyday lives. Although Tesco.com is online, orders are filled from local Tesco stores, so customers are served by their local shop, not an unfamiliar, distant corporate giant. Shoppers pay the same product prices in-store and online. Since the launch of Tesco.com, the company has repositioned itself as a mid-market grocer and its prices overall are higher than before. Accepted payment options are Electron card or credit card from Visa, MasterCard, American Express, Switch, Solo, Delta, or Clubcard Plus. Secure software encripts all transaction information. Tesco's 2003 online profits were £577 million (about US$650 million) on sales of £356 million (about US$576 million), an increase of 29 percent over 2002. In the first half of 2004, Tesco.com's sales rose 27 percent to £307 million and its profits increased 95 percent to £15 million.[3]

Shopping search sites Websites that provide comparative price and product information.

Many consumers are conditioned to be *price conscious* by retailers that regularly have sales and quickly mark down prices from their original, higher prices. These consumers resist paying full price because they know that if they wait, the price will soon drop. Price-conscious consumers are attracted to **shopping search sites,** websites that provide price and product information and make *price comparisons* easy and fast. This helps reduce *price information asymmetry,* the price information advantage previously enjoyed by sellers. Many loyal (and also price-conscious) apparel shoppers are attracted to Lands' End's (*www.landsend.com*) *Overstocks* clearances, where new markdowns are listed every Wednesday and Saturday and savings can reach up to 80 percent. Even greater discounts are posted on the company's *On the Counter,* which offers very limited quantities at substantial reductions. The already discounted prices are further reduced by 25 percent on Monday, by 50 percent on Wednesday, and by 75 percent on Friday. The prices are "fixed" but fall by a regular increment on a regular basis. This clears Lands' End's inventory of small-lot remainders and saves the company the cost of dealing with a liquidator.

Status-conscious consumers use price as an indicator of prestige; for them, a higher price makes a product more attractive. They may be drawn to such sites as eLuxury.com (*http://eluxury.com*), owned by LVMH (Moet, Hennessey, Louis Vuitton at *www.lvmh.com*), which guarantees the authenticity of all luxury brands it sells. Because counterfeiters target luxury brands for *knock-offs,* illegally branded cheap copies, the authenticity guarantee is a very powerful sales incentive to shop eLuxury.com. In this case, reliability, security, and prestige are a greater consideration than price.

Elasticity is a measure of consumer sensitivity to price changes. Although a reduction in price typically results in an increase in demand, the amount varies. This is critical information, because the degree of elasticity suggests how much of a price change is needed to generate the desired sales effect. Essential products, necessities, addictive products, products whose purchase cannot be delayed, and those with few substitutes typically exemplify *inelastic* demand. Demand is relatively *price insensitive,* and a 1 percent change in price results in less than a 1 percent change in demand; thus the slope of the demand curve is flatter. For example, if a salesperson must fly to Chicago unexpectedly and immediately to make a sale, he or she typically will pay whatever is necessary to get on the earliest flight. Let's say the airfare is US$862 for a ticket purchased the same day, whereas the same ticket would have cost only US$312 if purchased 30 days in advance. Under the circumstances, paying the higher price is understandable and reasonable. Demand insensitivity also suggests the salesperson will avoid online ticket auctions that require bidding for airline tickets over a several-day or several-week period and will instead go straight to Orbitz (*www.orbitz.com*) or another travel site to purchase the electronic ticket (eticket) that expeditiously will deliver him or her to Chicago.

Products characterized by *elastic* demand are not essential, can be delayed, are expensive, or have many substitutes, and demand for them is relatively *price sensitive.* Therefore, a 1 percent change in price will cause more than a 1 percent change in demand. For example, Ford Motor Co. (*www.ford.com*), General Motors Corporation (GM at *www.gm.com*), and DaimlerChrysler (*www.daimlerchrysler.com/dccom*) offered interest-free or very low financing of automobile purchases right after the 2001 terrorist attacks and into early 2002 to stimulate sales. This *hood money* resulted in a buying frenzy, and both GM and Ford saw over 30 percent sales gains in October 2001. For GM, this was the highest sales spike in fifteen years; it broke a thirty-four-year-old sales record at Ford. Unfortunately, however, it did not increase company profits, which illustrates that even significant price discounts may not compensate for other business factors that work against profit.[4]

Understanding the demand curve for different types of products and consumer sensitivity to price changes gives Internet marketers extremely useful information that can help them in setting and changing prices. At the same time, consumers can get price comparisons from many online competitors, so they can find alternatives to a price change designed to get them to increase or accelerate their purchases. The great marketing challenge is to use price effectively to satisfy buyers *and* achieve revenue, margin, profit, and/or inventory objectives.

CONSUMER CONFIDENCE

Businesses closely monitor consumer *primary demand* because it generates *derived demand* for enterprise products. Consumer spending gives businesses the confidence to invest and spend and hence fuels national economic growth. As consumers buy more, products are moved through channels, inventories are reduced, and production (typically) increases. Consumer spending drives the U.S. economy and represents two-thirds of U.S. gross domestic product (GDP), which reached over US$11.8 trillion in current dollars in 2004. National consumer purchasing sentiments are monitored monthly through the Conference Board's *Consumer Confidence Index* (*www.conference-board.org*) and the University of Michigan's *Consumer Sentiment Index* (*www.isr.umich.edu*); quarterly by the American Customer Satisfaction Index (ACSI at *www.theacsi.org/overview.htm*); and online by the Consumer Internet Barometer (*www.consumerinternetbarometer.us/*). Evidence confirms that the ACSI measure of customer satisfaction with previous buying experiences is a more accurate predictor of subsequent consumer spending than household income or debt, interest rates, or consumer confidence. Another predictor is the relationship of spending to movement in the price of single-family homes, the greatest investment most consumers will ever make.[5]

MANY FACTORS INFLUENCE PRICE

Many goals are set for price, and price can be influenced by a number of factors (Table 10-1). Whatever the goal, it must be clearly identified so that the *right* price can be identified and appropriate marketing tactics can be developed to support it. Internet price goals may be to use price to increase online sales (short-term revenue goal), to gain market share (long-term revenue goal), to match the competition's price moves (competitive goal), to pay current bills (short-term survival goal), or to drive traffic offline. Price targets may be consumers and/or enterprises and niches within these groups.

Some factors that influence price must be considered regularly, such as demand, competitors' actions, and channel member markups. Other factors exert infrequent or sometimes unique influences. Government regulations can constrain price setting, particularly in utilities. Geography can influence price setting because shipping products, particularly heavy or bulky ones, to distant or remote locations adds costs. Product life

Table 10-1 Factors Influencing Price	
Internal objectives	What goals are set for price online—to gain market share, drive web traffic, increase revenue, build brand equity, widen profit margins or other goals?
Buyer segments	What segments will be served? What do they want from the website, the product, and the company? What is their price sensitivity?
Product	Where is the product in its life cycle? What are its characteristics?
Demand	Is it elastic or inelastic?
Cost	What will it cost to produce and market the product, create and maintain the website, and fulfill product orders?
Economy	What is the state of the economy? Boom, bust, stagnation, other?
Consumer satisfaction	How satisfied are consumers with past purchase experiences?
Consumer confidence	Is consumer confidence driving online purchases?
Competitors	What are competitors' prices for comparable products?
Free alternatives	For content sites in particular, is anyone giving away the same content free? Are free alternatives readily accessible?
Channel members	What markups do channel members add and/or expect?
Government	What constraints does government place on prices?
Special events	Are the products sold at special events that can bear a higher price?
Seasons	If the product is seasonal, where in the cycle is it?
Promotions	Will promotions be run to stimulate demand?
Weather	If weather influences sales, what weather is expected?

cycle stage can greatly influence price. It can be set high when innovators and early-majority buyers are eager to purchase a new product and can be reduced later to attract late-majority and laggard buyers. Products that have been on the market for a long time and are nearing termination, returned or refurbished products, and merchandise and fixtures from liquidated companies require a *discount price*. Overstocks, remainders, cancelled orders, and discontinued products can be sold at bargain prices by sites such as Overstock.com (*www.overstock.com*), the online outlet store that sells name brands at clearance prices, up to 80 percent every day.

Many clicks-only businesses rushed online in the late 1990s, believing the hyperbole about first-mover advantage and the imperative need to attract buyers and crowd out potential competitors. Taking this as their goal, they set prices ridiculously low and piled on free shipping and handling (S&H), product freebies (free products), and special discounts. This strategy attracted extremely price-conscious bargain hunters, who are notoriously fickle about paying more than a discount price. As the first movers burned through their cash reserves and investors began withdrawing support, the pricing environment shifted, and pricing started becoming more rational. But for many dot-com businesses it was too late, as they suffered the crushing effects of believing this *Internet price fallacy*.

PRICE SETTING

Prices typically are set within a range. The *ceiling* is the highest price buyers can or are willing to pay for a product. It is also the price typically set by direct competitors for identical products. The *floor* is the lowest price that a business can afford to accept or is willing to accept. It may be the breakeven point, or it may be below breakeven when price is deliberately set at a low *penetration price* level to build market share quickly in a new market or drive traffic to a website, or when the product is a *loss leader*, offered at a discount or even at a loss to drive traffic or cross-sell. Restricted free shipping is a form of online loss leader. It attracts buyers and gets them to spend up to the limit that activates free shipping, but in reality, it significantly cuts the company's shipping costs. Amazon.com (*www.amazon.com*) recoups its free-shipping offer by getting buyers to agree to wait longer to receive their purchases. Amazon doesn't ship an order until it is completely filled and batches orders to get budget shipping prices. Also, the offer is good only on in-stock qualified products and thus helps clear inventory. The iTunes that Apple (*www.apple.com/itunes/*) sells for US$0.99 cents each are a loss leader for its iPod tune player. However, it's a profitable gambit because Apple sold over 70 million songs in its first year and more than 150 million tunes were purchased by mid-2004. In fiscal fourth quarter 2004, Apple reported sales of over 2 million iPods and iPod minis, six times its sales in the same quarter in 2003.

An *acceptable price* lies in the range between the ceiling and the floor. A *price indifference band* is within the acceptable range. It is the band within which buyers are (relatively) insensitive to price changes. The band varies for different product categories; for example, it is 17 percent for brand name consumer beauty products and only 0.2 percent for various financial products. Generally, prices should be set at the top of the acceptable range (and price indifference band) to boost profit margins. A recent study showed that as long as online products are priced within the acceptable range, customer response is unaffected. But competitors' responses must also be considered. If competitors undercut price, offer inducements such as free shipping and handling, or provide product enhancements, then products priced at the top will be punished unless there are mitigating factors. Ironically, a large number of online shoppers still do not take the time to compare prices, even though they have ample opportunity to do so. An estimated 89 percent of book shoppers make their purchase at the first site they visit; only 10 percent aggressively hunt for bargains.[6]

Price testing
Using dynamic online real-time changes in price to test buyer price sensitivity and demand.

The Internet environment is particularly well suited to real-time **price testing,** which consists of changing product prices in real time to determine buyer receptiveness, price sensitivity, and demand. In contrast to the offline pricing environment, prices can be changed instantly online and for different types or segments of buyers or even for individuals. Buyers can be segmented by their price sensitivity and targeted for different prices using a *differential price strategy.* Cookies and log files are used to identify visitors and link them to databases stocked with their characteristics, purchase histories, and familiarity with a web storefront. Product prices can be set to vary according to preselected variables; for example, a lower price may be offered to buyers making their first visit to the site or to buyers in a particular part of the country that will result in lower shipping costs. An alternative decision rule might be to offer a different price to every *n*th visitor. Consumer responses (purchases) are tracked in real time and used to adjust prices on the basis of buyer price tolerance (price sensitivity). If price testing shows that consumers will purchase at a higher price (that is, they are relatively price insensitive), then the higher price can be used instantly. However, if testing shows that consumers are highly price sensitive, then a lower price is advised. These tests are also used to predict inventory fluctuations. It is estimated that an online 1 percent price increase for most products can generate profit improvements of 11 percent or more. However, price testing can also land an Internet marketer in deep trouble with customers if the company's use of this practice becomes widely known and the target of chat room outrage, as Amazon.com found to its distress in 2000.[7]

Before the Internet, setting a price in most businesses was arguably more art than science, and too often it was a *seat-of-the-pants* intuitive decision or a simple cost markup calculation. Today, businesses with enormous databases full of buyer behavioral data and intelligence software that tracks price sensitivity and competitors' prices in real time can claim that, at least for them, setting a price is more science than art. Other businesses fall somewhere between the two. Some businesses let others set prices for their products in one of two ways: They may use a *parity price,* adopting the price used by direct competitors with substitute products, or they may use a *follow-the-leader* price, observing what price a market leader sets and setting their own price accordingly. Because it is easy to monitor competitors' price changes online in real time, parity and follow-the-leader price decisions can be made rapidly and accurately.

Setting a price should be a carefully considered, systematic process, but for too many businesses, pricing is a neglected or expediently used tool. This can be a costly mistake, particularly on the Internet. Price volatility is far greater online than offline, because price transparency often motivates competitors to respond immediately with price adjustments. Having the ability to change prices instantly is a powerful incentive for many businesses to do so. Few products remain priced at the same level for any appreciable time. Price volatility, particularly in consumer products, is more likely than the long-term price stability that is characteristic of many enterprise products, particularly most raw materials.

SUSTAINABLE COMPETITIVE ADVANTAGE

Survival is an overriding goal for businesses, be they global corporate giants or small local firms, and most seek a competitive advantage that is sustainable. Price contributes to a company's competitive advantage, but because it can be changed, matched, or bettered almost instantly online, it should be continuously monitored and adjusted appropriately. Relying exclusively on price as the only point of differentiation is very risky, however, because doing so undermines brand value and customer loyalty and can lead to price wars and margin erosion. Price must be used strategically with the other marketing mix tools to deliver what buyers need and want, sometimes even before they know they *have* a need or want. General Electric (GE at *www.ge.com*), for example, offers competitive prices, but it pairs price with an outstanding brand reputation, reliability, stability, innovations, and customer-centric marketing.

Retailers identified with prestige pricing, such as Tiffany (*www.tiffany.com*), sustain their advantage by offering unique high-quality products, superb online service, flawless delivery and return policies, and a clear focus on customer satisfaction. eBay is not primarily about price; it also offers entertainment and the allure of finding or selling treasure, even though what sells may be flea market fodder to some. Discounters such as Wal-Mart (*www.walmart.com*) attract price-conscious and bargain shoppers, as well as those who want the convenience of in-store returns for products purchased online. Targeting bargain hunters increases a web storefront's vulnerability to price transparency and downward price pressures. Online transparency and price volatility have the potential to make price less effective in building and sustaining a competitive advantage.

Issues Related to Price

Price touches most aspects of Internet marketing, from access price to product price. Price issues are complex, some are quite sensitive, and others help explain why many early dot-coms failed.

Price information asymmetry
Condition that exists when one party to the buyer–seller exchange has more information about price than the other.

Price information symmetry
Condition that exists when all buyers and sellers can access the same price information.

MAKING PRICE INFORMATION AVAILABLE

Initially the Internet was expected to be a price utopia, where free and complete knowledge of prices forced them down toward marginal costs. Sellers would experience a price squeeze, forcing them to compete on factors other than price. Enterprise buyers would be readily able to identify price discrepancies, then enter B2B exchanges (emarketplaces) and, through their informed buying power, force prices lower. Marketers would easily and rapidly monitor competitors' price changes and would respond and communicate price change information to their customers by email or immediately on their websites. Offline **price information asymmetry,** which puts buyers (particularly consumers) at a disadvantage because they lack comparative price information, would disappear online, and **price information symmetry,** in which all parties can access the same price information, would prevail.

The challenge for Internet marketers is to provide enough good, usable price information that satisfies buyers and, at the same time, to emphasize other parts of their value propositions. Progressive Insurance (*www.progressive.com*) is a company that understands the importance of value propositions. Progressive shares competitive price information about its own and competitors' prices for specific insurance offers because supplying this information (a) keeps customers on Progressive's site longer, which increases the probability of their making a purchase, (b) builds trust by demonstrating price honesty, and (c) de-emphasizes price while emphasizing services that Progressive provides and competitors may not. Online price changes can be matched instantly, but service and other value propositions take far longer to counter. This strategy is not appropriate for all businesses, but it works when price information is widely available and with commodities, where price transparency and communicating a value proposition can deliver a profit advantage.[8]

Progressive

Progressive helps customers make price comparisons while communicating its own value propositions.

Source: Copyright © 2005 Progressive Auto Insurance. Reprinted with permission, http://auto.progressive.com/auto1.asp.

PRICE COMPARISONS

Online price comparisons are available to anyone with the time, skill, and motivation to find them from general third-party shopping search engines such as PriceGrabber (*www.pricegrabber.com*) and Google's Froogle (*http://froogle.google.com*); reverse auctions such as Ariba (formerly FreeMarkets at *www.ariba.com*); and product-specific sites for such categories as insurance (*http://Insurance.com*), gasoline (*www.gaspricewatch.com*), computers and accessories (*www.pricewatch.com*), and books (*www.addall.com*). Froogle is one of the newest shopping search sites; CNET Networks's mySimon (*www.mysimon.com*) is one of the oldest. MySimon, uses intelligent agent software guided by the company's expert shoppers to collect price and product information from just about every online store, and it accepts data feeds from online merchants who pay a click-through fee if visitors reach their site from mySimon. The company has partnership deals with several thousand online retailers. It reports over 7.3 million unique users and averages more than 386,000 weekly page views. Key demographics show that men (59 percent) use the site more than women (41 percent) and that users are highly educated (69 percent have a college degree or higher), tend to be affluent (average household income US$87,000), and are business decision makers (63 percent).[9]

The popularity of shopping search sites, along with the availability of good product and price information online, has given rise to a model of *online–offline shopping complementarity.* Buyers search online for product and price information and then, armed with this information, go offline to complete the purchase in a store, through a catalog, or by telephone or fax. Consumers say they do this to avoid perceived Internet shopping risks, to avoid shipping and handling costs, or because a retailer does not sell online.

Initially, buyers had to be educated about shopping search sites, primarily through advertisements and onsite instructions, because they lacked experience with offline equivalents. To make offline price comparisons, buyers would have to contact each potential seller directly, visit stores, or search *Consumer Reports* (*www.consumerreports.org*) or other published sources for information on the product sought. Although price comparison shopping search sites are now more familiar, there still are drawbacks to their use. It takes time to initiate and wait for a search to be completed. A search can return an overwhelming amount of information. Some search sites *top-list* merchants that sponsor the site or buy onsite advertising, so price listings can be misleading and subjective. Product model differences can make direct price comparisons overly complicated or impossible. To get better results, buyers should perform multiple price searches, using at least three search sites; should sort lists by price with the lowest price listed first; and should determine whether the search site identifies sponsors and/or uses top-listing.

Price search sites and website price comparisons are having an impact as customers are becoming empowered by online price transparency. At the same time, price deliberations are complicated by such value propositions as brand loyalty, word-of-mouth recommendations, free shipping and handling, and websites that entertain as well as sell.

WEB UPDATE

For updates and more on this topic, visit the textbook student website at http://college.hmco.com/business/students and select Siegel, Internet Marketing, 2e. **Shopping Search Engines**

PRICE TRANSPARENCY

Price transparency exists when prices for competing products are visible and easily obtainable so that buyers, competitors, sellers, regulators, and others can readily make price comparisons. If price transparency exists, then all other things being equal (*ceteris paribus*), competitive pressure should drive prices down, act as a *price equalizer*, and reduce profit margins on transparently priced and widely available products. Price transparency can change some parity products into commodities and erode customer loyalty and brand value.

Price transparency and online anonymity (what's left of it) can combine to save buyers money. Take the case of women and minorities, who offline typically pay from US$45 to US$500 more for an automobile than white males pay. This difference disappears when women and minorities purchase online, because the Internet acts as an equalizer for offline price disparities that reflect a buyer's limited haggling (negotiating) skills or lack of information that can be used to negotiate.[10]

Online price transparency could be a solution to some *price gouging*, where prices are artificially inflated to increase seller profits. This complaint is frequently levied against oil companies when gasoline prices rise sharply. In a move designed to discourage price gouging, the Australian Competition and Consumer Commission (ACCC) considered proposals to list all petrol (gasoline) station fuel prices online on a public website. The goal is for online price transparency to drive down or stabilize offline prices. Any price increase would have to be posted on the site before it was

Price transparency
Condition that exists when prices for competing products are clearly visible and easily obtainable by anyone—buyers, sellers, competitors, and regulators.

charged. The state of Michigan has taken a different approach and uses one of its websites to collect complaints about gasoline price gouging (*www.michigan.gov/homeland/0,1607,7-173-23583_23713-64241—,00.html*), in another example of online–offline complementarity.

Price discrimination
An individual seller offering identical products to different buyers at different prices.

Transparency can highlight **price discrimination,** which occurs when the same seller sells identical products to different buyers at different prices. Sellers that knowingly collude in setting commodity prices for distributors and resellers could be in violation of the U.S. Robinson-Pitman Act of 1936, a highly complex law that outlaws price discrimination designed knowingly to injure the competition. Price discrimination is allowed if it reflects the true costs of offers to different buyers or is used to meet competitors' prices. Thus price skimming with new product introductions, charging more when demand fluctuates, and using premiums for price-insensitive buyers are generally acceptable practices.

The Internet encourages *price differentiation,* wherein buyers' price sensitivity becomes the basis for targeted price setting to segments and individuals. Differentiation is possible online because of the enormous amount of information collected about Internet users' buying habits and because of the availability of software that can mine these data.

Dell Computer (*www.dell.com*) differentiates when it charges different prices for the same computer depending on whether the buyer is an individual, business, government, hospital, or other entity, and on the quantity purchased. Price is based on buyer type (segment), which is taken as an indicator of willingness and ability to pay. Price differentiation also occurs when the same product is sold for different prices on different pop-up ads. In this case, price is based on sensitivity information housed in company databases and activated by cookie data stored on an individual's computer hard drive. Price differentiation is extremely common online and is an effective strategy for increasing revenues by charging buyers what the traffic will bear (that is, what they are willing and able to pay). However, this can only work *if* the business can tell its customers apart (segment them), identify the demand curve for products and buyers, and control the selling process. Price differentiation and the debate over online privacy are linked, because when buyers willingly surrender personal information to get a bargain or complete a purchase, their personal information is collected and used often without their knowledge. This makes them more susceptible to targeted price offers. Price differentiation makes Internet pricing more opaque, whereas price transparency makes it less so.[11]

INTERNET ACCESS PRICING

Internet access price
The price paid to a service provider for a connection to the Internet.

Before commercialization, users idealized the Internet as an unrestrained environment characterized by free and open access for all. However, even at the beginning, users had to pay a price to go online. The **Internet access price** is what consumers, and enterprises without direct Internet access, pay a service provider to connect to the service and Internet. Initially, U.S. access pricing was metered and users paid based on time spent online, which often meant paying long-distance charges. Today, access is almost universally purchased at a basic, fixed flat rate, a monthly fee that guarantees unlimited use. And sometimes, access is free.

Dial-up, DSL, ISDN, and cable prices vary among vendors, plans, and buyer groups and with the availability of special temporary price promotions. They also differ for consumers and enterprises. Access prices vary worldwide. In many countries, access is still metered and very expensive, which is detrimental to the growth of Internet use. This cost clearly plays a role in the relatively low Internet adoption rates in some Eastern European and Latin American countries, where access rates are very high compared to GDP per capita. By comparison, the Scandinavian countries have low access rates and high Internet use. From 2002 to 2003, an international wave of DSL price cuts lowered the cost of high-speed access in many countries. The cheapest broadband access prices are in the Asia Pacific region, followed by the United States, while prices remain high in many European countries.[12]

CONTENT PRICING

Content price

The price paid for access to content on a website.

Access is also what is sold in the case of **content pricing,** the price charged for access to content on a website. Content can be news articles, pictures, online games, stock trading information, money management assistance, downloadable music, software, videos, gambling, dating information, baseball broadcasts, genealogical information, pornography, and more. Willingness to purchase content depends on a number of factors, including who is paying. When an employer is paying, content is more likely to be purchased if the job requires it. This might include a subscription to the *Wall Street Journal Online* (*www.wsj.com*), which has one of the largest online paid subscription bases. Otherwise, content is more likely to be purchased only if the buyer really wants or needs it, there is no viable free alternative, it might help them make or manage money, they are involved with the product category, or the content is entertaining.

Some sites offer free content while trying to generate revenue from other sources, such as on-site paid advertising or sponsorships. Others use free content as a driver, pushing traffic to offline stores or salespeople. Some offer limited free public content and then charge by subscription or per unit for premium, private content. Paid content may be bundled with free content. Another alternative is an extranet, members-only site with no free public content and with access restricted to paid members.

Websites that charge for content must have something that buyers really value; otherwise, price will reduce or destroy site traffic. Over time, consumers have become more willing to pay for content. The Online Publishers Association (OPA at *www .online-publishers.org*) reports that U.S. consumers increased their spending for online content from US$1.3 billion in 2002 to US$1.6 billion in 2003. Online personals and dating services represent about 30 percent of all paid content. The most rapidly growing category is in content related to personal growth, including dieting sites.

Sites are advised to start out with a relatively low price and then raise it as content value is established. The *Wall Street Journal Online* was launched in April 1996. It initially offered an annual online subscription for US$49, which rose to US$59 in 1998 and to US$79 in 2004. Articles retrieved from the paper's archives are priced per copy for download. Journal subscribers are relatively price insensitive; few abandoned the site despite the price increases. The *Journal* is one of the most popular paid-content sites online, with over 701,000 subscribers who deliver an average of 158 page views per subscriber per month and spend an average of 62 minutes on the site; 15 percent of offline print edition subscribers also read the online edition. Each month over 5.8 million unique visitors access the site. In late 2004, the *Journal* began opening its paid content wall and letting visitors read several of its stories free. For five days beginning November 8, 2004 the site removed all its paid content restrictions and opened the entire site to enable visitors to learn about the site and the depth of its content. Analysts believe the move was designed to test traffic for a possible change to an advertising-supported site, perhaps with behaviorally-targeted ads.[13]

Consumer Reports Online (*www.consumerreports.org*), launched in 1997, is the largest online paid-content site, with over a million subscribers. Some content is free; most is not. In one especially valuable free area, visitors can check the latest recalls in a long list of products from appliances to vehicles. A subscription includes access to the magazine's archives with reports on product tests and prices. *Consumer Reports* brings its objective research and valuable brand name to its website. Because its reports save buyers money and search time, many consumers believe the value of its content justifies paying the site's nominal price. Subscribers can purchase annual or monthly access, and magazine subscribers are offered a special discounted annual price.[14]

Internet marketers should be cautious about charging for content. It is clearly not appropriate at some sites, including those that sell products such as apparel, toys, books, automobiles, appliances, computers, and software. Information and entertainment sites are more promising candidates. The *Wall Street Journal* and *Consumer Reports* show that charging for content can be done profitably. Other sites are having greater difficulty because comparable content is free. Some sites that feature adult content are highly profitable. Estimates in 2001 were that only 1.5 percent of all websites had adult content but they contributed 66 percent of all online content revenues; by 2003, adult content was an online industry worth over US$2.5 billion. Paid content (not including adult sites) reached over US$2 billion in 2003, an increase of 25 percent from 2002. It is forecast to increase more than 20 percent each year through 2007. Younger broadband users are driving the rise in paid-content revenues. Buyers 25 to 44 years old generate almost 50 percent of online paid-content revenues; 59 percent use broadband, and almost 25 percent report annual household incomes over US$100,000.[15]

PRICE FAIRNESS

A fair price is hard to define, but like pornography, buyers generally know it when they see it. A *fair price* is being asked when a product is perceived to be worth the price asked for it. It is the *perception* that the buyer is not being taken advantage of by an unscrupulous seller, and it is the opposite of *price gouging* (gross, undeserved overcharging). Generally, the perception is that the lower the price, the greater the fairness, *ceteris paribus*. However, a low price has negative connotations for prestige products, and for convenience and shopping products it can signal low quality. Of course, what one buyer perceives as a fair price another may perceive as a swindle. Price fairness is a highly subjective judgment unless unbiased evidence can be found to substantiate fairness and—more importantly—buyers accept it.

The Internet has leveled the price fairness playing field to a considerable extent, and with time, patience, and skill, consumers and enterprises can obtain timely comparative price information and make informed judgments about fairness. This even extends to works of art, which are notoriously difficult to price and are often subject to price gouging. AskArt.com (*http://askart.com*), The American Artists Bluebook, offers comparative price information and lists recent sale prices for the hundred best-selling artists, topped by prices near US$30 million. It also has information and price lists for regional artists, practitioners in different styles (such as cartoonists and sculptors), and art books. The site offers both free content and subscription services. Although online art price information may help an experienced buyer, a new buyer is still vulnerable to price asymmetry when purchasing paintings, sculpture, and other unique art works online.

StrongNumbers.com (*www.strongnumbers.com*), an eBay partner, is a product and price reference guide to the fair market value of hundreds of thousands of popular consumer products. Its technology calculates prices on the basis of the results of more than 5 million weekly eBay auctions and furnishes fair market values and market trends. StrongNumbers provides a range of final sale prices, along with its own fair market value calculation, a regression line drawn through a sale price scatter plot. The site appears to be a valuable asset in trying to determine price fairness for many popular products sold at auction.

SHIPPING AND HANDLING (S&H)

Price fairness has yet another dimension. Consumers want to know the full price they will have to pay for purchases and particularly for shipping and handling (S&H), the cost of order fulfillment and product delivery. S&H should be disclosed early in the buying process so that it will not come as a shock later and precipitate shopping basket abandonment. Applicable taxes should also be identified. The marketer's problem is determining when to provide the information. S&H and taxes typically are not calculated until the buyer provides purchase information and is ready to check out.

S&H is a contentious issue. Initially, it generally was a free loss leader, an inducement for consumers to purchase online and half of an attractive price reduction duo—no sales tax, no S&H. With the dot-com meltdown and heightened emphasis on profitability and building revenue streams, companies moved away from free S&H and began charging. By mid-2001, the fifty most visited websites all charged for S&H. To illustrate the importance of S&H costs, consider that an estimated 63 percent of customers abandon their online transaction when they learn how much shipping adds to the price.

S&H pricing methods vary. The most common is a graduated scale, adding a fixed price calibrated to the purchase price. Landsend.com's standard shipping begins at US$5.95 for orders less than or equal to US$25 and tops out at US$22.95 for orders delivered UPS next day. A flat shipping rate is less common. Bluefly.com (*www.bluefly.com*) charges US$7.95 per order for standard ground shipping in the continental United States and Canada. Some sites still offer free S&H for purchases over a preset amount. Tiffany.com has free ground shipping to one address for orders of US$1,000 or more; Amazon.com offers free Super Saver Shipping on eligible orders of at least US$25.

The demise of free S&H raises a serious question: Do Internet marketers really want bargain shoppers who are so price sensitive that they abandon a site when they have to pay S&H? Remember the 80-20 rule. A better profit margin can be achieved with a smaller, more select, less price-sensitive customer base. It is unlikely that a small S&H charge will deter most buyers, particularly if it is perceived as fair and they can still avoid state sales tax and the added time, effort, and travel costs of offline shopping. Rising gasoline prices also favor online shopping.

There are risks to increasing the opacity of online pricing. Amazon.com got itself into hot water with consumers over a "free" shipping promotion in mid-June 2001. It offered buyers free shipping for orders of two or more books, music CDs, or videos. At the same time, Amazon increased some product prices and reduced others. To illustrate the power of price transparency and how rapidly price information can spread online, buyers checked Amazon's new prices against others at ISBN.nu (*http://ISBN.nu*), which lists comparative prices with and without shipping. Consumers cried foul, calling Amazon's offer of free shipping a price increase in disguise. They quickly spread the word through online chat rooms that buyers could "game the system" by ordering *The Book of Hope* at US$0.49 (used, US$0.02) as their second purchase to qualify for free shipping. Within twenty-four hours of Amazon's free shipping offer, *The Book of Hope* climbed from number 995 in sales to number 75 on Amazon's Top 100 Sellers list. A week later it was number 31. Of course, Barnes& Noble.com (*www.bn.com*) immediately matched Amazon's offer of free shipping, without being the target of similar negative comments. Within two weeks, Amazon abandoned what it claimed was a *price test to see whether consumers preferred to have S&H costs rolled into the purchase price.*[16] This is also an example of how closely competitors monitor price on each other's sites. Book prices at Amazon.com and Barnes&Noble.com tend to be the same or only pennies different. Regular online *price benchmarking* is something that even small businesses can and should do.

ILLEGAL PRICING PRACTICES

In a perfect world, all prices are fair and price fraud is nonexistent, but this is not the case either offline or on. Bait and switch, credit card fraud, investment fraud, loan fraud, discriminatory pricing, and other illegal practices that haunt offline transactions are lurking online as well. Buyers who use credit cards with dispute-protection clauses have more protection against losses from fraud. Online sellers face their own hazards. Not all buyers are authentic or honest. When an online seller encounters fraud, he or she typically absorbs 100 percent of any costs occasioned by the fraudulent transaction. Online fraud may be no more prevalent than offline fraud, just more visible and more often exposed.

Online retailers that accept credit card charges face a *card not present* situation with almost every transaction. A standard address verification search is not sufficient to guard against unauthorized charges. Etailers with high fraud rates may end up paying higher fees for their merchant accounts. Because the sale of digital products leaves a particularly thin paper trail, these sales are often the most vulnerable to *spoofing,* illegally using someone else's identity for a purchase. Sellers also lose when a buyer claims a fraudulent credit card charge and demands restitution. The charge-back to cover the original charge is a cost to the seller, and if the processing bank levies penalties, the final cost may be greater than the cost of goods sold (COGS). Fraud rules and screening software are helping large sites screen buyers (consumers and enterprises) to ensure that they fit an authenticity profile. These processes are currently too expensive for most small and midsize enterprises.

Price Models

Highly creative alternative Internet price models sprang up like weeds in the late 1990s, and many disappeared just as quickly. Most failed models defied all business common sense; others are still around in a modified form or with a new owner. Although some pricing models were transferred unchanged from offline practices, others were adjusted to better suit the virtual environment.

BASIC FIXED PRICE

Fixed price
A price posted by the seller that the buyer can take or leave, with no haggling.

Offline, new music CDs are traditionally sold in record stores for a basic **fixed price** posted at a particular point in time; there is no haggling, negotiating, or bargaining. Buyers cannot compile their own albums or create a personal jukebox of favorite tunes. They can do both online, where individual songs can be downloaded legally from Apple iTunes for a basic fixed price of US$0.99 each and where Rhapsody Music Service (*www.listen.com*) offers to *Turn Your PC Into a Jukebox* through a variety of basic fixed-price subscription plans for US$9.95/month to listen or US$0.79 per cut to burn. Amazon.com uses basic fixed prices for new books, Lands' End for apparel, AOL for Internet access, and the *Wall Street Journal* for online subscriptions.[17] Fixed or standardized basic prices have been the retail norm since the 1890s, when Fred Kohnle invented a machine that quickly printed price tags and attached them with a straight pin to individual product items. Sears & Roebuck Co. was among the first to offer a basic fixed price on products sold nationwide in its stores and catalogs. Fixed-price tags replaced *haggling* (bargaining or price negotiation).

Basic fixed prices predominate online and off. Offline fixed prices are far more static than online fixed prices, which can be extremely dynamic. There is a high labor cost involved in price changes offline, but changing them online entails almost no labor cost. In other words, even though a price is fixed, it can be (and often is) changed almost instantly online. A site that uses sophisticated data analysis techniques to determine real-time demand and customer price sensitivity can use that information to change price as demand shifts, particularly by lowering price to stimulate demand during non-peak use times. Fixed prices also change at clearance or with a sales promotion.

Fixed pricing simplifies the pricing process for small and midsize businesses that do not have the time, money, expertise, or need to negotiate or use dynamic pricing. Stable prices make price comparisons easier and more accurate and thus facilitate price transparency. Sellers with the tools and expertise to use dynamic pricing effectively gain an advantage by tailoring price to a target market. They create less transparent prices that competitors have a harder time tracking and matching.

Negotiated price
Price arrived at after buyer and seller bargain, or haggle, over price.

NEGOTIATED PRICE

Negotiated price is a price arrived at through bargaining between seller(s) and buyer(s). The process is as old as human history. In many cultures, a fixed price is nothing more than the starting point for bargaining. Americans traditionally have found bargaining somewhat undignified and uncomfortable, but that is changing as more Internet users negotiate price in online auctions and marketplaces. Negotiations open with a proposed or reserve price, and then participants counter until a mutually satisfactory price (typically the highest bid) seals the sale. Negotiations are common among channel members, and bargaining is traditional with agricultural products.

Although the Internet's interactive, dynamic environment appears ideally suited to negotiated-price models, it is unrealistic to think that negotiating appeals to all consumers or enterprises. Many prefer fixed prices because they do not want to deal with the stress and uncertainty of negotiations, because they lack information about quality or price fairness, or because they do not have the time or patience to auction. Others enjoy the thrill of negotiating and the prospect of getting a bargain.

AUCTIONS

Auctions certainly operate offline, but online they reach hundreds of millions more participants who can follow the bidding at their leisure. Governments auction surplus property online; police departments auction confiscated goods; individuals clear their attics of trash and treasure; and charities and churches auction donated goods to fill their coffers. The author's university even sold its used bowling alley equipment on eBay! Online auction sales reached US$556 million in 2001, up from US$223 million in 2000. Forrester Research expects online auction sales to reach over US$48 billion in 2006 and US$54 billion by 2007. eBay, the world's largest online auction, dominates with an over 60 percent market share. Its Q3 2004 profits amounted to US$182 million, an increase of well over 77 percent from Q3 2003.[18]

General auctions accept items from many different product categories. eBay is a general auction trading center that accepts just about any item imaginable, although it prohibits the sale of animals, human parts and remains, stocks and other securities, guns, and many other items whose sale is illegal or objectionable. Other auctions are *product-specific,* such as PotteryAuction.com (*www.potteryauction.com*). Most auctions are for profit; some are run by charities and are non-profit. Classic *forward auctions,* where participants bid up a price and the highest bidder wins, are the most common. *Reverse auctions,* where the lowest bid wins, also are common among enterprise buyers. Other types include pooled, private, reserve price, and Dutch (multiple-product) auctions.

DEMAND COLLECTION OR NAME YOUR OWN PRICE   Priceline.com (*www .priceline.com*) pioneered the method where buyers name their own price in an anonymous reverse auction. Buyers lock in their bid price for a particular product and guarantee it with their credit card. Conditions are restrictive, and consumers cannot pick brands, sellers, and/or product features. Priceline.com contacts suppliers that bid to close the deal from their excess inventory. Sellers generate incremental revenue without affecting their existing distribution network or retail price structure. Buyers learn the details of their purchase only after the deal is closed because they do not know the identity of the sellers bidding for their business; that is, the seller's brand is shielded.

Priceline initially sold everything from gasoline to hotel rooms but later, after a brutal retrenchment, pared its product categories and currently offers cheap airfares, hotels, rental cars, cruises, and package vacations. In 2004, Priceline.com shifted to a dual price strategy that allows buyers to name their choice of flights, times, and airlines at a higher price while retaining its name-your-own-price model to satisfy more bargain-conscious shoppers.[19]

BARTER

Barter
A nonmonetary exchange of things of value between two or more parties that trade goods, labor, or other products.

Barter, also known as reciprocal trade or countertrade, is a nonmonetary exchange of things of value between two or more parties (individuals, businesses, or other enterprises) that trade goods, labor, travel, supplies, advertising, or other products. The U.S. Department of Commerce estimates that about 30 percent of business worldwide is barter-based; an estimated US$16 billion was bartered in the United States in 2003. Barter is widely used in media promotions, where radio or television advertising time is exchanged for the products being advertised. Hotels and resorts trade unused rooms for barter units taken in trade for advertising and supplies. Many smaller companies that need to conserve cash, have excess inventory, and are willing to take the time to find partners consider barter a desirable option.

When products of roughly the same value are traded one for one, the transaction is a *direct barter*, which typically is arranged without "middleman" fees. *Network pool barter* occurs through a barter marketplace where members do not trade directly but sell their products for barter units (trade credits, tokens) that are credited to their accounts and used to make purchases. The risk is that the barter units may not be widely accepted. Most barter marketplace sites offer free memberships, and some collect transaction fees. TradeFirst (*www.tradefirst.com*), the Trade Exchange of America, is a business barter network where its more than 5,000 enterprise members can trade goods and services.

Some online barter sites are run strictly for individuals. The Sporting Swap Shop (*www.less-stress.com/swap*) is a free international barter listing service for men and women who want to swap hunting, shooting, or fishing trips. Recent offerings were for *estuary wildfowling in South Wales, deep sea saltwater fishing in Florida,* and *sea angling in Scotland.* The site is very careful to post the following disclaimer: *It is incumbent upon people using this page to satisfy themselves about the nature of the exchanges being offered and to make their own detailed arrangements. The publishers of Sporting Swap Shop cannot accept any responsibility for any consequences arising from the use of the facilities of this website, which is provided on a goodwill basis only.*[20]

Priceline

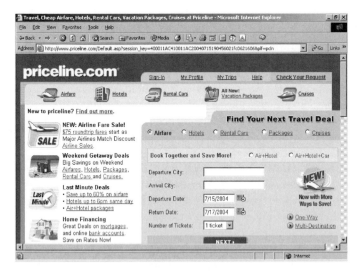

Priceline pioneered the name-your-own-price model.

Source: Courtesy of Priceline.com (www.priceline.com/customerservice/faq/ howitworks/howitworks.asp?session_key= 410011AC420011AC200406292127719675080927648).

CHANNEL PRICING

Uniform cross-channel pricing
Using the same price across all channels in which a product is sold.

Clicks-only sellers use a single channel of distribution, so they do not have to worry about the consistency of their prices in different channels. Bricks-and-clicks sellers operate through multiple channels, so *multichannel pricing* is a concern. Price transparency has forced many companies to adopt **uniform cross-channel pricing,** using the same price for a product across all the channels in which it is sold. This model assumes that the same price is justified across all channels. It is easier to administer and runs less risk of angering customers when they discover that prices vary across channels. It can also avoid buyers' encountering different prices for the same product when a different channel is used for a return. Some marketers sidestep the issue by offering some products exclusively in one channel. Williams-Sonoma, Inc. (*www.williams-sonoma.com*), a multibrand, multichannel retailer, markets its products through 5 retail concepts, 516 branded stores, 8 catalogs, 5 websites, and an online bridal registry. Its main brands are Williams-Sonoma, Pottery Barn, Pottery Barn Kids, and Hold Everything. The company didn't launch its first website until 1999 because it wanted to integrate its channels fully and link its company websites directly to its catalog infrastructure. Some products are web, store, or catalog exclusives; others are the same across channels, as are their prices. About a third of Williams-Sonoma's FY 2004 sales of US$2.74 billion were catalog- and web-based. Extremely sophisticated software systems are needed to track and adjust prices for companies with multiple product lines and channels.[21]

Variable channel pricing
Using different prices in different channels.

An alternative model is **variable channel pricing,** in which product prices are not the same in all channels. This model, which proposes that channels and markets are sufficiently different to justify different prices, was the most widely used model in the late 1990s. It is based on an idealized pricing strategy of first-degree price discrimination, wherein sellers should charge exactly what the market will bear.[22]

Multitier pricing
Charging different prices for different levels of service or product types at a website.

Multitier pricing entails charging different prices for different levels of service or product types. Content sites often use multitier pricing where content in the entry level, or public level, is free and content on the next level is accessed by subscription or by paying a per-unit price.

DYNAMIC AND TEST PRICES

Dynamic pricing
Pricing a product at a higher or lower price depending on buyer characteristics, demand, and inventory level.

Dynamic pricing occurs when price adjustments are made online in real time on the basis of buyer characteristics, demand, and product inventory level. Dynamic pricing requires highly sophisticated software to adjust prices as visitors shop the site. Price can be mass-customized when inventory levels trigger a change. As a result, visitors are offered a lower price on a product that is not selling as expected or a higher price on one where demand is great and inventory is low. Lower prices may be offered as loss leaders for new buyers or as rewards for loyal ones. Because dynamic pricing can be individualized for one-to-one pricing in real time, it raises privacy concerns about personal data collection and use. Buyers offline rarely realize that differential pricing occurs, because they cannot easily perform price comparisons; thus price nontransparency (opacity) is the norm. This is not the case online. Price transparency reveals price discrepancies, which leaves dynamic pricing open to a consumer backlash. The key is whether buyers perceive price differences as fair.

Customized pricing is common in credit cards, airline tickets, and apparel. Customers are differentiated by their preferences or characteristics and by their willingness to pay. Bargain hunters receive lower prices and reduced services; service hunters are offered more services at a higher price. Large sizes pay more for many clothing lines. Magazines have preferred subscription rates for educators. IBM (*www.ibm.com*) is testing dynamic pricing on its server lines. Hewlett-Packard (*www.hp.com*) is using it in a strategy it calls *contextual pricing*, where prices change as customers add multiple items to a specified promotion. These companies look on customized pricing as a way to reduce inventories and optimize profits. Zip code demographics can be the basis for customized pricing. Consumers in affluent zip codes receive catalogs with higher prices; those in less affluent zip codes receive the same catalog with lower prices. Victoria's Secret (*www.victoriassecret.com*) has used this strategy successfully for years. Customized or differential pricing is rational under the Pareto (80-20) Principle, where distinctions are made between customers on the basis of the revenue stream they generate, the cost to serve them, and the profit they produce.[23]

BARGAIN PRICES

The Internet is filled with bargain hunters looking for discounts. Some shop discounts at *house clearances* such as Lands' End's, where small quantity first-quality Lands' End branded products are sold at up to 80 percent off. Others head for Overstock.com, a *discount consolidator* that purchases first-quality excess inventory from such brands as Sony, Toshiba, Kodak, Remington, Samsonite, and Waterford and then sells it online at 40 to 70 percent off. Brand names often sell excess inventory to a consolidator to avoid having sale items on their own sites at the same time as they are trying to sell regular-price merchandise.

Another type of discounter is the *remainder liquidator* that takes merchandise from bankruptcies, receiverships, freight claims, and other distress situations to sell at radically reduced prices. LiquidationWorld.com (*www.liquidationworld.com*) is an asset recovery liquidator that expanded its offline business to the Web, where it offers liquidated, clearance, closed-out, and distressed merchandise.

CyberRebate.com (*http://cyberrebate.com*) pioneered a failed *free-after-rebate* discount model. Up to 100 percent of the purchase price of books, toys, housewares, and other products was rebated to the buyer. About 30 percent of the site's inventory was offered at a whopping 100 percent rebate. Highly price-sensitive customers paid for their purchase, took delivery, and then had to apply for the rebate. As many as 10 percent never collected rebates, and because the markup prices were high, CyberRebate profited from their loss. It also used the float, collecting interest on the purchase price before rebates were delivered. This was not enough to keep the company afloat. CyberRebate.com filed for Chapter 11 bankruptcy on May 16, 2001, amid millions in unfilled rebates.[24]

Another failed discount model was that applied by iDerive.com. Its motto was *Save or get paid*. The buyer named the price, which was locked in. iDerive.com agreed to find a seller at that price by a certain date or pay the buyer a predetermined amount of cash. This was essentially a put option, where suppliers had until the delivery date to sell the merchandise for more than the bid price. It was a complicated model that most buyers were not willing to endure, particularly when shopping search sites could find the same product at a comparable or lower price.[25]

LastMinute.com (*www.lastminute.com*) is the perfect site for European procrastinators, buyers faced with a last-minute trip, and the romantically inclined looking for spontaneous adventure. Products include hotels, restaurants, flights, holiday travel, car hires, vacation rentals, and skiing. Its prices are sometimes far lower, but travel times are often off-peak and subject to availability. This is a bucket shop for tour companies eager to fill seats on already arranged trips by offering a significant price discount.

ESTIMATORS

Home improvements are highly popular yet prone to escalating costs, as most people who have survived a remodeling can confirm. Interactive estimators, or price wizards, help consumers calculate the probable price of a remodeling job. Price wizard software lets consumers pick design options and then make tradeoffs between alternatives, given their budget constraints. Parameters can be changed to get new estimates. Kitchens and bathrooms are the most frequent remodeling jobs, and more is spent on them than on other home improvements. Estimate prices are locally adjusted and include labor, materials, and installations. An example is ImproveNet's bathroom estimator (*www.improvenet.com/HomeOwner/ProjectTools/estimators/bathroom/*), which estimates costs on the basis of the type of job, size, and budget constraints—localized to the owner's zip code.

Another type of estimator works on home loans, personal loans, and insurance. Online loan estimation, application, and processing reduce sales pressure and human error, but not paperwork. MSN House & Home (*http://houseandhome.msn.com*) offers a loan payment estimator and an estimator for the present value of an existing home. The site determines whether the consumer qualifies for a loan and then calculates the cost of the best-price loans to match his or her financial situation. Mortgage production for home loans in 2003 was the highest in U.S. history, as Americans bought or refinanced homes worth over US$3.8 trillion. Generally, loan prices are comparable online and off, although some online lenders claim to offer lower rates. Online lenders began to report profits as buyers sought price advantages amid strong 2003–2004 home sales.[26]

EXTRANET PRICING

Extranets (Chapter 2) selectively allow approved visitors access to a company's intranet or to a specially constructed multicompany website protected by a firewall from unauthorized users. Companies use extranets extensively to identify their supply needs and post RFQs. Suppliers post price changes for their strategically important customers on extranet web pages, an approach that allows 24/7/365 access. Visitors can use internal price search engines to locate current price information. As prices change, real-time responses can be initiated. Before extranets, price and product updates were sent by email or fax during working hours, which varied by time zone. Extranet pricing is far more dynamic and accessible.[27]

GROUP SHOPPING

Demand aggregators
Intermediaries and technology that bring buyers together to form a group in order to gain volume price discounts through bulk buying.

The rationale behind **demand aggregators** is that a groups of buyers purchasing together can force prices down, because a group buying in bulk gets volume discount prices. Demand aggregators are intermediaries that bring buyers together to form a group and organize a reverse auction for the products they want to purchase. Dynamic group buying online for consumers has not worked particularly well. Promised deep discounts did not materialize, products got stale while waiting for more buyers to join the group, and groups often could not get sufficient numbers of buyers to sign up.

The two top consumer demand aggregators were Mercata and MobShop. Mercata went bankrupt in January 2001 when additional financing could not be found after the company lost US$36 million on sales of US$6 million. Mercata could not get the deep discounts that customers wanted, it had a limited number of products in some categories, and its prices were often higher than what shop bots could find. MobShop took a slightly different path. It closed its B2C operation, also in mid-January 2001, and began selling its demand aggregation technology B2B and to enterprises, including the U.S. General Services Administration (GSA), which uses it for online government volume purchasing in the eFAST sector of its site.[28]

Payment Strategies

Purchases must be paid for regardless of whether they are tangible goods, services, entertainment, or website content. Credit cards are used more in the United States than in other parts of the world. Consumers have expressed concern about using their credit cards online ever since they began web shopping. Doubts about privacy, safety, and security persist, but their effect on shopping appears to be lessening as more consumers have positive experiences online.

Nearly all web selling sites (99 percent) offer payment by general-purpose credit card; some (14 percent) offer their own private-label credit card. Gift cards are also available at 46 percent of sites, 41 percent allow some form of recurring billing (bill later), and a growing number offer PayPal (20 percent). Other options are debit cards, digital wallets, smart cards, and **echecks.** The more payment options offered, the higher the sales conversion rate. Sites with four or more payment options average sales conversion rates of 72 percent; those with three methods average 71 percent; those with one method average 60 percent. A growing number of sites are beginning to accept echecks, online electronic or virtual checks that include banking information and can be paid directly online or through a clearing house.[29]

echecks
Electronic or virtual checks that include banking information and can be paid directly online or through a clearing house.

CREDIT AND SMART CARDS

Credit cards have been around for almost three decades. They began as a way to speed customers through retail checkout lanes, and they are still one of the easiest ways to complete store, online, and cross-border payments. People who use them regularly, and most U.S. consumers do, are reluctant to abandon them unless something considerably better comes along.

Credit card authorizations are made over telephone lines, a relatively inexpensive data transfer method in the United States. European telephone charges have always

Smart cards
Stored-value credit cards that have more memory and are capable of performing additional operations, such as security encryption and decryption, data management, and authentication.

been much higher than in the United States, so U.S.-style credit cards are less popular. This contributed to the rapid adoption of **smart cards,** or smart credit cards, an advanced form of a combination credit-ATM-cash-debit-ID card. A smart card, or stored-value card, is an intelligent credit card. It is the same size as a standard plastic credit card but has an integrated circuit embedded in it. The typical plastic credit card can hold only about a hundred bytes of read-only memory (ROM). A smart card can store as much as 8K of information and can perform operations such as security encryption and decryption, data management, and authentication. Smart cards are also called chip cards, IC cards, and memory cards. Although they have become extremely popular in Europe, they have been slow to catch on in the United States.

American Express (*http://home4.americanexpress.com/blue/blue_homepage_nr.asp? Entry=0*) offers the Blue, a credit card with a Smart Chip. This microchip contains an authenticity certificate that provides additional security online for users by locking credit information on the smart chip.

The U.S. Department of Defense has issued more than five million interoperable smart cards to all active-duty and reserve personnel since 1999. Its Common Access Cards (CAC) cost US$6 to US$8 each—over US$250 million overall in FY 2003. The key benefit of CAC is in security, but the cards could conceivably extend someday to authenticating online purchases and collecting useful marketing information about the card holder.[30]

ALTERNATIVE PAYMENT SYSTEMS

Although smart cards may yet find a larger market in the United States, others are looking to alternative systems for safety and convenience. Yahoo! offers Yahoo! Wallet (*http://wallet.yahoo.com*), a free service that securely stores a user's credit card number and billing information but does not actually use them to make purchases. Instead, users pay Yahoo! merchants with the Wallet instead of their credit card. The Wallet is accepted for all Yahoo! features. A security key, like an ATM pin number, is the identifying number that allows users to access secured areas. It is actually a secure cookie that cannot be traced to the user's credit card number. Yahoo! Wallet is not accepted by nonparticipating merchants.

PayPal.com (*www.paypal.com*), an eBay company with over 50 million account holders in 45 countries, is by far the most popular ecurrency system and appears to be in the best position to replace many consumers' credit cards online by building on existing bank and credit card accounts, speeding transactions, and protecting consumers' personal information. PayPal was founded in 1998 and acquired by eBay in 2002. Initially, PayPal service was free for individuals and merchants. Since June 2000, vendors taking in more than US$100 in PayPal transactions have paid from 2.2 percent to 2.9 percent of each transaction, plus 30 cents for use of the PayPal process. An additional 2.5 percent is charged for multiple-currency transactions. This is still about 2 percent less than what most credit card companies charge merchant accounts. Like the other virtual-cash systems, PayPal can be used only with another member of the system, although member web shops now number over 42,000. PayPal is the market leader in Internet payments. Most PayPal transactions are small. About 60 percent of its business is from eBay transactions. In 2003, PayPal handled over US$17 billion in transactions. Some cities accept PayPal payments for taxes, a growing number of charities accept PayPal donations, and PayPal has gift vouchers. PayPal's revenues in Q1 2004, over US$155 million, were up 69 percent from Q1 2003.[31]

MICROPAYMENTS FOR TINY TRANSACTIONS

Micropayments
Online virtual cash systems that allow consumers to make extremely small payments, US$5 or less.

Unlike virtual currency designed for products moderate to high in price, **micropayments** are extremely small payments, US$5 or less, even pennies. They have been the promised salvation of online content providers since the mid-1990s, but their promise has largely gone unfulfilled. Many content providers want to charge a small amount for access. However, using a credit card for a small purchase will drive consumers away, which is why the concept of micropayments is so appealing.

Only Japan's NTT DoCoMo seemingly is having success with micropayments. Each time a customer accesses a wireless DoCoMo service, from cell phones to games, maps or photo sharing, a small charge is added to that customer's monthly subscriber bill. The charges range from US$0.85 to US$2.50. Wireless is the key, because PC users tend to think in terms of larger purchases and do not want more hassle in paying for them. Micropayments do not simplify the payment process. They also are not as secure as other forms of payment, so the potential for fraud is increased.

Honor systems
Processes whereby visitors can donate small amounts to their favorite websites.

Apple's iTunes selling for US$0.99 each is driving renewed interest in micropayments. PayPal, recognizing the potential, has reduced its merchant processing fees for music subscriptions and downloads to 2.5 percent plus US$0.09 per transaction. Other possible drivers for micropayments are ringtones, weapons upgrades for online games, and accessories for avatars. Whatever the micropayment system, it must be simple and secure to succeed.[32]

Amazon.com

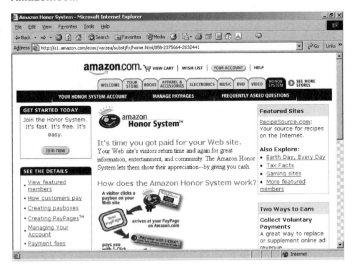

Amazon.com's honor system encourages voluntary payments to a favorite website.

Source: Courtesy of Amazon.com, Inc. All rights reserved. http://s1.amazon.com/ exec/varzea/subst/ fx/home.html/058-2375664-2632441.

PayPal and Amazon.com have both implemented micropayment **honor systems** for sites that have trouble generating revenue and do not want to hassle customers with credit card transactions for small amounts. Growing numbers of websites are asking visitors to donate, voluntarily, to their continued operation. The premise is that a visitor gaining value from the site should want it to survive, so dropping a few dollars into a paybox icon is fast and relatively painless. Amazon's cookie activates on any cooperating website, addressing the visitor by name, which some may find disconcerting. An Internet marketer signs up for the program at Amazon and follows directions to get registered and to have a paybox installed on the marketer's front page. Each website can personalize its message in the paybox. When one of Amazon's over 29 million customers visits the site, the Amazon cookie is activated, and the paybox addresses the cookie holder by name with a personal invitation to contribute. Amazon customers can turn off the use of their name at Amazon but cannot turn off the cookie unless they delete it in their browser's cookie file. Featured members include National Public Radio's *Lost and Found Sound* initiative, RecipeSource recipes from around the world, Andrew Sullivan's blog, and others. The paypage at Amazon records the contribution with Amazon's one-click payment. The site sends a customized thank-you to the customer.

Non-Amazon visitors who see a paybox and do not have an Amazon cookie can still click through to Amazon and contribute with a credit card. Amazon's fee is 2.9 percent and 30 cents per donation. Only Amazon knows the donor's identity. Contributions can be as low as US$1.00. Amazon's Honor System gives small web storefronts and content sites access to a revenue stream that can help some of them stay online.[33]

BILL PAYING ONLINE

A big obstacle that online bill paying must overcome is the reluctance of many consumers to change their banking habits. Bill-paying alternatives exist, but most consumers are not seeking them out. Intermediaries, bill managing companies such as PayTrust.com (*www.paytrust.com*) and StatusFactory.com (*www.statusfactory.com*), compete for bill payers, but thus far, banks offering this service appear to be drawing more users. Users must pay for bill management services, which can be as low as US$5.95 per month. Online bill paying is one of the biggest incentives for switching to online banking, and over a third of all U.S. banks were offering the option by 2004. The number of Americans who pay bills online will continue to grow from an estimated 35 million in 2004 to over 65 million by 2007. Many such payments are paid directly to the company issuing the bill.

This service has significant potential, given that every consumer pays between eight and fifteen bills each month and that even more monthly bills are paid and collected by enterprises. The advantages of online services include options for automatic payments for recurring monthly bills through debit accounts, reminders about due dates, bill tracking, security, and savings from not having to use postage stamps or drive to a post office. Enterprises gain through reduced bill-processing costs.

The United States Postal Service itself (*www.usps.com/paymentservices/welcome.htm*) anticipated the revenue potential of online bill payments and their effect on stamp sales. With partner CheckFree (*https://mybills.com/webpay*), the USPS initiated an online bill-paying system, USPS eBillPay, in April 2000 with the reassuring slogan, "Secure? Of course. It's the Postal Service." It discontinued the service May 1, 2004, without explanation, although revenue disappointment certainly is a credible explanation. As of 2001, the USPS was spending around US$33 million annually on its various online operations, while generating revenues of around US$2 million. Some critics maintain that the USPS has no business using taxpayer funds to develop services that directly compete with the private sector.[34]

Summary

The Fundamentals of Price

Marketing is the functional business activity directly responsible for generating revenue, and price is a key marketing mix tool used to achieve revenue goals. Price determines how much buyers must give up to take possession of or use a product. It allocates products, determining who can buy, possess, and use them, and clears markets via the law of supply and demand. Consumers may be price sensitive, price conscious, or status conscious. Businesses closely monitor consumer primary demand because it generates derived demand for enterprise products. Price is influenced by many factors. Prices typically are set within a range. The Internet is well suited to real-time price testing. With few exceptions, price alone cannot provide a sustainable competitive advantage.

Issues Related to Price

Price information is readily available online, and shopping search sites are having an impact. Price transparency makes prices for competing products clearly visible and easily obtainable; competitive pressure should drive prices down. The availability of good product and price information online has given rise to a model of online–offline shopping complementarity. Online price transparency should discourage price gouging. The Internet encourages price differentiation. An Internet access price must be paid to connect to a service provider and the Internet. Content pricing is another form of access price. Price fairness is a subjective judgment unless unbiased evidence can be found to substantiate fairness. Initially, free S&H was an inducement for consumers to purchase, as part of an attractive price reduction duo—no sales tax, no S&H. Online price fraud may be no more prevalent than fraud offline, just more often visible and publicly exposed.

Price Models

Highly creative alternative online price models sprang up like weeds in the late 1990s, and many quickly disappeared. When the seller sets a price and the buyer can take it or leave it, that price is a basic fixed or posted price. Fixed pricing online can be extremely dynamic, changing frequently. Negotiated prices involve bargaining over price. Online auctions are extremely popular. Barter is a nonmonetary exchange. Bricks-and-clicks sellers operate through multiple channels, so multichannel pricing is a concern. Price transparency has forced many companies to adopt uniform cross-channel pricing. Dynamic prices are price adjustments made online in real time on the basis of demand and product inventory level. The Internet is filled with bargain hunters looking for discounts. Interactive estimators help consumers calculate the probable cost of a home-remodeling job. Demand aggregators get groups of buyers together so that they can take advantage of group discounts.

Payment Strategies

Consumers have expressed concern about using their credit cards online ever since they began shopping there. Smart cards are an advanced form of the credit-ATM-cash-debit-ID card. A smart card, or stored-value card, is a card that has memory and is capable of performing additional operations. Smart cards are far more popular in Europe than in the United States. PayPal is the most popular ecurrency system. Micropayments are extremely small payments. Growing numbers of websites are asking visitors to donate to their continued operation through an honor system operated by Amazon.com. A big obstacle that online bill paying must overcome is the reluctance of many consumers to change their banking habits. Online payments significantly reduce the cost of processing bills and eliminate the need for the payee to stamp a return envelope.

Take Action!

Because you are well on your way to becoming an Internet marketing specialist, you have been asked to report on shopping search engines for your student newspaper. Begin by evaluating three shopping search engines to assess their usability and effectiveness. The product for your research is a DVD movie, *Return of the King* (2003), the third film in the *Lord of the Rings* trilogy. The engines are PriceGrabber .com (*www.pricegrabber.com*), Froogle (*http://froogle .google.com*), and mySimon (*www.mysimon.com*).

1. Before you begin your research, create a table with a column for each engine so that you can organize your work and report results. For each row, designate a measurable and important factor on which you will compare the engines. For example, the first row might be *price*. Check the price at each engine, and record the best one in the appropriate column. Another important variable is *shipping and handling*. You might consider including a row that indicates whether the search engine allows the user to *rank-order results* by price. Develop a list of no more than ten comparison factors.

2. Create a bullet list of the *best* store choices, according to the three engines, with the top choice as number one.

3. Write a newspaper article (750 words or less) in which you describe the use of shopping search engines, explain their value for consumers, identify problems with their use, describe the comparative research you conducted, state your conclusions, and identify which of the three engines you recommend and why.

Chapter Review Questions

1. Why is price often a lightning rod for consumer complaints?
2. Explain how consumer primary demand affects derived demand.
3. Explain why a prestige price offline retailer should also adopt a prestige price strategy online.
4. Why do marketers try to set a price near the ceiling?
5. What is price information asymmetry?
6. How do search sites drive consumers to retailers?
7. Explain the reason for "search online—purchase offline" behavior.
8. Explain the practice of content access pricing.
9. Who determines whether a price is fair?
10. What are the benefits of barter?
11. Why is dynamic pricing online vulnerable to consumer backlash?
12. Why didn't consumer demand aggregation work?
13. How do micropayments differ from virtual currency?
14. What are the advantages of online bill paying?
15. Who benefits from using Amazon's honor system?

Competitive Case Study

Going, Going, Gone at Goodwill

Online auction sales are forecast to reach US$54 billion by 2007, according to Forrester Research, and eBay will certainly take the major share if, as expected, it continues to dominate the online auction industry. Although eBay has cornered around 60 percent of the online auction market, that leaves 40 percent for others to share. Some competitors are very large companies such as Yahoo! (*http://auctions.yahoo.com*) and Amazon (*www.amazon.com/auctions*); others are smaller, but they still compete with eBay. Some sites serve important niches. One of these is ShopGoodwill.com (*www.shopgoodwill.com*). It was started by some entrepreneurs at Goodwill Industries in Orange County, California, in August 1999. These individuals decided to launch an online auction to convert donated items into cash to fund local community social service programs. Because a typical Goodwill store draws customers from a three-mile radius, going online vastly expanded the customer base. Their success prompted them to open the site to other local Goodwills, and by 2003, ninety-one were participating. The site has generated over US$9 million in sales since January 2002—and nearly all is profit. All proceeds benefit Goodwill's education, job-training, and job-placement programs for people with disabilities. Registration is free and the site is public. Over 5,000 items are listed from seventeen categories including antiques, art, books, records, cameras, electronics, collectibles, toys, and dolls. Collectibles is the hottest category. Because donations arrive regularly at Goodwill stores, the site constantly turns over new merchandise. Some buyers find real treasures at ShopGoodwill.com A signed Picasso etching that was gathering dust in a Goodwill store, where it was priced at only US$3, sold online for US$1,801. A lady's pendant brought US$4,651; Barbie dolls have sold for as much as US$500; and a John Wayne photo brought US$5. Goodwill has a considerable advantage over lesser-known sites: its integrity. Another advantage is its relative small scale, which makes the site less intimidating than larger sites. Finally, buyers are attracted by the idea of doing good for others while having the fun of auctioning.[35]

CHECK IT OUT

Charity auctions have also been held on eBay. It held an *Auction for America* in 2001 for the United Way's September 11 Fund, raising US$100 million in 100 days for disaster relief. Visit eBay and search for *charity auctions.* Take a look at some of the auctions in eBay's *Giving Works.* What charities benefit and how much do they receive? What products are being auctioned and for what prices? Do you think regular sellers might have a problem with these auctions? Note that some auctions are backed by different groups, such as MissionFish (*www.missionfish.org/About/aboutguarantee.jsp*) and Charity AuctionConcepts. What role do they play? Do you think Goodwill should also offer some items on eBay?

A GLOBAL PERSPECTIVE

Visit other English-speaking eBays—for example, eBay Australia (*www.ebay.com.au/*) and eBay UK (*http://ebay.co.uk/*). Do they also have charity auctions? If so, how are they like and how are they different from the U.S. eBay charity auctions?

Place in the Internet Marketing Mix

LEARNING OBJECTIVES

» To understand the role of place online
» To learn about enterprise emarketplaces
» To consider B2C channel issues
» To learn about etailing

Hotels Book Direct and Save

For many enterprises the Internet is a great direct-to-customer distribution channel and can often be their best channel. However, not all industries are benefiting equally from the advantages offered by Internet distribution. Segments of the travel and hospitality services industry are doing well, and many branded hotels already report significant savings from online reservations (bookings). Some major hotel brands receive 30 percent or more of their total revenues from online bookings, and direct reservations are increasing for both business travelers and consumers. In 2002, each direct online reservation saved Hilton Hotels Corp. (*www.hilton.com*) US$25 over a traditional travel agency booking and saved Hyatt Corp. (*www.hyatt.com*) US$6 over a call center or reservation office booking. An estimated 54 percent of hotel bookings in 2004 were made directly on hotel-owned websites. The lodging market is expected to generate US$15.5 billion in online bookings in 2006. At the same time, traditional travel agents have felt the sting of **channel shifting,** the transfer of business activities from one channel to another. They have lost business as hotel, airline, car rental, cruise,

and vacation package reservations have shifted to hotel and airline websites, travel suppliers, and self-booking corporate online systems. Direct inventory information and airline flight information that previously was restricted is now available online from companies such as Orbitz (*www.orbitz.com*) and WorldRes (*www.worldres.com*). Over 14 percent of all hospitality services revenues were generated online in 2003, 16 percent were generated online in 2004, and the figure is expected to be 24 percent by 2006. Consumers prefer dealing directly with online travel and hospitality service suppliers. Forrester Research reports that 69 percent of U.S. travelers prefer to buy online, whereas only 27 percent still prefer purchasing offline. Branded hotels are advised to shift more of their business to their own websites and away from online discounters and intermediaries who collect a fee for each reservation. Intermediaries such as Active Hotels' ActiveReservations (*www.activereservations.com*) make online booking easy. Active Hotels booked over £200 million (roughly US$246 million) in hotel rooms throughout Europe in 2004 at the rate of over 1.7 million hotel rooms per night. The ActiveReservations site search is configured with an intelligent technology that returns sensible suggestions even when a name is misspelled. The site posts unbiased feedback from thousands of recent hotel guests and connects with 7,000 European hotels ranging from luxury resorts to bed and breakfast inns (B&Bs). Company research indicates that 98 percent of ActiveReservations' customers are likely to recommend its web service to others. If hotel brands are to compete successfully, they must improve the website experience they offer in order to raise look-to-book (conversion) rates. The 2004 User Satisfaction and Hotel Web Site

Performance (RUSH) Report found that fewer than 19 percent of hotel website visitors reported an *excellent* experience and 17 percent rated their visit *fair* to *poor.* Hotel website visitors are consumers (56 percent) and business travelers (32 percent); are seeking information (34 percent), changing or making reservations (31 percent), and comparing rates (23 percent); and include more lookers (64 percent) than bookers (36 percent). The report also found business travelers more demanding and critical than either event planners or consumers seeking leisure travel.[1]

Channel shifting
Transfer of business activities from one channel to another.

Place
The marketing mix variable concerned with decisions about where to sell products and how to get them to the point of sale and delivered to buyers.

What is happening in travel and hospitality services illustrates the Internet's influence on **place,** the marketing mix variable concerned with decisions about where to sell products and how to get them to the point of sale and delivered to buyers. A considerable portion of Internet marketing is about place and how the Internet is changing many long-standing traditions related to place, shifting marketing channels, offering ways to make existing channels more efficient, creating new channels, and cannibalizing others. This chapter examines the fundamentals of place and considers online enterprise and consumer marketing channel issues. Place involves a wide array of participants and activities. One of the greatest effects of the Internet on place has been in traditional industrial sectors where manufacturers, suppliers, distributors, and logistics companies procure what is needed for production, collaborate with top-tier suppliers to make production more efficient, and use logistics to distribute finished products to buyers. That is where this discussion of place begins.

The Fundamentals of Place

It is not possible to address the question "What is marketing?" without considering marketing channels. Without them, production would grind to a halt, products would not be delivered, store shelves would empty, and online sales would cease. Most consumers are blissfully unaware of channel members and activities apart from the retail stores or etail websites where they shop and the delivery trucks that bring goods to their doors.

Marketing channels
Individuals and enterprises performing supply and distribution activities that make products available to buyers.

MARKETING CHANNELS

The two industrial revolutions and the subsequent rise of mass production and mass marketing widened the distances separating suppliers, producers, and users and created a need for specialized enterprises to fill the gaps. **Marketing channels** (Figure 11-1) consist of individuals and enterprises (independents or corporations and their busi-

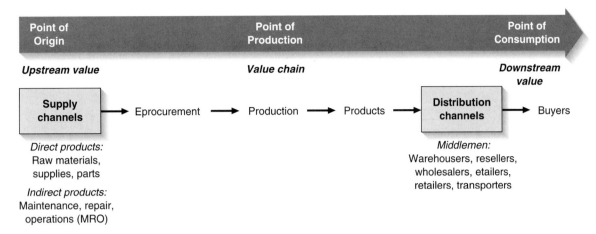

FIGURE 11-1   Marketing Channels Are Product Pipelines
Marketing channels consist of enterprises and individuals performing supply and distribution activities that ultimately make products available to buyers. Supply channels provide inputs to production and distribution channels make finished products available to end users.

Supply channels
Marketing channels that provide *upstream value* by bringing raw materials, supplies, and parts directly into production, and furnishing equipment, materials, and parts to maintain and operate the enterprise.

Distribution channels
Marketing channels that make finished products available to buyers and provide downstream value.

Channel members
Individuals and enterprises, principally businesses, that are members of supply and/or distribution channels and perform channel activities.

ness units), collaboratively performing supply and distribution activities that make products available to buyers and, in the process, add value. Buyers can be businesses, other enterprises, or consumers. Marketing channels are product pipelines consisting of *supply channels* and *distribution channels.* **Supply channels** provide *upstream value* by bringing raw materials, supplies, and parts directly into production and by furnishing equipment, materials, and parts to maintain and operate the enterprise. **Distribution channels** provide *downstream value* by making finished products available to buyers and end users. Channel members contribute value-added services at each transfer point in the channel through their specialized knowledge, skills, experience, and contacts. They perform valuable services that keep products flowing through the pipeline. Some channels are very tightly organized and exclusive; others are loosely organized and actively seek new members.

INTERNET BENEFITS AND DRAWBACKS

The Internet promises many benefits for **channel members,** the individuals and enterprises, principally businesses, that are members of supply and/or distribution channels and perform channel activities. An obvious channel benefit derives from the Internet's 24/7/365 *continuous availability:* Orders can be taken and modified electronically through automated online systems that are always at the ready. Channel members can share sales reports, demand forecasts, and other information instantly in real time, regardless of their time zone. If members are alert and flexible, they can make cost-saving, revenue-enhancing changes. They can benefit from the Internet's *reach,* which can expose them to more buyers and sellers, and to more competitors, worldwide. Revenues may be enhanced by expanding markets and increased market penetration. Competition can reduce costs and force enterprises to become more efficient. Channel members benefit from the Internet's *interactivity,* whereby they can collaboratively make decisions that streamline production, reduce inventories, and lower holding costs. Online conferencing facilitates group projects regardless of members' physical locations and can be used to include suppliers and distributors in production planning. Automated customer services can replace some service center personnel and can lower costs, allowing salespeople to be redeployed. Because the Internet operates on common standards, its *interoperable access* means that channel members can communicate and collaborate using different computer platforms and software. Proprietary legacy systems can communicate with different legacy systems. Because the Internet is a vast *information repository,* access to timely, accurate, relevant information facilitates price transparency, downward price pressure, greater customer satisfaction, and benchmarking.

Along with these benefits, there also are drawbacks. Continuous access can create a disadvantage for smaller businesses that cannot accommodate intense time pressures from dominant channel members. This can weaken channels rather than strengthen them. Reaching large numbers of unknown buyers and sellers can increase the firm's vulnerability to fraud and other illegal and unscrupulous activities. The low cost of entry online intensifies competition, which can lead to margin-eroding price discounting. Interactivity demands quick responses, and this can increase the need for customer service representatives and salespeople, adding human resource costs. Common standards are not a guarantee that older legacy systems will be interoperable, and changing standards typically mean costly upgrades that place a greater burden on smaller channel members. Information is a double-edged sword; too much information produces an unmanageable glut that undermines rather than aids decision making.

Smoothly operating, efficient channels are essential to business success, online or offline, but they are often expensive to create and maintain, and they are not always easy to operate efficiently. Marketing channels are one of the few remaining areas where businesses can still ferret out inefficiencies and reduce costs. That is why so much excitement was expressed initially about the potential of the Internet to streamline and automate channel activities and produce significant savings. Analysts promised that B2B **emarketplaces,** online trading platforms bringing enterprise buyers and sellers together to negotiate transactions, and eprocurement would reduce or eliminate paperwork, increase access to buyers and suppliers, lower supply and material costs, increase fulfillment efficiency, cut delivery times, reduce inventory and holding costs, close costly warehouses, and eliminate intermediaries ("middlemen"). Streamlined channels, agile and flexible, would raise productivity and fuel growth. Some of the promised benefits have been realized, but not as easily, rapidly, or widely as expected. Others have proved to be more fantasy than fact.

Emarketplaces
Online trading platforms that bring enterprise buyers and sellers together to negotiate transactions.

CHANNEL DECISIONS

Contemporary enterprises face complex, often costly decisions about place that are influenced—and sometimes made for them—by other channel members. If an enterprise is a member of an established, tightly organized marketing channel offline, or if it seeks to become a member of an established channel, it may be forced to go online if the channel's dominant member insists. There was no ambiguity in Wal-

Mart's (*www.walmartstores.com*) September 2002 command that its thousands of suppliers go online and communicate with the company electronically using Wal-Mart's Internet-operable proprietary software over its private industrial extranet, RetailLink (*https://retaillink.wal-mart.com*). Wal-Mart's clout is indisputable. It is the top brand in the United States and the world's largest retailer. In 2002, for every US$1 spent in any store in the United States (not including auto parts stores), an incredible 7.5 cents was spent in a Wal-Mart. It has a 30 percent share of the U.S. consumer staples market and a 15–20 percent share of music and video sales. Dial Corporation (*www.dialcorp.com*) generates around 28 percent of its sales from Wal-Mart, Del Monte Foods (*www.delmonte.com*) 24 percent. If Wal-Mart were a country and sales were its GDP, the company's US$256 billion (FY 2004) revenues would rank it thirtieth in the world, immediately after Saudi Arabia. Wal-Mart operates an incredibly tight marketing channel, a vast pipeline to global markets. The company's marketing power forces suppliers (vendors) to become leaner, flexible, and faster. If they cannot, they are likely to be dismissed or forced out. Wal-Mart applies pressure on its suppliers to improve constantly, drive out inefficiencies, lower costs, and help the company achieve its promise of "Always Low Prices. Always." This creates the *Wal-Mart effect* of falling prices. The company uses Internet-based communication to speed and simplify ordering processes. Its vendor-managed inventory management system has larger suppliers overseeing stock control and recommending store stocking alternatives to Wal-Mart buyers. Inventory controls reduce costs and, ultimately, prices. In early 2004, the company told its top one hundred (top-tier) suppliers to embed electronic RFID (radio frequency identification) product code tags on consumer goods pallets shipped to its stores by January 1, 2005, although it admitted that only about 65 percent could actually meet the deadline. The tags will identify items in the supply chain, and eventually Wal-Mart will be positioned to tap into a web-based service that tracks products from production to location on a store shelf and purchase. This will increase inventory efficiency by allowing manufacturers to reconcile purchase orders and deliveries with sales. Real-time information should result in better inventory management, reduce holding costs, and lessen stockouts (unavailable inventory). In the meantime, RFID is a costly technology that Wal-Mart's suppliers will have to adopt.[2]

Although some place decisions are made by a channel's dominant member, often in collaboration with top-tier suppliers, other decisions are made independently. An enterprise's industry segment, revenue, market share, competition, complexity, location, and other factors will help determine the *size* of the channel—that is, the number of suppliers, intermediaries, and others needed to move products through the pipeline. These factors will also affect the *form* the distribution channel will take: direct to customers, as in the case of Dell (*www.us.dell.com*), multichannel, as in the case of Lands' End (*www.landsend.com*), or a mix. And they will help determine channel *management:* whether the channel is tightly managed by a dominant leader (channel captain) like a Wal-Mart, or more loosely managed, which is more characteristic of smaller businesses in financial, logistics, and other services. Good communication is essential to good channel management. Internet-based communication can expedite and simplify ordering, fulfillment, inventory management, information dissemination, logistics, and after-sale support.

CHANNEL AGREEMENTS

Channel arrangements are regularly formed and frequently dissolved. Sometimes they do not work out even when they are initially successful. Channel members can become dissatisfied with their partners and, when negotiations fail, end up in court. For example, since 2000, Amazon.com (*www.amazon.com*) had successfully operated the Toys "R" Us website (*www.toysrus.com*) under a 10-year exclusivity agreement. Toys "R" Us had sought out Amazon after the 1999 holiday selling season, during which its own order fulfillment had failed to deliver some products in time for Christmas. Amazon agreed to the arrangement because that same season it was left with an unsold toy backlog. Under the channel agreement, Amazon handled order taking for Toys "R" Us, payment processing, and fulfillment. But in early 2004, after mediation failed, Toys "R" Us sued Amazon, claiming that Amazon-based third-party merchants were offering over 4,000 toys and other products that violated the exclusivity agreement. Toys "R" Us sought US$200 million in damages for the breach and the return of exclusivity fees. Amazon claimed the Toys "R" Us suit had no merit. In August 2004, a state judge ordered the two sides to work out their disagreements.[3]

INTERMEDIARIES

Intermediaries have different names and different relationships with producers and customers. They can be found online using Google or another search engine. *Agents* are independent businesses that have legal authority to act in the name of a manufacturer; thus they are manufacturers' representatives (reps). They may handle similar products for different manufacturers, selling them in different territories, but they do not directly handle competitive products in the same territory. They are field salespeople who often perform other valuable marketing and financial services. Reps typically work in only one industry segment—for example, in foodservices (see Manufacturers' Agents Association for the Foodservice Industry at *www.mafsi.org*). *Brokers* bring buyer and seller together, directly and often face to face, to negotiate a sale. Real estate brokers are intermediaries who facilitate the sale of real estate, travel agents are brokers for travel services, and financial services brokers transact stock and bond exchanges. Of all the intermediaries threatened by the Internet, brokers are the most vulnerable because, to varying degrees, their work can be duplicated by electronic exchanges. Travel agents that only sell airline tickets can easily be replaced by Internet travel sites, particularly for easily arranged point-to-point trips. Travel agents that add value in scheduling complex, multipoint trips and deliver personal service are more difficult to replace.[4]

DISINTERMEDIATION?

Disintermediation
The collapsing of channels, removing or reducing the number of intermediaries.

Disintermediation was initially associated with households removing their savings from low-paying bank accounts and investing in money market and mutual funds, where their money could earn higher interest rates. **Disintermediation** is the collapsing of channels—that is, the removing of intermediaries in order to reduce costs, increase efficiency and revenue, and better serve customer needs. It was once assumed that manufacturers would go online to sell their products directly from their own websites and cut retailers (and etailers) out of their channels. This turned out to be less of a threat than was originally feared, but some disintermediation has occurred.

Research shows that 70 percent of consumers perform product research online and make their purchase offline. Accordingly, many manufacturers make their websites rich in product information. It is a logical next step to sell directly from their sites to the consumers seeking information and cut out intermediaries—that is, to disintermediate. Polaroid (*www.polaroid.com*) is one firm that considered disintermediation, eliminating its trading partners and routing all sales through its website. This sounded like an enticing way to absorb dealer margins and gain complete marketing control over its products. Disintermediation was reconsidered, however, when the costs of taking over all customer billing and shipping were factored in. Although Polaroid now sells products from the Polaroid Online Store *Polaroid 2go* (*http://shopus.polaroid.com/shop/*), it also features an onsite dealer locator service with maps and encourages visits to a nearby retailer. This gives dealers online support and, rather than eliminating them, supports their sales. More manufacturers and product originators *are* selling directly from their websites, but those that have established distribution channels typically identify their channel partners and encourage customers to visit these businesses' websites and/or stores.

Some original pure-play cyberbrands, such as Amazon.com, are bucking the disintermediation trend. Amazon went online in 1994 as an online bookseller that only made transactions from its website, outsourcing everything else. Amazon's founder Jeff Bezos quickly realized he needed greater marketing control and built six huge robot-picking warehouses strategically located around the United States. Warehousing efficiency gives Amazon above twenty inventory turns each year, compared to below fifteen for the industry as a whole. The company went into the direct-mail print catalog business in 2000 when it purchased Tool Crib. This continued the repositioning of Amazon as a broad-based, general-purpose, multichannel merchant.[5]

SUPPLY CHANNELS

Suppliers

Individuals or enterprises that make up a supply channel and furnish others with direct and indirect products.

Suppliers are individuals and enterprises that make up a supply channel providing manufacturers and other enterprises with *direct products* that are used in production and *indirect products* needed for enterprise operations and sale. Traditional manufacturing supply channels are short, have few members, and are characterized by long-term commitments, personal relationships, negotiations, customized selling efforts, and extended supply contracts. It may take years to develop a satisfactory supply channel whose members fill supply needs and are reliable, flexible, and motivated to sustain efficient channel relationships.

Supply channels often are led by powerful manufacturers, channel leaders such as a General Electric (GE at *www.ge.com*), or dominant retailers such as a Wal-Mart. Leaders can issue orders to their suppliers and buyers, but most find that guidance, cooperation, and negotiation work best in getting members to adopt new business methods. GE Polymerland.com (*www.gepolymerland.com*) is an example of the latter approach. It was one result of GE's Internet initiatives to improve efficiency and cut costs. GE Polymerland.com went online in mid-1997 as the GE resins distribution site targeting plastics engineers, designers, and specifiers creating new products and reformulating old products. It is an electronic marketplace for a vertical market. According to the company, the site helps users "design products, research and select materials, cost and purchase resins, and troubleshoot production processes." Users can access data sheets on over 30,000 resins, participate in online seminars and industry discussion groups, and link to industry-specific pages. First-time users are shown how to place orders, check on product availability, place and track orders, and review their order status and history.

By 2000, GE Polymerland.com was the industry's leading B2B emarketplace. It began 2000 with online sales of US$5 million, and by year end it was generating US$50 million in weekly sales and contributing 25 percent of the company's total resin sales. In 2000 the site took in over US$1.5 billion in online orders and was a model for the digitization of other GE SBUs. By 2002, the site had 200,000 registered users and online sales of US$4 billion.

GE worked with some of its top-tier channel members in planning the site, which eased their transition to online ordering and reduced reluctance to adopt the technology needed to use the site. The website cuts GE's transaction and inventory costs, eliminates paperwork, speeds up ordering time, and expands customer service options. Customer questions are answered online, at a cost of about US$0.50 each, considerably less than the US$80 that the average personal service call can cost. In 2000, GE saved US$1.6 million through Internet-enabled efficiencies, including saving US$600 million through eprocurement at its online auctions. Another US$1 billion was saved through eproduction efficiencies in its twenty major SBUs.[6]

Dell, the world's leading computer systems company, maintains a constant, seamless flow of information with its small, tight group of suppliers over a secure extranet at *https://valuechain.dell.com* or one of the special extranets that Dell has created for its largest suppliers. They include Intel (*http://intel.com*) for processors and Sony (*www.sony.com*) for monitors. Dell was one of the first companies to automate its supply chain online completely and to manage interactions electronically with component suppliers, original equipment manufacturers (OEMs), distributors, system integrators, repair and support companies, service partners, logistics suppliers, third-party product providers, employees, and customers. Dell's suppliers are in constant contact with the company through exceedingly tight information links. The company uses its enterprise websites to provide performance report cards, share supply and demand forecasts, transmit engineering change orders, and report on parts quality. Real-time sales reporting means replenishment is closely tied to orders and ensures that Dell's four-day inventory supply is maintained. Dell has about sixty inventory turns a year. It also runs an extensive intranet for employees.[7]

DISTRIBUTION CHANNELS

Enterprise and consumer products traditionally have had different distribution channels, although this distinction is blurring as more of the same products are sold to both. Distribution channels deliver downstream value and products to end users; they also manage product returns. Enterprise distribution channels move finished products from producer to businesses, governments, educational institutions, health care facilities, or other enterprise purchasers. Enterprise distribution channels have few intermediaries—sometimes none if they are direct. Consumer distribution channels move finished products to consumers, either directly or indirectly through intermediaries such as retailers and etailers.

DIRECT DISTRIBUTION   Even in today's complex marketplace, many exchanges are still *direct*, one-to-one, seller-to-buyer without intermediaries. Dell has always used a highly successful direct channel for buyers, initially by telephone and catalog, and now also online. Dell has buyers configure and price systems, purchase, track orders, and receive technical assistance online. Their computers are made to order and delivered within one to two weeks. The speed of order taking, manufacturing, and delivery; low inventory stockpile costs; the avoidance of intermediaries; the fact that there is no need to tie up capital in retail stores, and aggressive pricing combine to give Dell a sustainable competitive advantage. Finished computers are shipped from one of Dell's manufacturing plants to a purchaser's home or business by FedEx Corp. (*www.fedex.com*) or United Parcel Service, Inc. (UPS at *www.ups.com*). In 2001–2002, Dell expanded into direct-mail brochures and selling products on QVC television home shopping and QVC's website (*www.qvc.com*). Low interest rates, falling computer prices, and aggressive online marketing solidified Dell's position as the PC market share leader. About two-thirds of Dell's sales (US$41.4 billion in FY-end 2004) are to large enterprises.

Dell embraced the Web early, launching a site in 1994. It began taking online orders in 1996; the next year it was processing US$1 million in orders each day, and by 1999 it had reached US$40 million in daily online sales. Five years later, Dell websites were processing one billion page requests per quarter from eighty-four country sites. About half its technical support and three-quarters of order-status transactions happen online. Dell maintains an industrial sales force that works with enterprises to design computer systems for their unique needs. These salespeople are key to maintaining Dell's price advantage. Customer support delivered online reduces costs and often is more satisfying to buyers than phone service, which is subject to delays. Dell's use of Internet marketing is a model for other products that can be mass-customized and sold direct. In 2002, Dell announced that it was extending its direct sales reach to ten-by-ten-foot multimedia web kiosks in select retail malls. Its first kiosk opened in Austin, Texas, and within two years, sixty-five kiosks were operating in ten states. Customers can try Dell's latest computers and accessories at a kiosk and ask salespeople questions, then place orders directly from the kiosk to *www.dell.com*. Dell also mails catalogs, but orders are taken only online or by telephone.

Dell has been highly profitable with its simplified direct distribution channel. The company closely integrates its online (website) and offline (telephone) sales and tightly controls its customer **touchpoints.** Touchpoints are the points of contact, or *customer facings*, where a customer interacts with the enterprise. In Dell's case they include websites, telephone salespeople, direct-mail catalogs, mall web kiosks and kiosk salespeople, and print and television advertising.[8]

INDIRECT DISTRIBUTION AND CHANNEL CANNIBALS   Some companies do not sell directly from their websites, often because they are reluctant to cannibalize sales of channel member partners, dealers, retailers, or other resellers. **Channel cannibalization** is the loss of sales in an existing channel when a new channel is

---

Touchpoints
Contact points (customer facings) where a customer interacts with the enterprise.

Channel cannibalization
Loss of sales in an existing channel when a new channel is introduced to sell the same product(s).

introduced to sell the same product(s). Sometimes it is *planned cannibalization,* where a business creates a competing channel, even though it undercuts sales in an existing channel, because it wants to block a competitor's sales or recognizes a revenue opportunity. *Unplanned cannibalization* is an unexpected loss in sales when a new channel is introduced.

P&G avoided cannibalizing existing channels and angering its retail distributors by restricting sales of Reflect.com (*www.reflect.com*) products to its website and not using the company name on the site. Ford and GM redirect online buyers to complete sales at their dealers in order to avoid cannibalizing dealer sales and undermining their dealer networks.

Levi Strauss & Co. (*www.levis.com*) initially sold its jeans online from a site launched in November 1999 and ordered its retailers not to sell Levi's products online from their websites. By January 2000, however, the company had reversed its strategy and stopped selling its jeans directly from its website. Although Levi's company officials will not admit that retailer pressure caused the reversal, they admit that a "little bit of tension" existed. Today, Levi's website is information-only. Site visitors are advised to go to one of Levi's retail partners' websites to make an online purchase. Links are to JC Penney.com (*www1.jcpenney.com*), Kohl's (*www.kohls.com*), Urban Outfitters (*www.urbn.com*), Sears (*www.sears.com*), and Macys.com (*www.macys.com*), among others.[9]

MULTICHANNEL DISTRIBUTION   Because it is well documented that customers

Multichannel distribution
The strategy of using more than one channel to reach consumers.

spend more when there are more channels where they can spend, **multichannel distribution** is common. This strategy uses more than one channel to reach consumers, providing products where consumers are willing to buy and it is profitable to sell. One channel might be direct: sales made directly to customers from the manufacturer's or producer's website. *Dual distribution* requires two channels. Multichannel distribution, more than two channels and up to five or more, is more difficult to manage because it involves more channel members and intermediaries. It may consist of *store-based* channels (department, outlet, discount, specialty, clubs, superstores, and the like) and *non-store* channels (mail order catalogs, telephone, mall kiosk, interactive television, and online—primarily through websites).

Lands' End (*www.landsend.com*), a direct merchant of traditionally styled clothing, went online in 1995 selling only one hundred items from its website. However, it had been a successful catalog direct merchant since 1962. Lands' End built its brand by working directly with mills and clothing manufacturers to ensure product quality. Because it had no middlemen (intermediaries), it could pass cost savings along to customers as lower prices. Today, Landsend.com is the world's largest apparel site in volume sold, and every product sold through the company's general and specialty catalogs is online—over 90,000 SKUs. It continues to sell through catalogs and its thirty branded stores in the U.S., UK, and Japan. In FY 2001, the company mailed 269 million catalogs. Since the company was acquired by Sears, Roebuck and Co. in June 2002, some Lands' End clothing has been sold in Sears stores, but initially, Lands' End clothing was not sold on the Sears website. By late 2004, some Lands' End inventory was also available from Sears.com with fulfillment by Lands' End. Lands' End clothing represents about 15–20 percent of the apparel sold at Sears stores. Landsend.com's online 2003 sales were $435 million, 28 percent of its total revenue, up from 21 percent in FY 2001. Twenty-five percent of its new customers in 2003 came from the Web, up from 20 percent a year earlier. Lands' End Custom, where customers can design their own pants and shirts, is available only online. This *web exclusivity* is credited with driving more new customers to the Landsend.com website.[10]

Digital distribution channels

Channels for the distribution of digital products to buyers electronically over the Internet, intranets, extranets, or other networks.

DIGITAL DISTRIBUTION Some products—such as music, airline tickets, hotel reservations, video games, magazines, newspapers, radio and television programs, information, entertainment tickets, and financial services—are digital products that can be distributed directly to end users on the Internet via **digital distribution channels,** channels for the electronic distribution of digital products to buyers over the Internet, extranets, or other networks. Although contemporary digital distribution is a new channel model (particularly in B2C markets), Electronic Data Interchange (EDI) systems predate Internet commercialization, and many businesses still use proprietary EDI to communicate with their channel members. However, EDI is limited to a one-to-one exchange, while Internet digital distribution channels are one-to-many.

Digital products can be *pushed* directly to many buyers instantaneously, automatically, and simultaneously. Many businesses can be sent an RSS feed simultaneously. Many business subscribers can simultaneously download articles from the *Wall Street Journal* in a *pull* strategy. Some digital service products require entry into users' computers in order to make on-site repairs or upgrades.

Digital distribution can be paperless, with purchase confirmation sent electronically by email, but many purchase confirmations are still sent the old-fashioned way by hard copy. Some businesses take no chances and send both. Fulfillment for digital purchases still requires a payment mechanism, and a growing number of businesses use PayPal as well as commercial credit cards, letters of credit, and other forms.

Underground distribution channels

Peer-to-peer (P2P) shared distribution of digital content and software, typically without regard to copyright.

Abandonware

Software or content distributed P2P that is no longer copy-protected or for which the copyright is not enforced.

UNDERGROUND DISTRIBUTION CHANNELS Speed and convenience are two great advantages of digital distribution; concerns about security, privacy, and legality are drawbacks. Music distribution is perhaps the classic case, which also illustrates problems of copyright, royalties, and controlled distribution. Most music is distributed through a tight band of major labels: Universal Music Group, Sony Music Entertainment, EMI Group, BMG Entertainment, and Time Warner. These companies failed to recognize the great opportunity and threat of online music distribution. Instead, it fell to file-sharing sites to take the lead, particularly the original Napster.com (*www.napster.com*). Napster facilitated the spread of peer-to-peer (P2P) music sharing that initially ignored copyrights and royalties, allowing individuals to share music freely—and free—over the Internet. Napster proved that demand exists for downloaded digital music.

Underground distribution channels are made up of individuals who share digital content (music, video), and software (operating and applications programs, games) P2P without regard to copyright. A far smaller amount of digital content distributed P2P is **abandonware,** software or content no longer copy-protected because the copyright has expired or is no longer being enforced. If the copyright is active, P2P distribution and multiple copying are illegal. Abandonware web rings openly distribute these products.

Although copyright holders vigorously protest the existence of underground distribution channels, others challenge the right of the copyright holder to encroach on product purchasers' rights. Some courts have ruled in favor of purchasers, saying that *for personal use,* they can make digital copies of what they legally own. This dispute also highlights the conflict between the concept of the Internet as an environment for the free sharing of information and content, on the one hand, and, on the other, the need for copyright protection and the desire for a paid-content model. The popularity of underground distribution is shown in a comparison between iTunes and Kazaa. The week after the Apple iTunes Store (*www.apple.com/itunes*) legally sold its millionth tune, over 2.5 million copies of Kazaa (*www.kazaa.com/us/index.htm*) P2P software were downloaded. Kazaa claims over 357 million downloads of its "100 percent legal" P2P software.

Distribution of pirated purchased software (illegal multiple copies) or pirated beta versions (almost-ready-for-release software that the developer wants others to review) rivals legitimate retail sales and has existed since the earliest days of personal computing. An estimated 30 percent of all software in the United States is pirated; in Asia, pirated software is used on 90 percent of all desktop computers. As much as 80 percent of all illegal software is distributed online.

Analysts predict that by 2009, several billion dollars' worth of music will be downloaded legally, about a third of total music industry sales. Underground P2P sharing will not end, but iTunes is showing that legal downloading can be profitable. It is also expected that legal P2P models may develop to link interactive television (TiVo at *www.tivo.com* or ReplayTV at *www.digitalnetworksna.com/replaytv/default.asp*) to a subscription file-sharing network where members legally share programs that others record.

Pressures on underground channels will come from three sources. Tougher enforcement of existing laws such as the Digital Millennium Copyright Act of 1998 (*www.copyright.gov/legislation/dmca.pdf*) and continued legal actions against large-scale P2P downloaders and software pirates will shrink some underground channels. Fair pricing for digital downloads will make even greater inroads, as shown by the iTunes example. Finally, expanding pay-as-you-use services by online application service providers (ASPs) over broadband connections that are always on will make software delivery affordable, efficient, and seamless. A better product, fairly priced, may encourage purchases and make poorer-quality illegal copies less desirable.[11]

LOGISTICS/PHYSICAL DISTRIBUTION   Logistics/physical distribution (PD) intermediaries store, handle, and move products through channels and ultimately to end users. *Supply distribution* moves raw materials and parts into production, and *physical distribution* moves products from producer to consumer. *Logistics* stores, handles, and moves products (raw materials, parts, supplies, unfinished and finished) from point of supply to point of production to point of sale.

UPS is a third-party logistics provider and the world's largest express carrier and package delivery service. Its employees, driving those ubiquitous brown trucks, make consumer deliveries and provide specialized logistics and physical distribution services for enterprises in more than 200 countries. UPS Supply Chain Solutions (SCS at *www.ups-scs.com/*) operates in 120 countries with logistics support, financial services, freight and mail services, and consulting on global supply chain performance. SCS is particularly attractive to small businesses that can turn to UPS experts for all their logistics and supply chain management needs. UPS OnLine Tools are server resident programs on UPS Internet servers for businesses to adopt so that their customers can track online purchases and select from an array of variously priced shipping options. More than 65,000 enterprises have embedded UPS shipping software in their websites. The company also handles returns (*reverse logistics*), which represent approximately 6 percent of all online purchases. Jupiter Media Metrix estimates that by 2005, U.S. online retail spending will reach US$118 billion and require 2 billion product deliveries, which could be an additional 36 million packages for UPS and its competitors to return.

UPS is a US$30 billion corporation that delivers 57 percent of all online purchases and receives more than 5 million online tracking requests daily; 93 percent of all its delivery orders are received online. Electronic bar code tags embedded in delivery packages allow tracking with an accuracy of about thirty feet. The company delivers to almost every U.S. address, and 13.6 million packages are delivered worldwide every day. UPS moves products from manufacturers to warehouses, shipping docks, trucks, planes, and trucks for delivery to buyers. It returns online purchases to manufacturers, warehouses, stores, service centers, and liquidators. UPS offers customers choices: faster air delivery or slower ground delivery; simple delivery services or storage, repair, and shipping. U.S. packages are routed through the UPS Worldport hub, the company's massive central warehouse and distribution center in Louisville, Kentucky, USA, which processes over 600,000 packages every night.

In 2004, UPS signed an agreement with AuctionDrop (*www.auctiondrop.com*) to accept eBay (*www.ebay.com*) auction items at any of over 3,400 locations of The UPS Store (*www.theupsstore.com*) in the contiguous United States. UPS ships the dropped-off items to AuctionDrop, where trained personnel take high-resolution photographs, evaluate and price the items, and write detailed eBay listings. They track auctions, answer prospective buyers' questions, and, when auctions close, process payment and ship items to purchasers by UPS. This makes auctioning far easier, particularly for people who really don't have the time or desire to do it themselves. No payment is taken by The UPS Store, but it shares in a variable commission charged by AuctionDrop.[12]

WIRELESS CHANNELS

The term *wireless channel* has multiple meanings. It refers to wireless networks that connect LANs within a corporation; to extranets that connect supply and distribution chain members; to the purchase of wireless cell phones online; to the geographic deployment of Wi-Fi routes around barriers such as trees, hills, and buildings, and the support of Wi-Fi hotspots; to wireless distribution channels for digital products using wired and wireless devices; and to the use of Bluetooth short-range and long-range satellite tracking in logistics. Wireless channels are considered in various places in this and other chapters, in the context of their various meanings.

Enterprise Emarketplaces

Businesses go online for many reasons. They do so to purchase materials used in making the products they sell. They go online to find services needed in their operations, to sell products, and to seek opportunities for franchising and licensing. They go online to recruit salespeople and brokers and to find liquidators that convert surplus assets to cash. Other enterprises, including governments and non-profits, do many of the same things online, often using the same channels as businesses and sometimes competing with them for buyers.

ONLINE B2B TRADE

Online B2B trade
Any sale between businesses where some part of the transaction or product configuration is made online.

Not all businesses are part of a tightly knit channel captained by a manufacturer or dominant retailer, but many of those that are not still participate actively in **online B2B trade,** any sale between businesses where some part of the transaction occurs online or some part of the product configuration is agreed upon online. B2B traders include, for example, such very small businesses as a home-based custom gift basket shop that goes online to purchase supplies needed to make its baskets and uses search engines to find business buyers to make bulk purchases of corporate gifts and sales incentives. It includes businesses that purchase office supplies online from Office Depot (*www.officedepot.com*), business insurance from Safeco (*www.safeco.com*), and merchant payment services from Wells Fargo (*www.wellsfargo.com/biz/products/ merchant/retail/retail.jhtml*). B2B trade takes place on manufacturers' websites and extranets, and through online trading platforms, shopping malls, auctions, and even some barter sites.

Around 95 percent of all online transactions are estimated to be B2B. However, reliable estimates of the sector's size are elusive, and it is difficult to determine the contributions of different types of businesses. Estimating B2B sales volume is also complicated by the fact that some businesses, just like many individuals, conduct product research online and then purchase offline.

B2B ecommerce in the United States is concentrated in manufacturing and among large wholesalers and retailers. Initial forecasts were that online B2B transactions would reach over US$6.3 trillion by 2004, up from US$600 billion in 2000 (less than 15 percent of total B2B sales), and that 25 percent of all B2B transactions would be online by 2003. The public Internet was expected to eclipse extranet and one-to-one EDI sales. Even though the original forecasts were overly optimistic, eprocurement has been growing steadily despite the dot-com crash, the 2001 recession, and the demise or consolidation of most public Internet trading exchanges, whose numbers were down from an estimated high of 2000 or more in 1999 to around 200 in 2004. Online B2B sales exceeded US$1.4 trillion in 2003 and were expected to reach US$2.3 trillion in 2004.

Emarketplaces
Online trading platforms that facilitate the transactions of enterprise buyers and sellers.

Growing numbers of businesses are buying and selling to one another on automated public exchanges, in private exchanges, and directly from business websites. **Emarketplaces** are online trading platforms that typically operate on a single software standard. They facilitate enterprise buyer and seller transactions by integrating buyer procurement systems with supplier fulfillment systems. This service is performed for a subscription fee, a transaction fee, or both.

Emarketplaces can be housed on the *public* Internet, often at third-party website exchanges run by intermediaries and open to anyone for a fee, or on *private* networks (extranets) often operated by a major buyer, manufacturer, or retailer. Extranets can be *vertical*—specific to an industry segment or product type—or they can be *horizontal*—general, comprising many segments and product types. Deals that previously were sealed with a handshake or telephone call, or on the golf course, are not easily moved online to horizontal emarketplaces. Many businesses fear becoming involved with suppliers or buyers they do not know, whose reliability and honesty they have not tested. Other concerns include reluctance to use public exchanges that may not be secure, where proprietary information can be exposed with slow online ordering; unresponsive technology that cannot accommodate unusual orders; technical problems that hinder order completion; and the dilemma of deciding which emarketplace technology to adopt.

Private emarketplaces are an increasingly important part of B2B transactions. They occur directly on supplier or buyer websites via special software, electronic catalogs, and online ordering processes. They also take place on private industry exchanges, on members-only auctions, through purchasing groups (aggregate buying), and at liquidators.

Most enterprises realize that going online can cut costs by reducing phone calls, faxing, and customer coddling and that direct, automated online transactions reduce ordering time and almost eliminate paperwork. Companies successfully using online B2B include grocery chain Kroger Co. (*www.kroger.com*) and Sun Microsystems (*www.sun.com*). Successful emarketplace survivors include Exostar (*www.exostar .com*), serving the aerospace and defense industry, GlobalNetXchange (GNX at *www.gnx.com*) for the global retail industry, and Quadrem (*www.quadrem.com*) for industrial maintenance, repair, and operating equipment (MRO) products in the mining and metals industry. Quadrem connects more than 11,012 suppliers and 274 buyers and processes over US$3.75 billion annually in order throughput (transactions).[13]

INDUSTRY EMARKETPLACES

B2B emarketplaces were undoubtedly the hottest online eprocurement trading sites before the dot-com bust. They were seen as one-stop shops where buyers and sellers could browse looking for good deals and sometimes long-term partners. Industry-run emarketplaces are among the most successful survivors. As vertical markets often operated by dominant manufacturers, they benefit from previously established relationships and known participants. An example is Covisint (*www.covisint.com*), the leading marketplace for suppliers and customers in the automotive industry. Covisint gives members a common platform to interact with their suppliers and customers. Originating partners were DaimlerChrysler, Ford, General Motors and Renault-Nissan. The platform went online in 2001. Covisint encourages members to *connect, communicate,* and *collaborate.*

INDEPENDENT VERTICAL EMARKETPLACES

Some independent emarketplaces also survived the dot-com bust. For example, LegFind (*http://legfind.com*) is an independent auction serving B2B aviation.

Launched in May 2000, during the dot-com bust, the charter service matches private jet plane space with businesspeople and enterprises that need transportation. It connects dispatchers worldwide through its centralized Internet database and enables owners to keep their planes flying rather than sitting idly at airports while their value depreciates. The service also fills return flights that otherwise would be empty. Company revenues grew to US$7 million in 2002 from US$1.2 million in 2001. To avoid risks associated with unknown customers and operators, the company prequalifies customers and checks operators through Federal Aviation Administration (FAA) documents.[14]

GENERAL B2B AUCTIONS

eBay is a popular general (horizontal) auction site where businesses can sell products to other enterprises as well as to consumers, some at a fixed price. eBay is a trading platform that facilitates exchanges between buyers and sellers in an open, public marketplace. At least twenty major brands, including Dell and IBM, use eBay to auction off surplus assets, overstocks, and used goods. Major brands represent about 3 to 4 percent of eBay sales and should rise to about 10 percent by 2005. B2B buyers can find products in many categories for their business operations or resale. B2B sellers are attracted to eBay because of the volume of its transactions and its reach worldwide. Small businesses are a rapidly growing segment of eBay's B2B buyers. Often they can find equipment and supplies on the site that otherwise they could not afford or would need a loan to purchase new.[15]

LIQUIDATOR EMARKETPLACES

B2B buyers and sellers also come together at liquidator sites and auctions, which understandably thrived during the recession and dot-com bust. Liquidity Services' Liquidation.com (*www.liquidation.com*) website runs bulk surplus asset auctions, and its Asset Recovery Division offers services to manage B2B asset sale transactions. The site turns surplus assets into cash through auctions of such items as consumer products, electronics equipment, industrial equipment, construction materials, office supplies, and aircraft parts. About 40 percent of this site's business is electronics. Its auctions and services are targeted to manufacturers, wholesalers, retailers, and professional buyers. The company was awarded a federal General Services Administration (GSA) contract in 2001 that allows federal agencies to sell surplus assets using Liquidation.com auctions.[16]

MULTILEVEL MARKETING

Multilevel marketing (MLM)
A form of direct selling involving many levels of distributors.

Considerable controversy surrounds multilevel marketing. Also known as network marketing, **multilevel marketing (MLM)** is a form of direct selling involving many levels of distributors that bring in new distributors to purchase products, sell to consumers, and recruit others who will also become distributors. It is a distribution system and personal selling structure that involves small businesses and individuals typically selling part-time.

Concern arises from the resemblance of multilevel marketing to pyramid schemes, which are illegal. Legitimate MLM distributors sell a product that fills a need and satisfies buyers. Distributors do not profit *solely* from recruiting others to become distributors. They sell products that work and are priced at fair market value. A pyramid scheme, by contrast, draws in naive people who believe they will get rich quick by recruiting other sellers. Profits derive from getting paid for recruiting new distributors and the distributors *they* recruit. The people at the top of the pyramid make money; most others do not.

The Internet's interactivity is a natural attractant for MLM activities because it is easy to build customer relationships online, and that is the foundation for MLM. Amway (*www.amway.com*) is the best-known global MLM. Founded in 1959, it currently has over three million distributors selling Amway products in over eighty countries. Retail sales in 2004 were US$6.2 billion generated through its global distribution network. Amway does not sell its products or directly recruit distributors from its website. Quixtar.com (*www.quixtar.com*), owned by Amway's founders, sells products online. To purchase any product from the site, consumers must contact an independent business owner (IBO) who gives them a referral number (IBO identification number) by email. Launched in September 1999, Quixtar is a member of the Alticor group of companies that includes Amway. IBOs refer clients and members to the site to make purchases and sponsor others who want to become IBOs. By not using the Amway name, Quixtar may attract customers who have negative impressions of Amway.

OTHER ENTERPRISE ONLINE CHANNELS

Businesses are not the only enterprises with online channels. Government, education, health care, and religious organizations use some of the same channels as businesses, as well as other channels that are very different. Many governments use online liquidators. Police departments use ThePropertyRoom's (*www.stealitback.com*) online auctions of confiscated property. Education systems and universities sell used assets online, many at eBay. Health care organizations have highly organized channels for obtaining supplies and personnel online.

B2C Online Channels

Many online channel strategies are evolutionary, not revolutionary. This is illustrated by Wal-Mart bringing its suppliers online and by Lands' End reinventing its catalogs on landsend.com. Many B2B and B2C channels overlap. Businesses, other enterprises, and consumers all go to Dell.com and purchase computers and accessories, along with related services. B2B and B2C traders use websites and emarketplaces (exchanges, auctions) to buy and sell products, reduce surplus inventory, and arrange product delivery and returns. Enterprises and consumers rely on digital distribution channels for digital content, digital products, and product information.

There are far more consumers than businesses online, and there are more B2C websites, but online B2B sales continue to be higher than total B2C sales. All web storefronts are more than just end points in the distribution chain. They are also sites where data about customers and prospects can be collected. They are service centers and can be drivers to offline stores. Internet marketers realize that not all websites are profitable, but some of those that do not themselves turn a profit have value as loss leaders to attract buyers. Thus they have value to their owners far beyond direct revenue generation.

MULTICHANNEL B2C INCREASES REVENUE

A business that sells to consumers can do so using various online distribution models. It can run a website off its own server, rent server space from an ISP or RSP, auction products on eBay or Yahoo!, sell directly by email with or without a website, store a hard-copy catalog on Google's Catalogs Beta (*http://catalogs.google.com*), or rent space at Yahoo!'s or Amazon's shopping malls. The business can use a single-distribution-channel strategy. This was the approach of the original first mover cyberbrands. A far more common alternative is to develop a dual or multichannel online approach or multichannel oneline distribution that combines online and offline distribution. Staples, Inc. (*www.staples.com*) exemplifies the latter approach. Staples, the world's largest seller of office supplies in terms of sales volume, has 1,500 retail stores, mostly in the United States, Canada, and a limited number of other countries, including the United Kingdom, Germany, the Netherlands, and Portugal. Its primary target markets are small businesses, consumers, and home office professionals, but it also sells to corporations, universities, hospitals, and other enterprises. The company is reducing its inventory of consumer products and increasing its inventory for corporate customers because the latter are more frequent and higher-volume purchasers. The company has operated a web storefront since 1998, along with a mail-order catalog business, web kiosks in over 1,000 of its stores, and a contract business. In 2003 it expanded into medical supplies. The Staples website offers 130,000 items and can be accessed in any U.S. Staples store that has a web kiosk. The company reported 2004 sales of US$13.2 billion. Staples's online revenues have steadily increased; worldwide sales were US$2.1 billion in 2003, an increase of 31 percent from 2002. Online sales were US$1 billion in 2001, up from US$512 million in 2000 and US$94 million in 1999.

Staples has found that rather than cannibalizing offline sales, its website increases sales. The average yearly spending of small business customers increased from US$600 to US$2,800 when they shopped online. When buyers shop all three of Staples's main channels, their purchases are 4.5 times greater than when they shop only one channel. Staples's experience is confirmed by Spiegel Inc.'s Eddie Bauer Unit (*www.eddiebauer.com*), which distributes through catalogs, retail stores, and online. The retailer reports that a consumer shopping in only one channel spends US$100 to $200 annually. For consumers shopping in two channels, sales increase to US$300 to $500 a year. A customer shopping in all three channels spends an average of US$1,000 a year. Most sales (70 to 75 percent) still come from retail stores, 25 percent from catalogs, and 5 percent online. A multichannel approach gives consumers the choice of when, where, and how they want to shop Eddie Bauer. Evidence also suggests that a shift from catalogs to online sales is underway as a result of increased website security and growing consumer preference for the convenience of shopping online.[17]

WHAT CONSUMERS WANT

According to Forrester Research's annual study for Shop.org, online retail sales exceeded US$114 billion in 2003, far surpassing industry and analyst expectations. This represents 5.4 percent of all retail sales, a dramatic increase from the typical average of slightly over 1 percent in the early 2000s. Profit margins collectively averaged 21 percent, and 79 percent of all online etailers were profitable. The rising importance of online sales to the retail industry and the pressure of growing competition emphasize the importance of knowing what customers want and delivering it. Understanding what consumers want in an online distribution channel is just as difficult as determining what they want in traditional offline consumer channels. Consumers are fickle; their needs and wants can change in a flash. They often do not know what they want, or they do know and are not truthful about it. Failing to *try* to understand them, however, can be a fatal marketing mistake.[18] Forrester Research also reports that consumers shop online primarily for *convenience* (84 percent) and greater *product depth* (41 percent), or because the *experience* is better than offline (36 percent), *content* is rich (31 percent), they receive *value* (26 percent), the *brands* they want are online (20 percent), they receive *customer service* (11 percent), *interactive tools* are available (7 percent), and they are attracted to the *novelty* of the experience (4 percent).

Convenience   Consumers want the convenience of "always-on" shopping. Dataquest Inc. confirms Forrester's conclusions and also reports that convenience is the top reason why consumers shop online (75 percent) and the number-one factor behind their online store choice. Online banking is exploiting the convenience advantage and giving customers 24/7/365 access to their accounts, where they can look up checking account balances, pay bills, and transfer money between accounts.

Consumers also want convenience in product returns. This gives bricks-and-clicks retailers such as Target (*www.target.com*) and Wal-Mart an advantage over clicks-only and bricks-and-clicks retailers that do not accept returns from online sales in their stores. Others, such as Nordstrom (*www.nordstrom.com*), have front-door delivery pickups for returns. This is an important issue for etailers, because returns will increase along with online sales, particularly as purchases increase for products that are more risky than books, airline tickets, and computers. Store returns for women's apparel, a high-risk product category, average 20 percent. Catalog return rates for women's apparel average around 33 percent, online returns nearly 40 percent. This is a serious concern; returns cost four to five times more than initial delivery. Because of this high cost, many etailers do not bother restocking returned items. They add them to clearance sales, remainder them to liquidators, or sell them on eBay. Others turn to web outlet malls that specialize in discounted first-quality merchandise, such as SmartBargains (*www.smartbargains.com*). Some companies outsource returns. Catalog companies with long histories of handling returns are in the best position to constrain online return costs.[19]

Product depth   Many businesses take their entire inventories online, whereas others offer only a limited number of items. Some web storefronts whose products are not particularly well suited to online sales use their sites to provide information that directs consumers offline to their retail stores. Larger businesses that can support offering all their inventories online will attract consumers who otherwise lack access to the products. However, the complete-inventory approach is costly, particularly if inventory is seasonal or requires frequent updating.

Experience   The online experience is an area that needs improvement. Many websites are not well designed, lack effective search capacities, are not secure, and are just generally not user-friendly. They seem to ignore the likelihood that while a bad experience loses sales, a good experience can increase them. Some sites, like Tiffany & Co.'s (*www.tiffany.com*), convey the offline store's ambience to give online buyers a "feel" for the store, in this case that of tasteful and expensive elegance. Many consumers want to duplicate the offline shopping experience, while also taking advantage of the interactivity that enables sites to provide feedback from other consumers and comparisons.

Content   Consumers want content. Product information is extremely important, particularly information about product availability and price, shipping and handling, purchase options, and delivery and returns. Consumers need better information about products, including accurate product pictures, close-ups, and multiangle views. Consumers expect brand manufacturers' sites to provide product and contact information, particularly toll-free telephone numbers and email. They are far less interested in games and time-wasting features. Consumers are willing to share product satisfaction information with the manufacturer, but they are not being asked to do so by most manufacturers.[20]

Value   Value-added services include speed itself and service, both before and after the sale. Some consumers highly value speed. Rather than wait three or four days for a purchase to arrive, they want same-day delivery. Kepler's Books and Magazines (*http://keplers.booksense.com/NASApp/store/IndexJsp*) partners with Ensenda and UPS to offer free same-day delivery on in-stock books to thirteen cities in the San Francisco Bay area for orders of US$50 or more. Even Amazon.com cannot deliver that rapidly. Other consumers are willing to pay extra for second-day delivery. Most are content to pay as little as possible and receive their purchases in around a week. Consumers trading online also want rapid access to exchange data and to their accounts. They want trades to be instantaneous.

Consumers value their privacy and transaction security. They want guarantees that any information they provide will not be shared without their permission. They need reassurance that sites are safe and secure. Consumers expect security statements on manufacturers' websites, but only 59 percent of such sites actually post them. Trust is a very important marketing tool at online storefronts—and particularly at auctions. eBay has been effective in reassuring the enterprises and consumers using its trading platform that it guards their privacy and is a secure emarketplace.

Service   Consumers want service: real people answering their email and providing assistance when requested. Lands' End understands the value of live customer service representatives. It offers consumers live chat or telephone assistance while online. It also has interactive finders, search engines that return clothing suggestions based on information provided by the consumer. Consumers can create their own virtual models, representing their body shapes, and can select clothing styles to try on the model. Timely responses to inquiries, informative content, and communication with a real person contribute to customer satisfaction. The payback is that 90 percent of satisfied customers say they will return; 87 percent recommend the seller to others. Amazon.com effectively uses customer recommendations as a sales-building service. Consumers want varying levels of service. Some are willing to pay more for it; others are willing to do more for themselves if they can pay less.

Interactive tools   Consumers want simple site technology that makes navigation easy. They need better-functioning in-site search engines. Most consumers are not technology sophisticates, so complex sites richly endowed with high-end bandwidth features can drive them off.

Novelty   As consumers become more accustomed to shopping online, the novelty wears off. Thus, of all the things consumers want, novelty is the least important.

AUCTIONS

Consumers have shown how much they like online auctions, the primary mechanism for consumers to become online sellers. Historically, traditional auctions have not been a big factor in balancing supply and demand or in consumer purchasing. They have been a factor in agriculture, other commodity markets, fine art, and antiques—markets that most average consumers never approach. eBay.com is by far the most popular and widely trusted public auction, offering its auction platform to consumers and enterprises. It performs a quality control function that reduces the risk of auctioning on its site.

Consumers like auctions because they offer an opportunity to clean out closets, garages, and attics at a profit. Many find them entertaining and exciting; some are addicted to them, while others have given up full time jobs to make auctions their business. The Internet opens online auctions to millions of people, and sophisticated software allows multiple interactions among large numbers of buyers and sellers. Online auctions are far faster and more convenient than visiting traditional auctions. However, they do not always result in lower prices or even in fair prices. Online auctions attract buyers and sellers from all sectors—consumers, businesses, governments, and other enterprises. As we noted in Chapter 10, there is more than one type of auction engaging buyers online. Forward, reverse, Dutch, pooled, and private auctions all are available.

Legitimate differences of opinion about the value of products cause some problems for online auctions. More serious problems include deliberate misrepresentations or fraud. Auction fraud continues to occur, but there are signs that it is beginning to abate. A number of online businesses offer services to make auctions less risky. Escrow companies such as Escrow.com (*www.escrow.com*) act as intermediaries in online B2B, B2C, and other auctions. As a third-party intermediary, it collects payment from the buyer and retains it until the buyer either accepts the purchase or returns it to the seller. SquareTrade (*www.squaretrade.com*) offers neutral third-party online dispute resolution for eBay disputes, the parties to real estate transactions, and other transactions. The company handles over 12,000 resolution cases each month with a worldwide network of more than 250 professional mediators and arbitrators. *Ask the Appraiser* at the CollectingChannel.com (*www.collectingchannel.com/cMart/cesATEIndex.asp*) takes a different approach, offering appraisals for auctions. Sellers submit a digital photo and short description of their auctionable item, pay US$19.95 per item, and receive a professional appraisal within three working days. These sites provide valuable services, but most consumers are unaware that they exist.

A distinguishing feature of successful auctions, etailers, and content sites is a powerful internal search engine. eBay's buyers and sellers initiate over thirty million searches daily, looking for products to bid on or to check bids. To keep transactions current, eBay needs search engine technology that continuously updates auction postings and bids. Lands' End uses data-mining search engine technology that pushes products to users that fit or are associated with the search term. Efficient search engines compensate for common misspellings and use dynamic technology to broaden searches beyond the initial request.

C2C CHANNELS

One of the remarkable successes of online marketing has been the encouragement of consumer-to-consumer distribution. It happens at eBay auctions and small shops on Yahoo! and Amazon.com. Although yard and garage sales and estate sales are offline equivalents, nothing offline can approach the magnitude of online C2C sales. In some cases, what begins as a hobby of selling online to others turns into a full-time job. The elusive nature of C2C sales makes it impossible to estimate them accurately. However, eBay's C2C auctions indicate C2C sales represent a considerable sales volume.

Internet Retailing (Etailing)

Internet retailing (etailing) has been called the third significant transformation of the retail industry. The first began in the 1950s with the introduction of shopping centers and malls. The second transformation began in the 1970s with the arrival of large discount stores and nationwide chains. Then, in the mid-1990s, came etailing.

THE INTERNET TRANSFORMATION

The Internet transformation is not just about the number of etail storefronts that have gone online since 1993. It is also about Internet-associated changes in offline retail stores. For example, best estimates are that there are well over 400,000 retail computer kiosks with touch screen menus in use worldwide and that there will be over 700,000 by 2007. Consumers use kiosks to check product availability, access and place orders from online gift registries, and order products that are in-store stockouts. Because kiosks are self-serve, they hold the promise of enabling stores to reduce staffing further. Not all kiosks are Internet-connected, but a growing number connect to a company's online websites. Office Depot has over 7,000 in-store web kiosks. Each store is equipped with eight movable wireless kiosks that consumers can use to order mass-customized personal computers and to check their shopping histories and loyalty points. Arch competitor Staples has about 6,000 web kiosks, four to six per store.

Total U.S. online retail sales are increasing and were expected to reach around US$144 billion in 2004. However, these figures still fail to count the large numbers of consumers who go online to *comparison shop.* In other words, they perform product research online and then go offline to complete the sale. Shop.org finds that 81 percent of consumers self-report they research gift purchases online, but only 18 percent purchase online. The gift purchases most frequently researched online are electronics (56 percent), toys (38 percent), and books and music (37 percent). Sears estimates that at least 10 percent of its store appliance sales are influenced by information downloaded from Sears.com. About two-thirds of automobile purchases offline are influenced by online product information.

B2C sales have seasonal peaks, just as offline sales do. The top selling seasons are Christmas, the back-to-school period, and various holidays. Top 2003 holiday sales categories were computers, electronics, and entertainment. Other strong categories were food and wine, gifts and flowers, and apparel.

Online customer acquisition costs are falling and currently average around US$12 per customer, down from US$20 in 2000. Conversion rates (look-to-buy ratios) are increasing, having grown from an average 1.5 percent in Q1 2000 to 2.3 percent in Q1 2001. Seasonality affects consumer conversion rates. Landsend.com has a conversion rate of 9 percent, JCPenney.com 8.9 percent, Gap.com between 2 and 4 percent, and luxury product storefront Ashford.com 0.7 percent.

Catalog merchants report online operating margins averaging 28 percent, an increase of 6 percent since 2002. They are the most profitable online sellers. Many web-only retailers became profitable for the first time in 2003, reporting operating margins averaging 15 percent, compared to –16 percent in 2002. Etailers are figuring out how to balance sales, customer acquisition and retention, and earning a profit.[21]

BRICKS-AND-CLICKS RETAILERS

For most clicks-only etailers, the first-mover advantage was myth, not reality. Later arrivals, such as traditional retailers Wal-Mart, Sears, and Target, learned from earlier dot-com mistakes. They have the advantage of brand name recognition, familiarity and trust, stores where products can be picked up or returned, and established distribution centers and delivery systems. They have learned to integrate their offline and online retail businesses successfully. Clicks-only and bricks-and-clicks etailers can generate multiple revenue streams. In addition to selling products online, they can also sell on-site advertising space, generate revenue from affiliate networks, host honor system payboxes, sell customer data (although this is not advised), and sell services such as order fulfillment, as well as proprietary software, to other storefronts.

Bricks-and-clicks retailers such as Circuit City (*www.circuitcity.com*) are creating new ways to simplify online shopping and to make it more convenient and less costly. The company offers *Express Pickup,* where consumers select a product online, select the nearest local Circuit City store from a pulldown menu, and (at the online checkout) select the store where they want to pick up the product. *Express Pickup* can be a significant money-saver for large products such as computers and television sets.

Catalogers are particularly well positioned to benefit from the Internet environment. Their advantages include experience in the postsale channel: dealing with returns, exchanges, and adjustments and providing customer service. Returns average about 8 percent of online purchases, compared with 5 to 6 percent for catalogs. Some product types, especially apparel, have higher return rates than others. More than

70 percent of catalogers with online storefronts are profitable. Lands' End has been profitable at least since 1998. Spiegel (*www.spiegel.com*) and L.L. Bean (*www.llbean .com*) also report profits online.

ETAIL DECISIONS

Going online forces retailers to make a large number of key decisions (Table 11-1). Staying online means these decisions must be continuously evaluated and adjusted to ensure that the website continues to serve the etailer's goals, that it satisfies customers, and that benefits are greater than costs. Online benefits include 24/7/365 accessibility, expanded customer reach, low rent on server space (compared with the high cost of opening and operating bricks-and-mortar stores), possible international sales, collection of data about customers, the website acting as a driver for offline sales, opportunities to test new merchandise lines and categories, and the generation of additional revenue. These potential benefits must be weighed against the costs of initial and continuing web maintenance, vulnerability to comparison shoppers, high product return rates, security breaches, consumer privacy complaints, and high customer service costs.

Table 11-1 Etailer Decisions	
Service level	Service provided by the etailer (full, limited) and the extent of self-service that the consumer will perform. Includes credit, delivery options, order tracking, packaging, gift registry, shopping assistance, and returns.
Products	Full product line (identical to catalog and/or store) or limited. Some products are not appropriate because of their bulk, low margins, and high delivery costs. Products with high inventory turns are preferred to those with low turns.
Product assortment	Width (different types of products) and depth (different alternatives within a product type) offered; product types include convenience, specialty, discount, brand, prestige, and so on.
Inventory turns	How often to change online products, same as offline or less/more frequently.
Prices	Discount, prestige, off-price, or other mixture of prices; same or different from retail stores.
Returns	By independent distribution company (UPS, FedEx) or USPS; to an outsourced return intermediary processor, to the seller, or to a return reseller.
Trust	Join TRUSTe, VeriSign, BBBOnline, or other enterprise that reassures consumers about seller trustworthiness; publish customer endorsements on the website.
Facilitation	Accept payment by credit card, easy installment payments, PayPal, or other payment system.
Aftermarket service	Postsale channel; service and support in-house or through an intermediary.

TOP ETAIL SITES

Etail destinations vary broadly from general merchants such as Amazon to specific-industry sector sites for travel and hospitality services and from mixed-product sites such as eBay and to single-product sites for insurance. The ClickZ Network Stats Toolbox (*www.clickz.com/stats/big_picture/stats_toolbox/*) collects data from various research sources and is useful in identifying what is happening in etail. The top shopping categories in December 2003 were apparel and clothing; toys and video games; consumer electronics; computer hardware and accessories; and video and DVD. The top etail destinations and their share of all online retail traffic volume (as of December 2003) were eBay (26 percent), Amazon.com (4.2 percent), Yahoo! Shopping (1.8 percent), Walmart.com (1.8 percent), BestBuy (1.6 percent), eBay Motors (1.4 percent), and Target (1.2 percent). A look at some top etail sites in various sectors highlights the diversity of etailing and the dominance of the major players. Within specific sectors, the highest-volume sites include

Apparel Blair.com, Victoria's Secret, Gap Online (July 2003)

Department stores Amazon, Wal-Mart, Target (August 2003)

Flowers and gifts Hallmark.com, 1-800-flowers.com, FTD.com (February 2004)

Games Yahoo! Games, Pogo, Sandboxer (January 2004)

Health eDiets, Weight Watchers, WebMD (January 2004)

Pharmacy Drugstore.com, MedcoHealth.com, Walgreens.com (October 2003)

Shopping search destinations Google, Yahoo!, MSN, AOL, Ask Jeeves (March 2004)

Travel Expedia, Travelocity, Orbitz (December 2003)

CONCERN OVER SHOPPING BASKET ABANDONMENT

Shopping basket
Software that lets customers make selections from throughout the site, compiling the data while they continue shopping and then completing the order.

Shopping basket abandonment
Leaving a shopping basket before purchase.

For every dollar spent online, five dollars are lost through shopping basket abandonment, according to DoubleClick (*www.doubleclick.com/us/*). A **shopping basket** is software that lets customers make selections from throughout the site, compiles the order while they continue shopping, and then completes the order of all products selected. Etailers are concerned about the high rate of **shopping basket abandonment,** because as many as 57 percent of consumers leave their basket before the sale is completed. The leading reasons for shopping basket abandonment are sticker shock at the total cost of the order and shipping costs. Over 40 percent of online customers experience technical problems at checkout. Others complain about overly complex ordering forms or forms that take too long to download. Consumers often do not find out that a product is not in stock until they are ready to pay for the order. Computers crash, the site will not accept their credit card, or they just decide at the last minute that they really do not want the product(s).[22]

Fear of shopping basket abandonment is getting in the way of etailers realizing that browsing consumers can also result in sales. Browsing is what many consumers find most pleasurable about retail shopping offline. Websites are short-circuiting browsing by sending consumers targeted emails with hot links to special offers that bypass the rest of the storefront. Etailers should remember that more than a third of consumers searching for gifts online purchase products that they happen to see while web browsing.

DROP SHIPPING

Drop shipping
Shifting fulfillment from an etailer to manufacturers or distributors (drop shippers) that fulfill orders sent from the etailer's site.

The Internet's low entry cost has lured large numbers of entrepreneurs and small businesses online to make their fortune. What many found were overwhelming demands imposed by the need to track and manage inventory, rent and organize warehouse space, ship and receive products, and accept product returns. One solution well known to catalog retailers is **drop shipping,** an arrangement between an online retailer (etailer) and the manufacturers or distributors (drop shippers) of products sold by the etailer that they, not the etailer, fulfill orders on sales made from the etailer's site. Drop shipping shifts fulfillment responsibilities to other channel members. It reduces or eliminates etailer warehouse costs and concern about unsold inventory. It relieves the pressure to develop new products and allows etailers to expand their product lines and test demand. It can also tempt them to fill a website with an excessive amount of products that differ from the site's core offerings.

When an etailer makes a sale, the details are emailed or automatically transferred to the drop shipper (manufacturer or distributor). The etailer has already charged the buyer the product's retail price plus shipping and handling (S&H). The drop shipper fills the order, packages it, readies it for shipping with the seller's packing label and invoice, and arranges delivery by a carrier. The drop shipper bills the etailer the product's wholesale price plus S&H. Because the etailer charged the buyer the retail price plus S&H, the difference is profit. Or so it appears. If the drop shipper is a distributor, this lowers the margin because the distributor has to pay the manufacturer and cover those costs by reducing what the etailer is paid. The etailer relies on the drop shipper's honesty, reliability, and promptness. The etailer's reputation and image depend on the drop shipper's ability and motivation to do a good job. Small etailers can become overwhelmed with the amount of electronic communications needed to manage the drop shipper relationship. However, drop shipping is a viable option if the drop shipper's references are checked carefully and if its performance and customer satisfaction are closely monitored.[23]

Summary

http://college.hmco.com/business/students

The Fundamentals of Place

Place is *where* buyers purchase products and *how* products get there. Marketing channels are supply channels and distribution channels. The Internet promises benefits for channel members but also has some drawbacks. Enterprises face complex decisions related to place that are influenced (and sometimes made) by other channel members. Channel arrangements are regularly formed and frequently dissolved. Intermediaries have different names and different re-

lationships with producers and customers. Logistics/physical distribution intermediaries store, handle, and move products through channels and ultimately to end users. Some disintermediation has taken place, particularly in financial services and hospitality. Distribution channels can be direct, dual, or multichannel. Some products are distributed digitally. Underground distribution is a persistent problem of digital distribution.

Enterprise Emarketplaces

Not all businesses are part of a tightly knit channel captained by a manufacturer or dominant retailer, but many that are not still actively participate in online B2B trade. Emarketplaces are online trading platforms that typically operate on a single software standard. They include industry exchanges, independent vertical marketplaces, general B2B auctions, and liquidator auctions. Multilevel marketing is a form of direct selling that involves many levels of distributors who themselves bring in new distributors. Government, education, health care, and religious organizations use some of the same channels as businesses, as well as others that are very different.

B2C Online Channels

Many online channel strategies are evolutionary, not revolutionary. There are far more consumers than businesses online, and there are more B2C websites, but online B2B sales are higher than B2C sales. A business selling to consumers can do so using various online distribution models. Consumers shop online for convenience, greater product depth, the experience itself, rich content, value, brands, service, interactive tools, and to a lesser extent, novelty. Auctions are the primary mechanism by which consumers become online sellers. One of the remarkable successes of online marketing has been the encouragement of consumer-to-consumer (C2C) distribution.

Internet Retailing (Etailing)

Internet retailing (etailing) has been called the third significant transformation of the retail industry. The Internet transformation is not just about the number of etail storefronts that have gone online since 1993; it is also about Internet-associated changes in offline retail stores. Bricks-and-clicks etailers have many advantages online. Catalogers are particularly well suited to the Internet environment. Going online forces retailers to make a large number of key decisions. Etail destinations vary broadly. Shopping basket abandonment is a serious problem for many etailers. Drop shipping is a popular arrangement used by etailers for fulfillment.

Take Action!

Let's assume that a major marketing research company has hired you to be a website mystery shopper. The client sponsoring the research is a well-known branded hotel. Your job is to evaluate two branded competitors, Hilton Hotels Corp. (*www.hilton.com*) and Hyatt Corp. (*www.hyatt.com*).

1. Consider what features make a hotel industry website effective—for example, search engine efficiency, availability of local maps, description of local tourist attractions, price range, and discounts. Once you have identified ten features, create a table of three columns and eleven rows. In the first column, name the heading *Features* and in the remaining ten rows, list the features, one to a row. The second column heading is *Hilton* and the third column heading is *Hyatt.*

2. Select any major U.S. city as your destination, and choose a day and time when you need a room. Your stay will be for five nights over a weekend, and you need a double room. Based on your experience in trying to find a room and your evaluation of each website, evaluate the two sites for each feature listed in the table. Use a scale of 0 to 10 (where 0 means the feature is absent and 10 means the website is extremely effective in offering this feature) to record your observation of each site.

3. Review your results, and prepare a business letter to the research company explaining how you conducted the research and summarizing your results. Judging on the basis of your research, what should a good hotel etailer do to satisfy customers? (If you need assistance in writing a business letter, most word processing programs have macros for standard business letter form.)

Chapter Review Questions

1. How has channel shifting affected traditional offline travel agents?
2. Why is place such an important element of the marketing mix?
3. What are marketing channels?
4. Identify Internet-related channel benefits.
5. Why would a business cannibalize its own channels?
6. Could automatic replenishment be a valuable consumer online etail strategy? For what types of etailers?
7. Is speed important to all consumers?
8. What are Internet kiosks? How are they used?
9. Is shopping basket abandonment really a problem?
10. What might an etailer do to avoid shopping basket abandonment?
11. What is drop shipping?
12. What are underground distribution channels? Are they legal?
13. Explain the various meanings associated with the term *wireless channels.*
14. For what reasons do businesses go online?
15. What is MLM and why is it controversial?

Competitive Case Study

The Expedia Experience

Expedia, Inc. (*www.expedia.com*) is the world's top on-line travel service and the eighth largest travel agency in the United States. It is also the number one seller of hotel rooms online, with 10,000 hotel partners and a record booking rate of almost 70,000 rooms in a single day. It is a very customer-oriented company that has positioned itself as the traveler's trusted advisor, offering not just flights, hotels, or cars but experiences. However, its dynamic search engine does allow users to search for the best rates and fares, as well as to build complete multistop trips and download maps and destination guides with travel information on 150 different locations. Expedia has an agreement with the Sabre Travel Network to send a portion of Expedia bookings through the Sabre Global Distribution System (GDS). The site has received many awards, including one in January 2004 from *PC World* that voted it the best travel site on the Web. Expedia has websites in Canada, Germany, Italy, the Netherlands, the UK, and (as of 2004) France. An agreement with Ticketmaster (*www.ticketmaster.com*) lets Expedia travelers pur-chase event tickets while they are in the process of making trip arrangements. Microsoft (*www.ms.com*) was initially a major stakeholder in the company but sold its share to InterActiveCorp. (IAC) in 2002. In 2003 IAC purchased the remaining Expedia shares and took the company private. Expedia's year-end 2002 sales were US$590.6 million.[24]

CHECK IT OUT

How valuable are Expedia's destination guides? Visit *Destinations & Interests* (*www.expedia.com/daily/guides/default.asp?rfrr=-1071*) and check it out. Select any of the destination guides and evaluate it from multiple perspectives: that of leisure traveler, that of business traveler, and that of Expedia competitor. Is this the type of feature that other hotel and travel sites should offer?

A GLOBAL PERSPECTIVE

How is Expedia doing internationally? Link to any of its international sites and examine how Expedia markets its experiences in that market.

12

Promotion in the Internet Marketing Mix

LEARNING OBJECTIVES

» To understanding the fundamentals of marketing promotion
» To identify issues related to online promotion
» To consider the role of online advertising and paid search
» To learn about online sales promotions and email marketing

Kraft's Candystand.com: A Candy-Loving Gamer's Dream

One of the most popular gaming sites on the Internet is owned by Kraft, a company whose origins date to 1767, when a company named Bayldon and Berry began selling candied fruit peels in York, England. Today, Kraft Foods' North American subsidiary (*www.kraft.com*) is the number-one food business in the United States. Part of the Altria Group of companies (*www.altria.com*), Kraft owns the world's largest branded cheese (Kraft Cheese at *www.kraftfoods.com*) and Nabisco (*www.nabiscoworld.com*), the world's largest cookie and cracker maker. Kraft's 2003 sales topped US$31 billion, up 4.3 percent from 2002. LifeSavers is far from being Kraft's top-selling brand, but LifeSavers's Candystand.com (*www.candystand.com*) is one of the Internet's top game destinations. Candystand went online in March 1997, and its free games quickly began drawing millions of visitors, who stayed an average thirty minutes per visit. The site has received many awards for the excellence of its games and its creative use of **advergaming** to promote Kraft products and brand-build using its

custom-designed online games. On-site pitches for LifeSavers candy and other Kraft brand sponsors, such as Jell-O, Milk-Bone, and Planters peanuts, help cross-sell the company's products. *Advertising Age* credits Candystand with saving the LifeSavers brand, boosting sales 15 percent over the two years following its launch. Candystand has been called one of the two most successful online marketing promotion efforts since Internet commercialization began, the other being the pop-under campaign for the X10 wireless camera (*www.x10.com*). Candystand's blend of product placement and entertaining Flash-based games immerses visitors in a total, unique brand experience that can succeed only in a digital environment. As a destination site, Candystand is well positioned for use in seamless *oneline* promotions. An example is the 2004 co-sponsorship by Kraft Foods and Universal Games (VU Games at *www.vugames.com*) of a nationwide promotion, *Crash & Spyro Adventure World*. Offline, ninety-six unique trading cards were placed in 10 million specially marked packages of various branded Kraft Foods products. Each coded card directed customers to Candystand.com to unlock six *Crash & Spyro* exclusively online games created from the *Crash*

Bandicoot & *Spyro the Dragon* computer videogames. *Crash Bandicoot,* played on Nintendo Game Boy, has sold over 30 million copies since its 1996 release. The online games were housed in a special locked area of the Candystand site accessible only with the unique code written on each card. While Candystand gets visitors to stay and play, other *advergames* are pop-up instant plays. Advergames have high click-through and conversion rates, entertain participants, and can capture the email addresses of visitors with highly desirable demographic characteristics and drive offline purchases. As for selling Kraft products, 10 million units is not an unreasonable goal, considering the popularity of the games and the passion of online game players. Online advergaming revenues will reach over US$800 million in 2005, up from US$134 million in 2002. Advergaming has even been used successfully in B2B trade shows.[1]

Promotion is the marketing mix variable of planned, persuasive, targeted, and goal-driven marketing communication. Effectively executed and targeted marketing communication can brand-build, differentiate a product from its competitors, make a sale, and nurture customer relationships. This chapter examines promotion fundamentals, explores issues that concern marketers, and considers popular online promotion models.

The Fundamentals of Promotion

All promotions are advertising, right? Not really, although it certainly appears so to many observers and advertising revenues exceed those of other promotion forms. Traditional marketing promotion includes advertising as well as sales promotions, personal selling, publicity/public relations, and direct marketing. Marketing communication in contemporary American life is inescapable. The average person is bombarded with hundreds—if not thousands—of commercial messages each day in the morning newspaper, on television and radio, through telephone sales calls and direct mail, and on clothing and store signs, company news releases read on television, highway billboards, bus signs, truck panels, and the Internet. This barrage of information has made everyone an expert on marketing promotion and has bred vocal critics. Internet promotion, like Internet commercialization, is in its formative years and currently represents only a fraction of total promotion revenue. Many promotion approaches are being tried; some have already been found wanting while others, like paid search advertising, are yielding significant returns. The Internet encourages creativity, and although some online promotions are irritating, others can be entertaining and involving.

Advergaming
A type of marketing promotion that uses custom-designed, entertaining web games to promote a brand.

Promotion
The marketing mix variable of planned, persuasive, targeted, and goal-driven marketing communication.

Message
Communication contents used in marketing promotion.

Feedback
Audience responses to marketing communication.

THE MARKETING COMMUNICATION PROCESS

Marketers use promotion to send a **message**—that is, communication contents, including the words, images, sounds, and symbols *encoded* by a sender, conveyed through a channel to a receiver, *decoded* by the receiver, and either acted on immediately or stored in the receiver's memory for later use. Audience responses provide **feedback,** comments and actions related to the message, channel, or product that can be used to refine the message and/or alter the channel or product.

Noise

Whatever distorts or blocks the message during the marketing communication process.

Incentive

A short-term inducement to move a target audience immediately toward a purchase.

Noise can distort or block the message at any point in the marketing communication process. It can result from mechanical processes—for example when the sender's or the receiver's computer crashes, when the receiver's computer takes forever to download rich media advertisements (ads), when a server crashes, or through Internet transmission slowdowns. It can also be a function of human noise that can occur when the receiver is distracted while viewing an animated banner ad, is multitasking, or trashes commercial email messages before reading them.

Marketing communication can also be an **incentive,** a short-term inducement to move a target audience immediately toward a purchase. It can be an online cents-off coupon, product sample, two-for-one special, sweepstakes, or other short-term stimulus. With sales force promotions, the goal is to increase productivity. Senders (marketing communicators) create and convey a message that is typically paid for by an identified sponsor. Ideally, the promotion delivery channel (media vehicle) distributes the message and/or incentive where and when it is most relevant to the audience. This does not always occur as planned, and as a result, many marketing communications underachieve the goals set for them.

Traditional mass-market communication is a *one-to-many* distribution process. The same message or incentive is delivered simultaneously and unchanged to a mass audience, perhaps as they watch the Super Bowl on television, or it is delivered repeatedly to catch an audience at different times over a week, month, or longer. The designation *mass market* is somewhat misleading. Even though advertisers at a televised World Cup Soccer Finals reach over a billion viewers worldwide, the audience is targeted because they share a common interest in soccer.

Internet marketing communication has the potential to be *one-to-one,* although most businesses are not trying to achieve this desirable yet costly goal. The largest enterprises are the ones most likely to invest in the technology needed to personalize or customize promotion. Many websites *mass-customize* online messages and incentives that deliver personally relevant messages to site visitors who fit specific targeting criteria. Cookies can be used to identify website visitors and if their purchase histories and other personal data sort them into the targeted group, they receive "personal" electronic messages and/or incentives that appear to be one-to-one. Customization and personalization are desirable advantages of Internet promotion; however, they also raise serious privacy concerns (see Chapters 5 and 7).

The Internet is primarily a *pull environment* where users take the initiative and link to a website, then pull specific content back to their computer or wireless device. It can also be a *push environment,* where content is pushed to the user's computer from a website without a specific request, as in pop-up ads, or by an initial request followed by periodic and unobtrusive updating. For example, when a user signs up for a financial news update, customized weather report, or rich site summary news aggregator (RSS) feed, the updated content is pushed to his or her computer without the user making any additional requests. Updated pushed content like email newsletters and RSS feeds often contains embedded advertisements (ads) and sponsorship buttons. A weather site may include travel ads along with the weather report, and a travel site may include a weather button ad. Netscape.com (*http://my.netscape.com*) invites visitors to make the Netscape homepage their *start page* and to personalize page settings, content, and layout by creating their own *My Netscape.* If they do, each time they boot up and go online, their personalized *My Netscape* page is the default page and their gateway to the Web. Ads embedded in the page also appear. Content and promotions are pushed to their computer, but if a user wants detailed information, he or she must click through on the hypertext link. This is a *push–pull hybrid* that combines elements of both models. Getting a user to accept a site as a default page gives the site owner an opportunity to initiate a long-term relationship as well as collect useful customer data and push customized ads.

PROMOTION GOALS

Promotion can serve a variety of goals including to sell products, build awareness and loyalty, brand and rebrand, position and reposition products, drive traffic to sponsors' websites and/or offline stores or salespeople, add value, build goodwill, and entertain. If promotion ceased, how would users know that websites are offering special services, new content, or enhanced information? How would they learn about special offers, discounts, coupons, sales, contests, or free samples? How would interested buyers become aware of new and improved products, product line extensions, or new movies and music? Promotion communicates important marketing information to target audiences, and online, increasingly it is designed to entertain.

Promotion should be supported by all marketing mix variables working together, though often it is not. The very best promotion is a good *product* sold at a fair *price* in a readily accessible *place* that benefits the buyer. Satisfied customers talk about good products, and their positive word-of-mouth recommendations are priceless promotion. An outstanding promotion, however, cannot deliver repurchases for a bad product, an unfairly priced product, or a good product that is unavailable. The quickest way to kill a bad product is with good promotion that moves an audience to product trial, then dissatisfaction, and negative comments to friends or millions of strangers at Internet chat rooms and complaint sites.

The line between promotion and entertainment online is rapidly blurring. Many promotion formats are designed to *soft-sell* products rather than use *hard-sell*, in-your-face pressure. Minifilm ads and webisodes, streaming web advercasts, and floating animated ad overlays are **advertainment,** enticing online promotion that draws viewers to it. Candystand shows that product placement in advergames sells products.

Burger King (BK) used a pop counterculture approach to reach its desired demographic, ad-resisting teens, tweens, and 18- to 34-year-old men, to sell TenderCrisp chicken sandwiches. The BK Subservient Chicken (*http://subservientchicken.com*) Flash-powered site was launched April 7, 2004, and within ten days registered 20 million hits, each visit lasting an average of seven minutes. Chatter about the compliant Chicken, also called the *Porno Hen* because of its garter-belted costume, lit up blogs, chat rooms, instant messages, and emails, drawing millions of visitors to the site. The resulting clamor illustrates the power of **viral marketing,** directed word of mouth that gets customers and others to spread the word about a site, product, or brand at little or no cost to the company. The term has nothing to do with the idea of a destructive computer virus; it merely suggests that the news spreads as rapidly as a virus. Initially there was speculation that the Subservient Chicken site couldn't possibly be sponsored by BK. Advertising specialists called it a failure for not clearly identifying

Advertainment
Enticing online promotion that draws viewers to it.

Viral marketing
Directed word of mouth; getting customers and visitors to spread the word about a site, product, and/or brand.

the brand and product. Geeks were inspired to backward-engineer site code to get the Chicken to do naughty things that the original site forbade. However, the company says that TenderCrisp chicken sandwiches sales rose, although BK would not release sales figures for before and after launch of the site. Marching around a deliberately grainy and tacky-looking, claustrophobic living room, the lingerie-clad Chicken let visitors *Have It Your Way,* an innuendo-laden application of BK's classic slogan. A human in a chicken suit followed the typed-in commands of visitors, throwing pillows, break dancing, sleeping, or whatever the visitor requested—within limits. The controversial, offbeat, peepshow-like site was supported by thirty-second television spots on MTV, Comedy Central, Spike, and BET. Love it or hate it (and many parents did hate it), the site hit its target and had the desired traffic results, but it was also a big risk for BK, which wisely decided not to have the Chicken go mainstream. This is certainly not an appropriate or recommended approach for the vast majority of products, but it illustrates how the Internet's unique attributes can lead to unexpected marketing applications.[2]

THE PROMOTION MIX

Promotion mix
A conceptual framework for the strategic use of advertising, personal selling, direct marketing, sales promotions, and publicity/public relations.

The marketing mix is a conceptual framework for understanding the strategic use of the 4Ps. The **promotion mix** is a conceptual framework for understanding the strategic use of promotion tools (advertising, personal selling, direct marketing, sales promotions, and publicity/public relations) to communicate marketing messages and/or deliver incentives to target audiences. Marketing promotion is funded by a *promotion budget,* an amount allocated for planning, implementing, and evaluating promotion. A typical large-scale promotion *campaign* includes many forms of promotion implemented concurrently or sequentially, often online and offline in a complementary, integrated, and *synergistic effort.* A campaign is a single-themed, goal-directed mix of promotions that extends over a specified time period. Synergistic promotion requires that all promotions deliver the same consistent, integrated message, design, and feel. This is not always easy to accomplish, but when it works, the impact on the audience is far greater than when promotions deliver uncoordinated, conflicting messages and images. Synergistic promotion is often referred to as **integrated marketing communication (IMC),** a planned, coordinated, integrated campaign that uses more than one promotion tool and has one voice, one look, and one feel. For example, The Milk Processor Education Program (*www.milkpep.org*) began a US$40 million IMC in 2004 tied to the long-running Milk Mustache campaign but targeted to dieters with the slogan *Milk Your Diet. Lose Weight!* The MilkPEP.org campaign used extensive advertising, public relations, events in a 100-city Milk Mobile Moustache tour, and an online sweepstakes called *Show Off With The Top Down* that awarded twenty-four VW Beetle convertibles in twenty-four days from its *www.2424milk.com* website. The same message was used in multiple promotion vehicles in multiple markets, multiple times to raise awareness of milk's importance in diets.[3]

Integrated marketing communication (IMC)
Using more than one promotion tool in a planned, coordinated, integrated campaign that has one voice, one look, and one "feel."

Offline ads can be highly effective at directing consumers to websites and raising awareness of companies and products. Amazon.com (*www.amazon.com*), eBay (*www.ebay.com*), Yahoo! (*www.yahoo.com*), and AOL (*www.aol.com*) could not have become household words without massive offline promotion campaigns. E*TRADE rebranded itself E*TRADE Financial (*https://us.etrade.com/e/t/home*) during Super

Bowl XXXVI in 2002 through ads and sponsorship of the halftime show. Its dancing monkey ads and sponsorship built awareness of the rebranded company and drove traffic to its website and associated offline services. E*TRADE also had considerable success with its 2001 Super Bowl monkey ads that raised top-of-mind awareness of the company's brand name 64 percent.

Promotion points of contact
Interfaces where an audience comes into contact with something that communicates image or brand message or is a web driver.

Promotion points of contact (also called touch points or customer facings) are interfaces where an audience comes into contact with something that communicates image or brand message or acts as a web driver. These facings may not be directly included in a promotion budget or considered traditional promotion mix tools. Points of contact offline can drive customers online. Examples include a website URL printed on a cash register receipt and store signage or employee uniforms that display a URL. Even a building can help define a brand. An example is the corporate headquarters of the Longaberger Company (*www.longaberger.com*). The building is constructed to look like one of the company's handwoven Medium Market baskets. It is a seven-story, US$30 million basket with two handles, each weighing seventy-five tons, constructed of steel, stucco, and wood that was grown, harvested, and installed by the company itself. The building is a striking eye-catcher that promotes the company and its products long after visitors have left. Promotion points of contact are important for communicating marketing messages, particularly building website awareness, promoting brands, and driving traffic. They should always be considered in the planning and management of promotion programs, yet typically they are not.[4]

The Longaberger Company

The Longaberger Company's corporate headquarters is a seven-story steel, stucco, and wood basket.

Source: Courtesy of Elevator World, www.elevator-world.com/magazine/archive01/9908-002.html-ssi.

Internet promotion is rapidly evolving. There is a great deal to be gained from the effort to find promotion that works well, capitalizes on the Internet's unique characteristics, and creates a satisfactory return on the promotion investment (p-ROI). Even though all tools in the promotion mix are used online, some exploit the Internet's unique environment far more effectively than others, and a number of them are controversial. The following section briefly introduces each promotion tool and illustrates online applications. Advertising, paid inclusion search engine promotion, sales promotions, and permission email marketing are discussed at greater length later in the chapter.

Internet advertising
Paid, nonpersonal persuasive messages by identified sponsors.

ADVERTISING   Internet advertising is paid, nonpersonal persuasive messages by identified sponsors. This most visible type of Internet promotion includes those ubiquitous, often inescapable banner ads, sponsorships, interstitials and other rich media ads, pop-ups, pop-unders, onscreen floating overlays, classified ads, in-stream and gateway webcast ads, minimovies, webisodes, advergames, paid search, and other formats. Internet ads are commercial and sometimes noncommercial messages distributed on the public Internet, intranets, and/or extranets, primarily on websites and via email and email newsletters. The sponsor's message is included in host web pages exactly as created and is clearly recognized as a paid-for message by an identified advertiser. Hypertext links directly deliver audience members to the advertiser's site *if* they click through. Target audiences rarely distinguish between marketing promotion forms and usually call everything advertising, online or off. Unlike static offline advertising, online interactive advertising (like traditional direct advertising) can quickly stimulate sales. **Search engine advertising,** which is paid inclusion advertising on search engines that is designed to drive traffic to a website, has no direct offline equivalent and is currently the hottest form of online advertising and promotion.

SALES PROMOTIONS   **Internet sales promotions** are temporary inducements to direct a desired behavior. They are used to stimulate demand, increase storefront traffic and/or sales, encourage distribution channel members to distribute, stock, or purchase a product, and raise salesforce sales. Websites run contests or sweepstakes, offer downloadable discount coupons for purchases made at offline retailers, supply free product samples, or provide memberships in product clubs. Discount coupons can be distributed by email. Offline print catalogs often include dollars-off coupons for purchases made from the company's website in an effort to drive customers online and therefore reduce offline call center costs.

PERSONAL SELLING   Personal selling occurs when a salesperson interacts with potential or current customers face-to-face, door-to-door; or by telephone, by fax, or on the Internet, intranets, or extranets by email, instant messaging, live chat, or telephony. Salespeople are trained to provide information, answer questions, make offers, counter objections, overcome resistance, complete the sale, and provide service after the sale. Personal selling plays a key role in enterprise promotion, although the cost per contact is very high and is rising. Personal selling electronically on an extranet or website is far less expensive than personal selling offline and can be as effective as traditional methods, particularly with relatively uncomplicated products. Some salespeople use email to make sales pitches directly to enterprise end users in an effort to bypass purchasing departments. Many websites provide sales service by email. IBM (*www.ibm.com*) combines online information with offline sales negotiations for its high-end enterprise computer systems. Landsend.com's *Lands' End Live* (*http://live .landsend.com/callFrameACD.html?query=http%3A%2F%2Flandsend.com*) has salespeople standing by to help online customers anytime in text chat rooms or by email, phone, or fax.

PUBLIC RELATIONS (PR) AND PUBLICITY   Like advertising, public relations (PR) has an identified sponsor that pays for the development and implementation of PR programs to create and maintain a favorable image and goodwill, persuade an audience, and/or generate traffic, which is often referred to as *identity building*. PR includes community-based events, open houses and plant tours, and other activities to create a favorable impression. Many enterprises host live chats with company officials

Search engine advertising
Paid inclusion advertising on search engines that is designed to drive traffic to a website.

Internet sales promotions
Temporary inducements, offered on the Internet, to stimulate demand.

or schedule online events to launch new products or embellish the company's image. Some companies, such as Coca-Cola (*www.vpt.coca-cola.com/vpt_index.html*) and Crayola Crayons (*www.crayola.com/factory/preview/factory_floor/crayon_mfg.htm*), host entertaining and educational virtual plant tours.

Volvo North America (*http://volvocars.com*) held the first solely digital automobile launch in September 2000. Its S60 model was introduced online with no national television or national print support. Deals were made with banner and column ads placed on general-interest and special-interest pages in AOL's auto and men's areas and on MapQuest (*www.mapquest.com*). AOL subscribers received special free-option offers worth up to US$2,100 on the S60, and giveaways occupied prime space on AOL's homepage. More than 500,000 promotional CD-ROMs showcasing the car were mailed to current Volvo owners and top prospects. Targeted print advertising appeared in *Motor Trend* and *Car & Driver.* Volvo initiated the launch online because 89 percent of its Model 2000 owners are Internet users, and a past purchase is a good predictor of a future purchase. Being the first to have an online automobile launch generated great interest and considerable free media coverage, and it was also far cheaper than a traditional offline launch. The *elaunch* did not sit well with some Volvo dealers, however, who felt that prospective buyers should have been directed to their showrooms, not to the Web. Undeterred, Volvo next used personal digital assistants (PDAs) and Internet handheld wireless devices to determine which media pulled best results for Volvo ads shown during 2001 NCAA basketball games. All messages directed receivers to a special website where they could enter a contest to win a Volvo S60. The cost of the two-week campaign was estimated at US$400,000 to US$600,000. Volvo turned to the Internet again in 2004 when it launched its S40 Sedan. An online sweeps (sweepstakes) was part of the US$3 million tour that showcased the new model and generated publicity. The winner of the estimated US$75,000 online sweeps received a trip for four to Sweden and London—and an S40. Volvo, a division of Ford Motor Company (*www.ford.com*), is aggressively testing new media channels, anticipating that their importance will grow.

Publicity is promotion that provides information to the media for use in a hard or soft news story or in an editorial. When a press release is distributed to third parties, the reporters who receive it can use all, some, or none of the information provided. The message may gain credibility and believability if it is not directly paid for by an identified sponsor, but the sponsor loses control over the message, and media distortions or misreporting can produce unwanted and sometimes unexpected results. The press release may even be totally ignored.[5]

Most corporate websites maintain pressrooms with archived press releases that can be picked up and used for publicity purposes. Others send press releases by email to media targets—newspapers and magazines (online and offline), radio, and television. Online pressrooms such as Forrester Research's (*www.forrester.com/ER/Press/0,1772,0,00.html*) offer press releases that describe what the company is doing and provide information about current research that marketing students may find useful. Forrester also emails press releases to media in the expectation that greater exposure will lead to increased sales of its proprietary reports. PR Newswire (*www.prnewswire.com*) is a United Business Media Company that posts and emails targeted press releases to interested audiences. Its PRN Press Room (*http://media*

.prnewswire.com) is a free resource for journalists looking for stories. It is also a useful channel for businesses disseminating information. Few press releases, of course, are very objective. Enterprises put positive spin on press releases particularly when the news is bad, so they must be read with caution. As a means of raising awareness and disseminating information, they can play a useful promotion role.

DIRECT MARKETING   Promotion on the Internet typically is interactive, creates a direct contact with audience members, and can result in an immediate response. This is also the definition of *direct marketing.* For this reason, many marketers regard all Internet promotion as direct marketing. Traditional offline direct marketing forms include catalog sales, direct-mail letters, bill stuffers, direct-response television ads, and telemarketing.

PROMOTION DELIVERY CHANNELS

Promotion delivery channels

Pipelines for delivering marketing promotions to target audiences.

Before the Internet's commercialization, promotion generally was delivered through traditional **promotion delivery channels,** pipelines for delivering marketing promotions to target audiences. They include face-to-face personal selling, electronic mass media (television, radio), print media (magazines, newspapers), outdoor media (billboards, kiosks), and direct media (advertising, mail). Newer channels include promotion delivered on computer disks and on facsimile (fax) machines, bill stuffers and door hangers, automobile and bus wraps, grocery store floor and shopping basket ads, and even print ads placed on public toilet stall doors and toilet tissue. Some of the same delivery channels are used online in electronic form, others differ in certain respects, and a number are impossible to use in an electronic environment. Some channels link the offline and online settings; consider those Net-ready ad-flashing gasoline pumps that allow customers to view interactive Internet ads while filling up. Another example is Clear Channel's Video-Interactive Displays' (Vert VID at *www.vert.net*) Taxi Media, a web server that displays ads from taxi-top electronic billboards. The small billboards are mounted on taxi roofs and continuously display eye-catching ads. They represent the integration of wireless Internet, global positioning system (GPS) technology, and video. The advertising message changes as the taxi moves from one city block, neighborhood, or zip code to another. In a financial district the billboard may deliver streaming stock quotes, and near a medical center the ad may be health-related. Messages are in color and are displayed on high-resolution, bright screens.[6]

Companies use the Internet to create *buzz,* encouraging word-of-mouth communications (viral or guerrilla marketing) whereby consumers communicate among themselves about products. Yahoo! (*http://buzz.yahoo.com*) measures search behaviors or online buzz on its *Buzz Index—Buzz Log,* identifying buzz *movers* and *leaders* of the moment on Yahoo! Google does the same with its Google Zeitgeist (*www.google.com/press/zeitgeist.html*), measuring the general direction of users' current interests in the U.S. and the major foreign markets Google serves. Identifying what is hot in a culture can help others decide what movie to see, what DVD to buy, or what television program to watch. Buzz can also be dangerous if it is negative or misinterpreted.

PROMOTION TARGETS

Target markets are consumer and/or enterprise audiences that need or want a product and have the authority to make a purchase, as well as an acceptable payment mechanism to complete the exchange. Because marketing promotion often casts a very large net, it also reaches sometimes hostile audiences that are not interested in the message and are irritated by its delivery. This is promotion *waste*. Reaching the wrong audience with the wrong message is far less costly online, but it can still result in hard feelings and negative word of mouth about the message sponsor on blogs, chat rooms, and instant messages.

Promotion sponsors do not want to waste their money sending messages to oblivious or inappropriate targets, so they attempt to select audiences receptive to their market offers. Targets can be defined broadly (U.S. men aged 30 to 45 years) or narrowly (male college graduates aged 45 to 55, white-collar professionals living in urban areas of one million or more population, married with two children under the age of 15, avid golfers who recently spent US$200 or more on golf equipment online). The narrow (*niche*) definition relies on purchase history and on demographic and psychographic (lifestyle) data to identify targets for email commercial messages or customized online ads.

Targets can also be part of a mass undifferentiated online market, just as in mass marketing offline. An example is the campaign for the X10 wireless video camera. Ads for this product were online everywhere throughout 2001 and 2002 as half-screen persistent pop-unders that spawned their own window underneath the viewer's browser screen. The low cost of online advertising facilitated the delivery of virtually unlimited numbers of ads to an increasingly irritated mass market of receivers. However, the mass-market approach was effective, and the X10 gained awareness and clickthroughs. X10.com (*www.X10.com*) was fourteenth on the list of most popular web destinations in April 2001, just three places below eBay. It had practically disappeared by 2003 and that same year, the company declared Chapter 11 protection because of severely reduced revenues and the loss of a lawsuit related to its technology.[7]

Consumers are the principal targets of most online promotion. However, commercial email is targeted to both consumers and enterprises, and the amount of enterprise B2B email is growing rapidly. Its ability to reach receivers at work is unsurpassed. Some web advertising (such as that for airline tickets) is targeted both to consumers and to enterprises where they shop or info-search for products they purchase. Enterprise intranets are used for

Advertising Council

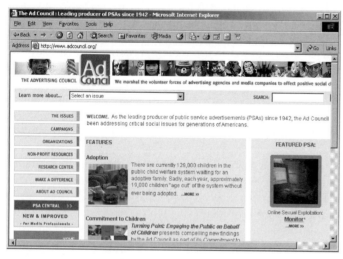

The nonprofit Advertising Council promotes its PSA campaigns on the Web.

Source: Reprinted by permission, www.adcouncil.org.

promotions targeted to a company's employees, motivating them to sell more, urging compliance with safety rules, or encouraging enrollment in training classes. Promotion is targeted on extranets to select channel members. B2B ads have a powerful advantage online because they can reach workers during business hours when they are online and able to take immediate action. B2B ads can be personalized based on tracking information stored on the worker's hard drive.

Marketing promotion is also performed by nonprofit organizations, governments, causes, and individuals. Nonprofit organizations such as the American Red Cross (*www.redcross.org*) use online promotion to increase awareness about their activities, collect relief donations, arrange gifts or planned giving, recruit volunteers, and generate goodwill. The nonprofit Advertising Council (*www.adcouncil.org*) targets individuals and enterprises with public service announcements (PSAs) via television, radio, newspapers, magazines, and the Web. Memorable Ad Council slogans include "Friends don't let friends drive drunk" and "A mind is a terrible thing to waste." Online banner PSAs are created *pro bono* by some of the country's top advertising agencies and placed on space donated by various web page owners. Recent PSAs were developed for HIV/AIDS education and prevention, domestic violence prevention, colon cancer detection and prevention, crime prevention, drunk driving prevention, and fire safety.

PROMOTION DIRECTS BEHAVIOR

Promotion decisions are often based on the assumptions of a hierarchy-of-effects model first proposed in the 1960s. The model proposes that promotion, particularly advertising, helps move some target audience members through steps that culminate in purchase and repurchase. Promotion makes an audience *aware* of a brand or product. After simple awareness, they develop product *knowledge* through repeated exposures to product messages. Then, the advertiser hopes, the audience develops *liking, a preference* for the brand, and *conviction* that it is the best one for them, which leads to a *behavioral intention.* All things being equal, intention should lead to *purchase* and *repurchase,* although this certainly does not always happen. This is a rational model based on high audience involvement with the product. Some members of the target audience will not respond to promotion or move through the steps, regardless of the effectiveness of the campaign. Others will start moving through the steps but break off before they complete a purchase. Repurchase is what most marketers strive for, because customer retention is far less costly than acquiring new customers.

Most products, however, are not involving and represent a casual choice between comparable (parity) products. Rather than a rational, stepwise approach to purchase, these product decisions rely more on emotions and feelings. Yet the Internet is a low- or no-emotion environment, so generating emotional content in online promotions is not easy. Some online promotion, such as the dynamic flash-based banner ads used for gambling sites, is exciting. Classmates (*www.classmates.com*) makes an appeal to aging baby boomers to *Rediscover Your Past!* by registering and locating classmates from high school. The site and its banner ads show pictures of 1960s and 1970s high school students. This approach is involving because viewers can relate to people like themselves in situations (high school graduation photos) that they also have experienced.

Involvement is another indicator of whether an ad will register with an audience. If customers are involved with a product or buying situation, or if they feel emotional about the sender, they tend to be more engaged with an associated ad. This principle also applies to website content. If a customer is highly involved with compelling website content, there is a greater chance that he or she will maintain contact with the site. To increase awareness, ads should be relevant to site content like ads for food and food preparation equipment on recipe, health, and nutrition sites. Ideally, visitors should access the ads in separate pop-up boxes without leaving the content site.

PROMOTION PLANNING

Effective promotion requires planning by in-house marketers, specialists with an outside promotion agency, or both working together. Promotion planners must consider the target audience: their characteristics, their preferences, and how and where to reach them. Cost is a major consideration, because online promotion can be expensive to create, implement, and evaluate although it is often less costly than similar offline promotion. Another factor is the economy, as a downturn often results in sharp reductions in promotion budgets at a time when promotion is most needed. This was certainly the case during the 2001 recession. Planners should evaluate how the competition is promoting its products, whether government or industry self-regulation will affect or restrict a promotion form, whether any cultural or legal constraints exist, and the availability of alternate promotion distribution channels. Planning should include strategies for developing synergy by integrating online and offline efforts. It should also consider the risk of a backlash if promotion exceeds standards of what is acceptable.

Promotion Issues

The Internet has the potential to intensify the promotion message, achieving one-to-one intimacy that is rare offline, and to improve accountability through directly measurable results such as click-throughs and conversion rates. At the same time, the Internet has limitations that can weaken some promotion forms. Two singular problems of online promotion are clutter and the Internet's emotionless environment.

CONSUMERS IN CONTROL . . . MAYBE OR MAYBE NOT!

Consumers have always had the power to ignore marketing promotion, throw away junk mail, or turn off the radio or television. They can opt out of direct marketing lists by registering with the Direct Marketing Association (*www.the-dma.org/cgi/offmailing listdave*), the national trade association of direct marketers. This will not stop all direct marketing contacts, but it should reduce their numbers. Consumers can control telemarketing calls by using caller identification technology that screens out unknown, unwanted callers. Television viewers can use remote controls to channel-surf during commercials or tape programs and later avoid commercials entirely by fast-forwarding. It is still problematic whether the Can-Spam Law will reduce spam, but a national consumer opt in *Do Not Spam* list might. New browsers with potent anti-spam options are expected within the next few years, which will also help lessen the spam problem.

At the same time that consumers try to exert control, marketers try to counter their evasive efforts. When there were only three national television networks, advertisers could set up *roadblocks,* showing the same commercial on all three networks at the same time to capture channel-changing consumers. Today, the proliferation of cable and television channels makes a roadblock extremely expensive and difficult, if not impossible, to implement. This can, however, be accomplished online. **Web page roadblocks,** or *portal takeovers,* occur where one advertiser purchases all available advertising space on a page or a site owner serves only house ads (ads for the site owner's products). The online component of the "All New 2003 Ford Expedition" launch included portal homepage takeovers (roadblocks) on May 6, 2002, at MSN.com, AOL.com, and Yahoo!, as well as the creation of an online destination site (*www.fordvehicles.com*) for a themed sweepstakes. Banner ads were placed on pages within the portals and on auto sites Edmunds.com (*www.edmunds.com*) and the Kelley Blue Book (*www.kbb.com*). The Explorer IMC campaign also included integrated television, print, and outdoor ads.[8]

Consumers and enterprises can avoid roadblocks or any online ads by clicking past or installing ad-blocking software such as AdSubtract.com (*www.adsubtract.com*) or WebWasher.com (*www.webwasher.com*). AOL subscribers and Windows users can access their Marketing Preferences commands to block pop-ups. For those who see the ads, a roadblock can raise their awareness, but unless the advertiser tracks viewers and avoids multiple viewings (which Ford did), repetitions will become irritating.

More websites are resorting to aggressive tactics to corral visitors. In addition to spawning ads such as pop-ups and persistent pop-unders that launch an ad upon the viewer's entering, exiting, or triggering a command, some sites "mousetrap." A mousetrapped visitor is forced to stay on the site, unable to advance, retreat, or exit. Often the only resort is to reboot. Instant streaming audio is a variant of mousetrapping. Fear of audience backlash has convinced some advertisers to back off host-initiated instant streaming audio. In this technology, an endless audio loop begins broadcasting as soon as a visitor downloads a hosting page. A reboot is often the only way to stop the loop, unless the visitor has installed audio-blocking software. Even though these technologies are available, advertisers need to think carefully about whether their use is appropriate and desirable. In short, advertisers should have access to consumers but must avoid irritating them needlessly.

Adware and spyware (also called sneakware or malware) pose much more serious problems. As discussed in Chapter 8, adware is a variant of spyware, although not all adware is spyware. Spyware software is secretly transferred to a user's computer operating system in downloaded shareware or freeware, through email or from web pages. These independent programs can monitor, track, and report just about anything that occurs on an infected computer. Adware, or *advertising supported software,* is ad-serving software. It gathers information secretly from a user's computer, primarily tracking Internet behaviors, and reports it for advertising purposes so that targeted advertising can be directed to the user's browser based on the user's browsing habits. These programs can interfere with the user's computer to the extent that it becomes inoperable. Spyware and adware can be so malicious and damaging that marketers are well advised to disavow their use. If the online advertising industry doesn't respond by banning their use, calls for government intervention may lead to regulations that, if enforceable, could negatively affect other Internet promotion activities.[9]

Web page roadblock
A portal takeover, which occurs when one advertiser purchases all available advertising space on a homepage or a site owner serves only house ads.

CLUTTER

Promotion clutter
The glut created by the growing volume of online promotion, email messages, websites, and pages.

Promotion clutter is the glut created by the growing volume of online ads, email messages, sales promotions, websites, and pages. This is often the result of site owners monetizing their sites with advertising, bigger and more intrusive ads, more ads per page, and more sites going online. Sites increasingly use *house ads* (own-site ads), sell space to other advertisers, and advertise on other sites. **Email clutter** is growing because of the increasing volume of commercial email and richer messages with high-bandwidth streaming audio and video. The average user must sift through an almost overwhelming amount of clutter to locate personally meaningful and useful marketing communications. Web clutter also makes it more difficult to drive traffic. As clutter grows, marketers are beginning to recognize the effectiveness of clutter-cutting search engines for paid inclusions (text ads).

Email clutter
The glut of commercial email, particularly spam.

CRITICISMS

Internet marketing promotion is highly visible and intrusive, often blocking a user's view of page content, clogging an email box, slowing download time, mousetrapping, or embedding malicious spyware or adware in their hard drive. Small wonder that it is so often criticized. Longtime Internet users complain that promotion clogs the Internet, accelerates commercialization, and is offensive. Promotion is criticized for targeting children, teens, compulsive gamblers, and other vulnerable audiences. Criticisms are directed particularly at email spam and advertising, and now at spyware and adware that can destabilize and crash computers. Complaints about advertising focus on scams (deceptive promotions), promotion that targets vulnerable audiences such as children and the elderly, visual blight from ads cluttering websites, tasteless advertising that some find offensive, privacy issues that arise with customizing ads and sales promotions, and advertising supported software. Online coupon fraud is also a growing concern.

Despite all this criticism, promotion is defended as playing a key role in letting buyers know about marketing offers. It provides information that increases competition, which exerts downward pressure on prices. Advertising revenues subsidize content sites and help keep most content free or nominally priced. Web PSAs are a public service, although they are not widely distributed. Promotion also provides employment, directly and indirectly, for hundreds of thousands of people in the United States and worldwide. It can be entertaining and diverting, as shown by the millions of visitors who flocked to BK's Subservient Chicken and various advergaming sites.

Internet promotion is monitored and controlled by government at the federal, state, and local levels. The Federal Trade Commission (FTC at *www.ftc.gov*) hears complaints, investigates, and can mandate change, levy fines, or close sites. The FTC is particularly alert to email scams and supports legislation to limit junk email. Consumer protection laws extend to the prohibition of unfair advertising practices online and off, and cross-border ecommerce complaints. Promotion is regulated by state attorneys general and trade associations and by the American Association of Advertising Agencies (*www.aaaa.org*), the Interactive Direct Marketing Association (*www.the-dma.org*), the Better Business Bureau (*www.bbb.org*), and others.

Online Advertising and Paid Search

It is important to remember that Internet advertising, just entering its second decade, is still experiencing growing pains. Advertisers are sorting out what works and what does not, and inventing new forms in the process.

AD STATS

Internet advertising revenue in the United States for the entire year of 2003 was just under US$7.3 billion, up 21 percent from 2002. It was the first yearly increase since 2000. DoubleClick (*www.doubleclick.com*) and Nielsen Media Research (*www .nielsenmedia.com*) conclude that 2003 was the year that online advertising made its comeback, but it was also a year of change. Online ad spending in 2003 outperformed spending on spot television, outdoor, and network television advertising. Online represented about 5.7 percent of all U.S. advertising spending in 2003 that fell just short of US$130 billion. In the first six months of 2004, online advertising revenues reached US$4.6 billion, an increase of 39.7 percent over the same period in 2003, and was on track to reach US$9 billion by year's end. Internet advertising spending is growing at the expense of offline spending. It is increasingly credited with being more cost effective for branding and generating sales, and as a result, online advertising budgets are growing.

Advertisers continue to experiment with formats. In the Internet's infancy, most advertising was in a banner display format. Banners represented almost 60 percent of total Internet ad spending in 1997. By 2003, display ads continued their steady decline, accounting for only 21 percent of advertising spending, down from 29 percent in 2002. At the same time, spending on keyword search advertising increased to 35 percent of all online ad revenues, up from only 15 percent in 2002. From 2003 to 2004, search advertising grew 97 percent in absolute dollar terms. Its popularity is based on its capacity to deliver targeted audiences, its simplicity, low cost, controllability, and accountability. Search ads drive traffic, but it is so far unclear whether they can also build brands.

Spending on other online advertising formats is mixed. Classified ad spending increased to 17 percent in 2003, up from 15 percent in 2002. Rich-media ads represented 8 percent of 2003 spending, up from 5 percent the year before, an increase of 27 percent in absolute dollar terms. Spending on sponsorships continued to fall (8 percent in 2003 compared to 12 percent in 2002). Email ad spending reached only 3 percent in 2003 and interstitials only 2 percent, down from 4 percent and 5 percent, respectively, in 2002. Interstitials are now considered a rich media format.

Consumer brands were the heaviest advertisers in 2003 (37 percent of all online ad spending), and within the consumer category, the leading advertisers were in retail (41 percent), automotive (21 percent), and travel (17 percent). After consumer brands, the next top categories for ad spending were computing (20 percent) and financial services (12 percent). Online ad revenues continue to be concentrated in these categories and in the top ten ad-selling agencies.

Advertising volume increased 49 percent from Q1 to Q4 2003 for the Internet's top publishers, marketers, and ad agencies. In 2003, the volume of ad spending by mature cyberbrands Amazon.com, Classmates, AOL, X-10 Wireless, eBay, and other 2002 advertising leaders fell dramatically. They reduced spending, particularly on banner ads, because their brands were already established and web driving display ads were less vital. Telecommunication services, credit card, mortgage, and debt consolidation advertisers picked up some of the slack.

Ads grew larger in 2003 in an effort to capture attention and make a more lasting impression. The average covered area reached 71,834 pixels, compared to a standard banner size of 26,280 pixels (468 by 60). A pixel is a *picture* element, the smallest element in a picture image. The largest ad formats, the skyscraper (160 by 160) and large rectangle (300 by 250), grew by 106 percent and 263 percent, respectively, while the use of standard banners fell 13 percent. Use of wide leaderboards that span the top of a web page grew 900 percent in 2003. More than 78 percent of the major web publishers now use leaderboards.

Rich media ads
Advertisements made more dynamic with the use of Flash, streaming audio and video, or other features.

Because more people have broadband, more **rich media ads** are being served. These ads are more dynamic because they use Flash, streaming audio or video, or other enhanced features. They are not static .gif (Graphic Interchange Format image file) or .jpeg (also .jpg or Joint Photographic Experts Group) compression images. However, rich media ads can crash underpowered computers, and they require broadband to avoid painfully slow downloads. There is a direct correlation between the rise in use of broadband and the increase in the number of rich media ads served.

Pop-ups and pop-unders are the formats that consumers hate most. They rank slightly below spam in generating consumer irritation. Wisely, advertisers appear to be pulling back from them, and their use did not grow in 2003. Although such ads have been effective for financial services and travel advertisers, Fortune 500 companies for the most part avoid using them.

Response rates are declining for most ad formats. Initially, online click-throughs averaged 5 percent (5 viewers clicked on the ad for every 1,000 views). During 2003 the average declined to 0.6 percent and, in the fourth quarter, fell even more, to 0.4 percent. This reflects growing ad clutter, as well as more ad-cutting software in use and increased consumer indifference as the novelty has worn off. Even rich media click-throughs declined to 1.2 percent, although rich media ads are still four times more likely to be clicked on than static ads. Rich media ads were also twice as effective in getting sale conversions; 1.78 percent of consumers who clicked on a rich media ad continued on to make a purchase.[10]

Banner ads
Online interactive billboard-style marketing communication messages on or linked to web pages and designed to raise awareness, build a brand, rebrand, and remind consumers about a product, brand, and/or website.

ADVERTISING FORMATS

Internet advertising comes in a variety of different formats. While banner ads were initially the most popular format, the current favorite is search ads. The only certainty is that other formats will be developed and will eventually replace search ads as online advertisers' top choice for reaching target markets.

BANNER ADS   Online **banner ads** are interactive billboard-style messages that are on or linked to web pages and that raise awareness, build a brand, and remind consumers about a product, brand, and/or website. Banner ads can also be used as a directed path to a purchase. The first web banner ads were placed by IBM on the low price travel site Hotwire (*www.hotwire.com*) in 1994. At least in part because of their uniqueness, they generated a 30 percent click-through rate. By 2002, banner ads had become commonplace and average banner click-through rates had declined to between 0.3 and 0.75 percent. Although click-through rates obviously are decreasing, that does not mean banners are ineffective. They are useful in branding and raising awareness, and their low cost and broad reach (number of people exposed to the ad) make them highly attractive for those purposes. Cost per thousand (CPM) ranges from a low of US$1 to over US$60, depending on host site traffic, conversion rates, and other factors.

Banners come in many sizes and shapes. Although attempts at standardization continue, ad sizes vary and are dictated by site property owners. If standardized banner ad sizes become widely accepted, advertisers will be able to place the same banner on multiple sites without costly resizing. The Interactive Advertising Bureau's (IAB at *www.iab.net*) Ad Unit Task Force has issued voluntary guidelines for **interactive marketing unit (IMU)** ad formats used by web publishers. The guidelines (*www.iab.net/standards/adunits.asp*) are optional, and publishers can choose to adopt, adapt or disregard them.

Interactive marketing unit (IMU)

Advertising size formats used by web publishers to standardize ads.

Visitors are increasingly exposed to skyscrapers, large rectangles, and big boxes on web pages. Big, aggressive, flashy ads build awareness, and larger ads with greater visual exposure are more likely to increase branding effectiveness. Studies have found that skyscraper and large rectangles can increase brand awareness for a single exposure by as much as 40 percent. Flash and DHTML (Dynamic HTML) lift branding metrics as much as 19 percent. Large rectangles are over 52 percent more effective than page pop-ups. Interstitials increase brand metrics over 194 percent. With more Internet users on fast connections, larger and more rich-media ads will be less irritating to download, which increases the probability that advertisers will use them. An exception is persistent pop-unders. Although they attract attention and may drive a mass audience to a website, the gains in traffic do not convert to purchases. So many factors determine advertising effectiveness that size alone cannot be relied on as the single deciding factor. However, it does appear that, all other things being equal, size is important and bigger is better, at least until consumers get bored and tune out or block online advertising entirely.

Banners are placed at various locations on a page. Initially, they appeared mostly at page top or bottom. Today they are positioned on all four sides, as well as in the middle with wraparound text and even as floating ad overlays that pop-up somewhere on the page and then float to another area. While on screen, they block content, although many have *close* options. Preliminary evidence suggests that a top placement may draw more viewers. Expandable banners allow the viewer to get more information or even make a purchase, all without leaving the original site, through the use of pop-up minipages. Banner ads that pop-up or pop-under a page can be persistent or self-closing after several seconds.

No universally applicable banner ad rules can possibly apply to all situations and products. However, some attributes can make banners more effective. Banner content should be simple if branding is the objective. Banners should be surrounded by white or blank space to highlight the ad and focus attention on its content. Because the Internet is an information-intense medium, high information content is appropriate in many product categories and particularly in B2B banner advertising. Banners should be unexpected—placed where receivers least expect them. Excessive use of animation or distracting creative elements can undermine awareness and branding effectiveness. The company or brand logo should be prominent. Repetition works, and at least five impressions per banner may be optimal for awareness, although this varies by industry. A human face in banners increases interest and forges an otherwise missing emotional link. Attention is drawn to branding characters, cartoons, or clever action figures whose dimensions, colors, or actions can be changed with a click. Banner ads should send users to the right place if they click through. All too often, click-throughs land users far from where they can make a purchase. Many offline ads strive for humor, but humor can be risky online, particularly if ads are directed toward an international audience. An exception is when the ad effectively uses a well-known humorist like Jerry Seinfeld, who starred with Superman in highly effective five-minute webisodes for American Express.[11]

Sponsorships
Web page ads, usually the size of a small button banner ad, placed adjacent to content related to the sponsor's product.

SPONSORSHIPS   **Sponsorships** are web page ads, usually the size of a small button banner ad, placed adjacent to content related to the sponsor's product. For example, Nestlé Carnation Infant Nutrition sponsors YourBabyToday.com (*www.yourbabytoday .com/afronet/index.html*). The sponsorship announcement reads *We would like to thank our sponsor [Nestlé] for enabling us to produce this independent editorial program.* The tie-in between company and web content is obvious. The company helped prepare this special web editorial but is not mentioned in the contents. The sponsored content was offered without charge to site owners with related content and ran on Baby Place (*www.baby-place.com*) and similar-content portals. Site owners benefit in two ways by hosting sponsored content. It encourages their viewers to stay on the site longer to read the content, and advertising space on the page(s) can be sold by the site owner. Sponsorships are also used for games and interactive tools such as currency, size, and mortgage calculators.

Most sponsorship button ads are interactive but not intrusive. They are not rich media, so they can be viewed by anyone with a graphical browser. They capitalize on the goodwill that viewers express for sponsors that provide useful content, and they are particularly attractive to large corporations, which use them for public relations purposes. Even so, sponsorships are declining in popularity. In 1998 they generated 40 percent of all advertising revenue; by 2003 their share of revenue had fallen to 8 percent. It is generally agreed that sponsorships increase awareness and are more cost-effective than banner ads. However, there are no standards for sponsorship deals, so each arrangement has to be negotiated between the sponsor and the site property owners that host the content.

Interstitials
Rich media ads that closely resemble slimmed-down television commercials or print ads in a magazine.

INTERSTITIALS   **Interstitials** are rich media ads that closely resemble slimmed-down television commercials. They are flashy, intrusive audio, animation, and video ads that last from five to thirty seconds. More than five to ten seconds on the Internet is a very long time, so interstitials must be scheduled sparingly. They can be extremely annoying to people trying to use the Web as an information source because they block content. They also require fast connections, so it is important to run them on pages likely to attract viewers who use the latest browsers and high-bandwidth connections on DSL, cable, or a T-1 at work. Interstitials play between web pages, much as print ads in a magazine do. Viewers complain that because interstitials block the screen, they slow access to a site.

Minimovies
Very short, cinema-like ads filmed specifically for Internet showing.

Webisodes
A push technology that uses streaming video or other techniques to push multi-episode animated cartoons, advertisements, music videos, or other content to the user.

MINIMOVIES AND WEBISODES   Although they are more expensive to produce, **minimovies,** very short, cinema-like ads filmed specifically for Internet showing and **webisodes,** animated cartoons, short television-like ads, music videos, and other vehicles that use Flash and other technologies, are appearing online in direct relationship to the growing adoption of broadband. Automobile company BMW North America has been recognized for its highly effective short cinema ads (*www.bmwfilms.com*), which took far longer to create than any website banner ad and were much more expensive to produce. The five- to six-minute short DVD-like movies, *The Hire Film Series*, were filmed by top international directors (John Frankenheimer and Ang Lee, among others) for the Internet. Each stand-alone minifilm shows BMW automobiles in exciting situations and are short on plot but long on car chases. The minimovies were launched with an IMC campaign of television, print, and web ad support, along with viral marketing and public relations. Each film stars a different BMW automobile. The cinema ads also ran on the Independent Film Channel (IFC) and Bravo as paid media buys. The media fed on this launch, loading it with coverage in the entertainment and business presses. The web strategy was driven by studies indicating that 85 percent of BMW buyers researched their car purchase online before visiting a dealer's showroom. BMW and its agency, Fallon Worldwide (*www.fallon.com*), found that more BMW drivers spent time in contact with BMW promotions online than were reached by BMW television ads. Unlike traditional advertising, where more is spent on media placement than on the creative component of advertising, this web advertising spent more on creative than on media. The minifilms are estimated to have cost around US$15 million. The films are not interactive. Between April 2001, when the films were launched, and July 2001, they were downloaded over 10 million times. Visitors stayed on the site an average of sixteen minutes.[12]

Many webisodes are shown only online and they often run in a series like episodes in a television situation comedy, hence the name *webisode*. In early 2004, American Express (AmEx) launched a series of soft-sell webisodes starring Jerry Seinfeld and his pal Superman. Unlike traditional television product placement where the product is placed within the program's content, AmEx built content around the product. The webisodes cleverly integrated a live-action celebrity (Seinfeld) with an animated cartoon character (Superman) in humorous, everyday situations designed to build interest in the brand. AmEx is at the forefront of companies directing their ad dollars away from television and into other forms, particularly the Internet. While the company spent 80 percent of its advertising dollars on television in 1994, by 2003 its TV ad spending was reduced to only 35 percent. Terminix also takes a humorous approach in its continuing webisodes called *Bug's Eye View*, a monthly animated cartoon offered solely online.[13]

CLASSIFIEDS   Most newspaper sites run online classified ads. The *New York Times* (*www.nytimes.com/classified*) runs local ads and banner ads specific to the classified category for individuals and enterprises. Some classified ads are included as features on large sites or portals. Yahoo! (*http://classifieds.yahoo.com*) has classified ads in such categories as real estate, pets and animals, business opportunities, services, and personals. The search can be local or nationwide. Others are run on sites dedicated to classified ads C2C, B2B, and/or B2C. Google Local (*http://local.google.com*) encourages users to find local businesses online and includes directions and maps with the listings, and, where available, reviews of the products and services offered.

WEBCAST ADS   Webcasts are audio, video, or audio/video streaming broadcasts on the World Wide Web. Some are live, others are rebroadcasts, many are archived, and a large number are streaming audio from traditional radio stations such as the BBC (British Broadcasting Company at *www.bbc.co.uk/radio/*) and NPR (National Public Radio at *www.npr.org*).

Real.com (*www.real.com*) sells RealPlayer Plus, with links to more than 3,200 on-line radio stations worldwide and 60 ad-free stations. Copyright problems have forced many radio stations to stop broadcasting online. Until copyright payment issues can be resolved, growth in webcasts will be limited.

Webcasters generate revenue by selling in-stream ads within the streamed content and gateway ads that appear on the page that links to the webcast. Most webcasters sell a combination of forms, including sponsorships, in-stream ads, and gateway ads. Many advertisers are wary of webcast ads, and particularly in-stream ads, because they are so new and thus are not backed up by abundant measurement and rate standardization information. Top webcast advertisers are automotive companies, entertainment, music, and alcoholic beverages. Webcasting is also used by Wall Street analysts to broadcast information exclusively to larger institutional clients. It is unclear whether streaming audio will be an effective advertising channel because radio availability is already extremely broad. Dayparts are meaningless when it comes to the Internet, so using drivetimes and other radio metrics makes little sense in a virtual venue. [14]

Blogads
Paid advertisements, typically banners or sidebars, on blogs (weblogs).

BLOGADS   **Blogads** are paid banners or sidebar ads on blogs (weblogs). This format is beginning to show promise as some blogs, particularly those with political content, come to be more heavily read by self-selected readers. Blog readers are an attractive demographic. They are older (61 percent are over 30), more affluent than typical U.S. Internet users (40 percent have household incomes over US$90,000), more highly educated, and more likely to use broadband (60 percent). They purchase books (50 percent), plane tickets (47 percent), and click on blogads (67 percent). Some top political blogs (poli-blogs) already benefit from advertising placements and they are beginning to attract some mainstream product advertisers. One poli-blog, The DrudgeReport (*www.drudgereport.com*), is estimated to generate over US$1 million in annual ad revenue. Blogs lend themselves to text-based ads for niche products. However, attempts at using blog-like sites for product launches and brand building have thus far failed. Dr. Pepper tried to use a blog to launch a new milk drink. Its RagingCow blog was not a success, although it did generate considerable comment by media critics. Companies continue to experiment with blogs. General Motors launched a *Smallblock Engine Blog* (*http://smallblock.gmblogs.com*) in late 2004 to celebrate the fiftieth anniversary of the engine's creation, but it is also a soft-sell approach to draw car enthusiasts to the brand and solicit customer testimonials.[15]

INSTANT MESSAGING   Instant messaging is one of the five most popular online activities and is particularly hot among teens and young adults. Approximately 2.3 billion instant messages are sent daily on AOL; over 200 million instant message users are registered worldwide. Although the platform is very interesting to advertisers, they have not yet figured out how to use the format successfully. Unfortunately, spammers have and it's called *spim*, unsolicited commercial instant messages and it is a nuisance. However, network managers are rising to the challenge of developing controls that hopefully ensure spim never reaches the magnitude of spam.

PAID SEARCH

An estimated half-billion searches are performed daily using search engines. Understandably, advertisers want to go where there is traffic, which attracts them to search engines. Search engine advertisements are low-cost, highly relevant because they are inserted where consumer-initiated actions indicate their interest is high, and deliver measurable results. Search engines beat standard banner or button advertising in creating favorable brand impressions and directing visitors to websites. Search listings are more effective than banner or other ads in generating brand recall, favorable opinion, and purchase intention. Brand recall is three times better with search listings than with ads. Nine out of ten Internet users visit a search engine or use a search engine on a portal or community site. They also revisit at least five times monthly. Fifty-seven percent of Internet users search the Web daily, the second most frequent Internet activity after email (81 percent).

Paid search

Various formats used by advertisers to gain preferential placements in search listings or to insert text ads in listings relevant to their products.

Most search engines initially generated revenue by selling advertising space primarily for banner ads. When the online advertising market collapsed, search engines sought new revenue streams and today, even Google offers opportunities for paid-for sponsor text listings on its search results pages. **Paid search** includes various formats used by advertisers to gain preferential search listings or to insert text ads in listings that are relevant to their products. There are several types of paid search formats, and the differences among them are subtle. They include:

Paid placement   Also called pay-for-placement or bid-for-placement, results in search engine rankings that are artificially high because advertisers (companies, web owners, and third-party "search-engine-optimizing" companies) have bid and paid for the top listing. This is the opposite of *organic* listings, which are natural (objective) because the top-listed sites are those that the most visitors have actually used. Top paid-placement listings go to the highest bidder. Where a bidder is listed on a page depends entirely on how much they bid compared to the top bid.

Paid inclusion   Also called pay-for-inclusion or submit-URL programs, allows advertisers to insert their URL and keywords in a search engine's database or index. Pricing is based on the number of URLs listed, and sometimes a fee per click is charged. The advantage is that advertisers get listed faster and are guaranteed that their site is available in the search engine's index for the period of the contract. Paid inclusion means paying the search engine a set fee to ensure that a website's URL is included in the engine's database. It does not guarantee a top listing.

Sponsored links Where advertisers pay to have small text advertisements placed in clearly identified locations on a search listing page. Advertisers that sign up for Google's AdWords (*https://adwords.google.com/select/*) program create their own ads, select keyword descriptors that visitors are likely to use, and pay per click through—that is, advertisers pay the search engine for every click-through on the listing. Google clearly identifies these ads as Sponsored Links. Organic listings still appear below the sponsored links, and they typically are the links that other searchers have clicked on most often. These are the most objective and most trusted links.[16]

Paid placements are the paid search format most attacked by organizations that believe special bid fees undermine the validity of Internet searches and violate federal laws against deceptive advertising. Little if any screening is performed on the top-listed sites. Commercial Alert (*www.commercialalert.org*), a consumer activist watchdog group, says that by soliciting paid placement advertisers, search engines are abandoning their objectivity without letting users know how concealed fees affect rankings.

It is still possible to become highly ranked on search pages using *non-paid placement* strategies. Search engine optimization initially was accomplished principally by inserting metatags in HTML code to aid search engine indexing algorithms. Optimization can also be manipulated by inflating the number of hits on a site in order to fool a search engine into believing that the site is heavily trafficked. However, the only sure way of guaranteeing top listing is through some form of paid search or paid text advertising.

Most search engines and portals today are loaded with ads. Of the major search engines, only Google accepts no advertising on its front page. Google performs more than several hundred million searches per day and searches over 8 billion web pages. Its AdWords Select program offers cost-per-click (CPC) pricing that charges the advertiser only when a visitor clicks through on the ad. Ads can be changed as often as the advertiser wants and can be targeted by keywords, country, and language.

Not all businesses have an equal need to use search engine promotion. An IBM, Dell, Wal-Mart, or other well-known brand with a short, easy-to-remember URL is less likely to need help directing Internet users to its website. A mid-size national or regional brand is more likely to use bid search. A local brand with a very restricted geographical service area has even less need, because its customer base and reach are exceedingly small by Internet standards. Small local businesses can drive local traffic to their websites via local search, although some are expanding their reach by purchasing text ads on Google and other highly popular engines.

Google

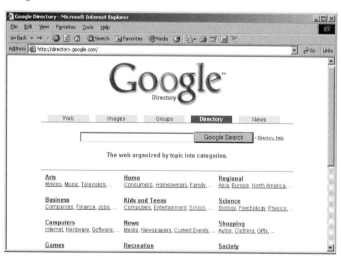

Google's local search is a popular advertising format for small businesses.

Source: Copyright © 2004 by Google.com. Reprinted by permission, http://local.google.com/lochp.

LOCAL SEARCH The Yellow Pages are directional advertising. People go to local print directories when they are actively seeking information and ready to purchase. The same is true online, where local search is drawing in visitors and small business advertisers. Local search through Yellow Pages and other directories represents about 7 percent of all online search. Google, Yahoo! (*http://local.yahoo.com*), and other companies already offer their own local search engines, often with maps to local businesses. Local spending on paid-search ads is forecast to grow from US$1 billion (2003) to US$2.5 billion in 2008. Leading online directories are YellowOnline.com (*www .yellow.com*), Verizon SuperPages (*www.superpages.com*), Yahoo! Yellow Pages (*http://yp .yahoo.com*), SBN.com (Superior Business Network at *http://SBN.com*), AOL (*http://yp.aol.com*), and Google Local. They are all localized; users access listings by zip code and/or city and state, and business category. Directories typically provide address information, telephone number, website link (if available), driving instructions, maps, and sometimes coupons. Most pages have localized display, banner, and/or pop-up ads. A considerable advantage of online directory listings is that they can be modified or corrected in real time. Changes to hard-copy directory listings are often delayed several months to a year until the next year's directory is printed.

PLACING ADVERTISING

An advertiser that wants to place its ads somewhere other than on its own website has several options. It can go to a well-known, heavy-traffic site such as AOL (*http://media space.aol.com*) or Yahoo! (*http://docs.yahoo.com/info/advertising*) and purchase advertising space directly from the site owner. It can purchase space on the website of a complementary product or category. For example, *BusinessWeek's* (*www.businessweek.com*) homepage recently ran house ads (ads for its own branded products) along with button ads for an ISP and Carnegie Mellon University's Tepper School of Business, and sponsored text links for five other companies. Nonprofits and government agencies may qualify for free banner ads and placements through the AdCouncil's online PSA program.

Most host sites have highly specific instructions for advertisers. AOL's instructions cover several pages and address such issues as file formats, maximum file sizes, color palette, animation, and sponsorship buttons. Advertising rates are often posted on the host's site or can be obtained from a placement service or a third party such as DoubleClick (*www.doubleclick.com/us/*).

Reciprocal advertising links
Free ad links swapped between cooperating host sites.

Less costly alternatives are available for small and midsize businesses. **Reciprocal advertising links,** or co-op links, are free ad banners and links swapped among cooperating host sites. A host site offers space for reciprocal hypertext linking. Advertisers that place ads on the host's site reciprocate. Reciprocal space is also available in some online magazines. MS-Links Exchange (*http://ms-links.com*) hosts a banner exchange where potential advertisers can link up their targeted banner ads. The problem with reciprocal advertising is lack of traffic. Although common interests may encourage visitors to visit reciprocally linked sites, low numbers limit their effectiveness.

Affiliate marketing is another way to monetize a site and in the process, advertise the facilitating site. Affiliate or associate programs are offered by most major sites that act as facilitators collecting payments for small sites. They include Amazon.com, AOL,

Yahoo!, and eBay. Affiliate advertising works to the advantage of the sponsor. Affiliate members receive a small fee for each site visitor who clicks through and buys something from the network sponsor. Of course, visitors leave the affiliate's site to make the purchase, which can rob the affiliate of a sale. The affiliate may gain a small revenue stream, but it is the sponsor that benefits from increased traffic. Some sites have adopted newer software that allows the visitor to link to the affiliate network owner and make a purchase without leaving the affiliate member's site.

RATES

The Internet and the Web are unique in their capacity to allow marketers to gather more information than other promotion channels, and at a remarkable depth and specificity, instantaneously. Some advertisers still want to know about hits and stickiness. Others realize the value of calculating conversion rates and return on advertising investment. What they seek are indications that their advertising spending is having the desired effect. Measurement accuracy is vital to negotiating fair rates. Advertisers must know how many impressions (views of an advertisement, typically as CPM) they can count by advertising on a site and how many of the viewer click-throughs will turn into sales (conversions). Pricing models for online advertising are fairly constant, with CPM/Impression (cost per thousand impressions) pricing dominating, although performance and some hybrid pricing models are attracting interest.

From about 1994 through 2000, demand for ad space was greater than supply, and host sites selling valuable space had the upper hand in setting rates. In market conditions where sellers had the advantage, they did not have to provide much information about audiences or effectiveness. With the dot-com meltdown at the turn of the century and the decline in advertising spending, power shifted to advertisers (ad space buyers), who became able to negotiate rates downward and to demand more information from a site owner about numbers of visitors served (impressions), how long they stayed, and their characteristics (demographics, spending, preferences). More information, however, is not necessarily better information. Measurement inconsistencies and, in some cases, deliberate overcounting resulted in erroneous measurements, particularly impression miscounts. Even as the advertising recovery gathered strength beginning in 2003, rates were still negotiable on most sites, and the listed or placed rate was not necessarily final. Quantity discounts are often given, depending on availability of space. Barter works online in the same way as offline.

Advertising rates generally are set by the web owner selling the space or by a third-party intermediary such as DoubleClick. Custom and competitive pressure, as well as economics, also influence rate setting. Sites that add value, sites that have more attractive audience statistics, and sites whose space is highly sought after obviously can charge higher rates. Space owners post their rates on their sites or provide a contact number for rate cards. Space brokers, advertising, and promotion agencies also provide rates.

Online Sales Promotions and Permission Email

Sales promotions, like cents off coupons, are a temporary incentive designed to move an audience quickly toward a desired action—principally a purchase. Permission email marketing directs marketing messages and incentives to audiences that agree (opt-in) to allow their names to be included on a commercial email distribution list. Sales promotions are a small but growing online promotion while email is being overused to the point where its value is rapidly being eroded. The vast volume of spam (unsolicited commercial email), well over 50 percent of all email and perhaps as much as 80 percent or more, is further undermining the effectiveness of advertisements placed in permission email and the willingness of customers to opt-in to commercial email and newsletters.

SALES PROMOTIONS

Coupons are the most highly visible sales promotion. Free-standing coupons distributed in newspapers and direct mailers continue to be the dominant form, and consumer package goods companies are the principal coupon issuers. Top retail coupon redeemers are Kroger, Wal-Mart, and Safeway. In 2002, 242 million Internet coupons were distributed, an increase of 111 percent over 2001. However, this represented less than 0.1 percent of the almost 340 billion coupons distributed in the United States yearly. According to coupon clearinghouse CMS, consumers printed 992 million Internet grocery coupons in 2003, a 365% increase over 2002.

The redemption rate for online coupons is about 3 percent, compared to 1.3 to 1.8 percent for offline coupons. Top product coupon categories are groceries (37 percent), health care (33 percent), beauty (37 percent), books (23 percent), and toys (23 percent). Women, larger families, and lower-income consumers are the most loyal coupon clippers. They are attracted to online coupons because they have a higher average redemption value (US$0.97) and a longer average life before expiration (4.8 months). Once coupon-receptive target audiences have been identified, a relationship based on interest in the product can be established and encouraged by continued contact. The risk is being too generous with coupons. Fraud is also a concern, because home-printed coupons are far harder to control than those printed on special high-gloss, multicolor paper.

Coupons made their way online in 1995. Now, more than 25,000 retailers participate in various online coupon programs. Coupons are particularly attractive to stores with their own private label products because private label profit margins average 40 percent higher than manufacturer brand products.

Coupons are distributed in several ways. Coupon sites such as ValPak.com (*http://valpak.com/index.jsp*) offer coupons in many categories that can be printed and redeemed in a variety of local stores. ValPak is also the largest offline coupon distributor, mailing print coupons in distinctive bright blue envelopes. ValPak went online in late 1998. In addition to grocery coupons, ValPak has rebates, online deals, and free samples. H.O.T.! Coupons (*http://Hotcoupons.com*) and ValPak ask visitors to type in their zip code or city. Coupons for that location are then shown onscreen. Localized screens also carry local retailers' banner ads in a stacked vertical banner or leaderboard at page bottom.

Coupon fraud is an increasingly serious online problem with offline consequences. This is an example of the negative effects of the integration of online and offline. In the summer of 2003, consumers flocked into grocery stores trying to redeem coupons for free Häagen-Dazs ice cream and deeply discounted Pepsi and Stouffer products. Some of these consumers knew they were trying to redeem counterfeit coupons; others did not. Homemade counterfeit coupons are appearing on eBay and are being distributed through web rings and chat rooms, as well as emails. They are for a variety of consumer brands, and most offer free items. Fraudulent coupons harm retailers, manufacturers, and innocent consumers who purchase them on auctions. eBay and other sites are cracking down on coupon fraudsters and are closely monitoring coupon activities. However, stopping the circulation of these coupons P2P is extremely challenging. Knowingly circulating counterfeit coupons is a criminal offense that can be prosecuted at the federal, state, and local levels. The coupon industry advocacy group, the Coupon Council (*www.couponmonth.com*), estimates total annual losses in the United States to all forms of coupon fraud at around US$500 million. This includes non-Internet, traditional coupon deceits.[17]

Contests also are a popular sales promotion. For example, General Mills (the sponsor) used the external promotion company Promotions.com (*www.Promotions.com*) to create and implement, as part of a national campaign with NASCAR legend Richard Petty, an Internet promotion for Pop Secret Microwave Popcorn called the "Guess Richard Petty's Favorite Paint Scheme" Sweepstakes. Participants had to guess which of three color combinations Petty preferred for his NASCAR Winston Cup car, driven by John Andretti in the Pop Secret Microwave Popcorn 400 race. The grand prize winner received a four-night, five-day trip for two to the race and $25,000. The website had games, instant prizes, and information about the drivers. Support for the Internet sweepstakes included store point-of-purchase (POP) displays, coupons in free standing inserts (FSI), promotions on 8 million packages of Pop Secret Microwave Popcorn, and events at state fairs nationwide.[18]

Many Internet users like giveaway sites where they can win cash or merchandise without making a purchase or buying a lotto ticket. Marketers like the sites because they offer the opportunity for one-to-one marketing, assembling house email lists, and collecting customer data. A recent Jupiter Communication study revealed that about 93 percent of all commercial sites offer some form of sales promotions using discounts, sweepstakes, giveaways, or other freebies. Marketers spent US$0.9 billion on Internet sales promotions in 1999 and US$1.8 billion in 2000 and are expected to spend US$14.4 billion by 2005. They report that sales promotions drive traffic, increase email contacts, build brand awareness, create customer relationships, and lead to purchase.

Perhaps surprisingly, product demonstrations are also presented online. Demonstrations increase awareness and help remove customer reservations about purchasing a product. Automobile manufacturers have simulations where visitors can experience driving a car. Many apparel retailers offer virtual dressing rooms where customers can see how they will look in various clothing combinations.

EMAIL MARKETING

Sales promotions are a short-term strategy designed to create an immediate inducement to purchase. Marketing by email, particularly using permission or opt-in email, is a long-term strategy designed to establish a meaningful relationship with customers. Thus it is unlike spam, which is a short-term strategy and does not ask permission.

Nearly all Internet users have one or (more commonly) two or more email accounts where they send and receive personal messages and receive commercial email. Personal messages are one of the great Internet success stories and remain the single most widely used Internet service. By the end of 2004, total annual email volume in the United States exceeded 1.5 trillion messages, and the volume of email continues to grow. Spam also continues to grow, clogging email boxes, blocking out legitimate marketing messages, overworking servers, and fraying nerves. **Spam filters,** software installed to block spam email, also frequently blocks legitimate email, particularly email containing attachments, which creates an additional problem for email marketers.

Spam filters
Software that blocks spam but also frequently blocks legitimate email.

Email can be a trusted marketing tool for those customers that sign up to receive it. An eMarketer study revealed that 66 percent of consumers who give permission (opt in) to receive commercial email trust the source while 95 percent of them distrust any email that is uninvited spam.

Marketers can counter spam. They can restrict the messages they send to only those messages that are most important, particularly those that extend a discount or special offer. They also should stop thinking of batch email as a *blast* and conceive of it, rather, as a one-to-one communication with valued customers who deserve to be treated with respect.

Commercial email
Promotion messages sent by email to enterprises and/or consumers with or without their permission.

Commercial email consists of marketing promotion messages and incentives conveyed by electronic mail. This interactive method for making an offer and initiating an exchange is widely praised by marketers who use it, because it can reach a highly segmented target market almost instantaneously at a far lower cost than other forms of direct marketing. It is denounced, however, by consumers and businesses whose email inboxes are clogged by unsolicited email messages they did not request and resent receiving. Some commercial email is less odious than others, particularly when the receiver has given the sender permission to deliver a promotion message or incentive. Such an opt in arrangement is more expensive for the marketer than opt out, but it is also far more desirable, because it avoids annoying receivers and reduces the waste of sending messages or incentives to receivers who lack all interest in the product or service being promoted.

Any company engaged in traditional direct marketing should find it relatively easy to use email marketing, which is actually much cheaper than the offline method. House lists can be used with email addresses collected through buyer information, online product registrations, website registrations, newsletter subscriptions, on-site contests, and other inducements. The challenge for most businesses is implementing the email marketing campaign. Many run their own email campaigns. The advantages of doing so include complete control over the list, message, timing, follow-up, and customization. Disadvantages include the time and technology required and the limited scope of house lists. That is why many companies, large and small, turn to outside vendors for their email campaigns.

Many businesses offer email services, including YesMail.Com (*http://YesMail .Com*), NetCreations.com (*http://w3.netcreations.com*), and PostMasterDirect.com (*http://rentals.postmasterdirect.com*). Most target U.S. and sometimes Canadian, but usually not international, audiences. E@symail Interactive (*www.easymailinteractive. com*), the oldest independent email list broker in the United States, represents over 1,500 unique domestic and international B2C and B2B lists, with more than 276 million opt-in email consumer addresses, 35 million B2B addresses, and 105 million international addresses. E@symail has select lists of opt-in audiences in such categories as *adventure outdoors, animals, antiques, shopping/online, real estate, sports, wedding, wireless,* and *weekend trips.* It offers only opt-in lists.

A marketer typically contracts with a list broker to rent a specified number of email addresses in a category and then creates the email pieces exactly as they will be distributed, text-only, HTML, or rich media. The email piece is then sent to the list broker and distributed to the designated opt-in audience. Tracking is performed in real time and/or within a prespecified time frame. Lists cost around US$0.10 to $0.50 cents a name, US$100 to $500 CPM (cost per thousand). Charges usually include list rental, email distribution, tracking, and final reporting. The obvious advantages of permission email marketing are greater reach at a lower price, more rapid distribution, real-time tracking of results, and more privacy for the audience. Costs can be reduced by sharing a list and sending a group mailing with other vendors, but that dilutes the impact. Traditional postal direct mail has about a 1 to 2 percent response rate. Permission email response rates have been as high as 30 to 40 percent, although the rate is declining.

Tracking the results of an email campaign is easier and more efficient than tracking those of an advertising campaign. When interactive messages are distributed, an identifier code number is placed in the email. When receivers click through, the code number tracks their reaching the site from the distributed email. Millions of email messages can be distributed simultaneously. The message sponsor can tell when the messages are received and acted on, because site traffic increases accordingly. Tracking is in real time and is highly accurate, providing both a unique visitor rate and a conversion rate.

Small and midsize businesses are particularly drawn to permission email because they can use it effectively at low cost. However, if a majority of the millions of small businesses in the United States began sending commercial email, the impact could be overwhelming. It has been suggested that if every employee spent an average of five minutes reading each email received, it would take four hours every workday to clear his or her email inbox. That is probably an underestimation.

Email got Google into considerable hot water in 2004 when the company announced it was testing a free web mail service called *Gmail.* Google offered users an enormous amount of storage space, far more than its rivals. However, the email came with a catch. Google's software would be reading the mail and inserting advertisements relevant to its content. If a Gmail user received an email from a friend, even if the friend was using a different email service, and the email contained references to a great vacation on Sanibel Island, Florida, Gmail might insert advertisements into the email for Sanibel eateries and condos. As expected, privacy advocates and Internet observers were mortified by this blatant invasion of privacy. Google responded by saying it would impose restraints and that it had established an internal standards board to set parameters for determining whether an email might not be a candidate for ad insertions. For example, no ads will be inserted on email that contains references to sex, guns, or drugs (even if the reference is to dating services or squirt guns). If Google's email service is a clearly superior product, it is likely that consumers will flock to use it. Because email is already susceptible to prying eyes at every stage on its Internet journey, they may believe that Google has enough integrity to be trusted with their email.[19]

The majority of sites take advantage of visitors by automatically capturing their email address when they enter the site, adding these addresses, without asking permission, to an email distribution list. Somewhere, hidden in such a site, there is a place where visitors can choose to **opt out**—that is, tell the site they do not wish to receive mailings. Depending on message quantity and content, unsolicited email can be a minor nuisance or a major annoyance. For businesses it can be extremely costly, because bulk email sent to many of their employees at once can crash their servers and waste employee time purging email inboxes of spam.

By far the better alternative is **opt in,** which asks permission for the marketer to make future contact. The address owner's consent is needed before he or she is added to an email distribution list. Opt in is less intrusive than opt out, but it also carries a risk. The relationship can be broken if email messages come too frequently, are too long, or fail to engage the visitor's interest. If this happens, "unsubscribe rates" rise. Even when permission is given, sometimes people forget and, when they receive the opt in mail, believe it is spam. This can poison a relationship.

Double opt in requires double agreement. First is the standard opt in permission. This is followed by a confirmation opt in to ensure that the holder of the email address is the same person who gave the original permission. This step also serves as a reminder and avoids the misperception of spam when the email arrives.

The best possible list is an opt in (or double opt in) compiled from a house list of the customers and/or visitors who have already interacted with the business. Compiled lists can be obtained from list brokers and email companies that specialize in providing lists of email addresses for people or enterprises that fit the purchaser's specifications. Lists can also be compiled from memberships, directories, and other sources with large numbers of addresses.

Businesses that use permission email marketing should adhere to some fundamental rules. They should send email only to those who have given their permission to receive it, keep the email short and to the point, and not send email too often. Probably the most important rule is *Don't spam!*

Opt out
A command whereby visitors to a website can have the site drop their names from the site's email list.

Opt in
A command whereby visitors to a website can request that their names be added to the site's email distribution list.

Web Update

For updates and more on this topic, visit the textbook student website at: http://college.hmco .com/business/students and select Siegel, Internet Marketing, 2e. **Email Marketing**

Summary

The Fundamentals of Promotion

Promotion is planned, persuasive, targeted, goal-driven marketing communication. Various promotion goals are to build awareness of brands, increase traffic to a sponsor's website, and generate sales. Traditional forms of promotion include advertising, sales promotions, personal selling, publicity/public relations, and direct marketing. Marketers use promotion to send a message and deliver an incentive. Most traditional promotion is a one-to-many distribution process. Internet promotion can be one-to-one. The Internet is primarily a pull environment but can also be a push environment. Multiple promotion goals may operate concurrently. Promotion should be supported by all marketing mix variables working together. The best promotion is a good product sold at a fair price in a readily accessible place. In addition to building awareness, marketing promotion can inform, persuade, and remind buyers about products, build goodwill and value, brand and rebrand, position and reposition products, and entertain. The line between promotion and entertainment online is rapidly blurring, giving rise to advertainment. Marketing promotion is funded by a promotion budget. Integrated Marketing Communication (IMC) requires a planned, coordinated, integrated campaign with more than one promotion tool that has one voice, one look, and one feel. Promotion points of contact are the ways in which an audience comes into contact with something that communicates image or brand message or is a web driver. Internet advertising is the most visible promotion form and includes banner ads, sponsorships, interstitials and other rich-media ads, pop-ups, pop-unders, classified ads, advergames, Yellow Pages, in-stream and gateway webcast ads, and other types of ads. Internet sales promotions are temporary inducements to stimulate demand, increase storefront traffic and/or sales, or encourage distribution channel members. In personal selling, a salesperson interacts with potential or current customers. Public relations (PR) has an identified sponsor that pays for the development and implementation of PR programs to create and maintain a favorable image and goodwill, persuade an audience, and/or generate traffic. Publicity is promotion that provides information to the media for use in a news story or editorial. Some marketers consider all Internet promotion direct marketing because it is interactive, personal, and encourages an immediate response. Promotion delivery channels vary and include face-to-face personal selling, electronic mass media (television, radio), print media (magazines, newspapers), outdoor media (billboards, kiosks), and direct media (advertising, mail). Newer channels include promotion delivered via computer disks, facsimile (fax) machines, bill stuffers and door hangers, automobile and bus wraps, grocery store floor and shopping basket ads, and other forms. Promotion can stimulate word-of-mouth communications, or buzz. Promotion targets can be narrowly or broadly defined and can even be a mass market. Promotion decisions are often based on the assumptions of a hierarchy-of-effects model. Effective promotion requires planning.

Promotion Issues

Two problems that plague Internet promotion are its lack of emotion and clutter. Consumers have always had the power to ignore marketing promotion. Web roadblocks, or portal takeovers, occur when one advertiser purchases all available advertising space on a page or a site owner serves only house ads. Consumers and enterprises can avoid online ads by clicking past or installing ad-blocking software. Promotion clutter is created by the growing volume of online ads, email messages, sales promotions, websites, and pages. Internet marketing promotion is highly visible and intrusive, often blocking a user's view of page content, clogging email boxes, slowing download time, or even mousetrapping, which helps explain why it is so often criticized. Promotion is nevertheless defended because of the critical role it plays in letting buyers know about marketing offers.

Online Advertising and Paid Search

Internet advertising is just entering its second decade and is still experiencing growing pains. Internet advertising revenue in the United States for 2003 was just under US$7.3 billion, the first yearly increase since 2000. In the Internet's infancy, most advertising was in the form of display banner ads. That has changed radically, and the fastest-growing segment of online advertising is paid search. The top-spending categories in 2003 were consumer brands (retail, automotive, travel), computing, and financial services. Ads have grown larger in an effort to capture viewers' attention and make a more lasting impression. Because more people have broadband, more rich-media ads are being served. Pop-ups and pop-unders are the ad formats that consumers hate most. Although the use of banner ads has declined, they still are used because they can raise brand awareness, and have low cost and broad reach. Visitors are increasingly exposed to skyscrapers, large rectangles, and big boxes on web pages. Banners are placed at various locations on a page. No rules for the use of banner ads can possibly apply to all situations and products. Banner ads should send users to the right place if they click through. Sponsorships are web page ads, usually the size of a small button banner ad, placed adjacent to content related to the sponsor's product. It is generally agreed that sponsorships increase awareness and are more cost-effective than banner ads. Interstitials are rich-media ads that closely resemble slimmed-down television commercials. Minimovies are very short, cinema-like ads filmed specifically for showing on the Internet. They and webisodes are beginning to appear online in direct relationship to the increased use of broadband. Webcasters generate revenue by selling in-stream ads within the streamed content and gateway ads that appear on the page that links to the webcast. Blogads are paid banners or sidebar ads on blogs. Blogs reach a highly attractive demographic, but advertising on blogs is extremely limited, primarily to political blogs. Attempts at using blog-like sites for product launches and brand building have failed. Instant messaging is very interesting to advertisers, but they have not yet figured out how to use the format successfully. Search engine listings and search engine advertisements are low-cost, targeted, and highly relevant. Search engines beat standard banner or button advertising in creating favorable brand impressions and leading visitors to websites. Paid search refers to various formats used by advertisers to gain preferential search listings or to insert text ads in listings. Search advertising is currently the hottest form of online ad.

Online Sales Promotions and Permission Email

Sales promotions are designed to move an audience quickly toward a desired action. Permission email marketing directs marketing messages and incentives toward audiences that allow their names to be included on a commercial email distribution list. Initial indications are that online sales promotions are still a very small factor online and that permission email is being overused to the point of burning out its desirable audiences. Coupons are the most highly visible sales promotion. Consumers printed 992 million Internet grocery coupons in 2003, a 365% increase over 2002. Consumers are attracted to online coupons because they have a higher average redemption value and a longer average life before expiration than offline coupons. Online coupon fraud is a problem with increasingly serious offline consequences. Contests are another popular sales promotion. Many sites have free offers, two-for-one specials, and other short-term incentives to buy products sold from their storefront. Internet users like give-away sites where they can win cash or merchandise without making a purchase or buying a lotto ticket. Marketers like the sites because they offer the opportunity for one-to-one marketing, assembling house email lists, and collecting customer data. Sales promotions drive traffic, increase email contacts, build brand awareness, create customer relationships, and can lead to purchase. Permission marketing by email is a long-term strategy designed to establish a meaningful relationship with customers, unlike spam, which is a short-term strategy and does not ask permission. Commercial email consists of marketing promotion messages and incentives conveyed by electronic mail. Tracking the results of an email campaign is easier and more efficient than tracking an advertising campaign. Small and midsize businesses are particularly drawn to permission email for its low cost. The majority of sites take advantage of visitors by automatically capturing their email address when they access a site and adding them to an email distribution list. The better alternative is opt in, which asks permission for the marketer to make future contact. Double opt in requires getting permission confirmed.

Take Action!

Clutter has been cited as a major problem online, interfering with the effective delivery of promotion to intended receivers. Your university's vice president for marketing and development has hired you to help him redesign the school's marketing homepage. He is particularly concerned that it is too cluttered.

1. Identify four universities or schools that are direct competitors to your university. Visit each school online and print screenshots of their homepages and of your own university's page. If possible, print in color so that you can evaluate the overall design effect of the homepage. With the screenshots in front of you, identify the elements that the pages have in common.

Create a table with the elements as column heads and the schools for rows. Use check marks to indicate which elements are present for each school.

2. On a separate page, create a bullet list of what you believe are the essential elements that must be on your university homepage, placing the most important elements at the top of the list.

3. In a one-page memo to your boss, describe your research, your conclusions about clutter, and your recommendations for developing a new homepage that is clutter-free. Attach the table and bullet list to the memo as appendices.

Chapter Review Questions

1. What is advergaming and what makes it so popular with viewers and marketers?
2. Explain what happens during the marketing communication process.
3. Explain how traditional forms of promotion and promotion points of contact work together.
4. Can word of mouth really be effective promotion online?
5. How can promotion direct behavior?
6. How can emotion be added to online promotions?
7. What types of promotion are particularly well suited to the Internet and Web?
8. What is promotion synergy?
9. Why should online and offline promotions be complementary?
10. Explain how the Internet may operate as both a push and a pull environment.
11. Why might top-of-page banner ads be more effective than those placed at the bottom of the page?
12. Are minimovies and webisodes effective online promotion forms?
13. Will webcasting ads be effective in the future? Explain.
14. Why do consumers like sales promotions?
15. Why do marketers like to use paid search?

Competitive Case Study

Nestlé Advergames, Too

Swiss-owned Nestlé SA (*www.nestle.com*) is the world's largest food company and the market leader in most of the segments in which it competes. It is known for instant coffee (Nescafé), bottled water (Perrier), chocolate, pet food (Ralston Purina), pasta (Buitoni), and many other food, cosmetic, and pharmaceutical products. Year-end 2003 sales were US$70.8 billion. The company employs over 250,000 people worldwide. Nestlé actively uses promotion to build brands and sell products. In early 2004, seven Nestlé USA candy brands launched an on-pack and online sweepstakes giveaway of music downloads and trips to visit with bands Crunch, SmashMouth, and (hip-hop band) B2K. The target markets are kids. The brands are Nestlé Crunch, 100 Grand, Butterfinger, Baby Ruth, SweeTARTS, Spree, and Shockers. Instant-win wrappers with game codes were placed on 64 million candy wrappers. Customers had to take the redemption codes online to determine whether or not they had won. Nestlé announced that it would give 50,000 winners 10 songs to download and that another 100,000 winners would get 5 free downloads. Nestlé also employs advergaming. It launched an advergaming site to raise brand awareness of its Vanilla Chocolate Milk in China using Gugule, its cartoon ambassador. Kids were encouraged to play over twenty minigames. The premise was that "Coco," a magical chocolate, had lost its vanilla character and ability to fly. A set of codes inserted into Nestlé product packages contained short-cut clues to pass through the challenges in the game and help Coco regain its flying abil-

ity. The game was promoted through print advertising and targeted kids and teens aged 8 to 15. The company claimed that the games not only were fun but also were an education tool because they taught children about the origins of vanilla. China is rapidly becoming the top Internet-using country in Asia. In Hong Kong, 93 percent of people between the ages of 10 and 24 have online access, and 40 percent play online games. Nestlé's targeting of kids and tweens illustrates one of the serious criticisms of promotion online and offline when it targets consumers and "consumers-in-training." Child advocacy groups and media critics deride this type of effort, saying it is unfair because the targets are unduly vulnerable to persuasive marketing communication.[20]

CHECK IT OUT

Visit the Nestlé-sponsored site YourBabyToday.com (*www.yourbabytoday.com*). Evaluate the site to determine whether Nestlé is identified anywhere other than in the boxed sponsorship announcement. Do you believe this is an effective promotion format for the company? Explain your answer.

A GLOBAL PERSPECTIVE

Visit some of the Nestlé country sites (*www.nestle.com/Header/Internet_Directory/Home+Internet+Directory.htm*). How does the company use .jpeg images to add interest to each site? Are the sites clean or cluttered? What common elements are used? What differentiates the sites?

Module IV

Internet Marketing Action Plans

Internet marketing takes place within a highly turbulent, challenging commercial and political environment. Marketing products in this environment necessitates attention to emerging trends, changing customer preferences, competitive pressures, and new technologies. In order to recognize and capitalize on opportunities and cope with threats to success, goal-driven marketing requires effective planning, implementation, and control processes. Marketing plans should be specifically designed to advance the goals and objectives of the enterprise by developing appropriate strategies and tactics. Plans, as discussed in Chapter 13, are blueprints for marketing activities but it requires implementation to put those plans into action. Operational decisions about website content, design, and construction—substance, look and feel, and functionality—is the subject of Chapter 14. Control completes the loop by measuring actual performance against expected performance, analyzing the results, and adjusting plans to correct shortcomings, respond to environmental changes, and amplify what's successful.

The Web Marketing Plan

LEARNING OBJECTIVES

» To explain the value of web marketing planning
» To identify the components of a web marketing plan
» To examine how web marketing plans are implemented and controlled
» To understand the role of a web marketing budget

Planning for Web Marketing

Kim has been operating a gift basket business from her home for the past two years. Before that, she wove baskets for family and friends and filled them with books, games, chocolates, and other treats tailored to the recipient and occasion. Family and friends loved her baskets and urged her to consider selling them to others. She took their advice and carefully planned how she could turn a satisfying hobby into a flexible, profitable home business. She began by thoroughly researching the gift basket industry and learned how to run a gift basket business by attending business-building seminars at the annual Philadelphia Gift Show, which is billed as the largest regional gift show in the United States. She recognized that her competitive advantages were twofold: the personalized designs painted on exterior basket surfaces and their handcrafted contents. For example, her highly prized baby baskets contain standard hair brushes and rattles purchased from a supplier, then hand painted with personalized designs customized for the customer. Because Kim has state and city business licenses, she qualifies to buy products from wholesalers nationwide. Customers can further personalize their baskets

by selecting from among her hand-knit caps and booties, crocheted crib blankets, embroidered bibs, and woodcut crib mobiles. They can also select a design that will be painted on the basket's exterior and the cloth basket lining. Other favorites are her Kentucky Derby and Mother's Day baskets. Kim offers standardized baskets as well as those that are custom-built, and price points are set by client, basket type and size, contents, and assembly time. Shipping is by USPS. She accepts credit card orders by telephone and fax, and she has also created a small print product catalog with color photographs of her baskets. The business has grown primarily through satisfied customer word of mouth, small display advertisements placed in the Yellow Pages of the local telephone directory, and bulletin board flyers. Kim has developed a cottage industry of women, mostly friends, who work from their homes creating the handmade baskets and personalized contents. Now Kim is ready to take a giant step and launch a website to showcase her baskets, increase sales, expand her customer base, and reduce costs, particularly those associated with personally answering questions from potential customers. She knows that she can just go online and, for a nominal fee, use any of several new programs that can help the novice build and maintain a website. But Kim also realizes that she increases her probability of success if she develops a web marketing plan before the site is built and uses the plan (and its updates) to guide her web marketing decisions. Carefully planning her web marketing site can help her move her business to a new, more profitable level and avoid costly mistakes that could imperil her expansion.

Unlike the other chapter opening cases in this book, this case is a composite of several small businesses that, over the years, the author's students have assisted in planning their web marketing sites. Although Kim is fictional, the gift basket business definitely is not. It is an over US$3.5 billion industry made up largely of women entrepreneurs attracted to its flexibility and creativity. Gift baskets are sold in specialty shops, in department and grocery stores, by home-based and independent retailers, and now, online. *Gift Basket Review* reports that 72 percent of the gift basket companies surveyed had annual sales up to US$50,000, 23 percent had sales of US$100,000 to $199,999, and 27 percent had annual sales at or over US$200,000. Profits on average were 22 percent of sales, with markups averaging 78 percent. Although many gift basket businesses are home-based, other small businesses operate out of office buildings, retail stores, warehouses, or manufacturing complexes and have many more employees than just the owner–operator and several friends. According to the Small Business Administration (*www.sba.gov*), a *small business* is independently owned and operated and not dominant in its field of operation. Most have far fewer than five hundred employees, and many are owner-operated. Small businesses can also be agricultural. Many small home businesses are a silent, almost hidden part of the U.S. economy, yet they represent over 50 percent of all businesses and generate about 10 percent of the U.S. gross domestic product. The Internet is an attractive option for many of the country's estimated 23 million small businesses. These businesses also represent a promising business opportunity for companies such as Yahoo! (Yahoo! Small Business at *http://smallbusiness.yahoo.com* and Yahoo! Merchant Starter at *http://smallbusiness .yahoo.com/merchant/c1.php*), Microsoft (Small Business Services at *www.microsoft .com/smallbusiness/products/online/hub .mspx*), EarthLink (Business Resource Center at *http://start.earthlink.net/channel/ BUSINESS*), and others that offer basic small business website templates.[1]

Yahoo!

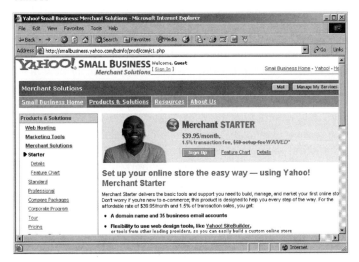

Yahoo! Merchant Starter offers online business solutions for a monthly fee and a sales transaction fee.

Reproduced with permission of Yahoo! Inc. © 2005 by Yahoo! Inc. YAHOO! and the YAHOO! logo are trademarks of Yahoo! Inc.

The Web has given small business owners unprecedented opportunities for worldwide exposure and growth. The low cost of creating, hosting, and maintaining a website has encouraged many small businesspeople to try their hand at web marketing. They can perform marketing intelligence online and assess their competition, follow industry trends, and identify gaps in the market that their offers might fill. Because the Web is a vast library, they can find resources that were previously inaccessible and can locate suppliers and partners, as well as new products and customers. At the same time, web marketing is a risky venture. A site can easily get lost in web clutter, or, at the other extreme, the business can be overwhelmed by orders it cannot fill. A well-designed and well-executed web marketing plan can increase the probability of success but cannot guarantee it. In this chapter we consider the development and implementation of a web marketing plan. We will discuss site content, design, and construction in Chapter 14.

The Fundamentals of Planning

Plans are blueprints for the future, written road maps designed to guide an enterprise as it moves from its current position to a desired future. Plans are partly visionary but mostly practical, and they should contain specific instructions for what should happen and when. Kim is new to the Web and her initial marketing plan focuses on getting started online, but other businesses with existing websites need marketing plans to guide their decisions as they consider expanding, updating, or refocusing their sites.

In large corporations, marketing planning is often left to professional planners trained to write multiple concurrent, comprehensive, complex, multifunctional plans. Salespeople, brand and product managers, advertising and public relations managers, and other marketers contribute information used for planning purposes. Marketing plans are more commonly found in larger enterprises, but size alone is no guarantee that a web plan will be written and implemented—or that it will be successful.

Although marketing planning should be conducted by enterprises of all sizes in all industries, it is often overlooked. Far too often, marketing activities are conducted on an ad hoc basis, guided by an idea that leaps from someone's mind into hasty implementation without a clear understanding of industry trends, market volatility, competitors, or customer preferences. Planning is something many people shy away from, claiming they lack the time, information, expertise, or need to do it. But planning is not as intimidating as it sounds, and good plans effectively implemented can reduce costs, increase receipts, and protect the enterprise against marketplace disruptions. Effective marketing planning is essential to creating and sustaining a competitive advantage online as well as offline.[2]

A NEST OF PLANS

Any business seeking financing from a bank or other lender must present a business plan that clearly and systematically documents how the business intends to operate. The lender wants evidence that the business can create a profitable revenue stream and repay the loan within a prescribed time. The dot-com crash and the 2001 recession dramatically limited financing opportunities, but even then money was still available to support well-conceived, carefully planned Internet ventures.

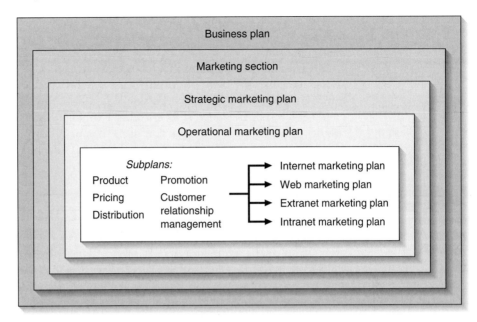

FIGURE 13-1 Nested Plans
Marketing plans are nested within other plans, starting with the business plan.

Marketing plan
An overall blueprint for how marketing mix strategies and tactics will be implemented to satisfy customer needs and meet business goals typically over a period of one year or more.

Strategic marketing plan
A marketing plan for a longer period of time, often three to five years or more.

Operational marketing plan
A detailed tactical blueprint for marketing goals and performances within a short period of time, usually up to one year.

A marketing section within the business plan generally addresses how marketing will be conducted to meet business plan goals, but it is not a marketing plan. Instead, a **marketing plan** is an overall blueprint for how marketing mix strategies and tactics will satisfy customers and meet business goals within a period of time, typically one year or more. Figure 13-1 illustrates how a marketing plan is nested within a business plan.

A **strategic marketing plan** presents a blueprint for marketing activities to be conducted over a longer period of time, often three to five years or more. It provides a vision for what marketing can accomplish during that period, although it lacks the fine details of an operational marketing plan.

An **operational marketing plan** is a detailed, month-to-month and sometimes week-to-week or even day-to-day tactical blueprint for marketing goals and performances within a short period of time, usually up to one year. It should be revised and updated on a regular basis, sometimes daily. It directs marketplace performances, establishes how those performances are evaluated, and provides specific tactical guidance. An operational plan contains detailed subplans for product management, pricing, distribution, and promotion and for customer relationship management (CRM).

A **web marketing plan** moves marketing planning from the traditional to the Internet environment. The web plan can be freestanding for clicks-only businesses that market only on the Web, or it can be part of a traditional marketing plan for businesses with both offline and online operations (bricks-and-clicks). A web marketing plan identifies goals, objectives, strategies, and tactics for web marketing, along with expected performances and outcomes. It serves business plan goals and reflects the

Web marketing plan
A detailed plan or set of instructions for how web marketing will be conducted.

Internet marketing plans
Marketing plans that expand coverage to include all Internet marketing activities (the Web, intranets, and extranets) and other Internet services.

mission statement. Ideally, all plans should be integrated, coordinated, and complementary. When they are not, significant problems can arise for a business and its managers.

Internet marketing plans expand coverage to include all aspects of Internet marketing, including the Web. Marketing plans may be written solely for an intranet or extranet if sufficient marketing activities occur there. Intranet marketing may target employees or stakeholders such as investors. Extranet marketing targets suppliers, distributors, and customers who are part of the company's extranet. Internet marketing plans should also complement offline marketing. Our discussion focuses on public web marketing planning because that is where online marketing activity is significant and growing.

WHO IS RESPONSIBLE FOR WEB MARKETING PLANNING?

In large corporations, marketing managers simultaneously run multiple marketing plans. Plans can be written for brands, product lines, product categories, target markets, or served geographical areas. They are written for Internet, intranet, extranet, and web marketing, as well as for offline traditional marketing. Many corporate marketing managers run sophisticated computer programs and data warehouses that enable them to create highly detailed, numerically rich plans whose implementation can be electronically tracked in real time. They can forecast demand and sales receipts, simulate the effects of price changes, and develop cost projections. They may use data mining to develop descriptive and predictive models.

Small businesspeople typically lack the resources, time, and energy to develop extremely detailed, highly sophisticated formal marketing plans, but this does not mean they should ignore writing a web marketing plan. Lack of planning is one of the principal reasons why so many dot-coms failed in 2000–2001. Planning requires the business to confront key issues that affect its success and survival. The process of writing the plan requires organization and an objective assessment of the business's readiness to engage in Internet and web marketing.

Corporate marketing managers writing operational web marketing plans are often isolated from customers, the marketplace, and the specialists who design and implement websites and pages. In small businesses, the same people who write the web marketing plan are likely to interact directly with customers as well. They answer questions by telephone and fax and correspond with customers by email, so they are personally familiar with customer questions, complaints, purchases, and suggestions. They may update web content themselves, work directly with local ISP technicians who maintain their sites, or contract with an online company that builds and maintains sites. They may sell inventory using listings at various online shopping malls, such as Amazon.com's Amazon Marketplace (*www.amazon.com*), which allows sellers to list their inventory beside Amazon's products, and eBay (*www.ebay.com*), which encourages small businesses to set up auctions on its site for a nominal transaction fee.

Small business web marketing is often personal and immediate, which can be a considerable advantage when plans are developed for a volatile Internet environment that requires nimble responses to rapid changes. Another advantage is that small businesses have few if any management levels, so plans can be revised or sites updated without seeking multiple approvals at successively higher management levels. Small businesses can also avoid the interdepartmental friction that sometimes arises from resistance to web marketing or conflicting goals for a web marketing site. Because small business owners are closer to the customer and marketplace, they can personally monitor the environment and their competitors and can make quick changes in response to emerging trends. Speed can be a considerable competitive advantage online, even more so than offline. A disadvantage is that small businesspeople may lack the time to systematically use the information they have at hand to respond to marketplace changes.

INITIAL QUESTIONS

Answering several key questions will help marketers set web marketing plan boundaries. The answers will differ, depending on the type and size of the enterprise and on the environment it faces.

Why is this business going online?   One common answer is that everyone else is doing it. Although this answer hints at competitive reasons for going online, marketers are well advised to identify clearly the goals that they expect the web marketing site to achieve for their business. Effective goals are hard but reasonable, specific, measurable, relevant, and stated with benchmarks and time limits. Commonly expressed web marketing goals include to gain awareness, sell products, build brands, position or reposition products, increase profits, drive customer traffic to an offline storefront or salespeople, clear stale inventory, provide information, entertain, service customers, reduce costs, create goodwill, spread a message, maintain parity with the competition, or collect customer data.

Who is responsible for website marketing?   If the business is a small, owner-operated business, the owner may take responsibility or work closely with a consultant (online or offline) to create, host, and refresh the site on a regular basis. In larger enterprises, this task can be done in-house, outsourced to external service consultants, or performed by a combination of the two. Many companies use a combination of in-house experts and outside service consultants. Website marketing may be solely a marketing responsibility or a team effort involving members from other functional areas of the business with a stake in the success of the website. Depending on the enterprise, they may include representatives from advertising, public relations, sales, computing services, human resources, corporate management, finance, production, information technology, and others. Alternatively, each department or brand may support its own website. A related question concerns personnel within the marketing department who will work on the plan. Will their web responsibilities be added to their regular marketing duties, or will these people be shifted totally to the Web? If so, can their vacated positions be filled? If it is not possible to use existing personnel to create, run, and manage the website, will permission be given to hire new people or will current personnel be retrained? Launching and maintaining a website creates a series of sometimes thorny human resource problems. These problems are exacerbated during a recession, when hiring is frozen, or at times when people with needed skills are in short supply.

How difficult will it be to gain cooperation for the web marketing effort?   In a very small business, it is assumed that the owner–operator supports the concept of web marketing; otherwise, it would not be attempted. In any business with more than one employee, it should be a top priority to gain the cooperation of everyone directly involved with the web marketing effort who can benefit from it or might imperil it. In a larger business, this includes getting support from other departments that, although they may not be directly involved in or benefit directly from the web marketing effort, could block resources and undermine web marketing success. If the web marketing effort is not viewed as important to corporate goals, it may require powerful persuasion to get doubters to cooperate.

How will the website be financed?   In some cases, website costs are carved out of the existing marketing budget. In other cases, the enterprise has to seek additional internal funds or external loans to launch and maintain the site until it is self-sufficient or profitable. Because sites can make other contributions to the bottom line, like drive traffic offline to a retail store, it may be run as a loss leader and not be expected to directly generate revenue. Loss leaders can add value by expanding the processes currently applied in customer relationship management, by providing enhanced public relations capacities, or by driving visitors offline to company stores or salespeople. For example, web grocers have historically operated at a loss; however, the survivors realize that a money-losing online service can still be a powerful competitive advantage for their offline retail business. Many customers like online ordering and home delivery. It increases their loyalty to the grocer, online and offline. This may become more important as the Internet-savvy baby-boom generation ages. In this case, it is an investment in the future.

Do we need a full-scale web marketing site?   Initially, many small businesses may test the Internet waters by listing products at a shopping mall, through email direct marketing that drives prospects to a telephone or fax number, or by selling on eBay or another auction site. However, for as little as US$39.95 per month (2004 cost), a small business can have a company such as Yahoo! set up site hosting, domain registration, product catalogs, secure shopping cart and online credit card processing, inventory management, sales reporting, and so on.

MARKETING PLAN FORMATS

Most marketing students are familiar with the components of a traditional marketing plan and realize that there is no single standardized format. Most plans generally cover the same topics but vary by enterprise type, size, and industry. Marketing plan formats and examples of completed marketing plans, as well as the software used to create them, are accessible online at such sites as Bplans.com (*www.bplans.com*) and Bizplans.com (*www.bizplans.com*). Palo Alto Software Inc.'s Marketing Plan Pro (*www.paloalto.com/ps/mp/*) provides an online guided tour that outlines the steps in marketing planning and provides examples.

The Web Marketing Plan

Web marketing plans focus on how marketing will be accomplished on the business's website and, if there is a bricks component, on how the two will work together. The parts are much like those of a traditional marketing plan, but the focus is specifically on web marketing.

Every web marketing plan is unique, its format and details tailored to enterprise characteristics, its operating environment, resources available for developing the plan, and the company's reason(s) for going online and/ or maintaining a web presence. Each plan should include, at the least, the following elements:

Elements of the Web Marketing Plan
Web marketing plan formats vary but generally, at the least, have these parts.

Web Marketing Plan
1. Company Situation and Market Analysis
   Company and Industry Overview (Including Trends)
   Market Analysis
   Online Environmental Analysis
   General Environmental Analysis
2. Web Marketing Mix Analysis and Strategies
   Goals and Objectives
   Strategies and Tactics
3. Web Marketing Action Plan
4. Financial Analysis
5. Control and Feedback Processes

1. A company situation and market analysis that evaluates the company, market, customers, competitors, and relevant online/offline environments, industry characteristics, and trends
2. Marketing mix analysis and strategies
3. An action plan that implements (operationalizes) the marketing mix
4. A financial analysis that projects expected expenses, revenues, breakeven point, and profits
5. Control and feedback processes that determine how well the site and plan are performing, perform risk analysis, and provide guidance for how plan and site should be revisited and revised (see the accompanying outline, "Elements of the Web Marketing Plan").

COMPANY, MARKET, AND ENVIRONMENTAL ANALYSIS

The company analysis considers (a) what unique benefits and value the company can offer its target market(s) online, (b) how the company can benefit from web marketing, and (c) its readiness to do so. A company's web offer should add value. For example, an office supply website adds *convenience value* by selling reasonably priced home office supplies delivered directly to the customer's home office. A bank's website adds *time value* by letting customers access their checking accounts online 24/7/365 and pay bills online, thus avoiding postage. A game site provides *entertainment value*. A travel site offers *price value*. All websites should provide *information value*.

This analysis should identify the benefits of web marketing for the business as well as for its customers. For example, a business may benefit because its website generates additional revenues from new customers; gets current customers to purchase more items, to purchase more frequently, or to buy higher-priced products (up-selling); or facilitates cross-selling. Other businesses may want to enter new markets with new (for them) products or to serve existing customers better and strengthen their loyalty. Alternatively, the goal may be to drive web traffic to an offline salesperson who can answer customer questions or to reduce customer service costs by posting catalogs and frequently asked questions (FAQs) online. Benefits should be clearly stated and quantified. On-site testimonials are very helpful for highlighting how customers benefit from the company's offer.

Readiness is examined from management, cost, and human resource perspectives. Ideally, web marketing should be supported by all parts of the enterprise and not become a focal point for conflict. It is important to determine whether managers in other functional areas support web marketing and whether web marketing requires that funds be taken from their budgets. Few managers surrender resources willingly. If web marketing clearly benefits all parts of the company, making this clear can help build support for the web marketing effort companywide.

Costs are a key consideration, particularly in view of the fact that poor planning and high start-up and maintenance costs drove many first movers off the Web. Cost projections should be prepared so that they can be compared with expected benefits using cost/benefit analysis. The business must determine whether it has sufficient resources to initiate and maintain the web effort in the short term or needs to seek outside funds. If outside funds are sought, does the company have the stability and track record to support its application and get funded?

From a human resource perspective, the web effort requires web-savvy marketers and technology system specialists working together. Technology responsibilities can be outsourced or can be an in-house effort.

The industry overview examines (1) how similar companies are using the Internet in their marketing efforts and (2) industry trends, including Internet use trends in the industry. Many industries have trade associations with websites that may have case studies of other companies' experiences with Internet marketing. They often can be located through a Google (*www.google.com*) search.

Market analysis examines the present state of the company's specific market, including its size and number of buyers, customer demographics and purchasing characteristics, numbers of competitors and their distribution (clicks-only, bricks and clicks, bricks and mortar), trends, and identification of principal online direct and indirect competitors. Marketing intelligence should be gathered about main competitors, including information about their strengths and weaknesses. Their websites should be visited and evaluated and their market offers studied. Products and prices should be analyzed, along with shopping baskets usability (for selling sites), return policies, site navigation, feedback options, and use of new technology. The analysis should specify the extent of direct and indirect online competition, and whether the market is saturated or there is a gap to be filled; if competitors have a synergistic online/offline marketing effort and/or a competitive advantage. Answers to these questions should indicate positioning opportunities. A useful resource for online competitive marketing intelligence is DMOZ, The Open Directory Project (*http://dmoz.org/Business/*), which has links to websites in many different industries, including toy retailers, retail hardware stores, home furnishing retailers, etailers, store planners, picture framers, and gift baskets (*http://dmoz.org/Shopping/Gifts/Gift_Baskets/*).

Market analysis is of served *and* prospective target markets. If the business has an offline presence, offline customers should also be considered, particularly if they can be moved online. Marketing research can answer questions about how difficult it will be to persuade target markets to become Internet users if they are not already; what customers want and expect to find on a website; what promotions will move customers to visit the site and purchase; and customer price sensitivity, particularly to shipping and handling costs. Website marketing requires getting inside customers' heads and trying to understand what motivates them and how to appeal to them and build long-term relationships. As important as marketing research is, it can be costly, time-consuming, and beyond the capacities of some very small businesses.

A SWOT analysis (strengths, weaknesses, opportunities, threats) is commonly used in marketing planning and can help assess web readiness. An analysis of strengths and weaknesses directly addresses the business's resources, including the managers' commitment to developing a successful web marketing site. An assessment of opportunities and threats evaluates environmental factors. These include the economy, technology, and competition, all of which can either jeopardize the web marketing effort or present opportunities for growth and expansion. An opportunity analysis should identify gaps in the web market that the business can fill.

Some marketing academics question the value of a SWOT analysis. They consider the time and effort needed to conduct one a drain on company resources, and they claim that there is no evidence that a SWOT analysis directly affects profitability. However, the *process* of conducting a SWOT is unquestionably valuable. It causes planners to focus on issues that require attention and to identify issues that are not so important. Systematically addressing issues that underlie the SWOT categories may not be *directly* linked to increased profits, but to ignore them entirely could be short-sighted and, in the long run, costly.

ANALYSIS OF THE WEB MARKETING MIX

Marketers manage the marketing mix variables (the 4Ps) and use them to make offers that target markets find attractive. Goals and objectives for what the website is to accomplish are established early in the planning process. A goal is broader than an objective and sometimes may overlap several marketing plans. For example, a typical website marketing goal is to increase profits. Specific and often multiple objectives are stated for how the goal will be achieved. For the profit goal, objectives may include instituting stringent cost controls for website operations and getting customers to buy more at the site. Objectives should be stated in measurable terms as performance outcomes. Performance and outcome objectives may include sales objectives, site traffic objectives, customer service objectives, cost reduction objectives, and personnel reduction objectives.

Objectives stated numerically with time limits provide performance benchmarks that can be monitored to see whether they are achieved. Multiple objectives can be operationalized simultaneously. Whatever the objectives are, they should be stated simply, clearly, measurably, and with time limits. Large corporations can have hundreds of marketing plans, each with multiple objectives, operating concurrently. Our hypothetical basket business owner Kim and other home-based small business owners may state only one or two website objectives. Kim's sales objective is to increase sales receipts by 10 percent in the first three months after going online. A cost reduction objective is to get 5 percent of her offline customers to order online within the next three months. This will reduce the amount of time she has to spend on the telephone taking orders and the time cost of diverting attention from filling gift basket orders. She also wants to increase the number of her corporate customers by 10 percent within six months. These objectives are clear, simple, achievable, measurable, and time-based.

Strategies are broadly stated activities and performances for the marketing mix variables (4Ps), for customer relationship management, and for website content, design, and technology (Figure 13-2). Marketing mix and technology strategies must be customer-centric—designed to make the web experience positive for customers and to satisfy their needs and wants with the company's product offer.

Strategies should flow from customer insight based on an analysis of customer characteristics, buying preferences, and interaction history. Marketers that believe in the marketing concept make customer satisfaction a central premise for their web marketing effort. To do this, they need to know their customers and what satisfies them. In our gift basket example, the following questions about the company's customers should be answered.

Who Are They?   What are customer demographics and psychographics, and who are the heavy-user 20 percent? How many purchases are new buys and how many are repeat purchases? Gift baskets are most likely to be purchased by individual consumers and corporations, and by customers in the South, Midwest, and Northeast. The individual gift basket giver is more likely to be a moderate- or upper-income woman, 35 to 49 years of age, purchasing for herself or on behalf of a man in her life. Their purchase averages US$45 to $50 for a single basket. Corporate buyers represent about a third of the gift basket market. They buy year-round and at holidays. Other target markets are professionals (doctors, lawyers, and others), other enterprises (medical centers, hospitals, universities, and government bodies), and nonprofit groups (Chambers of Commerce and clubs). Gift baskets are particularly popular among real estate agents, who give them to clients at sale closings.

FIGURE 13-2 Web Marketing Strategies
Strategies are approaches designed to accomplish objectives. Strategies should be developed for the marketing mix variables, for customer relationship management, and for the web marketing site.

Why Do They Buy?   Some customers purchase baskets for themselves, as a pick-me-up or reward for an accomplishment. Most individuals purchase baskets for family members or friends for birthdays, new babies, funerals, weddings, special events, anniversaries, housewarmings, or to express thanks or send get-well wishes. Corporate buyers purchase baskets to give to their own customers, to reward employees, to recognize promotions or retirements, or as thank-you's.

When Do They Buy?   Are purchases concentrated around religious or secular holidays or events such as graduations? If so, promotions should be "heavied up" prior to the time when customers make their decisions. Permission email campaigns should be timed to hit just before purchase decisions are made. If purchases are made for family events, email reminders can be sent prior to the events. About half of all gift basket sales coincide with holidays—principally Christmas, Valentine's Day, Easter, and Mother's Day. Some gift basket businesses send emails to their customers at the beginning of each month to remind them about the baskets and about the gift-giving events coming up during that month. Kim needs to look closely at her sales records over the past two years to identify the most popular occasions for basket purchases and then plan her promotions accordingly.

What Do They Buy?   What types of baskets, in terms of contents and price, are most popular? What custom designs are ordered most often? Most gift basket businesses offer both standard and custom options. Custom baskets cost more and typically have a greater markup. They also take more time to assemble.

How Much Do They Spend?   Corporate customers are more likely to make volume purchases of multiple baskets for special events. They may have very long gift lists that can keep a business quite busy year-round. Pricing options can be developed on the basis of past spending patterns as well as industry averages.

How Do They Buy?   What payment forms are preferred? Most online customers still use credit cards, so the most popular cards must be accepted online as a customer service. Yahoo! Merchant Solutions offers storefront options that small businesses can use to set up online payment options.

How Did They Find You?   Most gift basket businesses advertise using word of mouth, networking, telephone directory display advertisements and listings, direct mail, brochures, and (less frequently) local newspaper advertisements. Online gift basket sites use sponsored links on Google, Yahoo!, and other sites, as well as email direct marketing. A recent search on Google for *gift baskets* returned 3.6 million results, a clear indication of the popularity of web marketing in this industry. Kim advertises in the local hard-copy Yellow Pages and pays for small display ads in the local newspapers around Christmas. However, most customers find her business through referrals from friends. Kim needs to know what proportion of customers find her from each online and offline contact point so that she can use this information as a basis for future promotion decisions.

Once Kim has systematically evaluated her current customers, she must develop strategies to meet her objectives and tactics to implement her strategies. For example, one of her sales objectives is to increase sales receipts by 10 percent in the first three months after the website is launched. Judging on the basis of her current monthly offline sales receipts, Kim must generate US$3,249.99 in sales in order to achieve this objective. Considering the average price of her baskets, that is around a total of forty to forty-five baskets sold from the website in three months. Kim's strategies rely on driving traffic to the website, products, pricing, order fulfillment, promotions, CRM, and website characteristics. Tactics are the details—that is, the short-term tasks designed to implement the strategies. In the case of our gift basket example, they include the following.

TRAFFIC   Kim must develop tactics for getting customers to her site. Offline, she will send mailers to current customers offering a 10 percent one-time-only, one-basket discount for web purchases. She will add an additional 10 percent discount for any current customer who gets a friend to make a purchase from the website. The discount will eat into her profits, but added traffic will increase sales. Online, she will register with search engines, join web rings and gift communities, add reciprocal links, and use email permission marketing to announce her website launch to consumers and corporate buyers. She will hire a website positioning company for search engine optimization or use Web Site Traffic Builder (*www.intelliquis.com*), which can register her domain name with more than nine hundred search engines.

PRODUCTS   Kim needs to showcase her products in the best possible light. This means displaying her entire product line in clear, high-definition, enlargeable, multi-view pictures accompanied by descriptive text and testimonials from satisfied customers. She will offer free gift wrap and cards with purchases over US$100, because her offline customers always want them.

PRICING   To stimulate corporate sales, Kim will offer multipurchase corporate discounts for web purchases. She will post the price of each product in U.S. dollars. Initially, she will not sell her products to buyers from other countries, which eliminates the need for currency converters and dealing with currency fluctuations. She will provide clear explanations of shipping and handling costs, and of transportation options. Free shipping will be offered for purchases of US$200 or more to the same address in the continental United States. She will contract with major U.S. credit card vendors for payment fulfillment.

FULFILLMENT   Order fulfillment will be in-house, and shipping will be handled by the United States Postal Service (USPS). USPS package tracking is a popular service that customers appreciate.

PROMOTION   Kim's promotion strategy is to use as many free or reciprocal promotion devices as possible. She will pay for Google AdWords (*https://adwords.google.com/select/*) listings. Her site will be interactive, with email going from customers directly to Kim's home computer so that she can answer email personally. She plans to contract with a permission marketing company to send email announcements of her online business to corporate executives who opt in to receive promotions about corporate gift offers by email. She will place her web URL on her business cards, business stationery, product catalogs, sales invoices, gift cards, and directory listings.

CUSTOMER RELATIONSHIP MANAGEMENT   Because her customers value privacy, Kim will have a clear, concise, simple privacy statement on the website front page assuring them that no information will be sold to third parties. All ordering and payment information will be encrypted. Data collected from customers will be used to contact them in the future, with their permission. She will offer an email reminder service for customers. With their permission, Kim will contact them by email with a reminder of the approach of any date on which they have purchased gift baskets in the past.

WEBSITE DYNAMICS   Kim has found that her customers are not interested in games or other distractions when they are shopping online. Therefore, she will not clutter her website with anything that distracts from the shopping experience. She will make sure that shoppers can find what they want quickly, order it securely, and track package delivery. She also knows they are interested in how the gifts are crafted, so several pages of information will be linked to the website front page, showing Kim and her friends painting baskets and assembling the contents. Kim will work with her ISP technology consultant to ensure that the site design is clean, bright, uncluttered, and easy to navigate and has shopping basket software that works quickly, simply, and accurately.

THE WEB MARKETING ACTION PLAN

Action plan
A step-by-step blueprint for implementing tactics that will achieve marketing plan strategies.

An **action plan** is a step-by-step blueprint for implementing tactics that will achieve marketing plan strategies. Tactics are highly detailed tasks with deadlines that identify responsibilities and specify who will carry them out. For example, product tactics include Kim taking digital pictures of each type of basket she sells and writing detailed descriptions of the available contents and the images that can be painted on the wooden slats. Her ISP consultant will convert the digital pictures into web images for product page displays. Kim will contact current customers and ask them for short testimonials expressing their satisfaction with her gift baskets. The best statements she receives will be displayed on a *Satisfied Customers* web page, along with pictures of the baskets that these customers purchased. She will get signed releases from them for the use of their statements and initials on the website. Kim will select an email list broker for a permission email mailing to announce the launch of the site and will choose an online marketing firm to register her site with the most popular U.S. search engines and reregister it when required. She will contact VeriSign's Network Solutions (*www.networksolutions.com*) and register an appropriate domain name for her site.

An action plan should be sufficiently detailed so that a stranger can pick it up and immediately know what has to be done, within what time frame, and by whom. It should not be cluttered with documentary materials that belong in an appendix to the web marketing plan. It should be realistic about what can be achieved with the number of people and the resources available. Most of the technology will be left to her technology consultant, but Kim can use the action plan to identify how the website will function. An action plan should be revisited and revised as it is implemented.

FINANCIAL ANALYSIS

By now the marketer should be able to forecast what it will cost to create, launch, and maintain the website. Expected costs, revenues, profits, and losses should be projected.

Several scenarios should be developed for different levels of demand. If demand is higher than expected, what are the implications for fulfillment, receipts, costs, and profits? If demand is lower than expected, how will losses be covered? What sales levels trigger alarms that require revisions to the plan? What is the breakeven point?

Creating and maintaining a website, even if it is a static, information-only site, carries a cost. Most businesses tend to underestimate costs, and when they are selling online, they overestimate revenues (and profits). These distortions are a function of the relative youth of the online environment, coupled with a lack of experience on the Web. As more businesses reach profitability online, case histories of financial successes will become models for others to follow.

CONTROLS AND FEEDBACK

Control

The process of identifying and implementing measures that will be used to compare actual marketing performance and outcomes to projected performance and outcomes.

Marketers use control processes to track implementation of the marketing plan and to determine how well it is working. **Control** processes identify measures that will be used to compare actual marketing performance and outcomes to projected performance and outcomes. The purpose is to evaluate whether web marketing objectives have been met, and if not, to determine why. Control, like planning and implementation, is a systematic process. Controls should be in place to measure the performance of each tactic.

Performance must be monitored continuously because of web, environment, competitor, and customer volatility. Depending on the results, alterations should be made to the plan in order to bring actual performance in line with the ideal (projected) performance. Control processes must be developed along with the plan and implemented with site launch.

Control tracking systems apply yardsticks to collected data. As we have noted, Kim's sales objective is a 10 percent increase in sales over the first three months, and her cost reduction objective is to get 5 percent of her offline customers to order online during the same time period. These objectives are measurable benchmarks. The control mechanism in this case is to take actual sales and costs in three months and determine how they compare with the objectives. If both exceed the objectives, Kim is doing something right. Missing the objectives is a clear signal that adjustments are needed.

Some controls run continuously, particularly those that track unique site traffic and sales. They can be reported daily or summary statements can be prepared weekly. Given the Web's volatility, monthly or quarterly reports are too infrequent to be of real value. Web marketers must decide when control information is needed—and how much is needed—in order to control marketing activities without causing information overload. With the technology available, the volume of information generated and distributed can easily overwhelm the ability of any marketer to analyze and use it.

Feedback can be an important indicator of how well the web marketing plan and site are working. However, any site that invites customer contact and feedback must also be prepared to respond in a timely manner. This can present serious problems for the very small business whose owner–operator is frequently otherwise occupied. Prompt attention to email feedback can promote future sales.

Implementing the Plan

Implementation
The process of activating or operationalizing marketing plans.

Web marketing plans are meaningless until they are activated. This process is known as **implementation,** where resources (people and money), technology, and materials are brought together in an organized way to execute plan tactics and achieve web marketing strategies, objectives, and goals. Planning, implementation, and control are the three interrelated, unified marketing management processes that occur in all enterprises. They are identified and managed formally in large corporations. Small businesses also use these processes, although they may not be identified by name.

TIMELINE

Launching and maintaining a web marketing site in large corporations involves many functional specialists who work full-time on narrowly defined tasks. Web marketers in small or midsize businesses typically multitask, tending to other responsibilities while overseeing the total web marketing effort, or outsource these tasks to others. Regardless of enterprise size or resources, time has a tendency to slip away, which makes a timeline important to successful plan implementation. A timeline should specify dated deadlines by which specific tasks are to be accomplished, along with the identity of who will take responsibility for them. For example, Kim sets a deadline of six weeks from the start of implementation to her receipt of testimonials and signed releases from satisfied customers. When she has received these documents, she can check this task off the list. Within that period of time, she will be performing other tasks, which also have deadlines, and her ISP consultant will be developing the website's backend processes. Timelines should be maintained on charts or computer spreadsheets so that tasks can be checked off as they are completed, and deadlines should be noted so that work can be planned to meet them.

SITE CONSTRUCTION AND MANAGEMENT

An important part of plan implementation concerns website construction and management. Small businesses are likely to outsource the technical work involved. Selecting, hiring, and working with a technical system consultant or firm requires collaboration and the constant exchange of information. Arrangements vary, but technical consultants can help create web marketing plans or can concentrate solely on website design, construction, hosting, and management. Decisions about content, design, site navigation, usability, and other site-specific issues should not be left solely in the hands of any consultant. If the site is to capitalize on the customer insight developed in the process of web marketing planning, then plan developers must collaborate to ensure that the site accomplishes its customer relationship marketing purposes. Alternatively, construction and maintenance can be handled in-house. Many businesses host websites that offer assistance for the do-it-yourselfer. For example, Staples Business Center (*www.staples.com/BizServices*) offers sales and marketing help that includes many facets of website planning, implementation, and maintenance.

A web marketing site is a constant *work in progress.* Content must be refreshed on a regular basis. Prices must be changed as needed. Design standards change and nothing is worse than a stale, old-fashioned website design. If external links are used, they must be checked regularly to ensure that they are still active. Site management details *must* be resolved before the site is launched.

PLAN REVISION

Control data can flag problems early so that changes can be made in time to avert disaster. They can also show what is effective so that resources can be redirected to support successful offers. A website without controls leaves the marketer in the dark. Haphazardly implemented controls give untrustworthy, unusable results. Excessive control data can cause an information glut. If results are good, the response may be to maintain the status quo. If results are bad, action must be taken or the situation will probably get worse. This often means revising web marketing action plans and/or reconstructing all or parts of the website.

The Web Marketing Budget

Web marketing budget
A blueprint for how funds are allocated to various web marketing activities.

A **web marketing budget** is a blueprint for how funds are allocated to various web marketing activities. As a policy statement, it is a detailed plan that identifies priority spending areas and indicates how marketing will be conducted to achieve its performance goals. It is a projected profit and loss statement for the year, linked to financial reporting periods. In large businesses, it is also an evaluation tool for measuring a manager's performance.

In large businesses and corporations, marketing managers receive a marketing allocation and then distribute it through a marketing budget. Many small businesses do not budget for marketing, let alone for web marketing. They get trapped in a race to survive week to week and month to month, moving funds from one account to another, paying bills as they collect receipts, always worried about covering their costs and making margins. Funds for marketing activities are provided on an ad hoc basis, which typically means whatever is left over after the bills are paid. Others write budgets but never follow them. Even those businesses that follow budgets rarely have enough money to do everything they want to do. Instead, they have to choose among alternatives on the basis of costs, estimated benefits, projected revenue, and available funds. Regardless of business size, all marketers should create a reasonable web budget tied to performance outcomes that serve web marketing goals. They should stick to a marketing budget, yet be flexible enough to revise it when necessary.

THE WEB BUDGET IN THE MARKETING BUDGET

A marketing budget is an integral part of the business's operating budget. A web marketing budget may be a component of the marketing budget or a separate entity. It may be carved out of other budgets, which can generate conflict if other departments do not support the web marketing effort. A budget should state expenses (fixed and variable costs), projected sales, breakeven point, and projected net profit.

EXPENSES, REVENUES, AND PROJECTED NET PROFIT

Web marketing expenses include both website and related offline fixed and variable costs. A comprehensive expense estimate includes initial website development and launch costs, as well as estimates of the costs of site maintenance and upkeep, marketing, and promotion. Costs should be kept in line through the use of controls that monitor actual expenditures, compare them with projected expenditures, and signal cost overruns.

Some costs are fixed and recurring; others are variable. Initial creation and launch costs are associated with content, design, technology, and promotion activities. Some costs continue after launch, as the site is maintained. Others will appear again when the site is refreshed or relaunched. Most sites can take advantage of multiple revenue streams. Even if the site is not a web storefront, affiliate marketing and selling on-site advertising can generate revenue. Some sites add revenue by selling their email lists, a practice that results in customers getting unwanted email. Obviously, online sales are a prime revenue source for many sites. What is less clear is how to account for offline sales by customers who first use the website for information and direction offline. Revenue streams may include advertising, affiliate marketing, product sales, paid subscriptions, and the sale of customer lists.

The budget is incomplete without a final calculation of breakeven and projected net profit. Breakeven is the exact point where total costs equal total revenues. Profit is total sales (minus cost of sales) minus total expenses. The website generates profit if sales are greater than expenses; it operates at a loss if they are not. Some sites are not meant to be profit centers. Whether they are designed to run at a loss is another issue.

Summary

http://college.hmco.com/business/students

The Fundamentals of Planning

Plans are blueprints for moving an enterprise from its current position to a desired state in the future, with specific instructions for what should happen and when. The marketing section within a business plan is not a marketing plan. A marketing plan is a detailed, comprehensive, exhaustive blueprint for how marketing will be conducted. A strategic marketing plan presents a blueprint for a longer period of time, often three to five years or more. An operational marketing plan is a detailed, month-to-month (and sometimes week-to-week or even day-to-day) tactical blueprint for marketing performances within a short period of time, usually one year, with subplans for the marketing mix. It should be revisited regularly for revision and updating. A web marketing plan can be freestanding or can be integrated into a traditional marketing plan or an Internet marketing plan. It is a detailed set of instructions for how web marketing will be conducted, with expected performances and outcomes. Plans are written for Internet, intranet, extranet, and web marketing. Even before the planning process begins, marketers must address some key questions whose answers set plan boundaries: Who is responsible for the plan? Why is the business going online? Do we need a website? There is no single, standardized marketing plan format.

The Web Marketing Plan

Every web marketing plan is unique, with format and details specific to the enterprise, its environment, and its reason(s) for going online and/or maintaining a web presence. Each plan must consider the company, market, and environment, must set goals for the website, and must present strategies to achieve them. An action plan operationalizes strategies with highly detailed tactics. Financials project expected costs, revenues, and profits. Feedback and control processes determine how well the site is performing and provide insight into how the plan and site should be revised. The company analysis considers (1) what unique benefits and value it can offer its target market, (2) how it expects to benefit from web marketing, and (3) its readiness to do so. Readiness should be examined from management, cost, and human resource perspectives. A SWOT analysis can be valuable in assessing web readiness. The costs of web marketing are a key consideration. Market analysis examines the market and trends, what competitors are doing, and demand. Objectives consist of what the website is to accomplish for the enterprise. Frequently used objectives are related to sales, traffic, service, cost reduction, and personnel reduction. Objectives stated numerically and associated with time limits provide performance benchmarks. Strategies are approaches that will be used to achieve objectives. They integrate the mission and its policies and actions into a cohesive whole. Before trying to develop strategies to satisfy them, web marketers should know who their customers are, why they buy, when they buy, what they buy, how they buy, and how they found the website. An action plan is a step-by-step blueprint for implementing tactics, which are highly detailed, short-term tasks with associated deadlines. The marketer should be able to forecast what it will cost to create, launch, and maintain the website. Expected revenues, breakeven, profits, and losses should be projected. Marketers then use controls to track the progress of marketing plan implementation.

Implementing the Plan

Web marketing plans are meaningless until they are activated (implemented). Planning, implementation, and control are interrelated, unified marketing management processes. A timeline should be constructed with dated deadlines by which specific tasks are to be accomplished. Plan implementation includes website construction and management. A web marketing site is a constant work in progress. Control data can flag problems early so that changes can be made and resources can be redirected. Control tracking systems apply yardsticks to collected data. Controls can run continuously, particularly those that are tracking site traffic and sales.

The Web Marketing Budget

A web marketing budget is a blueprint for how funds are allocated to various web marketing activities. It is a detailed statement that identifies priority spending areas and indicates how marketing will be conducted to achieve performance goals. It includes a projected profit and loss statement for the year, linked to financial reporting periods. In large businesses, it is also an evaluation tool for measuring managers' performance. A marketing budget is an integral part of the business's operating budget. Some costs are fixed and recurring; others are variable. Initial creation and launch costs are associated with content, design, technology, and promotion activities. Multiple revenue streams, including advertising, affiliate marketing, product sales, and subscriptions, can generate receipts for the site. The budget is incomplete without the final calculation of projected net profit.

Take Action!

Kim needs help. It's clear that she is stretched too thin to develop a comprehensive marketing plan, so she asks the local university for a marketing student to take a cooperative education placement with her for the semester. That's you!

1. Perform a search at Google, Yahoo!, and one other search engine of your choice for *Kentucky Derby gift baskets.* Construct a table in which you have a column for each of the search engines and a row for each of the top ten sites that *all* the engines list. Identify the top listed site with an asterisk.

2. Evaluate any three Kentucky Derby gift basket sites using the competitive intelligence tools developed in this and other courses. Develop a table for reporting the results. Name the sites in the columns and include their URLs. In the rows, identify items that will help Kim develop her website. Divide them (via subheadings) in

terms of whether they fall in the category of content, design, or construction (technology). For example, one content issue is providing sufficient product information, one design issue is presenting attractive product pictures, and one construction (technology) issue is having working navigation bars.

3. On the basis of your evaluation of the three sites, prepare a business memorandum for Kim in which you bullet-list a series of content, design, and construction recommendations for her site. Be prepared to defend your recommendations in class.

Chapter Review Questions

1. Why are small businesses so important to the U.S. economy?
2. Explain why all businesses should have a marketing plan.
3. Contrast a strategic and an operational marketing plan.
4. Why is it important to assign responsibilities in a web marketing plan?
5. Is the marketing section in a business plan the same as a marketing plan? Explain.
6. How can a marketing plan help a dot-com get financing?
7. What major headings are typically found in a web marketing plan?

8. Why is an environmental analysis conducted during marketing plan development?
9. What does web marketing readiness mean?
10. How detailed should strategies be in a web marketing plan?
11. What financials should be included in a web marketing plan?
12. Timelines are useful tools. Why?
13. Is a website ever finished? Explain.
14. What costs should be included in a website expense statement?
15. Why are some websites deliberately constructed not to be profit centers?

Competitive Case Study

Corporate and Independent Gift Basket Sellers

There are thousands of gift basket sellers online, and one of them—perhaps surprisingly—is Sears, Roebuck and Company, which offers a list of web-exclusive gift baskets

available only online. The company's 2003 year-end sales were US$41 billion, and it is obviously better known for its appliances, tools, and Lands' End apparel, but nevertheless, Sears is a competitor in the online gift basket business. Gift baskets are an almost miniscule part of its annual sales, but Sears.com obviously considers them important enough to offer several pages of gift basket choices. The advantages that Sears enjoys in this business include its almost universally known and respected brand name, reliability, and prices, which are highly competitive. Its disadvantages include its products, the fact that it offers only standardized baskets, and its size, which is a handicap among customers who prize customization, creativity, flexibility, and personal attention. For our hypothetical gift basket seller Kim, a more directly competitive site is GothamBaskets.com, which also operates as TheGiftedOnes.com (*www.thegiftedones.com*). GothamBaskets began as a home-based online business started by a bored Wall Street entrepreneur looking for an online business opportunity. Dissatisfied with being a drop-site website, with high advertising costs that ate into profits, and with working in isolation, this owner–operator sought out a nearby established gift basket retailer, The Gifted Ones, that didn't have a website. The two businesses merged and launched a new site, TheGiftedOnes, on September 1, 2003. Both URLs take the visitor to the same site; GothamBaskets is maintained because of its search engine rankings. Combined, the two sites daily average around 1,000 visitors, many driven to the sites by Google AdWords advertising. The resulting high conversion rate helped double revenues within two months of the launch. AdWords is the partners' only advertising. Their advice is to focus on personalized service, not to worry about what the big companies do, maintain quality products and service, respond immediately to emails, and call the customer if there is a question about an order.[3]

CHECK IT OUT

Read *About Us* at TheGiftedOnes.com (*www.thegiftedones.com/index.asp*). Consider how the site creates an image that suits gift basket customers. How would you rate the site on its content, design, and construction (technology)? What could a novice online gift basket marketer learn from this site? Does it have a Kentucky Derby gift basket? If not, is that a gap for this etailer to fill?

A GLOBAL PERSPECTIVE

Are gift baskets solely a U.S. market? Go to Google UK (*www.google.co.uk/*) and search for *gift hampers.* Next, go to Google France (*www.google.fr/*) and search for *paniers de cadeau*; to Google Spain (*www.google.es/*) and search for *cestas del regalo*; to Google Germany (*www.google.de/*) and search for *geschenkkörbe;* and to Google Italy (*www.google.it/*) and search for *cestini del regalo.* Even though the languages differ, explore several websites linked from each national Google site and look for product pictures. Are there similarities to U.S. gift baskets? What is your conclusion about the global popularity of gift baskets online?

14

.COM

Marketing Site Development: Content, Design, and Construction

LEARNING OBJECTIVES

» To examine initial website development decisions
» To identify content issues that affect website development
» To understand how website design can advance site marketing goals
» To consider the impact of construction issues on website effectiveness

Adobe at the Forefront of Website Development

Adobe Systems Inc. (*www.adobe.com*), the second-largest PC software company in the United States, was a leader in imaging products long before web commercialization and the company's rise to prominence in desktop publishing. The company was founded in 1982 by computer scientists John Warnock and Charles Geschke, both former employees of Xerox Corporation's Palo Alto (California) Research Center (PARC at *www.parc.xerox.com*). Today, Adobe is known worldwide for its printing, publishing, and graphics software, including Photoshop, Illustrator, and PageMaker for web and print publishing; GoLive for web design; and InDesign for professional publishing. Adobe is also participating in deployment of the Semantic Web (*www.w3.org/2001/sw/*). Adobe offers product training using books, videos, online tutorials, seminars, and customized support. Year-end 2003 sales were US$1.295 billion (US$266 million in earnings), an increase of over 11 percent from 2002, and the company employs almost 4,000 workers worldwide. With over half a billion copies of its free electronic document

exchange software in use, Adobe Acrobat portable document format (PDF) files are the global standard for document sharing. The latest Acrobat versions have strong encryption to protect order forms and other interactive enhancements. Acrobat also supports 2D barcode technology for new forms processing. The company has created a highly customer-centric website with free downloads and many how-to features for site developers. Adobe Studio has easy-to-follow tutorials and demonstrations of how professionals have used Adobe products to create some remarkable web effects. The site exemplifies many principles of customer-centric web content, design, and construction. It is clean, clear, easy to access, searchable, and helpful. The type font is a very readable sans serif black on a white background with red highlights and few illustrations other than product pictures. Illustrations match products and are used appropriately but not excessively. It is remarkable for its lack of gratuitous animations. Adobe's website is an example of what good designers can create with exceptional products and an understanding of the *reason why* visitors come to the site.[1]

Even though new software and web hosting services have made website development far easier, faster, and cheaper than ever before, some businesses still don't need a website. They can achieve their marketing goals by selling products at auction on eBay or by using online directory listings and promotions to drive traffic offline to traditional marketing channels. However, for the vast majority of businesses, the Internet is a powerful marketing tool for selling products, providing information, satisfying customers, and achieving company goals. Customers have come to expect a business to be online, and not having a website can be commercial suicide—a costly mistake that drives customers to competitors that *are* online.

The Fundamentals of Website Development

An enterprise shows its face to the public through its website, which emphasizes the importance of making the right website development decisions. A site should reflect the enterprise's goals and image in a clear, positive way. Sites should not promise more than they can deliver, yet they must be rich enough to attract customers, serve them, and bring them back. Sites are developed through a series of interrelated, coordinated *content, design,* and *construction* (CDC) decisions. Some decisions are guided by past best practices; others are guided by the results of marketing research, data mining, and marketing intelligence. An unknown number are guided by what competitors do, and some even illegally duplicate all or parts of competitors' sites.

Although the focus of this chapter is marketing sites on the public Web, private intranets and extranets also have marketing sites that use web protocols and are developed through CDC decisions. Marketing occurs on many secure intranet sites without the majority of public Internet users being aware of their existence. Just like public sites, they too must be goal-driven and customer-friendly. Intranet websites focus internally and are often used for employee marketing. They provide information and incentives to the sales force, distribute corporate information, host newsletters and documents, and facilitate teamwork. Extranets focus both internally and externally, and facilitate communication with a select audience of joint venture partners, suppliers, preferred clients and customers, and other stakeholders. Some secured extranet websites allow one company's employees to make corporate purchases from another company's web marketing site. Some businesses create extranet marketing sites specifically for a single large corporate buyer.

THE EVOLUTION OF EARLY SITES

Information-only site
A web marketing site that provides information without interactions or online selling.

Observers of the Internet's first decade of commercialization saw a three-step pattern emerge as many websites evolved through distinct developmental stages. Initially, in the early to mid-1990s, most websites were static, **information-only sites** that provided information about the company and its products without interactions or online selling. Early sites consisted of traditional hard-copy product catalogs, brochures, or annual reports uploaded in their entirety to a web server. These sites were extremely text-intensive and remarkably free of advertising. Some sites today are still static, information-only sites that are used to reduce customer service costs and/or drive traffic offline to traditional marketing channels. By the mid- to late 1990s, as software became more sophisticated and Internet users increasingly went online with powerful computers and faster connections, many sites were quickly redesigned. Such interactive elements as email, search, and other functions were added, often along with pop-up and pop-under advertising, interactive banner ads, animation, and games. At an **interactive website,** customers can send email to the company, comment on products, search online catalogs, and participate in surveys, but they cannot directly purchase products from the site. Some business sites today use the Web to provide information and drive transactions to offline channels. By the late 1990s and early 2000s, however, large numbers of companies, including many small businesses, were selling products online from web marketing sites. For them, a **transaction website** is a highly interactive site where orders are taken and products are sold.

This three-step evolution of websites is less prevalent today. Now that web development and fulfillment software have become more user-friendly and less expensive, even small business newcomers that go online are likely to have transaction sites. Most follow one of several approaches to developing their website. *Do-it-yourselfers* use off-the-shelf web-editing software to construct the site in-house, set up their own merchant account, and then rent server space from a secure ISP host or other service provider that also helps with site registration and other tasks. *Self-maintainers* hire local consultants to build a site and create a **page template,** a predesigned web page that is set up as a model and can be easily updated with new text or images without a major redesign. Others sign up for merchant management services and web hosting offered by experienced companies such as Yahoo! Merchant Solutions (*http://smallbusiness.yahoo.com*) and are satisfied with a less unique site. After the site is online, the owner often self-maintains it, adding content and updating it as needed. This gives the owner complete control of content, keeps maintenance costs low, and facilitates budgeting for site operations. *Hands-offers* let someone else do it all, including maintenance. Whatever the site development approach, order management and fulfillment, inventory control and merchandising, and channel compatibility remain significant challenges, particularly for small businesses.

Businesses that operate by marketing concept principles put satisfying customer needs first, which in turn helps them achieve their business goals. Their customer-centric web marketing sites are developed from similarly oriented web marketing plans (Figure 14-1). They seek to satisfy customer needs and to achieve their online goals through the effective integration of website content, design, and construction. **Website content** is the core matter of the site and includes product and other information, special features, and services that customers want to access and the company needs to provide. **Website design** is the appearance and layout of the site—its style or pattern of text, graphics, and other elements constructed to function in a manner that is compatible with content and customer needs and serves the web marketing plan and enterprise goals. Design should reflect target market preferences and characteristics and should be compatible with content. **Website construction** is functionality—web technology, page coding, accessibility to multiple systems and platforms, links that work, navigation and searches that get customers where they want to go, efficient shopping baskets, inventory management, security, multimedia, page file transfers (FTPs) to web servers, server hosting and storage, and the integration of backend databases and warehouse functions with content and design processes.

Interactive website
A marketing website where customers interact with the enterprise but cannot purchase products online.

Transaction website
A highly interactive marketing website where products are sold.

Page template
A predesigned web page that is used as model and can be easily updated with new text or images without a major redesign.

Website content
The substance of the site: product and other information, special features, and services that customers want to access and the company needs to provide.

Website design
The appearance and layout of the site, a pattern of text, graphics, and other elements.

Website construction
The technical processes of a website that make the site accessible, usable, and operable.

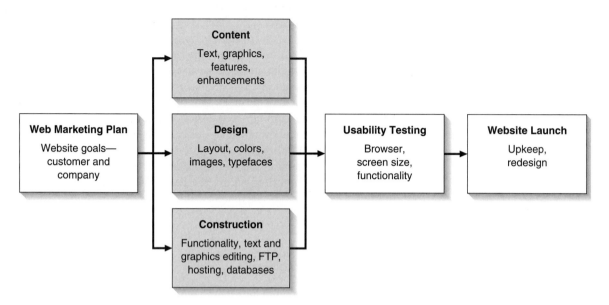

FIGURE 14-1 Developing Web Marketing Sites
Web marketing plans should direct decisions related to the development of web marketing sites. Website development decisions are about making content, design, and construction serve target market needs and achieve business goals. Design and construction are dependent on content, must be compatible with content, and should be developed concurrently with content in order to facilitate effective integration and coordination.

INITIAL SITE DEVELOPMENT DECISIONS

CDD decisions should be made concurrently because they are interrelated and mutually dependent. Content decisions are about what content is needed, who provides it, and who maintains and updates it. Content responsibilities should be primarily in-house, where product and customer knowledge are greatest. In larger businesses, designers, site architects, and database managers should be included in the decision-making process, because their responsibilities are content-related. Design and technology responsibilities are frequently outsourced to individuals and businesses that have the expertise and resources to construct or redesign sites quickly.

WEBSITE UPFRONT AND BACKEND

Upfront
The public website that the site visitor sees and directly experiences.

Web marketing sites are composed of two linked sectors: upfront and backend. **Upfront** is the public website—what the customer sees and directly experiences. Upfront is determined by customer needs, site goals, and resources available for content acquisition, design, site construction, and maintenance. Some upfronts are small-scale, essentially static product brochures (brochureware) that require little backend support and infrequent maintenance. These sites may be what customers want, principally 24/7/365 access to collateral materials, brochures, or product catalogs that they can scroll through page by page. Large-scale upfronts are far richer in media, content breadth and depth, interactivity, and features that can make a site visit come alive. However, such sites are far more costly to build and maintain, and they entail greater risk, particularly if the site is overdone with excessive, superfluous interactivity that irritates customers. Highly enhanced interactive, media-rich sites are slower to download even with broadband, can cause confusion because so much is happening at once, overload and often crash older browsers, and frustrate visitors who want information or products quickly. It is easy for web designers to become infatuated with animated .gifs, Flash, or other enhancements. Unless the website is a designer's site, it is wise to avoid giving customers more than they want or need in the way of animation, text, or features like games, contests, and downloads.

The interface is where upfront and backend interact. It is a seamless and invisible link between the public frontend and order fulfillment, data collection, and relationship management activities managed through the backend. Both are essential to smooth operations.

Whereas upfront is important in initiating and sustaining customer contact, getting customers to return and repurchase relies to a great extent on backend efficiency. **Backend** operations are hidden from public view. Backend is the functional foundation technology that supports content and design. It includes working navigation, product and information searches, order processing and fulfillment, dynamic content, data gathering, and databases that run shopping baskets, service centers, and other customer-centric operations, inventory and merchandise management, and other services. Initially, backend software was custom-coded, took a long time to create, and was very expensive. Today, the widespread availability of relatively inexpensive backend software means that backend coding is often purchased "off the shelf" and, as a result, is less expensive. It is now cost-effective for sites that at first were solely information providers to become interactive and/or transaction storefronts.

Backend
Site operations hidden from public view; the foundation technology that supports content and design, including the functionality of navigation, product and information searches, order processing, and fulfillment.

SITE DEVELOPMENT COSTS

Website development costs vary greatly, depending on such factors as the site's content and content sources, size (number of pages and amount of file space), features (forms, search, counters, inventory management, shopping baskets, and the like), activities (online sales, registration, subscription, file downloads, discussion groups, and so on), and complexity. That's why a product such as Yahoo's Merchant Solutions, with its standard monthly rate and variable transaction fees, is attractive to many web newcomers as well as established online businesses. Yahoo! offers end-to-end plans that include a platform for creating a website; managing inventory, search engine and email marketing, and dynamic cross-selling options; processing orders and payments; and tracking site performance. Its Store Editor software is menu-driven with options for creating pages and also allows users to upload pages designed in other software, such as Macromedia's Dreamweaver (*www.macromedia.com*).

Development costs for an information-only site can be as low as the cost of purchasing and learning to use a web editing program (around US$100) plus a monthly web hosting fee for a merchant DSL account of around US$40 for 250MB of disk space, 25 email accounts, and 10GB of data transfer per month. Set-up fees vary by host. Holly Hill Inn's website is typical of many information-only restaurant sites. It is a simple, attractive site with several pages for menus, a wine list, events, directions, interesting information about the restaurant, and contact information. Note the consistency of the page design and the clarity with which information is presented.

Holly Hill Inn

Holly Hill Inn in Midway, Kentucky, has an information site that invites visitors to contact the restaurant directly to make a reservation.

Copyright © 2004 by Holly Hill Inn. Reprinted with permission.

Talbot's

Talbot's primarily targets women interested in classic apparel.

Source: Courtesy Talbots.

Development costs rise as sites become more complex, adding goals, target markets, content, time-sensitive material, pages, features, and interactivity. A low-end transaction site can cost as little as US$1,500 to create and US$100 per month for hosting with 350MB of disk space, 75 email accounts, and 30GB of data transfer per month. On the other hand, sites developed by global corporations such as Microsoft (*www.microsoft.com*), Pfizer (*www.pfizer.com*), and IBM (*www.ibm.com*) cost millions and sometimes hundreds of millions of dollars to develop and maintain.

In the following paragraphs, we discuss the factors that affect development costs.

GOALS Single-goal sites generally are cheaper to develop than multi-goal sites. Multiple goals increase the number of pages required, as well as their size and complexity. Sites will disappoint visitors if the enterprise ignores their goals for visiting. Too many websites are designed for the organization (or site designers) rather than for the customer. One website that has avoided this error is Walmart.com (*www.walmart.com*). It is not a flashy site, nor does it offer cutting-edge web technology. Instead, it is highly utilitarian and tightly integrated with Wal-Mart stores. Its goals are to complement store sales by adding product depth, to test to see what products customers want, and to drive visitors to its ubiquitous stores.

TARGET(S) Targets are the site's audience, whom or what the site is designed to reach (enterprises, consumers, shareholders, or the like) and the products (goods, services, or information) they seek. Enterprise sites typically are more expensive to construct and maintain than most consumer sites. Targeting multiple buyer segments and offering multiple types of products increase costs. Talbot's (*www.talbots.com*) is a multichannel apparel retailer that primarily targets women, although men and children are secondary targets. It hosts a less complex site than Macy's (*www.macys.com*), a multichannel retailer with the same targets, but one that offers a greater product assortment of housewares, furniture, and beauty products along with apparel.

CONTENT   Content consists of the substance of the site (text or media-rich or both) and the ease or difficulty of obtaining it. Text is far cheaper than formats rich in photos, graphics, and animations. Content interactivity, transactivity, and other enhancements add complexity and cost. The *Wall Street Journal Online* site (*http://online .wsj.com/public/us*) is heavily text-based; gambling sites typically are rich in animations, color, and images.

SIZE   Size is the number of pages planned for the site, along with page and file size. More pages and larger file sizes increase costs and download times. Costs obviously are far greater for a Landsend.com (*www.landsend.com*) site, with its hundreds of pages, than for a ten-page restaurant site.

TIMING   Frequency of upkeep is an issue of timing. Static information sites need maintenance and redesign far less frequently than interactive and transaction sites. News, sports, weather, and financial services are examples of sites that require constant updating. Weather radar feeds and stock tickers may be updated in real time via continuous feeds. More frequent maintenance, redesign, and updating increase costs. CNN.com (*www.cnn.com*) has time-intensive content, hosting live radio feeds for news updates, email opt in breaking news updates, local weather updates, a stock ticker, and sports scores. Its text-based content is updated less frequently.

BUDGET   A web budget is a policy statement that specifies funds allocated for site development, maintenance, and redesign, as well as provision for web drivers. Commitment to website development is meaningless unless sufficient resources are allocated to support it. A constrained budget can force decision makers to contain costs and reduce or eliminate features that customers expect. Budget decisions also include whether advertising or other revenue-generating features will be used on the site and how to allocate the costs of promoting the site online and offline through various web drivers.

BACKEND   Greater backend development increases costs. Proprietary backend software is more costly than off-the-shelf software. Highly complex, multifunctional transaction sites are more expensive to construct, maintain, and refresh than static, information-only sites.

WEB DRIVERS   If you build it, they will not necessarily come—unless effective web drivers are deployed. For site owners selecting an end-to-end development service such as Yahoo! Merchant Solutions, various web drivers are included. The Merchant Professional option includes listings in shopping destinations, search engine pay-for-performance listings, search engine submissions and optimization, and email marketing (*http://smallbusiness.yahoo.com/bzinfo/prod/com/c3feat.php*).

TASKS   Tasks concern whether the site will be designed, implemented, and maintained in-house or outsourced. Outsourcing can reduce costs if little experience in site development is available in-house. Do-it-yourself development can lead to costly mistakes and/or longer development time. In other cases, outsourcing can increase costs, particularly if decisions about consultants and contracts are not made wisely.

Online website cost calculators such as those at GenTek Solutions, Inc. (*www.gentek .net/gentek/webcalc.html*) estimate development costs for sites with various combinations of pages, images, and features. Other cost calculators can be found by using a Google or Yahoo! search for *website development costs*.[2]

Site owners often fail to realize that maintenance costs typically far exceed development costs. Like development costs, maintenance costs also vary. Some sites need relatively little maintenance because they offer static information that does not require frequent updating. However, any site that goes several months without an update becomes stale and risks losing customers. Interactive and transaction sites and sites with time-sensitive content require more costly and more frequent maintenance—some monthly and others weekly, daily, or even multiple times during the day.

Maintenance, like development, ranges from totally *do-it-yourself* to *hands-off*. Maintaining a simple, small site can cost as little as several hundred dollars a year. Maintenance of a medium-sized site can cost from US$5,000 to US$14,000 and more. Larger, highly complex site maintenance can cost in the millions and hundreds of millions of dollars annually. Content management software can be used to simplify maintenance and, in some cases, to automate it.[3]

ENSURING PRIVACY AND SECURITY

Privacy and security are prime concerns of consumer and enterprise buyers alike. Some sites post short privacy statements on their front page; most have links from the front page to privacy statement pages within the site. Although these statements will not drive traffic to a site, it can potentially drive customers *from* a site if privacy assurance is absent or misleading. Two-thirds of active web users state that they leave a site if they are asked for personal information. Equally worrisome are the 21 percent who enter false information to gain access. Consumers are far more likely to stay on a site and surrender some personal information when prominent privacy and security statements are displayed.[4]

Because Internet users are sensitive to the collection of information about themselves and their site visits, all sites should have a clear, understandable privacy statement and should adhere to it. Privacy statement content is site-specific. A growing number of site owners adhere to TRUSTe (*www.truste.org*) privacy standards and post privacy seals on their front pages as further evidence of their commitment to privacy and to reassure visitors that an impartial third party has certified their truthfulness. Far too many sites have lengthy, obscure privacy statements that most buyers will not read or cannot decipher. Sites take this route at their own peril, for it may cost them the very visitors they are trying to convert into buyers. Some relief may be found in the Platform for Privacy Preferences Project (P3P at *www.w3.org/P3P/*) developed by the World Wide Web Consortium (W3). If it becomes widely adopted, it will become a standard for how users can gain greater control over the information collected about them when they visit a website. Sites participating in P3P will have an advantage with privacy-sensitive visitors.

Security has multiple meanings. For consumers, it is the safety of their online transactions, which requires Secure Sockets Layer (SSL) security for encrypting data transferred during online transactions and secure data storage. An Ipsos-Reid *Face of the Web* study confirms that consumer fear of credit card fraud is still keeping some people from shopping online. Credit card fraud against enterprises is a far greater threat than fraud against consumers. In 2003, consumer-not-present credit card fraud cost online merchants an estimated US$1 billion worldwide. Transaction site developers that accept credit cards must determine before site launch how backend processes can offer protection. Onsite fraud protection can be outsourced to companies such as VisualWare (*www.visualware.com/business/index.html*) and its AI Corporation's AuthentiShield (*www.smartauth.com/services/smartauth.shtml*), which provides fraud detection profiling integrated with standard credit card processing. Credit card security should be in place before any site is activated, monitored closely to make sure it is working, and replaced if it isn't.

Another security concern involves hackers and crackers. Site defacement, denial-of-service attacks, theft of data with credit card information, and other illegal acts should concern all site owners and administrators. Strong firewalls carefully checked and maintained are a necessity for transaction sites in order to ensure that stored customer data are protected. Like credit card security, firewalls must be in place before a site is activated. Most ISP hosts offer firewall protection on their servers. Web administrators should determine whether this protection is available and, if so, whether it is sufficient.

USABILITY

Usable site

A site that is easy for visitors to learn to use, is suitably constructed for its purpose, employs appropriate technology, and is user-friendly.

Most enterprises want a user-friendly, customer-centric site. That having been said, designing and implementing a usable site is more difficult than it might appear. A **usable site** is one that is easy for visitors to learn to use; has content that customers want and need; is suitably designed for its purpose; employs appropriate, efficient, and sufficient technology; and generally is user-friendly. A usable site must be designed from the start with knowledge of customers' needs, preferences, experiences, limitations, and reasons for visiting the site. This is why so many large enterprise sites use focus groups regularly to develop and test their sites. Doing so helps them avoid the *self-reference* problem, where a site is designed for the developer(s) instead of the user(s).

A different usability issue arises in connection with Section 508 of the Americans with Disabilities Act (ADA), which requires accessibility to federal agencies' electronic and information sites by people with disabilities (*www.section508.gov*). Information on accessibility issues worldwide for people with disabilities can be found at the W3C's Web Accessibility Initiative (WAI at *www.tracecenter.org/world/web/#awsg*).

Usable sites generally have features and design elements that are familiar to users from previous experience online. For example, headers should take up no more than about 25 percent of the page and should be clearly differentiated from footers. A logo should be flush left in the header masthead. Navigation bars are placed vertically on the left side of the page in a table or frame with sidebar links, in a horizontal strip across the top of the page (below the mast), and/or in the footer at the bottom of the page. A search should be offered in a standard small, rectangular search box placed onscreen in a highly visible location, usually at page top right or center right. It makes no sense to change the style and force visitors to search for the search box. A home linking icon is placed header left. Modification date, copyright date, privacy links, disclaimers, and additional contact links go in the footer. Primary links are placed first, followed by secondary links. This is not an exhaustive list; it merely suggests how many usability features site developers must consider.[5] Consistency, another usability factor, demands uniformity of elements throughout a site. If a left-hand vertical navigation bar is used on the front page, it should be used throughout the site on the left-hand side of the screen. In the past, frames were not recommended because most browsers could not read them. That has changed, however; today's browsers can read frames and the antiframe bias is fading. Typeface and font size, colors and page width, and image types and sizes should be standardized, or at least be complementary, on every page. Consistency makes it easier for visitors to use the site, reinforces the site's visual identity, and reassures them that they are still on the site even when they have traveled several pages within it. This is also why page titles should be used as page markers.

Usability testing

A process in which testers actually use and report on site functions to ensure that a site is usable and that all features work as planned.

Although usability consultants are readily available, and they generally offer expensive testing alternatives, usability testing can be performed inexpensively in-house. **Usability testing,** in-house or outsourced, requires using the site, testing its features, and making sure the site operates as expected. Current site visitors and customers can help with usability testing, systematically using site features to ensure that everything works as planned. After all, who is better able to determine whether a site is easy to use than the people who are already customers or visitors? The Motley Fool's (*www.MotleyFool.com*) usability manager brings in a group of site users every two weeks to observe how they move through the site and interact with its financial service features. With their help, problems are quickly pinpointed and resolved. The key to effective testing is to do it often with the right subjects while the site is under development, when it is launched, and throughout its use and eventual redesign. In-house testing can be highly cost-effective.[6]

Free-form testing consists of asking individuals (customers and others) to surf the site without a specific task to complete and then collecting their comments. In *directed* or *task-based* testing, users are given specific tasks to perform and then are monitored as they perform them. Testers attempt to determine how easily users interact with the site. They observe whether users encounter difficulties, get lost, or become frustrated because they can't find a product. They want to know what users like and what they hate. For example, a women's apparel site might direct testers to search for a woman's short-sleeve pink cotton turtleneck sweater, size medium. The testers' keystrokes and movements through the site are observed as they search for the product, use the shopping basket, and complete the order. Individuals testing a financial services site might be directed to set up a portfolio and purchase selected

Drill down

Moving from the front page through successive pages in the site to the page(s) where the task is completed.

quantities of several stocks. These processes require significant **drill down**—that is, the user has to move from the front page through successive pages to the page(s) where the task is completed. The *three-click rule,* which suggests that a visitor should be able to reach his or her destination page in only three to four clicks, is often used as a measure of design efficiency. In reality, however, reaching the destination often takes far more drilling. Testing can determine whether drill down is excessive, and analysis can identify click reduction strategies. Excessive drill down drives away prospective customers.

Selecting the right participants for a usability test is critical. Usability testing of existing or relaunched sites should be conducted with current customers. For prelaunch testing, a visitor relationship management company or online marketing research and website evaluation company such as SurveySite (*www.surveysite.com*) can assemble panels of testers. Once a site is launched, server logs record what pages and features visitors click on and help identify problem areas. The points at which shopping baskets are abandoned can be exposed through server log file analysis, but further study is needed to determine *why* buyers break off before completing the transaction. Usability testing is an ongoing process at large sites.

Alternatively, a web development team can identify the site's target markets and run simulations of their site usage. This requires personifying representative users, developing scenarios for how they use the site, and testing the site by assuming visitor characteristics and using the site as users would. This technique is called a *pluralistic walkthrough.* It can be helpful in identifying problem areas, particularly prelaunch.[7] It can also give misleading results, because it relies heavily on the ability of developers to second-guess buyers.

The 80-20 rule also applies to usability. In this context, it reminds us that 80 percent of the time, only 20 percent of the pages in a site are heavily used. Server log files can identify these pages. They are the core content pages, the ones that must be the most user-friendly and the freshest.[8]

SITE REDESIGN

Initially, the Web was such a new environment that few early sites were anything more than just rough sketches or visions in developer's heads of how pages might be linked together. New pages were added without regard to a master plan, which in many cases did not exist. Sites sprouted branches in all directions, with pages that displayed *Under Construction* signs and others that deadended. Within a relatively short time, particularly as sites evolved, disorganization became more glaring and irritating to visitors. Some site administrators realized sooner, and others later, that a site redesign was necessary. Customer feedback, focus group results, and server log files that indicate declining or stagnant site use can indicate when a redesign is required. Web competitive marketing intelligence can indicate when competitors have redesigned their sites, which often triggers other sites to redesign. However, reactive redesign is less desirable than proactive redesign initiated because the site needs it. Widespread adoption of larger monitors, faster connections, updated graphical browsers, and new applications software, as well as changes in competitor's sites, are valid triggers for site redesign.

The extent of site redesign varies from a simple touchup of several pages to a complete site overhaul and relaunch. Touchups or simple maintenance may simply require changing product or price lists, updating contact information (phone, fax, address), or reducing typeface size. Static billboards may need nothing more than a copyright date rollover. Overhauls are more extensive and involve content, site architecture, design, and backend operations. Transaction sites typically revise products, prices, and information on a regular basis. Some products are seasonal, so updates occur when seasons change or for sales. Other sites offer information that must be changed daily or multiple times each day. News sites in particular require continuous upkeep, as do financial sites that offer real-time stock market updates and weather sites that broadcast *weather maps in motion.*

As sites evolve, they usually need an overhaul and integration between online and offline operations, upfront and backend. Although a large-scale redesign may be necessary, customers will not necessarily like it. Some resist learning how to navigate a redesigned site and resent having to do so. Sometimes an incremental redesign, rolled out over several months, is less disturbing than an immediate radical makeover that changes an old friend into a complete stranger.

Some sites undergo continuous design modification. For example, InfoWorld (*www.infoworld.com*) went online in late 1999 and had hundreds of design adjustments within its first months of operation. These changes were driven by visitor email comments, survey and online focus group results, and customer tracking. Market research showed that InfoWorld served at least three diverse markets: hard-core tech-savvy programmers, high-level strategic nontech managers, and a large middle-ground audience seeking technology news. Site redesign efforts for this user-centric business began with developing scenarios for each key target market. These users were personified as *Mike the Mad Manager, Pete the Powerful Programmer,* and *Ned the (Tech) Newshound.* The challenge was to create a site that served the needs of all three markets. Site developers also realized that even when the site was redesigned, they could not let it get stale, so redesign was built into the budget and corporate culture. In March 2003, InfoWorld announced a top-to-bottom site redesign based on research that identified what its magazine subscribers and site visitors wanted, primarily "breaking news and analysis, independent product reviews, shared best practices among peers and aggregated information on specific technologies and products." The new site has improved navigation and interactivity, an elegant new look, and increased advertising potential. Substantial investment was made in both its frontend and backend.[9]

Redesign plans should reflect what visitors value in a site and what frustrates them, as well as their buying behaviors. First, visitors need to be able to find the site. Next, they need to be able to find what they want in three to four clicks, or they will abandon the site. Most visitors (over 80 percent) cite ease of use and navigation as their top concern. Other concerns include fast downloads, quality content, fresh information, accessible customer service, organized content, search engines (on large sites), front page look (and feel), and overall site aesthetics. Animated graphics are the least important design element.[10]

Rapid site redesigns sometimes occur because of unexpected events. This happened at news sites on Tuesday, September 11, 2001, when terrorists hijacked four passenger aircraft, flying two into the World Trade Center buildings in New York City, one into the Pentagon in Washington, and another into a field in Pennsylvania. Record site traffic levels were recorded at CNN.com (*www.cnn.com*), MSNBC (*www.msnbc.msn.com*), and ABC (*http://abcnews.go.com*) after the attacks. MSNBC counted over 12.5 million unique visitors in the next twenty-four hours. MSNBC stripped its homepage of all graphics and contracted with third parties to rent additional server space in order to shorten download times and allow more visitors access to the site. CNN did the same. At that time, the site normally served 14 million visitors, but on the day of the attacks, it was receiving about 9 million visitors *an hour,* which rose to 19 million an hour by Wednesday. *USAToday* (*www.usatoday.com*) took a different approach. It did not strip its pages but instead created an entirely new homepage devoted just to the unfolding tragedy. These sites removed advertising entirely or greatly reduced it. The *Wall Street Journal Online* (*www.wsj.com*), which normally restricts access to many of its pages to subscribers, opened its entire site to all visitors from 10 p.m. Tuesday through 6 p.m. Wednesday in response to the emergency, as did the *New York Times Online* (*www.nytimes.com*).[11]

Website Content

On the Web, content is king. Content is what visitors seek at a site, and fresh content keeps them coming back. Content online comprises both verbal (text) and nonverbal elements. Verbal content includes product descriptions, newspaper and magazine stories, dictionaries, travel schedules, and the like. Nonverbal content includes images and graphics, as well as such interactive devices as insurance and mortgage calculators; currency converters; news, weather, and sports real-time tickers; and electronic slot machines. A site's market offer is made through its content. Some offers are heavily text-based; others use multimedia, text, and nontext elements. Content decisions both drive and must be integrated with design and construction decisions.

Content "shelf life" varies. Reference materials that rarely need updating, such as topographical maps and dictionaries, have a long shelf life. Content on financial, weather, and news sites has an extremely short shelf life and requires dynamic updating several times a day or, in the case of stock market tickers, real-time streaming content. Content with a medium shelf life is updated weekly, monthly, or within a six-month period. The challenge is to keep content fresh enough to satisfy customers without overwhelming content providers and web administrators and precipitously increasing costs.

Although the Web is a multimedia environment, many sites are heavily text-based. Web writing is not the same as writing for print newspapers or magazines. Web text should be shorter, more concise, useful, and interactive where appropriate, but not gratuitously so. Information should be *chunked*—that is, broken into small, related, more easily digested segments separated by headings and subheadings. For example, the *Wall Street Journal Online* (*www.wsj.com*) front page has a prominent box with large type that reads "What's News." The font size and box draw the visitor's eye to a section of news headline teasers with links to longer articles on pages within the site. Teasers are used to link headlines to full articles. Teasers are also used on other sites. Google (*www.google.com*) uses "New!" in a bright red teaser for new services. Amazon.com (*www.amazon.com*) has a "What's New" right-hand sidebar box on its homepage.

KISS (Keep It Simple Stupid) is advised for most but not all web writing. This is not meant to imply that visitors are stupid, only that many find reading online tiring, so they tend to scan rather than concentrate. As a result, web text should be scannable, which saves the reader time. In most cases, web text should be objective, not puffery or hype, and should use accessible language, not technical jargon.[12]

The Web's interactivity and browser support of colors, sound, visual images, animation, and other features makes nonverbal content prominent on many websites. The tendency with animation is overkill: wretched excess that overwhelms the visitor and clutters the screen, moving images and floating advertisements that distract and irritate rather than entertain or drive a purchase. Images should be used sparingly and for a clear purpose that advances site and page goals. Original photographs or drawings are preferred to overused clip art. Streaming audio and video should be used sparingly and only if research has indicated that the target markets in question use browsers and fast connections that can access the files. Server log files can determine what browser most visitors and (especially) preferred customers are using, and this information should carry significant weight in decisions about using streaming files. Streaming video is still a problem for many people who use slow connections. For them, images are jerky, with action and sound often not synchronized. As speedier connections become the norm, this will become less of a problem. KISS is also advised for nonverbal content. The major exceptions are gambling and game sites, where animation, blinking images, loud colors, and blaring sound excite the visitor and stimulate greater interaction with the site. Sites targeted to children are also more likely to be rich in graphics, colors, and animation.

FINDING CONTENT

Content decisions are about what to offer on a site, where to find it, and who will provide it. Site developers should create a *content catalog* that identifies what content it must offer, where that content can be found, and how often it should be refreshed (updated). Content depends on site goals and on the *reason why* customers are there. A small pet-grooming business with an information-only site has an extremely simple, limited content requirement. The purpose is to have an online presence as a driver to its offline location. The site is no more than several pages, which provide a description of services offered, operating hours, prices, contact information, pet tips, and a map to the business. It has a relatively long shelf life and will not need frequent redesign. Content at other sites is far more complex and spread over multiple pages—sometimes hundreds or even thousands nested in directories and subdirectories, with different refreshment schedules.

Most marketing departments in large enterprises regularly generate original content for advertising copy, sales promotions, collateral materials, direct marketing, public relations, events, publicity, and sales manuals. Content may be taken without alteration from these sources or produced uniquely for a site, or it may be assembled using a combination of these approaches. Hard-copy brochures scanned and converted to HTML and then uploaded to a web server are still used on brochureware sites. In this case, little or no content is unique to the site.

Some sites have onsite interactive catalogs for easy reference and ordering. For example, the apparel company Coldwater Creek (*www.coldwatercreek.com*) has a catalog quick-order search where a customer can order from one of the company's currently circulating mail catalogs. Hard-copy catalogs are presented online with few if any alterations. Customers enter the catalog item number and are sent directly to an order form. Alternatively, a customer can also search for products in an interactive online catalog.

Other sites have content that is completely original, without an offline equivalent. In some cases, content that originates online is later reproduced in an offline catalog. Eziba (*www.eziba.com*) offers handcrafted products sourced worldwide. Originally, it was a clicks-only site with completely original content. Today, it also has a mail catalog that reproduces some online content in hard copy, as well as a growing number of retail stores.

Content sometimes is stolen from other sites. Copying online content is so easy that it encourages theft. Bold copyright statements posted on website front pages will not stop a committed thief. Relatively few sites follow up and prosecute content theft; most site owners don't have the resources to track down and sue offenders. Images are the most tempting targets, but lines of text and sometimes entire pages and whole sites are stolen.

Content can be legally obtained from content providers, sometimes without cost but more often for a one-time use or subscription fee. A site can link to a weather ticker without charge by joining Weather.com's (*www.weather.com*) *Weather on Your Site* affiliate program. Dynamically generated content (*Weather Magnet* or *Weather Viewer*) is inserted on a page with just a few lines of cut-and-paste HTML code. Tickertech.com (*www.javaticker.com/home.mpl*) offers stock and sports tickers, charts, news, and other content. As its name implies, Cartoonlink.com (*www.cartoonlink .com*) has email cartoons as well as cartoons for web pages. Dr. Wilson's weekly syndicated marketing tips *Web Marketing Today* (*www.wilsonweb.com*) appear on over 350 subscribing sites.

Content can be purchased from freelancers and professional service providers. EffectiveContent.com (*www.effectivecontent.com*) offers content for real estate, automotive, finance, and travel sites. In the real estate area, it lists over 500 separate pages of information on a wide variety of topics. A site can select specific topics or purchase entire packages. Under the heading *Buying a Home*, pages are available for *Financial Preparation, Finding a Home, Building a Home, Home Inspections*, and related topics. This type of service may be too expensive for some small businesses, but the benefits are obvious for those sites that can afford it. The problem with syndicated content is keeping it fresh. When too many sites in the same industry use identical syndicated content, duplication conveys a negative impression.

MANAGING CONTENT

Content management
An organized system for identifying what content is needed, procuring it, determining when and how content should be changed, and implementing the changes.

All sites need **content management,** an organized system for identifying what content is needed, procuring it, determining when and how content should be changed, and implementing the changes. Small sites, particularly static information-only sites,

Content audits
Monitoring the site and its pages on a regular basis to identify, remove, and replace outdated content.

can manage content manually in-house through **content audits,** monitoring the site and its pages on a regular basis to remove and replace outdated content. Customer comments can be extremely helpful in identifying new content that should be added or in pinpointing problem spots.

Content management can become overwhelming as sites evolve, grow, and add pages. Links get broken and users begin to complain about receiving annoying 404 error messages. Dynamic content makes the task even more daunting. Site complexity and/or large numbers of pages make it impossible to manage manually. Site owners and web administrators often turn to automated processes or outsource content management when it no longer is possible to visualize the entire site. This also occurs when a site evolves to a transaction stage, when it is personalized, has many different types of content, and when it requires frequent design changes.

ORGANIZING CONTENT

Web storyboarding
A process that identifies what text and visual content will be contained on web pages and how the pages will be linked.

Smaller businesses that are developing or refreshing website content may use a marketing communication technique known as **web storyboarding.** Storyboarding identifies what text and visual content, design elements, and enhancements will be contained on web pages and how the pages will be linked. Storyboarding can be developed manually or with the help of storyboarding software such as BoardMaster (*www.boardmastersoftware.com*) or electronic presentation software such as Power-Point (*http://office.microsoft.com/en-us/FX010857971033.aspx*).

Some site developers storyboard using three-by-five-inch Post-it Notes or notecards, with each card representing one web page. This process begins with brainstorming what content is needed for the site, starting with the front page and creating cards for every page nonsequentially. Once content has been placed on separate cards, the cards are sorted, laid on a flat surface, and moved around to represent relationships and hypertext links.

Another approach to storyboarding is using PowerPoint slides, with each slide representing a different web page. The slides are printed, separated, and then sorted into the appropriate order. This can also be accomplished electronically by using the PowerPoint program and shuffling slides in the slide editor, but doing so can be more difficult to visualize than shuffling tangible cards.

Template pages
Pages that serve as models for the consistent use of text, graphics, and layout.

Storyboarding offers important advantages for those developing a site or involved in its upkeep. It forces developers to concentrate on content, identify key information that must be included, and design a clear path through the pages. Examining the laid-out storyboard should bring any omissions to light. Designers and technical people can contribute their expertise at this point, making suggestions that unify page content and head off problems that might otherwise arise later in the development process. Storyboarding should lead to the development of **template pages,** pages that serve as models to encourage the consistent use of text, graphics, and layout. By duplicating the basic elements of each page, site developers maintain consistency and facilitate usability.

Storyboard pages typically include detailed information that guides HTML coding. Each page should be identified with a descriptive title that will become the web page title. Text elements, image captions, links, and other relevant pieces of information are on the cards or attached to notes. An important note for each page should be to add a copyright statement, typically of the form ([© date]), and a disclaimer that the site owner is not responsible for the content of external sites linked from the owner's site.

THE POWER OF THE FRONT PAGE

As soon as visitors reach a site, the front page should clearly let them know what the site is about. The front page is also called a splash, home, or entry page. Highly stylized, ambiguous front pages frustrate and confuse visitors, often speeding their departure from the site. It is important to get to the point and make it easy for visitors to move from the front page to their destination with as few clicks as possible. Ideally, but often not realistically, visitors should be able to get to the reason why they came to the site within three or four clicks.

The front page should be customized with a logo, contact information (address, phone, fax, and the like), navigation bar, and an appealing image that reflects the enterprise and its goals. It should be a single screen with no scroll down or scroll across. The most important content should be displayed within the top 350 pixels of the screen, where visitors look first and often make a split-second decision about whether to stay or go.

Website Design

Design is the way a site looks (visual images) and how a visitor experiences it (its feel). Good design rules differ depending on the type of site, the industry it is in, and its size, goals, and target market. Good design reflects attention to detail, functionality, and creativity, all based on user needs and the reasons why they visit the site. Design also applies to a website's structure and organization and (increasingly) to its aural appeal. It is a plan for how content will be organized and presented on the front and subsequent pages with text, graphics, animation, and other features. Website design is a combination of aesthetics and usability.

Unlike books, magazines, and other traditional hard-copy materials, websites are *nonlinear*. Visitors can jump within a page from one place to another, within a site from one page to another, or from one site to another. A visitor can easily become disoriented and, after several jumps, be unsure of his or her present location. This discontinuity underscores the importance of design consistency. Taking pains to achieve the same look and feel on the front and subsequent pages provides a visual anchor that orients visitors and helps clarify their location. It also emphasizes the importance of always using page titles as site identifiers.

Most pages should be designed for skimming unless the site is educational, contains reference material, or is used for training. Lengthy text that scrolls on for multiple screen lengths stands an excellent chance of never being read. The sound-bite generation, weaned on *Sesame Street* and MTV delivery speeds, is less receptive to text-intensive pages. Seniors, who are more likely to be readers, often need larger text that makes pages appear longer. Although the user can change font size, page designers cannot rely on visitors' making this adjustment. Language should be appropriate to the audience and jargon-free.

Site developers should create a *visual catalog* that identifies what logos must be used, color palettes, font choices, graphics, and other design elements. They also need to develop a hierarchy of importance, identifying the most important page elements and giving them primacy.

Navigation is a design as well as a construction issue. Navigation includes the visual interface that visitors access and the actual linking. Functional navigation icons are essential and must be readily identified as *hot,* or hypertext-linked. The standard for identifying hot icons is a blue frame around a graphic, underlined blue text font, and a hand that appears when the mouse moves across either. These visual cues are the default cues on most browsers and should be adhered to for the sake of consistency and to avoid confusing visitors.

Users have a significant amount of control over website design. They can adjust the size of their screen and font size by using browser preference menus. They can influence colors by not calibrating their screens to show web-safe colors. If they copy a page, it typically loses all formatting. Some people turn graphics off to speed download times and see the site as text only. Others turn off sound cards. Slow connection speeds and insufficient computer memory can limit access to enhanced site features. The user's browser default font selection overrides special fonts used on a website unless the font is a graphical image.

WEBSITE ATMOSPHERICS AND FLOW AESTHETICS

Web Update

For updates and more on this topic, visit the textbook student website at http://college.hmco .com/business/students and select Siegel, Internet Marketing, 2e.
Good Website Design

A retail store establishes a mood and sustains its image through such features as color schemes, product displays, floor layouts, dressing room fixtures, music, flooring, salesperson uniforms and attentiveness, products, promotions, and pricing. Differences in store atmospherics are readily apparent right from the front door. An upscale department store such as Neiman Marcus (*http://neimanmarcus.com/index.jhtml*) is obviously very different from a Target (*www.target.com*), although both promote style. The same customers may shop both, but their expectations for experiences at each store will differ sharply. Their expectations are often confirmed from website atmospherics—design elements used site-wide to establish a mood and consistent image. A site can be visualized as a landscape on the Web, or a *webscape.*

Consistency is achieved by adopting a page model and replicating it for each page in the site. This template specifies primary, secondary, and complementary colors; font type and size; graphics; navigation bars, buttons, marks, and icons; and other elements standardized site wide, although page content will vary. Consistency also requires the use of only one logo on all pages. Screen size should be set either at no more than 590 pixels for a 640-pixel-wide screen or at no more than 760 pixels for an 800-pixel-wide screen. The navigation icons, buttons, bars, or lines should appear at the same place on each page. Ideally, navigation will include *breadcrumbs,* a tracer that shows where the visitor is and how he or she got there. On an apparel site, they might take the form: <u>Home</u> > <u>Products</u> > <u>Clothes</u> > <u>Sweaters</u>.

Feng Shui, or the Chinese art of arranging objects harmoniously, offers many insights for site designers. *Web Shui* suggests that there should be a flow to each page, an energy that comes from the compatible arrangement of elements. In the virtual environment of the web page, visitors should be able to move easily from one feature to the next as their right brain processes graphical images and their left brain absorbs alphanumeric text, merging the two to provide an intuitive understanding of the site. Even the U.S. government advocates the concept of Web Shui, where a good website is one that satisfies users, not designers.[13]

Flow is apparent in bricks-and-mortar stores when customers are so familiar with the store layout and the location of frequently purchased products that they can navigate the space easily without conscious effort. Websites should be designed so that customers can do the same online—that is, so that they can navigate the space at a low level of cognitive processing because of its familiarity and flow.

LAYOUT ISSUES

Layout is a plan for the way design features relate to one another on a page and for the arrangement of the pages in a website. Layouts differ according to site goals, target audiences, and resources. Sites in the same product or industry category often share some layout characteristics, but a quick look at their site maps shows how pages differ. For example, website front pages of print broadsheet newspapers typically have a masthead with the same logo used on the hard-copy version and text blocks three to four columns wide with organization similar to the print version. Little if any animation appears in stories, although some may be used in advertising, often within vertical skyscrapers and increasingly with floating pop-ups. Text is black on a white background, and pictures are relatively small. On the other hand, gambling sites use a generous amount of flashy animation, reverse type (white on a black background, gold on a dark purple background), and bold colors, in an effort to convey the excitement of casino gambling. Government sites are very conservative, use black text on white backgrounds, are text-intensive and not very colorful, and generally emphasize functionality over creativity. Layout and design tips can be found at a number of websites, including the Web Style Guide (*www.webstyleguide.com/index.html?/contents.html*) and Useit.com, Jakob Nielsen's site (*www.useit.com*).

In the following paragraphs, we consider some layout recommendations.

PAGE SAFE AREA   New desktop and many laptop browsers generally display a 800-by-600-pixel screen, and sometimes wider. The safe screen area for displaying and printing a web page is slightly smaller (760-by-410 pixels). Users can control page size by engaging their browser's *fit-to-page* option. Most users don't know that this option exists. Pages that are too wide require side-to-side scrolling; too long pages require top-to-bottom scrolling. Neither is desirable on most transaction sites.

HEADER AND FOOTER   A front page should begin with a heading (masthead), which typically includes a logo, graphic, and other identifying information. Key information should be top loaded—placed within the first 350 pixels so that visitors can see it without scrolling down. A footer should contain basic information about the page owner, copyright and contact information, a privacy statement, a disclaimer, and (often) a logo or graphic that reinforces the header.

TYPEFACE   In the context of the Web, the term *typography* refers to electronic type composition (letterforms) measured in pixels. It is the design of letters, numbers, and symbols. Choices for online typeface are far more limited than for mechanical type. Certain type families are recommended because they are read unchanged by the majority of graphical browsers. Georgia, Verdana (also Arial), Chicago, Courier, Times New Roman (also Times), and Geneva are popular online fonts. Although a site may be constructed in one of these typefaces, a browser will not read them as such unless it stores that particular typeface. Instead, the site will appear in the browser's default font, usually Times or Times New Roman. Typefaces can be read unchanged by browsers if they are created as a graphic in a design program such as Adobe Photoshop. Excessive mixing of typefaces on a page is not recommended, but a sans serif font (such as Verdana or Arial) is often used for headlines to contrast with a serif font (such as Times New Roman or Georgia) used for body text (see Figure 14-2). Overly large and overly small fonts should be avoided. Capital (upper-case) letters should be used sparingly and only where appropriate. Words that appear in all capitals, other than company logos, scream at visitors and are more difficult to read than a mixture of upper case and lower case. A text-only option should be available for visitors without graphical browsers, people with visual disabilities who are using digital readers, and those who want to speed downloads. Notice of the availability of a text-only option should appear in the header or at the beginning of the body on the front page. There are at least 1,900 available language fonts from Abkhasian to Zuñi (*www .linguistsoftware.com*).

ALIGNMENT   Text should be left-justified. Avoid center-aligned and right-justified text layouts, which are harder to read. The exception is the navigation bar that is often centered at the bottom of a page, a logo centered at the top of a page, and a search box at center page or page right.

TEXT BLOCKS   Text blocks should be broken into smaller segments or more readable chunks. Text block chunks can be used as design elements separating information presented in other formats and layout sectors. Lengthy text should be separated into pages linked from a table of contents or introductory page. Chunk information into

---

THIS IS 12-POINT SANS SERIF (Folio)
It has no cut marks (tiny flat areas) at the end of the lines and looks clean

THIS IS 12-POINT SERIF (Palatino)
It has cut marks (tiny flat areas) at the end of the lines and is easier to read

---

FIGURE 14-2 A sans serif typeface is often used for headlines and a serif typeface for body copy.

segments that appeal to visitors and allow them to select what they want to read. Visitors typically will not tolerate more than a ten-second download time, which is a strong incentive to avoid overly long and graphics-rich pages.

TABLES   Tables are often used as design elements and arranged to anchor text and graphics on a screen. Avoid lengthy tables that can spread across two or more typed pages. They are difficult to read; remember that table headers disappear when the user scrolls down past the first page. It is better to use several smaller tables than one extremely large table. Another option is to use cells within a table to set off content.

FRAMES   Although frames are more acceptable with newer browser versions, many browsers still cannot read them. Therefore, it is better to use tables to anchor layout elements than to use frames, at least for now.

SITE MAP   A site map should be used for sites with twenty or more pages. It is a road map or interactive overview of the pages in a site and their organization. Google has a particularly clear site map at *www.google.com/sitemap.html*.

COLORS   Color, a design element that conveys messages, creates contrasts, and stimulates emotions, is a powerful tool for the website designer. Color schemes involve the selection of primary, secondary, and accent colors. Primary colors are darker and bolder than secondary colors. Accent colors are darker and bolder than either primary or secondary colors. Overly rich, bold background colors and designs increase download times and distract visitors from the text. Because type should contrast with background color, the darker the background color, the lighter the type. Bear in mind that reverse type (light type on a dark background) is harder to read, particularly when it is very small. Some color combinations, including yellow type on a blue background, red type on a green background, and green type on a red background, are extremely difficult to read.

LINKS   All pages should link back to the homepage via a wagon wheel design. No page should deadend. Pages should have bidirectional links that go backward, perhaps to the homepage, and forward to another page. Links should be checked regularly to ensure that they still work. Link checks can be performed manually or automatically with link-checking software (see *http://home.snafu.de/tilman/xenulink.html*).

SEARCH   Search boxes typically are placed in the top part of a web page in the header or just under it. They should be simple, load quickly, and provide instructions for simple and advanced searches.

ORGANIZATION   Pages are arranged in hierarchical, radial tree, wagon wheel, or other form. The first page is the home, splash, or entry page. This page shapes the first impression a visitor forms of a site and links to content pages. Sites should avoid being too shallow, with too many top-level content pages, or too deep, with top-level content pages that lead to large numbers of second-level pages.

MENUS   A menu is a list of links or submenus for other pages in the site. It can be pulldown, rollover, or another form. Menus should function as categorized mini-site maps.

FAQS   Where appropriate, sites should include a Frequently Asked Questions (FAQ) page. Visitor comments and questions can be used as FAQ content.

VISUAL AXIS   Most target audiences in the Western hemisphere read from top to bottom and from left to right. Page layout should reflect this preference. The top of the screen is dominant for such readers.

FEEDBACK   Feedback options, particularly email, are typically offered on a separate content page. They include response forms, guest books, requests for information, and surveys.

GRAPHICS AND ANIMATION

Some of the flashiest sites are targeted to gamblers and children. Filled with bold colors, bright contrasts, and lots of movement, they are designed as attention grabbers, not for lengthy reading. These sites deliberately break the generally accepted rule of limiting animated graphics to one or two per page.

Some sites still display far too many horizontal rules, bullets, flashing icons, pulsating text, buttons, and other embellishments. Page fade-ins and Java script text scrolling have also been overdone. They were used extensively in the early days of web commercialization, but now they look outdated and unprofessional. Contemporary web design emphasizes the use of small, appropriate graphics. Randomized graphics are a useful method for displaying an array of images without cluttering a page. The images appear in a box and change at regular intervals to give the site a fresh appearance. This technique is often used on university homepages to show a constantly varying montage of campus life scenes.

Many website owners cannot afford custom graphics. Instead, they rely on far cheaper, off-the-shelf images. The declining cost of digital cameras has also reduced the expense of creating custom images. Royalty-free web-ready digital stock pictures are available online at such sites as GettyImages's Photodisc (*http://creative.gettyimages.com/photodisc*) and Picturequest (*www.picturequest.com*).

Simple is best for most graphics decisions. What is interesting when new and fresh becomes irritating when old and overdone. For that reason, it is best to avoid using hit counters on a front page. They are meaningless additions in any case, because gross duplicated hits are highly inaccurate traffic counts. If they show a very low count, it implies that the site is an unvisited backwater. If a hit counter must be used, it should be invisible to visitors.

Web users are notoriously short on patience. A widely used rule of thumb for how long visitors are willing to wait for a page to download is ten seconds. To apply the ten-second rule, be sure the front page is no larger than 100 kilobytes so that the page can download in several seconds. For the same reason, avoid excessive use of large size graphics. Because most browsers can read no more than 72 pixels per inch (PPI), higher-resolution graphics are a waste of space and cause unnecessarily slow downloads.

Under Construction warnings and animated .gifs showing construction workers in hard hats are tiresome and unnecessary. Fortunately, their use is diminishing. Another irritant is overly large 404 error messages that stridently blame the visitor for making an address mistake. It is better to custom-design an error message clearly stating that the error is not the visitor's fault, explains why it occurred, and outlines the alternatives for finding the requested page.

The last several years have seen the introduction of streaming audio and video, Flash animation, video clips, and other new forms. Not all browsers can open these files. Often they require downloading a plug-in, which some visitors will not or cannot do, so the impact is lost. In the case of Portable Network Graphics (PNG), which was designed to replace older graphics formats, most older browsers cannot read PNG-8 or PNG-24, so a broken icon appears on the browser screen. At this time, PNG is probably not a desirable option unless the site's target audience is highly likely to be operating up-to-date browsers.

SPECIAL CONSIDERATIONS

Some target markets and visitors need special consideration. For example, the numbers of online visitors who do not speak English are increasing. If a site's target audience includes such readers, consideration should be given to providing translations or mirror sites in their language.

People with disabilities are another audience that is frequently overlooked. They include people with visual impairments, people who are deaf, and people with limited motor skills. People who are colorblind cannot process color images and therefore cannot distinguish colored icons from a colored background. Because colors appear gray to them, icons should include text descriptors to avoid leaving such readers stranded on a page. Users with impaired hearing may need visual readers to interpret streaming audio.[14] The alt tags in HTML can be used to provide explanations for how graphics function so that site visitors using digitized speech software will hear the contents of a web page. This underscores the importance of providing text captions for all pictures and images.

If seniors are a site's target market, they may also need special attention. Because older people frequently have some visual impairment, readability can be improved by using a sans serif typeface and at least twelve- or fourteen-point type. Text should not be written completely in capital letters but in both upper case and lower case. As we have noted, text is easiest to read when it is left-justified; center alignment is the most difficult to read. The colors yellow, blue, and green should be separated because older people often have difficulty discriminating among them. Patterned backgrounds and reverse type (white on dark backgrounds) are particularly difficult to read and should be avoided.[15]

Website Construction

Construction requires using technology, software, and databases to create web pages and sites and install them on web servers. The early years of web commercialization were marked by a tidal wave of new technologies, which made website development more difficult because it required constantly learning new software and mastering new techniques. The learning curve was very steep, and development time and costs were high for sites striving to be on the cutting edge. Today, the technology is even more complex, but developers are more experienced and better trained, a happy circumstance that partially accounts for decreasing website development costs.

It is beyond the scope of this book to explore web construction in great depth or to deal with such issues as which platform to use—Windows NT, Macintosh, or Linux. Realistically, few corporate marketing or brand managers, salespeople, advertising or sales promotion professionals have more than a nodding acquaintance with such issues, and most leave construction to the experts. Small and medium-size enterprise (SME) marketers are more likely to be personally involved with website development and with the technical professionals who do the construction that makes content and design work as planned.

PREPARING CONTENT

Content must be coded before pages can be transferred and stored on a web server. Website developers who spend their professional lives constructing pages and sites typically write HTML code. Large, complex sites have teams of programmers constructing pages. SMEs that create sites in-house are far less likely to have developers writing HTML. Their alternative is to use image-editing software, such as the professional graphics standard Adobe Photoshop (*www.adobe.com*) or Macromedia Fireworks (*www.macromedia.com*), and web page editors such as Adobe's GoLive or Macromedia's Dreamweaver.

Web pages carefully coded or created by popular page editors can still be a problem for some browsers. Not all browsers interpret code the same way and this can lead to broken links, missing graphics, and unreadable text. Anyone who is creating pages should check them on all current browsers. Each page should be closely examined in both Netscape and Microsoft Explorer, and on Windows and Macintosh operating systems, at the least, before being transferred to a server. Pages should be viewed with a text-only browser or a graphical browser with images and sound turned off. Most developers do not transfer pages directly to a server without first checking them in a staging area, a place on the server that is closed to public view.

BACKEND CONSTRUCTION

Marketers typically are not directly responsible for constructing or installing backend systems that manage inventory and fulfillment, but they do contribute to determining what data will be collected and used. They also manipulate databases once these are established. Marketers have pushed for the use of personalization as a customer retention tool, and personalization requires establishing a comprehensive database, warehouse, and mining rules. Using the Internet to sell, up-sell, and cross-sell means establishing dynamic databases that can be entered and manipulated.

Dynamic web pages, customer relationship management, interactive searching, and communication require constant management and upkeep of databases and data warehouses. Large corporations have information technology or information systems specialists to capture, scrub, store, manipulate, retrieve, and use data. SMEs with interactive sites are more likely to outsource these tasks. As small businesses become transaction sites, they will need well-designed, dependable, simple shopping baskets that simplify and speed up transaction processing.[16]

Web marketers must be assured that transactions and sites are secure. This is a construction, technology, and policy issue. It requires a total commitment to firewalls, encryption, credit card verification, and related processes for ensuring privacy and online safety. Sufficient resources must be committed to ensure that customers can interact and transact on the site with confidence and that site owners are protected as much as possible against customer fraud. Likewise, electronic payment mechanisms must be available for online ordering. These processes must be acceptable and usable, flexible enough to accommodate multiple options, and available nonstop.

A website is not online until page files have been transferred to a web server for storage. Servers may be owned and maintained in-house or outsourced to an ISP or other web-hosting business. Each site has dedicated space assigned to it on its host's web server(s). This space is identified with the site's unique URL. Most files are electronically transferred to the server and stored in the addressed space using a File Transfer Protocol (FTP). Various versions of FTP can be downloaded free. The FTP program allows the user to put files on the server, modify them, and delete them from the server.

Summary

http://college.hmco.com/business/students

The Fundamentals of Website Development

Many early websites evolved through three stages, beginning as information-only sites, then becoming interactive, and finally maturing into transaction sites. Today, many more sites begin their web presence as interactive or transaction sites. All sites require site design and redesign. Customer-centric web marketing sites focus on satisfying customer and enterprise goals through effective integration of website content, design, and construction (CDC). Private intranets and extranets also have marketing pages and sites that use web protocols and are developed through CDC decisions. The best web marketing sites evolve from a clear vision of what they are designed to accomplish for the enterprise and its customers. Web marketing sites are composed of two linked sectors: upfront and backend. Website development costs vary with site content, size, features, complexity, and other factors. Maintenance costs also vary. Consumer and enterprise sites should contain relevant, appropriate privacy and security statements

and should adhere to them. A usable site is one that is easy for visitors to learn to use, is suitably constructed for its purpose, and employs appropriate technology. Usability testing involves actually using the site, testing features, and making sure the site operates as expected. It is important to maintain a consistent look and "feel" by ensuring the uniformity of elements throughout a site. Site redesigns are needed for a variety of reasons and vary from a simple touchup of several pages to a complete site overhaul and relaunch.

Website Content

Content is what visitors seek at a site and fresh content keeps them coming back. Content shelf life varies. Many sites are still heavily text-based. Web text should be scannable, which saves the reader time. Content decisions include what to offer on a site, where to find it, and who will provide it. Content depends on the goal of the site and on customer needs. Web content may be taken without alteration from in-house marketing materials prepared for other purposes, but many sites have content that is prepared specifically for the web marketing effort. Some firms have stolen content from other sites. Content can be legally obtained from content providers, sometimes without charge. All sites need some form of content management—an organized system for identifying what content is needed, procuring it, determining when and how content should be changed, and implementing the changes. Web storyboarding is used to describe web page content (both text and nontext), the design elements, any enhancements, and how pages will be linked. The website front page should clearly let visitors know what the site is about.

Website Design

Design is the way a site looks and feels—its structure and organization and its visual and (increasingly) aural appeal. It is a plan for how content will be organized and presented on the front page and subsequent pages via text, graphics, animation, and other features. Website design should achieve both aesthetic appeal and usability. Websites are nonlinear, and most pages should be designed for skimming. Navigation is a design issue as well as a construction issue. Users have a considerable amount of control over website design. Website atmospherics are design elements that are used sitewide to establish a mood and a consistent image. A site can be visualized as a webscape. Each page should have a "flow," an energy that comes from the compatible arrangement of elements. Layout is a plan for the way design features are related to one another on a page and for the arrangement of the pages in a website. Simple is best for most graphics decisions. Some target markets and visitors need special consideration or accommodation in the design of a website.

Website Construction

Construction requires using foundation technology, software, and databases to create web pages and sites and to install them on web servers. Content must be coded before pages can be transferred and stored on a server. Even web pages carefully coded or created by popular page editors can be a problem for some browsers that are unable to read them. Marketers typically are not directly responsible for constructing or installing backend systems that manage data, but they do contribute to determining what data will be collected and used. Web marketers must be assured that transactions and sites are secure. A website is not online until page files have been transferred to a web server for storage. Most files are electronically transferred to the server and stored in the addressed space using a File Transfer Protocol (FTP).

Take Action!

Web storyboarding is a useful technique for small and midsize (SME) businesses developing and redesigning their websites. To illustrate how easy it is to apply this technique, create six storyboard cards for a small business going online for the first time. Block out what will appear on the front page and the five additional pages that will constitute the site. Post-it Notes (three-by-five-inch size) are large enough to contain necessary content information and can be moved around easily. Once the notes are complete, lay them out on a flat surface on top of two pieces of paper placed side by side (Figure 14-3), and draw links between pages.

The hypothetical business is *Kim's Baskets* from Chapter 13. Conveniently, it is located in your city, so you can create a realistic address, phone number, fax

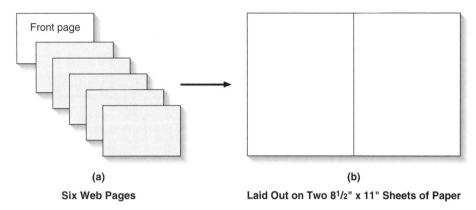

(a)

Six Web Pages

(b)

Laid Out on Two 8¹/₂" x 11" Sheets of Paper

FIGURE 14.3 Storyboarding Kim's Baskets

number, and email address. Kim has been making baskets for more than ten years as a hobby and for several years as a business operating from her home. Her logo is the name of her company written in Comic Sans MS typeface placed within an oval.

1. Using information from Chapter 13 about Kim's business, storyboard Kim's website for her.

2. Prepare an oral presentation in which you describe the website, using the storyboard, and explain the basic aspects of its content, design, and construction.

Chapter Review Questions

1. Are transaction sites also interactive? Explain.
2. Should all sites be transaction sites?
3. Explain the statement "An enterprise shows its face to the public through its website."
4. Why should CDC decisions be made concurrently?
5. Who should make content decisions?
6. Why should usability testing be conducted?
7. Why is customer input an important part of site redesign?
8. Do information-only sites have the same security concerns as transaction sites?
9. Why is content king on the Web?
10. Does all content have to be original?
11. What does KISS stand for, and why is it such good advice for website developers?
12. Can there be too much dynamic content on a front page? Explain.
13. What is web storyboarding, and how does it contribute to the website development process?
14. Websites are nonlinear. How does this affect design?
15. Once pages are made, why should they be viewed in different browsers and platforms?

Competitive Case Study

Web Development the Macromedia Way

When it comes to software generally, Adobe faces aggressive competition from Microsoft, among other companies. When it comes to multimedia web publishing software, Adobe's principal competitor is Macromedia (*www.macromedia.com*). Although Macromedia is a far smaller company, with fiscal 2004 year-end sales of US$369.8 and only 1,405 employees, its Dreamweaver MX is a strong competitor to Adobe's GoLive and is the product that many developers prefer because it is powerful and relatively simply to master. Others prefer GoLive because it has a thick hard-copy manual and offers online help; Dreamweaver MX's documentation is electronic, which can be inconvenient. Dreamweaver MX is credited with having a cleaner workspace that relies on docked work panels instead of screen-cluttering palettes. Both products are WYSIWYG (*what you see is what you get*) editors that allow for the visual construction of web pages and for full-screen previews of design and code views. Dreamweaver MX is tightly integrated with Fireworks and Flash. Both products offer site management facilities. GoLive is considered more usable for developing pages for wireless products.[17]

CHECK IT OUT

See for yourself whether or not Adobe has designed a customer-centric website. Begin at the Adobe homepage (*www.adobe.com*). What downloads does it offer without charge? Search for *GoLive.* Was the search quick and accurate? Read some "Customer Stories" (*www.adobe.com/products/golive/customerstories.html.*) What is the marketing value of testimonials? What is a *Tryout?* Is it product sampling? Is this an effective tactic to convert visitors into buyers? What is going on in *Adobe Studio?* What does Adobe offer visitors in its *Learn* section? Is it accurate to say that Adobe assumes an educational role on the site? Explain the marketing strategy behind this approach. Can Adobe products be purchased online? Is Adobe a transaction site? Is it interactive? Contrast Adobe's and Macromedia's offers. Which product might a novice user prefer?

A GLOBAL PERSPECTIVE

Adobe products have been creating traditional print materials for over twenty years. Today, Adobe products are used to design some of the Web's best sites. Thus everywhere you look, you'll find Adobe products hard at work. Adobe *online stores* are in twenty-four countries (*www.adobe.com/store/main.jhtml*). Adobe products can be purchased worldwide offline and, now, online. Compare and contrast Adobe sites in the United States with Adobe sites in several other countries. What are their similarities and differences? Is Adobe truly a global company?

Chapter 1

1. Paul S. Piper, "Google Spawn: The Culture Surrounding Google," *Searcher,* June 2004, www.infotoday.com/searcher/jun04/piper.shtml, accessed 11/04; Staff, "How Google Works," *The Economist,* 16 September 2004, www.economist.com/science/tq/displayStory.cfm?story_id=3171440, accessed 11/04; Susan Kuchinskas, "Google Search Hits the Desktop," InternetNews.com, 14 October 2004, www.internetnews.com/ent-news/article.php/3421671, accessed 10/04; Michelle Delio, "Google's Gaggle of Discussions," Wired News, 11 December 2001, www.wired.com/news/culture/0,1284,49016,00.html, accessed 10/04; Chris Sherman, "Happy Birthday, Google!", SearchEngineWatch, 8 September 2003, http://searchenginewatch.com/searchday/article.php/2160731, accessed 10/04; Bill Thompson, "Is Google Too Powerful?," BBC News, 21 February 2003, http://news.bbc.co.uk/1/hi/technology/2786761.stm, accessed 10/04; Staff, "Google," Wikipedia, 11 November 2004, http://en.wikipedia.org/wiki/Google, accessed 11/04; Josh McHugh, "Google vs. Evil," Wired News, January 2003, www.wired.com/wired/archive/11.01/google.html, accessed 11/04; John Battelle, "Watch Out Google! Amazon Gets Search," *Business2.0,* 14 September 2004, www.business2.com/b2/web/articles/print/0,17925,697177,00.html, accessed 11/04; Simon English, "Free Google e-mail Raises Privacy Fears," *Telegraph Group Ltd.,* 14 April 2004, www.money.telegraph.co.uk/money/main.jhtml?xml=/money/2004/04/14/cngoog14.xml&sSheet=/money/2004/04/14/ixfrontcity.html, accessed 11/04; Jon Udell, "The Google PC Generation," *InfoWorld,* 18 June 2004, www.infoworld.com/article/04/06/18/25OPstrategic_1.html, accessed 10/04.

2. Patricia Buckley and Sabrina Montes, "The Evolving Online Environment," in *Digital Economy 2002,* U.S. Department of Commerce, Economics and Statistics Administration, February 2002, pp. 9–21; Richard Williamson, "Dot-Com Failures Pass 700," *Interactive Week,* 31 October 2001, www.ecruitinginc.com/news/news.asp?ID=107, accessed 7/04; James Surowiecki, "The Financial Page: Let the Bad Times Roll," *The New Yorker,* 3 September 2001, p. 34.

3. Avivah Litan, "Anthrax Scare Spikes Interest in Already Surging e-Billing," Gartner Group, 5 November 2001, www4.gartner.com/DisplayDocument?doc_cd=102155, accessed 7/04; Staff, "Online Shopping Will Grow to $11 Billion This Holiday Season," Forrester Research, 16 October 2001, http://www.forrester.com, accessed 6/02; Staff, "Jupiter: Online Holiday Shopping to Grow 11 Percent," *San Francisco Business Times,* 31 October 2001, http://sanfrancisco.bizjournals.com/sanfrancisco/stories/2001/10/29/daily36.html, accessed 7/04.

4. Irving Fang, "Timeline of Communication History," University of Minnesota, www.mediahistory.umn.edu/time/alltime.html, accessed 7/04; "History of the Information Revolution and Communications Technology: A Timeline of Technology," San Jose State University, myron.sjsu.edu/caesars/COMM.HTM, accessed 7/04.

5. Katie Harrow, "A Brief Guide to the History of the Written Word," in *New Archeology,* 2003, www.newarchaeology.com/articles/writing.htm, accessed 7/04; Special Collections Department, "History of the Written Word," University of South Florida, 17 February 2000, www.lib.usf.edu/spccoll/wrtword.html, accessed 1/01.

6. "The Invention of Printing Gutenberg (1450?)" and "The Gutenberg Press," Printer's Mark, Inc., printersmark.com/Pages/Hist2.html#Anchor-The, accessed 7/04; "Gutenberg.DE, The Time of Gutenberg," www.gutenberg.de/english/zeit.htm, accessed 7/04; Eva-Maria Hanebutt-Benz, "Gutenberg and Mainz," www.gutenberg.de/english/zeitgum.htm, accessed 7/04.

7. Peter Drucker, "Beyond the Information Revolution," *The Atlantic Monthly,* October 1999, www.theatlantic.com/issues/99oct/9910drucker.htm, accessed 7/04.

8. Phil Shannon, "The Short Inspiring Reign of King Ludd," review of Kirkpatrick Sale, *Rebels Against the Future: The Luddites and Their War on the Industrial Revolution* (Cambridge, MA: Perseus, 1996), www.greenleft.org.au/back/1996/254/254p28.htm, accessed 7/04; Felix Silverio, "The Luddites," 28 September 1999, www.gober.net/victorian/reports/luddites.html, accessed 7/04.

9. Charles Babbage Institute, "Who Was Charles Babbage?" CBI, 23 July 2003, www.cbi.umn.edu/exhibits/cb.html, accessed 7/04; David Crane, "The Great Unsung Victorian Machine-Maker," *The Spectator,* 13 May 2000, p. 32; Ada, "About the Ada Home: Mission," 2 May 1998, www.adahome.com/HBAP/mission.html, accessed 7/04.

10. Mary Bellis, "Herman Hollerith–Punch Cards," About.com, http://inventors.about.com/library/inventors/blhollerith.htm?terms=Herman+Hollerith+, accessed 7/04.

11. Martin H. Weik, "The ENIAC Story," Ordnance Ballistic Research Laboratories, Aberdeen Proving Ground, January–February 1961, http://ftp.arl.mil/~mike/comphist/eniac-story.html, accessed 7/04; "The Emerging Digital Economy," Chapter One, "The Digital Revolution," U.S. Department of Commerce, April 1998, www.technology.gov/digeconomy/danc1.htm, accessed 7/04; Rachel K. Sobel, "Faulty Memory," *U.S. News & World Report,* 11 February 2002, p. 70.

12. United States Bureau of the Census, "World Population Today: World POPClock Projection," 20 July 2004, www.census.gov/cgi-bin/ipc/popclockw, accessed 7/04; David Levine, "World Population Today," University of North Carolina, www.ibiblio.org/lunarbin/worldpop, accessed 7/04; United States Bureau of the Census, "Historical Estimates of World Population," 30 April 2004, www.census.gov/ipc/www/worldhis.html, accessed 7/04.

13. Joyce L. Morris, "The Technology Revolution," in D. Schon, *Beyond the Stable State* (New York: Norton, 1971), www.uvm.edu/~jmorris/comps2.html, accessed 7/04.

14. U.S. Department of Commerce, "The Emerging Digital Economy II: Executive Summary," www.esa.doc.gov/TheEmergingDigitalEconomy.cfm, accessed 7/04.

15. Bob Schaller, "The Origin, Nature, and Implications of Moore's Law," GMU, 26 September 1996, www.iso.gmu.edu/~rschalle/moorelaw.html, accessed 7/04; Staff, "Moore's Law," Intel, www.intel.com/research/silicon/mooreslaw.htm, accessed 7/04; Dori Jones Yang, "Leaving Moore's Law in the Dust," *U.S. News & World Report,* 10 July 2000, www.usnews.com/usnews/issue/000710/moore.htm, accessed 2/01.

16. Steve Schoenherr, "The Cold War Begins," University of San Diego, 19 May 1999, history.acusd.edu/gen/20th/coldwar0.html, accessed 7/04; "Sputnik," University of Michigan, www.windows.umich.edu/space_missions/sputnik.html, accessed 7/04; Roger D. Launius, "Sputnik and the Dawn of the Space Age," NASA, 11 August 1999, www.hq.nasa.gov/office/pao/History/sputnik/, accessed 7/04; Sputnik recording at www.hq.nasa.gov/office/pao/History/sputnik/sputnik.wav; New York Times on AOL, "The Times Looks Back: Sputnik," *New York Times,* 1997, www.nytimes.com/partners/aol/special/sputnik/, accessed 7/04; sound file www.nytimes.com/partners/aol/special/sputnik/sputnik.rm; Michael Wright, "Beep, Beep, Beep . . . Here Comes Sputnik!," 16 March 2002, www.batnet.com/mfwright/sputnik.html, accessed 7/04.

17. Ibid.

18. Charles M. Herzfeld, "On ARPANet and Computers," Defense Technical Information Center, inventors.about.com/library/inventors/bl_Charles_Herzfeld.htm www.dtic.mil/summit/ma02%5F1a.html, accessed 7/04.

19. Barry M. Leiner, Vinton G. Cerf, David D. Clark, Robert E. Kahn, Leonard Kleinrock, Daniel C. Lynch, Jon Postel, Larry G. Roberts, and Stephen Wolff, "A Brief History of the Internet, Version 3.31," last revised 10 December 2003, www.isoc.org/internet/history/brief.shtml, accessed 7/04; Robert H. Zakon, "Hobbes' Internet Timeline v.7.0," 2004, www.zakon.org/robert/internet/timeline/, accessed 7/04.

20. Ibid.

21. John Naughton, "The Man Who Wove the Web," *The Spectator,* 16 October 1999, pp. 45–56; Tim Berners-Lee, "Biography," World Wide Web Consortium, 2 July 2004, www.w3.org/People/Berners-Lee/, accessed 7/04; Tim Berners-Lee, "The World Wide Web: A Very Short Personal History," World Wide Web Consortium, 7 May 1998, www.w3.org/People/Berners-Lee/ShortHistory.html, accessed 7/04.

22. CIA World Factbook, "U.S. Economy 2004," www.cia.gov/cia/publications/factbook/geos/us.html, accessed 7/04.

23. U.S. Census Bureau, "2002 E-Commerce Multi-Sector Report,," U.S. Department of Commerce, 15 April 2004, www.census.gov/eos/www/papers/2002/2002finaltext.pdf, accessed 7/04; Patricia Buckley and Sabrina Montes, "The Evolving Online Environment," *Digital Economy 2002,* U.S. Department of Commerce, Economics and Statistics Administration, February 2002, www.esa.doc.gov/DigitalEconomy2002.cfm, accessed 7/04.

24. University of Texas, Austin, and Cisco Systems, "January 2001 Internet Economy Indicators," Center for Research in Electronic Commerce, www.internetindicators.com/internetindic.html, accessed 7/04; Cyrus Afzali, "Internet Pumps $507 Billion into U.S. Economy," ClickZ Network, 3 November 1999, www.clickz.com/stats/markets/professional/article.php/5971_227421, accessed 7/04; Associated Press, "Millions of Web-Slingers," ABCNews.com, more.abcnews.go.com/sections/business/dailynews/internetjobs000606.html, accessed 9/03.

25. Patricia Buckley and Sabrina Montes, "The Evolving Online Environment," *Digital Economy 2002,* U.S. Department of Commerce, Economics and Statistics Administration, February 2002, www.esa.doc.gov/DigitalEconomy2002.cfm, accessed 7/04; U.S. Department of Commerce, "The Emerging Digital Economy II: Executive Summary," April 1998, www.esa.doc.gov/508/esa/TheEmergingDigitalEconomyII.htm, accessed 6/02; Jessica Schneider Davis, "Internet Drives U.S. Economy," Cisco Systems, May/June 2002, business.cisco.com, accessed 9/03.

26. Staff, "Users Still Resistant to Paid Content," ClickZ Network, 11 April 2003, www.clickz.com/stats/markets/retailing/article.php/6061_2189551, accessed 7/04; ZDNet, "Europeans Spending More Online," Nua.com, 4 March 2003, www.nua.ie/surveys/index.cgi?f=VS&art_id=905358734&rel=true, accessed 7/04; eMarketer, "Worldwide B2B Revenues to Pass One Trillion," Nua.com, 1 April 2003, www.nua.ie/surveys/index.cgi?f=VS&art_id=905358753&rel=true, accessed 7/04; News.com.au, "Australian Businesses Increase Online Revenue," Nua.com, 29 November 2002, www.nua.ie/surveys/index.cgi?f=VS&art_id=905358618&rel=true, accessed 7/04; AsiaBizTech, "Over 50 Percent of Japanese Population Online," Nua.com, 17 March 2003, www.nua.ie/surveys/index.cgi?f=VS&art_id=905358740&rel=true, accessed 7/04.

27. Mortimer B. Zuckerman, "Tensions on the Net," *U.S. News & World Report,* 24 April 2000, p. 75.

28. Gary S. Becker, "How the Web Is Revolutionizing Learning," *BusinessWeek,* 27 December 1999, p. 40; Mary Lord, "Suddenly, E-Commerce Is the Hot New Specialty," *U.S. News & World Report,* 10 April 2000, pp. 62–64; Jacqueline L. Savukinas, "e-Learning: Impacts of IT on Education," *Digital Economy 2002,* U.S. Department of Commerce, Economics and Statistics Administration, February 2002, http://www.esa.doc.gov/DigitalEconomy2002.cfm, accessed 7/04.

29. Randall E. Stross, "Digital Divide Hooey," *U.S. News & World Report,* 17 April 2000, p. 45.

30. Greg R. Notess, "Search Engine Features Chart," Search Engine Showdown, 7 September 2003, www.searchengineshowdown.com, accessed 7/04; Greg R. Notess, "Freshness Issue and Complexities with Web Search Engines," *Online Magazine,* November 2001, www.onlinemag.net/OL2001/net11_01.html, accessed 7/04; Linda Barlow, "The Spider's Apprentice," Monash Information Services, 17 May 2002, www.monash.com/spidap.html#ratings, accessed 7/04; Danny Sullivan, "Search Engine Sizes," Search Engine Watch, 2 September 2003, searchenginewatch.com/reports/article.php/2156481#current, accessed 7/04; Linda Barlow, "In-Depth Analysis of Popular Search Engines," Monash Information Services, 17 May 2002, www.monash.com/spidap3.html, accessed 7/04; Staff, "Google Grabs Globe, U.S. to Yahoo!," ClickZ Network, 1 May 2003, www.clickz.com/stats/big_picture/applications/article.php/1301_2200171, accessed 7/04; Danny Sullivan, "Nielsen NetRatings Search Engine Ratings," 14 July 2004, www.searchenginewatch.com/reports/article.php/2156451, accessed 7/04; Danny Sullivan, "comScore Media Metrix Search Engine Ratings," Search Engine Watch, 1 August 2003, www.searchenginewatch.com/reports/article.php/2156431, accessed 7/04.

Chapter 2

1 Cisco Systems, 2003 Annual Report, Cisco Systems, www.cisco.com/warp/public/749/ar2003/online/, accessed 8/04; Stephen Lawson, "IBM, Cisco Help Networks Help Themselves," NetworkWorldFusion, 10 October 2003, www.nwfusion.com/news/2003/1010ibmcisco.html, accessed 8/04; Erin Bergamo, "Industry Leaders Create Mobile Wireless Internet Forum," Cisco Systems Press Release, 2 February 2000, www.cisco.com/warp/public/146/pressroom/2000/feb00/sp_020200.htm, accessed 8/04; Wylie Wong, "Cisco Sets Its Sights on Software," CNET News, 23 May 2000, http://news.cnet.com/news/0-1004-202-1933855.html, accessed 8/04; Network World Fusion, "Cisco," NW Fusion, 1999, www.nwfusion.com/power99/power99-cisco.html, accessed 8/04; Scott Thurm, "Cisco's Orders Strong; Options Move Rankles Some," *Wall Street Journal,* 14 September 2003, p. B4; Scott Thurm, "Servers Turn to Networking," *Wall Street Journal,* 18 September 2003, p. B4; Nancy Singer, "Cisco

Systems and U.S. Small Business Administration E-Learning Program Empowers Growing Companies to Utilize Internet for Business," Cisco Systems Press Release, 19 July 2000, www.cisco.com/warp/public/146/pressroom/2000/jul00/smb_071900.htm, accessed 8/04; David Kirkpatrick, "Cisco Still Bets on the Net," *Fortune,* 15 October 2001, www.fortune.com, accessed 11/01.

2 ISP-Planet Staff, "Top 22 U.S. ISPs by Subscriber: Q1 2004," ISP-Planet, 20 May 2004, www.isp-planet.com/research/rankings/usa.html, accessed 8/04; Staff, "ISP Report," Security Space, 1 July 2004, www.securityspace.com/s_survey/data/man.200406/ISPreport.html, accessed 8/04; Goli Ameri, "The Evolution of the ISP Market as a Model for Public Wi-Fi," Telephony Online, 23 May 2003, telephonyonline.com/ar/telecom_evolution_isp_market/, accessed 8/04.

3 The Bandwidth Report, "US Broadband Penetration Jumps to 45.2%—US Internet Penetration Nearly 75%—March 2004 Bandwidth Report," Web Site Optimization, 19 June 2004, www.websiteoptimization.com/bw/0403/, accessed 8/04; Staff, "Broadband Use Up in U.S.," Federal Communications Commission, 14 August 2001, www.nua.net, accessed 6/02; Raymond Reid, "Canada Trumps US in Broadband Use," comScore, 17 March 2003, www.comscore.com/press/release.asp?id=312, accessed 10/03; Robyn Greenspan, "What They're Doing Down Under," ClickZ Network, 10 October 2003, www.clickz.com/stats/big_picture/geographics/article.php/5911_3090361, accessed 8/04; Staff, "More Than Half of U.S., Canada Online," ClickZ Network, 2 May 2003, www.clickz.com/stats/big_picture/geographics/article.php/5911_2200601, accessed 8/04.

4 BBC News, "Internet Takes a Break," BBC Online Network, 23 February 1999, http://news.bbc.co.uk/hi/english/sci/tech/newsid_284000/284702.stm, accessed 8/04; Staff, "Major Power Outage Hits New York, Other Large Cities," CNN, 14 August 2003, www.cnn.com/2003/US/08/14/power.outage/, accessed 8/04; Robert MacMillan, "Internet 1, Blackout 0, *Washington Post,* 15 August 2003, www.washingtonpost.com/ac2/wp-dyn/A62497-2003Aug15?language=printer, accessed 8/04.

5 Staff, "Software," LearnThat, 2004, www.learnthat.com/define/view.asp?id=56, accessed 8/04; Staff, "Software," Free On-Line Dictionary of Computing, wombat.doc.ic.ac.uk/foldoc/index.html, accessed 8/04.

6 Jill Hecht Maxwell, "Special Technology Report: Inside Story," *Inc.,* April 2002, www.inc.com/magazine/20020401/24048.html, accessed 8/04; Amy Cortese, "Here Comes the Intranet," *Business Week,* 16 June 1997, www.businessweek.com/1996/09/b34641.htm, accessed 8/04; Gerry McGovern, "Intranet Return on Investment Case Studies," *New Thinking,* 18 November 2002, www.gerrymcgovern.com/nt/2002/nt_2002_11_18_intranet_roi.htm, accessed 8/04; Toby Ward, "Measuring the Dollar Value of Intranets," *Intranet Journal,* 25 April 2001, www.intranetjournal.com/articles/200104/ii_04_25_01a.html, accessed 8/04.

7 Staff, "Andreessen Foresees the Extranet," News.com, 20 September 1996, www.news.com/2100-1001-230435.html?legacy=cnet, accessed 8/04; Heidi Anderson, "The Rise of the Extranet," *PCToday,* 1997, www.pctoday.com/editorial/goingonline/970235b.html?guid=Okewm1d0, accessed 6/02.

8 MasterCard International, Annual Report 2003, MasterCard, www.mastercardintl.com/corporate/index.html, accessed 8/04; Staff, "About MasterCard Online," MasterCard, https://hsm2stl101.mastercard.net/public/login/ebusiness/aboutmastercardonline.jsp, accessed 8/04.

9 Vinton Cerf, "The Internet Is for *Everyone:* How Easy to Say—How Hard to Achieve!" 10 May 2000, The Internet Society, www.isoc.org/isoc/media/speeches/foreveryone.shtml, accessed 8/04; Robyn

Greenspan, "Internet Not for Everyone," ClickZ Network, 16 April 2003, www.clickz.com/stats/big_picture/demographics/article.php/5901_2192251, accessed 8/04.

10 Thomas E. Weber, "Terrorist Attacks Raise the Issue of How Best to Protect the Internet," *Wall Street Journal E-World,* 8 October 2001, p. A15; Dorothy E. Denning, "Cyberterrorism: Testimony before the Special Oversight Panel on Terrorism Committee on Armed Services, U.S. House of Representatives," Georgetown University, 23 May 2000, www.cs.georgetown.edu/~denning/infosec/cyberterror.html, accessed 8/04; Staff, "Increased Potential for Distributed Denial of Service (DDoS) Attacks," National Infrastructure Protection Center, Advisory 01-026, 2 November 2001, www.nipc.gov/warnings/advisories/2001/01-026.htm, accessed 8/04.

11 David L. Margulius, "Who Runs the Internet Anyway?" InfoWorld.com, 21 November 2003, www.computerworld.com.au/index.php/id;807983703];relcomp;1, accessed 8/04; Harry Hochheiser and Robin Rice, "Who Runs the Internet?," Computer Professionals for Social Responsibility, 3 May 1998, www.cpsr.org/onenet/whoruns.html, accessed 10/03; Robert W. Lucky, "Who Runs the Internet?" IEEE, 2002, ieee.cincinnati.fuse.net/reiman/02_2003.html, accessed 8/04.

12 TRUSTe, "Building a Web You Can Believe In," www.truste.com, accessed 8/04; National Association of Boards of Pharmacy, "Verified Internet Pharmacy Practice Sites (VIPPS)," http://vipps.nabp.net/verify.asp, accessed 8/04; BBB Online, "About the Reliability Program," www.bbbonline.org/reliability/index.asp, accessed 8/04.

13 CERN, "How the Web Works," European Organization for Nuclear Research, 2002, public.web.cern.ch/public/about/achievements/www/howworks/howworks.html, accessed 8/04; Marshall Brain, "How Web Servers Work," HowStuffWorks, Inc., 2004, computer.howstuffworks.com/web-server.htm, accessed 8/04.

14 Staff, "Internet Littered with Abandoned Sites," CNN.com, 3 November 2003, www.cnn.com/2003/TECH/internet/11/03/deadwood.online.ap/, accessed 8/04; Jared Sandberg, "At Thousands of Web Sites, Time Stands Still," *Wall Street Journal,* 11 March 1997, pp. B1, B3.

15 Roger Clarke, "Domains: A Primer on Internet Technology, 3.3 The Domain Name System (DNS)," Australian National University, 5 March 2004, www.anu.edu.au/people/Roger.Clarke/II/IPrimer.html#ProtDNS, accessed 8/04; Staff, "InterNIC FAQs—The Domain Name System: A Non-Technical Explanation Why Universal Resolvability Is Important," InterNIC, 5 October 2002, www.internic.net/faqs/authoritative-dns.html, accessed 8/04.

16 Robert H Zakon, "Hobbes' Internet Timeline vol. 7.0," 1 January 2004, info.isoc.org/guest/zakon/Internet/History/HIT.html, accessed 8/04.

17 Avery Comarow, "Just What's Dot Next?" *U.S. News & World Report,* 16 October 2000, p. 50.

18 Internet Corporation for Assigned Names and Numbers, "Preliminary Report, Meeting of the ICANN Board in Yokohama," ICANN, 16 July 2000, www.icann.org/minutes/prelim-report-16jul00.htm, accessed 8/04; Staff, "InterNIC FAQs on New Top-Level Domains," InterNIC, 25 September 2002, www.internic.net/faqs/new-tlds.html, accessed 8/04.

19 Staff, "The Value of IDNs," Verisign, 2003, verisign.com/nds/naming/idn/value, accessed 8/04; David L. Margulius, "Who Runs the Internet Anyway?" ComputerWorld.com, 21 November 2003, www.computerworld.com.au/index.php/id;807983703];relcomp;1, accessed 8/04.

20 Matt Lake, "Get Your Own Domain Name," CNN.com, 8 June 2000, www.cnn.com/2000/TECH/computing/06/08/get.own.domain.idg/, accessed 8/04.

21 Paul M. Eng and Marsha Johnston, "Get Your Hands Off My .Com," *Business Week,* 28 July 1997, p. 88.

22 Dow Jones Newswire, "Julia Roberts Wins Control of Domain Name on Web," *Wall Street Journal,* 1 June 2000, p. B12; Staff, "James Bond Zaps Cybersquatter," CNN.com, 1 September 2003, www.cnn.com/2003/TECH/internet/09/01/web.brosnan/, accessed 8/04.

23 Doug Isenberg, "Anticybersquatting Consumer Protection Act," GigaLaw.com, 2004, www.gigalaw.com/library/anticybersquattingact-1999-11-29-p1.html, accessed 8/04; "S 1255 IS, Anticybersquatting Consumer Protection Act," *Tech Law Journal,* www.techlawjournal.com/cong106/cybersquat/s1255is.html, accessed 10/03.

24 Catherine Yang, "Still the Master of Its Domain," *Business Week,* 13 March 2000, pp. 104–105.

25 The Internet Corporation for Assigned Names and Numbers, "ICANN-Accredited Registrars, 10 October 2003," ICANN, www.icann.org/registrars/accredited-list.html, accessed 8/04.

26 Ryan J. Foley, "FCC Blesses New Wireless Technology," *Wall Street Journal,* 17 October 2003, p. B2; Don Clark, "Intel Quickens Wireless Race," *Wall Street Journal,* 15 September 2003, p. B3; Colin C. Haley, "Acotel Targets U.S. Carriers, Media Companies," InternetNews.com, 20 October 2003, www.internetnews.com/xSP/article.php/3095781, accessed 8/04; Hae Won Choi, "Running Your Bathtub, Stove, and Microwave by Cellphone," *Wall Street Journal,* 16 September 2003, pp. B1, 15; Robert X. Cringely, "How Ultra-Band May or May Not Change the World," PBS, 24 January 2002, www.pbs.org/cringely/pulpit/pulpit20020124.html, accessed 8/04; Staff, "Wireless LANs Gaining Popularity in Asia-Pacific Region," *Pacific Business News,* 14 January 2003, pacific.bizjournals.com/pacific/stories/2003/01/13/daily19.html, accessed 8/04; Staff, "Wireless LANs," Wireless LAN Association, 2003, www.wlana.org/index.html, accessed 8/04; Reuters, "It's a Wireless World in Japan," *Wired,* 20 June 2000, www.wired.com/news/culture/0,1284,37099,00.html, accessed 8/04; Staff, "84 Million People in the United States Will Plug into Wireless Internet by 2005," IDC, 17 October 2001, www.idc.com/communications/press/pr/CM101701pr.stm, accessed 11/01; Robyn Greenspan, "Consumers Calling for Better Wireless Support," ClickZ Network, 9 September 2003, www.clickz.com/stats/markets/wireless/article.php/10094_3074371, accessed 8/04; Staff, "Cutting the Ties That Bind," *The Economist Technology Quarterly,* 21 September 2002, pp. 6–7; Staff, "Making the Web World-Wide," *The Economist,* 28 September 2002, p. 76; Michael Pastore, "Wireless Looks for a Lift to Clear Adoption Hurdles," ClickZ Network, 16 March 2001, www.clickz.com/stats/markets/wireless/article.php/10094_715841, accessed 8/04; Intermarket Group, "Eighteen-fold Growth for Wireless Net," Nua, 26 October 2001, www.nua.net/surveys/index.cgi?f=VS&art_id=905357341&rel=true, accessed 8/04; Peter Hadfield, "I Need I-mode, Do You Need I-mode?" *U.S. News & World Report,* 9 October 2000, pp. 47–48; Ephraim Schwartz and Cathleen Moore, "E-Commerce on the Go," *InfoWorld,* 23 October 2000, pp. 1, 29; Stephen H. Wildstrom, "Wireless Gets Easier and Faster," *BusinessWeek,* 29 May 2000, p. 34.

27 Walter S. Mossberg, "Tracking the Elusive Hot Spot," *Wall Street Journal,* 5 November 2003, p. D4; Scott Thurm and Nick Wingfield, "How Titans Swallowed Wi-Fi, Stifling Silicon Valley Uprising," *Wall Street Journal,* 8 August 2003, pp. A1, 10; Staff, "WiFi," FOLDOC, 2 September 2003, wombat.doc.ic.ac.uk/foldoc/foldoc.cgi?query=WiFi, accessed 8/04; Steven J. Vaughan-Nichols, "802.11 vs. 3G," *WiFi-Planet,* 31 January 2003, www.wi-fiplanet.com/tutorials/article.php/1577551, accessed 8/04; Larry Mittag, "Guide to IEEE 802.11 Wireless LAN Standards," ChipCenter, 3 June 2002, www.chipcenter.com/wireless/tn002.html, accessed 10/03; Junko Yoshida, "HP's Bluetooth Enables Wireless Printing, Nokia Signs On," *EE Times,* 13 October 2003, www.commsdesign.com/news/market_news/OEG20031013S0036, accessed 8/04; Dean Takahashi, "Nokia to Engage Gamers with New N-Gage," NWANews.com, 13 October 2003, www.nwanews.com/adg/story_Business.php?storyid=44387, accessed 10/03; Staff, "UPS Uses WiFi & Bluetooth Together to Manage Packages at Shipping Hubs," MobileInfo.com, December 2002, www.mobileinfo.com/News_2002/Issue47/UPS_WiFi_Bluetooth.htm, accessed 8/04; Janet Rae-Dupree, "Bluetooth Lets Gadgets Speak in One Language," *U.S. News & World Report,* 15 May 2000, pp. 58–59; Stephen Baker, "A Revolution Called Bluetooth," *BusinessWeek,* 18 September 2000, pp. 62–64; Don Clark, "Intel Makes Risky Bet on New Wireless Brand," *Wall Street Journal,* 11 March 2003, pp. B1, 4; Kesse Drucker, "Beyond Starbucks? Verizon Offers Wi-Fi You Can Tote Around," *Wall Street Journal,* 1 October 2003, pp. D1, 12; Karen Lowry Miller, "Is Wi-Fi Just a Bubble?" *Newsweek,* 29 September 2003, pp. E22–24.

28 Yardena Arar, "Five Reasons Not to Go Wireless," PCWorld, November 2003, p. 140; Staff, "Wireless Update," *T.H.E Journal,* October 2003, p. 24; Sean Captain, "Warp-Speed Wireless," PCWorld, November 2003, pp. 125–140; Matt Moore, "Some Cell Phones Susceptible to 'Bluejacking'," *Lexington Herald-Leader,* 13 November 2003, p. A7; Jeanette Borzo, "The Wireless Web," *Wall Street Journal,* 17 April 2000, p. R46; Michael Pastore, "Wireless Looks for a Lift to Clear Adoption Hurdles," ClickZ Network, 16 March 2001, www.clickz.com/stats/markets/wireless/print.php/10094_715841, accessed 8/04.

Chapter 3

1. Dow Jones Business News, "Apollo Posts Sharp Increases in Earnings, Revenue," Hoover's Online, 18 December 2003, www.hoovers.com/apollo-group/—ID__42338,ArticleID__NR20031218460_b1ce000b3b0e2432—/free-co-news-detail.xhtml, accessed 1/04; William Symonds, "University of Phoenix Online: Swift Rise," *BusinessWeek,* 23 June 2003, www.businessweek.com/magazine/content/03_25/b3838628.htm, accessed 9/04; Staff, Apollo Group, Inc., Corporate Information, www.apollogrp.com, accessed 9/04; Staff, "University of Phoenix Online—The Nation's Leading Online University," Peterson's Guide, 2003, www.petersons.com/distancelearning/articles/uop.asp, accessed 9/04; Rachel Hartigan Shea, "E-Learning Today," *U.S. News & World Report,* 28 October 2002, www.usnews.com/usnews/edu/elearning/articles/02phoenix.htm, accessed 9/04; James M. Pethokoukis, "E-learn and Earn," *U.S. News & World Report,* 24 June 2002, www.usnews.com/usnews/edu/elearning/articles/020624elearning.htm, accessed 9/04.

2. Staff, "Trends in Europe and North America: The Statistical Yearbook of the Economic Commission for Europe 2003," United Nations Economic Commission for Europe, 2003, www.unece.org/stats/trends/, accessed 9/04; Staff, "Internet Users Will Top 1 Billion in 2005, Wireless Internet Users Will Reach 48% in 2005," Computer Industry Almanac, Inc., 21 March 2002, www.c-i-a.com/pr032102.htm, accessed 9/04; Staff, "Broadband Revolutionizing Europe's Internet Behavior," Nielsen/NetRatings, 29 May 2003, www.nielsen-netratings.com/pr/pr_030529_uk.pdf, accessed 9/04; Staff, "Europe Online: A. Internet Users Worldwide," eMarketer, 2003, www.emarketer.com, accessed 1/04.

3. SBA Office of Advocacy, "Small Business Frequently Asked Questions," U.S. Small Business Administration, 25 April 2003, www.sba.gov/advo/stats/sbfaq.html#q2, accessed 9/04; U.S. Small Business Administration, Office of Advocacy, "2002 Small Business

Profile: UNITED STATES," SBA, www.sba.gov/advo/stats/profiles/ 02nation.pdf, accessed 9/04.

4. Ibid 3; U.S. Small Business Administration (SBA), "Small Business Economic Indicators for 2002," SBA Office of Advocacy, June 2003, www.sba.gov/advo/stats/sbei02.pdf, accessed 9/04; U.S. Census Bureau, "Statistics of U.S. Businesses: 2001," U.S. Census Bureau, www.census.gov/epcd/susb/2001/us/US—.HTM, accessed 9/04.

5. Stewart Adam and Kenneth R. Deans, "Inter-Study Comparison of Small Business Internet Use in Australia and New Zealand," AusWeb01, Seventh Australian World Wide Web Conference, April 2001, http://ausweb.scu.edu.au/aw01/papers/refereed/adam/ paper.html, accessed 9/04; Staff, "II. The Importance of Small Business in Canada," Strategis, 7 October 2003, http://strategis.ic .gc.ca/epic/internet/insbrp-rppe.nsf/vwGeneratedInterE/ rd00022e.html, accessed 9/04; Staff, "Barclays Small Business Survey," Barclays, epolitix.com/data/companies/images/Companies/Barclays -Bank/sbs.pdf, accessed 9/04; Staff, "Small and Medium-sized Enterprise (SME) Statistics for the Regions, 2001," SBS Press Release, 3 April 2003, sbs.gov.uk/default.php?page=/press/ news119.php, accessed 9/04.

6. Staff, "D&B Survey Finds Optimism Among Small Businesses: 21st Annual D&B Small Business Survey Also Reveals Continued Growth of Computers and Internet Among Small Businesses," Dunn & Bradstreet, 22 April 2002, www.corporate-ir.net/ireye/ir_site.zhtml ?ticker=DNB=410=9=299272, accessed 1/04.

7. Ann Zimmerman, "To Sell Goods to Wal-Mart, Get on the Net," Wall Street Journal, 21 November 2003, online.wsj.com, accessed 1/04.

8. Staff, "Use of E-government in Britain Increasing—But Still Lags Far Behind Global Average," TNS News Centre, 12 September 2003, www .tns-global.com/corporate/Doc/0/V5SBQVTD7OK4LCEE9U13628B75/ GovOnline_UKrlseDec2003.pdf, accessed 9/04; Michael Pastore, "Citizens Taking Government Business Online," CyberAtlas, 10 January 2002, cyberatlas.internet.com/markets/professional/article/0,,5971 _952531,00.html, accessed 9/04; Staff, "E-Government May Not Mean Efficiency," CyberAtlas, 27 November 2001, cyberatlas.internet.com/ markets/professional/article/0,,5971_929471,00.html, accessed 9/04.

9. Roy Mark, "School Web Access Soars, Digital Divide Still Remains," CyberAtlas, 13 November 2003, cyberatlas.internet.com/markets/ education/article/0,,5951_3101281,00.html, accessed 9/04; Robyn Greenspan, "Reading, Writing, Pointing-And-Clicking," CyberAtlas, 18 July 2003, cyberatlas.internet.com/markets/education/article/ 0,,5951_2237481,00.html, accessed 9/04.

10. Staff, "49% of Physicians Writing a New Rx for Pharmaceutical Marketing," Manhattan Research, 6 August 2003, www.manhattanresearch.com/ePharma%20Physician%20v3 %20(08062003).pdf; accessed 9/04; Brian Morrissey, "Doctors Like Web for Drug Info, Still Want Perks," CyberAtlas, 26 August 2003, cyberatlas.internet.com/markets/healthcare/article/0,,10101 _3068941,00.html, accessed 9/04; Grace Ada Ajuwon, "Computer and Internet Use by First-Year Clinical and Nursing Students in a Nigerian Teaching Hospital," BioMed Central, 18 September 2003, www .biomedcentral.com/1472-6947/3/10/abstract, accessed 9/04; Staff, "Health on the Internet Foundation," HON Foundation, 10 June 2002, www.hon.ch/Survey/Spring2002/support.html, accessed 9/04.

11. U.S. Census Bureau, "POPClocks," Population Division, 1 January 2004, www.census.gov/main/www/popclock.html, accessed 9/04; Staff, "The Top 25 Countries in Internet with the Highest Penetration Rate (Percentage of the Population Using the Internet)," 10 November 2003, InternetWorldStats.com, www.internetworldstats.com/ stats.htm#top20, accessed 9/04; Staff, "The Internet Top 25 Countries with Highest Number of Users," InternetWorldStats.com, 10

November 2003, www.internetworldstats.com/stats.htm#top25, accessed 9/04.

12. Michelle Conlin, "Unmarried America," BusinessWeek, 20 October 2003, www.businessweek.com/magazine/content/03_42/b3854001 _mz001.htm, accessed 9/04; Nicholas Kulish, "Census 2000: The New Demographics," Wall Street Journal, 15 May 2001, p. B1; Vanessa O'Connell and Jon E. Hilsenrath, "Advertisers Are Cautious as Household Makeup Shifts," Wall Street Journal, 15 May 2001, pp. B1, B4.

13. Mary Madden, "The Changing Picture of Who's Online and What They Do," Pew Internet & American Life Project, 22 December 2003, www.pewinternet.org/reports/pdfs/PIP_Online_Pursuits_Final.PDF, accessed 9/04; Staff, "comScore Media Metrix Announces Top 50 U.S. Internet Property Rankings for November 2003," Media Metrix, 17 December 2003, www.comscore.com/press/release.asp?id=386, accessed 9/04; Rick Cook, "Internet Not Just for Kids Anymore," E-Commerce Times, 4 April 2000, www.ecommercetimes.com/ news/articles2000/000404-2.shtml, accessed 9/04; Roger O. Crockett, "A Web That Looks Like the World," BusinessWeek e.BIZ, 22 March 1999, pp. EB 46–47; eStats, "User Demographics: Introduction/ Overview," eMarketer, 14 September 1999, www.emarketer.coml, accessed 1/01; Michelle Nelson, "Who's Going Online?" PCAlmanac Reference Series, December 2000, vol. 4, no. 4, pp. 24–27; Lee Rainie and Dan Packel, "More Online, Doing More," Pew Internet & American Life Project, 18 February 2001, www.pewinternet.org/ reports/toc.asp?Report=30, accessed 9/04.

14. Staff, "comScore MediaMetrix Announces Top 50 U.S. Internet Property Rankings for November 2003," MediaMetrix, 17 December 2003, www.comscore.com/press/release.asp?id=386, accessed 9/04; Mary Madden, "The Changing Picture of Who's Online and What They Do," Pew Internet & American Life Project, 22 December 2003, www.pewinternet.org/reports/pdfs/PIP_Online_Pursuits_Final.PDF, accessed 9/04; Staff, "Web Use and Communication Activities," Pew Internet & American Life Project, www.pewinternet.org/reports/ reports.asp?Report=106=ReportLevel1=Level1ID=467, accessed 9/04; eMarketer, "U.S. Public Schools Are Online," TechSoup.org, 21 May 2001, www.techsoup.org/news_article.cfm?newsid= 591&btcfile=news_article, accessed 9/04.

15. Robyn Greenspan, "Europe, U.S. on Different Sides of the Gender Gap," CyberAtlas, 21 October 2003, http://cyberatlas.internet.com/ big_picture/demographics/0,,5901_3095681,00.html, accessed 9/04; Staff, "European Women on the Web," Nielsen//NetRatings, 24 June 2003, http://banners.noticiasdot.com/termometro/boletines/docs/ audiencias/nielsen-netratings/2003/0603/netratings_pr_030624_uk.pdf, accessed 9/04.

16. Staff, "The Top 25 Countries in Internet with the Highest Penetration Rate (Percentage of the Population Using the Internet)," InternetWorldStats.com, 10 November 2003, www.internetworldstats.com/stats.htm#top20, accessed 9/04; Staff, "The Internet Top 25 Countries with Highest Number of Users," InternetWorldStats.com, 10 November 2003, www.internetworldstats.com/stats.htm#top25, accessed 9/04.

17. Alfred Hermida, "UN Summit Pledges Net for All," BBC News, 12 December 2003, news.bbc.co.uk/1/hi/technology/3314921.stm, accessed 9/04; Staff, "WSIS: The World Summit on the Information Society First Phase: Geneva, 10–12 December 2003," WSIS, December 2003, www.itu.int/wsis/, accessed 9/04.

18. Staff, "Bridging the Digital Divide: Internet Access in Central and Eastern Europe," Center for Democracy and Technology, 2003, www.cdt.org/international/ceeaccess/, accessed 9/04.

19. Corry Bregendahl and Cornelia Flora, "Native American Business Participation in E-Commerce: An Assessment of Technical Assistance and Training Needs," U.S. Department of Agriculture, December 2002, www.ag.iastate.edu/centers/rdev/pubs/contents/ecommercebook.pdf, accessed 9/04; Kade Twist, "A Nation Online, But Where Are the Indians?," World History Archives, 12 March 2002, www.hartford-hwp.com/archives/41/402.html, accessed 9/04.

20. Jon Gunderson, "World Wide Web Accessibility to People with Disabilities: A Usability Perspective," MOSAIC/Web Access Project, University of Illinois at Urbana/Champaign, www.staff.uiuc.edu/~jongund/access-overview.html, accessed 1/04; Staff, "Designing Web Pages for People with Disabilities," Links from Valle Verde Library, 23 October 2003, www.epcc.edu/vvlib/webada.htm, accessed 9/04; Barbara Marquand, "Designing for the Disabled Online," Office.com, 8 June 2000, www.office.com/global/0,2724,505-18123-18417,FF.html, accessed 1/01; Washington Post, "Better Electronic Access for the Disabled," Nua Internet Surveys, 25 August 2000, www.nua.ie/surveys/index.cgi?f=VS&art_id=905355999&rel= true, accessed 9/04.

21. Staff, "Daily Internet Activities," Pew Internet & American Life Project, 22 October 2003, www.pewinternet.org/reports/chart.asp?img=Daily_Activities_11.7.03.htm, accessed 9/04.

22. Mary Madden, "America's Online Pursuits: The Changing Picture of Who's Online and What They Do," Pew Internet & American Life Project, 22 December 2003, www.pewinternet.org/reports/pdfs/PIP_Online_Pursuits_Final.PDF, accessed 9/04.

23. Mary Madden, "America's Online Pursuits: The Changing Picture of Who's Online and What They Do," Pew Internet & American Life Project, 22 December 2003, www.pewinternet.org/reports/pdfs/PIP_Online_Pursuits_Final.PDF, accessed 9/04.

24. Carnegie Mellon University, "Carnegie Mellon Study Reveals Negative Potential of Heavy Internet Use on Emotional Well-Being," 1998, homenet.hcii.cs.cmu.edu/progress/pressrel.html, accessed 9/04; Susannah Fox, "Wired Seniors," Pew Internet & American Life Project, 9 September 2001, www.pewinternet.org/reports/toc.asp?Report=40, accessed 9/04.

25. Staff, "Retail E-Commerce Sales in Third Quarter 2003 Were $13.3 Billion, Up 27.0 Percent from Third Quarter 2002, Census Bureau Reports," U.S. Department of Commerce News, 21 November 2003, www.census.gov/mrts/www/current.html, accessed 9/04.

26. Consumer Internet Barometer, "Shipping Charges, Giving Away Credit Card Numbers Top Consumers' List of Internet Frustrations," NFO World Group and The Conference Board, 17 December 2003, www.consumerinternetbarometer.us/press.cfm, accessed 9/04; Graeme Wearden, "Men Have a Grand Time Shopping Online," ZDNet UK, 7 November 2003, http://news.zdnet.co.uk/internet/ecommerce/0,39020372,39117710,00.htm, accessed 9/04.

27. Max Heineman and Grace Kim, "Kids Account for One Out of Five Internet Surfers in the U.S.; More Than 27 Million American Kids Connect Online, According to Nielsen//Netratings," Nielsen//NetRatings, 21 October 2003, www.netratings.com/pr/pr_031021.pdf, accessed 9/04.

28. Jed Kolko, Michael E. Gazala, and Charles Q. Strohm, "Gays Are the Technology Early Adopters You Want," Forrester Research, 24 June 2003, www.forrester.com/ER/Research/Brief/Excerpt/0,1317,17004,00.html, accessed 1/04; Jeff Bounds, "Forrester: Gay Tech Users Worth Targeting," Dallas Business Journal, 28 July 2003, www.bizjournals.com/dallas/stories/2003/07/28/newscolumn2.html, accessed 9/04.

29. Staff, "iTunes Music Store Downloads Top 25 Million Songs," Apple.com, 15 December 2003, www.apple.com/pr/library/2003/dec/15itunes.html, accessed 9/04; Michael Singer, "iTunes Music to Apple's Pocketbook," Ecommerce News, 5 May 2003, http://ecommerce.internet.com/news/news/article/0,,10375_2201561,00.html, accessed 9/04; John Borland and Ina Fried, "iTunes for Windows Goes Live," ZDNet News, 17 October 2003, http://news.zdnet.co.uk/internet/ecommerce/0,39020372,39117193,00.htm, accessed 9/04; Daniel B. Wood, "Forget the CD: Consumers Now Buy Music Online," Christian Science Monitor, 17 July 2002, www.csmonitor.com/2002/0712/p01s03-ussc.html?related, accessed 9/04.

30. Robyn Greenspan, "Gamers Growing Up," CyberAtlas, 29 August 2003, cyberatlas.internet.com/big_picture/demographics/article/0,,5901_3070391,00.html, accessed 9/04; Robyn Greenspan, "The Digitization of Home Entertainment," CyberAtlas, 31 March 2003, cyberatlas.internet.com/big_picture/applications/article/0,,1301_2172571,00.html, accessed 9/04.

31. Elizabeth Millard, "The Future of Online Gambling," E-Commerce Times News Network, 29 October 2003, www.linuxinsider.com/perl/story/31962.html, accessed 9/04; Staff, "Adult Content Industries," Caslon Analytics, 2003, www.caslon.com.au/xcontentprofile.htm, accessed 9/04.

32. Carnegie Mellon University, "Carnegie Mellon Study Reveals Negative Potential of Heavy Internet Use on Emotional Well-Being," 1998, homenet.hcii.cs.cmu.edu, accessed 9/04; Norman H. Nie and Lutz Erbring, "Internet and Society: A Preliminary Report," Stanford Institute for the Quantitative Study of Society (SIQSS), 6 July 2001, www.stanford.edu/group/siqss/Press_Release/internetStudy.html, accessed 9/04.

33. Peter Mitchell, "Internet Addiction: Genuine Diagnosis or Not?," The Lancet Interactive, 19 February 2000, www.thelancet.com/journal/vol355/iss9204/full/llan.355.9204.news.2083.1, accessed 9/04; Tori DeAngelis, "Is Internet Addiction Real?" Monitor on Psychology, vol. 31, no. 4, April 2000, www.apa.org/monitor/apr00/addiction.html, accessed 1/04.

34. Tony Pugh, "Online Complaints Empower Consumer," Lexington Herald-Leader, 26 April 2000, pp. A3, 11.

35. AsiaPulse/Yonhap, "Disgruntled Consumers Have Giants in Their Sites," Asia Times Online, 11 January 2000, www.atimes.com/media/BA11Ce02.html, accessed 9/04; Marcia Stepanek, "Now, Companies Can Track Down Their Cyber-Critics," BusinessWeek, 7 July 2000, www.businessweek.com/bwdaily/dnflash/july2000/nf00707g.htm, accessed 9/04.

36. Sally Alt, "Apollo Group, Inc. Fact Sheet," Hoover's Online, 2003, www.hoovers.com/apollo-group,-inc./—ID__42338—/free-co-factsheet.xhtml, accessed 1/04; Sally Alt, "DeVry, Inc. Fact Sheet," Hoover's Online, 2003, www.hoovers.com/devry/—ID__15303—/free-co-factsheet.xhtml, accessed 1/04; Staff, "DeVry University Online," www.uc411.com/getprofile.asp?profileid=481, accessed 9/04; Staff, "DeVry University Online Graduate Business Programs," U.S. News & World Report, Fall 2003, www.usnews.com/usnews/edu/elearning/directory/elearn2mba_H322.htm, accessed 9/04; Rachel Hartigan Shea, "E-learning Today," U.S. News & World Report, 28 October 2002, www.usnews.com/usnews/edu/elearning/articles/02phoenix.htm, accessed 1/04; William Symonds, "University of Phoenix Online: Swift Rise," BusinessWeek Online, 23 June 2003, www.businessweek.com/magazine/content/03_25/b3838628.htm, accessed 9/04.

Chapter 4

1. Alex Biesada, "Wal-Mart Stores, Inc.," Hoover's Online Fact Sheet, 2003, www.hoovers.com/co/capsule/0/0,2163,11600,00.html, accessed 9/04; Ann Zimmerman, "To Sell Goods to Wal-Mart, Get on the Net,"

Wall Street Journal, 21 November 2003, online.wsj.com, accessed 2/04; Charles Fishman, "The Wal-Mart You Don't Know," *FastCompany,* December 2003, www.fastcompany.com/magazine/77/ walmart.html, accessed 9/04; Robyn Greenspan, "Many Unhappy Returns," ClickZ Network, 4 September 2003, www.clickz.com/stats/ markets/retailing/article.php/6061_3072761, accessed 9/04; Erin Joyce, "Your Checks Are Good at Walmart.com," E-Commerce News, 23 July 2003, http://ecommerce.internet.com/news/news/article/ 0,3371,10375_2239011,00.html, accessed 9/04; Staff, "2003 Global Most Admired Companies," *Fortune,* 2003, www.fortune.com/fortune/ globaladmired, accessed 9/04; Staff, "2003 America's Most Admired Companies," *Fortune,* 2003, www.fortune.com/fortune/mostadmired, accessed 9/04; Parija Bhatnagar, "Walmart.com Looking to Stir Things Up," CNNMoney, 30 October 2003, money.cnn.com/2003/10/29/ news/companies/walmart/, accessed 9/04; James Maguire, "Case Study: Walmart.com," E-Commerce.Internet.com, 15 November 2002, ehttp://ecommerce.internet.com/news/insights/trends/article/ 0,3371,10417_1501651,00.html, accessed 9/04; Jessica Davis, "Wal-Mart Brings Remodeled Web Site Back Up—E-commerce Outlet Enlivened in Time for Holiday Season," *InfoWorld,* 6 November 2000, www.findarticles.com/cf_dls/m0IFW/45_22/66680312/p1/ article.jhtml, accessed 1/04; Mike Troy, "Better Late Than Never for Traditional Stores," *Discount Store News,* 13 December 1999, www .findarticles.com/cf_0/m3092/23_38/58381767/p1/article.jhtml?term= Wal-Mart.com, accessed 2/04; Staff, "A Leader Beyond Bricks and Mortar," *Discount Store News,* October 1999, www.findarticles.com/ cf_0/m3092/1999_Oct/57578942/p1/article.jhtml?term=Wal -Mart.com, accessed 2/04; Wal-Mart Stores, Inc., Corporate Site Information, www.walmart.com, accessed 9/04; Thane Peterson, "Walmart.com's Jeanne Jackson: 'A Foundation-Building Year,' " *BusinessWeek,* 30 October 2000, www.businessweek.com/bwdaily/ dnflash/oct2000/nf20001030_321.htm, accessed 9/04; Chet Dembeck, "Wal-Mart Spins Off E-Commerce Operations," E-Commerce Times, 7 January 2000, www.ecommercetimes.com/story/2250.html, accessed 9/04; Wendy Zellner, "Wal-Mart.com's Second Grand Opening," *BusinessWeek,* 29 September 2000, www.businessweek.com/bwdaily/ dnflash/sep2000/nf20000929_472.htm, accessed 9/04; Keith Regan, "Kmart, Wal-Mart Rein in E-tail Units," E-Commerce Times, 24 July 2001, www.ecommercetimes.com/perl/story/12229.html, accessed 9/04; Staff, Four-Part Series on Wal-Mart, National Public Radio, June 2003, www.npr.org/news/specials/walmart/, accessed 9/04.

2. Alan Greenspan, "The Challenge of Central Banking in a Democratic Society: Remarks by Chairman Greenspan at the Annual Dinner and Francis Boyer Lecture of the American Enterprise Institute for Public Policy Research, Washington, D.C.," Federal Reserve, 5 December 1996, www.federalreserve.gov/boarddocs/speeches/1996/ 19961205.htm, accessed 9/04; Staff, "Robert J. Shiller, Irrational Exuberance (Review)," *The American Journal of Economics and Sociology,* July 2000, www.findarticles.com/p/articles/mi_m0254/ is_3_59/ai_65348070, accessed 9/04.

3. Lydia Lee, "Boo Hoo!" Salon, 18 May 2000, http://dir.salon.com/ tech/log/2000/05/18/boo/index.html, accessed 9/04; Alexander Drobik, "Dot-coms Learn a Lesson from Boo.com," c/net News.com, 18 May 2000, news.com.com/2100-1017-240772.html?legacy=cnet, accessed 9/04; Jennifer DiSabatino, "Boo.com Failure Raises Questions About Online Boutiques," *Computerworld,* 12 June 2000, www.computerworld.com/news/2000/story/0,11280,45735,00.html, accessed 9/04.

4. Richard A. Wright, "A Brief History of the First 100 Years of the Automobile Industry in the United States—Chapter 1, A Century Whittles Auto Makers to 3," TheAutoChannel.com, 1996,

www.theautochannel.com/content/mania/industry/history/chap1.html, accessed 9/04; Mel Moffitt, "The Duryea Automobile—For Historic Truth Web Site," Duryea-Peoria.com, 2002, www.duryea-peoria.com, accessed 9/04.

5. Staff, "eZiba Announces Significant Sales Increase Due to Expansion into Multi-Channel Retailing," eZiba.com. October 2001, http://eziba.com/about_eziba_news_article.asp?XSL=xsl/about_eziba _news_press_release_16.xsl, accessed 9/04; Keith Regan, "Customer Service: The Good, the Bad and the Ugly," E-Commerce Times, 17 July 2000, www.ecommercetimes.com/story/3790.html, accessed 9/04; Business Editors, "eZiba.com Reports Record Sales for Holiday Season; E-Tailer of Handcrafted Goods Surpasses Own Aggressive Plan," *Business Wire,* 11 January 2001, www.findarticles.com/cf_dls/ m0EIN/2001_Jan_11/69010479/p1/article.jhtml, accessed 9/04.

6. Staff, Press Releases - 2001 to 2004, E°TRADE FINANCIAL website, https://us.etrade.com/e/t/home, accessed 9/04; Megan Barnett, "Getting Real," *The Standard,* 13 November 2000, www.findarticles .com/cf_0/m0HWW/48_3/67050951/p1/article.jhtml, accessed 9/04.

7. SBA, "Selecting the Legal Structure for Your Business," U.S. Small Business Administration, www.sba.gov/library/pubs/mp-25.pdf, 1 February 2002, accessed 2/04; SBA, "The U.S. Small Business Administration's Small Business Startup Kit," U.S. Small Business Administration, 9 February 1999, www.sba.gov/starting/ regulations.html, accessed 9/04.

8. Robyn Greenspan, "Small Biz Worried About Success," ClickZ Network, 1 October 2003, www.clickz.com/stats/markets/smallbiz/ article.php/10098_3086191, accessed 9/04; Staff, "Citigroup Expands Big-Business Advantages for Small Business at Bizzed.com," Citigroup Press Release, 15 November 2000, www.citigroup.com/citigroup/ press/2000/001115b.htm, accessed 9/04.

9. David Shook, "Jeff Bezos: Finally Relaxing?" *BusinessWeek,* 1 October 2002, www.businessweek.com/technology/content/oct2002/ tc2002101_9694.htm, accessed 9/04; Charles Fishman, "Face Time with Jeff Bezos," *FastCompany,* February 2001, www.fastcompany. com/magazine/43/bezos.html, accessed 9/04; Chip Bayers, "The Inner Bezos," *Wired,* March 1999, www.wired.com/wired/archive/7.03/ bezos.html, accessed 9/04.

10. U.S. Census Bureau, North American Industry Classification System (NAICS), 14 January 2004, www.census.gov/epcd/www/naics.html, accessed 9/04; U.S. Census Bureau, *Statistical Abstract of the United States,* 2002, www.census.gov/prod/www/statistical-abstract-02.html and www.census.gov/prod/2003pubs/02statab/business.pdf, accessed 9/04.

11. Judi Hasson and Graeme Browning, "Dot-Gov Goes Retail," Pew Internet & American Life Project, 30 May 2004, www.pewinternet .org/pdfs/PIP_FCW_Dot-gov_retail.pdf, accessed 9/04; Janet Kornblum, "Uncle Sam Wants You to Shop on the Net, *USA Today,* 29 May 2001, www.usatoday.com/tech/news/2001-05-29-ebrief.htm, accessed 9/04.

12. Michael Wilson, "Police-Loot Is Online and Yes, It's a Steal," *New York Times,* 4 January 2004, www.nytimes.com/2004/01/04/nyregion/ 04AUCT.html, accessed 9/04; Trudy Walsh, "Move Over, eBay: Police Auction Seized Goods over the Web," Government Computer News, July 2001, www.gcn.com/state/vol7_no7/tech-report/1082-1.html, accessed 9/04.

13. Business/Technology Editors, "Circle.com Turns American University's Business School Web-centric; Over 95% of Prospective Student Applications Submitted via School's Web Site," *Business Wire,* 25 April 2000, www.findarticles.com/cf_0/m0EIN/2000 _April_25/61638384/print.jhtml, accessed 9/04.

14. Odvard Egil Dyrli, "Web-Based Virtual Campus Tours," *Matrix,* June 2000, www.findarticles.com/cf_0/m0HJE/1_1/65014396/print.jhtml, accessed 9/04; Olive L. Sullivan, "Internet Speeds Up College Admissions Process," *Morning Sun,* 11 April 2003, www.morningsun.net/stories/041103/loc_20030411020.shtml, accessed 9/04.

15. Rachel Hartigan, "Surfing for Schools: How Students Can Use the Web to Research Colleges," *U.S. News & World Report, America's Best Colleges 2001,* http://static.elibrary.com/u/usnewsampworldreport/ september112000/surfingfortherightschool/, accessed 2/04.

16. Heather O'Mara, "Improve Training, Cut Costs with E-Learning Programs," *Los Angeles Business Journal,* 20 November 2000, www.findarticles.com/cf_0/m5072/47_22/67939556/print.jhtml, accessed 9/04.

17. Elena Larsen, "CyberFaith: How Americans Pursue Religion Online," Pew Internet & American Life Project, 23 December 2001, www.pewinternet.org/pdfs/PIP_CyberFaith_Report.pdf, accessed 9/04; Genia Jones, "Hallelujah, It's the Internet! Religion Is Proving to Be More Popular on the Web Than Online Auctions or Banking, According to a New Study," *PCWorld,* 23 December 2000, www.pcworld.com/news/article/0,aid,37024,00.asp, accessed 9/04.

18. Eileen Rivera, "Let There Be Websites," TechTV, 4 March 2002, www.g4techtv.com/techtvvault/features/36854/Let_There_Be_Websites.html, accessed 9/04; Berta Delgado, "Church Adding Dot.Com to Name as Ministry Tool,"*Lexington Herald-Leader,* 3 February 2001, www. kentuckyconnect.com/heraldleader/news/020301/ faithdocs/dotcom03.htm, accessed 2/01.

19. Samuel Flint, "Building Your Nonprofit Organization Through the Internet," The Alford Group, May 2000, www.donornet.com/ general/articles/may00flint.htm, accessed 6/02; Tom Watson, "A Watershed Moment for Online Fundraising," TechSoup, 7 August 2002, www.techsoup.org/howto/articlepage.cfm?ArticleId=406=10, accessed 2/04; Todd Cohen, "Seeking Big Donors," *The NonProfit Times,* 1 January 2004, www.nptimes.com/Jan04/cyberfrontier.html, accessed 9/04; Harry Lynch, "What Your Mother Can Teach You About Online Fundraising," On Philanthropy, 24 October 2003, www.onphilanthropy.com/tren_comm/tc2003-10-24.html, accessed 9/04.

20. Carol Ebbinghouse, "Avoiding Charity Fraud and Misinformation from Non-Profits on the Internet," *Searcher,* July/August 2000, pp. 58–63; Carol Ebbinghouse, "Deliberate Misinformation on the Internet?: Tell Me It Ain't So!" *Searcher,* May 2000, pp. 63–67.

21. Pew Trusts, "Charitable Groups Discover New Revenue in Retailing Goods via Their Own Web Sites," *New York Times,* 27 March 2000, www.pewtrusts.com/news/news_subpage.cfm?content_item_id=85& content_type_id=13&page=nr2, accessed 9/04; Robert Travis, "Shop-for-a-Cause Web Sites: Conclusions and Speculations," NCIB's Wise Giving Guide, Fall 1999, www.give.org/guide/index.asp, accessed 6/02.

22. Business Wire Features, "Shopping Online for the Holidays Helps Raise Money for Charities; Commission Junction's Technology Allows Consumers to Donate to Charities Online," *Business Wire,* 14 December 2000, www.findarticles.com/cf_0/m0EIN/2000_Dec_14/ 68013336/print.jhtml, accessed 9/04; Beth Kaner, "Exploring Online Fundraising for Nonprofit Arts Organizations," Idealist.org, www.idealist.org/beth.html, accessed 9/04; Patricia Berry, "Scams Swiftly Follow Terrorist Attacks: Beware of Cons Tied to Tragedy," AARP, November 2001, www.aarp.org/bulletin/consumer/Articles/ a2003-07-01-scams_terr.html, accessed 9/04.

23. E-Commerce Times, "Final Whistle Blows for Sports Retailers," *Nua,* 8 February 2001, www.nua.net/surveys/index.cgi?f=VS&art_id= 905356435&rel=true, accessed 9/04; Troy J. Strader and Sridhar N.

Ramaswami, "The Value of Seller Trustworthiness in C2C Online Markets," *Communications of the ACM,* December 2002, pp. 45–50.

24. ClickZ Network Staff, "Top Searches of 2003," ClickZ Network, 31 December 2003, www.clickz.com/stats/big_picture/traffic_patterns/ article.php/5931_3293581, accessed 9/04; Holly Aguirre and Sonya A. Donaldson, "Celebrities Online," *Black Enterprise,* July 2002, pp. 45–46.

25. Jodie T. Allen, "Unconfident Consumers," *U.S. News & World Report,* 12 February 2001, www.usnews.com/usnews/issue/010212/econ.htm, accessed 9/04.

26. Staff, "Holiday Online Sales on Fire," *Money,* 29 December 2003, money.cnn.com/2003/12/29/news/companies/holiday_online/?cnn=yes, accessed 9/04; Staff, "Happy e-Christmas: UK Online Sales Up 70% to £2.5b," inSourced, 2 February 2004, www.in-sourced.com/article/ articleview/1198/1/1/, accessed 9/04; Laura Rush and ClickZ Network Staff, "Women, Comparison Shopping Help Boost E-commerce Holiday Revenues," ClickZ Network, 15 January 2004, www.clickz.com/stats/markets/retailing/article.php/6061_3299531, accessed 9/04.

27. Eric Palmer, "Computers, Internet Blamed for Higher Gas Prices, Shortage," *Kansas City Star,* 5 February 2001, www.kentuckyconnect. com/heraldleader/news/020501/nationaldocs/05Close-up.htm, accessed 2/01; John L. Micek, "Internet Blamed for California Power Emergency," News Factor Network, 18 January 2001, http://crm-daily. newsfactor.com/perl/story/6817.html, accessed 9/04.

28. Tom Spring, "Terror, Tragedy of Attacks Ripple to the Net," *PCWorld. com,* 11 September 2001, www.pcworld.com/resource/ printable/article/0,aid,61604,00.asp, accessed 9/04; Dwight Cass and Matthew Crabbe, "September 11: Dealing with the Aftermath," *Risk Magazine,* October 2001, www.riskwaters.com/risk/latest/oct01/ cover01.htm, accessed 11/01; Randy Barrett and *Interactive Week* Staff, "Safety Net," *Interactive Week,* 17 September 2001, www.interactiveweek.com/print_article/0,3668,a%253D14477,00.asp, accessed 11/01.

29. ClickZ Network Staff, "U.S. Web Usage and Traffic, December 2003," ClickZ Network, 27 January 2004, www.clickz.com/stats/big_picture/ traffic_patterns/article.php/5931_3301321, accessed 9/04; Laura Rush and ClickZ Network Staff, "Women, Comparison Shopping Help Boost E-commerce Holiday Revenues," ClickZ Network, 15 January 2004, www.clickz.com/stats/markets/retailing/article.php/ 6061_3299531, accessed 9/04; Robyn Greenspan, "Many Unhappy Returns," ClickZ Network, 4 September 2003, www.clickz.com/ stats/markets/retailing/article.php/6061_3072761, accessed 9/04.

Chapter 5

1. Katie Dean, "New Napster Off to a Solid Start," Wired News, 3 November 2003, www.wired.com/news/digiwood/0,1412,61023,00. html, accessed 9/04; Jefferson Graham, "Napster Goes Legit This Week," *USA Today,* 5 October 2003, www.usatoday.com/tech/news/ internetprivacy/2003-10-05-napster_x.htm, accessed 9/04; Bill Mann, "Napster's Back," The Motley Fool, 10 October 2003, www.fool.com/ News/mft/2003/mft03101008.htm, accessed 9/04; Matt Richtel, "Napster Is Told to Remain Shut," *New York Times,* 12 July 2001, www.nytimes.com, accessed 9/04; Warren Cohen, "Napster's Rap Sheet," *U.S. News & World Report,* 8 May 2000, p. 45; Staff, "Napster's Musical History," *The Standard,* 12 February 2001, www.thestandard.com/article/article_print/0,1153,22139,00.html, accessed 6/02; Dan Goodin, "Can Napster Change Its Tune?," *The Standard,* 18 February 2001, www.thestandard.com/article/ article_print/0,1153,22296,00.html, accessed 6/02; Scott Rosenberg,

"The Napster Files," Salon, 4 February 2000, http://dir.salon.com/tech/col/rose/2000/02/04/napster_swap/index.html, accessed 9/04.

2. Henry H. Perritt, Jr., "The Internet Is Changing the Public International Legal System," *Chicago-Kent Law Journal,* 2000, www.kentlaw.edu/cyberlaw/perrittnetchg.html, accessed 9/04.

3. Staff, "Status of Conventions and Model Laws," United Nations Commission on International Trade Law (UNCITRAL), 8 April 2004, www.uncitral.org/en-index.htm, accessed 9/04; Staff, "UNCITRAL Model Law on Electronic Commerce with Guide to Enactment," UNCITRAL, 1996 (additional article 1998), www.uncitral.org/english/texts/electcom/ml-ecomm.htm, accessed 9/04; Dave Reddick, "Electronic Signatures Take Hold in U.S.," *eCommerce Times,* 17 February 2000, www.ecommercetimes.com/perl/story/2535.html, accessed 9/04; Arent Fox Kintner Plotkin & Kahn, PLLC, "Electronic Signatures in Global and National Commerce Act," FindLaw, 2000, http://library.lp.findlaw.com/articles/file/00077/000250/title/Subject/topic/Communications_Wiretapping/filename/communications_1_294, accessed 9/04.

4. Staff, "Day 5: Conference Ends Without Consensus," World Trade Organization, 14 September 2003, www.wto.org/english/thewto_e/minist_e/min03_e/min03_14sept_e.htm#statement, accessed 9/04; WTO Briefing Note, "Electronic Commerce: Work Programme Reflects Growing Importance," World Trade Organization, http://www.wto.org/english/tratop_e/ecom_e/ecom_briefnote_e.htm, accessed 9/04.

5. FTC and OECD, "Electronic Commerce. Selling Internationally: A Guide for Business," Federal Trade Commission, March 2000, www.ftc.gov/bcp/conline/pubs/alerts/ecombalrt.htm, accessed 9S/04.

6. Lisa M. Bowman, "Global Treaty—Threat to the Net?," ZDNet.com, 22 June 2001, http://news.zdnet.co.uk/internet/0,39020369,2089815,00.htm, accessed 9/04; Elizabeth Hurt, "Border Disputes Simmer," 30 April 2001, *Business2.0,* www.business2.com/articles/web/print/0,1650,15697,FF.html, accessed 6/02; Peter Griffin, "Global Web Law a Thorny Issue," *New Zealand Herald,* 16 July 2001, www.nzherald.co.nz/storydisplay.cfm?storyID=200279, accessed 9/04.

7. Juliet M. Oberding and Terje Norderhaug, "A Separate Jurisdiction for Cyberspace?," *Journal of Computer Mediated Communication* 2, no. 1 (June 1996), www.ascusc.org/jcmc/vol2/issue1/juris.html, accessed 9/04.

8. United Nations, "Convention on the Law of the Sea," UN Division for Ocean Affairs and the Law of the Sea, 2001, www.un.org/Depts/los/convention_agreements/convention_overview_convention.htm, accessed 9/04.

9. Staff, "Jurisdiction," LawInfo.Com, 2004, http://resources.lawinfo.com/index.cfm?action=dictionary&show=main, accessed 9/04.

10. Christopher Wolf, "Internet Jurisdiction," FindLaw.com, 1999, http://profs.lp.findlaw.com/netjuris/index.html, accessed 9/04; Staff, "Zippo Mfr. Co. v. Zippo Dot Com, Inc., 952 F. Supp. 1119 (W.D. Pa. 1997) Case Abstract, The Berkman Center for Internet & Society, Harvard Law School, 1997, http://cyber.law.harvard.edu/property00/jurisdiction/zipposum.html, accessed 9/04; Doug Isenberg, "Zippo Manufacturing Company v. Zippo Dot Com, Inc., U.S. District Court, Western District of Pennsylvania," 1997, www.gigalaw.com/library/zippo-zippo-1997-01-16.html, accessed 9/04; Staff, "Civil Action No. 96-397 Erie, United States District Court for the Western District of Pennsylvania, 952 F. Supp. 1119; 1997 U.S. Dist. LEXIS 1701; 42 U.S.P.Q.2D (BNA) 1062, 16 January 1997, Chicago-Kent School of Law, www.kentlaw.edu/legalaspects/zippo.html, accessed 9/04.

11. Roy Whitehead and Pam Spikes, "Determining Internet Jurisdiction," *CPA Journal,* 7 March 2003, www.nysscpa.org/cpajournal/2003/0703/features/f072403.htm, accessed 9/04; Doug Isenberg, "The Legal Side Effects of Internet Jurisdiction," GigaLaw.com, August 2001, www.gigalaw.com/articles/2001-all/isenberg-2001-08-all.html, accessed 9/04; Baila H. Celedonia and Joel Karni Schmidt, "Internet Jurisdiction: The Global Issue of Liability for Trademark Infringement on the Web," CLL, 21 November 2002, www.cll.com/articles/article.cfm?articleid=151, accessed 9/04.

12. Staff, "Global Survey: U.S. Companies More Concerned About Internet Jurisdiction Than European and Asian Companies," American Bar Association, 2 April 2004, http://www.abanet.org/media/releases/news040204_1.html, accessed 9/04; Michael Geist, "Survey of Global Internet Jurisdiction," CircleID, 7 April 2004, www.circleid.com/article/560_0_1_0_C/, accessed 9/04: Michael Geist, "World Resists One-Size-Fits-All Web Laws," *Toronto Star,* 5 April 2004, www.thestar.com/NASApp/cs/ContentServer?pagename=thestar/Layout/Article_Type1&c=Article&cid=1081116610792&call_pageid=968350072197&col=969048863851, accessed 9/04.

13. Robin Peek, "Customizing the World on the Web," *Information Today,* May 2000, www.infotoday.com/it/may00/peek.htm, accessed 9/04; Darrel Menthe, "Jurisdiction in Cyberspace: A Theory of International Spaces," *Michigan Telecommunication Technical Legal Review,* 23 April 1998, www.mttlr.org/volfour/menthe.html, accessed 9/04.

14. Martin Stone, "Japanese Court Ruling Could Impact Internet Law," *Newsbytes PM,* 23 March 1999, www.findarticles.com/p/articles/mi_m0HDN/is_1999_March_23/ai_54201297, accessed 9/04.

15. John Burgess, "Amazon Reverses on Hitler Book," *Newsbytes,* 18 November 1999, www.exn.ca/Stories/1999/11/18/01.asp, accessed 9/04.

16. Stephen Lawson, "Judge Dismisses French Case Against Yahoo," IDG News Service, 9 November 2001, www.pcworld.com/news/article/0,aid,70323,00.asp, accessed 9/04; Staff, "Landmark Ruling Against Yahoo! in Nazi Auction Case," *The Guardian,* 20 November 2000, www.guardian.co.uk/freespeech/article/0,2763,400491,00.html, accessed 9/04; Peter Sayer and Sarah Deveaux, "Jurisdiction in Cyberspace," *PCWorld.com,* 28 July 2000, www.pcworld.com/news/article/0,aid,17868,00.asp, accessed 9/04.

17. Nick Hasell, "Sportingbet Tipped to Gain from WTO Ruling," TimesOnline, 26 March 2004, http://business.timesonline.co.uk/article/0,,8211-1051558,00.html, accessed 9/04; Mark Berniker, "Antigua May Fight U.S. Online Gambling Ban Plan," InternetNews, 25 March 2003, www.internetnews.com/ec-news/article.php/2169921, accessed 9/04; Matt Richtel, "Trade Group Says U.S. Ban on Net Gambling Violates Global Law," *New York Times,* 26 March 2004, http://nytimes.com, accessed 4/04; David Colker and Jason Whong, "E-Commerce Taxation in California: A Look at Nexus and Entity Isolation for Sales and Use Taxes," GrayCary, May 2002, www.gcwf.com/gcc/GrayCary-C/News—Arti/Articles/052002.2.doc_cvt.htm, accessed 9/04; Elizabeth Hurt, "Border Disputes Simmer," 30 April 2001, *Business2.0,* www.business2.com/articles/web/print/0,1650,15697,FF.html, accessed 9/04.

18. Staff, "Bush Asks Senate Approval to Ratify Convention on Cybercrime," U.S. Department of State, 17 November 2003, http://usinfo.state.gov/gi/Archive/2003/Nov/18-773753.html, accessed 9/04; Staff, "Entry into Force of the Council of Europe Convention on Cybercrime," Council on Europe, 18 March 2004, http://press.coe.int/cp/2004/135a(2004).htm, accessed 9/04; Rick Perera, "30 Countries Sign Controversial Cybercrime Treaty," *PCWorld.com,* 26 November 2001, www.pcworld.com/news/article/0,aid,72903,00.asp, accessed 9/04; Council of Europe, "Convention on Cybercrime, ETS no. 185," 23 November 2001, http://conventions.coe.int/Treaty/en/Treaties/Html/185.htm, accessed 9/04.

19. Raven Taylor, "The Patriot Act," *PBS The News Hour,* 12 February 2003, www.pbs.org/newshour/extra/features/jan-june03/patriot.html, accessed 9/04; Staff, "EFF Analysis of the Provisions of the USA Patriot Act That Relate to Online Activities," Electronic Frontier Foundation, 27 October 2003, www.eff.org/Privacy/Surveillance/ Terrorism/20011031_eff_usa_patriot_analysis.php, accessed 9/04; D. Ian Hopper, "New Law Lets U.S. Nab Foreign Hackers," Associated Press, 26 November 2001, http://lists.econ.utah.edu/pipermail/ rad-green/2001-November/001773.html, accessed 9/02; Jessica Reaves, "Antiterrorism Bill Becomes Law," *Time.com,* 26 October 2001, www.time.com/time/nation/printout/0,8816,181437,00.html, accessed 9/04.

20. Staff, "Bill Summary and Status for the 107th Congress–H.R. 3162," U.S. Congress, 2001, http://thomas.loc.gov/cgi-bin/bdquery/ z?d107:h.r.03162:, accessed 9/04; Charles Lane, "U.S. May Seek Wider Anti-Terror Powers," *Washington Post,* 8 February 2003, http://foi.missouri.edu/domsecenhanceact/usmayseek.html, accessed 9/04; Stephen Gardner, "EU Must Guard Against Security Creep," EuroObserver, 14 April 2003, www.euobserver.com/index .phtml?print=true&sid=9&aid=10925, accessed 9/04.

21. IDC Research, "Worldwide Net Traffic to Rise," Nua Internet Surveys, 23 March 2003, www.nua.com/surveys/index.cgi?f= VS&art_id=905358733&rel=true, accessed 9/04; Staff, "Internet Users Will Top 1 Billion in 2005. Wireless Internet Users Will Reach 48% in 2005," *Computer Industry Almanac,* 21 March 2002, www .c-i-a.com/pr032102.htm, accessed 9/04.

22. Staff, "Retail E-Commerce Sales In Second Quarter 2004 Were $15.7 Billion, Up 23.1 Percent From Second Quarter 2003, Census Bureau Reports," Economics and Statistics Administration, Census Bureau, 20 August 2004, www.census.gov/mrts/www/current.html, accessed 9/04; Bob Sullivan, "Just How Bad Is Online Fraud?," MSNBC, 25 June 2001, www.cardcops.com/msnbc/msnbc1.htm, accessed 9/04; Jaikumar Vijayan, "Fears of Online Fraud Rise as Shopping Season Begins," *Computerworld,* 1 December 2003, www.computerworld .com/securitytopics/security/privacy/story/0,10801,87602,00.html, accessed 9/04; Olaf Jüptner, "Online Fraud Not as Bad as You Think," e-Gateway (European Commission), 19 June 2001, www.e-gateway .net/infoarea/news/news.cfm?nid=1679, accessed 9/04; Mathew Schwartz, "Busting B2B e-commerce Fraud," *Computerworld,* 19 February 2001, www.itworld.com/Tech/2409/CWSTO57770/ pfindex.html, accessed 9/04.

23. Staff, "National and State Trends in Fraud and Identity Theft: January–December 2003," Federal Trade Commission, 22 January 2004, www.consumer.gov/sentinel/pubs/Top10Fraud2003.pdf, accessed 9/04; Ryan Naraine, "FTC: Online Fraud Losses Hit $473 Million," Internet.com, 23 January 2004, www.internetnews.com/ bus-news/article.php/3302971, accessed 9/04.

24. Patricia Berry, "Scams Swiftly Follow Terrorist Attacks: Beware of Cons Tied to Tragedy," *AARP Bulletin Online,* November 2001, www.aarp.org/bulletin/consumer/Articles/a2003-07-01-scams _terr.html, accessed 9/04.

25. Staff, "Businesses Better Understanding Online Fraud," *ClickZ Stats,* 3 December 2001, www.clickz.com/stats/markets/retailing/ print.php/6061_932941, accessed 9/04; Staff, "New Report Reveals Latest Internet Fraud Trends, Statistics, and Hotbeds," National White Collar Crime Center, www.nw3c.org/2001_media.html, accessed 9/04; Joanna Glasner, "FBI: Net Fraud Reports Rising," *Wired News,* 13 June 2001, www.wired.com/news/politics/ 0,1283,44452,00.html, accessed 9/04.

26. Staff, "Judge Dismisses eBay Fraud Case," ZDNet News, 19 January 2001, www.zdnet.com/zdnn/stories/news/0,4586,2676115,00.html,

accessed 9/04; Margaret Mannix, "Sure It's a Great Deal. But Is It Real?," *USNews.com,* 11 December 2001, www.usnews.com/ usnews/home.htm, accessed 9/04.

27. Fraud Protection Network, "New Web Site Helps E-Tailers Combat Online Fraud," Worldwide E-Commerce Fraud Protection Network," 15 January 2001, www.merchantriskcouncil.org/press.php?p _press_id=3, accessed 9/04; Sharon Curry, "E-Commerce Fraud," *Internet ScamBusters* 39, 31 August 2000, www.scambusters.org/ Scambusters39.html, accessed 9/04.

28. Jakob Nielsen, "Deep Linking Is Good Linking," Jakob Nielsen's Alertbox, 3 March 2002, www.useit.com/alertbox/20020303.html, accessed 9/04; Mike France, "Did 'Deep-Linking' Really Get a Green Light?," *Business Week* Online, 31 July 2000, www.businessweek.com/ ebiz/0007/ep0731.htm, accessed 9/04.

29. Doug Mellgren, "Teen-age Computer Whiz Scares Hollywood, Inspires Hackers," *Lexington Herald-Leader,* 25 February 2001, p. A11.

30. George A. Chidi, "Akamai, Digital Island Will Square Off in Court," *InfoWorld,* 8 February 2001, www.infoworld.com/articles/hn/ xml/01/02/08/010208hncourt.xml, accessed 4/04; Damien Cave, "Patently Absurd?," Salon, 3 March 2000, www.salon.com/tech/feature/ 2000/03/03/patent/print.html, accessed 9/04; Scott Rosenberg, "Amazon to World: We Control How Many Times You Must Click!," Salon, 21 December 1999, www.salon.com/tech/log/1999/12/21/ bezos/, accessed 9/04; David Sims, "Amazon.com Patents Enemy-Making Process," *The Standard,* 28 February 2000, www.thestandard .com/article/display/0,1151,12377,00.html, accessed 6/02.

31. Saul Hansell, "Surging Number of Patents Engulfs Internet Commerce," *New York Times* Online, 11 December 1999, www.nytimes.com/library/tech/99/12/biztech/articles/11web.html, accessed 9/04; Karen Rodriguez, "Dot-coms Scramble for Patent Protection in Record Numbers," *Silicon Valley Business Journal,* 8 September 2000, http://sanjose.bcentral.com/sanjose/ stories/2000/09/11/story8.html, accessed 9/04; Jonathan Krim, "Patenting Air or Protecting Property?," Information Age Invents a New Problem, *Washington Post,* 11 December 2003, p. E01, www.washingtonpost.com/ac2/wp-dyn/A54548-2003Dec10 ?language=printer, accessed 9/04.

32. Maxine Lans Retsky, "Trademark Applications Simplified," *Marketing News,* 14 February 2000, www.findarticles.com/cf_0/m4313/ 4_34/61493365/print.jhtml, accessed 2/01.

33. Michael L. Baroni, "Diluting Trademark Protection on the Web," GigaLaw.com, May 2003, www.gigalaw.com/articles/2003-all/baroni -2003-05-all.html, accessed 9/04; William Mears, "Victoria's Secret Case Tests the Power of a Name," CNN.com/Law Center, 9 November 2002, www.cnn.com/2002/LAW/11/08/scotus.trademark/, accessed 9/04; Jill Priluck, "The Reel.com Deal," *The Industry Standard,* 10 May 2000, www.thestandard.com/article/display/ 0,1151,14946,00.html, accessed 6/02.

34. Staff, "James Bond Zaps Cybersquatter," CNN.com/Technology, 1 September 2003, http://www.cnn.com/2003/TECH/internet/09/ 01/web.brosnan/, accessed 9/04; Doug Isenberg, "The Year in Net Law," *Internet World,* 15 December 2000, www.findarticles.com/ cf_0/m0DXS/24_6/68155732/p1/article.jhtml, accessed 4/04.

35. Andy Sullivan, "Cybersecurity Liability Seen Increasing," CNET News.com, 28 March 2004, http://investor.news.com/Engine ?Account=cnet&PageName=NEWSREAD&ID=969530&Ticker =RSAS&SOURCE=N28200065, accessed 9/04; Lee J. Johnson, "Offering Medical Advice on the Web," *Medical Economics Archive,* 10 July 2000, www.memag.com/be_core/content/journals/m/ data/2000/0710/lee143.html, accessed 9/04.

36. Roy Mark, "FTC Concludes Annual Holiday Web Surf," Internet.com, 2 December 2002, http://boston.internet.com/news/article.php/ 1550251, accessed 9/04; Carol Ebbinghouse, "Webmaster Liability: Look Before You Link, and Other Admonitions for Today's Webmaster," Searcher, February 1998, www.infotoday.com/searcher/ feb98/sidebar.htm, accessed 9/04.

37. Rusty Dornin, "House Passes Digital Signature Bill," CNN.com, 31 January 2000, www.cnn.com/2000/TECH/computing/01/31/ esignatures/, accessed 9/04; Benjamin D. Thomas, "Bad Signs," LinuxSecurity.com, 25 October 2000, www.linuxsecurity.com/ articles/general_article-1823.html, accessed 9/04.

38. Patty Edfors, "Your John Hancock Goes Digital," *Communications News,* December 2000, www.comnews.com/stories/articles/ c1200guest.htm, accessed 9/04.

39. Jennifer LeClaire, "Companies Largely Ignore Web Sites Lambasting Them," *Sacramento Business Journal,* 7 November 2003, www.v -fluence.com/resources/hatesites.html, accessed 9/04; Peter Crush, "Out to Get You," *Management Today,* November 2000, www.clickmt.com/index.cfm, accessed 6/02.

40. Allen Wastler, "Kiss Your Taxless Net Goodbye," CNN Money.com, 27 February 2004, http://money.cnn.com/2004/02/25/commentary/ wastler/wastler/index.htm?cnn=yes, accessed 9/04; TechWeb News, "States Move to Tax Internet Sales," InternetWeek.com, 4 March 2004, www.internetweek.com/e-business/showArticle.jhtml ?articleID=18202028, accessed 9/04; Michael Greve, "Sell Globally, Tax Locally," American Enterprise Institute Online, December 2003, www.taemag.com/issues/articleID.17771/article_detail.asp, accessed 9/04; Roy Mark, "End of the Beginning: Internet Sales Tax," Internet.com, 13 November 2002, www.internetnews.com/ec- news/article.php/1499501, accessed 9/04; Andrew Caffrey, "States at Odds over Web Taxes," *Wall Street Journal,* 7 March 2001, p. B3; Jason Anders, "Pressure Grows to Allow Web Sales Taxes," *Wall Street Journal,* 15 March 2001, p. B12.; Linda Rosencrance, "Online Sales Continue to Climb," *PCWorld,* 21 February 2002, www.pcworld.com/ news/article/0,aid,85424,00.asp, accessed 9/04; L. J. Martinez and Jon Weisman, "Bush Signs Off on Extension of Net Tax Ban," *E-Commerce Times,* 29 November 2001, www.ecommercetimes .com/perl/story/15021.html, accessed 9/04

41. AP, "Bush to Sign Bill Extending Net Tax Ban," *USA Today,* 16 November 2001, www.usatoday.com/tech/news/2001/11/16/net -taxes.htm, accessed 9/04; Grant Gross, "Senate Extends Internet Tax Moratorium," IDG News Service, 30 April 2004, www.cbsnews.com/ stories/2004/04/30/tech/main614855.shtml, accessed 9/04.

42. AP, "Arizona Senator Plans to Push Internet Gambling Bill Again," *USA Today,* 29 January 2004, www.usatoday.com/tech/news/ techpolicy/2004-01-29-net-gambling-bill_x.htm, accessed 9/04; Staff, "Should Online Gambling Be Banned in the U.S.?," Casino World, 2004, www.gamblingmagazine.com/articles/37/37-21.htm, accessed 9/04; Elsa Wenzel, "What Are the Odds of Legal Online Casinos?," *PCWorld.com,* 29 April 2003, www.pcworld.com/news/article/0 ,aid,110508,00.asp, accessed 9/04; Beth Cox, "Could Online Gambling Be Banned?," InternetNews.com, 13 March 2002, www.internetnews .com/ec-news/article.php/4_990891, accessed 9/04; Marci McDonald, "Online Gambling Proves Addictive–Even to the Big Casinos," *U.S. News & World Report,* 16 October 2000, pp. 44–46; Beth Cox, "Could Online Gambling Be Banned?," InternetNews.com, 13 March 2002, www.internetnews.com/ec-news/article.php/990891, accessed 9/04.

43. Staff, "Bill Summary and Status for the 108th Congress," U.S. Congress, 2004, http://thomas.loc.gov/cgi-bin/bdquery/z?d108:s.00627, accessed 9/04; Richard Waddington, "Antigua Claims Win over U.S. in Gaming Dispute," Reuters, 25 March 2004, www.msnbc.msn.com/

id/4594859/, accessed 9/04; Brian Krebs, "U.S. Internet Gambling Crackdown Sparks WTO Complaint," *Washington Post,* 21 July 2003, www.washingtonpost.com, accessed 9/04; Matt Richtel, "Trade Group Says U.S. Ban on Net Gambling Violates Global Law," *New York Times,* 26 March 2004, www.nytimes.com, accessed 9/04.

44. Steve Kroft, "Porn in the U.S.A.," *60 Minutes,* CBS News, 21 November 2003, www.cbsnews.com/stories/2003/11/21/60minutes/ main585049.shtml, accessed 9/04; Bill Keveney, "Hollywood Gets in Bed with Porn," *USA Today,* 16 October 2003, www.usatoday.com/ life/2003-10-16-porn_x.htm, accessed 9/04; Jeordan Legon, "Sex Sells, Especially to Web Surfers," CNN.com, 11 December 2003, www.cnn .com/2003/TECH/internet/12/10/porn.business/, accessed 9/04; Melba Newsome, "The Plastic Police Are Cracking Down," *Red Herring,* 1 September 2000, www.redherring.com/mag/issue82/mag-pornography -82.html, accessed 4/04; ABC News, "Porn Pullout," ABCNews.com, 7 May 2001, http://abcnews.go.com/sections/business/DailyNews/ yahooporn010507.html, accessed 9/04.

45. Edvard Pettersson, "Porn Entrepreneur Gives Inside Look at Profiting Online," *Los Angeles Business Journal,* 27 November 2000, www .findarticles.com/cf_0/m5072/48_22/67643185/p1/article.jhtml, accessed 9/04; Erik Gruenwedel, "Tricks of the Trade," *Brandweek,* 30 October 2000, www.findarticles.com/cf_0/m0BDW/42_41/ 66705311/p1/article.jhtml, accessed 9/04; John Buskin, "The Web's Dirty Little Secret," *Wall Street Journal,* 17 April 2000, p. R54; Keith Regan, "Online Porn Profits Still Lurk in Shadows," E-Commerce Times, 31 January 2002, www.ecommercetimes.com/perl/story/ 16088.html, accessed 9/04.

46. Brian Hindo, "Playboy Survives Its Mid-life Crisis," *Business Week Online,* 20 August 2003, www.businessweek.com/bwdaily/dnflash/ aug2003/nf20030820_1555_db014.htm, accessed 10/04; Stephen Lacey, "Playboy.com IPO Has the Harder Core Eyeing Public Marts," *Investment Dealers' Digest,* 4 October 1999, www.findarticles.com/ cf_0/m3628/1999_Oct_4/66164381/print.jhtml, accessed 3/01; Playboy Enterprises, 2001 10K SEC Filing, Playboy Enterprises, Inc., 21 March 2002, www.corporate-ir.net/ireye/ir_site.zhtml?ticker= PLA&script=700, accessed 9/04.

47. Lisa Shuchman, "Teach Your Children Well," *The Standard,* 13 November 2000, www.findarticles.com/cf_dls/m0HWW/48_3/ 67050928/p1/article.jhtml, accessed 9/04.

48. American Marketing Association, "Code of Ethics for Internet Marketing," AMA, 2004, www.marketingpower.com/, accessed 9/04.

49. Federal Trade Commission, "How to Comply with the Children's Online Privacy Protection Act," FTC, November 1999, www.ftc.gov/ bcp/conline/pubs/buspubs/coppa.htm, accessed 9/04; Michael Pastore, "Children Likely to Reveal Information Online," ClickZ Network, 24 May 2000, www.clickz.com/stats/markets/advertising/article.php/ 5941_379511, accessed 9/04.

50. Staff, "Teens Have Easy Cigarette Access Online," American Cancer Society, 9 October 2003, www.cancer.org/docroot/NWS/content/ NWS_2_1x_Teens_Have_Easy_Cigarette_Access_Online.asp, accessed 9/04; David McGuire, "Net Tobacco Sales Pose Threat to Minors," Biz Report, 10 December 2001, www.bizreport.com/ article.php?art_id=2632, accessed 9/04.

51. Staff, "Right of Privacy: Access to Personal Information," Legal Information Institute, Cornell University, 2004, www.law.cornell.edu/ topics/personal_information.html, accessed 9/04; Staff, "Right of Privacy: Personal Autonomy," Legal Information Institute, Cornell University, 2004, www.law.cornell.edu/topics/personal _autonomy.html, accessed 9/04.

52. Declan McCullagh, "Court Says Anti-Smut Law Illegal," *Wired,* 22 June 2000, www.wired.com/news/politics/0,1283,37171,00.html,

accessed 9/04; Keith Perine, "De-COPA-tated," *The Standard,* 26 June 2000, www.thestandard.com/article/article_print/0,1153,16352,00.html, accessed 6/02.

53. Staff, "Privacy in Cyberspace: Rules of the Road for the Information Superhighway," Privacy Rights Clearinghouse, August 2003, www.privacyrights.org/fs/fs18-cyb.htm, accessed 9/04.

54. Heather Green, "Your Right to Privacy: Going . . . Going. . . .," *Business Week,* 23 April, 2001, p. 48; Glenn R. Simpson, "The Battle over Web Privacy," *Wall Street Journal,* 21 March 2001, pp. B1, B4; Christina Le Beau, "Mountains to Mine," *American Demographics,* 1 August 2001, www.americandemographics.com/, accessed 10/01.

55. Christopher Saunders, "EU OKs Spam Ban, Online Privacy Rules," Privacy Rights Clearinghouse/UCAN, August 2003, www.privacyrights.org/fs/fs18-cyb.htm, accessed 9/04; Staff, "The European Union Directive on the Protection of Personal Data," Federal Trade Commission, www.ftc.gov/reports/privacy/APPENDIXb.htm, accessed 9/04; Peter K. Yu, "An Introduction to the EU Directive on the Protection of Personal Data," GigaLaw.com, July 2001, www.gigalaw.com/articles/2001-all/yu-2001-07a-all.html, accessed 9/04.

56. Harris Interactive, "Website Privacy Policies Need Plainer English," *Nua,* 4 December 2001, www.nua.net/surveys/index.cgi?f=VS&art_id=905357471&rel=true, accessed 9/04.

57. Grant Gross, "Is the Can-Spam Law Working?" *PCWorld,* 13 January 2004, www.pcworld.com/news/article/0,aid,114287,00.asp, accessed 9/04; Declan McCullagh, "Bush OKs Spam Bill—But Critics Not Convinced," CNET News.com, 16 December 2003, http://news.com.com/2100-1028-5124724.html?part=dtx&tag=ntop%20, accessed 9/04; Jennifer Barrett, "When Crooks Go 'Phishing,' " *Newsweek,* 26 January 2004, p. 66; Scott Woolley, "A New Low," *Forbes,* 27 October 2003, p. 4; Brad Stone, "Soaking in Spam," *Newsweek,* 24 November 2003, pp. 66–69; Martin Stone, "Two Spam-Scanners Sentenced for Web Fraud," *eMarketer,* 3 January 2001, www.findarticles.com/p/articles/mi_m0NEW/is_2001_Jan_3/ai_68713210, accessed 9/04.

58. Kevin J. Delaney, "Will Users Care If Gmail Invades Privacy?," *Wall Street Journal,* 6 April 2004, pp. B1, B3; Staff, "Twenty-Eight Thirty-One Privacy and Civil Liberties Organizations Urge Google to Suspend Gmail," Privacy Rights Clearinghouse, 6 April 2004, www.privacyrights.org/ar/GmailLetter.htm, accessed 9/04; David W. Bard, "Google Not Fooling Around: Launches Gmail," News Factor, 1 April 2004, www.newsfactor.com/story.xhtml?story_title=Google_Not_Fooling_Around__Launches_Gmail&story_id=23589, accessed 9/04.

59. Kevin Featherly, "AMA Releases Online Med-ethics Guidelines," *Newsbytes,* 22 March 2000, www.findarticles.com/p/articles/mi_m0NEW/is_2000_March_22/ai_60583455, accessed 9/04; Margaret A. Winker, Annette Flanagin, Bonnie Chi-Lum, John White, Karen Andrews, Robert L. Kennett, Catherine D. DeAngelis, and Robert A. Musacchio, "Guidelines for Medical and Health Information Sites on the Internet: Principles Governing AMA Web Sites," *Journal of the American Medical Association* 283, no. 12, 22 March 2000, http://jama.ama-assn.org/cgi/content/full/283/12/1600, accessed 9/04.

60. Zachary Rodgers, "TRUSTe Launches Wireless Privacy Guidelines," ClickZ Network, 20 February 2004, www.clickz.com/news/article.php/3315811, accessed 9/04; Stephanie Olsen, "Privacy Group to Put Seal on Spam," CNET News.com, 31 January 2002, http://news.com.com/2100-1023-826747.html, accessed 9/04.

61. Staff, "Apple's iTunes Hacked," News.com.au, www.news.com.au/common/story_page/0,4057,7971893%255E15321,00.html, accessed 9/04; John Borland, "DeCSS Programmer Turns Attention to iTunes,"

ZDNetNews.com.UK, 25 November 2004, http://news.zdnet.co.uk/internet/security/0,39020375,39118097,00.htm, accessed 9/04.

62. Gregor Freund, "Hacking 2003: The New Agenda," CNET News.com, 13 May 2003, http://news.com.com/2010-1071_3-1001016.html?tag=fd_nc_1, accessed 9/04; Steven Levy, "Hey, You've Got Worms," *Newsweek,* 9 February 2004, p. 9; Dennis Fisher, "Feds Escalate Warning About e-commerce Hacks," ZDNet.com, 8 March 2001, www.zdnet.com/eweek/stories/general/0,11011,2694098,00.html, accessed 9/04.

63. Paul Roberts, "Microsoft.com Falls to DOS Attack," IDG News Service, 15 August 2003, www.infoworld.com/article/03/08/15/HNmsfalls_1.html, accessed 4/04; Hiawatha Bray, "Saboteurs Hit Spam's Blockers," *Boston Globe,* 28 August 2003, www.boston.com/news/nation/articles/2003/08/28/saboteurs_hit_spams_blockers/, accessed 9/04.

64. Bob Trott, "Virus That Hits Word and Excel Discovered," *InfoWorld,* 1 September 1998, www.infoworld.com/cgi-bin/displayStory.pl?98091.wnshiver.htm, accessed 9/04.

65. Colin C. Haley, "Interest in Online Banking Grows," ClickZ Network, 30 December 2003, www.clickz.com/stats/markets/finance/article.php/3292041, accessed 9/04; Thor Olavsrud, "Consumers Still Wary of Online Security," 20 May 2003, InternetNews.com, www.internetnews.com/ec-news/article.php/2209641, accessed 9/04.

66. FTC Consumer Alert, "Going Shopping? Go Global! A Guide for E-Consumers," U.S. Federal Trade Commission, October 2001, www.ftc.gov/bcp/conline/pubs/alerts/glblalrt.htm, accessed 9/04; FTC and AOL, "Guide to Online Payments," U.S. Federal Trade Commission and America Online, March 2003, www.ftc.gov/bcp/conline/pubs/online/payments.htm, accessed 9/04; MasterCard, "More Ways to Shop Smart," MasterCard International, 2002, www.mastercardintl.com/newtechnology/set/bestpractices.html, accessed 4/04; National Consumers League, "Be E-Wise: How to Shop Safely Online," National Consumers League, 2004, www.nclnet.org/BeEWISEbroch.html, accessed 9/04.

67. Roy Mark, "Music Downloading Demand Dramatically Declines," ClickZ Network, 5 January 2004, www.clickz.com/stats/big_picture/applications/article.php/3295201, accessed 9/04; Spencer E. Ante, "What Price Online Music?," *Business WeekOnline,* 17 October 2003, www.businessweek.com/technology/content/oct2003/tc20031017_1991_tc078.htm, accessed 9/04; Staff, "'New Napster Faces Serious Competition," iafrica.com, 16 October 2003, http://cooltech.iafrica.com/technews/278364.htm, accessed 9/04; Bryan Chaffin, "iTMS Beats Napster 5:1 in Head-to-Head Sales," The Mac Observer, 7 November 2003, www.macobserver.com/article/2003/11/07.10.shtml, accessed 9/04; Mike Langberg, "Reborn Napster Faces Strong Competition," *Mercury News,* 6 November 2003, www.siliconvalley.com/mld/siliconvalley/7196297.htm, accessed 9/04.

Chapter 6

1. Staff, "Yahoo! Reports Second Quarter 2004 Financial Results," Yahoo, 7 July 2004, *http://yhoo.client.shareholder.com/news/Q204/YHOO070704.pdf,* accessed 10/04; Gerry Khermouch and Diane Brady, "Brands in an Age of Anti-Americanism," *BusinessWeek,* 4 August 2003, pp. 69-78; Staff, "A Perfect Market," *The Economist,* 15 May 2004, pp. 3–5; Press Release, "Yahoo! Reports First Quarter 2004 Financial Results," Yahoo!, 7 April 2004, *http://yhoo.client.shareholder.com/news/Q104/YHOO040704-942134.pdf,* accessed 10/04; Staff, "Google Still the World's Leading Search Engine," SearchEngineJournal, 7 May 2004, *www.searchenginejournal.com/index.php?p=536,* accessed 10/04; Mylene Mangalindan, "Yahoo

Agrees to Acquire Overture," *Wall Street Journal,* 15 July 2003, pp. A3, 6; Ben Elgin and Ronald Grover, "Yahoo! Act Two," *BusinessWeek,* 2 June 2003, pp. 70–76; Amy Schein, "Yahoo! Inc.," *Hoover's Online,* 2004, *www.hoovers.com,* accessed 10/04; Staff, "Yahoo to Kick-Off Global Expansion Strategy," The CalTrade Report, 25 March 2004, *www.caltradereport.com/eWebPages/page-two -1080228475.html,* accessed 10/04; Mylene Mangalindan, "Yahoo Breaks Dot-Com Mold, Sees a Rebound," *Wall Street Journal,* 15 January 2003, pp. B1, 12; Mylene Mangalindan, "Yahoo Gets Set to Give Google Run for Money," *Wall Street Journal,* 8 January 2004, pp. B1, 2; Staff, "Searching for Relevance," *The Economist,* 19 July 2003, p. 52; Mylene Mangalindan, "Rising Clout of Google Prompts Rush by Internet Rivals to Adapt," *Wall Street Journal,* 16 July 2003, pp. A1, 6; Nick Wingfield and Mylene Mangalindan, "Yahoo Will Close Europe Auctions, Promote Rival eBay on Site Instead," *Wall Street Journal,* 28 May 2002, pp. A3, 4.

2. Staff, "Beyond the Bubble," *The Economist,* 11 October 2003, pp. 3–7; Robert Hobbes' Zakon, "Hobbes' Internet Timeline v7.0," Zakon Group LLC, *www.zakon.org/robert/internet/timeline/,* accessed 10/04; Nick Wingfield and Connie Ling, "Unbowed by Its Failure in Japan, eBay Will Try Its Hand in China," *Wall Street Journal,* 18 March 2002, pp. B1, 6; Beth Cox, "eBay Enters Taiwan Market, Exits Japan," Silicon Valley Internet.com, 26 February 2002, *http://siliconvalley .internet.com/news/article.php/981061,* accessed 10/04; Cynthia L. Webb, "EBay Hops the Fast Boat to China," *Washington Post,* 22 April 2004, *www.washingtonpost.com/wp-dyn/articles/A33683 -2004Apr22.html,* accessed 10/04; Robert D. Hof, "The eBay Economy," *BusinessWeek,* 25 August 2003, pp. 125–128.

3. Jennifer Banke, Fiona Paua, and Xavier Sala-I-Martin, "The Growth Competitive Index: Analyzing Key Underpinnings of Sustained Economic Growth," World Economic Forum, 2004, *www.weforum.org/ pdf/Gcr/GCR_2003_2004/GCI_Chapter.pdf,* accessed 10/04; Staff, "U.S. Tops Rankings in Global Information Technology Report," U.S. Department of State, 9 December 2003, *http://usinfo.state.gov/gi/ Archive/2003/Dec/09-632414.html,* accessed 10/04; Klaus Schwab, "Preface: Global Information Technology Report," World Economic Forum, 2004, *www.weforum.org/pdf/Gcr/GITR_2003_2004/ GITR_Preface_03_04.pdf,* accessed 10/04; Soumitra Dutta, Bruno Lanvin, and Fiona Paua, "Executive Summary: The Global Competitiveness Report 2003–2004," World Economic Forum, *www .weforum.org/pdf/Gcr/GITR_2003_2004/Executive_Summary.pdf,* accessed 10/04; Soumitra Dutta and Amit Jain, "The Networked Readiness of Nations," Global Competitiveness Report 2002–2003, INSEAD and World Economic Forum, *www.weforum.org/pdf/ Global_Competitiveness_Reports/Reports/GITR_2002_2003/GITR _NRI_02_03.pdf,* accessed 10/04; Bob Tedeschi, "Developing Nations," *New York Times,* 24 November 2003, *www.nytimes.com,* accessed 6/04; Pattarasinee Bhattarakosol, "IT Direction in Thailand: Cultivating an E-Society," National Electronics and Computer Technology Center, September/October 2003, *www.nectec.or.th/ pressnews/pdf/f5016.pdf,* accessed 6/04; Michael Tarm, "Estonia Blazes Internet Trail," Government Technology, 25 April 2003, *www.govtech.net/news/features/news_feature.phtml?docid=2003.04 .25-48816,* accessed 10/04; Staff, "Progress at a Snail's Pace," *The Economist,* 11 October 2003, p. 43; Staff, "Beyond the Bubble," *The Economist,* 11 October 2003, pp. 3–7; Martyn Williams, "North Korea Develops Internet," ComputerWeekly.com, 3 July 2003, *www .computerweekly.com/Article123734.htm,* accessed 10/04.

4. Staff, "E-readiness," *The Economist,* 1 May 2004, p. 106; Staff, "The 2004 E-readiness Rankings," *The Economist* Intelligence Unit, *http://graphics.eiu.com/files/ad_pdfs/ERR2004.pdf,* accessed 10/04;

Eric Chabrow, "U.S. Internet Leadership Is Slipping," InformationWeek, 23 April 2004, *www.informationweek.com/story/ showArticle.jhtml?articleID=19200096,* accessed 10/04.

5. Staff, "The Mobile Telecommunications and Internet Index, 2002," *The Economist,* 21 September 2002, p. 96; Staff, "Hong Kong (China) and Denmark Top ITU Mobile/Internet Index," International Telecommunication Union, 17 September 2002, *www.itu.int/ newsarchive/press_releases/2002/20.html,* accessed 10/04; Lara Srivastava, Joanna Goodrick, Tim Kelly, Tad Reynolds, and Yoshihisa Takada, "Internet for a Mobile Generation: Executive Summary," International Telecommunication Union, September 2002, *www.itu.int/ osg/spu/publications/sales/mobileinternet/execsumFinal.pdf,* accessed 10/04; Larry Press, "Wireless Internet Connectivity for Developing Nations," FirstMonday, Vol. 8, no. 9 (September 2003), *http:// firstmonday.org/issues/issue8_9/press/index.html,* accessed 10/04; Staff, "Ringing the Changes," *The Economist,* 17 April 2004, p. 62; Scott Banerjee, "Ringtone Rumble Brewing in U.S.," Reuters, 16 May 2004, *www.reuters.com/newsArticle.jhtml?type=musicNews& storyID=5156335,* accessed 6/04; Geoffrey A. Fowler, "What Separates Man and Ape These Days Is the Thumb Action," *Wall Street Journal,* 17 April 2002, pp. A1, 6; Staff, "Dough in Downloads," Asia Intelligence Wire, 25 May 2004, *www.hoovers.com,* accessed 6/04; Jeanette Borzo, "Almost Human," *Wall Street Journal,* 24 May 2004, pp. R4, 10.

6. Staff, "Population Explosion!," ClickZ Network, 10 September 2004, *www.clickz.com/stats/big_picture/geographics/article.php/5911_151151,* accessed 10/04; Robyn Greenspan, "Three-Quarters of Americans Have Access from Home," 18 March 2004, ClickZ Network, *www.clickz.com/stats/big_picture/geographics/article.php/3328091,* accessed 10/04; Michael Pastore, "Global Internet Population Moves Away from U.S.," ClickZ Network, 11 January 2001, *www.clickz.com/stats/big_picture/ geographics/print.php/5911_558061,* accessed 10/04.

7. CIA World Factbook, "Field Listings—Languages," 2004, *www.cia.gov/cia/publications/factbook/fields/2098.html,* accessed 10/04; Staff, "Global Internet Statistics (by Language)," Global Reach, 30 March 2004, *www.glreach.com/globstats/index.php3,* accessed 10/04.

8. Sally Beatty, "Fashion Tip: Get Online," *Wall Street Journal,* 31 October 2003, pp. B1, 3.

9. Peter Loftus, "Internet Turns Firms into Overseas Businesses," *Wall Street Journal,* 16 December 2003, pp. B4; Staff, "About Us," BlueTie, Inc., 2004, *www.bluetie.com/about/facts.asp,* accessed 10/04.

10. Nick Wingfield, "EBay Will Close Japan Auction Site as Sale Rates Remain Below Normal," *Wall Street Journal,* 27 February 2002, *http://online.wsj.com/article/0,4287,SB101476587328351190,00.html,* accessed 10/04; Tiffany Kary, "eBay Exits Japan, Moves into Taiwan," C/Net News.com, 22 February 2002, *http://news.com.com/2100-1017 -845099.html,* accessed 10/04; May Wong, "Online Auction Powerhouse eBay Expands to China," *Detroit News,* 19 March 2002, *www.detnews.com/2002/technology/0203/19/technology-443762.htm,* accessed 10/04; Mark Berniker, "eBay Acquires Chinese Shopping Site EachNet," InternetNews.com, 12 June 2003, *www.internetnews.com/ec-news/article.php/2220991,* accessed 10/04.

11. Theodore Levitt, "The Globalization of Markets," *Harvard Business Review,* 1 May 1983, *http://harvardbusinessonline.hbsp.harvard.edu/ b01/en/common/item_detail.jhtml?id=83308,* accessed 10/04.

12. Staff, "UCLA Releases First Findings of World Internet Project," Center for Digital Government, January 2004, *www.centerdigitalgov .com/international/story.php?docid=85067,* accessed 10/04; Reuters, "New Study Shatters Internet 'Geek' Image," CNN.com, 14 January 2004, *www.cnn.com/2004/TECH/internet/01/14/geek.study.reut/,*

accessed 10/04; Robyn Greenspan, "Europe, U.S. on Different Sides of the Gender Divide," ClickZ Network, 21 October 2003, *www.clickz.com/stats/big_picture/demographics/article.php/3095681*, accessed 10/04.

13. Ned Desmond, "Let's Underwrite Broadband," *Business2.0*, February 2003, p. 56; Ken Belson, "The Express Lane to the Internet, Now with Fewer Bumps," *New York Times*, 30 May 2004, *www.nytimes.com*, accessed 6/04; Staff, "Broadband Revolutionizing Europe's Internet Behavior," Nielsen//Net Ratings, 29 May 2003, *www.nielsen-netratings.com/pr/pr_030529_uk.pdf*, accessed 10/04; Mark Russell, "High-Speed Internet Had Advantages for Korea," *Billboard*, 2 August 2003, Vol. 115, n. 31, pp. AP–1, 2; ComScore Networks, "Canada Trumps US in Broadband Use," Nua, 8 April 2003, *www.nua.ie/surveys/?f=VS&art_id=905358758&rel=true*, accessed 10/04; Staff, "Seriously Wired," *The Economist*, 19 April 2003, p. 7; Timothy J. Mullaney, "At Last, the Web Hits 100 MPH," *BusinessWeek*, 23 June 2003, pp. 80–81; Leslie Walker, "High-Speed Users Move Into the Majority," *The Washington Post*, 22 August 2004, *www.washingtonpost.com/wp-dyn/articles/A20674-2004Aug21.html*, accessed 10/04; Grant Goss, "U.S. Broadband Users Triple In Less Than Three Years," InfoWorld, 9 September 2004, *www.infoworld.com/article/04/09/09/HNusbroadband_1.html*, accessed 10/04.

14. Staff, "Making the Web World-Wide," *The Economist*, 28 September 2002, p. 76; Staff, "The Jhai PC and Communication System," The Jhai Foundation, 2004, *www.jhai.org/jhai_remoteIT.htm*, accessed 10/04; Amy Waldman, "Indian Soybean Farmers Join the Global Village," *New York Times*, 1 January 2004, *www.nytimes.com*, accessed 6/04.

15. Victoria Shannon, "Online Music Industry Is Focusing on Europe," *New York Times*, 26 January 2004, *www.nytimes.com*, accessed 6/04; Mark Landler "For Music Industry, U.S. Is Only the Tip of a Piracy Iceberg," *New York Times*, 25 September 2003, *www.nytimes.com*, accessed 6/04.

16. Staff, "Global Internet Statistics (by Language)," *Global Reach*, 30 March 2004, *www.glreach.com/globstats/index.php3*, accessed 10/04; James Ledbetter, "Making a Global Web Audience Count," *The Industry Standard*, 22 March 1999, *www.thestandard.com/article/0,1902,3785,00.html*, accessed 7/02; Adam Lincoln, "Localisation Services May Be Key to Crossborder Revenues," *The Economist* Intelligence Unit, 19 April 2001, *www.ebusinessforum.com/index.asp?layout=printer_friendly&doc_id=3141*, accessed 10/04; Ipsos-Reid Study, "U.S. No Longer Dominates Net," Nua Internet Surveys, 17 May 2001, *www.nua.net/surveys/?f=VS&art_id=905356771&rel=true*, accessed 10/04.

17. Connie Ling, "Learning a New Language," *Wall Street Journal*, 12 March 2001, p. R18.

18. Lynda Radosevich, "Going Global Overnight," CNN.com, 21 April 1999, *www.cnn.com/TECH/computing/9904/21/global.ent.idg/*, accessed 10/04; Staff, "Business Protocol: China," *Asia Business Today*, *www.asiabusinesstoday.org/travel/bp_china.cfm*, accessed 10/04; Staff, "Business Protocol: India," *Asia Business Today*, *www.asiabusinesstoday.org/travel/bp_india.cfm*, accessed 10/04; Andrew Marlatt, "Can One Site Appeal to All?," *Internet World*, 16 November 1998, *www.findarticles.com/cf_0/m0DXS/1998_Nov_16/53250776/print.jhtml*, accessed 7/02.

19. StudentsCount, "Are You Driven by Numbers?," Certified General Accountants of Ontario, *www.studentscount.com/unlucky/scary.shtml*, accessed 7/02; Kylie Hsu, "Lucky and Unlucky Numbers," California State University Los Angeles, *www.calstatela.edu/faculty/khsu2/cartoon3.html*, accessed 10/04.

20. Staff, "Business Protocol: China," *Asia Business Today*, *www.asiabusinesstoday.org/travel/bp_china.cfm*, accessed 10/04; Staff, "Business Protocol: India," *Asia Business Today*, *www.asiabusinesstoday.org/travel/bp_india.cfm*, accessed 10/04.

21. Leo Deegan, "Writing Dates in Chinese," University of California, Berkeley, *www.stat.berkeley.edu/users/deegan/dates.htm*, accessed 10/04.

22. Dow Jones Newswires, "US-Sanctioned ICANN Defends Internet Stewardship Role," *Wall Street Journal*, 26 March 2004, *http://online.wsj.com*, accessed 6/04; Staff, "Swiss Fudge," *The Economist*, 13 December 2003, pp. 60–61; Jennifer L. Schenker, "Digital Divide to Be Big Issue at UN Summit on Internet," *New York Times*, 7 December 2003, *www.nytimes.com*, accessed 6/04; Staff, "Time for UN Intervention?," *The Economist*, 1 November 2003, pp. 59-60.

23. Mei Fong, "The Spam-China Link," *Wall Street Journal*, 19 March 2004, pp. B1, 2; David Bank, "Mydoom Virus Can Turn You into a Spammer," *Wall Street Journal*, 29 January 2004, *http://online.wsj.com/article/0,,SB107531592990914207,00.html*, accessed 6/04; Staff, "E-Mail Spam: How to Stop It from Stalking You," *Consumer Reports*, August 2003, pp. 12–15.

24. Investor Relations, "Harrah's Entertainment Reports Fourth-Quarter, Full-Year Results," Harrah's, 4 February 2004, *http://investor.harrahs.com/news/20040204-128092.cfm*, accessed 10/04; Bradley Vallerius, "Harrah's Unveils Subscription Based I-Gaming Operation," *Interactive Gaming News*, 12 November 2003, *www.igamingnews.com/index.cfm?page=artlisting&tid=4666*, accessed 10/04; Reuters, "Challenge on Ban to Net Gambling Upheld," C/Net News.com, 30 April 2004, *http://news.com.com/2100-1028_3-5203388.html*, accessed 10/04; Shailagh Murray, "Internet-Gambling Curbs Face Long Odds," *Wall Street Journal*, 22 August 2003, p. A4; Staff, "Flutter Away," *The Economist*, 10 May 2003, p. 49; Ryan Pearson, "MGM Opens Casino on Web," *Lexington Herald Leader*, 4 October 2002, p. C2; John Horn, "Point and Bet," *Newsweek*, 28 October 2002, pp. 50–51; Scott Miller, "Does U.S. Ban on E-Gambling Violate WTO?," *Wall Street Journal*, 28 January 2004, pp. B1, 10; Scott Miller and Christina Binkley, "U.S. Ban on Web Gambling Breaks Global Trade Pacts, Says WTO," *Wall Street Journal*, 25 March 2004, p. A2; Matt Richtel, "U.S. Steps Up Push Against Online Casinos by Seizing Cash," *New York Times*, 31 May 2004, *www.nytimes.com*, accessed 6/04.

25. Matt Gallaway, "French (Dis)Connection," *eCompanyNow*, 4 December 2000, *www.ecompany.com/articles/web/print/0,1650,8943,00.html*, accessed 7/02; Matt Gallaway, "International Jurisdiction Soup," *eCompanyNow*, 27 February 2001, *www.ecompany.com/articles/web/print/0,1650,9579,00.html*, accessed 7/02; Randall E. Stross, "Pardon My French," *U.S. News & World Report*, 12 February 2001, p. 41.

26. Jason Dean, "China Issues 'Trial' Online Ad Licenses in First Step Toward Regulating Sector," *Wall Street Journal*, 1 June 2000, p. B18; Staff, "Google Bows to Chinese Censorship," CNN.com, 27 September 2004, *www.cnn.com/2004/TECH/internet/09/27/google.china.ap/*, accessed 10/04; Jonathan Zittrain and Benjamin Edelman, "Empirical Analysis of Internet Filtering in China," Berkman Center for Internet & Society, Harvard Law School, 20 March 2003, *http://cyber.law.harvard.edu/filtering/china/*, accessed 10/04.

27. Staff, "Progress at a Snail's Pace," *The Economist*, 11 October 2003, p. 43; Thomas Crampton, "Beijing Uses Cyberspace to Widen Control," *International Herald Tribune*, 24 March 2001, *www.iht.com/articles/14484.html*, accessed 10/04.

28. Glenn R. Simpson, "U.S. Officials Criticize Rules on EU Privacy," *Wall Street Journal*, 27 March 2001, p. B7; Robyn Weisman, "U.S.

Lawmakers Blast EU Internet Privacy Rules," NewsFactor Network, 9 March 2001, *www.osopinion.com/perl/printer/8079/*, accessed 7/02; Brian Krebs, "U.S. Businesses Slow to Adopt EU Safe Harbor Agreement," Infowar.com, 4 January 2001, *www.infowar.com/law/01/law_010501a_j.shtml*, accessed 7/02; Brandon Mitchener, "Microsoft Plans to Sign Accord on Data Privacy with the EU," *Wall Street Journal*, 16 May 2001, p. A14; Staff, "TRUSTe Approves First Web Site Under EU Safe Harbor Privacy Program," PR Newswire, 12 February 2001, *www.findarticles.com/cf_0/m4PRN/2001_Feb_12/70354892/print.jhtml*, accessed 7/02.

29. Staff, "Chinese Search Engine to Compete with Google, Yahoo," *Inquirer*, 26 December 2003, *www.theinquirer.net/?article=13341*, accessed 10/04; Staff, "China Search Engine Feud Continues—Baidu.com Wins Second Round, 3271 Appeals Again," Interfax, 27 April 2004, *www.interfax.com/com?item=Chin&pg=0&id=5716962&req=*, accessed 10/04; Staff, "Baidu.com Beats Google.com to Rank Fourth in Terms of Web Traffic," Interfax, 31 May 2004, *www.interfax.com/com?id=5727264&item=Chin*, accessed 10/04; Juliana Liu, "China's Web Search Engines Set to Take on Google," Reuters, 10 March 2004, *www.forbes.com/technology/newswire/2004/03/10/rtr1292819.html*, accessed 10/04.

Chapter 7

1. Matt Saucedo, "WPP Group plc," Hoover's Online, 2004, www.hoovers.com/wpp-group/—ID__43120—/free-co-factsheet.xhtml, accessed 10/04; Joe Bramhall, "The Kantar Group," Hoover's Online, 2004, www.hoovers.com/kantar-group/—ID__103898—/free-co-factsheet.xhtml, accessed 10/04; Joe Bramhall, "Millward Brown Group," Hoover's Online, 2004, www.hoovers.com/millward-brown/—ID__111228—/free-co-factsheet.xhtml, accessed 10/04; Staff, "Millward Brown IMPACT: Still Going Strong After 20 Years," Asia Intelligence Wire, 14 May 2004, www.hoovers.com, accessed 6/04; Staff, "Media Consumption Study Confirms Internet's Role as Leading Daytime Medium," Millward Brown, 12 May 2003, www.millwardbrown.com/scripts/news/press_releases.asp?txtAction=Next&txtPage=3, accessed 6/04; Online Publisher's Association, "At Work Internet Audience Media Consumption Study," OPA and Millward Brown, May 2003, www.online-publishers.org/opa_media_consumption_050203.pdf, accessed 6/04; Staff, "ESPN.com's Big Impression Ad for Universal Pictures' 'The Mummy Returns' Three Times More Impactful Than Traditional Banner Ad, According to Millward Brown Intelliquest," ESPN.com, 30 May 2001, http://sports.espn.go.com/espn/print?id=1207465&type=story, accessed 10/04.

2. Staff, "Facts About P&G 2003–2004 Worldwide," Procter & Gamble, 2004, www.pg.com/content/pdf/01_about_pg/01_about_pg_homepage/about_pg_toolbar/download_report/factsheet.pdf, accessed 10/04; Cliff Peale, "P&G Fuels Marketing Machine With Science," *Cincinnati Enquirer*, 4 May 2003, www.enquirer.com/editions/2003/05/04/biz_labtoshelf.html, accessed 10/04; Staff, "P&G Annual Report 2003," P&G, 2004, http://www.pg.com/investors/annualreports.jhtml, accessed 10/04; Thomas K. McCraw, "P&G: Changing the Face of Consumer Marketing," Harvard Business School—Working Knowledge, 2 May 2002, http://hbswk.hbs.edu/item.jhtml?id=1476&t=marketing&noseek=one, accessed 10/04; Charles L. Decker, "Winning the P&G Way," IndiaInfoline.com, 4 December 2003, www.indiainfoline.com/bisc/br13.html, accessed 10/04; Cliff Peale, "P&G Retrenches on Research," *Cincinnati Enquirer*, 2 September 2001, www.enquirer.comeditions/2001/09/02/fin_p_g_retrenches_on.html, accessed 10/04; Dan McGraw, "Building

Strategic Partnerships," PRISM Online, February 1999, www.asee.org/prism/february/html/Partnerships.html, accessed 10/04; Mark Thompson, "There's More to These Soap Stocks Than Suds," MSN.Money, 5 April 1999, http://moneycentral.msn.com/articles/invest/sectors/3137.asp, accessed 10/04.

3. Staff, "White-Hot Trend: Teeth Whiteners Brightening Up Retail Sales," NACS Online, 2 May 2003, www.nacsonline.com/NR/exeres/000041e6uqxhzyncgqtdbdqq/NewsPosting.asp?NRMODE=Published&NRORIGINALURL=%2fNACS%2fNews%2fDaily_News_Archives%2fMay2003%2fnd0502036%2ehtm&NRNODEGUID=%7b06A0A244-0A97-477D-ABF7-869D06E058C3%7d&NRQUERYTERMINATOR=1&cookie%5Ftest=1, accessed 10/04; Paul Demery, "Manufacturers Solve Their Online Dilemma," Internet Retailer, November 2003, www.internetretailer.com/article.asp?id=10545, accessed 10/04; John Gaffney, "How Do You Feel About a $44 Tooth-Bleaching Kit?," *Business2.0*, September 2001, www.business2.com/articles/mag/print/0,1643,16977,FF.html, accessed 7/02; Crest Dental ResourceNet, "Professional Crest Whitestrips," 2001, www.dentalcare.com/soap/cws/pgintro.htm, accessed 10/04; Ron Lieber, "P&G Has Something to Smile About," *Fast Company*, August 2001, www.fastcompany.com/lead/lead_feature/pg2.html, accessed 7/02.

4. Staff, "Robert Merton," *The Economist*, 15 March 2003, p. 81.

5. Jeff Walkowski, "Smart Shopping," Quirk's Marketing Research Review, December 2001, www.quirks.com/articles/article.asp?arg_ArticleId=747, accessed 10/04; Casey Sweet and Jeff Walkowski, "Online Qualitative Research Task Force: Report of Findings," Quirk's Marketing Research Review, December 2000, www.quirks.com/articles/article_print.asp?arg_articleid=643, accessed 10/04.

6. Peter Lloyd, "The Basics of Brainlining," *Geocreate*, 2001, www.gocreate.com/articles/abl101.htm, accessed 10/04; Kim T. Gordon, "Creative Brainstorming Techniques," Entrepreneur.com, 2 December 2002, www.entrepreneur.com/article/0,4621,304962,00.html, accessed 10/04.

7. Staff, "IdeaStation Online Brainstorming Sessions," Greenfield Consulting Group, 2004, www.greenfieldgroup.com/ideastation.asp, accessed 10/04; Staff, "Online Brainstorming," Buzzback.com, 2001, www.buzzback.com/case_studies.asp, accessed 7/02.

8. Staff, "WETI - Global Qualitative Research through New Web-Enabled Technique," Greenfield Online, 2004, www.greenfieldgroup.com/weti.asp, accessed 10/04.

9. Staff, "Software Digs Up Buzzwords Old and New," CNN.com, 16 March 2003, www.cnn.com/2003/TECH/internet/03/14/word.bursts.ap/, accessed 10/04; Michelle Locke, "Which Buzzwords Are Buzziest?," *Lexington Herald Leader*, 14 March 2003, p.C2.

10. Brian Faler, "Dean Leaves Legacy of Online Campaign Use of Internet to Raise Funds, Organize Rallies," *Washington Post*, 20 February 2004, www.washingtonpost.com/wp-dyn/articles/A55846-2004Feb19.html, accessed 10/04; Marilyn Domas White, Eileen C. Abels, and Neal Kaske, "Evaluation of Chat Reference Service Quality," *D-Lib Magazine*, February 2003, www.dlib.org/dlib/february03/white/02white.html, accessed 10/04; Dylan Tweney, "Analyzing Chat," *Business2.0*, 20 April 2001, www.business2.com/b2/web/articles/0,17863,513479,00.html, accessed 10/04; David Orenstein, "Hidden Treasure," *Business2.0*, July 2001, www.business2.com/articles/mag/0,1640,14841,FF.html, accessed 7/02.

11. Staff, "Surveys and You," CASRO, Council of American Survey Research Organizations, 2004, www.casro.org/survandyou.cfm, accessed 10/04; Troy Janisch, "Talking 'Bout My Generation: The Evolution of Online Marketing Research," Wisconsin Technology

Network, 26 October 2003, www.wistechnology.com/article.php ?id=304, accessed 10/04.

12. Maryann Jones Thompson, "Market Researchers Embrace the Web," *The Standard,* 26 January 1999, www.thestandard.com/article/display/ 0,1151,3274,00.html, accessed 7/02; Jon Rubin, "Online Marketing Research Comes of Age," *Brandweek,* 30 October 2000, http:// articles.findarticles.com/p/articles/mi_m0BDW/is_42_41/ai_66705290, accessed 10/04.

13. Peter Coy, "Harris Interactive: A High Opinion of Online Polling," *BusinessWeek Online,* 11 January 2000, www.businessweek.com/ technology/content/0001/ec0111.htm, accessed 10/04.

14. Staff, "The Deep Web," University Libraries State University of New York at Albany, 13 October 2003, http://library.albany.edu/internet/ deepweb.html, accessed 10/04; Reuters, "Search Engines Grapple with Constant Web Growth," CNN, 27 March 2000, www.cnn.com/2001/ TECH/internet/03/27/search.engines.reut/index.html, accessed 3/01.

15. Dru Sefton, "Sociologists Lurk on Net to Examine Our Behavior," *USA Today* Tech Report, 7 June 2001, www.usatoday.com/life/ cyber/tech/cth732.htm, accessed 6/02; Jeffery R. Young, "Committee of Scholars Proposes Ethics Guidelines for Research in Cyberspace," *Chronicle of Higher Education,* 11 October 2001, http://chronicle .merit.edu/free/2001/10/2001101102t.htm, accessed 6/02.

16. Troy Janisch, "Talking 'Bout My Generation: The Evolution of Online Marketing Research," Wisconsin Technology Network, 26 October 2003, www.wistechnology.com/article.php?id=304, accessed 10/04; Erin White, "Market Research on the Internet Has Its Drawbacks," *Wall Street Journal,* 2 March 2000, p. B4; David Lake, "Online Research Market to Hit $230 Million," 24 January 2000, www.thestandard.com/article/0,1902,10101,00.html, accessed 7/02; Dana James, "The Future of Online Research," *Marketing News,* 3 January 2000, www.findarticles.com/cf_0/m4313/1_34/61538777/ print.jhtml, accessed 3/01; Larry Gold, "Online Research," ICONOCAST, 14 September 2000, www.iconocast.com/dotcom/ marketing/research.html, accessed 7/02; Staff, "Harris Interactive Announces 40% Increase in Its Internet Client Base," Harris Interactive, 13 April 2000, www.harrisinteractive.com/news/ allnewsbydate.asp?NewsID=81, accessed 10/04; Jon Rubin, "Online Marketing Research Comes of Age," *Brandweek,* 30 October 2000, www.findarticles.com/cf_0/m0BDW/42_41/66705290/print.jhtml, accessed 10/04; CASRO, "Market Trends: Online Research Growing," Greenfield Online, 2002, www.greenfield.com/research_solutions/ rsrch_solns_main.htm, accessed 7/02.

17. Melaney Smith, "Where Marketers Go for Information," ClickZ Network, 9 March 2004, www.clickz.com/experts/crm/analyze_data/ article.php/3322401, accessed 10/04; Staff, "Business-to-Business E-procurement Finding a Reinvigorated Market," Software Spectrum, Spring 2004, www.softwarespectrum.com/intouch/industry.asp ?subsection=Spectrum3, accessed 10/04; Staff, "Forrester Research Asks, 'Where Is Google Headed?,'" Forrester Research, 8 March 2004, www.forrester.com/ER/Press/Release/0,1769,906,00.html, accessed 10/04; Staff, "Forrester Research Ranks Credit Card Providers' Efforts to Drive Customers Online," Forrester Research, 24 February 2004, www.forrester.com/ER/Press/Release/0,1769,905,00.html, accessed 10/04; Joe Bramhall, "Forrester Research, Inc.," Hoover's Online, 2004, www.hoovers.com/forrester-research/—ID__52441—/free -co-factsheet.xhtml, accessed 10/04.

Chapter 8

1. Staff, "The World's Top 100 Brands," *BusinessWeek,* 4 August 2003, www.businessweek.com/pdfs/2003/0331_globalbrands.pdf, accessed 11/04; Staff, "About IBM," IBM, 2004, www.ibm.com/ibm/us/, accessed 11/04; Staff, "IBM Archives," IBM, 2004, www-1.ibm.com/ ibm/history/index.html, accessed 11/04; Staff, "Fast Facts," IBM, 2004, www-12.ibm.com/press/PressServletForm.wss?MenuChoice=fastfacts &TemplateName=ShowFastFactsList&Menichoice=fastfacts& ApplicationSequence=#8, accessed 11/04; Josh Lower, "International Business Machines Corporation," Hoover's Online, 2004, www .hoovers.com/ibm/—ID__10796—/free-co-factsheet.xhtml, accessed 11/04; Martin Rowe, "Big Servers at Big Blue," *Test and Measurement World,* 1 June 2004, www.reed-electronics.com/tmworld/article/ CA420485?text=big+servers+at+big+blue, accessed 11/04; Stephen Shankoand, "IBM: On-Demand Computing Has Arrived," C/Net News, 12 November 2003, http://news.com.com/2100-7784_3-5106577.html, accessed 11/04; Neil Gross, "IBM's Mark Bregman: 'The Immediacy of Data' Will Change How We Work," *BusinessWeek,* 22 May 2000, www.businessweek.com/2000/00_21/b3682042.htm, accessed 11/04.

2. Staff, "Measuring the Data Mountain," *The Economist,* 6 December 2003, p.10; Peter Lyman and Hal R. Varian, "How Much Information?," 2003, University of California at Berkeley, www.sims.berkeley.edu/ research/projects/how-much-info-2003/, accessed 11/04.

3. Robert Barker, "Will a Larger Chico's Look as Sharp," *Newsweek,* 12 April 2004, p. 112; Staff, "Annual Report 2003," Chico's FAS, 2004, www.chicos.com/store/investor_press_release.asp?release_id=84, accessed 11/04; Staff, "Catalog and Internet Sales Boom for Chico's FAS," *Direct,* 5 March 2002, www.directmag.com/ar/marketing _catalog_internet_sales/, accessed 11/04; Staff, "Chico's Investor Relations," Chico's FAS, 2004, www.chicos.com/store/investor _relations.asp?n=sb&, accessed 11/04; Elizabeth Cornell, "Chico's FAS, Inc.," Hoover's Online, 2004, www.hoovers.com/chico's-fas/ —ID__16010—/free-co-factsheet.xhtml, accessed 11/04; Staff, "Chico's FAS: How It Got Its Groove Back," *BusinessWeek,* 14 June 2001, www.businessweek.com/smallbiz/content/jun2001/ sb20010614_250.htm, accessed 11/04.

4. Caroline Kvitka, "Data Warehouses Go Big," *Oracle Magazine,* May/June 2004, www.oracle.com/technology/oramag/oracle/04-may/ o34news.html, accessed 11/04; Mohit Sahgal, "Big Data Warehouse, Small Budget: What's a Company to Do?," *DM Review Magazine,* November 2002, www.dmreview.com/article_sub.cfm?articleId=5985, accessed 11/04; Regoma Kwon, "Data Warehousing's Big Sleep," eWeek, 13 August 2003, www.eweek.com/article2/ 0,1759,1489755,00.asp, accessed 11/04.

5. Bill Miles, "Slick Move," *Darwin Magazine,* 1 June 2001, www.darwinmag.com/read/060101/headfirst.html, accessed 11/04; Sean Porcher, "Pacific Coast Jiffy Lube Navigates the Network Infrastructure with POPnetserver," *DM Review Magazine,* April 2002, www.dmreview.com/article_sub.cfm?articleId=4965, accessed 11/04.

6. Todd Wasserman, "Mining Everyone's Business," *Brandweek,* 28 February 2000, http://articles.findarticles.com/p/articles/ mi_m0BDW/is_9_41/ai_60805315, accessed 11/04; Joseph McKendrick, "Mining Specification Promises Rich Returns," *ENT,* 12 April 2000, vol. 5, no. 6, p. 44; Joaquim Menezes, "Database Makers Deepen Mining Capabilities," *Computing Canada,* 30 July 1999, http://articles.findarticles.com/p/articles/mi_m0CGC/is_29_25/ ai_55330813, accessed 11/04.

7. Heather Green, "Sensor Revolution: Bugging the World," *BusinessWeek,* 25 August 2003, pp. 100–101; Staff, "Smart Tools," *BusinessWeek,* Spring 2003, www.businessweek.com/bw50/content/ mar2003/a3826072.htm, accessed 11/04; Chris Murphy, "Market- Leading Wal-Mart Leads the Way with RFID," *InformationWeek,* 11 June 2003, www.informationweek.com/story/showArticle.jhtml ?articleID=10300791, accessed 11/04; Jon Dougherty, "Shopping to

Go High-Tech?," WorldNetDaily, 19 July 2003, www.worldnetdaily
.com/news/article.asp?ARTICLE_ID=33647, accessed 11/04; Julie
Rawe, "Supermarket Smackdown," *Time* Online Edition, June 2004,
www.time.com/time/insidebiz/article/0,9171,1101040503-629402,00
.html, accessed 11/04; Owen Thomas, "Lord of the Things,"
Business2.0, March 2002, www.business2.com/b2/web/articles/
0,17863,514502,00.html, accessed 11/04.

8. Elizabeth Cornell, "J. Crew Group, Inc.," Hoover's Online, 2004,
www.hoovers.com/j.-crew/—ID__40243—/free-co-factsheet.xhtml,
accessed 11/04; Staff, "Web Sales at J. Crew Take a Slide as the
Company Restructures," Internet Retailer, 5 December 2003,
www.internetretailer.com/dailyNews.asp?id=10795, accessed 11/04;
Rick Whiting, "Retailer Seeks Success in How Customers Dress: J.
Crew Uses Data Warehouses and Data Mining App to Analyze Sales
Trends from All Operations," *InformationWeek,* 26 November 2001,
www.informationweek.com/story/IWK20011120S0010, accessed
11/04; Ann Bednarz, "Holiday Prep: J. Crew Analyzes Web Buyers,"
Network World Fusion, 18 December 2001, www.nwfusion.com/
news/2001/1218jcrew.html, accessed11/04; Business/High Tech
Editors, "J. Crew Deploys digiMine Data Mining Solutions," *Business
Wire,* 13 November 2001, www.findarticles.com/p/articles/
mi_m0EIN/is_2001_Nov_13/ai_80004308, accessed 11/04.

9. John MacAyleal, "The Black & Decker Corporation," Hoover's
Online, 2004, www.hoovers.com/free/co/factsheet.xhtml?ID=10214,
accessed 11/04; Staff, "Black & Decker Nails a 40 Percent Increase in
Visitor Registration," NetIQ, 2004, www.netiq.com/library/
study.asp?cid=20020512140934OMGQ, accessed 11/04.

10. Jim Sterne, "Web Metrics versus Web Analytics," MarketingProfs,
16 March 2004, www.marketingprofs.com/4/sterne14.asp, accessed
6/04; Bryan Eisenberg, "How to Choose a Web Analytics Solution,"
ClickZ Network, 4 April 2003, www.clickz.com/experts/design/
traffic/article.php/2174241, accessed 11/04; Bryan Eisenberg,
"What Should You Measure?," ClickZ Network, 27 September
2002, www.clickz.com/experts/design/traffic/article.php/1471031,
accessed 11/04; Staff, "Gartner Says Analytics Will Be a Hot Career
Choice," Gartner, 14 May 2001, www4.gartner.com/5_about/
press_room/pr20010514a.html, accessed 11/04; Staff, "Got
Analytics? You're Hired!," Advisor.com, 23 May 2001, www.advisor
.com/Articles.nsf/aid/SMITT245, accessed 11/04; John Webster,
"Staffed for Web Analytics," *InfoWorld,* 15 October 2001,
www.infoworld.com/articles/pe/xml/01/10/15/011015peanalytics
.html, accessed 11/04.

11. Sean Michael Kerner, "SMBs Poised to Spend on CRM," eCRM
Guide.com, 4 June 2004, www.ecrmguide.com/article.php/3363991,
accessed 11/04; Staff, "SearchCRM.com Asked Paul Greenberg About
His Predictions for CRM Technology and eCRM in 2003,"
SearchCRM, 20 December 2002, http://searchcrm.techtarget.com/
ateQuestionNResponse/0,289625,sid11_cid510304_tax285177,00.html,
accessed 11/04; George S. Day and Katrina J. Hubbard, "Customer
Relationships Go Digital," CRM Today, February 2002, www
.crm2day.com/library/EpVpulykVuKbzZiCVD.php, accessed 11/04;
Roger Marsden, "Managing Customer Information from Cradle to
Grave," *Customer Inter@Ction Solutions,* vol. 20, no. 3 (September
2001), pp. 30–33; Michael Pastore, "Most CRM Projects Remain in
Planning Phase," ClickZ Network, 29 May 2001, www.clickz.com/
stats/big_picture/applications/article.php/1301_774831, accessed
11/04; Michael Pastore, "Benefits of CRM Justifying Costs," ClickZ
Network, 13 June 2001, www.clickz.com/stats/big_picture/
applications/article.php/1301_783781, accessed 11/04; Michael
Pastore, "CRM to Lead Market for Analytical Applications," ClickZ
Network, 24 January 2001, www.clickz.com/stats/big_picture/

applications/article.php/1301_569511, accessed 11/04; Joanne
Cummings, "Study: CRM Is Done Wrong 85% of the Time,"
eBusiness IQ, 4 May 2004, www.ebusinessiq.com/news/1089
-eBusinessIQ%20News.html, accessed 11/04; Staff, "Online Selling
and eCRM," eMarketer, www.ebusinessforum.gr/content/downloads/
rr0009.pdf, accessed 11/04.

12. The Customer Respect Group, "The 10 Rules of Online Customer
Respect," The Customer Respect Group, Inc., 2003, www
.customerrespect.com/upload/Ten_Rules.pdf, accessed 11/04; Business
Editors, "The Customer Respect Group Announces 2004 Publication
Schedule of Online Customer Respect Studies of Top 100 U.S.
Companies and 13 Industry Sectors," *Business Wire,* 16 January 2004,
http://articles.findarticles.com/p/articles/mi_m0EIN/is_2004_Jan_16/
ai_112241918, accessed 11/04; Business Editors, "P&G Tops
Customer Respect Rating Online," *Business Wire,* 18 October 2003,
www.businesswire.com, accessed 6/04.

13. Stephanie Stahl and John Soat, "Feeding the Pipeline,"
InformationWeek, 24 February 2003, www.informationweek.com/
story/showArticle.jhtml?articleID=8700568, accessed 11/04; Staff,
"Who We Are," P&G, 2004, www.pg.com/company/who_we_are/
index.jhtml, accessed 11/04; Traci Purdum, "Beyond Bells & Whistles,"
IndustryWeek Value-Chain, 1 February 2002, www.iwvaluechain.com/
Features/articles.asp?ArticleId=1198, accessed 11/04.

14. Rob Enderle, "Fighting Terrorism Through Technology,"
TechNewsWorld, 19 April 2004, www.technewsworld.com/story/
33460.html, accessed 11/04; Gene J. Koprowski, "The Future of
Human Knowledge: The Semantic Web," TechNewsWorld, 28 July
2003, www.technewsworld.com/story/31199.html, accessed 11/04;
Susan Warren, "I-Spy," *Wall Street Journal,* 14 January 2002,
http://online.wsj.com, accessed 6/04; Mubarak Dahir, "Getting the
Dirt," *The Standard,* 26 June 2000, www.thestandard.com/article/
display/0,1151,16201,00.html, accessed 7/02; Timothy M. Maier,
"Corporate Snoops Sharpen Skills," Insight on the News, 31 August
1998, www.insightmag.com/news/1998/08/31/Nation/Espionage
.Corporate.Snoops.Sharpen.Skills-208839.shtml, accessed 11/04.

15. Staff, "Google Woos Its Froogle Web Shoppers," *Wall Street Journal,*
30 March 2004, p. D2; Staff, "Over 6 Billion Items to Search on
Google," eMarketer, 18 February 2004, www.emarketer.com, accessed
6/04; Staff, "Prime Clicking Time," *The Economist,* 31 May 2003,
p. 65; Lee Gomes, "Is It Possible Google Is Just the Bling-Bling of the
Nethead Crowd?" *Wall Street Journal,* 3 May 2004, p. B1; Mylene
Mangalindan, "Playing the Search-Engine Game," *Wall Street Journal,*
16 June 2003, pp. R1, 7; Danny Sullivan, "How Search Engines Work,"
SearchEngineWatch, 14 October 2002, http://searchenginewatch.com/
webmasters/article.php/2168031, accessed 11/04; Danny Sullivan,
"Search Engine Features for Webmasters," SearchEngineWatch,
5 December 2002, http://searchenginewatch.com/webmasters/
article.php/2167891, accessed 11/04; Curt Franklin, "How Search
Engines Work," HowStuffWorks, 2004, http://computer.howstuffworks
.com/search-engine3.htm, accessed 11/04; Staff, "Google Has Many
Fans," eMarketer, 10 June 2004, www.emarketer.com, accessed 6/04.

16. Alison Diana, "Special Report: Search Engines Critical to E-Business
Success," E-Commerce Times, 16 April 2004, www.ecommercetimes
.com/story/33441.html, accessed 11/04; Pamela Parker, "Amazon
Unwraps A9 Search Portal," ClickZ Network, 14 April 2004,
www.clickz.com/news/article.php/3340581, accessed 11/04; Stefanie
Olsen, "Amazon Unveils Search Tool," CNET News.com, 14 April 2004,
http://news.com.com/2100-1038_3-5191661.html, accessed 11/04; Steven
Levy, "Welcome to History 2.0," *Newsweek,* 10 November 2003, p. 58.

17. Sean Michael Kerner, "Marketers: Look Past Paid Search to News,"
InternetNews.com, 12 May 2004, www.internetnews.com/ec

-news/article.php/3352721, accessed 11/04; Jeanne Jennings, "RSS: A Medium for Marketers," ClickZ Network, 11 September 2003, www.clickz.com/experts/em_mkt/opt/print.php/3074951, accessed 11/04; Danny Sullivan, "Making an RSS Feed," SearchEngineWatch.com, 2 April 2003, www.searchenginewatch.com/sereport/article.php/2175271, accessed 11/04.

18. Yochi J. Dreazen, "Consumers Are in the Dark on Web-Site Privacy," *Wall Street Journal*, 25 June 2003, p. D3.

19. George V. Hulme and Thomas Claburn, "Tiny, Evil Things," 26 April 2004, InformationWeek, www.informationweek.com/shared/printableArticle.jhtml?articleID=19200218, accessed 11/04; Staff, "Cookies and Privacy FAQ," CookieCentral, 2004, www.cookiecentral.com/content.phtml?area=4&id=10, accessed 11/04; Staff, "Amazon.com Privacy Notice,"Amazon.com, 3 April 2003, www.amazon.com/exec/obidos/tg/browse/-/468496/104-3648062-6041503, accessed 11/04; Staff, "Cookies," Electronic Privacy Information Center, 5 November 2002, www.epic.org/privacy/internet/cookies/, accessed 11/04.

20. Staff, "Yahoo! Web Beacons," Yahoo!, 2001, http://privacy.yahoo.com/privacy/us/pixels/details.html, accessed 11/04; Jack M. Germain, "Spam Wars: Fighting the Mass Mail Onslaught," TechNewsWorld, 10 June 2004, www.technewsworld.com/story/34366.html, accessed 11/04; Mark Glassman, "Tracking the E-Mail You Sent," *International Herald Tribune*, 5 June 2004, www.iht.com/articles/523394.html, accessed 11/04; Staff, "Web Bug Standards to Be Developed: NAI Announces New Program to Address Important Consumer Privacy Concerns," Network Advertising Initiative, 4 October 2001, www.networkadvertising.org/aboutnai_news_pr100401.asp, accessed 11/04.

21. Ted Bridis, "Spyware, Viruses Plague Computers in Most Homes," Lexington Herald-Leader, 25 October 2004, pp. A1, 9, 11; Staff, "Largest In-Home Study of Home Computer Users Shows Major Online Threats, Perception Gap," National Cyber Security Alliance, 25 October 2004, www.staysafeonline.info/news/NCSA-AOLIn-HomeStudyRelease.pdf, accessed 11/04; Cade Metz, "Spyware – It's Lurking on Your Machine," *PC Magazine*, 22 April 2003, www.pcmag.com/article2/0,4149,994086,00.asp, accessed 11/04; Staff, "What You Can Do About Spyware and Other Unwanted Software," Microsoft, 29 September 2004, www.microsoft.com/athome/security/spyware/spywarewhat.mspx, accessed 11/04; AP, "Feeling Sluggish? It Might Be Spyware.," CNN.com, 22 June 2004, www.cnn.com/2004/TECH/internet/06/22/spyware.qa.ap/, accessed 11/04; Amit Asaravala, "Tired of Spam? Prepare for Adware," *Wired News*, 7 May 2004, www.wired.com/news/technology/0,1282,63345,00.html, accessed 11/04; Adrienne Newell, "Anti-Spyware Law Proposed," 26 February 2004, *PC World*, www.pcworld.com/news/article/0,aid,114999,00.asp, accessed 11/04; David McGuire, "House Panel Moves to Criminalize Spyware, Net Piracy," *Washington Post*, 8 September 2004, www.washingtonpost.com/wp-dyn/articles/A6091-2004Sep8.html, accessed 11/04.

22. Charlie Morris, "Traffic-Building Ideas From Your Log Files," *Web Developer's Journal*, 22 April 2000, www.webdevelopersjournal.com/articles/site_promotion/site_promotion_logfiles.html, accessed 11/04; Thomas Dowling, "Lies, Damned Lies, and Web Logs," *Library Journal*, 15 May 2001, www.libraryjournal.com/article/CA106218, accessed 11/04.

23. Janis Mara, "Google Responds to Gmail Privacy Concerns," ClickZ Network, 2 April 2004, www.clickz.com/news/article.php/3335481, accessed 11/04; Kevin J. Delaney, "Will Users Care If Gmail Invades Privacy," *Wall Street Journal*, 6 April 2004, pp. B1, 3; Dow Jones Newswire, "Consumer Watchdogs Tear into Google's New E-Mail Service," *Wall Street Journal*, 6 April 2004, http://online.wsj.com, accessed 6/04.

24. Seth Shafer, "Microsoft Corporation," Hoover's Online, 2004, www.hoovers.com/microsoft/—ID__14120—/free-co-factsheet.xhtml, accessed 11/04; Rob Enderle, "Linux vs. Longhorn: The Battle Is Joined," TechNewsWorld, 10 May 2004, www.technewsworld.com/story/33707.html, accessed 11/04; Mike Magee, "Internal Memo Confirms IBM Move to Linux Desktop," *The Enquirer*, 7 January 2004, www.theinquirer.net/?article=13485, accessed 11/04; Michael Kanellos, "It's Linux for IBM Supercomputer Project," C/Net News.com, 24 October 2002, http://news.com.com/2100-1001-963285.html, accessed 11/04.

Chapter 9

1. Staff, "Santa's Helpers," *The Economist*, 15 May 2004, pp. 5–7; Nick Wingfield, "Amazon goes for Gold with Discount Jewelry," *Wall Street Journal*, 22 April 2004, pp. B1, 2; Susan Kuchinskas, "Amazon Price-Cuts to Q1 Profit," InternetNews.com, 23 April 2003, www.internetnews.com/ec-news/article.php/3344441, accessed 11/04; Staff, "Amazon Hits Record Q1 Sales of $1.5 Billion," Internet Retailer, 23 April 2004, www.internetretailer.com/dailyNews.asp?id=11808, accessed 11/04; Nick Wingfield, "A Web Giant Tries to Boost Profits by Taking on Tenants," *Wall Street Journal*, 24 September 2003, pp. A1, 10; Janelle Chester, "Amazon.com, Inc.," Hoover's Online, 2004, www.hoovers.com/amazon.com/—ID__51493—/free-co-factsheet.xhtml, accessed 11/04; Chip Bayers, "Amazon Gets the Last Laugh," *Business2.0*, September 2002, pp. 86–93 and www.business2.com/b2/web/articles/0,17863,514955,00.html, accessed 11/04; Nick Wingfield and Joe Pereira, "Amazon Issues 'Faux' Recommendations for Its Clothing," *Wall Street Journal*, 4 December 2002, pp. B1, 3; David Colker, "Bought It From Amazon? You Can Sell It There, Too," *Kansas City Star*, 23 March 2003, www.kansascity.com/mld/kansascity/business/5434042.htm?1c, accessed 11/04; Nick Wingfield and Amy Merrick, "Amazon to Offer Retailers' Apparel to Online Buyers," *Wall Street Journal*, 30 October 2002, pp. A3, 8; Nick Wingfield, "Amazon Delivery Delays Rile Some Buyers," *Wall Street Journal*, 9 January 2003, pp. B1, 4; Stefanie Olsen, "Amazon Powers Up Internet Search Engine," c/net News.com, 15 September 2004, http://news.com.com/Amazon+powers+up+Internet+search+engine/2100-1024_3-5367133.html, accessed 11/04; Jeffrey Rorhs, "Google Drops Restrictions on AdWords; Amazon's A9 Launches," SearchEngineWatch, 15 April 2004, http://searchenginewatch.com/searchday/article.php/3340461, accessed 11/04.

2. William H. Janeway, "The Fifth Great Wave Is Breaking Now," *The Spectator*, 18 October 2003, pp. 50–51; Edmund A. Mennis, "Technological Revolutions and Financial Capital: The Dynamics of Bubbles and Golden Ages," The National Association for Business Economists, 2003, http://articles.findarticles.com/p/articles/mi_m1094/is_4_38/ai_111856317, accessed 11/04.

3. Staff, "E-Commerce Takes Off," *The Economist*, 15 May 2004, p. 9; Staff, "E-Stats," U.S. Department of Commerce, 15 April 2004, www.census.gov/eos/www/papers/2002/2002finaltext.pdf, accessed 11/04; Staff, "Online Sales Skyrocket as Profitability Jumps," *The Business Journal*, 4 June 2004, www.business-journal.com/archives/20040604OnlineSalesSkyrocketasProfitabilityJumps.asp, accessed 11/04; Keith Regan, "Report: Online Sales Top $100 Billion," E-Commerce Times, 1 June 2004, www.ecommercetimes.com/story/34148.html, accessed 11/04; Robyn Greenspan, "Q1 '04 U.S. E-Com Sales = $15.5B," ClickZ Network, 1 June 2004, www.clickz.com/stats/markets/retailing/article.php/3361411, accessed 11/04; Staff, "US B2C E-Commerce to Top $90 Billion in 2003," CRM Today, 2 May 2003, www.crm2day.com/news/crm/EpVElVAFpupMUkesaQ.php, accessed 11/04.

4. Staff, "E-Commerce Takes Off," *The Economist*, 15 May 2004, p. 9; Staff, "E-Stats," U.S. Department of Commerce, 15 April 2004, www.census.gov/eos/www/papers/2002/2002finaltext.pdf, accessed 11/04; Staff, "Statistics: E-Business Trends—B2B," Shop.org, 2004, www.shop.org/learn/stats_ebizz_b2b.html, accessed 7/04; Staff, "Auto B2B Sales Rev Up Online," eMarketer, 28 January 2003, www.emarketer.com/Article.aspx?1002014, accessed 11/04; Robyn Greenspan, "EU B2B Expected to Explode," ClickZ Network, 28 August 2002, www.clickz.com/stats/markets/b2b/article.php/1453831, accessed 11/04.

5. Jack Aaronson, "Mass Product Customization, Part II," ClickZ Network, 30 October 2003, www.clickz.com/experts/crm/crm_strat/article.php/3101011, accessed 11/04; Jack Aaronson, "Personalization Meet Mass Customization," ClickZ Network, 16 October 2003, www.clickz.com/experts/crm/crm_strat/article.php/3091931, accessed 11/04; Toby B. Gooley, "Mass Customization: How Logistics Makes It Happen," Logistics Management, 1 April 1998, www.manufacturing.net/lm/article/CA125126, accessed 11/04.

6. Staff, "Reflect.com Broadens Scope," *Women's Wear Daily*, 2 March 2001; Reflect.com About Us In the Press, www.reflect.com, accessed 7/04; Erik Linden, "Procter & Gamble-backed Dot-com Puts on a Happy Face As It Hires Engineers to Buoy Growth," *Silicon Valley Business Ink*, 4 May 2001, www.svbizink.com/headlines/article.asp?aid=1563, accessed 7/02.

7. Bruce Nussbaum," The Best Product Designs of the Year: Winners 2004," *BusinessWeek*, 5 July 2004, pp. 60–68; Pui-Wing Tam, "Apple's iPod Drawing New Uses," *Wall Street Journal*, 8 June 2004, p. D6; Walter S. Mossberg, "Dressing Up Your iPod," *Wall Street Journal*, 23 June 2004, pp. D1, 3; John Borland, "Apple Unveils Music Store," C/net News.com, 28 April 2003, http://news.com/2100-1027-998590.html, accessed 7/04; Steven Levy, "Owning the Music," *Newsweek*, 29 December 2003, p. 20; Nick Wingfield, "Apple to Introduce a Cheaper iPod," *Wall Street Journal*, 6 January 2004, pp. D1, 2; Steven Levy, "Pumping Up the Volume," *Newsweek*, 27 October 2003, pp. 52–53; Ethan Smith and Nick Wingfield, "Online Music Rings Up New Sales with Outtakes, Mixes," *Wall Street Journal*, 1 March 2004, pp. B1, 4; Peter Burrows and Ronald Grover, "Steve Jobs, the Music Man," *BusinessWeek*, 28 April 2003, p. 38; Steven Levy, "Not the Same Old Song," *Newsweek*, 12 May 2003, p. 54; Walter S. Mossberg, "Apple's iPod Just Keeps Getting Better as Top Digital Player," *Wall Street Journal*, 1 May 2003, p. B1; Pui-Wing Tam, "Apple Launches Online Store Offering Downloadable Music," *Wall Street Journal*, 29 April 2003, p. B8; Walter S. Mossberg, "Music That You Don't Have to Steal," *Wall Street Journal*, 30 April 2003, pp. D1, 5.

8. Melvin T. Copeland, "Relation of Consumers' Buying Habits to Marketing Methods," *Harvard Business Review* Vol. 1, no. 3 (April 1923), pp. 282–289.

9. Jeffrey A. Trachtenberg, "The Plot Thickens," *Wall Street Journal*, 12 January 2004, p. R6; Staff, "College Books Move Online," *Wall Street Journal* 23 April 2004, p. B3; Staff, "Electronic Displays," *The Economist*, 17 May 2003, p. 72.

10. Staff, "IDC: Online-Banking in Westeuropa 2003–2007," SYSTEMSworld.DE, 30 May 2003, www.systems-world.de/id/8283/CMEntries_ID/10997, accessed 11/04; Reuters, "Sweden Turns to Banking Online," *ZDNet.com*, 2 January 2002, www.zdnet.com/filters/printerfriendly/0,6061,5101155-2,00.html, accessed 7/02.

11. Lisa Vickery, "Change of Tune," *Wall Street Journal*, 17 July 2000, p. R40.

12. Laura Landro, "Push Grows for Online Health Data," *Wall Street Journal*, 11 March 2004, p. D6; Matthew Rose, "More Subscribers After Time Ends Free Web Access," *Wall Street Journal*, 11 August 2003, pp. B1, 3; Saul Hansell, "Baseball Hopes to Score on Webcasts," *Lexington Herald-Leader*, 7 February 2003, p. C2; Ryan Naraine, "Paid Content Market to Soar," ClickZ Network, 24 March 2003, www.clickz.com/stats/markets/advertising/article.php/2169131, accessed 11/04.

13. Keith Regan, "Ebay Launches B2B Marketplace in Challenging Climate," E-Commerce Times, 29 January 2003, www.ecommercetimes.com/story/20603.html, accessed 11/04; Lynn Ward, "The New Face of B2B E-Commerce," E-Commerce Times, 22 May 2003, www.ecommercetimes.com/story/21569.html, accessed 11/04; Lesley Hensell, "The True Path of B2B E-Commerce," E-Commerce Times, 31 October 2003, www.ecommercetimes.com/perl/section/b2b/, accessed 11/04; Staff, "A Perfect Market," *The Economist*, 15 May 2004, pp. 3–5; Staff, "WWRE Overview," WorldWide Retail Exchange, 2004, www.worldwideretailexchange.org/cs/en/about_wwre/overview.htm, accessed 11/04; Michael Pastore, "Digital Marketplaces Deemed Crucial to Strategy," ClickZ Network, 18 December 2000, www.clickz.com/stats/markets/b2b/print.php/10091_539051, accessed 11/04; Michael Pastore, "E-Procurement Gaining Converts Among Mid-Sized Businesses," ClickZ Network, 6 December 2000, www.clickz.com/stats/markets/b2b/print.php/10091_528481, accessed 11/04; Staff, "B2B E-Commerce Will Survive Growing Pains," ClickZ Network, 28 November 2001, www.clickz.com/stats/markets/b2b/print.php/10091_930251, accessed 11/04.

14. Julia Angwin, "Renaissance in Cyberspace," *Wall Street Journal*, 20 November 2003, p. B1; Julia Angwin, "Used-Car Auctioneers, Dealers Meet Online," *Wall Street Journal*, 20 November 2003, pp. B1, 13; Staff, "Auto B2B Sales Rev Up," eMarketer.com, 28 January 2003, www.emarketer.com/Article.aspx?1002014, accessed 11/04.

15. Joab Jackson, "Loans Going, Going, Gone at FDIC Auction," Government Computer News, 7 May 2004, www.gcn.com/vol1_no1/daily-updates/25847-1.html, accessed 11/04; Genelle M. Hoban, "Going Once, Going Twice, Going Online," Stateline.org, 18 May 2004, www.govpro.com, accessed 7/04; Karen Schwartz, "Government Auctions Grow Up," *InformationWeek*, 22 December 2003, www.informationweek.com/story/showArticle.jhtml?articleID=16700550, accessed 11/04; Anne Marie Squeo," Military Surplus Sales Soar As Avid Net Buyers Bid for It," *Lexington Herald Leader*, 23 June 2004, pp. C1, 3; Brandon Ortiz, "Some Auction Items Stored in Kentucky," *Lexington Herald-Leader*, 23 June 2004, p. C1; Lori Enos, "U.S. Government Tops Amazon in Online Sales," E-Commerce Times, 29 May 2001, www.ecommercetimes.com/perl/board/mboard.pl/ecttalkback/thread656/656.html, accessed 11/04; Lori Enos, "Uncle Sam Moving Its Yard Sales to eBay," E-Commerce Times, 27 April 2001, www.ecommercetimes.com/story/9288.html, accessed 11/04; Pew Internet & American Life Project, "US Government Is Behemoth of Online Retail," Pew Foundation, 30 May 2001, www.pewinternet.org/releases/release.asp?id=23, accessed 7/02.

16. Wanda Cummings, "Online Branding: Developers and Designers Hold the Key," *WebReference Update Newsletter*, 27 April 2000, www.webreference.com/new/branding.html, accessed 11/04; Staff, "eBranding Index Introduced by Corporate Branding," 14 January 2000, www.corebrand.com/forum/release_ebranding01.html, accessed 11/04; Staff, "The Top 100 Global Brands," *BusinessWeek*, 4 August 2003, www.businessweek.com/pdfs/2003/0331_globalbrands.pdf, accessed 11/04; Staff, "Google Voted Best Brand of 2003," BBC News, 3 February 2004, http://news.bbc.co.uk/1/hi/business/3456363.stm, accessed 11/04; Staff, "Traffic Patterns," May 2003, ClickZ Network, 20 June 2003, www.clickz.com/stats/big_picture/traffic_patterns/

article.php/5931_2225361, accessed 11/04; Staff, "U.S. Web Usage and Traffic, March 2004," ClickZ Network, 18 May 2004, www.clickz .com/stats/big_picture/traffic_patterns/article.php/3355351#table2, accessed 11/04.

17. Brian Milligan, "Toys "R" Us Sues Amazon.com," CNN Money, 24 May 2004, http://money.cnn.com/2004/05/24/technology/ amazon_toysrus/, accessed 11/04; Keith Regan, "Toys "R" Us Sues Amazon for $200 Million," E-Commerce Times, 25 May 2004, www.ecommercetimes.com/story/33993.html, accessed 11/04.

18. Brian Milligan, "Transportation and the Internet: Brand-Name Recognition Problem Raises Its Head," Purchasing.com, 2 November 2000, www.manufacturing.net/pur/article/CA139279, accessed 11/04.

19. Kevin Lee, "Branding Metrics for Search Engine Marketing," ClickZ Network, 4 July 2003, www.clickz.com/experts/search/strat/ article.php2230621, accessed 11/04; Christopher Saunders, "Study: Online Ads Focus on Building Brand, Not Clickthroughs," ClickZ Network, 8 November 2000, www.clickz.com/news/print.php/ 12_506671, accessed 11/04; Christopher Saunders, "Study: Search Listings Better at Branding, Sales Than Banners," ClickZ Network, 13 February 2001, www.clickz.com/news/print.php/12_587751, accessed 11/04; Jim Meskauskas, "Branding Online Is Possible . . . Now What?" ClickZ Network, 11 September 2001, www.clickz.com/ experts/archives/media/plan_buy/article.php/881651, accessed 11/04.

20. Michael Carlon, Marc Ryan, and Risa Weledniger, "The Five Golden Rules of Online Branding," *AdRelevance and 24/7 Advertising*, 23 October 2000, www.nyecomm.org/Misc/docs/Five_Golden_Rules.pdf, accessed 11/04.

21. Nick Wingfield, "Racing Barnes & Noble for Same-Day Delivery in New York," *Wall Street Journal*, 3 June 2004, http://online.wsj.com, accessed 6/04; Staff, "Barnes & Noble and Barnes & Noble.com Merger Completed," Barnes & Noble Press Releases, 27 May 2004, www.barnesandnoble.com, accessed 7/04; Jim Milliot, "Solid Sales Gains at Amazon, B&N.com," *Publishers Weekly*, 3 May 2004, www.publishersweekly.com, accessed 7/04; Staff, "Barnes & Noble Announces First Quarter Results," Barnes & Noble Booksellers, 1 May 2004, www.barnesandnoble.com, accessed 7/04; Lindsey Arent, "Amazon, B&N's Mutual Hissy Fit," *Wired News*, 22 October 1999, www.wired.com/news/business/0,1367,32068,00.html, accessed 11/04; Tara Murphy, "Barnes & Noble to Take Online Unit Private," Forbes.com, 7 November 2003, www.forbes.com, accessed 7/04; Staff, "Amazon Settles Barnes & Noble Patent Suit," *Seattle Post-Intelligencer*, 8 March 2002, http://seattlepi.newsource.com, accessed 7/04.

Chapter 10

1. Staff, "U.S. Customer Satisfaction Highest Since 1995, Fueling Consumer Demand," American Customer Satisfaction Index, 18 February 2004, www.theacsi.org/press_releases/0204q1.PDF, accessed 11/04; Staff, "At the Drop of a Hammer," *The Economist*, 15 May 2004, pp. 12–14; Staff, "A Perfect Market," *The Economist*, 15 May 2004, pp. 3–5; Robert D. Hof, "The Constant 'Challenge' at eBay," *BusinessWeek*, 30 June 2004, http://businessweek.com/ technology/content/jun2004/tc20040630_3302_tc121.htm, accessed 11/04; Staff, "New Pact to Ease Hassles of eBay," *Wall Street Journal*, 17 June 2004, pp. D1, 2; Josh Wardrip, "eBay Inc.," Hoover's Online, 2004, *www.hoovers.com*, accessed 11/04; Staff, "Santa's Helpers," *The Economist*, 15 May 2004, pp. 5–8; Cynthia L. Webb, "EBay Hops the Fast Boat to China," *Washington Post*, 22 April 2004, www .washingtonpost.com/ac2/wp-dyn/A33683-2004Apr22, accessed 11/04; Nick Wingfield, "Hitching a Ride on eBay," *Wall Street Journal*,

20 October 2003, pp. R4, 5; Robert D. Hof, "The eBay Economy," *BusinessWeek*, 25 August 2003, pp. 125–128; Margaret Kane, "eBay Picks Up PayPal for $1.5 Billion," c/netNews.com, 8 July 2002, http://news.com.com/2100-1017-941964.html, accessed 11/04; Nick Wingfield, "Stock of eBay Acts Like...eBay," *Wall Street Journal*, 22 April 2003, pp. C1, 3; Nick Wingfield, "As eBay Grows, Site Disappoints Some Big Retailers," *Wall Street Journal*, 26 February 2004, pp. A1, 2; Nick Wingfield and Karen Lundegaard, "EBay Is Emerging As Unlikely Giant in Used-Car Sales," *Wall Street Journal*, 7 February 2003, pp. A1, 8; Staff, "eBay Announces Third Quarter 2004 Financial Results," eBay.com, 20 October 2004, http://investor.ebay.com/financial.cfm, accessed 11/04.

2. Corey Rudl, "Payment Options for Online Shoppers," Entrepreneur .com, 6 January 2003, www.entrepreneur.com/article/ 0,4621,305676,00.html, accessed 11/04; Darren Allen, "eConsumers: Get Lots of Credit," eMarketer, 20 June 2001, www.emarketer .com/analysis/ecommerce_b2c/20010620_b2c.html, accessed 7/02.

3. Alex Biesada, "Tesco PLC," Hoover's Online, 2004, www.hoovers.com, accessed 11/04; Staff, "Tesco PLC Annual Review and Summary Financial Statement," Tesco PLC, 2004, http:// 81.201.142.254/presentResults/results2003_04/Prelims/site/pdf/review/ 09_delivering_value.pdf, accessed 11/04: Jeff Canon, "How a Supermarket Can Be a Corner Shop," crmGuru.com, 23 January 2003, www.crmguru.com/features/2003a/0123jc.html, accessed 11/04; Laura Cohn, "How Tesco Lives Not by Bread Alone," *BusinessWeek*, 20 October 2003, www.businessweek.com/magazine/content/ 03_42/b3854086_mz054.htm, accessed 11/04; Andy Reinhardt, "Tesco Bets Small—And Wins Big," *BusinessWeek eBiz*, 1 October 2001, pp. EB25–32; Staff, "Q&A with Tesco.com's John Browett," *BusinessWeek e.Biz*, 1 October 2001, www.businessweek.com/ magazine/content/01_40/b3751626.htm, accessed 11/04; Staff, "Tesco PLC Interim Results 2004/5, Tesco, 21 September 2004, http://tesco.com/corporateinfo/, accessed 11/04.

4. Staff, "October Auto Sales Soar," *Money*, 1 November 2001, http://money.cnn.com/2001/11/01/companies/carsales, accessed 11/04; Staff, "Ford Warns on Q4," *Money*, 17 October 2001, http://money .cnn.com/2001/10/17/companies/ford/, accessed 11/04.

5. Staff, "Consumers Going Online Before Going on the Road," Consumer Internet Barometer, The Conference Board, 28 June 2004, www.conference-board.org/economics/consumerBarometer.cfm, accessed 11/04; Charles J. Whalen, "Consumer Confidence No Crystal Ball," *BusinessWeek*, 19 March 2001, p. 65.

6. Dave Chaffey, "The E-marketing Mix Part 1," Marketing Insights, 2003, www.marketing-insights.co.uk/wnim0602.htm#_Toc12064588, accessed 11/04; Walter L. Baker, Eric Lin, Michael V. Marn, and Craig C. Zawada, "Getting Prices Right on the Web," *McKinsey Quarterly*, 2001, no. 2, pp. 54–62; Keith Regan, "Harnessing the Power of Online Pricing," *E-Commerce Times*, 22 March 2001, www.ecommercetimes.com/story/8370.html, accessed 11/04; Luc Carton, "How to Set the Best Price on the Internet," *eMarketNews*, 3 April 2001, www.emarketnews.com/archives/2001- 6/ecommerce.htm, accessed 11/04.

7. Walter L. Baker, Eric Lin, Michael V. Marn, and Craig C. Zawada, "Getting Prices Right on the Web," *McKinsey Quarterly*, 2001, no. 2, pp. 54–62; Robert Drescher, "Price Matters: Live Price Testing Helps eRetailers Capture Profits," eRetail News, 2001, www.eretailnews .com/Features/0105pricing.htm, accessed 11/04; Linda Rosencrance, "Customer Outrage Prompts Amazon to Change Its Price-Testing Policy," *ComputerWorld*, 13 September 2000, www.computerworld.com/industrytopics/retail/story/0,10801,50153,00

.html, accessed 11/04; Todd R. Weiss, "Amazon Apologizes for Price-Testing Program That Angered Customers," *ComputerWorld,* 28 September 2000, www.computerworld.com/industrytopics/retail/story/0,10801,51392,00.html, accessed 11/04.

8. Jared Blank, "Coping with Price Transparency," ClickZ Network, 16 June 2003, www.clickz.com/experts/brand/capital/article.php/2221951, accessed 11/04; Mohanbir Sawhney, "Profit from Transparency," *CIO Magazine,* 15 June 2000, www.cio.com/archive/061502/netgains.html, accessed 11/04.

9. Staff, "MySimon: Informed, Educated, Upscale Shoppers," c/netNetworks, 2004, http://img.com.com/i/cn/specs/mysimon_details.pdf, accessed 7/04; Danny Sullivan, "Search Engine Watch 2003 Award Winners, Part 3," ClickZ Network, 3 March 2004, www.clickz.com/experts/search/opt/article.php/3319991, accessed 11/04; Margaret Kane, "Google Searches Out an E-Tail Niche," c/net News.com, 12 December 2002, http://news.com.com/2100-1017-977042.html, accessed 11/04.

10. Ronald Roach, "Study Says Minorities Get Better Auto Deals Online," Black Issues in Higher Education, 3 January 2002, www.findarticles.com/cf_0/m0DXK/23_18/82472609/p1/article.jhtml, accessed 11/04; Andrew Quinn, "Minorities Get Better Car Deals on Internet—Study," *Reuters,* 11 December 2001, www.nua.ie/surveys/index.cgi?f=VS&art_id=905357491&rel=true, accessed 11/04 and www.mklink.com/email/december2001.html#four, accessed 11/04.

11. Staff, "They're Watching You," *The Economist,* 16 October 2003, www.economist.com/displaystory.cfm?story_id=2137947, accessed 11/04; Ropert Goodwins, "Privacy's a High Price for a Bargain," ZDNet UK, 4 August 2003, http://news.zdnet.com/2100-9595_22-5059377.html, accessed 11/04; Brian Bergstein, "Web Price Discrimination Possible," *Daily Texan,* 8 August 2003, www.dailytexanonline.com/news/2003/08/08/News/Web-Price.Discrimination.Possible-493028.shtml, accessed 11/04.

12. Graeme Wearden, "Broadband Prices Tumble Worldwide," ZD Net UK, 20 October 2003, http://news.zdnet.co.uk/communications/broadband/0,39020342,39117243,00.htm, accessed11/04; Noah Elkin, "How to Beat the High Cost of Internet Access," *eMarketer,* 19 December 2001, www.emarketer.com, accessed 7/02.

13. Mark Glaser, "Journal Takes Broader View with Online Inclusion," *Online Journalism Review,* 11 November 2003, www.ojr.org/ojr/glaser/1068601595.php, accessed 11/04; Business Editors, "The Wall Street Journal Announces New Integrated Print and Online Sales and Marketing Initiatives," *BusinessWire,* 3 November 2003, www.businesswire.com/webbox/bw.110303/233075695.htm, accessed 11/04; Stefanie Olsen, "Extra! Wall Street Journal Gives Away Content," c/netNews.com, 22 October 2004, http://news.com.com/Extra!+Wall+Street+Journal+gives+away+Web+content/2100-1025_3-5423054.html, accessed 11/04.

14. Michael Totty, "Web Sites Learn How to Charge for Information," *Wall Street Journal,* 3 March 2004, http://166.70.44.66/2004/Mar/03282004/business/151617.asp, accessed 7/04; Timothy J. Mullaney, "Sites Worth Paying For?," *BusinessWeek e.Biz,* 14 May 2001, pp. EB10–EB12.

15. Robyn Greenspan, "Paid Content Paying Off," ClickZ Network, 24 September 2003, www.clickz.com/stats/markets/retailing/article.php/3082081, accessed 11/04; Staff, "Revenues from Paid-for Web Content to Rise 25 Per Cent in 2003," MacUser, 24 March 2003, www.macuser.co.uk/ news/news_story.php?id=40238, accessed 11/04; Reuters, "Online Adult Entertainment," Hoover's Online, 1 February 2003, www .hoovers.com/global/report/detail.xhtml?RID=75974, accessed 11/04.

16. Nick Wingfield, "Amazon.com's Free-Shipping Promotion Has Customers Crying, 'Price Increase,' " *Wall Street Journal,* 27 June 2001, p. A3; Greg Sandoval, "Amazon Stops Shipping Goods for Free," c/net News.com, 6 July 2001, http://news.com.com/2100-1017-269534.html?legacy=cnet, accessed 11/04.

17. Maureen Ryan, "Music Rental May Be the Wave of the Near Future," *E-Commerce Times,* 8 June 2004, www.ecommercetimes.com/story/34304.html, accessed 11/04; Owen Thomas, "Amazon.com Tests the Notion of Fixed Prices," eCompany.com, 28 September 2000, www .business2.com/b2/web/articles/1,17863,512692,00.html, accessed 11/04.

18. Ron Barnett, "Churches Cash In on Auctions," *Greenville News,* 28 June 2004, http://nl.newsbank.com/nl-search/we/Archives?p_action=doc&p_docid=1038B5DC84DDDC57&p_docnum=1, accessed 7/04; Patricia A. Michaels, "Shop Goodwill Online at the ShopGoodwill.com Auction Site," AuctionBytes, 27 July 2003, www.auctionbytes.com/cab/abu/y203/m07/abu0099/s04, accessed 11/04; Nielsen NetRatings, "Auction Sites Ever More Popular," Nua Internet Surveys, 28 June 2001, www.nua.ie/surveys/index.cgi?f=VS&art_id=905356927&rel=true, accessed 11/04; Corey Rudl, "Profiting from Online Auction Sites," Entrepreneur.com, 6 October 2003, www.entrepreneur.com/article/0,4621,311268,00.html, accessed 11/04; Staff, "E-Bay Third Quarter Net Surges 77% As Listings Rise," Bloomberg.com, 20 October 2004, http://quote.bloomberg.com/apps/news?pid=10000103&refer=us&sid=a90brcgdJgeU, accessed 11/04.

19. Janis Mara, "Priceline.com Trumpets Its Shift in Strategy, Offerings," ClizkZ Network, 16 January 2004, www.clickz.com/news/article.php/3300651, accessed 11/04; Ephraim Schwartz and Brett Mendel, "Auctions Preserve Pricing," *InfoWorld,* 18 October 1999, http://ww1.infoworld.com/cgi-bin/displayArchive.pl?/99/42/t23-42.12.htm, accessed 11/04.

20. Neal Aldine, "Company Uses Barter System Instead of Cash," *Detroit News,* 10 July 2003, www.detnews.com/2003/business/0307/10/c02-213892.htm, accessed 11/04; Laura Bailey, "Barter Systems Put the 'Trade' in Trade Group," CrainsDetroit.com, 21 April 2003, www.crainsdetroit.com/cgi-bin/article.pl?articleId=22480, accessed 11/04; Staff, "Barter Is Booming," Entrepreneurial Connection, 2004, http://entrepreneurialconnection.com/skills/module6/businesses.asp, accessed 11/04; Lynn Ward, "The New Face of B2B E-Commerce," *E-Commerce Times,* 22 May 2003, www.ecommercetimes.com/story/21569.html, accessed 11/04; Staff, "Industry's First Online Hotel Booking Barter System Launches Ibart 4.0 Designed to Help Beleaguered Travel Industry Capitalize Excess Capacity," Hospitality Net, 6 March 2002, www.hospitalitynet.org/news/4011134.print, accessed 11/04.

21. Eric Wahlgren, "Williams-Sonoma: Safe at Home?," *BusinessWeek,* 5 March 2004, www.businessweek.com/bwdaily/dnflash/mar2004/nf2004035_5506_db014.htm, accessed 11/04; Julie Kreppel, Williams-Sonoma, Inc., Hoover's Online, 2004, www.hoovers.com/williams-sonoma/—ID__15167—/free-co-factsheet.xhtml, accessed 11/04; Staff, "Cooking Good—Tactics of Williams-Sonoma," *Direct,* 15 November 2000, www.findarticles.com/p/articles/mi_m3815/is_15_12/ai_67720564, accessed 11/04.

22. David P. Hamilton, "The Price Isn't Right: Internet Pricing Has Turned Out to Be a Lot Trickier Than Retailers Expected," *Wall Street Journal,* 12 February 2001, http://update2.wsj.com/public/current/articles/SB981489999136217335.htm, accessed 7/02.

23. Alexis Gutzman, "Personalized Pricing Still Makes Sense," EC Tech Advisor, 26 July 2001, http://ecommerce.internet.com/news/insights/ectech/article/0,,10378_809541,00.html, accessed 11/04;

Kevin Featherly, "Personalized Pricing—Online Retail's Next Trend?," BizReport.com, 26 April 2000, http://exn.ca/stories/2000/04/26/03, accessed 7/02; Craig Bicknell, "Online Prices Not Created Equal," *Wired News,* 7 September 2000, www.wired.com/news/business/0,1367,38622,00.html, accessed 11/04; Michael Vizard, "Suppliers Toy with Dynamic Pricing—Users Face Prospect of Daily Server Pricing Changes as Industry Pursues Profits," *InfoWorld,* 11 May 2001, http://iwsun4.infoworld.com/articles/hn/xml/01/05/14/010514hndynamic.xml, accessed 7/02.

24. Peter Edmonston, "One Web Retailer's Watchword: 'Free After Rebate,' " *Wall Street Journal,* 5 March 2001, pp. B1, B5; Tom Mainelle, "CyberRebate.com Goes Bankrupt," *PCWorld,* 24 May 2001, www.pcworld.com/news/article/0,aid,50964,00.asp, accessed 11/04.

25. Thomas E. Weber, "Priceline Woes Suggest Novelty Isn't Enough to Succeed on the Web," *Wall Street Journal,* 16 October 2000, p. B1; Steve Baldwin, "IDerive.com," Ghost Sites: The Museum of e-Failure, 24 May 2004, http://disobey.com/ghostsites/show_exhibit/iderive, accessed 11/04.

26. Karen M. Kroll, "Strong Spring Home Sales Will Inflate Prices," BankRate.com, 2004, www.bankrate.com/brm/news/real-estate/buyerguide2004/best-worst-markets.asp, accessed 11/04; Business Editors, "ImproveNet Unveils Lavatory Laboratory: Online Bath Estimator Helps Homeowners Make Most of Powder Rooms," *Business Wire,* 14 January 2000, www.findarticles.com/cf_0/m0EIN/2000_Jan_14/58575345/print.jhtml, accessed 11/04; June Fletcher, "The Great E-Mortgage Bake-Off," *Wall Street Journal,* 2 June 2000, p. W12; T. Mullaney, "Don't Expect Miracles," *BusinessWeek,* 16 April 2001, pp. EB8, 10.

27. Staff, "Newer RAM Launches Extranet Site for Up-to-Date Pricing and Product Information," *PR Newswire,* 18 May 2000, www.prnewswire.com/cgi-bin/stories.pl?ACCT=104&STORY=/www/story/05-18-2000/0001222765&EDATE=, accessed 11/04.

28. Keith Regan, "Allen-Backed Mercata Bows Out," *E-Commerce Times,* 5 January 2001, www.ecommercetimes.com/story/6492.html, accessed 11/04; John Cook, "Venture Capital: Where Mercata Led, Shoppers Were Unwilling to Follow," *Seattle Post–Intelligencer,* 12 January 2001, http://seattlepi.nwsource.com/business/vc122.shtml, accessed 11/04; Greg Sandoval and Dawn Kawamoto, "Group-buying Site Mercata to Shut Its Doors," c/net News.com, 4 January 2001, http://news.cnet.com/news/0-1007-200-4372403.html?pt.ecompany.srch..ne, accessed 11/04; Bruce Gottlieb, "Does Group Shopping Work?," Slate, 26 July 2000, http://slate.msn.com/id/86925/, accessed 11/04; Bob Liu, "MobShop Discontinues Customer Service," InternetNews.com, 15 January 2001, www.internetnews.com/ec-news/article.php/560081, accessed 11/04; Joellen Perry, "Bulk Buying on the Web Rewards Togetherness," *U.S. News & World Report,* 21 August 2000, p. 62; Dick Kelsey, "Bulk Buying Site Mercata Heads South," Newsbytes, 4 January 2001, www.findarticles.com/cf_0/m0NEW/2001_Jan_4/68876776/p1/article.jhtml, accessed 11/04; James Turner, " 'Group Buying': Bogus Bargains?," *Christian Science Monitor,* 1 May 2000, www.csmonitor.com/durable/2000/05/01/p20s2.htm, accessed 11/04; Bob Liu, "MobShop Discontinues Consumer Service," 15 January 2001, InternetNews.com, www.internetnews.com/bus-news/article.php/3_560081, accessed 11/04; Kevin McCaney, "Strength in Numbers," *Government Computer News,* September 2000, www.gcn.com/vol19_no25/procurement/405-1.html, accessed 11/04.

29. Staff, "Payment Choices Lead to More Sales Online," eMarketer.com, 28 May 2004, www.emarketer.com/Article.aspx?1002819, accessed 7/04; Corey Rudl, "Payment Options for Online Shoppers,"

Entrepreneur.com, 6 January 2003, www.entrepreneur.com/article/0,4621,305676,00.html, accessed 11/04; Staff, "What is echeck?," eCheck Initiative, 2004, www.echeck.org/overview/what.html, accessed 11/04.

30. Matthew French, "DOD's Most Popular Card," FCW.com, 22 March 2004, www.fcw.com/fcw/articles/2004/0405/pol-cac-04-05-04.asp, accessed 11/04; Nancy Ferris, "Smart Cards: A Step Ahead, or a Step Backward?," FCW.com, 29 March 2004, www.fcw.com/fcw/articles/2004/0329/pol-smart-03-29-04.asp, accessed 11/04; Adam Bryant, "Plastic Is Getting Smarter," *Newsweek,* 16 October 2000, p. 80; Tim Selby, "Smart Cards, E-Checks, and ACH Online Payments Increasing Dramatically," ActivMediaResearch.com, 27 September 2000, e-mail alert, received 9/00; Tim Miller, "How Smart Are Smart Cards?," Entrepreneur.com, 11 March 2002, www.entrepreneur.com/article/0,4621,297984,00.html, accessed 11/04.

31. Staff, "Paying Through the Mouse," *The Economist,* 20 May 2004, www.economist.com/finance/displayStory.cfm?story_id=2693526, accessed 11/04; Staff, "Dreams of a Cashless Society," *The Economist,* 5 May 2001, vol. 360, no. 8220, p. 65; Staff, "PayPal Files $80.5M IPO," CNN Money, 1 October 2001, http://money.cnn.com/2001/10/01/deals/paypal, accessed 11/04; Nick Wingfield and Jathon Sapsford, "Ebay to Buy PayPal for $1.4 Billion," *Wall Street Journal,* 9 July 2002, p. A6.

32. Ryan Naraine, "PayPal Slashes Micropayments Fees," InternetNews.com, 8 December 2003, www.internetnews.com/ec-news/article.php/3286391, accessed 11/04; Anne Eisenberg, "A Virtual Cash Register Rings Up Tiny Transactions," *New York Times,* 7 January 2004, www.nytimes.com/2004/01/07/technology/circuits/08next.html?ex=1089172800&en=7c4b93bded5ea8db&ei=5070, accessed 11/04; Vin Crosbie, "Past Is No Prologue for Micropayments," ClickZ Network, 9 June 2004, www.clickz.com/experts/design/freefee/article.php/3365061, accessed 11/04; Geoffrey Smith, "A Penny-Ante Business Worth Billions," *BusinessWeek Online,* 23 April 2001, www.businessweek.com/technology/content/apr2001/tc20010423_871.htm, accessed 11/04; Joseph Nocera, "Easy Money," *Money,* August 2000, p. 71; Julia Angwin, "And How Will You Be Paying for That?," *Wall Street Journal,* 23 October 2000, p. R37.

33. Jane Bryant Quinn, "Web Sites Can't Demand Money, So They Ask for It," *Lexington Herald Leader,* 15 July 2001, p. H3; Carol King, "Amazon Honor System Draws Scrutiny," InternetNews.com, 6 February 2001, www.internetnews.com/ec-news/article.php/4_580621, accessed 11/04; Troy Wolverton, "Amazon Debuts Honor System," c/net.com, 6 February 2001, http://news.com.com/2102-1017-252122.html?legacy=cnet&tag=pff, accessed 11/04.

34. Linda Rosencrance, "Brief: USPS to Halt Online Bill-Paying Service," ComputerWorld, 17 November 2003, www.computerworld.com/managementtopics/ebusiness/story/0,10801,87224,00.html?from=story_picks, accessed 11/04; Mellody Hobson, "Bills, Web-Style," ABC News, 3 June 2004, http://abcnews.go.com/sections/GMA/MellodyHobson/Online_Bill_Paying_040603-1.html, accessed 7/04; Mindy Charski, "Online Bill Paying Is Still Waiting for the Big Payoff," *U.S. News & World Report,* 6 March 2000, p. 57; Dean Foust, "The Check Is in the e-Mail," *BusinessWeek,* 30 October 2000, pp. 120–122; Staff, "Postal Service Cancels Some Electronic and Financial Services Products: Should Cancel More," IRET Congressional Advisory, 19 March 2004, ftp://ftp.iret.org/pub/ADVS-167.PDF, accessed 11/04.

35. Patricia A. Michaels, "Shop Goodwill Online at the ShopGoodwill.com Auction Site," AuctionBytes.com, 27 July 2003, www.auctionbytes.com/cab/abu/y203/m07/abu0099/s04, accessed 11/04; Nicole Lewis, "Charities Find Perfect Place for Odd Donations:

Online Auctions," *Chronicle of Philanthropy,* 4 April 2002, www.missionfish.org/About/News/art_040402.jsp, accessed 11/04; Damon Darlin, "Goodwill Hunting," *Business2.0,* 29 May 2001, www.business2.com/b2/web/articles/0,17863,528877,00.html, accessed 11/04; Mario Cacciottolo and Lindsay Wood, "Charities Work for Disabled Workers," Goodstaff.com, 2000, www .goodstaff.com/employers/articles/charties_workers.html, accessed 11/04.

Chapter 11

1. Max Starkov, "Hotel Websites Have Much to Do to Increase User Satisfaction and Customer Loyalty," WiredHotelier.com, 28 June 2004, www.wiredhotelier.com/news/154000473/4019328.html, accessed 11/04; Max Starkov and Jason Price, "Now Is the Time to Fight Back with a Smart Direct-to-Consumer Internet Strategy," Hospitality Net, 3 February 2004, www.hospitalitynet.org/news/ 4018427.html, accessed 11/04; Staff, "Active Hotels Launches New Web-Site to Meet Increased Consumer Demand," Hospitality Net, 20 June 2004, www.hospitalitynet.org/news/4019902.html, accessed 11/04; Hospitality eBusiness Strategies, Inc., "Online Distribution vs. Traditional Distribution Channel - HeBS Report," Hospitality Net, 16 December 2002, www.hospitalitynet.org/news/4014141.html, accessed 11/04; Gunjan Bagla, "Travel Buying Has Changed Forever: Parts I and II," Hotel Marketing Newsweekly, 10 June 2004, http://www.hotelmarketing.com/triedtrue_article/4132_0_7_0_M/, http://www.imediaconnection.com/content/3615.asp, and http:// www.imediaconnection.com/content/3625.asp, accessed 11/04; Jason Price and Max Starkov, "Hoteliers Are Still Behind the Curve in Online Distribution," Hospitality Net Industry News, 18 March 2003, www.hospitalitynet.org/news/4015182.html, accessed 11/04.

2. Bob Brewin, "EPCglobal Sets Up RFID Product Code Management System," *ComputerWorld,* 16 January 2004, www.computerworld .com/industrytopics/retail/story/0,10801,89135,00.html, accessed 11/04; Jeff Hwang, "A Wal-Mart Monopoly?," The Motley Fool, 29 December 2003, www.fool.com/News/mft/2003/mft03092917.htm, accessed 11/04; Charles Fishman, "The Wal-Mart You Don't Know," *FastCompany,* December 2003, www.fastcompany.com/magazine/ 77/walmart.html, accessed 11/04; Scott McGregor, "Like It or Not, RFID Is Coming," *BusinessWeek,* 18 March 2004, www.businessweek .com/technology/content/mar2004/ tc20040318_7698_tc121.htm, accessed 11/04; Robert Mullins, "Smaller Retailers Might Feel Wal-Mart Tech Squeeze," *Sacramento Business Journal,* 23 April 2004, www.bizjournals.com/sacramento/stories/2004/04/26/smallb3.html, accessed 11/04; Beth Bacheldor, "Wal-Mart Kick-Starts RFID," Enterprise Apps Pipeline, 25 May 2004, www.enterpriseappspipeline .com/howto/showArticle.jhtml?articleId=21100077&pgno=2, accessed 11/04; Staff, "bTrade Offers Wal-Mart Suppliers Free 'TDAccess Wal-Mart Edition,'" bTrade, Inc., 16 October 2002, www .btrade.com/PDF/bTrade_PR2002-10.pdf, accessed 11/04; Anthony Bianco and Wendy Zellner, "Is Wal-Mart Too Powerful?," *BusinessWeek,* 6 October 2003, www.businessweek.com/magazine/ content/03_40/b3852001_mz001.htm, accessed 11/04.

3. Keith Regan, "Toysrus.com Sues Amazon for $200 million," *E-Commerce Times,* 10 July 2004, www.ecommercetimes.com/story/ 33993.html, accessed 11/04; Troy Wolverton, "Toys R Us Sues Amazon.com," TheStreet.com, 24 May 2004, www.thestreet.com /_tscs/stocks/troywolverton/10161980.html, accessed 11/04; Reuters, "Toys R Us Online Unit Sues Amazon.com," c/net News.com, 24 May 2004, http://news.com.com/Toys+%22R%22+Us+online+unit +sues+Amazon/2100-1038_3-5219330.html?tag=nefd.top, accessed

11/04; Jeffrey Gold, "Judge Orders Amazon and Toys "R" Us to Work Together," AP - *GrandForksHerald.com,* 12 August 2004, www .grandforks.com/mld/grandforks/business/9384433.htm, accessed 11/04.

4. Mark W. Vigoroso, "Online Travel Success Forces Offline Agents to Adapt," *E-Commerce Times,* 10 September 2001, www .ecommercetimes.com/perl/printer/13426/, accessed 11/04; Rob Spiegel, "Middlemen Join List of Endangered Species," eCommerce Business, 20 November 2000, http://graffiti.virgin.net/www3.org/ newintermediaries.htm, accessed 7/01; Larry Keller, "Endangered Careers: On the Aloha Tour," CNN.com, 2 October 2000, www.cnn .com/2000/CAREER/trends/10/02/travel.agents/, accessed11/04.

5. Paul Demery, "Manufacturers Solve Their Online Dilemma," InternetRetailer.com, November 2003, www.internetretailer.com/ article.asp?id=10545, accessed 11/04; Beth Stackpole, "Channel Crossing," *CIO Magazine,* 15 February 2001, www.cio.com/archive/ 021501/ecomm.html, accessed 11/04; Frederic Jallat, "Disintermediation in Question: New Economy, New Networks, New Middlemen." *Business Horizons,* March 2001, www.sciencedirect.com/science/ article/B6W45-4379G5Y-9/2/e6ad1f87ed3be63bb0c6944f3aace28c, accessed 11/04; Moira Pascale, "Acquisitions: Amazon Gets Back to Basics, *CatalogAge,* 1 January 2000, http://catalogagemag.com/mag/ marketing_acquisitions_amazon_gets/, accessed 11/04.

6. Joseph Pryweller, "Omnexus Ready to Take on the World," PlasticsNews.com, 6 July 2003, www.plasticsnews.com/ebiz/news2 .html?id=994444374, accessed 11/04; Ann M. Thayer, "Chemical E-Business: Are We There Yet?," *Chemical and Engineering News,* 10 February 2003, http://pubs.acs.org/cen/business/8106/8106bus1 .html, accessed 11/04; Annual Report 2000, "Business Review: Plastics," General Electric Co., 2001, www.ge.com/annual00/business/ plastics.html, accessed 11/04; Staff, "B2BWorks Signs Strategic Advertising Alliances with GE Services Network," B2BWorks, 27 March 2001, www.b2bworks.com/corporate/pressrelease.cfm ?releasenum=30&year=2001, accessed 7/02; Bob Tedeschi, "GE Has a Bright Idea," ZDNet, 14 May 2001, http://techupdate.zdnet.com/ techupdate/stories/main/0,14179,2711901,00.00.html, accessed 11/04; Alex Frangos, "Just One Word: Plastics," *Wall Street Journal,* 21 May 2001, p. R20; Staff, "Older, Wiser, Webbier," *The Economist,* 30 June 2001, vol. 359, no. 8228, p. 10.

7. James Maquire, "Case Study: Dell Computer," Internet.com, 3 March 2003, http://ecommerce.internet.com/news/insights/trends/article/ 0,,10417_2013731,00.html, accessed 11/04; Kenneth Kraemer and Jason Dedrick, "Dell Computer: Using E-Commerce to Support the Virtual Company," University of California at Irvine, June 2001, www .crito.uci.edu/GIT/publications/pdf/dell_ecom_case_6-13-01.pdf, accessed 11/04; Staff, "Build-to-Order Model for Success, Part II," The Manage Mentor, 2003, www.themanagementor.com/kuniverse/ kmailers_universe/manu_kmailers/scm_build2order2.htm, accessed 11/04; David Joachim, "Dell Links Virtual Supply Chain," InternetWeek.com, 2 November 1998, www.internetweek.com/ news1198/news110298-3.htm, accessed 11/04; Barry Silverstein, "Is It Time for a Customer-Driven Extranet?," ClickZ Network, 11 February 2000, www.clickz.com/experts/archives/b2b_mkt/b2b_strat/ article .php/821061, accessed 11/04.

8. Associated Press, "Dell Bringing Mall Kiosks to California," *Detroit News,* 15 June 2004, www.detnews.com/2004/technology/0406/15/ technology-183572.htm, accessed 11/04; Dell Press Room, "New Austin Dell Direct Multimedia Kiosk Gives Consumers First-Hand Experience with Dell Products," Dell, 27 June 2002, www.dell.com/ us/en/gen/corporate/press/pressoffice_us_2002-06-27-aus-000.htm, accessed 7/02; John H. Sheridan, "Dell Courts Customers Online,"

Industry Week/IW, 3 April 2000, www.industryweek.com/
CurrentArticles/asp/articles.asp?ArticleID=795, accessed 11/04; David
Shook, "The Winner of the PC Price Wars: Dell," *BusinessWeek Online,*
1 May 2001, http://www.businessweek.com/bwdaily/ may2001/
nf2001051_655.htm, accessed 11/04; Andrew Park and Peter Burrows,
"Dell, the Conqueror," *BusinessWeek,* 24 September 2001, pp. 92–102.

9. Paul Demery, "Manufacturers Solve Their Online Dilemma,"
InternetRetailer.com, November 2003, www.internetretailer.com/
article.asp?id=10545, accessed 11/04; Stacy Perman, "Why the Web
Can't Kill the Middleman," *Business2.0,* April 2001, www.business2
.com/articles/mag/0,1640,9600,FF.html, accessed 7/01; Jason Anders,
"Sibling Rivalry," *Wall Street Journal,* 17 July 2000, p. R16.

10. Elizabeth Cornell, "Lands' End, Inc.," Hoover's Online, 2004,
www.hoovers.com/lands'-end/—ID__10883—/free-co-factsheet.xhtml,
accessed 11/04; Staff, "2004 Internet Retailer Best of the Web: The
Top 50 Retailing Sites," InternetRetailer, December 2003, www
.internetretailer.com/article.asp?id=10752 and www.internetretailer
.com/article.asp?id=10758, accessed 11/04; Davide Dukcevich,
"Lands' End's Instant Business," *Forbes,* 22 July 2002, www.forbes
.com/2002/07/22/0722landsend.html, accessed 11/04.

11. Lorraine Woellert, "Piracy Wars: Hollywood Turns Its Guns on Tech,"
BusinessWeek, 19 July 2004, p. 45; Jack M. Germain, "Global Piracy:
Illegal Software Markets Endure," TechNewsWorld, 4 June 2004,
www.technewsworld.com/story/33327.html, accessed 11/04; Peter
Lewis, "Drop a Quarter in the Internet," *Fortune,* vol. 149, no. 6 (22
March 2004), pp. 56–58; John Borland, "Free vs. Fee: Underground
Still Thrives," c/net News.com, 30 May 2003, http://news.com.com/
2009-1027-1009541.html, accessed 11/04; David McGuire, "The
Future of Music Distribution," *Washington Post,* 24 May 2004, www
.washingtonpost.com/wp-dyn/articles/A44961-2004May21.html,
accessed 11/04.

12. Bob Brewin, "IT Drives the UPS Machine," *ComputerWorld,* 19 April
2004, www.computerworld.com/softwaretopics/software/story/
0,10801,92273,00.html, accessed 11/04; Dean Foust, "Big Brown's
New Bag," *BusinessWeek,* 19 July 2004, pp. 54-56; Chuck Salter,
"Surprise Package," *FastCompany,* February 2004, www.fastcompany
.com/magazine/79/ups.html, accessed 11/04; Charles Haddad, "UPS
versus FedEx: Ground Wars," *BusinessWeek,* 21 May 2001, pp. 64–68
and www.businessweek.com/magazine/content/01_21/b3733084.htm,
accessed11/04; Faith Keenan, "Warehouse Trouble," *BusinessWeek,*
20 November 2000, pp. 125–126; UPS, "AuctionDrop Takes eBay
Drop-Off National Through 3,400 The UPS Store Locations," UPS
Pressroom, 22 June 2004, www.theupsstore.com/about/062904
_press_release.html, accessed 11/04; Chris Isidore, "Still Time to
Deliver the Goods," *Money* at CNN.com, 16 December 2003, http://
money.cnn.com/2003/12/15/news/companies/holiday_shipping/,
accessed 11/04; UPS, "2003 Annual Report," 2004, www.shareholder
.com/ups/downloads/2003_Annual_Report.pdf, accessed 11/04; Galen
Gruman, "UPS vs. FedEx: Head-to-Head on Wireless," CIO, 1 June
2004, www.cio.com/archive/060104/ups.html, accessed 11/04.

13. Ephraim Schwartz, "E-marketplaces Make a Comeback," *InfoWorld,*
23 April 2004, www.infoworld.com/article/04/04/23/HNemarkets
_1.html?SUPPLY%2520CHAIN%2520MANAGEMENT, accessed
11/04; Siobhan McBride, "E-marketplaces Make a Comeback,"
ComputerWorld, 30 April 2004, www.computerworld.com.au/index
.php?id=249272367&fp=16&fpid=0, accessed 11/04; Sarah Z.
Sleeper, "B2B Exchanges See Growth in Transactions and Revenue,"
SAP, 26 May 2003, www.sap.info/public/en/article.php4/Article
-267523ea91865c7a55/en, accessed 11/04; Emory Thomas, "Armed
with a Dose of Realism, Online Marketplaces Stage a Comeback,"
MCI, 2003, http://global.mci.com/de/resources/articles/35/B2B.xml,

accessed 11/04; Mary Hillebrand, "B2B Explosion Anticipated in
2000," *E-Commerce Times,* 12 December 1999, www.ecommercetimes
.com/story/2069.html, accessed 11/04; Antonio Davila, Mahendra
Gupta, and Richard Palmer, "Slow Growth for Business-to-Business
Online Buying," Stanford Graduate School of Business, September
2002, www.gsb.stanford.edu/news/research/ecommerce
_b2b growth.shtml, accessed 11/04; Staff, "E-Commerce in
Developed Countries Continues on Strong Growth Path," United
Nations Conference on Trade and Development, 11 November 2003,
www .unctad.org/Templates/webflyer.asp?docid=4253&intItemID
=2261&lang=1, accessed 11/04; Lesley Hensell, "The True Path of
B2B E-Commerce," *E-Commerce Times,* 31 October 2003, www
.ecommercetimes.com/story/32000.html, accessed 11/04; Lynn Ward,
"The New Face of B2B E-Commerce," *E-Commerce Times,* 22 May
2003, www.ecommercetimes.com/story/21569.html, accessed 11/04;
Keith Regan, "Blueprint for Building a Viable B2B Site," *E-Commerce
Times,* 15 May 2003, www.ecommercetimes.com/story/21522.html,
accessed 11/04; Jonathan M. Roenker, "Online Sales and E-Commerce
Taxation at Kentucky Businesses," University of Kentucky, Gatton
School, 2001, http://gatton.uky.edu/CBER/Downloads/Roenker01
.htm, accessed 11/04.

14. Mark Micheli, "Business Takes Off," *Boston Business Journal,* 24
January 2003, http://boston.bizjournals.com/boston/stories/2003/
01/27/smallb2.html, accessed 11/04; Keith Regan, "Blueprint for
Building a Viable B2B Site," *E-Commerce Times,* 15 May 2003,
www.ecommercetimes.com/story/21522.html, accessed 11/04.

15. Gerry Blackwell, "eBay for Small Business (Part I)," Small Business
Computing, 7 April 2003, www.smallbusinesscomputing.com/
biztools/article.php/2176641, accessed 11/04; Gerry Blackwell, "eBay
for Small Business (Part II)," Small Business Computing, 28 May
2003, www.smallbusinesscomputing.com/emarketing/article.php/
2212951, accessed 11/04; Gerry Blackwell, "eBay for Small Business
(Part III)," Small Business Computing, 28 July 2003, www
.smallbusinesscomputing.com/emarketing/article.php/22402, accessed
11/04; Staff, "eBay Redraws Retailing's Map," InternetRetailer, January
2003, www.internetretailer.com/article.asp?id=8316, accessed 11/04.

16. Rob Spiegel, "No Downturn for Liquidation," Electronic News, 2
September 2002, www.reed-electronics.com/electronicnews/article/
CA241770?pubdate=9%2F2%2F2002, accessed 11/04.

17. Staples, Inc., "Staples, Inc. Reports Record Fourth Quarter and Fiscal
2003 Results," Staples, http://investor.staples.com/ireye/ir_site.zhtml
?ticker=SPLS&script=410&layout=-6&item_id=501520, accessed
11/04; Staples, Inc., "Securities and Exchange Commission Filings:
Form 10-K," 2004, http://secfilings.nasdaq.com/edgar_conv_html
%2F2003%2F03%2F05%2F0001047469-03-007679.html, accessed
11/04; William C. Symonds, "Can Office Depot Clip Staples?,"
BusinessWeek, 30 June 2004, www.businessweekasia.com/bwdaily/
dnflash/jun2004/nf20040630_9483_db035.htm, accessed 11/04; Gene
Marcial, "Listening to the Staples Story," *BusinessWeek Online,* 23
April 2002, www.businessweek.com/bwdaily/dnflash/apr2002/
nf20020423_9778.htm, accessed 11/04; Sarah L. Roberts-Witt, "A
Singular Focus," *PC Magazine,* 25 September 2001, www.pcmag.com/
print_article/0,3048,a=12672,00.asp, accessed 11/04; Jason Anders,
"Sibling Rivalry," *Wall Street Journal,* 17 July 2000, p. R16; Joellen
Perry, "The Best of the Web," *U.S. News & World Report,* 8 October
2001, pp. 59–60; Michael Pastore, "Consumers Shift from Catalogs to
the Web," ClickZ Network, 10 December 2001, www.clickz.com/stats/
markets/retailing/print.php/6061_937191, accessed 11/04.

18. Shop.org, "Online Retail Sales and Profitability on the Rise: The State
of Retailing Online," About.com, 25 May 2004, http://retailindustry
.about.com/od/seg_internet/a/bl_nrf052504.htm, accessed11/04.

19. Bob Tedeschi, "Online Retailers Grapple with the Age-Old Problem of Handling Returned Merchandise," *New York Times*, 28 May 2001, p. C6.

20. Michael Pastore, "Brand Web Sites Come Up Short with Many Consumers," ClickZ Network, 24 April 2001, www.clickz.com/stats/markets/advertising/print.php/5941_751271, accessed 11/04; Emily Nelson, "Shoppers Find Web Sites Fail to Satisfy Them," *Wall Street Journal*, 20 April 2001, p. B8.

21. Staff, "Office Depot to Roll Out More Than 7,000 Wireless In-Store Web Kiosks," KioskMarketplace.com, 7 July 2004, www.kioskcom.com/articles_detail.php?ident=2275, accessed 11/04; Ronald J. Bauerly and Paul Thistlewaite, "Retailing 2010: The Potential Impact of the Internet," Marketing Management Association, 2000, pp. 27–32; William M. Bulkeley, "What's Ahead for . . . Retailing?," *Wall Street Journal*, 25 June 2001, p. R16; Stephanie Miles, "Netkey Transforms Kiosks into E-Salespeople," *Wall Street Journal*, 17 May 2001, p. B6; Michael Mahoney, "Report: Despite Sales Slump, E-Tailers Turning More Surfers into Buyers," *E-Commerce Times*, 7 June 2001, www.ecommercetimes.com/perl/story/11070.html, accessed 11/04; Michael Totty, "Making the Sale," *Wall Street Journal E-Commerce*, 24 September 2001, p. R6; Keith Regan, "Customer Conversion in Spotlight at eTail2003 Conference," TechNewsWorld, 12 August 2003, www.technewsworld.com/story/31318.html, accessed 11/04; James Maguire, "Experts Speak Out on Improving Sales Conversions, Part 2," Internet.com, 2 July 2004, http://ecommerce.internet.com/how/customers/article/0,,10363_3376771,00.html, accessed 11/04.

22. Sean Michael Kerner, "Onsite Search Drives Sales, Cart Abandonment Unabated," ClickZ Stats – Retailing, 3 November 2004, www.clickz.com/stats/markets/retailing/article.php/3430671, accessed 11/04; Bryan Eisenberg, "20 Tips to Minimize Shopping Cart Abandonment," ClickZ Network, 8 August 2003, www.clickz.com/experts/crm/traffic/article.php/2245891, accessed 11/04.

23. Corey Rudl, "Using Drop Shippers for Your Online Store," Entrepreneur.com, 20 January 2003, www.entrepreneur.com/article/0,4621,306132,00.html, accessed 11/04; Laurie Gieson, "Picking Up Drop Shipping," Internet Retailer, June 2004, www.internetretailer.com/article.asp?id=12110, accessed 11/04.

24. Expedia, "Expedia, Inc. Announces Expanded Relationship with Sabre Travel Network," Expedia, Inc., 5 May 2004, www.expedia.com/daily/press/releases/2004-5-5Sabre_Expedia.asp, accessed 11/04; Julie Krippel, "Expedia, Inc.," Hoover's Online, 2004, www.hoovers.com/expedia/—ID__61378—/free-co-factsheet.xhtml, accessed 11/04; Staff, "Expedia Arrives in France (L'Arrivée d'Expedia Bouscule les Voyagistes en Ligne Francais)," Europe Intelligence Wire, 12 July 2004, www.hoovers.com, accessed 7/04; Christopher Saunders, "New Expedia.com Ads Debut in Advance of Orbitz Launch," ClickZ Network, 31 May 2001, www.clickz.com/news/article.php/776641, accessed 11/04; Press Release, "Expedia Achieves Hotel Industry Milestones," Expedia.com, 6 June 2003, www.expedia.com/daily/press/releases/HotelMilestones.asp, accessed 11/04.

Chapter 12

1. Barbara Murray, "Kraft Foods Inc.," Hoover's Online, 2004, www.hoovers.com/kraft-foods/—ID__103392—/free-co-factsheet.xhtml, accessed 12/04; PR Newswire, "Vivendi Universal Games Partners with Kraft Foods to Launch Crash & Spyro Adventure World Promotion," Yahoo! Business, 18 May 2004, http://biz.yahoo.com/prnews/040518/latu025_1.html, accessed 7/04; Staff, "Kraft's $600 Million Marketing Boost Holds Despite Slow Growth," *Promo Magazine*, 22 April 2004, http://promomagazine.com/news/marketing_krafts_million_marketing/index.html, accessed 12/04; Sean Carton, "Applications, Not Ads," ClickZ Network, 19 May 2003, www.clickz.com/experts/ad/lead_edge/article.php/2208261, accessed 12/04; Catherine Arnold, "Once B-to-B Clients Try Advergaming, Marketers Have a Captive Audience," *Marketing News*, 15 May 2004, pp. 1–2 and http://search.epnet.com/direct.asp?an=13218188&db=buh, accessed 12/04; Tessa Ergert, "Advergaming Catches On," ClickZ Network, 24 July 2003, www.clickz.com/experts/media/media_buy/article.php/2239071, accessed 12/04; Tessa Ergert, "Games Pop Up in Ads," ClickZ Network, 17 July 2003, www.clickz.com/experts/media/media_buy/article.php/2235891, accessed 12/04; Hassan Fattah and Pamela Paul, "Gaming Gets Serious," *Advertising Age*, May 2002, pp. 38–44 and http://search.epnet.com/direct.asp?an=6580965&db=aph, accessed 12/04; Venus Lee, " 'Advergaming' Your Way to Online Brand Building Success," *Media Asia*, 5 September 2003, pp. 15–18 and http://search.epnet.com/direct.asp?an=10874094&db=buh, accessed 12/04; Staff, "Online & Mobile Gaming Market, United States, May 2004," JETRO, May 2004, www.jetrosf.org/fp/Gaming%20Report_2004.pdf, accessed 12/04; Bob Liu, "X10 Pops Into Bankruptcy," InternetNews.com, 23 October 2003, www.internetnews.com/bus-news/article.php/3097651, accessed 12/04; MediaPost, "Online Gaming Explosion Creates New Opportunities for Advertisers, Marketingvox.com, 20 July 2004, www.marketingvox.com/archives/2004/07/20/advergaming_hits_half_billion_mark/, accessed 12/04; Denise Garcia, "Advergaming's Big Moment," Electronic Gaming Business, 28 January 2004, www.findarticles.com/p/articles/mi_m0PJQ/is_2_2/ai_112655766, accessed 12/04.

2. Janis Mara, "Burger King Hen Whets Chicken Yen," ClickZ Network, 16 April 2004, www.clickz.com/news/article.php/3341301, accessed 12/04; Chrus Ulbrich, "Porno Hen Hawks for Burger King," *Wired News*, 14 April 2004, www.wired.com/news/culture/0,1284,63053,00.html, accessed 12/04; Press Release, "Subservient Chicken Strikes Again with Spicy Tendercrisp Chicken Sandwich," Burger King Corp., 15 April 2004, www.burgerking.com/CompanyInfo/onlinepressroom/index.aspx, accessed 12/04; Nichola Groom, "Burger King Says Web Chicken Won't Go Mainstream," *USAToday*, 12 May 2004, www.usatoday.com/tech/webguide/internetlife/2004-05-12-chicken_x.htm, accessed 12/04; Catharine P. Taylor, "Playing Chicken," *Adweek*, 19 April 2004, pp. 19–21 and http://search.epnet.com/direct.asp?an=12985136&db=buh, accessed 12/04; Rod Gustafson, "Burger King Opts for Chicken a la Porn," Parents Television Council, 14 May 2004, www.parentstv.org/PTC/publications/rgcolumns/2004/0514.asp, accessed 12/04; Bob Garfield, "Subservientchicken.com is Virally Cool, But Still a Failure," *Advertising Age*, 26 April 2004, pp.103–108 and http://search.epnet.com/direct.asp?an=12945128&db=aph, accessed 12/04; Matthew G. Nelson, "Fast Is No Longer Fast Enough," *InformationWeek*, 5 June 2000, www.informationweek.com/789/web.htm, accessed 12/04.

3. Larry Riggs, "Draft Chicago Tapped for Milk Promotion," *Direct*, 1 June 2004, www.directmag.com/ar/marketing_draft_chicago_tapped/, accessed 7/04; Betsy Spethmann, "Milk Promos Multiply in $30 Million Push," Promo Xtra, 20 May 2004, Promo@Xtranewsletters.primediabusiness.com, received May 2004.

4. Julie Krippel, "The Longaberger Company," Hoover's Online, 2004, www.hoovers.com/the-longaberger-company/—ID__48112—/free-co-factsheet.xhtml, accessed 12/04; Maria Mallory, "...A Tasket?," *U.S. News & World Report*, 17 November 1997, p. 65.

5. Karen Lundegaard, "Volvo Plans Online Ad Campaign for Latest Launch," *Wall Street Journal*, 25 September 2000, p. B14; Suzanne Vranica, "Volvo Campaign Tests New Media Waters," *Wall Street Journal*, 16 March 2001, p. B5; Betsy Spethmann, "Volvo Launches S40 in $3 Million Push," *Promo Magazine*, 17 February 2004, http://

promomagazine.com/campaigns/marketing_volvo_launches_million/, accessed 12/04.

6. Alexei Barrioneuvo, "Chevron and BP Amoco Test Web Ads at Pumps," *Wall Street Journal,* 12 June 2000, p. B6; Staff, "The Sizzle: What's Up in Digital Marketing and Advertising," *Business2.0,* April 2001, www.business2.com/articles/mag/0,1640,14635,FF.html, accessed 7/02; Staff, "Taxi Tops 'Go Live,'" American Country ROADwise, Summer 2002, www.amctry.com/AmCountrySummer2002.pdf, accessed 12/04.

7. Nora Macaluso, "Pop-Under Ad Strategy Could Backfire," *E-Commerce Times,* 26 July 2001, www.ecommercetimes.com/story/12290.html, accessed 12/04; Thomas E. Weber, "Can You Say 'Cheese'? Intrusive Web Ads Could Drive Us Nuts," *Wall Street Journal,* 21 May 2001, p. B1; DoubleClick, "Year in Online Advertising 2003," DoubleClick, March 2004, www.doubleclick.com/us/knowledge_central/documents/trend_reports/dc_2003yearinonline_0403.pdf, accessed 12/04; Bob Liu, "X10 Pops Into Bankruptcy," InternetNews.com, 23 October 2003, www.internetnews.com/bus-news/article.php/3097651, accessed 12/04.

8. Sara Wilson, "Ford Revs Up Internets Online," iMediaConnection, 14 August 2003, www.imediaconnection.com/content/1402.asp, accessed 12/04; News Release, "Ford Expedition Ads Illustrate No Boundaries Thinking," Ford Motor Co., 6 May 2002, http://media.ford.com/products/press_article_display.cfm?article_id=11844&vehicle_id=950&make_id=92, accessed 12/04.

9. Amit Asaravala, "Sick of Spam? Prepare for Adware," Wired.com, 7 May 2004, www.wired.com/news/technology/0,1282,63345,00.html, accessed 12/04; Ian Cunningham, "Spyware and Adware Removal," *PC Review UK,* 27 September 2004, www.pcreview.co.uk/article-7086.php, accessed 12/04; Brian Morrissey, "Judge Says AdWare Is Legal," ClickZ News, 8 September 2003, www.clickz.com/news/article.php/3073741, accessed 12/04; Ariana Eunjung Cha, "Computer Users Face New Scourge," *The Washington Post,* 10 October 2004, www.washingtonpost.com/wp-dyn/articles/A20665-2004Oct9.html, accessed 12/04; Paul Roberts, "New Trojan Kills Awdare," IDG News Service, 7 October 2004, www.pcworld.com/news/article/0,aid,118098,00.asp, accessed 12/04.

10. PricewaterhouseCoopers, "IAB Internet Advertising Revenue Report," Internet Advertising Bureau, April 2004, www.iab.net/resources/adrevenue/pdf/IAB_PwC_2003.pdf, accessed 12/04; DoubleClick, "Year in Online Advertising 2003," DoubleClick, March 2004, www.doubleclick.com/us/knowledge_central/documents/trend_reports/dc_2003yearinonline_0403.pdf, accessed 12/04; Staff, "Internet Advertising Riding High," CNN.com, 24 May 2004, www.cnn.com/2004/TECH/biztech/05/24/internet.ads.ap/index.html, accessed 12/04; Nielsen News Release, "U.S. Advertising Spending Rose More Than 7% in Q1 2004, Nielsen Monitor-Plus Reports," Nielsen Media Research, 26 May 2004, www.nielsenmedia.com/newsreleases/2004/M+Q1-2004.htm, accessed 12/04; Staff, "U.S. Advertising Market Exhibits Strong Growth in 2003," TNS Media Intelligence/CMR, 8 March 2003, www.tnsmi-cmr.com/news/2004/030804.html, accessed 12/04.

11. John Buskin, "Imagine This," *Wall Street Journal,* 14 January 2002, http://online.wsj.com, accessed 2/02; Jeffery Graham, "Internet Advertising Best Practices," Clickz.com, 23 October 2000, http://clickz.com/print/jsp?article=2651, accessed 12/04; Katherine Hobson, "Ads That Just Don't Click—No, Literally," *U.S. News & World Report,* 12 March 2001, p. 56; Seth Stevenson, "It's a Bird! It's a Plane! It's a . . . Webisode?," Slate, 19 April 2004, http://slate.msn.com/id/2099152/, accessed 12/04.

12. Sean Carton, "Applications, Not Ads," ClickZ Network, 19 May 2003, www.clickz.com/experts/ad/lead_edge/article.php/2208261, accessed 7/04; Aaron Barnhart, "BMW Car-Chase Ads Raise the Standard for Internet Movies," *Lexington Herald-Leader,* 25 June 2001, p. 19; Anthony Vagnoni, "Action Mini-Movies Feature Top Actors and Cool Cars," *AdAge,* 23 July 2001, www.adage.com/news.cms?newsId=32430, accessed 7/02.

13. Seth Stevenson, "It's a Bird! It's a Plane! It's a . . . Webisode?," Slate, 19 April 2004, http://slate.msn.com/id/2099152/, accessed 12/04; Rick E. Bruner, "Amex Launches 5-Minute Seinfeld Webisodes," MarketingVox.com, 31 March 2004, www.marketingvox.com/archives/2004/03/31/amex_launches_5minute_seinfeld_webisodes/index.php?rss1, accessed 12/04; American Express, "Seinfeld and Superman Return to the Web Today With Their Highly Anticipated Second Webisode," AmericanExpress.com, 20 May 2004, http://home3.americanexpress.com/corp/pc/2004/webisode2.asp, accessed 12/04; Terminix, "A Bug's Eye View Webisode," Terminix.com, 2004, www.terminix.com/BugsEye/index.cfm?fuseaction=episode&clipID=23, accessed 12/04.

14. Michael Pastore, "Webcasters Spread the Gospel of Webcast Advertising," *CyberAtlas,* 9 May 2001, www.cyberatlas.com/stats/markets/advertising/print.php/5941_762271, accessed 12/04; Carol Pickering, "Live! From Merrill Lynch?," *Business2.0,* May 2001, www.business2.com/articles/mag/0,1640,14703,FF.html, accessed 7/02.

15. Rick E. Bruner, "Blogging is Booming," iMediaConnection.com, 5 April 2004, www.imediaconnection.com/content/3162.asp, accessed 12/04; Jeffrey Henning, "Persus Blog Survey," Perseus Development Corp., 2003, www.perseus.com/blogsurvey/thebloggingiceberg.html, accessed 1/04; Amanda Lenhart, Deborah Fallows, and John Horrigan, "Reports: Online Activities and Pursuits," Pew Internet & American Life Project, 29 February 2004, www.pewinternet.org/report_display.asp?r=113, accessed 12/04 Nat Ives, "Advertisers Learn From Candidates," *New York Times Online,* 2 November 2004, www.nytimes.com/2004/11/02/business/media/02adco.html?ex=1101704400&en=fbc0a734cf7a3b76&ei=5070, accessed 12/04; Rob McGann, "The Blogsphere By the Numbers," ClickZ Stats, 22 November 2004, www.clickz.com/stats/sectors/traffic_patterns/article.php/3438891, accessed 12/04 .

16. DoubleClick, "Year in Online Advertising 2003," DoubleClick, March 2004, www.doubleclick.com/us/knowledge_central/documents/trend_reports/dc_2003yearinonline_0403.pdf, accessed 7/04; eMarketer, "Online Ad Update: Search Supreme on the Race to $10B," eMarketer.com, 17 December 2003, www.emarketer.com/Article.aspx?1002600, accessed 7/04.

17. Lorraine Gallaher, "ACP State of the Coupon Industry," Association of Coupon Professionals, May 2003, www.couponpros.org/html/2_news&conferences/4_ezine/2003-05%20Ezine.htm, accessed 12/04; Staff, "Albertsons, Publix Reject Coupons Printed from the Internet," *InternetRetailer,* 30 September 2003, www.internetretailer.com/dailyNews.asp?id=10306, accessed 12/04; James P. Santella, "Coupon Trend Reports," Santella and Associates, www.santella.com/Trends .htm, accessed 7/04; Patricia Odell, "Counterfeit Coupons Flood the Internet," *Promo Magazine,* 27 August 2003, http://promomagazine .com/coupons/marketing_counterfeit _coupons_flood/, accessed 12/04; Karen Holt, "Coupon Crimes," *Promo Magazine,* 1 April 2004, http:// promomagazine.com/mag/marketing_coupon_crimes/, accessed 12/04.

18. Business Editors, "General Mills Launches Integrated Promotion to Enhance Pop Secret Brand Online; Promotions.com Chosen to Develop Integrated Internet Promotion for Leading Consumer Foods

Company," *BusinessWire,* 26 June 2000, www.findarticles.com/
cf_0/m0EIN/2000_June_26/62915915/print.jhtml, accessed 12/04.

19. Saul Hansell, "The Internet Ad You Are About to See Has Already
Read Your E-Mail," *New York Times,* 21 June 2004, http://nytimes
.com/2004/06/21/technology/21google.html, accessed 12/04;
eMarketer, "Amid Woes, E-Mail Volume Continues to Grow,"
eMarketer, 23 June 2004, www.emarketer.com/Article.aspx?1002881,
accessed 12/04; Keith Regan, "Building a Better E-Mail Blast,"
E-Commerce Times, 16 December 2002, www.ecommercetimes
.com/story/20252.html, accessed 12/04; David Ferris, "Drowning in
Email Overload? Ferris Research Forecasts It Will Only Get Worse,"
Ferris Research, 31 July 2000, www.ferris.com, accessed 7/01; Theresa
Forsman, "Are You Serving Spam?" *BusinessWeek,* 29 May 2001, www
.businessweek.com/smallbiz/content/may2001/sb20010529_737.htm,
accessed 12/04; Tom Yager, "Customer, May I? Getting the OK to
Sell," *InfoWorld,* 22 January 2001, www.itworld.com/Man/2695/
IW010122tcpermission, accessed 12/04; Dylan Tweney, "Radically
New E-mail Marketing Campaigns," eCompany.com, 30 November
2000, www.business2.com/articles/web/0,1653,8925,00.html, accessed
7/02; Jakob Nielsen. "Jakob Nielsen's Alertbox Mailing List Usability,"
eCompany.com, 20 August 2000, www.useit.com/alertbox/20000820
.html, accessed 12/04.

20. Barbara Murray, "Nestlé S.A.," Hoover's Online, 2004, www.hoovers
.com/nestl%c3%a9/—ID__41815—/free-co-factsheet.xhtml, accessed
12/04; Staff, "All About Nestlé," Nestle.com, 2004, www.nestle.com/
All_About/All+About+Nestlé.htm, accessed 12/04; Betsy Spethmann,
"Nestlé Candies Sweeps Touted on 64 Million Wrappers," *Promo
Magazine,* 20 January 2004, http://promomagazine.com/games/
marketing_nestl_candies_sweeps/, accessed 12/04; Venus Lee,
"'Advergamin': Your Way to Online Brand Building Successes,"
Media Asia, 5 September 2003, pp.15–18 and http://search.epnet.com/
direct.asp?an=10874094&db=buh, accessed 12/04; Haymarket
Publications, "Nestlé Game Targets Young Drinkers of Dairy Farm
Milk," Media Online Weekly Email Bulletin, 2 April 2003, http://
mako.resonance.com.sg/media/mailer020403.htm, accessed 12/04.

Chapter 13

1. Gwendolyn Bounds, "Programs Are Helping Uninitiated Build Web
Sites," *Wall Street Journal,* 11 May 2004, p. B4; Laura Tiffany, "Gift
Basket Service," Entrepreneur.com, 22 February 2001, www
.Entrepreneur.com/article/0,4621,287009,00.html, accessed 10/04;
SBA, "Guide to Size Standards," United States Small Business
Administration, 15 July 2002, www.sba.gov/businessop/standards/
guide.html, accessed 10/04; Joanne H. Pratt, "Homebased Business:
The Hidden Economy," Small Business Research Summary, Number
194, March 2000, US SBA, www.sba.gov/ADVO/research/rs194.pdf,
accessed 10/04; Staff, "How to Make Executive-Level Earnings with
Gift Baskets," Home Based Business Opportunities, 2004, www
.home-based-business-opportunities.com/library/giftbaskets.shtml,
accessed 10/04; JoAnna Gilford, "A Gift Basket Business the 'Punkin'
Way!," Home Biz Tools, 2001,
http://homebiztools.com/ideas/gift_basket.htm, accessed 10/04.

2. Roger Brooksbank, "Essential Characteristics for an Effective
Marketing Plan," *Marketing Intelligence & Planning,* vol. 9, no. 7,
1991, pp. 17–20; Laura Tiffany, "How to Create a Marketing Plan,"
Entrepreneur.com, 27 August 2001, www.entrepreneur.com/article/
0,4621,291706,00.html, accessed 10/04.

3. Beth Cox, "From Wall Street to Gift Baskets: An E-commerce
Entrepreneur's Tale," Internet.com, 30 October 2003, http://
ecommerce.internet.com/news/insights/trends/article/0,,10417

_3101951,00.html, accessed 10/04; Staff, "Retail & Floral Gift
Businesses," Hoover's Online, 2004, www.hoovers.com/floral-&-gifts
-retail/—HICID__1534—/free-ind-factsheet.xhtml, accessed 5/04.

Chapter 14

1. Rachel Meyer, "Adobe Systems Incorporated," Hoover's Online, 2004,
www.hoovers.com, accessed 5/04; Jay Lyman, "Adobe's Geoff Baum
on Merging Paper and Electronic Docs," TechNewsWorld, 16 May
2004, www.technewsworld.com/perl/story/33128.html, accessed 10/04;
Harry McCracken, "Adobe's Story Retold," *PCWorld.com,* 18 October
2002, www.pcworld.com/news/article/0,aid,106079,00.asp, accessed
10/04; Gene J. Koprowski, "W3C Standards to Usher In Era of
Reliable Searching," TechNewsWorld, 11 February 2004, www
.technewsworld.com/perl/story/32833.html, accessed 10/04.

2. Jay Lyman, "Ups and Downs of Building an E-Commerce Site,"
E-Commerce Times, 18 November 2002, www.ecommercetimes.com/
perl/story/20006.html, accessed 10/04; Lynn Ward, "Hidden Costs of
Building an E-Commerce Site," *E-Commerce Times,* 28 April 2003,
www.ecommercetimes.com/perl/story/21368.html, accessed 10/04;
Matt Carmichael, "Time to Build: Development Costs Have
Dropped," *BtoB: The Magazine for Marketing and e-Commerce
Strategists,* 14 May 2001, www.btobonline.com/cgi-bin/article.pl
?id=5972, accessed 5/04.

3. Matt Carmichael, "2001's Median Prices for Full-Site Development,"
BtoB: The Magazine for Marketing and e-Commerce Strategists,
14 May 2001, www.btobonline.com/webPriceIndex/, accessed 5/04.

4. Michael Pastore, "Privacy Remains a Concern for Online Consumers,"
CyberAtlas, 11 June 2001, www.clickz.com/stats/markets/advertising/
print.php/5941_781741, accessed 10/04.

5. Staff, "Methods for Designing Usable Web Sites," U.S. Government
Department of Health and Human Services, 2004, www.usability.gov/
methods/usability_testing.html, accessed 10/04; Jakob Nielsen, "Jakob
Nielsen on Usability and Web Design," useit.com, 2004, www.useit
.com, accessed 10/04; Darlene Fichter, "Designing Usable Sites: A
State of Mind," *Online,* January 2001, www.findarticles.com/cf_0/
m1388/1_25/68656987/print.jhtml, accessed 7/02.

6. Elizabeth McLachlan, "User Testing for Web Site Usability,"
Netscape, http://wp.netscape.com/computing/webbuilding/studio/
feature19980909-3.html, accessed 10/04; Alexei Oreskovic, "Testing
1-2-3," *The Industry Standard,* 5 March 2001, www.findarticles.com/
cf_0/m0HWW/9_4/71561484/print.jhtml, accessed 10/04.

7. Darlene Fichter, "Testing the Web Site Usability Waters," *Online,*
March 2001, www.findarticles.com/cf_0/m1388/2_25/70910893/
print.jhtml, accessed 7/02.

8. Alison J. Head, "Demystifying Intranet Design: Five Guidelines for
Building Usable Sites," *Online,* July 2000, www.findarticles.com/cf_0/
m1388/4_24/63568431/print.jhtml, accessed 7/02.

9. Laura Wonnacott, "Web Site Design Is a Combination of Both
Science and Art That Satisfies Many Users," *InfoWorld,* 31 January
2000, www.infoworld.com/articles/op/xml/00/01/31/000131opsavvy
.xml, accessed 5/04; Press Release, "IDG's InfoWorld Makes Sizable
Investment in New Website to Improve Technology Buying
Decisions," *InfoWorld,* 3 March 2003, http://archive.infoworld.com/
about/abt_prs_rel_03032003.html, accessed 5/04.

10. Staff, "What Are WebEnhancementServices?," *WebEnhancementServices,*
31 January 2000, www.marketingtactics.com/English/Services/Web/
WebEnhancement.html, accessed 10/04; Bryan Eisenberg, "End the
One-Page Site Visit," ClickzNetwork.com, 26 March 2004, www.clickz
.com/experts/design/traffic/article.php/3330541, accessed 10/04.

11. Melinda Patterson Grenier, "Traffic to News Web Sites over Two Days Sets Records," *Wall Street Journal Online,* 13 September 2001, http://interactive.wsj.com/articles/SB100037289444669854.htm, accessed 7/02.

12. Janet Bingham Bernstel and Hollis Thomases, "Writing Words for the Web," *Bank Marketing* vol. 33, no. 2 (March 2001), pp. 16–21.

13. Diane Frank, "Government Web Sites Focus on Satisfying Users, Not Designers," Federal Communications Commission, 19 May 2003, www.fcw.com/fcw/articles/2003/0519/pol-firstgov-05-19-03.asp, accessed 10/04; Michael Heim, "The Feng Shui of Virtual Worlds," *Computer Graphics World,* January 2001, http://cgw.pennnet.com/Articles/Article_Display.cfm?Section=Archives&Subsection=Display&ARTICLE_ID=89345&KEYWORD=The%20Feng%20Shui%20of%20Virtual%20Worlds, accessed 10/04.

14. Anne Clyde, "Bobby Approves—Web Accessibility for the Print Disabled," *Teacher Librarian* 28, no. 4 (April 2001), pp. 52–54.

15. Staff, "Tips for Creating a Senior-Friendly Web Site," *Geriatrics* 56, no. 6 (June 2001), p. 17.

16. ActivMedia, "Website Technical Sophistication Succeeds; Smoke & Mirror Sites Fail," Research LLC, 7 August 2001, www.activmediaresearch.com/magic/pr080701.html, accessed 7/02.

17. Rachel Meyer, "Adobe Systems Incorporated," Hoover's Online, 2004, www.hoovers.com, accessed 5/04; Rachel Meyer, "Macromedia Inc.," Hoover's Online, 2004, www.hoovers.com, accessed 5/04; Jesse Nieminen, "Battle of the WYSIWYGs: Adobe GoLive vs. Macromedia Dreamweaver MX," *Digital Web Magazine,* 26 February 2003, www.digital-web.com/articles/battle_of_the_wysiwygs/, accessed 10/04; Susan C. Daffron, "Choosing Web Site Creation Software," Computer Companion, 2004, www.computorcompanion.com/LPMArticle.asp?ID=132, accessed 10/04; Carol S. Holzberg, "Design, Build, Master," *Small Business Computing,* 16 January 2002, www.smallbusinesscomputing.com/webmaster/article.php/956821, accessed 10/04.

Index